To Be a Friend of Christ

To Be a Friend of Christ

THE LIFE OF MARION D. HANKS

Richard D. Hanks

SIGNATURE BOOKS | 2024 | SALT LAKE CITY

To Maxine Lehua Christensen Hanks

RichDHanks@gmail.com

Signature Books is a registered trademark of Signature Books Publishing, LLC. Printed in the USA using paper from sustainably harvested sources.

Join our mail list at www.signaturebooks.com for details on events and related titles we think you'll enjoy.

All images provided by the Hanks family unless noted otherwise.

FIRST EDITION | 2024

LIBRARY OF CONGRESS CONTROL NUMBER: 2024943808

Hardback ISBN: 978-1-56085-472-2
Ebook ISBN: 978-1-56085-490-6

Contents

THEIR ORDINARY LIVES

GROWING AMIABLE RELATIONSHIPS

SPIRITUAL STRENGTH

A FOCUS ON FAITH AND DOING THE NEEDFUL

CHANGE AND GROWTH

I bless you that your name shall be held in honorable remembrance throughout all the generations of your posterity, who shall be led by a consideration of your good works to glorify God with labors of righteousness.

—From the patriarchal blessing of Marion D. Hanks

Preface

Follow the Christ, the King,
Live pure. Speak true. Right wrong,
Follow the King—
Else, wherefore born?
—Alfred, Lord Tennyson, *Idylls of the King*

Marion Duff Hanks was a believer.

He loved the Savior and the restored gospel and chose to honor Heavenly Father by serving Him and His children in the best way he could.

Duff was born with an incredible gift to inspire others. He spoke from pulpits and podiums around the world—from great audiences in auditoriums and on television—to smaller gatherings of students at universities—from overflowing classrooms to individual families at weddings and funerals. But it was his countless hours spent focused on the individual that truly defined his life.

His message was one of encouragement and mercy, and the cultivation of faith. A friend once told him, "Yours is a ministry to the turbulent of soul." In thousands of letters, cards, and expressions of love received during his life, the overwhelming single sentiment repeated over and over was, "You will never know the difference you made in my life."

It was this ability to change the course of an individual life on a personal level that perhaps best defined him. He mingled with presidents and world leaders and was comfortable among the greatest souls and the most brilliant minds. But he seemed to find his greatest joy assisting and encouraging individuals in their search for happiness and truth. He had great confidence in the innate decency and goodness of people. He often reminded us, "The eternal well-being of the individual is our purpose."

Although he was presented with many honorary awards, there was really nothing "honorary" about either Duff or his wife, Maxine C. Hanks. They were the real deal. Once he was asked by one of their children, "Dad, what is the key to service?" He replied, "Less talk, more action." On more than one occasion, he came home from speaking at a conference only to pull on his old coat, hat, and boots, and shovel out a snowbound neighbor. Two of his favorite aphorisms are readily applied to him: "Preach the gospel all the time; when necessary, use words,"[1] and "If you were accused of being a Christian, would there be enough evidence to convict you?" He was the epitome of a "doer" and not just a "sayer" of the word.

Duff followed his conscience, fearless of the consequences when the right course was before him. Interestingly, both his patriarchal blessing[2] as a young man and a special blessing from church president David O. McKay invited him to let his voice be heard, even if the Holy Spirit led him counter to accepted norms. He was both a leader and a follower, but he was not a blind follower. His light gray suits in a sea of black ones among church leaders at general conferences were not so much a rebel stance as they were an invitation and a beacon to others who didn't see the gospel "just so." He always spoke up. He was not afraid to champion the unpopular cause or the unpopular person. He fought many a quiet battle to bring peace to his fellowman and to ensure fair judgment of a person or a problem.

He was a favorite speaker of many firmly within the church, but he also embraced those on the fringes. He reached out to both saint and sinner. He sought out the disenfranchised. He ministered in hundreds of hospital rooms, in prisons, and even in the jungles of Vietnam during the war there. He created the church's early-morning seminary program for teenagers. He championed Boy Scouting, serving at all levels in the organization and eventually on BSA's executive committee. He even led the creation of one of its merit badges. He loved the temple and its relationship to Christ. He started non-proselyting humanitarian service by LDS missionaries in refugee camps in Southeast Asia. He dug gardens and wells in Africa, blessed the sick in India, and comforted families in Idaho. He inspired a whole generation of youth, was a beloved mission president in England, a temple president in Salt Lake City, and an area president in Asia.

While church leadership was his calling, he could have served in numerous other venues and appointments. On multiple occasions he was recruited by others to leave his position with the church to become a professional speaker, the national leader for youth in the US government, a corporate business executive, a university president, and on at least two occasions to run for office as a US Senator.

In describing Duff, one of his friends from youth said, "When he was six, he was sixty." At fifteen he was a Sunday School teacher. At seventeen, Duff gave his first talk (in June Conference) in the Tabernacle.[3] At nineteen, he was a youth board member of his stake.[4] At twenty-six he was asked to be the commencement speaker at the high school he had graduated from just nine years before. When he was called as a general authority of The Church of Jesus Christ of Latter-day

1. Attributed to St. Francis of Assisi.

2. See "Patriarchal blessing" in the Glossary of Terms. See also Appendix B for Duff's blessing.

3. Held until 1975, June Conference was an annual gathering of the church for young men and women and their leaders, conducted by general church leaders.

4. A Latter-day Saint "stake" is a group of five to ten smaller congregations called "wards," totaling about three to five thousand members. Also, see the Glossary of Terms.

Saints at age thirty-one, another general authority, Elder Richard L. Evans, said of him, "It is surprising how early a true leader's abilities and deepest devotion manifest themselves in his life."

Duff served as a general authority for almost forty years, during which time he led almost every major department of the church. Because of his longevity as a general authority, people didn't usually comprehend the span of time and changes he witnessed. In a recent conversation, a friend questioned what church leadership looked like when Duff was called. I gave him a few examples. Gordon B. Hinckley was called as a general authority five years after Duff. One of Duff's early stake conference assignments as a visiting general authority was to the Pasadena California Stake while Howard W. Hunter was the stake president. Both Hinckley and Hunter later became church presidents. Duff was the mission president of many young missionaries, including two who became apostles, Elder Jeffrey R. Holland and Elder Quentin L. Cook.

And yet Duff was never "a counter." Frankly, he would not have liked my listing his many accomplishments in this preface. He never mentioned how many years he served as a general authority, had no idea how many countries he'd visited, stake conferences conducted, marriages performed, missionaries set apart, and so forth.

There were several titles I considered for this biography that described Duff:

- My Specialty Is Mercy
- An Example of the Believers
- Stay Inside and Lift
- Championing Christlike Service
- Reaching the One

But I found the most applicable title from a response he once gave to an audience member who asked about his personal goals. He replied,

"My strongest desire is to qualify to be a friend of Christ."

It was in preaching Christlike attributes and living a life of Christlike service that he spent most of his life.

A PERSONAL NOTE

It is dangerous to write a book about one's dad. I had several major concerns.

The natural tendency to let hero worship creep into every page is overwhelming. But that was not my main reticence in writing Dad's biography. Rather, my main concern was my inability to truly capture the life of the most remarkable man I've ever known. It is a daunting task. I took a shot. I know it's never going to accurately portray his incredible life. Any mistakes are mine, not his.

On the first page of each of his many copies of the Book of Mormon, Dad wrote these words by Goethe: "I can promise to be sincere, but not impartial." Similarly, in this book I too can promise to be sincere, but not impartial. I was tempted to take a more prosaic, analytically sterile approach to this biography, but I changed my mind because Duff Hanks did not lean toward being simply prosaic or analytical in his life. When he was made an emeritus general authority, the *Salt Lake Tribune*'s headline called him the "Poet-Soul" of the church.

Another concern I had about writing this biography had to do with the logistics of time. Because he was the youngest sibling in his family, one of the youngest general authorities called in modern times, and lived to almost ninety years of age, most of the people I would have liked to interview for this biography are deceased—in fact, Duff spoke at many of their funerals.

Fortunately, Phyllis Peterson Warnick, Duff's beloved secretary, saved many of the thousands of letters he wrote and received. Over the years, she typed up his dictated journal entries, sporadic as they were. And she saved newspaper and magazine clippings, photographs, and meeting programs from some of the thousands of talks and trainings he gave all over the world.

While there is a fairly comprehensive record of his formal church talks, devotionals, and trainings, there is little or no typed record of the massive number of talks and trainings that represent the largest expenditure of time over his ministry—that is, addresses given at thousands of stake conference meetings and trainings, hundreds of temple marriages performed, seminary and Institute classes taught, firesides presented, Boy Scout trainings given, and Rotary International trainings carried out. And of course, he kept no records of the details of countless confidential counseling sessions he had with individuals.

I recognize that additional information may come to light about incidents recounted in this book and that other opinions may exist, possibly even contrary to some that I've shared. Because of the need to rely on some secondary sources and people's memories, including Dad's, the potential for a blurring of reality is possible. Nothing of that sort was done on purpose. I love what Edward L. Kimball wrote in the preface of his book about his father, Church President Spencer W. Kimball, which I will adapt as if his words were my own.

As the son of Marion D. Hanks, I acknowledge that I cannot write a biography completely free of bias, but I have had a determination to tell the story as fairly as I can. That the anecdotes presented in this biography almost all illustrate good character comes not by conscious selection but because Duff was, on all the evidence, a truly good man.[5] Notwithstanding that, I think it fair to assume that there is an inherent bias in the letters he received and in my memory of conversations with him.

A final concern in writing this book is that in order to cover such a productive life in a single, reasonably sized volume, one's natural inclination is to succumb to the temptation to make it read like long lists of his accomplishments. But that

5. See Edward L. Kimball, *Lengthen Your Stride: The Presidency of Spencer W. Kimball* (Salt Lake City: Deseret Book, 2005), xiii.

problem is not with the author—that problem is with the subject. Marion D. Hanks was a true Renaissance man. In addition to the many things already mentioned, he loved Shakespeare, loved cutting wood, wrote the lyrics for a hymn, recommended the *Christus* statue for placement at Temple Square, won athletic championships as both a young man and old, authored hundreds of articles and multiple books, loved singing, and on and on. After the first draft of his obituary, my sisters and I had to cut, and cut, and cut, and it still ended up being really long. He participated and excelled in so many different things that a watered-down, generalized recounting of his history would be a disservice to the wonderful life he led. Accordingly, I have tried to include most aspects of his life, even while having to summarize subjects that could have been given full chapters of their own.

And finally, Dad would be the first to suggest that any praise or credit accorded to him should be directed to God and the Lord Jesus Christ. Dad planted a lot of seeds, but "God gave the increase" (1 Corinthians 3:6).

If you find this book helpful, I invite you to find someone who could use your individual love and attention today. That would make Dad happiest.

Richard D. Hanks
September 1, 2024

Editorial Notes

This book is a record of not only what Duff did but what he believed, which is best expressed by what he taught. Therefore, the hybrid form of this book diverges occasionally from the traditional chronological approach of most biographies to dive deeper into specific themes that were important to him and interwoven into his life.

Many quotations are lifted verbatim from among hundreds of letters to Duff and Maxine. I have sometimes listed the author's name in the text and not always duplicated it in a footnote. For some correspondence that included privileged or confidential information, I have chosen not to cite the author's name in this book.

Copies of all of the letters to and from Duff, his journals, scrapbooks, talks, interviews, and articles that are quoted herein are in the author's possession. The originals (with rare exceptions) have been donated to the Church History Library of the Church of Jesus Christ of Latter-day Saints (CHL).

In a few places, I have chosen to italicize specific words to accentuate a point that Duff emphasized in his notes or in the audio of a talk or that I believe he would have emphasized. I have been careful not to change the original meaning and have indicated in the corresponding source notes when such italics are mine.

Several terms commonly used during most of Duff's life were not considered racist or offensive at the time, but they are considered offensive now. For example, at that time, the words *Negro*, *Indian*, *handicapped*, *Oriental*, and others were used by all people, including those to whom the term was applied. I have replaced such terms when I could do so without affecting the reading of the sentences they were in. But that has not been possible in all cases. I apologize if this usage causes offense; none is intended.

The Merriam-Webster dictionary allows for both *proselytize* and *proselyte* to be used as a verb describing missionary work. Although *proselyte* is listed second, it has historically been the version used most frequently among Latter-day Saints, so I have chosen to use that form.

The term "temple meeting" as used throughout the book almost always refers to leadership meetings of general authorities that occur weekly in the Salt Lake Temple.

Abbreviations

BUW	Duff's book *Bread upon the Waters*
BYU	Talk given in any venue at Brigham Young University
CHL	LDS Church History Library
D&C	Doctrine & Covenants
GS	Duff's book *The Gift of Self*
GC	Speech given at a general conference of The Church of Jesus Christ of Latter-day Saints
LDS, Mormon	Either a member of The Church of Jesus Christ of Latter-day Saints or the church itself. Although recently deemphasized, the term "Mormon" was widely and routinely used throughout the time covered by this book.
MDH, Duff	Marion Duff Hanks
NF	Duff's book *Now and Forever*

SOURCES IN THE AUTHOR'S POSSESSION AND IN THE CHURCH HISTORY LIBRARY:

MDH-A	Article, writings, or quotations by Marion D. Hanks
MDH-JE	Journal entry written by Marion D. Hanks
MDH-L	Letter written by Marion D. Hanks
MDH-R	Recorded interviews of Duff and Maxine Hanks by Stephen Sorenson, Duff's nephew
MDH-T	Talk given by Marion D. Hanks

Acknowledgments

If it takes a village to raise a child, it takes a metropolis to create and publish a book of this nature. At the risk of missing someone, I would like to single out the following for grateful thanks:

Liz Hanks, my wife, best friend, confidante, and counselor.

Our children, Emily Hanks Aldrich, Daniel Duff Hanks, and Katherine Hanks Allen, who, along with their spouses, Jon, Becca, and Matt, kept prodding me to write this book about their grandpa.

My sisters (and their husbands, Paul, John, Spencer, and Chris) with whom I shared most of this journey: Susan Maughan, Nancy Baird, Ann Clawson, and Mary Clifford. Special recognition to Susan and her son Michael for their detailed and helpful reviews.

Duff and Maxine's nephew Stephen Sorenson, who conducted and recorded hours and hours of interviews with Duff and Maxine and also wrote the definitive biography of our ancestor Francis Marion Lyman.

Duff and Maxine's nephew Richard Olsen, for his helpful edits and for all the family history and other genealogical contributions over the years.

Maude Frame Hanks, Duff's mother and our grandmother, for raising Duff, serving as such a wonderful example, and recording her diaries and "Treasures of Truth."

Our grandfather Stanley Alonzo Hanks for his journal, and his life of integrity and grit.

Jeffrey R. Holland, Quentin L. Cook, Richard Whitehead, Hyrum Smith, Robert Garff, and many other missionaries and friends for their many years of support and love given to our parents.

Phyllis Peterson Warnick, Duff's secretary, who kept the trains on time for over forty years. What a blessing and friend she was to our family.

Those who read through drafts and provided valuable feedback including family members, Duff's former missionaries, friends, Ben Whisenant at the Church History Library, my incomparable editors, Devan Jensen and Suzanne Brady, and my publisher, Barbara Jones Brown.

And especially Mom and Dad for their lives, teachings, example, and love. We, and our children after us, call you blessed.

BEGINNINGS

MARION DUFF HANKS FAMILY

GRANDPARENTS

Alfred F. Hanks
1856–1935

Ellen T. Lyman
1861–1881

Archibald Frame
1842–1923

Helen Duff Dick
1845–1938

C. O. Christensen
1872–1958

Clara Larsen
1874–1951

Nathaniel Boothe
1873–1953

Eunice J. Wickham
1879–1947

PARENTS

Stanley A. Hanks
1878–1924
[Stanley had one brother]

Maude Frame
1883–1967
[Maude had 16 half siblings]

Elwood L. Christensen
1900–1983
[Elwood had two brothers]

Arva E. Boothe
1903–1979
[Arva had 10 siblings]

BROTHERS & SISTERS

Lincoln F. Hanks
1905–1968

Maurine H. Busath
1907–1992

Jeannette H. Sorenson
1910–1971

Beulah H. Olsen
1913–1971

S. Bruce Hanks
1915–1989

Maude May Hanks
1917–1919

Marion D. Hanks
1921–2011

Lowell Haruo Christensen
1923–2002

Maxine L. Christensen
1925–2018

Janet C. Wyman
1936–2007

Paul E. Christensen
1940–2005

CHILDREN

Susan G. Hanks
1950– , m. Paul G. Maughan

Nancy M. Hanks
1951– , m. John K. Baird

Ann E. Hanks
1954– , m. Spencer H. Clawson

Mary L. Hanks
1956– , m. Christopher J. Clifford

Richard D. Hanks
1960– , m. Elizabeth W. Hanks

1

A Rich Family Heritage

What from your father's heritage is lent, earn it anew to really possess it.[1]

The "D" in Marion D. Hanks stands for Duff. The name was given to him in honor of his maternal grandmother, Helen Duff Dick Frame. Helen was born to Helen Muir and Samuel Duff in 1845, the fifth of twelve children, and raised in Hillhead, Glasgow, Scotland. Her father worked in the iron mines, and the children learned under the tutelage of a local Irishman. At one time, Helen was declared to have a "brilliant future in school," but unfortunately at that time it was not considered necessary for girls to be as well educated as boys. Though her brothers later became professors, and one of them a fine musician, the girls stayed home and worked. One of Helen's daughters, Maude, would later recall of her, "Mother still carries the marks of the yoke she wore carrying water from the village."[2]

In Glasgow, Helen became acquainted with Janet Dick, who was nine years her senior. Janet worked in the wealthy Frame household for twelve years as a dressmaker and hatmaker, while Helen worked for the Frame family as a governess.

Janet and Helen became friends, and Janet taught Helen about Mormonism. Helen went secretly with Janet to attend meetings and would run all the way home to avoid her parents finding out. "Helen was convinced of its truthfulness beyond all doubt, and once Mother is convinced, she never wavers," Maude later wrote of her mother. "She had more faith by far than some who carried the gospel message to her."

Helen's family was bitterly opposed to the "terrible Mormons." One night her father, walking past her hanging coat, felt something hard strike his shoulder. He looked into her pocket and found an LDS hymnbook. When he questioned Helen about what she knew of "those people," she told him she believed what they taught.

Helen was baptized a member of the Church of Jesus Christ of Latter-day Saints in 1866, after dark, by a local ecclesiastical leader (branch president). Upon learning of the baptism, her father declared, "I no longer have a daughter named Helen."

---

1. Johann Wolfgang von Goethe, *Faust.*

2. "Sketch of the Life of Helen Duff Dick Frame," undated manuscript attributed to Maude Frame Hanks, in author's possession.

HELEN DUFF AND DAVID DICK

During visits to Janet's home, Helen met Janet's brother, David Dick. After a year of courtship, Helen and David were married in 1867. Deciding to gather with their fellow Latter-day Saints in "Zion" (Utah), they saved money for a year, and then in June 1868 they crossed the Atlantic in the ship *Constitution,* one of the last passenger sailing vessels to cross the Atlantic Ocean. David's parents made the trip with them, and against all advice, Helen and David sailed with their twenty-day-old son. Before their leaving, one of Helen's friends gave her a beautifully gift-wrapped package with a complete outfit they could use for a baby's burial at sea. As they sailed away, an old woman stood on the dock, screaming, "All you miserable, filthy Christian apostates will die when the ship sinks in the ocean."

The *Constitution* sank on its return voyage to England.

They encountered horrific storms on the way. According to Helen, the ship "tossed like a cork on the waves."[3] They were sick all the way across the Atlantic. Helen recounted that during the first storm she was afraid they were going to sink, and during the succeeding storms she was so sick she was afraid they were *not* going to sink.

After forty-four days at sea, they landed in New York and took the train to the rail terminus at Benton, Wyoming. There they joined John Gillespie's company and traveled toward the Salt Lake Valley by ox team and wagon.

After an arduous journey, David and Helen's group reached Echo Canyon, Utah, in August 1868. Many of the men, including David, left the wagon company there to work on the railroad. Helen and David lived in a dugout created by digging a hole in the side of a hill and making furniture from empty kegs used in blasting. To keep out the elements, they hung a strip of old carpet for the door.

Eventually, the growing family moved to the Salt Lake Valley. David took employment at the Magna smelter, then later at the lime kiln north of Warm Springs, and then at the smelter in Murray. Unfortunately, due to workplace exposure, David died of lead poisoning in 1881, at the age of only thirty-three.

When his elderly mother, Elizabeth Dick, was told of his death, she exclaimed, "Oh my God!" and went into a coma, dying a few hours later. A double funeral was held in Taylorsville, and Helen was left a widow with seven children to raise.[4]

ARCHIBALD AND JANET FRAME

Following David's untimely death, Helen and her children were invited to temporarily live in the four-room, Taylorsville home of her close friend and sister-in-law, Janet Dick Frame, and Janet's husband, Archibald Frame.

Archibald was born in Larkhall, Scotland, in 1842. His father, William Frame, was a contractor and builder. At fifteen, Archibald was apprenticed to a man who

---

3. "Sketch of the Life of Helen Duff Dick Frame."

4. Maude Frame Hanks, life sketch in her "Treasures of Truth" scrapbook, vol. 1., in author's possession.

taught him carpentry, masonry, stonecutting, and rock laying. Archibald would later cut stone for the Salt Lake Temple.

In the course of time, Archibald met Janet Dick, who worked for his mother. Archibald and Janet married in 1864, when he was twenty-two years old and she nineteen. Though he did not know when they married that she had been baptized a Mormon a few weeks earlier, he joined the church himself only a month later. The couple eventually had nine children.

In April 1865, three years before Helen and David's emigration, Janet and Archibald had moved to Salt Lake City, sailing from Liverpool, England, in the ship *Belle Wood.* Their voyage was a miserable thirty-one days at sea, pumping water the entire way. The boat "sailed when the wind blew and drifted when it didn't," Archibald recalled. "During the trip, the captain was abusive to the sailors, who endured it until they landed, at Castle Garden, New York, and then gave him a good thrashing, which … he richly deserved." They would have been guilty of mutiny if they had attacked him on the ship.[5]

The young couple then took the train to Nebraska, switching there to oxcart for the remainder of the journey to Salt Lake City. It took them three months to cross the plains. About a month into their journey, their first son was born. The wagon train halted for just one hour for the birth of the baby and then moved on. Fortunately, there was a doctor in the company, and in return for his services during the birth, Archibald took care of his cattle while crossing the plains.

Archibald and Janet lived in various places in the Salt Lake area while he worked at his trade. He built homes and schools downtown and in Salt Lake City's Avenues neighborhood, including a home that stood for many years at 838 East South Temple. While living in Salt Lake, Archibald was known to walk the entire eleven-mile distance to Taylorsville and nail a row or two of shingles on a roof before breakfast. Eventually, Archibald moved his family to Taylorsville, where he built many of the early homes, schools, and other buildings.

Archibald was a true pioneer. The trades he learned in the old country in his youth were a great advantage to him and to others whom he taught. He was known as a skilled craftsman who made beautiful things in his shop. His daughter Maude would later remember, "I used to watch my father do the same things that little Jesus saw his father do, because his father was a carpenter too." Several of Archibald's descendants have worked in construction, in the trades, or as woodworker hobbyists, and have taken special interest in his work.

Archibald served his church, family, and community with distinction. He served for thirty-two years as the superintendent of the Sunday School and then for twenty-one years as the choir director in his ward (congregation). He also served as a beloved patriarch of his stake in Taylorsville for many years. An entire book could be written about him.

---

5. Maude Frame Hanks, "Short Sketch of the Life of Patriarch Archibald Frame," n.d., in author's possession.

POLYGAMY AND THE EARLY LIFE OF MAUDE FRAME

After the widowed Helen Duff Dick and her seven children were taken in by Archibald and Janet in the early 1880s, Archibald built Helen a two-room brick house on the lot next to his own and deeded it to her.

At that time, polygamy was being practiced by Latter-day Saints in Utah. Archibald and Janet's son James recalled, "My mother wrote a little note to father suggesting to him that he marry Auntie Helen, as 'he was keeping her anyway.' So, he did, and from this marriage we got our sister Maude."[6] Maude later wrote that her Aunt Janet "told my father in a small note that she wanted him to marry Mother and raise her brother's children—a brother that she adored."[7]

Duff recorded, "Grandfather married Helen after her husband died, and they had a seventeenth child—my mother—and [the two women] remained friends all their lives. Archibald Frame had these two wives and families, and they were, as I used to carefully explain … 'not plural wives, but rather, they were plural families.' They were treated equally, and all given a chance at education, and they were all musical.… The two families lived together, and these two tribes remained friends and loved ones forever."

Although born into a polygamous household in 1883, Maude was the only child of her parents, with sixteen half siblings: nine on her father's side and seven on her mother's. Her siblings were also cousins to each other, which sometimes caused confusion. Once, she attended a dance with her half brothers, Robert Frame and James Dick. Maude remembered, "Rob introduced me to a barber named Vic from Murray and said, 'Vic, I'd like to introduce you to my sister.' Vic replied, 'Why, it is only a few minutes since Jimmie introduced her to me as his sister.' [Vic] said, 'You must be an awfully sweet sister; will you be mine too?' It was hard to convince him that I really was a sister to them both and then, looking at them, he said, 'Well, what relation are you two fellows?' When they said they were cousins, he threw up his hands."[8]

Archibald loved Maude dearly and cared for her. Because of Helen's previous temple sealing to David, he expressed concern that he might not get to be Maude's dad in heaven.

None of Archibald's extended family in Scotland ever joined the Church of Jesus Christ of Latter-day Saints. Two of Maude's half-brothers went on missions to Scotland and tried to teach them, but they were not interested. One member of the family, however, had heard about proxy temple work and asked to have his done, saying he'd "run the risk."[9]

Despite her father disowning her upon her conversion decades before, Helen returned to Scotland in 1891, at age forty-five, for a visit. Her father, then in his

6. James Frame, personal life sketch, in author's possession.
7. Hanks, "Treasures of Truth."
8. MDH-R, Nov. 8, 2000.
9. See "Temples and temple work" in the Glossary of Terms.

Helen Duff Dick Frame, Duff's grandmother, age 73 in 1918. She joined the church in Scotland and immigrated to Utah.

eighties, stood at the corner of the picket fence as his daughter approached, his white hair blowing in the breeze, and wept, saying, "Helen, my Helen." She remained in Scotland for four months and, in her words, had a "most delightful visit," gathering hundreds of names of her ancestors for temple work.

Helen was often called on to bless other women. Maude wrote, "It was her delight for years and years to do this, and the mothers are many who have received the most wonderful testimonies through her ministration. As long as I remember anything, I will recall people coming to her bedroom window to ask her to come to someone who was ill, and never did I hear her refuse, no matter how far it was, how deep the snow, nor how the blizzard was raging."[10]

Janet Frame died in 1902. Archibald lived another twenty-one years, and when he died in 1923, Helen said, "Well, I'll be going soon too." To which her son-in-law Stanley Hanks (Duff's father) replied, "No, you will live 15 more years." Stanley himself died about a month later, and Helen died exactly fifteen years later to the day.

At the end of her life, Helen lived with Maude for four years until she died in their home (in Duff's arms) in 1938. Duff loved telling people about his grandmother,

10. MDH-R, Nov. 8, 2000.

a true pioneer who crossed an ocean and a continent because of her desire to join with the Saints in Utah. Helen Duff Dick Frame, revered by generations to follow, was buried in the Salt Lake City Cemetery next to her first husband, David.

GROWING UP IN TAYLORSVILLE

Maude's childhood in Taylorsville was typical of close-knit, loving families. Maude loved her own mother, Helen, and her Aunt Janet. "We were taught to honor and respect both mothers." Maude loved her siblings and their great faith, hard work, good humor, and musical talents, freely shared. She loved the little community schoolhouse. She loved the church choir and meetings and socials. Duff wrote, "Like other youngsters of the time and place, she was terrified of the [federal] deputies who arrived periodically to search for polygamists, but she learned to appreciate faith and loyalty and sacrifice—qualities she never forgot."[11] Maude transferred these qualities, feelings, and faith to her children and to those around her.

The Frame family's life in the early years was in a rural setting within an urban surrounding. The family had eight cows, and it was Maude's responsibility to milk "two and sometimes three" of them. She remembered, "You can scarcely imagine just how cold it was early in the morning to milk. And there were other pressing issues. Every night when I said my prayers, I asked for protection from the deputies and from Chicken Charlie. Folks depended a lot on their chickens for both eggs and meat. Charlie was the name given to a notorious chicken thief who made visits to the coops around the settlement and, in spite of dogs and men, was never caught that I recall."[12]

Maude and her childhood friends had few toys. They played community games and roasted potatoes in big bonfires. They jumped rope, rode horseback, and occasionally made homemade ice cream. In the winter they skated on frozen ditches, built snow houses and snowmen, and did a lot of sleigh riding.

As a young woman, Maude attended LDS College in Salt Lake City[13] where she planned to study to become a teacher, but eventually changed her focus to business, learning shorthand and typing. She recalled, "I was a green little country girl, had never been anywhere, had known the same people, seen the same things, and I was very timid when I entered school, but it was not for long. It changed my life. I was full of life and good nature and loved it so much."[14] She described having "many dates, and many beaus."

AMASA LYMAN

Though Maude did not know it yet, Stanley Alonzo Hanks had a heritage of no less impressive faith and endurance. His great-grandfather Amasa M. Lyman

11. MDH-A, *Gifts from a Mother* (Salt Lake City: Deseret Book, 1978), 3.
12. MDH-R, Nov. 8, 2000.
13. Later renamed Ensign College.
14. MDH-R, Nov. 8, 2000.

was one of the 143 people who entered the Salt Lake Valley with Brigham Young's wagon company in July 1847.

Amasa was born in 1813 in New Hampshire and showed very little interest in religion until 1832, when two Mormon missionaries, Lyman Johnson and Orson Pratt, began preaching in his neighborhood. He was baptized by Lyman and confirmed by Orson. At age nineteen he journeyed seven hundred miles to Ohio to meet the young Latter-day Saint prophet Joseph Smith. About that meeting, he said, "The still small voice of the Spirit whispered its living testimony in the depths of my soul, where it has ever remained, that he was The Man of God."[15]

Amasa was ordained an apostle—at the age of twenty-nine—and served as a counselor to Joseph Smith in the First Presidency. He was known as an eloquent and convincing public speaker and a devoted friend of Joseph Smith. In November 1838, he, along with others, was imprisoned with the prophet and informed they would be executed the following morning. They were saved by the heroic refusal of Alexander Doniphan to obey the execution order.

Seven years after Joseph Smith's assassination in Nauvoo, Illinois, and four years after Smith's successor, Brigham Young, led the exiled Latter-day Saints into the Salt Lake Valley, President Young called Amasa and fellow apostle Charles C. Rich to establish an outfitting post in the San Bernardino Valley in California. San Bernardino progressed rapidly under Amasa's leadership.

Amasa also served several missions for the church, including presiding over the European Mission. There he began preaching sermons that questioned a few core doctrines of the church, specifically the Atonement of Jesus Christ. He was brought before his colleagues in the Quorum of the Twelve Apostles several times over the ensuing years, and despite confessing his error and apologizing, he continued to preach similar tenets publicly. As a result, Amasa was stripped of the apostleship in 1867 and excommunicated in 1870. It is not clear why he decided to value his desire to publicly teach his questionable doctrines over keeping his good standing in the church. Following his excommunication he gained a renewed activism, teaching liberal doctrines and spiritualism, and embracing the Godbeite movement. He died in Fillmore, Utah, in 1877.

In 1909, church president Joseph F. Smith posthumously reinstated Amasa's church membership and temple blessings, partly persuaded by some who asserted that Amasa had suffered from mental illness.[16]

FRANCIS MARION LYMAN

The eldest of Amasa's sons, Francis Marion Lyman (who was called Marion by his family and friends), was Stanley Hanks' grandfather.[17] Marion was one of

15. Andrew Jenson, *Latter-day Saint Biographical Encyclopedia*, 4 vols. (Salt Lake City: Andrew Jenson History Co., 1901–36): 1:97

16. Loretta L. Hefner, "From Apostle to Apostate: The Personal Struggle of Amasa Mason," *Dialogue: A Journal of Mormon Thought* 16, no. 1 (Spring 1983): 103.

17. Stephen J. Sorenson, *Francis Marion Lyman: A Rock in the Faith* (self-pub., 2020), 2.

Francis Marion Lyman, Duff's great-grandfather

the most important leaders of the church in the nineteenth century. In 1848, at eight years of age, he helped drive a yoke of cattle and a wagon across the plains to the Salt Lake Valley. At eleven, Marion began driving animals in freighting trips from Salt Lake to San Bernardino, California. At sixteen, Marion received the Melchizedek Priesthood and was called on a mission to Great Britain. The outbreak of the Utah War prevented him from going at that time, so Lyman married Rhoda Ann Taylor on November 18, 1857. He built a cabin for his wife and young son in Beaver, Utah, and then left on his delayed mission in 1860.

When he returned home, Brigham Young asked Marion to settle in Fillmore, Utah, where he remained for fourteen years, serving as a leader in church, politics, and business. He was a multiple-term member of the Utah Territorial Legislature, superintendent of schools, prosecuting attorney, and county clerk and recorder. In 1873, Marion was called on a second mission to England. He returned to Utah along with 300 immigrating Latter-day Saints in October 1875.

In general conference in October 1880, Francis Marion Lyman was called and sustained as an apostle. He wasn't in attendance because he had been sent on a mission to survey parts of southern Utah, Nevada, and Arizona. His journal records: "On October 15th, I put up at A. A. Kimball's in Kanab. After supper, I called on my friend, Collins R. Hakes. He handed me a two-week-old copy of the *Deseret News* from October 1, which contained a report of Sunday's general conference. I had been chosen one of the Twelve Apostles!"[18]

---

18. Albert R. Lyman, early draft of *Francis Marion Lyman: Apostle*, 428, Richard R. Lyman Papers, L. Tom Perry Special Collections, Harold B. Lee Library, Brigham Young University.

From 1901 to 1903, Marion again lived in England, where he served as president of the European Mission, presiding over at least nine nations where organized branches of the church were operating. His first wife, Rhoda, accompanied him to Liverpool in 1901, but returned home after fifteen months due to her health and family concerns. Marion traveled extensively to many countries during his presidency, including dedicating the lands of Finland, Poland, and Russia for the preaching of the gospel. In 1902, he visited Palestine and offered, in prayer on the Mount of Olives, the sixth known dedication of the Holy Land.

Marion spent his life serving God and his fellow man. During his time as an apostle, church membership more than tripled to about 477,000 members. When he died in 1916, Heber J. Grant succeeded him as the president of the Quorum of the Twelve Apostles.

STANLEY A. HANKS

Stanley Alonzo Hanks was born December 3, 1878, in Tooele City, Utah, to Alfred Fredrick Hanks and Ellen Taylor Lyman, daughter of Rhoda and Francis Marion Lyman.

Stanley's young life was spent in Tooele, attending school and doing whatever he could to earn a few cents. He set gopher traps and cut peaches and apples to dry, working all day for fifty cents. Herds of sheep would pass by their home, and Stanley was sometimes given little lambs who could not keep up with the herd. He raised these lambs, and they grew into fine sheep.

Stanley's mother, Ellen, was twenty-one years old with two sons when she suffered a severe toothache. A dentist pulled the tooth, but the abscess became infected and turned into lockjaw, which led to her death. The family was convinced that the instruments had not been sterilized and the doctor was inebriated. Stanley's father, Alfred, was twenty-four years old and left with two little boys. He was brokenhearted. Over the years, he suffered intensely with his teeth but wouldn't let a dentist touch him.

Francis Marion Lyman, upon the death of his daughter, went right out, bought dental instruments, and learned how to extract teeth. "Grandfather Lyman carried these instruments with him throughout the Church and found many who needed their teeth extracted," Maude would later write of Stanley's grandfather. "I recall a sign in their home which read, 'Teeth pulled without pay, but not without pain.'"[19]

When he reached the age of nineteen, Stanley was called to the Southern States Mission. Francis Marion Lyman had encouraged Stanley to serve a mission, and on June 15, 1898, he set apart his oldest grandson as a missionary.

Stanley's future son Duff would later say of him, "I thought of my sainted father, . . . how he went into the missionary field at the call of the Lord, in his late teens, carrying copies of the Book of Mormon with testimony and conviction,

19. Hanks, "Treasures of Truth."

and yet without adequate knowledge to defend his viewpoint in the eyes of the world. He had only his testimony, his faith, and the book."[20]

Letters from Francis Marion Lyman to his grandson Stanley contained the usual uplifting and spiritual sentiments that missionaries need and love to receive. But they also included such practical advice as "avoid those given to vulgarity if you cannot restrain them," "Avoid the use of words that you need to consult the dictionary to know the meaning of them," "Take pride in writing a letter that no one can find a misspelled word in," and "Come home and get married and you will have no trouble getting along in life. You cannot amount to much until you have a wife."[21]

An entry in Stanley's journal is indicative of his missionary experience: "We went on the street to preach the gospel. We first started to sing and as people passed, they stopped to listen. Then, we offered up a prayer and addressed them on whatever subject inspired.... We have endured many hardships because of a lack of money, and often have to walk 20 miles or more in a day. There are very heartening and also very discouraging experiences, but we feel to thank God for the kind of people he raised up to feed and shelter us."[22]

COURTSHIP AND EARLY HOME LIFE

After returning from his mission, Stanley was eager to attend school, so he went to LDS College in Salt Lake City. And then, "sometime in 1902, I met for the first time my future and now beloved wife, Maude Frame of Taylorsville."[23]

One day in the school hallway, Maude passed the newly returned missionary, who asked a girl near him who she was. "He liked me right straight," Maude later related. "He said it was my hair hanging down my back in great braids that he loved before he even saw my face. But he made his feelings too obvious. Everyone teased me about him and told me things he said."

Put off, Maude said that "when he asked for a date, I was always busy." She had plenty of boys to go out with, and she saw no reason to "bother with anyone I did not care for."

But Maude eventually relented, recognizing that Stanley "was a very fine speaker, who was chosen as one of the five representative students of the school." She was also impressed with Stanley's extended family, noting his family's "deep affection for him. I, of course, got the inside view of his background and learned his worth. Then too, he was intently in love with me and did not let me doubt it for a minute."[24]

After several years of dating, Maude and Stanley were sealed in the Salt Lake Temple in February 1905. Stanley bought the wedding ring on the way to the temple, having overlooked that detail until then.

20. MDH-T, "Just One Boy," Conference Report, Oct. 1959, 24–26.

21. Francis Marion Lyman to Stanley Hanks, July 16, 1900, letter in author's possession.

22. Stanley Hanks, missionary journal, 1899, in author's possession.

23. Stanley Hanks, 1912–15 journal, Aug. 15, 1913, in author's possession.

24. Hanks, "Treasures of Truth."

Stanley A. and Maude F. Hanks

Earlier, Stanley had given his valuable sheep herd of "about 25 or more" to his father. "His father asked Stanley to let him have the sheep to help finish their home," Maude wrote. "Stanley agreed, and his father promised that when we got married, he would give us something fine. Do you know what he gave us? Four dollars toward a heating stove."

Stanley and Maude began their life together, living humbly, making plans. They had a total of seven children, three boys—Lincoln, Bruce, and Marion Duff, and four girls—Maurine, Jeannette, Beulah, and Maude May.

Stanley took a job working at Cutler Brothers retail store downtown. One day, while he was trying to retrieve a trunk from a high shelf, the trunk fell and injured his back. That was the beginning of a lifetime of pain and suffering. For the last years of his life he wore a plaster-cast brace to help alleviate the pain. After Stanley's death, the brace remained in Duff's backyard during his boyhood to remind him of the endurance of his father, who never drew a breath without pain.

Stanley worked hard at his studies, attended law school, and was admitted to practice law in 1907. Three years later, in 1910, Stanley was elected to a two-year term as justice of the peace and city coroner for the Salt Lake precinct. That was perhaps the best time financially for the young couple, and they were able to pay off debts and improve their surroundings a bit.

On November 2, 1912, Stanley wrote in his diary, "I might have been elected justice of the peace again, if I had been so inclined, but I have not one regret that I am not. I have found more peaceful pursuits and particularly my increased love for the gospel, and less liking for contention and petty troubles of selfish people."

He practiced law the rest of his life and specialized in doing charity work. Fellow attorneys sent indigent clients to him because they knew Stanley would help them. His level of care and professionalism remained consistent for all clients, regardless of their ability to pay.

Life was not easy for the Hanks family, but they remained stalwart and positive. Without much money, Maude stretched the family's resources. She made the children's clothes from old clothes. She sat up nights to sew when the children were asleep. She painted and repaired furniture and did whatever else needed to be done. In his journal in September 1912, Stanley wrote, "My wife needs clothes, my children too, and I am almost a disgrace, I look too taggy. My wheat bin is empty; so is my coal bin. The light company has been threatening us with darkness if I don't pay up, [but] I see rays of light coming." A year later, on his thirty-fifth birthday, Stanley wrote, "We are struggling a little. But we enjoy a struggle."

MARION DUFF HANKS IS BORN

It was into this family of faith and trust in God that Marion Duff Hanks was born, the youngest of seven children. Maude and Stanley's children were spread out over sixteen years. Duff's next oldest sibling, Maude May, had died two years before he was born. After her birth, the doctor warned Maude that she must not have any more children, saying it would end "disastrously." When Maude later went to see him and told him she thought she was pregnant again, the doctor stood and nervously paced the floor. Maude finally said, "Well, doctor, if conditions are as bad as you think, I should be doing the pacing, don't you think?" He apologized and left the room, returning with a doctor who specialized in high-risk pregnancies, who took care of Maude until the baby was born.

Maude relates, "During my time of waiting, Stanley had a sort of vision, that we were to be blessed with a special spirit." Maude also had a dream in which she saw a specific scene of a baby sitting on the kitchen table. After Duff was born, this scene happened exactly as she dreamed it.

Marion Duff Hanks was born on October 13, 1921. Given his mother's situation, the doctors described him as a miracle baby. He was the largest of her babies, and when the doctor carried him in to show him to his parents, Maude asked, "Is it twins?"

ARCHIBALD AND STANLEY BOTH PASS AWAY

In December 1923, Maude was called to the bedside of her father, Archibald Frame. He had been cutting down trees in his front yard and sawing them into firewood when he strained his heart. He was very ill for several days and passed away on December 20, 1923, at age eighty-one. Maude wrote, "In his passing, I lost one of the best fathers. He was not very demonstrative, and didn't talk much, but he was sincere in what he said. He was steady, dependable and would not stoop to anything mean or low. He was a grand old Patriarch."

At about the same time, one day as Stanley was shaving, he had a severe stomach pain. By the time the doctor arrived to examine Stanley, he was feeling better, probably because his appendix had ruptured. Returning later that night, however, the doctor said he needed to go to the hospital immediately. Stanley refused and suffered all night at home. When the surgeons opened him up the next day, they described his bowels as "swimming in pus."

Maude wrote that when she went into his room at the hospital, Stanley begged her to go into another room and pray to "take him out of his awful misery." Maude replied, "Oh, I can't do that." Stanley turned his head and said, "I know it is you who is holding me here, and I can't endure this any longer." Maude prayed and told the Lord if He would not heal Stanley, to take him.

Stanley A. Hanks died of a burst appendix on January 21, 1924, at age forty-five, just one month after Archibald Frame died. Duff Hanks was only two years old.

Maude wrote, "Many times, I have wondered if I was not a bit hasty in saying, 'Thy will be done.' But I had watched him suffer physically for 19 years. I knew of his disappointment in his life's plan. I knew of his ambitions and the terrible sorrow that resulted when we realized that those ambitions were not to be. He had a remarkable brain and would have gone far, but his accident at work ended all of those plans. Who can say? We did retain our membership in the Church. We did retain our faith in God. We did raise a wonderful family, who bear an honorable name and are an honor and credit to us and are our crowning glory."[25]

Upon Stanley's passing, many people honored his name. One friend wrote, "Someone has said, 'He is truly great who can have tragedy in his heart and comedy in his head at the same time.' Stanley A. Hanks possesses in full measure this kind of greatness. Stanley was a heroic soul. In early manhood, he possessed abounding health and stood erect. But a cruel affliction sapped his strength and wrenched and bent his beautiful body. But this suffering did not break his brave spirit. With undaunted courage he grasped the broken blade and fought a better battle than most of us do with unbroken steel. He was my friend. I miss him."[26]

The stress of losing a child four years before, then her father, and then her husband a month later took a toll on Maude. The difficulties of raising children alone, coupled with her many church, political, and civic duties, caused her to suffer anxiety and mental and physical exhaustion. Acutely aware of her anxiety, she talked about it openly in her journals, sometimes making light of it. On one occasion, following the death of one of Duff's little boy pals, she lay in bed with "nervous exhaustion," with no one around but Duff. "I kept calling him over to be sure he was still alive," Maude wrote, "and he would come trotting in to see what I wanted." After this happened several times, Duff put his hands on his hips, looked his mother in the eye and said, "If I were the mother, and you the little

25. Hanks, "Treasures of Truth."

26. Nephi Jensen tribute, in author's possession.

boy, I would say, 'Now, laddie, you run out and play, and don't keep coming in and bothering me.' He was a philosopher even then," Maude recalled.[27]

STANLEY VISITS

One night, as Maude lay weeping, Stanley came from beyond the grave to visit. On his deathbed, Stanley had promised Maude he'd come back in spirit as much as he could. Maude later wrote in a letter to Duff, "One morning when you awoke, you told me you had seen Papa in the night and that he had played with you. You were three. I believe you saw him; he loved you so."

Duff later recalled, "He leaned over my bed and tucked me in, took my face in his hands and spoke to me. He told me of his love for all of us, expressed his sorrow that we were not able to be together for a time, said that I had a special purpose as the last child and that I was to comfort and love my mother. He made some reference to my future opportunities. Then he turned to speak to her privately, and that was the end of my experience, other than being aware that he was there. It seemed normal enough ... and I went to sleep as he spoke with her."

The next morning Duff's first words upon awakening were, "Momma, Papa was here last night." She said, "Oh. What did he do? What did he say?" The little boy replied, "Oh, he just tucked me in, patted my head, and gave me a little kiss, and then told me some things about you, and that you're going to be alright."

Sometime years later, Duff went to Maude and asked, "Did this really occur, or is it my imagination?" Maude got out a little blue notebook in which she had written the events of the night in question. Duff said, "Mother had written my exact memories, that Stanley had come, and he had said that he was there to bring her comfort, and then turned to me and explained that my birth had not really been expected, and that 'Heavenly Father sent you, after we thought we would not likely have any more children, and you have a purpose here.'"[28]

27. Hanks, "Treasures of Truth."
28. MDH-R, Nov. 29, 2000; MDH-L to Vicky Rasmussen, Apr. 22, 1982.

2

Family and Growing Up

She gave her children everything money could not buy.[1]

With children to feed and no husband, Maude dug deep into her reservoir of courage and determination, fashioning a heroic life worth emulating.

As a widowed mother of six living children, Maude Hanks served as her ward's Relief Society president for six years and then her stake's Relief Society president for ten more years. At the same time, she was heavily active in local politics. She never remarried and valiantly raised her children by herself, living for forty-five years as a widow until she died at the age of eighty-five. She was the most influential person in Duff's life.

"As a little boy, we lived without things," he remembered. "It was Depression time. But we did not know that we were poor. We had a mother who had a great heart and knew how to use her limited resources to the point that we did not have any consciousness of not having things. I knew my breeches were not as new as my friend Irving's and I knew that I did not have a quarter to get my hair cut sometimes. But none of that seemed to matter."[2]

At her funeral, a former bishop gave her the ultimate compliment, saying, "Maude Frame Hanks gave her children everything money could *not* buy."

Both Maude's frugality and testimony were famous. She often quoted a little phrase, "Don't worry about material things; just worry about keeping your testimony; then God will take care of you."[3]

Duff recalled that his family's "little adobe house, on 180 West Fourth North in Salt Lake, was where everything worthwhile occurred, because Mother was there." The house had a kitchen, dining room, front room, and three small bedrooms. In the kitchen there was an old coal stove with a water jacket that fit into it, providing the home's only hot water. A pipe ran under the floor from the stove into the small bathroom, which had a bathtub, sink, and toilet until a small shower was added much later.[4]

1. John Longden, remarks at Maude Hanks' funeral, Oct. 23, 1967.
2. MDH-T, "Make It a Good Day," BYU, Sept. 27, 1966, 8–9.
3. Larue Longden to MDH.
4. MDH-R, Nov. 8, 2000.

Young Duff Hanks about age ten, ca. 1931.

In spite of these humble circumstances, "the fondest memories of my early childhood," Duff said, were

> related to home and the little hearth in front of the tiny fireplace that seemed a symbol of security in the midst of very limited material comforts, and to the cozy kitchen warmed by a coal stove and filled with the smell of fresh bread and Mother's special vegetable pie. From this sanctuary we would venture forth at bedtime into cold bedrooms to be enveloped in frigid covers that soon warmed to our shivering bodies. We were a one-parent family. Mother did all the work raising us, and she had responsibilities in Relief Society, but they were only a formalized part of her humanity. I sensed then and certainly know now that much of her strength and some of her capacity to care for us temporally, came through the principle of sending forth succor on the waters and having it return in added measure.[5]

SURVIVING AS A FAMILY

The late 1920s through the 1930s was a tough time to grow up. Later memorialized by images of soup kitchens, the Dust Bowl migration, and bread lines, the Great Depression left more than thirty million Americans without jobs. With Stanley gone, Maude told her children, "We will now do what we can with what we have." Duff remembered having rabbits and chickens and rhubarb out back, a grape arbor, and a family garden.

"Along with my brothers and sisters," Duff later wrote, "I would like my life to be a monument to her integrity and devotion under trying conditions." When

5. MDH-A, chapter in *Woman* (Salt Lake City: Deseret Book, 1979), 107.

Maude was serving as ward Relief Society president during the Depression, the Hanks kitchen often was filled with vegetables, cans of milk, and loaves of bread to be distributed to the needy. Duff remembered: "It was hard for us to understand why, in our own difficult circumstances, we were never allowed to eat a vegetable or keep a loaf of bread. Sometimes we were sent to the store to buy bread when there were several dozen loaves right there on the table waiting to be distributed to others. We thought, surely just one loaf would not be missed, but we were never permitted to have a taste of it."[6]

Fiercely independent, Maude refused to accept help from the government and felt reluctant to receive help from anybody else. Though the church's formal welfare program was not established until 1936, Maude provided welfare as her congregation's Relief Society president. Distributing food up and down the neighborhood in his little red wagon, young Duff considered himself to be an arm of the Relief Society's assistance. One of his earliest times philosophizing had to do with a simple question, "What does one have to do to be considered poor?"

These early experiences taught Duff to be genuinely Christlike toward others throughout his life. In his late seventies, he received a letter informing him that a church member in Washington state had named an award after him to celebrate young people who had done an unselfish act. The letter recounted a story in which Duff was delivering newspapers when he came across a boy sitting on the sidewalk, crying and shaking. Beside him in the gutter was a broken bottle of milk. The little boy explained to Duff that when he returned home, he would be beaten for losing the milk. Knowing the boy's father had a violent reputation, Duff took the little boy back to the store and from his own meager funds bought him a new jug of milk.

Many years later, Duff was in Washington when he was rushed by a man who embraced him in a bear hug. The man said, "I've always loved you, Duff Hanks, ever since you saved me from the pain of a whipping and replaced a bottle of milk."[7] This man was the letter writer who had created the award in Duff's name.

The Depression had a profound impact on Duff. As his children would attest, it affected him his whole life. "Things" were not sought for and resources were conserved. Duff and Maxine had a difficult time throwing anything away.

Duff remembered the transients who frequented his childhood home, always receiving what they needed from Maude. They would come up from the train tracks and knock on the front door. She would invite them in, and they always left with something. It was confounding to Duff that they always stopped at his house but not at the rich folks' homes up the street. Later he learned that the transients had marked one of his family's front trees—a common practice of the time—so that other transients knew the hospitable door to knock on.

---

6. MDH-R, Nov. 8, 2000.
7. Loren Chapman to MDH, Oct. 19, 1996.

DUFF'S SIBLINGS

Duff described each of his siblings and their sacrifices for the family: "Lincoln was 17 years older, and had quit high school to work two jobs. After he got married, in the dark days of the Depression, he used to drive by and honk his horn, at maybe six o'clock, on his way to work. Then, he would always stop at the house on the way home with a day-old loaf of Wonder Bread or a fifteen-cent gallon of buttermilk. We learned to drink buttermilk and enjoy it. He was trying to survive with his own young family in some pretty hard times—but very conscious of us."[8]

As the children grew older, each stepped up to help the family. Maurine succeeded Lincoln as the chief wage earner with a good salary at the telephone company. "Maurine, I remember very well, of course, but she too was gone before I was very old. LaMar Busath came courting and took me for a ride on his motorcycle and later his Model A. He and Maurine were very kind to me."

After Maurine married LaMar, next-oldest Beulah continued to help support the family by working for the gas company. Like Maurine, Beulah unselfishly brought home a large part of her paycheck to help take care of the family for years.

Duff continued, "My brother Bruce was six years older. He was an extraordinarily strong, wonderful athlete, and a good role model on the Washington School playgrounds, where there were almost no others. Nobody messed with Bruce Hanks." Bruce excelled at any sport he played, including football, basketball, baseball, boxing, swimming—even handball when he was older. In track and field he held state records in the half-mile run and in discus. "He was my hero," Duff said.[9]

The hardest person for Duff to talk about was his sister Jeannette, whom Duff described as "my angel sister, the most Christlike and least selfish human being I ever knew." In order to save the dime for train fare, "Jeannette walked each day to and from home to the Church Office Building for seventeen years, where she was secretary to the Quorum of the Twelve [Apostles]." Recalling Jeannette's many years of sacrifice, Duff said that if he hadn't insisted otherwise, she would have stayed home and never married, feeding the family until she died.[10] "Jeannette worked tirelessly for everybody else. I remember her scrubbing the floor and grating the carrots and squeezing the pulp to get the juice, which was said to be good for mother's nerves." When their brother Bruce served a full-time LDS mission, Jeannette "was his chief support, even though it meant delaying her own marriage. When it came time for me to go on a mission, there were few funds available, so Jeannette offered to delay her marriage again. I wouldn't allow it."

It was a happy day when Jeannette finally accepted her beau's marriage proposal. Apostle and lyricist Orson F. Whitney, knowing Jay Sorenson was pursuing her, wrote:

---

8. MDH-R, Nov. 8, 2000.
9. MDH-R, Nov. 8, 2000.
10. MDH-R, June 20, 2000.

Duff and his siblings: Maurine, Bruce, Maude, Jeannette, Lincoln, (unknown child), Beulah, and Duff ca. 1938.

Jeannette, hard to get.
But once she's gotten,
Someone sad will feel glad.
Though the rest will feel rotten.

The Hanks children were poor but later didn't recall being ashamed or even really conscious of it. Through all the trials they faced, the family stuck together, cheered for each other, helped each other, and prayed for each other. Every child pitched in to keep the family afloat. Far from being sad for what they lacked, they were grateful and felt blessed.

GROWING UP

Duff's neighborhood, just northwest of downtown Salt Lake City, was a mixture of extremely poor and somewhat affluent people. The most important people in the neighborhood were those who drove Union Pacific trains, which ran on tracks only a couple of blocks away.

Some of the people who lived in his part of town led difficult lives, but he never heard his mother say anything negative about them. She was full of love and good sense. Duff wrote, "She would cry with sinners and damaged innocents, but she would never condemn or hurt anyone. Not even Brother Parrot. He was not well mentally and never had been, and he bedeviled my boyhood with his strange, and threatening, and sometimes nasty ways. But whenever Mom spoke of him, she would only say, 'Poor Brother Parrot.'"

The local kids played typical neighborhood games like tag, kick the can, run sheepy run, and slips. In the winter they tied barrel stays on their shoes and skied down the neighborhood hills. They had no access to expensive boots or newly invented bindings. Candy bars were a nickel or a dime. When they weren't playing sports, Duff would play with his friends on the playground or go to ball games or church. Occasionally, they went to the movies, where ten cents bought a balcony seat.

Some of his experiences were not as mild: "We were taught some rather rough things by some big boys behind the school, and we were tough and ready to have combat with other neighborhoods, but nobody was really violent," Duff said. "Everybody knew when it came time to quit our nonsense."

Mostly Duff experienced a happy childhood in a good neighborhood.

Duff loved to read. He especially liked Charles Dickens, all of whose books he read as a boy. He described his two favorite early books as "Richard Halliburton's *Adventures Across the World*" and the book *Larry*, "which is about a 19-year-old young man from back East who came out West to work on a ranch and lost his life. The book described his thoughts and feelings and very seriously affected my life. I also loved the Bible and Book of Mormon which my mother taught us about."

Duff began to love music at an early age, listening to the few records that his mother had loved, such as those by famous Scottish singer Harry Lauder and opera star Enrico Caruso. As a boy and throughout his adulthood, he loved to sing along with the records, including one favorite, "I've written a letter to Santa Claus, and I've asked my daddy to mail it. I told him I wanted a little toy boat, and a pond where I could sail it."

Duff's favorite music was sung while sitting at the piano with his mother, who played Stephen Foster, church hymns, and patriotic songs while everyone sang together. Duff had a beautiful voice and sang heartily all his life.

Christmas and other holidays required some care and ingenuity for the family, given their lack of financial resources. They didn't have much, but Christmas was a season full of lights and homemade decorations and presents carefully saved for and wrapped. Duff's favorite holiday treat was the Scottish shortbread his Grandmother Frame made.

One Christmas Eve, Duff's brothers carried in a combined record player and radio for Maude. She was astonished and overwhelmed by the lovely music it played. Duff remembers her wearing it out over the years. She always said that was the biggest surprise of her life—she never expected to receive anything that grand. Several friends had purchased it and given it to her for Christmas.[11]

Maude was deeply interested in literature, music, and every beautiful thing. She played the piano and organ and was an expert painter. She taught her children to love poetry and good books. She kept scrapbooks of all the important things that happened in each child's life. She was an excellent cook and seamstress.

Duff's niece Jill Heyes wrote about Grandma Hanks' home in later years: "It

11. MDH-R, Nov. 21, 2000.

was warm and friendly and full of memories. Grandma was usually in the dining room. The table seemed messy, full of letters, books, papers and pens, and newspaper clippings or a vase of flowers. Now I understand why, knowing her love of literature, writing, and her children's scrapbooks."

About sixty-five years later, Duff responded to a letter he received from a childhood friend who sent him a box of apricots for Christmas. He said, "You may be interested to know that I have had an attitude toward apricots for a long time. When I was a little boy, I had a friend whose parents were wealthier than anyone else in the neighborhood, and they always had good food and goodies. I was exposed there to oranges, bananas, and candy not enjoyed in abundance at our house."

One day, Maude greeted young Duff after a lengthy absence from home and suggested that perhaps he should go and stay with his friend's family because he obviously liked it better there than his own home. Duff was shocked but not without response. Years later, Maude told him that his immediate reaction was to resist the move and declare that he just couldn't live there because their aunt, who lived with them, pronounced "ape-ricots" as "*app*-ricots." Duff's letter playfully explained, "Evidently, I said I just could not live with anybody who said *app*-ricots. These many years later, my current feeling is that I would make some sacrifice in pronunciation if I could have *ape*- or *app*-ricots like these you have sent."[12]

Duff had several dogs when he was a boy. His favorite went with him on his paper route every night, where it would engage larger dogs in barking contests and then run behind Duff's legs when the other dogs advanced. Duff learned to expertly swing his newspaper bag full of folded papers to protect his dog from some "pretty fierce beasts."

Duff's family never owned a car while he was growing up. As a kid, he and his friends would pay a dime to ride the streetcar to get around.

He later described the eleven-mile journey to Taylorsville to see his grandparents as being as challenging and full of uncertainty as it was to visit refugee camps in Asia forty years later. The first car he ever rode in was a Model A Ford that belonged to his sister Maurine's boyfriend. It was an adventure when LaMar drove them out to a park at 4800 South and Redwood Road in Taylorsville. Automobiles were new, and no one ever considered getting a driver's license. The first car he ever owned was an old Buick he bought in college.

SCHOOLTEACHERS

Duff described his elementary and junior high schools as "wonderful, with excellent teachers who were interested in us as kids" and several who became his personal tutors and mentors, remaining his friends until they died. His memories of them are colorful:

12. MDH-L Oct. 18, 1989.

Miss Bird really liked me and kept liking me until she died, and I said at her funeral that she was the best teacher I ever had because I knew she really cared about me. For years, my small triumphs were rewarded by a note or a call from her. One day, many years later, I overtook her walking on the street—we held hands, and I promised once again to speak at her funeral and say that she'd lived a happy life, because she was a teacher and had loved lots of children, especially since she had none of her own. . . .

Miss Franke scared me but liked me because I knew some answers.

Mrs. Kiser had a long bony finger and stuck it in my back when I told someone an answer in arithmetic class. She hurt me, and I swung at her, a disgraceful thing, but I did not equate telling answers with cheating in those days; I have always been on questionable grounds where justice and mercy meet.

Miss Bond, the scariest lady alive, with an upper front that looked like a tank, was the principal, and I was her pet, until I was reported riding my sleigh down the school slopes at night, contrary to the rules. She kept me after and didn't like me anymore.

Miss Dysart sprayed the front row when she talked, and she was as large as a walrus, but she was devoted, and kind. I was conscious of her funny shoes and manner, but knew she was genuine. I wiped my eyes once after she was near, and she laughed and asked if I needed an umbrella. We became friends.[13]

WARD TEACHERS

Without a father in the home, Duff and his brothers and sisters came to rely on the men who were assigned to be their ward teachers.[14] When illness struck or help was needed, they relied on these good and decent men to help the family. Duff wrote, "I have clear memories of Jeannette saying to me, 'You'd better run and get the ward teachers; mother is ill.'

"They would come, often late at night, and give mother a blessing, and that was that. There was no doctor on call; that was just the way it was done. When they were through with the blessing, I just climbed into my bed and went to sleep—everything was going to be all right now. That kind of thing was bred in us, really."[15]

THE NINETEENTH WARD

Duff had fond memories of the ward he grew up in. "The people were, as I look back, incredible," he said. One example of this was the outstanding plays and "road shows" the ward members produced. Later in his life, when he was asked to speak at one ward member's funeral, Duff noticed the man's wife sitting in the congregation looking incredibly sad.

When Duff stood to speak, he said, "Ardell, do you remember some of the plays your husband was in?"

---

13. MDH-L to family, "A Life-Sketch," Nov. 7, 1980.
14. See "ward teachers" in the Glossary of Terms.
15. MDH-R, June 27, 2000.

Duff wins the Salt Lake City marble championship, 1933.
Duff is third from left. *Courtesy Deseret News*

She brightened and said, "Yes."

Duff said, "Would you like to hear a song I grew up singing from one of those plays?"

Her face beaming, the woman answered, "Yes."

So as the funeral goers waited "with great anticipation for Michael Ballam Hanks," Duff later quipped, he drew a deep breath and sang:

> Though my real name is Reuben, they all call me Bud.
> And the reason for that is as simple as mud.
> In a garden of Reubens so handsome and tall,
> You can see I'm the handsomest Bud of them all.

"The woman just outright giggled," Duff said. "That's the kind of thing we grew up learning. It was high-quality fun."[16]

THE CITY MARBLE CHAMPIONSHIP

Duff was a natural at any sport or game he played. At Washington Elementary, he played the typical childhood neighborhood games, the sandlot team sports, skied on homemade skis in the winter, played horseshoes, did pull-ups, and played tennis. He was also an accomplished marbles player. He ended up in the finals of the Salt Lake City Marbles Championship at twelve years old.

In the final match, the judge was a young man whose little brother was playing opposite Duff. Shooting first, Duff hit the end marble, sending it out of the ring,

16. MDH-R, June 27, 2000. Michael Ballam (1951–) is a famous Latter-day Saint opera singer.

where it hit the foot of the judge, who promptly kicked it back into the ring. Everyone in attendance saw it.

Duff recalled, "So, I began to take my next shot, and the judge said, 'You're not shooting. It didn't go out of the ring.'"

Looking at the judge with absolute incredulity, Duff answered, "I saw it, you saw it, and everybody else saw it."

Duff declared, "From that point on in my life, I never got over hating unfairness."

Despite the brazen attempt at cheating him out of the victory, Duff eventually won the match and the title. On arriving home for supper, he put on an act and looked glum at the table. Everyone kept asking, "Who won?" Finally, he admitted that he had won and was the new champion.[17]

EARLY WORK AND JOE WOOD'S STORE

As Duff grew older, he was happy to help with the family's needs as his older siblings had. He did typical young boy jobs like mowing lawns and raking leaves. In junior high, he got a job working in Joe Wood's store, delivering groceries. He worked three and a half hours each weekday and fourteen hours on Saturday. Once, Duff accidentally dropped a pickle from the pickle barrel onto the sawdust-covered floor. Joe charged him five cents for it but later washed the pickle off and put it back in the barrel. "I suppose the nickel was for the sawdust getting wet," Duff said cynically.

The seventy-five cents Duff earned each week went directly to his mother. When he graduated from West Junior High at age fourteen, Maude took him to the ZCMI department store to buy him a suit. They decided on a "lovely green suit," which cost so much that Duff was sure they couldn't afford it. He tried to tell her he didn't really need that suit and would rather have a different, cheaper one. Maude could tell that wasn't so, and she bought the green suit.

"When it came time to pay, Mother took out a purse and paid cash and proudly told the lady that I had earned every cent of this money working as a delivery boy. She had saved that money in her great extremity and bought that suit for me. It was typical of Mother and her life."

One time, Maude asked Duff to run down to Joe Wood's store to get a pound of hamburger for a vegetable pie. He ordered the hamburger and reached for the dollar bill in his pocket, only to find it missing. After unsuccessfully searching the parking lot and his path all the way home, "I went around the coal shed and knelt and talked to Heavenly Father, saying: 'I can't afford to lose Mother's dollar.' I turned around, went down, and picked it up off the grass right there. I paid Joe his 15 cents and took Mother the change," Duff recalled. "I was so simple, and I still am, that if I lose something I don't give up looking for it until I ask the Lord for a little help, because that was a significant lesson for me."[18]

---

17. MDH-R, June 27, 2000.
18. MDH-R, June 27, 2000.

Maude worked far into the night after her many household chores were done and the children were safely in their beds, preparing her literary, social science, or homemaking arts lessons for Relief Society or her Gospel Doctrine lessons for Sunday School. "We learned from her that proper performance entails careful and devoted preparation," Duff said. Maude often quoted the words of Phoebe Cary's poem "Obedience":

> If you're asked to do a thing,
> And mean to do it really;
> Never let it be by halves;
> Do it fully, freely!

HONESTY

When Duff was ten or eleven, he chopped and sold wood, cutting it into kindling and filling gunny sacks. He noticed that if he piled it in the gunny sack loosely, he could fill the sack without needing as much wood. One day, Maude asked him how much he was selling the kindling for. He replied, "Thirteen sacks for a dollar."

"But they're not really getting a dollar's worth of wood, are they?" Maude responded. "Wouldn't it be better, wouldn't you feel better, if you stacked it neatly so you could fit more wood in there?"

Duff remembered, "After that, forever, I stacked it neatly."

DO IT RIGHT THE FIRST TIME

Duff's brother Bruce had cut the Carr family's lawn in the neighborhood for years, and when Bruce left on his mission, Duff inherited the job. Sister Carr would have him in for breakfast with a big plate of eggs and toast and a big glass of orange juice and insist he finish it all. Duff knew his work had to be good, so he went over the lawn in multiple directions, including diagonally, until he thought he had done a 'good enough' job. He was paid one dollar, the same as his older brother had been.

Duff wrote, "When I went by later, just to check on it, there was Brother Carr, out there, re-mowing the lawn. Gee, what awful embarrassment. I just said to myself, 'You will never have to do that again, if I have to get down on my knees and clip it all with scissors.'"

JUNIOR HIGH BASKETBALL

Duff remembered playing for a good team at West Junior High and that he was as tough or tougher than anyone he ever guarded. After injuring his ankle in the first half of one game, his coach wrapped his ankle so tight during halftime that Duff could not feel it. Then the coach "sent me out to 'do or die' for old West Junior High," he recalled. "I can't remember if I did any good or not, but I do remember not being able to feel my foot, and wondering if dying or walking on a gimpy ankle for the rest of my life was worth it. It wasn't.

"I went out and suffered for the purple and gold that night, but for decades since, I've been reminded of that night as I had to wrap my ankle before every game I've played since then—basketball, handball, racquetball, squash—high school, college, and AAU."[19][20]

THE PAPER ROUTE

To help with family expenses and begin saving for his mission, Duff had an extensive paper route of more than two hundred papers. He picked up his papers on Salt Lake City's North Temple and Main Street, then delivered them all over Capitol Hill. Duff carried them every day, beginning in junior high and continuing all the way through high school.

Despite being an excellent athlete, Duff was often unavailable to play in games because the family needed the money he was making. He recalled one incident when the man who coached both football and baseball stopped him in the hall and said, "They tell me you can hit the ball farther than Skillicorn, who is our best batter, and that you were a quarterback playing up on the Capitol grounds. I'm told you could have helped our teams, but you are always too occupied to do it."

"Coach Ryan," Duff replied, "Do you know what I'm doing? I'm delivering papers every night. I can get away with playing one sport [basketball], but I can't lose my job. I'd very much like to play, but I have to work."

Duff didn't tell him that if he didn't carry that paper route, "our family would have been in trouble financially. So, I never got to play [baseball or football] in school."[21]

MISCHIEF AND MEMORIES

Duff got good marks in school, but he wasn't always a perfect angel. On occasion, he and his friends would break into the Washington School to play. "We'd all go in and play 'slips' up and down those corridors and climb up on the big pipes that heated that big old school," he said. "'Slips' is like 'hide and seek,' and it was a mark of honor to be able to slip away and hide and evade [the others]. It became a test of speed, will, and intrigue. Mom never got after us. But she didn't really know we were up there."

Duff also recalled climbing an apple tree in the yard of Judge Johnson, who was known as a very difficult man for boys to deal with. Duff said, "I didn't mind so much his turning the hose on me while I was in the tree, because it was summer. However, when he kept up a steady, forceful stream, it did unnerve me slightly to the point where I almost dropped out of some higher limbs, which could have caused serious consequences, I suppose."[22]

In his reminiscing, Duff described the occasional "watermelon-swiping trips"

19. MDH-R, Nov. 8, 2000.
20. The Amateur Athletic Union is an amateur sports organization based in the United States.
21. MDH-R, Nov. 21, 2000.
22. MDH-L Feb. 13, 1991.

he and his friends took to Bountiful. He wrote, "For some reason my callow morality didn't think of it as stealing to purloin a farmer's produce from his field."

Another memory involved his older brother Bruce.

Bruce and Duff would play sandlot football against neighboring playground teams on the grounds of the state capitol, where they always won. Once, when he and Bruce were cutting their family's lawn and cleaning up the yard, Duff began to leave to go play football after doing what he thought was more than his fair share.

"Where do you think you're going?" Bruce said. "We're not through here yet."

"I am," Duff retorted, which led Bruce to come over to "torment" Duff. Duff picked up the rake, and "let him have it right across the top of his head, and the blood began spurting," Duff said. "I had to call a cab and take him to the doctor."

In spite of occasional squabbles like these, Bruce was a doting big brother to Duff. He got a job working at a gas station and would go to sleep early, purposely leaving the key to his old Ford V-8 where the underage Duff could find it. Duff wrote, "So, I took it up Wall Street, starting down at Victory. I'd start there, and go up that hill, shifting from low to second, and I'd be going about 60 miles an hour by the time I shifted again. That's where I learned how to drive a car."[23]

Duff remembered another funny incident when his bishop gathered all the boys in a room after somebody stole a big cake intended for a ward party. The bishop went around the room, asking each boy, 'Was it you? Was it you?' Duff wrote, "I was scared of him anyway, and by the time he got to me, I blurted out, 'I'm not going to tell on Blaine!' This was unfortunate because Blaine 'Dope' Openshaw beat everybody up, and he had actually stolen the cake."

"MARION"

Duff was named after his grandfather Francis Marion Lyman. But even back in the 1920s and '30s, Marion was not a very playground-safe name. He had the opportunity to defend it many times.

People in Duff's neighborhood "on the west side," were pretty tough, Duff said, "and if your name was Marion and you played the violin, you had to plan on a little action. The fact that my nose isn't more flattened than it is seems strange, because I was a little bit pugnacious."[24]

When Duff was twelve, he went on his first Scout hike to Lake Blanche, in Big Cottonwood Canyon east of the Salt Lake Valley. Preparing to go, his bishop had the boys lay out their overnight gear on the church driveway for inspection. By the time the bishop got to Duff and his homemade gear at the end of the line, he was frustrated with what the boys had brought. (One boy's mother, for instance, had sent him with four sheets folded neatly in squares, one for each day.) Inspecting Duff's items, including some sticks to hold up a tent, the bishop mockingly mimicked the way Duff's mother called him home for supper each night, saying

23. MDH-R, Nov. 8, 2000.
24. MDH-R, Nov. 8, 2000.

loudly, "Maaayyrrriooon, there are plenty of sticks where we are going." Everyone laughed, and the bishop walked away. Duff climbed over the wall to his house and sat down behind the coal shed, waiting for them all to leave.

In a few minutes, the bishop left the other boys to find him. Sitting down by him, he began asking questions about their makeshift basketball court. "Where do you shoot from?" "How many can you hit out of ten, shooting from there?" "How many can your big brother make?"

Eventually the bishop paused and, placing his big hand on Duff's knee, said, "Son, I made a bad mistake back there, and I'm sorry."

"That's OK, bishop," Duff answered.

"You know, the boys are all loaded up on that truck," the bishop said. "They're waiting. I've got them ready; nobody will wise-crack you, and I've apologized in front of them. They understand it was my mistake and your reaction was not inappropriate—and anyway, you didn't name yourself. Are you ready to go now?"

"Yes, sir," Duff answered.

He and the bishop rolled up Duff's pack "and off we went," Duff would later recall, "walking right past the back door where Mother didn't open the screen door, but bade us farewell with a smile. That bishop was typical of the quality of folks that lived in the old 19th Ward. He was a big man, top priesthood leader in the ward, and a successful fellow who lived in a big house. But all those things paled in comparison with the fact that he made that walk and apologized to a stubborn little twelve-year-old."[25]

Years passed. When Duff went to visit a stake priesthood meeting as a church general authority, there at the back sat Bishop LeCheminant. Duff had him come up to the front, related the story, and the two of them wept together.

While most of his family continued to call him Marion, sometime in his teenage years he transitioned to being called Duff.

GRANDMOTHER FRAME

Among other truths her children learned from Maude was a firsthand lesson in honoring one's parents. She truly honored her mother, Helen, in health and in sickness, in happiness and in trying circumstances.

Helen was always a part of their lives and remained Scottish through and through, right up to her ninety-third year. When suitors would come home with her granddaughters, she would summon them over to her where she would feel the cloth of their trousers and coat and then pronounce what material it was to everyone in the room.

On December 20, 1938, Duff was in the kitchen after school when he heard his mother cry out. While being honored by the Daughters of Utah Pioneers at a party in their front room, Grandmother Frame had collapsed. Duff carried her

25. MDH-R, June 20, 2000.

into the bedroom, where this grand old pioneer lady, Helen Duff Dick Frame, died in his arms.

"I'M WAITING FOR YOU"

Duff cherished his mother, and she loved Duff dearly. One night while he was attending college and still living at home, he returned just past midnight to find Maude's bedroom still bright. Duff went into her room and, sitting on her bed, jokingly chastised her a little for staying up so late.

"What are you doing with your light still on at this hour?"

"I'm waiting for you," she said.

"Oh," Duff replied, "and did you wait up for me every night while I was on a mission or in the South Pacific in the war?"

"'No," she said, "that wasn't possible. No, I just got on my knees and told the Lord how I felt about you, the kind of man you are, and my dreams and aspirations for you. I asked Him to preserve you from evil and to help you do your duty for your country courageously. Then I left you in His hands and went to sleep."

Duff kissed her, bade her goodnight, "and went to my own quiet place and to my knees and gave thanks to God for such a mother."[26]

26. MDH-A, *Gifts from a Mother* (Salt Lake City: Deseret Book, 1978), 1–3, 6, 10–13.

3

West High School

My own self, at my very best, all the time!
—Marion D. Hanks[1]

The Great Depression was vicious. Jeannette was supporting the entire family financially, including Bruce on his mission. Others were trying to help a little bit. Duff had to keep going with his paper route. He was making more than some grown men were.

Duff delivered two hundred newspapers each night until he went to college. Because of their shorter seasons, basketball and some tennis were the only sports he could play and keep up with his paper deliveries. He had to quit baseball, probably his best sport, because he couldn't find a dependable boy to carry the papers until he could run home after practice and finish the second half of the deliveries. When he quit, the coach said he'd let the team down, and the other players were angry. No one really understood, and Duff chose not to tell anyone about it. Basketball worked out better, and Duff was a star athlete by the time he hit his senior year. He also had a few other extracurricular activities: "I was elected editor of the West High School newspaper, the *Red and Black*. I also ran (unsuccessfully) for president of the school. I bought my own clothes. I had a nice sport jacket and trousers. I found out later that they all thought I was a little rich boy, because I was a good ballplayer and a leader."

One night, he was delivering papers when he ran around a corner into a group of what he described as the prettiest "top-notch" girls in the school. He wrote, "The look on their faces was one of absolute astonishment—Duff Hanks . . . is . . . a paperboy!?'"

For just a second, Duff wondered if he or they were going to be embarrassed by discovering his modest profession. Without thinking much further, Duff grabbed a newspaper, folded it into a square, and said, "Just watch this." He wound up and let it sail beautifully, landing right in the middle of a porch. Grinning, Duff bowed and said, "You'll never see that again unless you follow me," and ran off to the next house, throwing papers and chuckling out loud. "I was not

1. MDH-A, college composition book, 1941, in author's possession.

embarrassed, ashamed, or worried about what they would think," Duff said. "It was one of the times in my life where I was proud of the way I reacted, and it was on Center Street, facing those classy girls."

One of the girls in the group was Dorothy Davis, who was not of Duff's faith. When he saw her approaching in the school hallway the next day, he shyly ducked into the restroom. When the class bell eventually rang, he had to reappear, only to find Dorothy waiting there to ask him to the upcoming Girls' Dance. She said, "We all thought you were a rich family's son," she said, "and when we saw what you were doing and how well you did it and listened to you laugh all the way up the street—well, you will always have our respect."[2]

They had a fine time at the dance but no further dates. She went away to one college and Duff to another. Many years later, one of Duff's fellow general authorities returned from a stake conference in Los Angeles with a message from a woman in the congregation named Dorothy. "Please tell Duff," she said, "that I am now a member of the church, and I am a Relief Society president here, and I remember our friendship with joy."

HIGH SCHOOL BASKETBALL

Duff played on a championship West High basketball team. Their coach proclaimed it the best team in West High history. The team won every league game soundly, beating both their rivals, East High and South High, twice. They even journeyed to Ely, Nevada (the farthest Duff had ever traveled from home), where they handed the local high school two successive defeats. His West High team also defeated Westminster College and Henager Business College in Salt Lake.

One of Duff's favorite memories of high school basketball involved his mild-mannered coach, Bert Ballard and the rival coach at East High, Mickey Oswald. Oswald coached both football and basketball at East and was not a loser. One newspaper declared "he would beat the whey out of West High over a number of years."

Coach Ballard was gentle in nature, never yelled, and was always calm. But during one game with East High, West was finally ahead of East at halftime when Bert strolled into the locker room with something to say.

"That Mickey Oswald has been handing it to me year after year after year," Bert began, softly. "I've never had players before that could beat him," he said, then started building to a crescendo. But "now we're ahead—and we're going to win! You're going to beat the hell out of them! I want you to go out there and pour it on! Pour it on! POUR IT ON!"

"It was so unlike Bert Ballard," Duff said, "so we poured it on and won big."[3]

Another story from his high school basketball days was unknown to Duff until more than fifty years later, when he received a letter from a former classmate.

2. MDH-R, June 27, 2000.
3. MDH-R, Nov. 25, 2003.

Shooting a layup for West High Panthers, ca. 1939.

"I didn't try out for the West High team because I was too short," the classmate wrote. "My friend, Ralph, kept telling me to reach high for the backboard during a layup, rather than shooting directly from the floor. But I saw little value in it.

"One night, Ralph and I went to watch our varsity team play, and during warmups, Ralph told me to watch one particular player when he went for the hoop. He reached very high for the backboard on every shot and seemed to stretch far more than any other players.

"'Who is he?' I asked.

"'His name is Marion Hanks.'

"We watched him the rest of the game, giving his all with every shot and scoring effectively. Ralph chided me, 'With your height, that's how you should be doing it.' I did, and my game improved."[4]

TEACHERS

Duff remembered his high school teachers fondly, particularly two who had a significant effect on him. Jennie Thomas was the advisor for the *Red and Black* school paper. She loved her students, was personally interested in them, was an expert in her craft, and taught her students how to fulfill the duties of a high school newspaper staff. In Duff's yearbook, she wrote that she thought he had a gift for writing and that "whatever else [he] was going to do—write!"

4. Kent Donaldson to MDH, 1999.

Jennie spoke at Duff's mission farewell, an unusual thing for a high school teacher. "She influenced the day, the month, the years, and my entire life!" Duff said of her.

Duff's most influential teacher was Georgia Young, who taught English and literature at West High. "I never had a better or an equal of her," he said. "She was the cynosure and the high point of teaching—a dogged little soul, I'm sure she was not more than five feet tall—trying to impress us with the beauty and joy of Shakespeare."[5]

One of Duff's most important lessons came from Miss Young, who previously taught each of his brothers and sisters at West High. During his senior year, Duff's scholastic record and sports participation qualified him for consideration for a special athletic award at graduation, including a medal and a watch. On the final day of school, he went from class to class collecting the grades that would make a vital difference in his chances. After receiving an A in each class, he was sure he'd get a similar grade in Miss Young's as well, since he had been getting A's in her class all year.

But when he received his report card from Miss Young, Duff stared at it in disbelief. In the space alongside the English literature class was an E, a failing mark—with Georgia Young's signature next to it.

After the other students were gone, Duff approached her. She didn't raise her eyes when Duff laid his report card in front of her and said, "You have made a mistake."

She looked at the card and said, "You're right. I have made a mistake." She took the card, superimposed a large C over the E, and handed it back. "You don't deserve an 'E,'" she said. "That might keep you from graduating. So, I will give you a 'C.'"

"Miss Young," Duff pleaded, 'how can you do this to me? I have scored high on every test, and I am sure that in comparison with the other students I deserve an 'A.'"

"Yes," she replied, "you have done well on the tests and in the class. You came here well equipped to sail through this class, in part, no doubt, because of your wonderful mother's love of literature. You had already read much of what we have been studying. If I were marking you in comparison with all the other students, I would probably give you an 'A.' But I am not marking on that basis.

"I think you have not been fair with me," she continued. "Many times, you have been absent to prepare for ball games, and you have excused yourself because you thought the ball game was more important. You have not been conscientious in your responsibilities in this class. So, I am not grading you in comparison with all the other students. I am grading you based on what you could have done. You get a 'C.'"

Sobered and ashamed, Duff responded, "Miss Young, do you understand what this will do to me?" He had in mind losing the athletic award. She replied, her face pained but determined, "Yes, I know what this will do to you. I would

5. MDH-R, Nov. 21, 2000.

like you to know that I love you and have great hopes for your future and that I have been up all night thinking about this decision. You get a 'C'."

"Thank you, Miss Young," Duff said quietly and went his way. He did not receive the medal or the watch, and his name was not engraved on the plaque.

"I lived long enough to stand with a group of retired schoolteachers and recall this incident," Duff said many years later. "Sitting there among them was Georgia Young. I told our story, and I said at the end, 'I am glad I lived long enough to face Georgia Young and tell her, in the presence of her respectful peers, that the most important lesson I ever learned in school was the one she taught me that spring day. In the eyes of God and wise men, none of us will be judged in comparison with what others do with their time, talents, and opportunities; we will find our judgment with what we could have and should have done with ours.'

"As a teacher myself I have never had far from my mind and heart that incident in fifth-period English literature at West High School. I see clearly in my mind's eye that doughty little soul agonizing through the night making her decision with an eye to the future of a student she loved and cared about too much not to require his best."[6]

STIRRINGS OF PHILOSOPHY

Even as a youth, Duff was a philosopher—thinking and writing like a grown man. Here are two paragraphs from his handwritten journal he wrote at age seventeen, titled "Journal of My Trip to Lake Steiner Boy Scout Camp, as Leader of Troop 59, Salt Lake Council, 19th LDS Ward."

> Monday afternoon further advanced my attitude of disgust and blueness. After dinner, Sterl [Sterling Paul] and I went row-boating and then decided to hike to the nearest cliffs. We started the ascent immediately, hitting a fast pace all the way up. The higher we climbed, the lighter became the load on my troubled brain. By the time the crest of the hill had been gained, my blueness was gone, and an all-encompassing feeling of exhilaration existed in its stead. Never in my life has such a complete transformation occurred to me. My new feeling might be best described as happiness and restful contentment. It now seems silly to have felt as I did, but the lesson gained thereof is invaluable to me.
>
> My moral to the experience is this: When in the darkest hours of despair and unhappiness you are submerged, climb upwards on the rocks and hills of difficulty and hard work until you reach the peaks of clear and sane thinking, where, if you are sensible and wise, you can gain new wisdom and invaluable courage![7]

BEING TRUE

In 1994, Duff received a letter from a fellow Nineteenth Ward friend who also went to West High. "One day walking home from school fifty-seven years

6. MDH-A, "No Watch, No Medal, No Plaque," *Ensign*, June 1989, 68–71.
7. MDH-JE, July 22, 1939.

ago," wrote the friend, "I was with Aileen, and you were with three boys. One of the boys stumbled on the sidewalk and turned the air blue with his swearing. You made no comment, just turned, and walked away.

"The swearing boy cried out, 'Where's Duff going?' One of the other boys spoke up, saying, 'When are you going to realize you're going to have to clean up your mouth if you want Duff for a friend?'"

She continued, "You had decided what and who you would be. To be true to yourself and your Maker. To stand for what you believed in."[8]

GRADUATION

Graduation was traumatic. West High had the state champion debaters, but Duff had been unable to participate due to time constraints. As graduation approached in 1939, rumors around the school suggested that the graduation speakers had been pre-selected from among the debaters, before the tryouts even began. Duff detested cheaters and bullies of all kinds, so he went to the tryout and gave a preamble to his prepared speech, putting them all on notice that he didn't like cheaters. He then gave his prepared speech.

Duff was chosen as one of the speakers.

Looking back with the hindsight of decades, he said that the words of his graduation speech were presumptuous, but true. "Over the turbulent waters of the seas of democracy tonight," he declared, "there hover dark and threatening clouds." World War II was soon upon them, and many of Duff's friends in attendance at graduation would lose their lives in the conflict.

For graduation night, Duff borrowed a car from a friend, Ted DeBry, who had just had a gas station mechanic tune his car and change the oil. Duff and three others drove about sixty miles that night, first to the Saltair Resort on the Great Salt Lake, then north to Lagoon Amusement Park. The next day, the mechanic visited Duff with Ted, accusing Duff of burning up a full load of oil in one night and ruining the engine.

"The mechanic tried to get me to admit to some recklessness," Duff wrote, so he could blame me for somehow burning up six quarts of oil he'd [failed to replace] the day before. Ted didn't have the courage to face him down and didn't know his left foot from an oil stick." The mechanic "started out with a little mistake and was willing to make a bigger one at [my] innocent expense," Duff said. But then Duff's big brother Bruce showed up. "Bruce *did* know an oil stick from his left foot and was big enough to make his argument impressive. He quietly explained to the [mechanic] how things go in this world when threats and bullying do not stack up against facts." With Bruce's help, the gas station replaced Ted's engine.

Duff never forgot that experience. "I've taken on bullies every time," he later said. "I never felt all that brave, but I have hated bullies since birth. I have never bullied, not on the streets, not on a court, not in or out of the Church. I know

8. Adell Grimstad Call to MDH, July 11, 1994.

that hating is a sin. I am a sinner. I hate bullies. I understand some of them, but I don't like them—in a Brooks Brothers suit or sneakers."[9]

In the 1930s, formal education lasted eleven years. Because of the lack of employment opportunities during the Depression, graduating students were given an option to go back to high school for a third year. Duff stayed and used the extra year to his advantage in both athletics and in the LDS seminary program, where he served as the seminary president.

SCHOLARSHIP RECIPIENT

On September 29, 1939, the *Red and Black* newspaper announced, "The first journalism scholarship ever to be awarded in Salt Lake City was presented to Marion D. Hanks, a former student of West High." The twenty-five-dollar scholarship to the University of Utah was given by West High for his outstanding work in "the journalism department." Duff had originally hoped to attend Brigham Young University, studying under English Professor Harrison R. Merrill, who published hundreds of articles, stories, essays, and poems in magazines and newspapers and whose writing Duff loved. But after Professor Merrill died in the summer of 1938, Duff redirected himself to the University of Utah.[10]

9. MDH-L to family, "A Life-Sketch," Nov. 7, 1980.

10. In August 2012, Duff was posthumously inducted into the West High School Hall of Fame.

4

University of Utah

An acquaintance of Duff's family offered to pay for his schooling at Harvard along with that of his own son, Bob, if Duff decided to go there. That would have changed Duff's life forever, but after considering such a generous offer, he couldn't accept it. "Bob had gone with me to seminary, and that, plus Brother Judd's appreciation for my father, motivated this good man to offer me the big chance, but I couldn't accept because of my commitment to caring for my mother. I went to the University of Utah and did well enough."

Girls played only a small part in his pre-mission life. When he did date, Janet Booth and Elaine Anderson (later Cannon)[1] were the two girls he saw the most. "I had little money and little interest and didn't give it much energy," he explained.[2]

CLASSES

College courses were challenging, especially the two in which Duff was the only freshman: Shakespeare, and Greek and Latin vocabulary. Duff said, "I learned my 50 Shakespeare lines after work and practiced my words every spare minute. I got honors marks in both classes and decided I would never let words lead me around again." Even though Duff had the vocabulary to potentially dazzle and impress others, he made a conscious decision *not* to do so. He wrote, "Let others impress and confuse—I'll try and use what is understood. I remembered what was said about a columnist of the time, that he was 'Captured by his own cuteness.' I've always remembered that."

THE UNIVERSITY OF UTAH FRESHMAN AND SOPHOMORE TEAMS

Duff made the basketball team at the University of Utah his freshman and sophomore years. He said his chief asset was being able to jump really high. In one game, his team was winning, and so the opposing team sent in a big guy who knocked Duff about into the sixth row of the bleachers. "They sent him in to neutralize me," he said. "I took that as a compliment."

In a speech Duff gave years later at BYU, he reminisced about his Utah days playing in Provo: "I do love BYU, but when I visited here as a participating athlete,

1. Elaine Anderson Cannon later served as general president of the church's Young Women program from 1978 to 1984.

2. MDH-L to family, "A Life-Sketch," Nov. 7, 1980.

I did my best to ruin your reputation—and succeeded. I know what it means to play basketball in the old [Women's] Gym. Driving for a layup there took more courage than loading up the twin-forty guns during the war."[3]

Duff's coach was the famous Vadal Peterson, who from 1927 to 1953 recorded the most wins in University of Utah basketball history and led the "U" to its only NCAA tournament title in 1944 and the NIT crown in 1947. Peterson told the press Duff was the best prospect he'd had in years.[4]

But after a year and half on the team, Duff disappointed his coach when he told him he was leaving the team to serve a mission.

Furious, Peterson grabbed Duff by the shoulder strap and exclaimed, "You don't want to win bad enough!"

"Yeah, I don't think I want to win as bad as you, coach," Duff said, then walked away and never looked back. "But we stayed friends over the years."[5]

JOBS IN COLLEGE

College life was a huge challenge for Duff, partly because, in addition to his classes, he had to work two jobs to help support his family and keep alive his dream of paying for a full-time mission. He was also serving as president of the "M-Men" (young men's organization) of his stake.[6] He would leave for the university at 7:30 in the morning, attend classes until noon, then run for the streetcar that took him downtown to the Brooks Arcade Building on State Street and Third South, where he worked repairing vacuums for the Hoover Company. Duff wrote about one work experience that stood out to him as an especially important glimpse of how a good man and leader behaves.

During Duff's first hour on the job, the shop manager came out of his office, and took off his business jacket to demonstrate how to polish the synthetic, plastic-like cover of a vacuum's motor.[7] He turned on the powerful buffing wheel, put some compound on it, grasped the cover in his big hands, "and buffed it into shiny beauty," Duff said. "Then he cautioned me for a moment about catching a sharp edge on the wheel, explaining that the wheel was very powerful and that I should wear protective goggles and be cautious."

The manager went back to his office. Duff turned to the wheel, applied the compound, forgot the glasses, then brought an unpolished top to the wheel. "The wheel accepted it quickly, tore it from my too tenuous grasp, turned it into a flying mass of tiny sharp parts, and spit it back in my face," Duff said. "I went to the sink, washed the blood away from many small cuts, checked my eyesight, clenched my teeth, and headed back to the wheel."

3. MDH-T, "Welcome to BYU," BYU, Sept. 25, 1969, pp. 8–9.

4. "Vadal Peterson, Ex-Coach, Dies," *Deseret News,* Sept. 2, 1976.

5. MDH-R, Dec. 10, 1988.

6. The M-Men and Gleaners were the church's educational and social programs for, respectively, young men and young women ages eighteen to thirty. These programs were discontinued in 1974.

7. Bakelite was an expensive, brittle, and hard-to-repair plastic, rarely used anymore.

The manager came out of his office, checked Duff's wounds to assure there was no serious damage, then, saying nothing, took off his jacket, put compound on the wheel, picked up another unpolished top, grasped it strongly in his big hands, and burnished it to shiny brilliance. He then picked up his coat and walked back into his office. "He didn't say one word about my first performance, then or ever," Duff said. "I went back and began to buff tops and do the work." In the many months Duff worked at the shop before his mission, he did not lose another top.[8] Duff remembered his manager's lesson for the rest of his life—that he could be trusted and could acquire competence in his work.

From the Hoover Company, Duff walked five blocks to the old Deseret Gym, where he would shower and eat a sandwich that his mother Maude had made for him. He'd then walk down to Fifth South and State to the Rainbow Randevu Dance Hall, where he chipped ice and prepared food from 7:00 to 9:00 p.m., at which time he began to serve the guests who came to drink and dance.

Duff worked behind the counter as the college crowd danced away the evening. Many of the best bands in the country performed at the Rainbow. At 11:00 p.m., Duff would trade his white apron for a jacket and become a bouncer. He circulated in the table area, witnessing displays of lewd behavior, drunken vomiting, and a lot of fighting, and getting a first-rate object lesson on the horrible effects of liquor. At 1:00 a.m. he would finally walk home, memorizing another fifty lines of Shakespeare by streetlight. After catching a little sleep, he'd head to school again at 7:30 in the morning.

In the summers, Duff took the streetcar to the Saltair Resort, on the shores of the Great Salt Lake, which had the largest open-air dance hall in the world. There he ran a big soda fountain.

PEARL HARBOR

On December 7, 1941, Japan bombed Pearl Harbor, thrusting America into World War II. Duff was a student at the University of Utah working on a degree in English and history. The bombing was a great shock to Duff and his friends, who knew they would most likely be called up to serve in the war.

"We were shocked and angry and a bit grim about our own individual prospects," Duff remembered, "but I heard no conversation that would suggest anything but a total commitment to defending our country against an enemy who had delivered a cowardly blow to our military forces and to our safety."[9]

ENLISTMENT OR MISSION?

Partway into his second year of college, Duff thought seriously about whether he could serve an LDS mission. He didn't want his full-time service to cause his sister Jeannette to delay her marriage again to help support him. And Jeannette's

8. BUW, 103–4.
9. MDH, oral history interview with Mindy Clawson, Mar. 17, 1989.

fiancé, Jay Sorenson, had already been waiting patiently for years. The situation was a terrible dilemma for Duff, who had wanted to go on a mission since he was a child. Ultimately, he decided to do what he thought would be in Jeannette's best interest. He told his family he was going to enlist with the US Naval Air Force.

Duff recalled, "I said to my sister, 'I won't go on this mission if you aren't going to get married.' I had figured it all out. 'I'll make enough money in the Navy and send it all home, so if you and Jay are willing to get married and live with Mom, I'll go. I didn't know if I'd still be alive to help Mom anyway. It was the only way I knew to make sure that Mother would be taken care of, and that Jeannette would do what she should do."

Things didn't work out that way. By the time Duff tried to enlist, the Naval Air Force had temporarily quit enlisting, so Duff went to the Army Air Force recruiters, but they had stopped taking people in also.[10] While Duff waited for enlistments to open again, the family got together and determined that with Duff's savings, and with Lincoln, Maurine, Beulah, and Bruce each helping a bit, Jeannette could get married, and then she and Jay could live with Maude and take care of her.[11]

It was decided. Duff would go on his mission.

10. The surge in post-Pearl Harbor enlistment was so great that the government began limiting voluntary enlistment. This was to ensure that the industrial workforce that produced raw materials needed for war would not be compromised.

11. MDH-R, Dec. 10, 1988.

CHALLENGE AND TRIUMPH

5

Serving a Mission

Behold, I am a disciple of Jesus Christ, the Son of God. I have been called of him to declare his word among his people, that they might have everlasting life.
—3 Nephi 5:13

Duff was called to serve in what was then called the Northern States Mission, which included all the Great Lakes states and Iowa.

"I had a great missionary experience," Duff would later say of his mission. "We were not disposed to believe we could change the world, or the mission, but we had a mission president who was forward-looking and liberal in his views and was a great speaker who would wind people around [his] gnarled old fingers."[1]

PREPARATION

Duff had prepared all his life to serve a mission. He was initially reluctant to go because he feared his sister Jeannette would delay her marriage again in order to provide financial support while he was gone. But in terms of his own desire to serve, there was no ambivalence. He had saved much of the money himself, and with some help from his family he was able to go.

In preparation, he marched down to a clothing store, holding tightly to five twenty-dollar bills wadded together in his pocket. The hundred dollars represented a new suit and overcoat he would wear on his mission. Duff was startled when a man stepped in front of him and stretched out his hand. It was Anthon Alrich, an old friend of Duff's father and a fellow church member.

When Alrich asked where Duff was headed, he replied that he was going on a mission and was on his way to buy a suit. Brother Alrich invited Duff to go with him into the more expensive store across the street. Entering the store, Alrich insisted that Stanley Hanks' son was to have the best quality. Knowing that Brother Alrich didn't have much money, Duff protested, but Alrich seemed so pleased and anxious to buy Duff a suit that he finally relented and gratefully thanked him.

Brother Alrich said to him, "Let me tell you why this privilege means so much to me. I came to this country as an immigrant boy of fourteen. I didn't speak

1. MDH-R, May 1, 2001.

English, had no money, no job, and no friends. Someone sent me to Stanley Hanks, saying, 'He takes in strays.' Your father found me a job, brought blankets so I could sleep on a couch in his office, and brought food for me until I could buy my own. I have been waiting a long time to tell that story to Stanley Hanks' son and share a little of the bread your sainted father cast upon the waters for me many, many years ago."[2]

Duff wore that suit and coat for years after his mission.

FAREWELL

Duff's missionary farewell was held on February 22, 1942, in the 19th Ward chapel, next to his home where he had grown up and learned to love the Lord. His program included talks by his former bishop Eli LeCheminant, his high school teacher Jennie Thomas, and his LDS Institute teacher and future colleague Lowell Bennion. Duff spoke of his testimony, his mission preparation and love for God, and his beloved mother.

In one of his first letters home from his mission, Duff would write to her: "I meant to say something about my father at my farewell, but I couldn't for fear of breaking down. But I want you to know that if I knew nothing else about him, if I didn't know what an honest, courageous, great man he was, the fact that *you chose him* would be enough to qualify him for any honor that I might pay him."[3]

CINCINNATI, OHIO

Duff vividly remembered arriving at his mission headquarters in Chicago. At that point in his life, he had only seen Salt Lake City, Logan, and Ely, Nevada. He had never seen anything like the big city of Chicago. Once there, he met with his mission president, Leo J. Muir, and was immediately assigned to work in Cincinnati, Ohio.

The beginning of his mission was difficult. "I knew how to study, to teach, and to work, and that saved me," Duff said. "I didn't know how to be regimented or how to be lazy. I didn't know how to put in an apprenticeship as a junior missionary until some pompous senior leader decided I knew enough to do the job. My first supervising missionary was just like my first seminary teacher, a weak man who pretended to be something he wasn't. I defied him and his need to play Napoleon. Finally, I just went out alone [to find people to teach]."

Duff was able to go back to Cincinnati more than forty-five years later and dedicate its second stake center. While there he was invited to a special meeting with people who remembered him. In attendance were more than a hundred people, not only those who had known him as a missionary, but also their descendants. The then current stake Relief Society president had been a seventeen-year-old girl who was baptized with her mother while Duff was a young missionary. When

2. NF, 17–19.
3. MDH-L to Maude Hanks, ca. 1942.

Farewell Testimonial
in honor of

Elder Marion Duff Hanks
Prior to his departure to the
NORTHERN STATES MISSION
Sunday, February 22, 1942
NINETEENTH WARD CHAPEL
172 West 4th North
VOLUNTARY CONTRIBUTIONS

Duff's mission farewell program, 1942.

he had served as a young man, there had only been a little branch that met in a rented room of the YMCA. Now there were two full stakes, as well as others in the surrounding area.

Duff felt a deep love for Cincinnati and his recollections of life there as a new missionary. He later wrote that he had "never known more generous or loving or devoted Latter-day Saints than the members of the Cincinnati Branch."[4]

THE MAN FROM HAMILTON, OHIO

One day, Duff and his companion were on their way home, waiting for a streetcar transfer with no money in their pockets. As they stood there, they noticed a man walking hesitantly toward them, looking hungry and cold. Duff's first thought was that there was no way to help him because they had no money. But

4. Stanley Fish, Bradley J. Kramer, and Wm. Budge Wallis, *History of the Mormon Church in Cincinnati (1830–1985),* (self-published, 1997), 70.

he approached the man anyway and said, "I sense that you need help, but I have to tell you that we are missionaries, and we have no money."

Immediately apologetic, the man backed away, saying, "I didn't know that. I wouldn't ask missionaries for anything. Please forgive me. I live fifty miles away, in Hamilton, Ohio. I lost my job and came here this morning trying to find work. I have no way to get home. I have not eaten, and I don't have any money to call my family. I know my wife and children will be worrying and afraid."

Duff replied, "We cannot leave you here. We're not far from where we live. Please get on the streetcar with my companion and use my transfer. I won't be much longer than you getting there." Duff pressed the transfer into the man's hand and took off running. It wasn't a big speech. It was a young man's guileless expression of what he had learned all his life in a widowed mother's home.

Running fast, Duff got home a little ahead of his missionary companion and the man, and prepared some bread and stew. The missionaries' landlady had a room where their new friend could spend the night, and he was able to call home to his family in Hamilton.

The next morning, Duff called the local branch president, "a wonderful, gracious, Christlike man who built and refurbished homes," and told him the story.

"He can have a job starting this morning," President Gilliam replied.

Gilliam provided a place for the man to stay, "and soon, a place for his family, and he was on his way up," Duff later said. "I have nurtured in my heart for more than forty-five years a blessing I would have missed had we not helped this man."[5]

THE "UNSAVING"

One of Duff's earliest assignments was to some little villages in rural Ohio and Kentucky, where conditions were rudimentary at best. People lived in hovels, wore ragtag clothing, and had their own culture of music, food, and entertainment. They were also incredibly generous and full of faith.

One day a letter came to Duff in Cincinnati from a village named Georgetown, saying that a crisis had occurred in a family quite isolated from their Latter-day Saint congregation. One of the sisters in the family wrote in anguish to report that a "holiness preacher" had come through the week before and "saved" two of her sisters. She requested that the missionaries come right away and "unsave" them.

Reaching the family would require a bus ride and a long walk through the countryside. Duff's companion was nearing the end of his mission and didn't feel like making the journey, in a rainstorm, in the middle of the night. "Nonetheless, I felt obliged to go," Duff said, "and he was obliged to accompany me."

After the bus dropped them off, they began their trek into the hills, walking in the rain and mush all night until they arrived at the home at dawn. There, the father dried them off, wrapped them in blankets by candlelight, and escorted

5. BUW, 13–14.

them to a bed that had obviously been slept in by the man and his wife until just moments before. The missionaries resisted. The good folks insisted.

Snuffing out the candle, they sank exhausted into the still warm bed. Only seconds passed before Duff's companion spoke the horrible words in the dark, "Do you feel them?"

"Yes, I feel them!" Duff replied.

The two missionaries fumbled for a match, lit the candle, and beheld "a multitude of crawly, flat creatures—bedbugs—which had already begun to engorge themselves on our hides," recalled Duff. Tired as the missionaries were, they could not stand to stay in the bed, "coming from a spoiled generation of clean beds, bedsheets, and punctilious mothers." They "shook the blankets to death" and then Duff slumped on an end table against a wall, and his companion accepted the only chair with the other well-shaken blanket. After a restless couple of hours, the missionaries answered the call to breakfast, where "all was made well by a platter full of solid-grease pork, solid-grease eggs, solid-grease grits, then lathered by a little hot grease to tie it all together."

By candlelight later that night, Duff and his companion "preached the gospel of repentance and love," completed the "unsaving" of those who had strayed from their faith, and established the beginning of a relationship with others, including their host, who later became the first stake clerk of the new Cincinnati Stake of Zion.[6]

YMCA CAMP

Full-time missionary work was far less structured in the early part of the twentieth century than it is today. Athletic teams, music groups, and community volunteering were often used to try and introduce the missionaries in the cities they served. In that vein, Duff was assigned for a few weeks to serve as a camp director at YMCA Camp Mecham in Mentor, Kentucky. The invitation had come through his association with the Cincinnati YMCA, and he was invited to attend and supply a number of counselors for the camp.

Duff had eleven boys in his cabin, which they named "Duffy's Tavern." On the first night, after taps had sounded, eleven youngsters lay on their bunks, quiet and homesick. Duff invited them to kneel with him in a circle and asked if any of them could pray, but they only hung their heads in silence. So Duff spent a few minutes teaching them to pray. From then on, they said grace at the table in their camp and had regular morning devotionals, in which each boy learned to take part. Before their time at camp was over, all eleven boys had had their turn.

Later, Duff received a letter forwarded from the YMCA director in Cincinnati. The letter was from one of the boy's dad, a truck driver, thanking the YMCA for the experience his son Jimmy had had with an unnamed Mormon counselor. He noted that when his son came home the first night and the family started to

6. MDH, personal reminiscence, Apr. 1975.

eat, Jimmy had quietly asked if he could offer a word of grace first. At bedtime, they had a similar experience. The father was grateful.

THE LADIES SEXTETTE

The mission had previously formed several singing groups of missionaries to help break the ice and introduce the church to others. One of these groups was the "Mormon Ladies Sextette," which traveled around performing at various civic clubs and venues. The group of sisters sang, while a male missionary served as their administrative manager, master of ceremonies, and speaker at the performances. Duff had mostly been doing regular, proselyting missionary work for about a year when he received a call from his mission president asking if he would take over the management of the group. Duff responded by saying that if he was being assigned, the answer was yes. But if he was being asked to do it voluntarily, the answer was no. "I had been with them all week, and they are fine people," Duff wrote in his journal, "but they are all giggly and they were acting like some of the other mission quartets, which was not good." President Muir asked Duff to take the assignment and leave the next morning for Green Bay, Wisconsin.

Duff became the manager of the Sextette for nearly a year—a job he didn't want and tried to avoid but turned out to be a fabulous way to open doors for the missionaries to share their message. From that time on, performances took on a different tone, less "let us entertain you" and more "let us share our story with you."

Part of their performance included a message about the Restoration of the church, delivered by Duff. In fact, the Sextette would not take an assignment unless they had time allotted to deliver their message. Many potential venues would say, "This performance will be in our church, so we wouldn't want your preacher." To which Duff would respond, "That's the only reason we're singing."

Despite his serious approach, Duff was occasionally the object of good-natured teasing. As he would walk down the sidewalk with six sister missionaries, he would be asked if he were trying to rush the prophecy in Isaiah 4 concerning seven women laying hold of one man.

Duff became acquainted with the officials and business leaders of each area where they served. The Ladies Sextette performed in fifty-five different churches and filled more than seven hundred appointments during the year—to PTAs, Kiwanis Clubs, YMCAs, civic clubs, ladies' auxiliaries, and union meetings. Most of their performances were in Wisconsin; Cleveland and Cincinnati, Ohio; and Bloomington, Indiana. In Wisconsin, the team was invited to present a weekly radio broadcast for nine weeks.

The letters that poured in about the Sextette's performances and Duff's sermons are fascinating. They came from diverse sources, but were almost universal in their praise of the performers, Duff's speaking ability, and the church that produced young people like these.

Duff with the Ladies Sextette, Northern States Mission, 1942.

One example is an article in the Masonic *Scottish Rite Bulletin,* written by a Jewish scholar who had served as a secretary to President Woodrow Wilson.

> With the fall of the Venerable Master's gavel, there appeared upon the scene gracious young ladies comprising the Mormon Sextette, who were introduced by the Reverend M. Duff Hanks of that outstanding Church, it being the duty of the ladies to travel about the country for eighteen months entirely upon their own resources, Reverend Hanks also giving two years of his time under the same conditions, and bring a message of truth to all, irrespective of race, creed, or religion.... Round upon round of applause was received by the Sextette and Reverend Hanks.[7]

When the famous Tabernacle Choir organist Alexander Schreiner, who was a distant relative of the Hanks family, came to play a huge organ at a concert in Cincinnati, he asked Duff and the Ladies Sextette to sing and speak. When he got back to Salt Lake, he reported to Duff's sister, Jeannette, "Why, this young man speaks like a bank president and looks like one."

The year Duff spent with the Mormon Ladies Sextette was a wonderful experience for him. After their missions, Duff and the women of the sextette remained dear friends and a part of each other's lives.

7. Article in the *Scottish Rite Bulletin,* quoted in MDH memo, ca. Oct. 1942.

FELLOW MISSIONARIES

Duff felt blessed to serve with and around choice fellow missionaries.

One of his favorites was Wayne C. Booth. Wayne went on to become one of the preeminent literary critics of the latter twentieth century and a professor of English language and literature for thirty years at the University of Chicago.[8] Wayne struggled with some aspects of the church, and he and Duff spent hours discussing the gospel.

"Wayne was a dear guy, and it was he who tried to convert me," Duff remembered. When Booth came into the mission office, "he was astonished to find out that I'd read a book or two. I was the first missionary he had met who read very many books. So he thought I was worth saving. For Christmas he gave me a Tolstoy book and then was later shocked when he found out I'd stayed up all night reading it. He was one of the dearest, most ingenuous, pure persons." Mission president Muir even allowed Wayne to attend classes at the University of Chicago during his mission.

After serving together as missionary companions, Duff and Wayne remained dear if distant friends for the rest of their lives. On a postcard birth announcement in 1951, Wayne wrote, "I regret what life does in the way of enforced and insidious separations.... We've had our second child. It is a far cry from our Chicago days, when all I had to worry about was the state of my own soul and your opinion of me."[9]

Fifty-five years after they were companions, Duff received a handwritten note from Wayne that read, "Dear Duff, you never done tole' me that you have a hymn in the 1985 LDS hymnal. I just stumbled onto it this morning" while preparing for a Sunstone Symposium. "Sang it, loved it. Bravo!"[10]

As are most missionaries, Duff was blessed with a wide and varying slate of companions and colleagues during his mission. One of his companions would soak cucumbers in vinegar overnight, throw away the cucumbers the next morning, and drink the vinegar. Another was going to take home a young lady from the mission to marry, even though he had a fiancée back home. Duff talked him out of it, and he went home and married his fiancée. They later had a family of ten children.

MISSION PRESIDENTS

Duff had two mission presidents, Leo J. Muir and David L. Stoddard, each very different from the other. Both were significant in his life.

---

8. Margalit Fox, "Wayne C. Booth, Critic Who Analyzed Rhetoric, Dies at 84," *New York Times*, Oct. 11, 2005.

9. Wayne Booth to MDH, 1951.

10. Duff wrote the words to "That Easter Morn," *Hymns* (Salt Lake City: The Church of Jesus Christ of Latter-day Saints, 1985), no. 195. For more about the writing of this hymn, see pages 121 and 213.

Duff especially loved and respected his first mission president, Leo Muir. An eminent educator, he had survived during the Great Depression by selling apples on the street in Los Angeles.

President Muir was a teacher and a man of intellectual accomplishment in literature and language. He was compassionate, considerate, kind, and rarely tough. Duff called him by far the best speaker he ever heard. He challenged Duff's mind and his compassion. Though Duff was not inclined to hero worship, President Muir became a figure of almost monumental importance to him.

On one occasion, Duff wrote a scathing letter to President Muir without thinking of the ramifications. On a visit to Cincinnati, President Muir—hearing a false rumor—criticized Duff and the Ladies Sextette for "just being entertainers" and not sharing the gospel strongly enough. Duff and the young women had run themselves ragged from early in the morning till late at night performing over the previous eleven months. In his letter, Duff castigated President Muir and told him that they didn't deserve his comments. He wrote, "If I felt like you meant what you said, I'd catch the next train home."

President Muir had been misinformed and came to feel apologetic for what he had said. As he was preparing to end his mission, he called Duff into his office and took out Duff's letter, saying, "I think you may wish to keep this in your file; I would rather not have it in mine. Someday, when you are in a position to guide young people, and they do something that causes you heartache, you will remember this letter and be merciful."

He pushed the letter across the desk, and it was then that Duff noticed big, salty tear stains all over the letter. He wrote, "I have remembered."[11] They remained friends the rest of his life.

President Muir saw promise in young Duff Hanks and encouraged him throughout his mission and after. In fact, just before Duff was called as a general authority to the First Council of the Seventy (now the Presidency of the Seventy) in 1953, Muir sent him a letter predicting it would happen.

President David L. Stoddard was a man of exact opposite demeanor—very self-contained and rarely showing emotion. A banker who married the daughter of a congressman, Stoddard had adjusted and closed banks during the Depression. While serving in the mission office, Duff remembered a marked transition between the two mission presidents. "Our dinner table went from a bowl of soup (President Muir was very strapped economically) to standing rib roasts; and the conversational atmosphere of freedom changed—President Muir was always egging us on, talking about theme subjects, not the gospel all the time; he was a remarkably widely read and beautiful man. But President Stoddard, equally

11. MDH-T, "It Speaketh of Jesus, and Persuadeth Them to Believe in Him," BYU, Book of Mormon Symposium, Aug. 1986.

brilliant or more so in his own way, had suffered severe disappointment in some parts of his life, and [we could tell.]"

Because Duff served in the mission office at the end of President Muir's tenure and at the beginning of President Stoddard's, he became a bridge between the two administrations. Despite any of their human foibles, Duff "had a warm, special relationship" with both mission presidents and later spoke at both their funerals.[12]

RICHARD R. LYMAN EXCOMMUNICATION

While Duff was on his mission, his half great-uncle Elder Richard R. Lyman of the Quorum of the Twelve Apostles, was excommunicated for adultery on November 12, 1943. He had been in an intimate relationship for twenty years with a woman he had originally been assigned to counsel. The Quorum of the Twelve convened a disciplinary council to hear the case and Lyman's explanation. After the council, he was excommunicated. His wife, Amy Brown Lyman, was serving as the Relief Society general president at the time.[13]

Duff felt devastated. He wrote, "It is the easiest thing in the world to kick a man when he is down. I feel no bitterness, only sorrow, and I can't get it off my mind. However, my faith will never be disturbed by the default of men. It might reasonably be shaken, since I am a lad of doubts and incertitude, but no dereliction of duty by men will ever convince me that principles I have espoused are wrong."[14]

Eleven years later, Lyman sent a letter to a few relatives saying, "I am sure you will be glad to know that a most welcome message from President David O. McKay advises that I can be reinstated in the Church." Richard Lyman was rebaptized in 1954 at age eighty-three. Three years later, in September 1957, Lyman wrote a pleasant note to Maude. On the bottom of the note, he wrote a postscript: "In the nearly 87 years of my life, I have made no investment that I feel has paid me such rich and wonderful dividends as the small monthly contribution I made to help keep your Marion in the mission field."[15]

In a book he gave Duff at age eighty-nine, Lyman inscribed a note to him that said, "Congratulations on your adding honor to the name of your great grandfather, Francis <u>Marion</u> Lyman."

THE HOPE FAMILY

During his time in Cincinnati, Duff became dear friends with Len and Mary Hope. Len had joined the Church of Jesus Christ of Latter-day Saints under miraculous circumstances in Alabama, and Mary joined five years after marrying

12. MDH-R, May 1, 2001.

13. For more on the Lymans' life story, see Dave Hall, *A Faded Legacy: Amy Brown Lyman and Mormon Women's Activism, 1872–1959* (Salt Lake City: University of Utah Press, 2015).

14. MDH-JE, missionary journal, Nov. 24, 1943.

15. Richard R. Lyman to Maude Frame Hanks, September 24, 1957, in author's possession.

Len. By 1930, the couple had moved to Cincinnati along with many thousands of other Black Americans in a Great Migration from the Southern States to the North. But the Hopes were not welcomed to worship at the branch in Cincinnati because of the color of their skin. The branch president told them that white members felt uncomfortable when they attended.[16]

Duff and his companion spent a lot of time worshiping with the Hopes in their home on Sundays since they weren't welcome in the branch. During one visit, Duff became seriously ill and stayed with the Hopes for a few days while Mary nursed him back to health. She applied compresses to his forehead and gave him medicine for his sore throat. Duff recalled, "I never even thought of the color of her hand." Len and Duff spent hours discussing the gospel, and the two men grew to love each other.

When he had recovered sufficiently to travel, Duff left the Hope home in tears, as Len and Mary stood on their porch. As he was helped into the automobile, he looked back and saw them waving. He recounted, "Shortly thereafter, I received a letter from Brother Hope expressing affection and appreciation, even though they had been the ones doing the giving." When the car pulled away, Mary asked Len to sweep the snow from the front porch of their home. Len refused, saying, "Don't you know what the scriptures say? 'How beautiful are the feet of those who preach the gospel of peace' (Romans 10:15). Don't you ask me to sweep away that missionary's footsteps."[17]

When the Hopes came to Salt Lake for a visit, no hotel in Salt Lake City would accept them, so Duff's mom, Maude, had them stay in her home.[18]

STAY OR GO TO WAR?

Duff faced a tough decision between staying on his mission and going home early to enlist in the war. Contrary to many who do everything they can to stay out of the military during wartimes, Duff and his friends felt drawn to serve their country. The fact that some missionaries were leaving their missions early to serve their country in the war left Duff uneasy. While his friends were leaving to defend the country, he was still out preaching the gospel. He talked to his mission president, who convinced him that while the military might need him, they didn't need him as much as the people in his mission did.

In a letter home to his mother a few weeks later, he wrote: "If I am to continue

16. MDH, oral history interview, 2, 4, 6, MSS 7752, Charles Redd Center for Western Studies oral history project records, L. Tom Perry Special Collections, Harold B. Lee Library, Brigham Young University, Provo, Utah. See also Joseph R. Stuart, "Len Hope," Century of Black Mormons.

17. Len Hope, audio transcript, n.d.

18. MDH-R, May 1, 2001; MDH, note on the Hope family. For more information on the Hopes, see page 429. The Hopes' story is depicted in volume 3 of the *Standing on the Promises* historical fiction trilogy *The Last Mile of the Way* (Salt Lake City: Deseret Book, 2003), by Margaret Blair Young and Darius Aidan Gray.

to enjoy the philosophy of the Christian way of life, it is necessary that I fight to preserve the American way of life. Critics and cynics aside, I prefer to believe that if I must battle, it will be for practical ideals—freedom, democracy, and individuality—and *not* to protect the purse strings of warmonger capitalists who sell the lives of American boys for a reasonable profit."[19]

19. MDH-L to Maude, Jan. 12, 1944.

6

World War II

Here dead lie we because we did not choose to live and shame the land from which we sprung. Life, to be sure, is nothing much to lose; But young men think it is, and we were young.
—A. E. Housman

Near the end of his mission, Duff felt increasingly anxious about not serving his country in the war. Duff said, "Some of my close friends died. Ray Slight died fighting in Sicily. Dave Teerlink lies in a watery grave in the Pacific Ocean. Countless other friends, including Chick Winder and Doug Cahoon, also died. As the playwright once said, 'This liberty will look easy by and by when nobody dies to get it.'"[1]

One of Duff's saddest losses was that of his dear friend Elwin "Moose" Vogler. On a stopover during his service in the Air Force, Moose visited Duff on his mission in Chicago, spent the night in the mission home, and ate cold mush fried with Duff, which he loved. "I took him out to the airfield and then he took off in his plane, wagging his wings," Duff said. Just weeks later, Moose's plane went down in the Caribbean during a routine training mission and was never found. "Before I even got the news, I received a letter from Moose, with his tithing inside, asking me to give it to the church for him. His letter was anticipating the worst, but he bore his testimony and signed the letter to me, 'Your first convert.' I really suffered those next few months." Just seven months earlier, Moose had married his high school sweetheart, Margaret Cornwall, the daughter of Tabernacle Choir director J. Spencer Cornwall and choir member Mary Cornwall.[2]

Duff was honorably released from his mission in February 1944. "It was a good time for me. I worked hard," he later summarized. "I had repeated opportunities through those two mission presidents to share whatever it was I had to share. I had opportunities for service in a number of major cities, and enjoyed them and remember them, and am remembered by a few. Typical story. I enjoyed it and came home feeling that I had given what I went to give, and could have

1. Maxwell Anderson, *Valley Forge* (1937), act III.
2. Margaret Cornwall Richards obituary, dignitymemorial.com.

done a lot better, perhaps, but I did better when I sort of lightened up and got less grim and began to appreciate what it was that we were sharing."[3]

Duff hurried home from his mission to enlist in the armed forces. Knowing that some of his friends had already died in the war and not knowing whether he would share the same fate, he gave away all his clothes and athletic equipment. The most difficult moment was when he said goodbye to his mother, thinking that he might not see her again. Duff and Maude bid each other farewell at the old gate of their home. She called him her "little-man grown-up," feeling how hard it was to let him go. As Duff walked off into the predawn darkness to go to war, she whispered a few lines of a beautiful poem she had written about him, "And on the waves a ship is borne, laden with sailors in blue, One of them my own dear lad, whose eyes are of a heavenly hue."[4]

The letters Duff would receive from his mother during the war, afterward at school, and throughout his life, were always encouraging and uplifting, filled with a mother's loving expectations that he would do his part to honor his name, his family, his country, and his church.

SAN DIEGO NAVAL TRAINING CENTER

Duff was appointed LDS group leader of a contingent of young recruits from Utah, who headed by train to San Diego's United States Naval Training Center. On arrival, they were housed in large barracks with a comparable-sized group from Arizona, almost all of whom were also members of the LDS Church—in total about six hundred men.

As a group leader, Duff worked with two chaplains, whom he considered "two of the choice men of the earth." John Boud and Milton Hess had been law partners before joining the navy, leaving their firm to serve their country. Under their direction, Duff was responsible for organizing the LDS meetings and activities. He conducted LDS services in a general assembly on Sunday mornings, divided the group into classes, then followed it up with an afternoon meeting of about fifty to sixty returned missionaries.

Rulon T. Burton, one of the young men in Duff's group, later wrote an autobiography, *By My Own Hand*, in which he talked about his boot camp experience: "There I became closely acquainted with Marion Duff Hanks; five years older than I. Duff was a yeoman 3rd class and made a good impression on me. He has been the backbone of most of the meetings held on the base here and is a very fine fellow."[5]

Boot camp was as advertised in the movies. The entire process was to get the men indoctrinated, experienced with shooting firearms, in physical and mental shape, and focused on a new life. Duff rejoiced in the physical regimen after two

3. MDH-R, Dec. 10, 1988.
4. Jeffrey R. Holland to MDH, Nov. 3, 1967.
5. Rulon T. Burton, *By My Own Hand* (Draper, UT: Tabernacle Books, 2003), 148.

Duff in the navy, 1944.

years of absence from it on his mission. But he wasn't as keen on the temperament or attitudes of some of the instructors. He said, "Much of the lecturing was by people whose tongues and lives were mixed up with dirty stuff and this did not ever become comfortable for most of us. Nonetheless, these were seasoned men who had been in the navy for years and knew the working of a navy vessel and all that went with it."[6]

Duff did his best to be effective as the group leader. In a letter home, he wrote, "Last night was one of the most satisfactory experiences I've ever enjoyed. I preached the gospel for 2½ hours to a large group. Many were nonmembers [of the LDS Church]. Afterward, one of the boys said: 'You've made me appreciate the gospel more in one week than 10,000 people in my hometown have done in 18 years.' Several others said similar things. I went to bed and wept."[7]

"Say Hanks, Do You Believe in Christ?"

One Sunday, Chaplain Hamilton, the senior chaplain of the huge naval base, complimented Duff on the church service and invited Duff to meet with him. As an apprentice seaman in boot camp, Duff felt a bit intimidated, but Commander Hamilton greeted Duff by calling him "Mr. Hanks," seated him cordially, and talked with him as equals.

Hamilton had invited Duff to his office to discuss the possibility of his becoming a chaplain. After some additional conversation he said, "Before I recommend

6. MDH-JE, n.d.
7. MDH-L to family from San Diego, California, Naval Base, June 1944.

you to the Chief of Chaplains, talk to me about your experience in your Church, about what you think may help me recommend you."

And so, Duff began to try to tell Chaplain Hamilton what might qualify him to serve in that role. "I mentioned growing up in the Church, including family home evenings, prayer, etc." Hamilton began to fidget, and Duff knew that he was losing him. Becoming a little more anxious, he tried telling him "All about the Church and its programs, the early two-and-a-half-minute talks, Scouting, the deacon opportunity, the Sunday School teaching, and the mission."

After a time, Chaplain Hamilton's demeanor completely changed, and he finally interrupted Duff. "Say Hanks, do you believe in Jesus Christ?"

"Yes, sir," Duff replied. "Everything I believe relates to Jesus Christ. The name of the Church that I belong to is his name. My faith revolves around him as my Savior."

Hamilton, looking at his watch, said, "Well, you have been talking for seven minutes and you haven't said so."

It was an unforgettable lesson for Duff. Years later, he said, "I haven't made that mistake again."[8]

In the end, Duff was informed he wasn't eligible to become an official chaplain because he didn't yet have a college degree. On top of that, a lower-level officer in charge of granting exceptions told Duff, "I will never give an exception to a Mormon!" Duff ended up spending the war as an unofficial chaplain anyway because there was no official chaplain on his vessel.

After six months of training in San Diego, Duff graduated at the head of his class and was given the right to choose what kind of service at sea he wanted. He chose a submarine, but when his assigned vessel was delayed in commissioning, he was reassigned to a submarine-chasing patrol craft escort, the *USS PCE-868,* with a complement of around a hundred men.

"ACTING CHAPLAIN" HANKS

After only a few minutes on Duff's first day on the vessel, he was escorted to the office of the commanding officer—a lieutenant from Long Beach, California, named Captain L. M. Hoover. As they talked, he referred to Duff's service record, place of birth, and his mission. Hoover said he had known many Mormons and missionaries. He asked, "Were you a good missionary?" Duff replied in the affirmative. Hoover then appointed Duff as acting chaplain of the vessel. He also told him that he would be the psychiatrist and counselor, friend to the crew, and the active Christian head onboard the ship.

Shortly after being assigned, Duff found that the word had already spread all over the ship that the new chaplain was a Mormon from Salt Lake City. He was coming down from an upper deck when he spotted a group of men standing in his way.

8. MDH-T, "Was He Relevant?" (Dec. 17, 1968), in *Speeches of the Year* (Provo, UT: BYU Press, 1969), 2–3.

"Well, well, this is our new Mormon chaplain," smirked Schyler, the leader of the crowd. "He looks like a big bag of $#!%."

Duff stopped and, putting his "life on the chopping block," answered, "What was that you had in your mouth, a big bag of what? You don't care very much about the kind of things you have in your mouth, do you?" Then he walked on.

The next day in the bathroom, Duff had just started to brush his teeth when Schyler came in. Hearing the vulgar talk around them "getting ripe," Schyler spoke out, "Knock it off—Duff is here." Duff saw it as nothing less than a miracle.

As acting chaplain, Duff's religious duties involved holding a service in the ship's mess hall every Sunday and at other times. "I got some friends, the carpenter's mates, to build me a podium, and cleaned out the mess hall every Sunday morning," he said. "Little Bobby Mieunere, the Catholic from New York, played the organ, and Ensign Long, whose father was a minister in Boston, he'd read scriptures, and we'd sing, and I'd preach. We formed a church organization—a 'branch presidency,' as it were, and led some activities. Over time, I involved several enlisted men, some of whom became dear friends, and ultimately members of the Church. We'd get almost half the crew who were off duty to attend. I had them giving talks, which I helped them prepare, and I preached every Sunday."[9]

Other religious crew members included "a choice man of the Pentecostal faith," who "taught me more about our relationship with the Savior than I taught him," Duff said. "There was also the wonderful Christian Scientist whose mouth and mind were clean and who was like a beacon in the middle of a lot of dirt and darkness. I loved them, and respected them, and wished I were more like them in many ways, and yet shared with them some great truths they did not know."[10]

Duff earned the nickname of "the deacon" on the *USS PCE-868*. The ship was fast but not stable—vulnerable to the waves. "The deacon is on the fantail!" the sailors would cry as Duff threw up off the back of the ship some days. "I'd toss my cookies," Duff said. "I'd had a sort of stomach as a little kid that was susceptible. But I could handle it. All the baloney about it just being 'in your head' is just that—when we finally got out to deep waters and storms, *everybody* got sick." Years later, Duff's future wife, Maxine, would quip, "Maybe that's why Duff was so sympathetic whenever I was sick during pregnancy, because he knew exactly how I felt."

Duff soon experienced the challenges of life at sea. As rain poured down and waves tossed the ship around for days, morale onboard was low. Duff showed particular concern for two sailors who hadn't been able to eat anything since they left port and were vomiting blood. He tried cooking poached eggs for them, but it didn't do much good. Both men had previously submitted letters trying to get off the ship by reason of chronic seasickness, but the captain had not sent the

9. MDH-JE, and personal letter, Mar. 2003.

10. MDH-T, "Without Prejudice, without Bigotry," BYU devotional address, Mar. 30, 1965, speeches.byu.edu.

paperwork on before the ship left port. Duff wrote, "One of the boys has given up, but I have bullied the other one into getting up a little, even if he does have to regurgitate to do it, and he seems to be better. The living conditions are fearful. There isn't a man on the ship strong enough to clean out the head (bathroom) properly or to give the galley the delousing it needs. Both of the cooks are sick, though there hasn't been much eating, anyway."[11]

THE SHIP AND ITS SERVICE

The *USS PCE-868* was assigned as an escort vessel in the US Pacific Fleet. Their tour over the next few years included many of the island areas of the Pacific, including landing at Iwo Jima and at Eniwetok (now Enewetak) Atoll after the major fighting there had ended.

During general quarters (meaning "enemy approaching"), every man on ship was assigned to a station, battle ready. Duff served as the leader of a gun crew assigned to a three-inch, fifty-caliber gun, the ship's largest gun. Later he served in the Combat Information Center, plotting course and ship movement.

Because of the nature of his assignment onboard a submarine chaser, Duff never really knew the outcome of the munitions his ship dropped and fired overboard, directed at submarines below. He did see oil slicks and other activity on the surface, but since damaged submarines would sink, he was never sure whether they ever hit one.

Duff recalled his ship's involvement in several island battles with Marine landings. He called one "a big and terrible battle. I'm glad I don't remember it well," he said. "We stood out there and lobbed shells in, while the Marines went in and got killed. We went right behind them. That island was shredded from all the battle wagons and the ships and the aircraft pouring it in; there wasn't a tree left standing."

He later told a grandchild, "We didn't see any heroic action, but we dropped explosive tin cans off the back, and shot hedgehogs [all anti-submarine warfare devices]. We were constantly firing anti-aircraft guns at anything above us—twin-40's and twin-20's. Movies make it all look glamorous sometimes, but it was no place for anybody. I never hated anybody and always had an unhappy feeling about the whole prospect of war and all that goes with it."[12]

PHILOSOPHY ON COMBAT

While on his mission, and contemplating the prospect of going to war, Duff wrote, "The prospect of killing a man is not pleasant to me. But it is my understanding that this service I am required to give is in partial payment of the debt I owe for the great blessing that I have enjoyed in this citadel of liberty."[13]

Looking back at the war decades later, he wrote, "Shooting at people in the war didn't grab me, but it was what I had to do, consistent with the decision I

11. MDH-L, to Maude during the war, about 1944.
12. MDH, oral history interview with Mindy Clawson, Mar. 17, 1989.
13. MDH-L to Maude, about 1944.

Duff (center) with shipmates during World War II.

made to defend my country and all that means to generations ahead. I don't like remembering it any better than I did doing it, but it was something that had to be done to accomplish a greater purpose."[14]

LESSONS LEARNED FROM BEHAVIORS OF SHIPMATES

In addition to the potential of being killed and his distaste for the vileness sometimes shown by his fellow sailors, Duff also wasn't fond of what was colloquially called the military "caste system," in which officers hazed and browbeat enlisted men. He wrote home, "After all the arm-twisting, maltreatment, coercion, and general guff-handing-out that I've witnessed, I don't have any confidence in my rights as a citizen so long as they have me where they want me. If some officer says so, I am required to blow my nose left-handed, and if I don't like it, I can jolly-well tell him so, and get fined $50 dollars or maybe just get lined up and shot."[15]

Duff noted other less-than-admirable behaviors among his fellow shipmates. He noticed one young man whom he described as modest, able, and promising. Gradually, the daily pressures began to take their toll on him. In a far-off port, Duff saw him preparing to go ashore in the company of some shipmates who wanted to take him to town to show him a "good time." Duff tried to warn him that these men meant him no good, but he became defiant and told Duff that he was a "big boy" able to make up his own mind.

---

14. MDH-L to George Turner, Mar. 22, 1988.

15. MDH-L to Maude, Dec. 2, 1945; Edmund A. Gibson, "More About the 'Caste System,'" *United States Naval Institute Proceedings*, Sept. 1949, 559.

When he returned to the ship in the custody of the shore patrol, out of control, and over leave in wartime, he became subject to severe discipline. Duff wrote, "The charges against him were heartbreaking. I won't forget his tearful anguish as he said over and over, 'What will I tell my mom? What will I tell my girl?'"

Duff continued, "There is no bravery in evil, no true courage in behavior that can only result in deep disappointment."[16]

At other times, Duff was surprised by the nobility he saw in a man he had thought of as "mean and nasty." During one incident of general quarters, Duff and his gun crew were standing at their gun when a "hedgehog" (timed explosive) from their ship misfired, sputtered, and landed in front of them.

"Along came this boatswain's mate, who was the most amoral person I'd ever met," Duff remembered. "He ran right up, picked up the thing in his bare hands and threw it overboard. It exploded just below the water line and put a big dent in our ship, but not a hole. We'd all be dead as doornails if it weren't for him."

Duff continued, "I also saw him do the same for a mangy dog while we were in port. This dog got confused and fell into the water between the ship and the dock. This same fellow went down there and picked up the dog with one hand, and yelled, 'Get me out of here!' He was pulled up just in time to keep him from having flat legs."[17]

END OF THE WAR

When Germany surrendered on V-E Day, May 8, 1945, Duff's ship was at sea. The captain gathered all the men topside, and asked Duff to lead them in a prayer of gratitude to God that "this terrible thing is almost over."

But they still had to finish the war with Japan. The ship was ordered into drydock to be turned into a communications craft to accompany the amphibious forces preparing to invade the mainland of Japan. They had all the electronics installed, and quarters for an admiral to lead their part of the assault.

Unknown to Duff and his crew, on July 26, the *USS Indianapolis* delivered components of a secret new weapon to Tinian Island near Guam. There, the components were assembled to form two atom bombs. A West High School buddy of Duff's, David Teerlink, served on the *Indianapolis.* After delivering the ship's cargo, Teerlink must have felt eager to return home to see his wife and first baby, born six days before. He never made it. A Japanese submarine sank the *Indianapolis* on July 30. Of the 1,195 crew members, only 316 survivors were pulled from the water, marking the largest loss of life from a single ship lost at sea in US naval history.[18]

Because military leaders did not yet comprehend the unconventional power of the atomic bombs and how they would cause Japan's surrender, their original

16. MDH-T, "I Will Look unto the Lord," GC, *Ensign*, Nov. 1986.

17. MDH-R, May 15, 2001.

18. MDH-R, Dec. 10, 1988; Department of the Navy, Defense POW/MIA Accounting Agency, Personnel Profile for CPC David S. Teerlink, dpaa-mil.sites.crmforce.mil; "David Sander Teerlink" (1921–45), bbgenealogy.net.

plan was to invade Japan right after the bombings. Duff's ship was on its way to Japan to participate in that invasion when American planes dropped the atomic bombs on Hiroshima on August 6 and Nagasaki on August 9, initially killing some two hundred thousand people and changing the course of human history.

Though Duff and his shipmates couldn't have known that Japan was about to surrender, on August 11—two days after Nagasaki—Duff experienced an evening of peace aboard the ship. "For some time, I was practically alone on a lookout station on the bow of the ship," he wrote home. "The last rays of the sun on the peaceful, pleasant deep really made for a lovely sight. A youngster passing by stopped and after meditatively gazing with me at the scene, asked why it is that things grow so calm at night. I told him that I suppose all things understand that night-time means rest and quiet and ceasing from activity."[19]

After Japan announced their surrender on V-J Day, August 15, 1945, "We gathered on the fantail to again praise God," Duff said. Following a brief program, Duff once again led the whole crew in a prayer of thanksgiving.[20]

Back in his ship's home port of Pearl Harbor again, on August 30, 1945, Duff wrote to his family, "This morning we watched the setting out for home of another group of ships who've fought their way through the war and are on the way back to decommissioning. We've watched many submarines leave with their homeward bound pennants flying and their 'kill' banners strung out on lines all over the ship. Some of these subs appear to have [sunk upwards of 20 to 30] Japanese ships." As the vessels would leave the harbor to the playing of a sailor band, the men would line up on their ship and toss their hats into the water. "After what they've been through," Duff wrote, "they are really happy to be leaving for home."[21]

Duff and his shipmates weren't so fortunate. Their ship was ordered to remain on duty, outfitted to serve essentially as a floating signal when it was not in port. Aircraft flying overhead would get their bearings from Duff's ship in the middle of the ocean.

"While the war was not really over for us yet," Duff said, "we were thrilled to know that we likely would be going home before too long."[22] But then, they had to put back out to sea. Having to wait to go home even though the war was over was the toughest part of the entire ordeal.

At one point, he found himself "holding on for dear life on an upper level of the ship, which seemed close to foundering. The waters were frenzied, washing the decks on each side of the ship as we tilted almost out of control," he said. "There was incredible apprehension, but no place else to go." So Duff sat on an

19. MDH-L to Maude, Aug. 11, 1945.

20. Japan announced its surrender on August 15, 1945, and formally signed surrender documents on September 2, 1945.

21. MDH-L, to his family, Aug. 30, 1945.

22. Granddaughter Mindy Clawson, school paper.

empty ammunition locker and read from his small, serviceman's copy of the Book of Mormon. "I read from 2 Nephi 4:15–20 about the groanings of [the prophet Nephi's] honest heart. 'My God hath been my support; he hath led me through mine afflictions in the wilderness; and he hath *preserved me* upon the *waters of the great deep.*'"[23]

Another time, "as I sat in a little office one day, there came a knock at the door. This big, rugged man from the Bronx stepped through the door, turned and locked it, and said,

"Hanks, I don't know you very well, . . . but the fellows tell me that you know how to pray."

He showed Duff a letter from his wife, informing him that she and their children had left and were no longer interested in him.

"I don't know how to pray," the sailor said, "but I want you to help me."

Then "this big, tough man and I got down on our knees in a little office in a little ship in the middle of a big ocean," Duff said, "and he repeated the words of the prayer after me. He did something for me that I needed to have done. It had never occurred to me that it was a gift, a blessing to be able to get down on your knees and look to God with confidence for help."[24]

After months at sea with the constant stress of the ocean and tight quarters with fellow sailors, the PCE-868's visits to its home port of Pearl Harbor and a few days of R&R were always a welcome respite. It was during one of these stops in Honolulu that Duff first met nineteen-year-old Maxine Christensen. "The first moment I laid eyes on her," he said, "my heart flopped. She was beautiful, but it was not my eyes that were affected; it was my heart."[25]

---

23. MDH-T, "It Speaketh of Jesus, and Persuadeth Them to Believe in Him," BYU, Book of Mormon Symposium, Aug. 1986; emphasis added.

24. MDH-T, "Spiritual Constants in Our Changing Times," BYU, Jan. 4, 1961.

25. MDH-L to family, "A Life-Sketch," Nov. 7, 1980.

7

Meeting Maxine

The first moment I laid eyes on her, my heart flopped.
—Marion D. Hanks

Docked at Pearl Harbor, many of the men on Duff's ship jumped into activities that were anathema to Duff and offended his sensibilities. Rather than accompany his shipmates in their chosen debauchery, Duff attended church and visited with the local members, who offered a home-away-from-home to Latter-day Saint sailors in Hawaii. One such couple were Arva and Elwood Christensen.

Elwood and Arva had been in Hawaii for more than twenty years when Duff met them. They were in their early forties with four children and had an idyllic life in Honolulu. Originally from Brigham City and Honeyville, Utah, they had been youngsters (twenty-one and eighteen), dating and falling in love, when the bishop called them into his office. He asked them if they were serious about getting married and, if so, would they "speed it up a little," and accept a call to go as a couple on a mission to Japan.

Elwood and Arva talked over the bishop's proposal, said yes to everything, got married, and were sent to Japan in June 1922, two weeks after they were married. They were in for a culture shock. For example, when their first child, Lowell, was born in 1923 during their mission, because he was a male, the Japanese nurses and doctors laid him on the floor and danced around him, chanting "Banzai! Banzai!" They were wishing the baby a "long life," but the Christensens were surprised and had no idea what was going on.

The Christensens performed their missionary labors, mostly in Osaka, until 1924, when nationalistic fervor in Japan brought on political tensions, low numbers of convert baptisms, and the closing of the Japan Mission. Following their faithful missionary service, Elwood and Arva traveled home by ship, stopping in Hawaii for a few days en route. They loved the islands immediately.

After being home on the mainland for about six months, a friend asked Elwood if he would like to return to Hawaii and work with him at a savings and loan. Having just returned from a mission to a foreign land for two years, Arva was a bit reluctant, but Elwood was persistent. "Look, just come try it for six months, and if you don't like it, we'll go back home," he convinced her. For the

Maxine Christensen, Honolulu, age 20, 1945.

rest of his life, Elwood loved telling the story, finishing it by chuckling and saying, "We came for the summer, and the summer never ended, so we stayed." They are both buried in a beautiful cemetery on their beloved Oahu.

Their second child, Maxine, was born on November 4, 1925. She loved her childhood in Hawaii, which was a much different place from what it is today. Waikiki, for example, had only two hotels, and things were significantly less commercialized. The Christensen family made wonderful memories going to the beach almost every weekend. On holidays, the close and cohesive young Latter-day Saint community on the islands, including the Moodys, the Clissolds, the Woolleys, and the Lunts would celebrate together with big parties. In later years, Elwood purchased a place on the beach near Nanakuli on the far west side of Oahu—"out in the country." The families barbecued right on the beach.

Maxine attended Punahou, a private K-12 school in Honolulu. Founded in 1841, Punahou was the oldest school west of the Mississippi. Maxine was one of only two Mormon kids outside her family at the school.

Honolulu was a melting pot of nationalities. Maxine, her sister, and two brothers lived in a racially and religiously diverse neighborhood. Her best friend in junior high was a Korean girl, her next-door neighbors were Portuguese, and her family consistently had Japanese people in their home because of Arva and Elwood's experience in Japan. "My father was a wonderful missionary," Maxine said. "He was very knowledgeable about the gospel. He started the first Japanese Sunday School in the Islands, and most of his workers were Japanese, so he could speak to them in their own language, which made his construction business easier for him and for them."[1] Maxine always attributed her family's lack of racial prejudice to this diverse background. The children were never allowed to denigrate other races or nationalities in speech or action.

Maxine described her parents as "wonderful, good people." Her father was "very bright." Besides teaching mathematics in high school, he started his own real estate business in the 1930s. When he died in 1983, his company was the second oldest real estate company in Hawaii. Maxine's mother, Arva, grew up on a farm in a family of eleven children, "so she really knew how to work," Maxine said.[2]

In his later years, Elwood went swimming every night at Waikiki. Arva would pick him up at work each night at 4:00 and drive him down to the beach, where he would swim, walk, paddle, or just talk to tourists. One of his favorite stories involved a large family playing in the water near him. After some conversation, he found out they were a Mormon family from Ogden, Utah. He playfully asked, "Isn't that a suburb of Brigham City?" (Elwood's much smaller hometown north of Ogden.) The Osmonds—the famous family of singers—laughed and they enjoyed each other's company for another hour.[3]

More often than not, the tourists he talked with would complain about the large hotels and the concrete and commerciality. He would reply with, "Look, the ocean's the same, the sky and the water are still blue, the flowers are beautiful and fragrant." He wouldn't let anyone malign Hawaii, because he loved it so.

PEARL HARBOR

One of Maxine's most vivid memories was from Saturday, December 6, 1941, when she was sixteen. "Mother and Dad knew things were rumbling—everybody did," Maxine remembered. "Dad said, 'Let's drive down around the island,' which people did often." As they drove through Honolulu's Pearl Harbor, "I remember Dad saying, 'Look at all those ships. There are so many in the harbor. Isn't it unusual that there are so many in one place?'"[4]

The next morning, life in paradise changed dramatically when the Japanese conducted a surprise attack on the United States Naval Base at Pearl Harbor. Before that, the United States had been neutral. The attack led to its formal entry into World War II.

The US Pacific Fleet had been stationed at Pearl Harbor since April 1940. In addition to nearly a hundred naval vessels, including eight battleships, there were substantial military and air forces present.

1. MDH-R, Dec. 10, 1988.
2. MDH-R, Dec. 10, 1988.
3. Waikiki beach, ca. mid-1970s.
4. MDH-R, Dec. 10, 1988.

The first Japanese dive-bomber appeared over Pearl Harbor at 7:55 a.m. in a first wave of nearly two hundred aircraft, including torpedo planes, bombers, and fighters. Within a quarter of an hour, the various airfields at the base were under savage attack.[5]

During the attack, an American anti-aircraft artillery shell fell on the grounds of Punahou, Maxine's school, half a block away from their home. It caused Maxine to fall out of bed, and made such a terrible noise that the family wondered if they were being bombed. "As I reflect back, I think how frightened my parents must have been," Maxine said. "But because we were children, it was just exciting to us. We didn't really understand what was happening, but I'm sure it was terrible for them."[6]

Maxine climbed a hill with a neighbor friend to see what was going on. There, they watched another wave of Japanese planes fly over their heads, with the big red sun of the Japanese flag clearly visible.

She remembered that some of her friends' initial response to the situation was to naively say, "Oh good, no school for a while." But, as the day wore on, rumors flew, and as news came from Pearl Harbor, forty-five minutes away, the reality of what had happened, and the terrifying threat began to sink in. "We congregated with our neighbors on the lawn—all of us talking in whispered voices," Maxine remembered. When her family didn't hear from her brother Lowell for hours, Maxine said, "Mother and Dad were frantic."

A member of the ROTC, Lowell had recently learned to fly, and he had reserved a small plane for 7:30 a.m. that Sunday morning in order to log a few hours of flight time towards earning his license. But his church leader called and asked Lowell to help collect fast offerings (money for the needy) early that morning. Lowell chose to do so and sublet the airplane rental to two servicemen who were on leave that weekend. Some time after the Japanese attack began at 7:55 a.m., they were shot out of the sky.[7]

One of the worst things that day, and those that followed, was the lack of trustworthy information. The radios had gone silent, and people were in the streets sharing concerns and rumors and fears. Some said they had heard of Japanese parachutists who had landed. Many thought that at any moment the Japanese would be landing their ships and taking over the island.

The bombing of Pearl Harbor changed everything about daily life. Curfews were immediately put into effect. Everyone in their neighborhood who owned a truck was asked to go to Pearl Harbor to help remove the dead and injured. The day after the bombing, Maxine and her mother volunteered to help the wounded at the hospital, rolling and changing bandages and running errands. Her school

---

5. "Pearl Harbor," Britannica.com.
6. MDH-R, Dec. 10, 1988.
7. Marta Murvosh, "Man Recalls Attack on Pearl Harbor," *Daily Herald,* Dec. 8, 1999.

building was eventually taken over by the Corp of Engineers, so she went to school in a rented building on the University of Hawaii campus. From then on, she had to take a gas mask and identification card with her to school every day, and school was often interrupted with air raid drills. Every house was required to black out all their windows, so Maxine did her homework in the bathroom because it was the darkest room in the house, and light couldn't get out from the crack under the door.

Each family had to build a bomb shelter underground. Initially, the Christensens just dug a hole, but as the war went on, Elwood had his workers build one out of wood. The air-raid sirens would go off every two or three days, and no one was ever told whether they were real or not, because they wanted the people to be ready. The family would have a pile of blankets ready to go, and Maxine would run and fill the bathtub with water in case their water was later poisoned. "I filled the bathtub, and I would grab my little brother who was a year old, Mother would grab the blankets, and everybody did their part," she said. We would have to stay in our air-raid bomb shelter underground until the 'all clear' came.

"At night, our family all left our bedrooms and slept together on the floor in the living room. Mother gave me a pocketknife and said I was to carry it at all times. That really scared me. There were many false reports and rumors of untrue ship landings, etc."[8]

After a few months there began to be many shortages, including of food, since many supplies were shipped in from the mainland. Along with significant changes in everyday life, small changes also became the norm. For example, when Christmas trees were no longer shipped in, Elwood went into the mountains near their house, cut a few branches from an ironwood tree, and stuck them into a wooden dowel as a makeshift Christmas tree.

AN ABUNDANCE OF SUITORS

Many soldiers were stationed in Hawaii during the war. Some estimates placed the ratio at six hundred men for every woman. As a result, Maxine had so many dates that she used to wish she could stay home. People would sometimes tell the young women, "It's your patriotic duty to go out with these men."

Maxine recalled one memorable date with an army pilot in his airplane. Because it was against regulations to take her flying, the pilot had her wear navy blue pants and a white shirt with borrowed dog tags around her neck. In the air, they did so many vertical rolls, that when they finally landed after thirty minutes, Maxine was so sick that she got out and lay right down on the runway.

Maxine made an impression on more than one serviceman. "During the war, I was caught in the Christensens' charity net and was one of half a dozen GIs to go to their home for dinner," one of them remembered. "The Christensens had this

8. MDH-R, Dec. 10, 1988.

Hawaiian-born, fantastic teenage daughter named Maxine. I saw her only once and I still remember her graceful beauty."[9]

THE CHRISTENSEN HOME—AN OASIS

During an interview fifty years later, Duff described Elwood and Arva: "They were very generous people who opened their home and hearts and refrigerators to the onslaught of American servicemen. I don't know how many slept on their floors and ate their food. Over the years they were solicitous, as few people are, of visitors to the Islands. We have met scores who were approached by this pleasant, genial older man at the Waikiki Ward and then ended up either eating dinner at the Christensen home or being taken out to dinner. They were more Christian in their generosity than any couple I ever knew."

Duff first visited the Christensen home with friends, two prominent LDS servicemen, Marsden Durham and Crawford Gates. Duff later commented, "It was typical of young LDS servicemen to make a beeline to the Christensen home, because they were welcomed into a lovely home and treated like their own children. We loved them dearly, and almost every place I go, somebody will come forward who has partaken of the hospitality of the Christensens."[10]

THEIR MEETING—FIRST IMPRESSIONS

And so, against this backdrop of war and confusion and fear, came the fortuitous meeting of Duff and Maxine. One Sunday in church, Maxine was sitting by her dad when Duff stood and bore his testimony. Elwood leaned over to Maxine and said, "I'd like to hear that young man speak in church." Maxine said, "My ears perked up, and I figured if my dad thinks he's pretty good, he must be good."

Duff had a shipmate who had been a missionary with his brother Bruce but had "succumbed to the habits of the world." One Sunday in port, Duff persuaded him to come ashore with him to church. That Sunday afternoon between services they joined with other servicemen to take a short hike up to the falls of Manoa Valley. Maxine was also at the base of the falls, showing the servicemen where to go. Duff records, "This beautiful blonde girl and her little sister were there, and my eyes and ears were pleased by what I saw, and I became interested in a person for the first time in many years. It wasn't a big flash, but it was a genuine quickening of the heart."

Maxine's version was slightly different. "I didn't pay much attention to him. I mean, there were lots of handsome young men there, all wearing white dress uniforms. On the hike my little sister got tired, so I asked Duff if he would carry her. He picked her up and her muddy feet got all over his uniform, so that was our introduction."[11]

9. Coy Miles to Hanks' children shortly after Maxine's death, ca. Mar. 2018.
10. MDH-R, Dec. 10, 1988.
11. MDH-R, Dec. 10, 1988.

Maxine Christensen, from a park overlooking Waikiki Beach, Honolulu, ca. 1950.

Duff's version: "On the hike, I carried her little sister on my back wearing my beautiful white uniform, and she muddied me up. She almost got me court-martialed."[12]

In a letter home to his mother, Duff wrote of another encounter with Maxine: "Sunday, I had a very happy day. Waffles I ate, in the lovely home of some good people. It was after Church, and I went with the chaplains and a few other boys, and we had a great time. The young lady of the house asked me to her home. She is 19 and quite pretty. She wanted to find out what I was thinking in the depths of my deep, unfathomable blue-doored beezer, behind my inscrutable flint-chinned un-informing pan. I didn't want to tell her that I hadn't thought a damn thing and that my mind was a vacuum and that my blue eyes were gazing, not thoughtfully, but just staring into space."

In a letter to Maxine, weeks after they met, Duff wrote: "Dear Blondie: I enjoyed the acquaintance we managed to brew during my weeks in your beautiful Hawaii. I have nothing but happy thoughts as to the place and people in general, and *you* in particular."[13]

Interspersed in a long letter home during another stop in Hawaii, Duff made subtle references to Maxine: "Friday night I took my first timeout and went into

12. MDH-R, Dec. 10, 1988.
13. MDH-L to Maxine, Nov. 3, 1945.

the ward dance, walked my cute friend home, and enjoyed it.... There were about 25 servicemen there, and only two girls present, my friend and the daughter of a commander. The two girls were born and reared here and can hula real pretty like. I enjoyed it."[14]

In another letter to Maxine, weeks later, he wrote: "I am working hard out here to have some of the work done in advance so I can spend a bit more time on the beach this trip. The captain has been in twice to tell me that I am to get some liberty this time! I think I shall if I can find someone to keep me company. Know anyone I could approach about the project?"[15]

In a letter to Maude: "After Mutual, I walked home with Maxine. She's really a lovely girl and it may well be that my interest has been more than a modicum. She *SURE* is cute. At any rate, I am going, and she is sad."[16]

And finally in a letter to Maxine, Duff quoted an anonymous poem:

Yer eyes is like two butterballs,
Yer cheeks is red as ham,
Yer lips is like a jelly-jar,
Sister, pass the jam!

14. MDH-L to Maude, Dec. 2, 1945.
15. MDH-L to Maxine, Dec. 23, 1945.
16. MDH-L to Maude, Jan. 16, 1946.

8

After the War

When you realize you want to spend the rest of your life with somebody, you want the rest of your life to start as soon as possible.[1]

CONTINUING IMPACT

Over the years, Duff received several letters from shipmates and fellow servicemen he had met during the war. A representative letter from one of his shipmates arrived for Duff after he had departed for home: "I have met few with the good character you possess, and I am so impressed by your convictions. It is unfortunate that you were subjected to this life, for while it may have been a help to you in various respects, it was also an insult to you, your life, your ideals, and most of all your mother. Even in the trivial things that must have been very distasteful to you, I was proud of the fortitude you used and the patience you exerted in all cases. I am honored to have known you."[2]

POSITIVE OUTCOMES FROM THE WAR

Duff summarized, "The only stories I've told about the war concerned men who were touched by the Spirit and a few whose heroism burns brightly in my heart. I never intended to make a career for life out of my very modest contribution. "I went where I was told and did what I was assigned. Most of the danger I faced was wickedness, and under those temptations, I did not succumb. The 'hard' was always the good for me. The easy times have afforded me my least worthy contributions."[3]

He continued, "A few virtuous things came out of the war. I taught a lot of people the gospel and comforted many others. Some people joined the church, a lot changed their lives, a few became dear and permanent friends, *and* I met Maxine.

"After the war was over and we'd been cleaned off a bit from the muck we'd lived in, most of us reported to some school someplace. My place was the University of Utah."

---

1. *When Harry Met Sally* (Columbia Pictures, 1989).
2. "Bill," Duff's former shipmate, to MDH, Mar. 1946.
3. MDH-L, to family, "A Life-Sketch," Nov. 7, 1980.

By then, Jeannette had finally married Jay, and they'd moved into an apartment, so Duff was the only one living at home with his mother. Maxine came to Utah for college, and, as Duff said, smiling, "she decided for 'reasons unknown' that it would be the U instead of the Y for her."[4]

LAW SCHOOL

For want of a better choice, Duff walked into the law school on his first day of registration after the war. Because nearly one-third of his friends and classmates had been killed during the war, he was happy when he saw old friends Allen Jensen, Burton Miller, Frank Nelson, and others there too. Later he met Coy Miles, Russ Harris, and Bob Backman along the way.

After the war, it was difficult to get good teachers at the law school. Duff remembered a couple of very strong professors, but half a dozen who "didn't amount to much. One professor, who became the president of the school, was the next-to-the-poorest excuse I ever saw. He was a peripatetic philosopher who wandered around the classroom. I had one professor who went on and became the dean of the law school at Chicago. But he couldn't carry the load alone."[5]

A particular incident stood out in Duff's mind. One of his professors had a reputation of being a vigorous defender of the law against ignorant and callow students. After carefully preparing and presenting a legal brief of a consequential law case, Duff anxiously awaited the response of the professor and several students preassigned to critique his effort. The professor drily remarked, "Thank you, Mr. Hanks, for that thoroughly unnecessary delineation of the obvious," The class then undertook to consider the deeper meaning of the matter at hand.[6] Duff loved to tell that story and apply it to topics he was speaking about.

THE ALL-CHURCH BASKETBALL CHAMPIONSHIP

The church fielded teams for all kinds of sports in those days, basketball and softball being the two largest church-wide sports. The most prestigious event was the All-Church Basketball Championship, held annually at the Deseret Gym in Salt Lake. The All-Church tournament was billed as the final tournament of "the largest basketball league in the world." While it seems almost unimaginable today, it was a big enough draw in those days to cause two University of Utah players to leave that team to play for their local church team.

Duff loved church basketball. His ward didn't win when he was younger because they didn't have enough ballplayers. But after the war, the Nineteenth Ward fielded its best team ever. The *Church News* described the players: "All nine boys hold the priesthood. Two of the boys are former missionaries, three are Master M-Men. One serves as a guide on Temple Square, two are Sunday School board members, and seven saw active service in the war."

4. MDH-R, Nov. 25, 2003.
5. MDH-R, Nov. 25, 2003.
6. BUW, 3–4.

Lots of athletes love to reminisce about that singular event in their athletic career—either the one that got away or the one they won, providing them with a story to repeat over, and over, and over. For Duff Hanks, that event was the 1947 LDS All-Church Basketball Championship. His family got to hear about it—a lot.

Duff recalled, "We had a good team that year. Myron and I were the backcourt, and Ralph was the center, and Sterling and Clare scored all the points. If they didn't do well enough, then I went up and scored some, too. Nobody came close to beating us."

Duff's teammates watched a team from Oakland in the semifinal game, declaring them "big, square-shouldered, tough-looking guys." After trouncing the Salt Lake City Twenty-seventh Ward, the Oakland players went to the Hotel Utah (later the Joseph Smith Memorial Building) and had a drunken celebration.

The next night, while Duff's team was getting ready for the championship game, in walked the presidency of the young men's organization of the church, Elbert R. Curtis, Ralph Hardy, and Marvin Ashton.[7] Elbert Curtis told them about the drunken celebration the night before, "These guys can't be crowned champions," he said, "but the stands are filled. By the way, we also found out that only two of their players are LDS, and the rest are all ringers. They found the best ballplayers in the Oakland area and brought them here to win the Mormon Church championship. So, either you fellas beat them, or we call a forfeit. So … *can you beat them?* We'd hate to just send everybody home."

Even though the Oakland team was good, Duff's team had played together for years. They looked at each other, smiled, then told the leaders, "We think we can beat them."

The newspaper reported that the championship game was never close, as Duff's team pulled away to an early 20–0 lead, making it 24–2 at the end of the first quarter. The newspaper reported, "The 19th Ward limited the California crew to a pair of field goals in the first half and only six in the entire game. The final score was 49–15.[8]

Duff emphasized, "Remember, this was the final score in the All-Church Championship Game, where there was usually just a point or two separating the two final teams. And, boy, if ever you want to write a novel about right triumphing—or, at least, wrong not triumphing—you would think that this was it."[9]

Duff also played basketball in several other leagues, including All Star County Rec and AAU teams. As but one example, a newspaper headline declared, "Hanks' Basket Gives Rose Shop Victory." The body of the story reported that Duff scored sixteen of his team's thirty-seven points, "including a last-minute basket in the

7. The young men's organization at the time was called the Young Men's Mutual Improvement Association (YMMIA).

8. Ed McFadden, "19th Wins All-Church," *Salt Lake Tribune*, Mar. 9, 1947, B5.

9. MDH-R, June 20, 2000.

second overtime period that gave the Rose Shop a hard-fought win over the Holladay Merchants in the finals of the county recreation AA basketball league."

MOVING FORWARD

Eventually, Duff graduated from college, while he did everything else he wanted to do—teaching seminary several hours a day, serving on the stake Sunday School board, playing on an All-Church basketball team, working long hours on Temple Square—both leading tours and managing it—and dating Maxine. He said, "I was tapped to be a scholar and disappointed my 'tappers.' I started with all 'A's' and settled for a bit less later. I graduated from law school in two years, and three months, and I decided that I'd never practice law, although I honored the law and loved it."[10]

LONG COURTSHIP AND MARRIAGE

For Maxine and Duff, their introduction in Honolulu began their "association," as Duff put it. It was a slow and painful progression. Maxine transferred from the University of Hawaii to the University of Utah, where she obtained a BS in elementary education. After much back and forth and years full of Duff's commitment to his mother, but no commitment to her, Maxine finally decided to go back to Hawaii—after almost four years of dating—and move on with her life, without Duff.

At home, she composed a letter to Duff expressing her pent-up disappointment and frustration, effectively telling him that he had wasted four years of her life when she could have been dating others who would commit to marriage.

Maxine showed the letter to her father, who advised her not to send a letter that would end the relationship on a negative note. So Maxine wrote a different letter, thanking Duff for everything and saying goodbye.

Duff admitted, "We courted for four years, which was difficult for her because men are dumb, and I was first in that class." After receiving Maxine's letter, "I finally became impressed with the decisive need to make up my mind—I had just graduated from law school and was trying to plot the future. I was living with my mother, and there were some complications."[11]

Gathering his courage, Duff made a long-distance call to Hawaii and proposed to Maxine. They decided to get married in just a couple of weeks.

After the decision was made, time suddenly compressed. "Dearest Duff," Maxine wrote on August 21, 1949. "I just got home and it's about 12:45 am. Janice and Elva had the loveliest shower for me at their home for 30 people. It was such fun and I wish you were here so I could share it with you. . . . I wish you were going to be here to take me through the temple Tuesday night. We're having to kind of

10. MDH-L, to family, "A Life-Sketch," Nov. 7, 1980.
11. MDH-L, to family, "A Life-Sketch," Nov. 7, 1980.

After finally asking Maxine to marry him, Duff quickly flew to Honolulu.

rush things, but I'd rather do it now, than be separated any longer. I wish Wednesday would hurry and get here. I love you, Duff, and always will."[12]

Duff flew to Oahu, where they were sealed in the Laie Hawaii Temple on August 27, 1949. A few friends from the military and elsewhere surrounded the couple, along with all the Christensen friends and family. The reception was held at the Christensen home on the *lanai*,[13] amid the trees, orchids, other flowers, and Hawaiian music.

More than three decades later, Duff wrote in a brief life sketch, "The most important decision I have made in a lifetime of decisions was to call Maxine Lehua Christensen and ask her to be my bride.... We were married in the Hawaiian Temple and have lived happily ever after. Our marriage has been good all the way.

12. Maxine to MDH, Aug. 21, 1949.
13. A *lanai* is a covered porch in Hawaii.

Line at Maxine and Duff's wedding reception in Honolulu, August 27, 1949.

We are learning still, but we learned long ago to be happy and have had every reason to be, every day of our lives."[14]

HONEYMOON

The newlyweds had a brief honeymoon on Oahu and Maui. They stayed in the Hana, Maui, hotel for two nights when the room rate was just twenty-seven dollars a night.[15] It is touching that they stayed in Hana for their honeymoon. Forty-four years later, they would build a home just outside Hana in Muolea, where they spent a few months each year until they died.[16]

From Hawaii they flew to San Francisco, where they stayed in the St. Francis Hotel. Almost thirty years later, Duff and Maxine stayed at the St. Francis again. He wrote, "The place had a certain familiarity, but not a pleasant one." Before they left Honolulu on their honeymoon, a doctor there had given him a large dose of penicillin to treat a rash. Unfortunately, he was also allergic to penicillin and had a violent reaction for the next week.[17]

EARLY MARRIED LIFE

When they returned to Salt Lake from their honeymoon, Duff continued his work as a tour guide on Temple Square and as a teacher at West High seminary.

14. MDH-L to family, "A Life-Sketch," Nov. 7, 1980.
15. Rates now average $750/night.
16. For more on Hana see pages 232 and 546.
17. MDH-JE, June 4, 1977.

Duff and Maxine on their honeymoon, after flying into the old Hana, Maui, airport, 1949.

Maxine taught school until they had their first child. Though they were from very different economic backgrounds, that didn't seem to matter a whole lot. They both came from deeply committed Latter-day Saint families and shared a love of the gospel. They were partners from the beginning and companions, best friends, and sweethearts.

Even though they were barely surviving financially, they didn't worry much. Together, they agreed that their first money would go to the Lord through tithing, and then to help support Maude Hanks. "We just followed that pattern, and Mother didn't live in luxury, but the others were all contributing a little, and I think at that point we were probably contributing more than most," Duff said. "It was a wonderful resolution. All we had to do now was learn how to be happy and take care of [our] children who kept arriving for a couple of years."[18]

Their first apartment, on Third East in Salt Lake City, was so small that it only had room for a "Murphy bed," which folded down from the wall at night and back up during the day. From there they moved to an apartment on J Street, where, in July 1950, they brought home their first baby, Susan. In anticipation of Susan's birth, Duff wrote Maxine a poem, which concluded:

But *this is not* a valentine
Although, it *looks* that way;
It's in anticipation of
Our special Labor Day!

18. MDH-JE, June 4, 1977.

When their second child, Nancy, was born thirteen months later, they moved to a bigger apartment on DeSoto Street, where they lived next to Duff's sister Beulah and her husband, LeGrand, for a couple of years.

ALLEN-DUFF ASSOCIATES AND OTHER THINGS

While working at Temple Square and West High Seminary, Duff partnered with three friends on the side to form an ad agency, called Allen-Duff Associates. Fred Wolters was the company's artist, Coy Miles sold gifts for customers of General Motors, Allen Jensen was the front man, and Duff did the writing. "We had a number of first-class clients who paid first-class money for the few years we were in existence," Duff recounted. "For a while, we were really doing quite well financially."

Later, as the partners went their separate ways, the ad agency split up. They used the agency's last several thousand dollars to produce and sell LeRoy Robertson's *Book of Mormon Oratorio* album, receiving due credit on the label.[19]

FIRST HOME—EMERSON AVENUE

Duff and Maxine bought their first, modest home on Emerson Avenue—sold to them by Cal Rawlings, a member of the Democratic National Committee. They paid fifteen thousand dollars for the house.

When they toured the home, Cal pointed out a rug he had had especially made for his little study. It wasn't big, but it fit. As they walked from room to room, he asked, "Are you serious about buying, Mr. Hanks?"

"Yes, I'm serious," Duff responded, "but I'm going to have to borrow the money. We don't really have any money, and I work for the church as a teacher, but we'll raise it."

Then Cal would say something like, "There are a few troublesome things about the house. For example, I told you that rug was made for that spot, and I can't take it with me. So I must leave it for you. And that painting of the mountains in winter is not a world-beater, but it's one I love. I could take it, and I'm terribly tempted to, but we don't have a place for it in our new home. So, do you mind keeping that? Would that be all right?"

"Yes," Duff gratefully replied.

That's how it went around the whole house. They came to an agreement on the price of the house, and then "Cal ended up tossing in everything else." It was a lovely experience for Maxine and Duff as a poor young couple. Cal and his wife, Ruth, remained dear friends with Duff and Maxine the rest of their lives.[20]

THE NEW TEACHERS QUORUM ADVISOR

All was settled for Duff and Maxine. They had two daughters, he had a job

---

19. MDH-R, Nov. 29, 2000.
20. MDH-R, Sept. 26, 2000; Nov. 29, 2000.

teaching seminary and another job on Temple Square, and they had their first house. Then their bishop stopped by.

"Brother Hanks, we hear you do well with the young people you teach, and we hear stories of your ability to teach the gospel," the bishop said. "We have thirteen boys of teacher age here in the Wasatch Ward, and we can't keep a [Sunday School] teacher in place." How'd you like to quit the downtown Church on Sundays, join the ward, and do some good?'

Duff responded to his bishop, "The Temple Square shift after the choir broadcast on Sunday mornings is rare and coveted—I just accepted it and I am loving it. But if you, as my bishop, are asking me, I didn't learn any other answer but 'yes.' I'll have to rearrange my schedule, but I'll do it."

So, Duff went in with the thirteen boys. He bought them each a new copy of the triple combination (scriptures).[21] Then he made the boys two promises. He said, "I promise you that if you come here, two things will happen. One, we will beat Edgehill Ward and win the basketball championship. And the second promise is, if you are faithful and attend, you'll know about this book. You'll know for the rest of your life that it is true, and your life, therefore, will not be the same."[22]

Both promises came true.

Even with all the things Duff accomplished in his life, he always carried a special sense of love and pride in his teachers quorum from those early years. He watched them go on missions and get married and still talked about them years later. Similar to what he experienced with his seminary and institute students, as these young men spread out, he would meet them all over the world. It was one of his chief joys in life. In November 1976, for example, he flew to Atlanta, Georgia, to conduct a stake conference in the Sandy Springs Georgia Stake. After all the usual Saturday meetings, he was invited to speak at a Scout court of honor that evening. He wrote, "The court was presided over by Bob Sperry, one of my teacher's quorum boys from the Wasatch Ward. As he entered the room, I clouded up a little and so did he when we saw each other. I had a chance to brag about him, and then saw him in action in the Scout meeting and was thrilled."[23]

BECOMING KNOWN AS A SPEAKER

Duff was quickly becoming known as a particularly competent and engaging speaker with a terrific personality. Among the young men of his generation, few had a more profound knowledge of the scriptures. As his reputation spread, he was invited to speak at more and more events. Most months, Duff spoke five or six times. On many Sundays he had speaking engagements and firesides, sometimes two a night. And he was invited to speak at missionary farewells and seminary and institute graduations around the state.

---

21. The Book of Mormon, Doctrine and Covenants, and Pearl of Great Price.
22. MDH-R, Sept. 26, 2000; Nov. 29, 2000.
23. MDH-JE, Nov. 20, 1976.

He also began to get involved in community and civic organizations. He became chair of the Speakers Bureau of the Salt Lake County Community Chest. He spoke at the Optimist Club, became an officer of the Salt Lake City Sons of Utah Pioneers chapter, and served as an officer of the Utah State Handball Association.

TEACHING: HIS PASSION

9

Temple Square

One cannot have intimate acquaintance with these buildings day after day and not acquire in his soul an appreciation for them and for those who built them.
—Marion D. Hanks[1]

Duff's time on Salt Lake City's Temple Square was one of the highlights and most beloved times of his life. Just out of the US Navy, Duff had begun teaching seminary at West High School when he was invited by Ben Bowring, a counselor in a stake presidency with Duff's brother Lincoln, to come to Temple Square as a guide. The new guides learned on the job by going with the older guides. Duff started by doing several tours a week.

"I love Temple Square," he later said. "It provided the sweet opportunity of teaching the rudiments of the gospel and meeting wonderful people." Visitors came with all kinds of preconceived notions about the church, some positive and some negative. Once, when he was explaining what the nineteenth-century Latter-day Saint pioneers had accomplished, a woman said to her husband, "George, isn't it remarkable what ignorant people can do?"

Duff smiled and said, "Madam, the pioneers were not ignorant people; and they didn't cross the continent, suffering every human damnation on the way, because they were ignorant. They were inspired by the Lord. Brigham Young himself is now counted by knowledgeable people as one of the great colonizers in history. He did all that he did, not because he was ignorant, but because he was inspired."

He later added, "It has been a great blessing to be able to tell such good people, and many thousands like them, about the pioneers. They were people of courage and faith and dignity and initiative, who were always willing to give up conveniences and comforts but never their convictions."[2]

Duff served on Temple Square from 1946 to 1962, even after being called as a general authority. Many years later, as he spoke to a group about his love of Temple Square, he was surprised at how emotional he felt about it. "Scores and scores of good people joined the church—hundreds, to be honest—over the many years

1. MDH-T, "Monumental Gifts of the Church," GC, Apr. 1954.
2. GS, 30.

I had a chance to teach there. The story will never be written, but my children should know that except for some of my teaching opportunities, Temple Square probably constitutes the scene of whatever good I've done for the Lord."[3]

TOURS AND QUESTIONS

On the southeast corner of Temple Square, the guides greeted visitors from around the world. After showing a church filmstrip titled *Tops of the Mountains,* guides stood outside at the top of a few stairs leading into the old Bureau of Information and, with a spotlight shining on them, answered questions. "In front of that microphone and light," Duff recalled, "some of the most joyful occasions of my lifetime occurred. We'd have fun with them. I would answer a few questions, and that would usually generate others."

On most days, a few Latter-day Saint visitors in the crowd liked to 'help' the guides by asking 'set-up' questions like "Can everybody go in that temple?" After a session or two of that, Duff would give a cheeky response. "You are a member of the church, aren't you? Why don't you answer that question—here, come up and tell them the answer to the question and explain it." He knew he "was taking a real chance" in doing so.

Duff would invite those who wanted to learn more to meet in a smaller group where he could respond more personally to their questions. Usually, a decent-sized group would come, and ultimately out of that little group, some stood out who wanted to know even more.

Duff's scrapbooks are filled with scores of letters about his tours and teaching on Temple Square. Letter writers complimented him on his answers and the geniality of the conversation. Hundreds sought him out later to tell him they had become members of the church. One of these converts even came to Duff and Maxine's wedding reception in Honolulu. After passing through the reception line at the Christensen home he said to Duff, "You don't know me. I wasn't invited, but I came to see you. I'm the branch president in my branch. I was in a small group you taught on Temple Square in Utah, and you gave me a Book of Mormon. You wouldn't remember me, but I remember you. I came home, found the missionaries, and joined the church. When I saw your wife's picture in the Honolulu newspaper, and who she is marrying, I decided to come and thank you personally."[4]

Another experience occurred with an army colonel who took a tour from Duff on Sunday morning, July 16, 1950. Following an invitation to take a church pamphlet, he inquired, "Is your name in it, young man?"

"No," replied Duff.

"Well, I want to know it. Someday, I'll be hearing great things about you, and I want to remember when I was on a tour with you."[5]

---

3. MDH-JE, June 25, 1975.
4. MDH-R, Sept. 26, 2000.
5. MDH, personal notes, n.d.

Duff teaching as a guide on Temple Square in Salt Lake City, 1951. *Courtesy Deseret News*

After a crowd of 250 members of the United Travelers of America Tour visited, forty-two of them bought copies of the Book of Mormon. Five said they wanted to join the church. One commented to his group that the convention had been turned from an insurance convention into a religious convention. Another shared with a friend in Utah that in his thirty years of traveling across the country he had never had such a wonderful experience as his tour of Temple Square.

Another visitor was so impressed that he sent a letter to church president George Albert Smith. "Last night I heard a program on Temple Square that impressed me deeply," he wrote. "I am a Mormon, recently moved here from San Francisco. Last night, I heard the gospel presented with complete honesty and without compromising the truth and yet in a manner acceptable to the most sensitive of other denominations." The letter writer described Duff and commended the direct, simple, and sincere way he handled questions. "His manner of instruction might well be studied by all who carry our message to the world."[6]

GUIDES AND NON-GUIDES

Duff felt blessed to work with wonderful Latter-day Saint guides, some of the brightest and most committed young members of the church. Dr. Russell Nelson, a heart surgeon, was one of them. "I would often feel uneasy when he came. I would ask, 'Did you leave somebody with their heart open on the table?' and he would calm me down."

"No, you can be sure I didn't," Nelson responded. "I have associates, and I prepared." Russell M. Nelson later became president of the Church of Jesus Christ of Latter-day Saints.

Other wonderful people Duff worked with included future BYU religion professor Truman Madsen, Viola Clawson, and Jean Dunn. After a young man named Neal A. Maxwell gave a talk that Duff heard at the University of Utah, Duff invited him to share time with him every night, five nights a week, talking to three to five hundred people. Maxwell later became a Latter-day Saint apostle.

Duff wrote in his journal, "There were many people who were touched by this guide or that guide, but none, to my memory, like Dr. Marlowe, who was a veterinarian, and a wonderful man with a great spirit. He probably brought more people into the church than any other single guide." One day, a brilliant, well-dressed professor denigrated a few of the other guides and then demanded, "I want to talk to somebody who knows what he is talking about."

He then went out on a group tour led by Dr. Marlowe, after which Dr. Marlowe had to go back to work. The professor went to the Bureau of Information counter with tears in his eyes, "Where is that man? You have now caused me to spend an extra day here, because I can't leave without meeting him personally. I learned more about true religion in a half hour with him than I've heard in my life from my preacher." Dr. Marlowe arranged to come back and take the man to lunch.

Duff noticed with amusement at first, and then with wonder, the number of tourists who avoided the well-dressed guides and the receptionists with their identifying badges, and instead quietly cornered a gardener planting flowers or a plumber fixing a fountain to ask them questions. Somehow, they wanted to avoid what they conceived to be a professional—ready to answer and probably willing to give you a lot more than you want to know—and went to ask questions from regular people.

---

6. Robert B. Hansen to George Albert Smith, Aug. 23, 1950.

EVENING PROGRAMS

Some of the most effective presentations on Temple Square were the evening programs. Attendees included many who had been touched during a tour in the daytime and wanted to learn more. One program included a showing of the 1940 commercial film *Brigham Young*.

The *Brigham Young* film always elicited a certain amount of interest and surprise. It featured famous actors Tyrone Power and Dean Jagger along with Vincent Price as Joseph Smith. After the movie, Duff would stand in front of the stage lights and say, "Okay, I'm a real live Mormon, and I will accept any question you have to ask. I know some of you are going to go back to Iowa or New Jersey tomorrow and ask your friends there about the Mormons, but you have a chance to ask any question right now, and I'll answer all your questions honestly. Quite a few of the answers may be 'I don't know,' but I know how to say that readily, if it's required.'"[7]

Typical of Duff, he lavished praise on all those behind the scenes who made things run successfully. In his journal he talked about a man named LaMar Williams, who came every late afternoon to set up five hundred chairs and a screen contrived from a pipe frame to create a theater environment. He said, "I felt I ought to be there and help put the chairs up and down with LaMar, who never failed."[8]

ASSISTANT DIRECTOR

After Richard L. Evans, a general authority, became the director of Temple Square, Elder Evans invited Duff, along with Bob McKay, to serve with him as a presidency, with authority to call guides, set them apart, and lead operations.

Things changed dramatically at that point. Previously, for example, there had been a sign on the south gate that read, "These grounds will close at 6:30 and will be closed on holidays"—exactly the times when people were crowding the street to get in. That changed immediately, and they stayed as late as people wanted to come.

Duff recalled, "This led to a few excesses—I once met a bus at 2:00 a.m. They were a musical group, and they'd been delayed with flat tires and desperately wanted to see the inside of that building and hear the organ. So, we got Alex Schreiner out of bed, and he came and played the organ for them. I have a tearful letter from that man, saying, 'Our people would have gone home empty and broken-hearted. Thank you for your willingness to come down here.'"[9]

Duff loved Elder Richard L. Evans, who broadcast a message to the world each Sunday with the Mormon Tabernacle Choir. Elder Evans would personally write each week's message of *Music and the Spoken Word*. He was self-effacing and a practitioner of care and kindness. Duff described him as "philosophically remarkable, and a wonderful mentor."

---

7. MDH-R, Sept. 26, 2000; Nov. 1, 2002.
8. MDH-R, Sept. 26, 2000.
9. MDH-R, Sept. 26, 2000.

The visitor count continued to grow, and Duff felt blessed to routinely share his testimony. One day, a man representing the Israeli government visited Temple Square. Duff had a pleasant talk with him, answering questions and testifying of the truths of the Restoration. During the conversation, Duff told him that, in effect, they were cousins since he was of the lineage of Ephraim. The man leaned back, startled, and said, "Say again?" Duff repeated his lineage through Abraham, Isaac, Jacob, and Joseph to Ephraim, according to his patriarchal blessing. The man came back the next morning and said, "Tell me again." They had another wonderful conversation and remained in communication for years. The visitor said, "Well, I came to America to learn about agriculture. I came to Utah to learn about irrigation. I expected to learn many things, but I never expected to find the lost sons of Ephraim."[10]

POLYGAMY AND OTHER TOPICS

Some tourists would arrive having heard strange stories about the Mormons—especially in regard to the church's former practice of polygamy. Duff's approach was different from most. Rather than downplaying or being defensive about the topic, he'd say, "You're here with a worldly view of what plural families were all about—for their own lust and pleasure. But it wasn't like that. With few exceptions, that was not the motivating factor of the Mormon men who pursued the biblical example of what we were supposed to do. They didn't begin it out of any but the most wholesome of reasons. The president of the church, the prophet of God, told them that this was the way they were to live when they qualified through [worthiness] to care for another family. They didn't begin it out of some inappropriate motivation. The Lord told them to do it."

Duff began training the guides in a few simple things. He prepared a booklet providing a baseline background about Temple Square, the Mormon pioneers, and the church. Much of what he taught was a bit different from what the guides had been accustomed to teaching. Similar to his unique way of explaining polygamy, Duff had a different focus of emphasis on many other areas. Another example was his view of Temple Square's Seagull Monument, marking the miracle of the gulls eating the plagues of crickets and thus saving the pioneers' crops. Duff emphasized that the monument wasn't created in honor of seagulls, but rather "In Grateful Remembrance of the Mercy of God to the Mormon Pioneers," as stated on the monument's plaque.[11]

EXPERIENCES

Duff's experiences over two decades on Temple Square could fill volumes. A few other examples will provide a flavor for what he experienced day after day.

---

10. GS, 32.
11. MDH-R, Sept. 26, 2000.

"I Am Looking for Something More"

A man came in needing to understand "this feeling, this sense of dedication, this peace" that he said he had experienced among the Mormons. Duff described him as "a man of real loyalty to principle, whose mind and mouth and life are clean and decent, and who is seeking earnestly to do that which God would have him do. He said, 'I have been an active, loyal, participating member of my church, but I am looking for something more.' He came here to try to discover if that 'something' can be found here."[12]

"A Guide Who So Exuded Goodness"

Duff believed Temple Square exuded a special spirit that the guides and the employees carried with them. In January 1951, Duff received the following letter from a Montana woman about her guide. "Today I visited your Tabernacle and heard the organ recital. Words are inadequate to express my feeling, but most of all I was impressed with our guide, who so exuded goodness I am sure I will try to be a better person because of my sojourn in Salt Lake today."[13]

Baptism by Immersion

A man who had spent more than half a century in the ministry came to Salt Lake after having met two LDS missionaries in California. He wanted to find out if all the members of the church had what he felt in these two humble young men. The missionaries had not been able to reach him with scripture or reason. He had the academic degrees, the experience, and half a century at the pulpit. But they had reached him through a spirit he could not fail to feel and could not explain.

> We had a long talk, the heart of which came when I said to him, "Doctor, there is just one question I need to ask you. Have you been baptized by an authorized administrator for the remission of your sins?" He got a hurt look in his eye. He said, "Elder Hanks, after this wonderful experience of brotherhood and the feeling we've had together, are you telling me that you think I have to go down in a pond of water like a little child to make some kind of a covenant with God?"
>
> They read together from the Bible, "And Jesus answering said unto him, Suffer it to be so now: for thus it becometh us to fulfil all righteousness. Then he suffered him" (Matthew 3:15). That is, Jesus was baptized by John.
>
> Now this courteous, gracious, wonderful man almost struck the book from my hand. He said, "I know very well what that says, but nowhere is it explained what it means. Christ was sinless. What does it mean to fulfill all righteousness?"
>
> And I said, "It is, in fact, written in the Book of Mormon." And we read together where those very words are explained (2 Nephi 31).
>
> I watched a tear hit the carpet. And then I heard his voice, through the tears, say, "Elder Hanks, it appears there are some things we should talk about. Do you have

12. See *GS*, 203–4.
13. Letter to MDH, Mrs. O. G. Benson, Plentywood, Montana.

some time?" We sat in an office on Temple Square in Salt Lake City, and I taught him some answers he himself had been seeking for more than fifty years at the pulpit. After some time, he found those two young missionaries in California and went down like a child into the water and was baptized, received the priesthood, and, at the age of eighty-one, became a noble, courageous teacher of the gospel.[14]

Christmases on Temple Square

Duff's call as a general authority altered his Temple Square assignment, but he carried on until the day he and Maxine were called as mission presidents in England. He talked about his lengthy service:

"By then, I had been there Sunday mornings for how many general conferences, I don't know. I'd also go down every Christmas, and let one of the others go home, where they belonged. I had, in the first years, no wife and no children. But even later, after I was married, Maxine was a saint, and she'd come and bring our little people in their strollers, so it was nice."[15]

GROWING TEMPLE SQUARE AND THE *CHRISTUS*

With the number of visitors increasing and the resources of Temple Square's Bureau of Information woefully inadequate, Richard L. Evans and Duff began investigating how other tourist locations operated. They traveled back east several times, accompanied by others, including church architect Don Carlos Young. They visited the New York Stock Exchange. They reviewed the way a new visitors' center in Williamsburg, Virginia, used films to tell the story of the Revolutionary War.

On their visit to the Christian Science Center in Boston, they noticed that the focus of the tours there was on the buildings and statistics of Christian Science rather than on the beliefs and teachings of the church and Mary Baker Eddy. Both Elder Evans and Duff left reinforced in their shared belief that the message of Temple Square needed to be focused on the Savior and the faith that drove the Mormon pioneers to Utah. "Let's concentrate on the great and remarkable story we have to teach," Evans and Duff instructed the Temple Square guides after they returned.

One gleam in Duff's eyes over the years was a way to more clearly demonstrate to the public that Mormons were Christian. Over a period of many years, he had been pushing for some representation of Christ on Temple Square. Elder J. Reuben Clark opposed the idea, and Elder Evans declined to propose it again. Duff kept pushing. He wrote, "The day Richard was convinced to again propose it and permit me to offer testimony on behalf of the idea to the First Presidency was a great day."

In June of 1957, Richard L. Evans, Robert McKay, and Duff met with the First Presidency concerning proposed changes to Temple Square. As they were

14. BUW, 311–13.

15. MDH-R, Sept. 26, 2000.

The *Christus* statue and the North Visitors Center on Temple Square, which were initiated by Duff and Richard L. Evans. *Courtesy LDS Church*

entering the council room, Elder Evans turned to Duff and said, "How would you like to go down in history as the guy who messed up Temple Square?"[16]

Duff remembered, "We went in, and I made the proposal for the two new visitors centers we wanted to build on the Square, one over on the northwest corner where it now rests and one to be built where the old Bureau of Information was, with the [Native American] artifacts upstairs."

Duff then expressed their feeling that the church needed a representation of the Savior that would leave little doubt that Mormons were Christians. They wanted something that would be well known and be received without controversy. Duff then suggested Thorvaldsen's *Christus* in Copenhagen, Denmark. He said:

> What we would like is to get your authority to acquire a copy of that statue. President McKay listened to my idea, slapped his thigh, and said, "Why not!" before President Clark had a chance to deliver his "we don't believe in icons" response again.
>
> President McKay then turned to his first counselor, Stephen L Richards, and asked him if he didn't have access to acquire a statue from President Richard's friend that owned Forest Lawn Cemetery (who owned the right to make copies of the statue).
>
> President McKay asked, "Do you think they might let us make one?" President Richards said, "He's offered it, President. I've told you this before; I'm sure he would

16. MDH-T, "Principles and Procedures in Selecting a New Stake President," Teaching the First Quorum of the Seventy, Jan. 11, 1979, 3.

hand it to us at no charge." And he did. That's where all these statues of *the Christus* began. They're in many places now—in visitors' centers around the world.[17]

In April 2020, the church introduced a new symbol of the faith, which includes an image of the *Christus* statue.

RELEASE FROM TEMPLE SQUARE MISSION PRESIDENCY

In December 1965, the Temple Square Mission Presidency was released and the oversight of all church museums and visitors' centers was consolidated under one central organization.

"I left there assuming that neither I, nor Temple Square, would ever be the same. It was such an integral part of my life," Duff said. "But no one is indispensable; and if you want to know how indispensable you are, put your finger in a glass of water, pull it out, and see the hole it makes.

"I love Temple Square. I went through law school, and marriage, and became a general authority, and mission president, and many other things, but it was still home base to me."[18]

17. MDH-R, Nov. 25, 2003.
18. MDH-R, Sept. 26, 2000.

10

Teaching, Learning, and Education

Elder Marion D. Hanks is one of the greatest teachers on earth. When he teaches, he comes alive.
—Hyrum Smith[1]

No message to teachers of the church should be without reference to my dear friend Duff Hanks, one of the most effective and most loved teachers in the church.
—Thomas S. Monson[2]

Duff was a born teacher.

It's what made him tick. The venues varied, but the messages didn't—service, uplifting others, supporting the underdog, the worth of the individual, importance of the scriptures, forgiveness, mercy, and the Savior Jesus Christ.

Someone said, "Teaching isn't filling a bucket; it's lighting a fire." Duff lit fires. He was also known for being completely honest in his teaching and candid in his responses to challenging issues. When you asked him the really tough questions about life, you knew that he had asked them too.

His friend Professor Eugene England wrote, "Duff is that highest form of teacher whose students not only learn, but learn *how* to learn, who not only know truths but learn to assess how things are true and to change their minds to better truths—in other words, he is a teacher who produces good teachers."[3]

Elder F. David Stanley wrote, "My association with Elder Hanks has taken place over several decades on many occasions. I consider him to be the 'Master Teacher' of all mortal men I have been associated with."[4]

Duff's lifelong association with learning and education began at his mother's knee. Maude Hanks taught her children to love good and decent things. They

1. Hyrum W. Smith (1943–2019) was an author, public speaker, and founder of the productivity company Franklin Quest. He also served as a young missionary under Duff in England.

2. Thomas S. Monson to John Baird, Feb. 14, 2007.

3. Eugene England, "Marion D. Hanks: The Quality of Mercy," in *Teachers Who Touch Lives*, comp. Philip L. Barlow (Bountiful, UT: Horizon, 1988), 64. Eugene England (1933–2001) was an LDS professor, essayist, book author, and scholar.

4. F. David Stanley was a general authority from 1992 to 1997 and a colleague of Duff's as a member of the seventy.

Teaching at a stake training meeting.

Teaching in the Holy Land.

Teaching at the Institute of Religion, University of Utah.

Teaching troops in Vietnam.

Teaching at a family reunion.

Teaching grandchildren at the cabin.

were taught from the best books, listened to good music, and gained a real love of learning.

"How grateful I am for the Relief Society work my mother did in teaching literature and social science!" Duff said. "I first heard of Longfellow and Hawthorne, of Shelley and Shakespeare through her studies. My first acquaintance with the names of Sir Walter Scott and of Lewis and Clark came around the table as she prepared lessons. My first efforts to write poetry were based on her lovely poems, stimulated by her Relief Society labors."[5]

As a youngster, Duff had mixed experience with teachers, some very good and some not quite so good. The unprepared or robotic teachers bothered him and caused him to be less faithful in attendance than he should have been, because he was not comfortable with the teachers or the kind of teaching they did. Later on, after he had some outstanding teachers, he became more convinced that anybody who undertakes teaching ought to do some very serious thinking and preparation. He didn't know then that he would spend a major portion of his life teaching, but he did have some strong feelings about being a teacher.

THE CHURCH'S DOCTRINAL FOCUS ON EDUCATION

Part of Duff's natural attraction to teaching came from his considerable activity in the Church of Jesus Christ of Latter-day Saints. In the LDS tradition, education is not only a lifetime process but also an eternal one. The church teaches that God's purpose in creating people is so that they may gain eternal life—God's life. A big part of that process is the increase of knowledge that comes from education. In fact, a fundamental teaching of the church is that salvation itself depends on knowledge—that it is "impossible for a man to be saved in ignorance" and "if a person gains more knowledge and intelligence in this life through his diligence and obedience than another, he will have so much the advantage in the world to come" (D&C 131:6; 130:19). Latter-day Saint scriptures are replete with instructions on learning, study, and education.

SERVING THE INDIVIDUAL IS TEACHING'S PURPOSE

Duff believed that the purpose of teaching was to mold lives, develop character, challenge minds, and inspire souls. He proposed that the vocation of a teacher was to serve individuals by helping them develop their highest potential. He summarized that feeling in an instructional handout, in which he wrote that a teacher's responsibility to students is to:

- Lead them to purposeful, participating citizenship.
- Assist them to become contributing, worthwhile individuals.

---

5. GS, 48; In the early twentieth century, the Relief Society curriculum included lessons on literature, community improvement, home economics, nursing, modern social work techniques, advice on household management, maternity and child welfare, and the group ran an employment bureau for young women. See "Relief Society," churchofjesuschrist.org.

- Teach them to have honor, integrity, morality, responsibility.
- Inspire them with knowledge of God and a bright future.

Duff taught that influential teachers are in a position to do much more than teach lessons and tell stories. They can motivate and stretch students' minds and awaken in them a love of truth.

Reminiscing about their fifty-year friendship, chief justice Cliff Wallace of the US Ninth Circuit Court of Appeals said of Duff, "He was my teacher. Discussions with him were like being on a long journey through a hot desert and finding an oasis with shade and water. That's the best description I can give of his teaching."[6]

WHERE HE TAUGHT

Seminary and the Beginning of Early-Morning Seminary

After returning from war, Duff began teaching seminary at his alma mater, West High School. In the mid-1940s, the Salt Lake City Board of Education permitted "released time" classes during the school day for religious instruction. This resolution became useless, however, in the late 1940s when some states, including Utah and California, raised graduation requirements, leaving students no time in their school schedules for daytime seminary classes.[7]

As a solution, the church began offering seminary classes just before school started, usually from 7:45 to 8:30 a.m. But students involved in extracurricular school activities in the morning couldn't attend at that time, either. Several of them asked Duff if he could help them with this problem because they wanted to graduate from seminary. Duff said, "If you want to come at 6 a.m. and meet me, we'll get you involved for a year's credit." They agreed. It was not easy for Duff to teach that extra, early-morning class, because he was also a full-time college student in addition to his other seminary teaching load and his Temple Square responsibility.

The first students brought others, who brought others, and the class size grew throughout that 1948–49 school year.

At some point, Duff was summoned to meet with Dr. Franklin L. West, LDS Church commissioner of education, who asked him to describe what in the world he was doing at 6:00 a.m. at the West High Seminary.

"Well, we're teaching early morning seminary," Duff replied.

"Has this been up through the chain of command?" West asked, wondering if Duff had gotten approval from his supervisor.

"No, it's just young people wanting to learn the gospel and get credit so they can graduate from seminary."[8]

6. J. Clifford Wallace, "The Growth of My Little World," University of Utah College of Law commencement address, May 14, 2010.

7. "Early Morning Seminary Celebrates 60 Years," Sept. 27, 2010, churchofjesuschrist.org.

8. MDH-R, May 15, 2001.

BY THE DAWN'S EARLY LIGHT THIS SEMINARY CLASS CONVENES
Instructor Marion D. Hanks welcomes Mitzi Wahlen, Douglas Carpenter, LaVon Davis

Newspaper article describing Duff's early-morning seminary class at West High School in Salt Lake City, 1948–49 school year. *Courtesy Deseret News*

The early-morning seminary class proved so successful that the church decided to replicate it in Southern California, where a group of stake presidents had recently requested permission to hold seminary classes outside of school time. Duff was asked to begin the program there, but he had other commitments, and graciously declined. After six years, more than 9,000 students were attending. Eventually, early-morning seminary classes expanded across the country and around the world.[9]

That wasn't the only way that Duff's early morning class was pathbreaking. In those days, there was no set curriculum for seminary students, so Duff chose to use the Book of Mormon as the course of study, using the scriptures as textbooks. "As far as I know," Duff wrote, "this is the first time that there was an organized effort to teach the Book of Mormon." Though hard to imagine today, at that time, the Book of Mormon was not a regular part of the church's teaching rotation of annual study. As the church website records, "Marion D. Hanks, a young attorney, taught early-morning seminary in Salt Lake City, Utah, pioneering the use of the Book of Mormon."[10]

9. "Early-Morning Seminary Celebrates 60 Years," Sept. 27, 2010, churchofjesuschrist.org.

10. *By Study and Also by Faith—One Hundred Years of Seminaries and Institutes of Religion,*

Duff loved the Book of Mormon and studied it diligently, but there were few commentaries or scholars on the book at that time. He started writing up lesson plans and lessons of life taught in the scriptures. He would go on to author some of the church's earliest teaching aides, including a detailed chart showing the journeys in the Book of Mormon, and an outline of the different plates that make up the book. (see appendix E)

One of Duff's students, Toby Pingree, described the class. "Since this was an 'extra' class, Duff apparently felt he could be more flexible in his teaching methodology. Usually seminary classes were about events, persons, and historical context using selected scriptures, quotations from church leaders and other sources. In our Book of Mormon class, we started reading from 'I, Nephi,' verse by verse, until we were through Moroni. Sometimes we focused intensely on the text, and other times we read quickly. The atmosphere was different in this class from any other—every student was involved and active. Marion D. Hanks became a role model for us in so many ways. We emerged from that experience with a greatly expanded view of the message and meaning of the life of Christ."[11]

When Duff described his class in his meeting with Dr. West, West queried, "So, you are going to stand up there and read from the Book of Mormon?"

"Yes."

"They will never come!"

"But they do," Duff answered.

The class was a great success, and the students obviously enjoyed it, as evidenced by their sacrifice of sleep and willingness to brave the winter weather to attend. Many hearts were touched as they read through the Book of Mormon together. One student, Mary Ann Dickson, wrote, "I pray that soon I will be worthy enough to be baptized. I sincerely hope that other people will have the privilege of being in your classes so that they will learn to love the gospel as I do."

Commissioner West told Duff that he wanted Joy F. Dunyon, another leader in the Church Education System, to observe Duff's class for a couple of weeks.

---

chapter 2: "The Charted Course, 1936–1952," churchofjesuschrist.org. Before the late 1940s, teaching directly out of the scriptures did not occur much, and if it did, it was primarily from the Bible. In the early 1930s the seminary program came under attack from the Utah State Board of Education who challenged its legality, citing problems like joint registration, seminary photos in yearbooks, and so on. Much of the Bible curriculum was rewritten to remove all references to the other standard works of the church. A scan of seminary teaching materials over the next fifteen years listed titles such as "The Truth of Mormonism," "Questions and Answers," and "The Program of the Church," with the curriculum focused on teaching doctrines and principles rather than a study of scriptural text. As one historian wrote, "The period of 1934–1953 was a period in commotion.… Curriculum in this era focused primarily on a nonsectarian Bible approach which can be seen in the manuals 'The Old Testament and the Problems of Life' and 'The New Testament and the Problems of Life.'" Griffin Sorenson, "A History of Seminary Curriculum in The Church of Jesus Christ of Latter-day Saints: 1912–2016," 44–45, BYU ScholarsArchive (2017), scholarsarchive.byu.edu.

11. J. Frederick "Toby" Pingree, "Early-Morning Seminary at West High School" (unpublished essay).

After a few days, Joy approached Duff and said, "I won't be here anymore." With trepidation, Duff asked him what report he was going to make.

Brother Dunyon said, "I have a book full of notes about things I've never even thought about. I'm going to tell them that, and that you're the best and most unusual teacher in the church."[12]

Up to that point, Duff had been volunteer teaching just for the love of the kids. From this point on, he started to receive some compensation as a seminary teacher.

Institute of Religion, University of Utah

In 1950, two years after Duff's graduation from the U, the legendary Lowell Bennion invited him to teach institute—religious classes for college students—at the University of Utah. Duff taught classes called "Mormon Doctrine and Philosophy" and "Studies in the Book of Mormon."

By then, Bennion was famous for his writings and for his tactical and practical expressions of true charity, a sterling example of "pure religion … before God" (James 1:27). Additionally, Bennion had written many church teaching manuals. Duff felt that no one exceeded him in his capacity to influence naturally, persistently, and honestly.

Duff was pleased to join Bennion at the U's Institute of Religion along with T. Edgar Lyon and George Boyd. Lyon and Bennion had been teachers at the institute when Duff was a freshman at the University of Utah. They were highly compatible but quite different in style. An intelligent and engaging teacher, Lyon was a historian focused on facts. Some described him as an iconoclast or de-mystifyer. Bennion was well known for his writings and wisdom. He was also an idealist and motivator who practiced true religion and involved students in helping widows and the poor. Theologian and philosophy professor Sterling McMurrin described this group of institute teachers as "the finest religion faculty ever to grace the church." Duff later said, "I have never enjoyed anything more than my association with those three men. I suppose I tried to emulate all of them in a measure, but ultimately decided that I had to be myself."[13]

Besides being brilliant teachers and devoted to the church, they were known by their students as men who acted on what they taught. In a *Sunstone Magazine* article, Eugene England, one of their former students, described them as "having the unique authority of practicing Christians.… When that faculty told us the gospel was true, and that it called us to a life of selfless service, we believed them."[14]

A Beacon

Duff's role as a teacher was as a beacon of light to his students, who beat a

12. MDH-R, May 15, 2001.
13. MDH-L to Ed Lyon's grandson, Apr. 1988.
14. Eugene England, "The Achievement of Lowell Bennion," *Sunstone,* July 1988, 24–30.

path to his classroom doors. "It was such a warm and wonderful experience," he recalled. "I loved to teach, and I loved those kids." Every year until he died, he received hundreds of letters and cards from all over the United States from his former seminary and institute students. A common refrain in those letters was, "I still have my copy of the Book of Mormon that I used as you taught us."

One wrote, "Dear Elder Hanks, I attribute much of my testimony to your teaching and example at West High Seminary." Said another, "Outside of my family, you were the single biggest influence in my life. In my years of teaching seminary, I often quoted you and recalled many of your wonderful stories and examples."[15] Another said, "I am so grateful to have attended your institute classes, especially since I'm a convert to the church.... My parents didn't teach me about compassion, unselfishness, humility, and forgiveness. I am grateful to have learned something of them from you by example, as well as words."[16]

After his call as a general authority, Duff continued to teach his seminary classes through the end of the 1953–54 school year. He continued to teach his institute classes at the University of Utah Institute for another sixteen years, until December 1969.

In 1965, Duff's institute students gave him a plaque that read

> A persuasive voice who has spoken to us with a gentle might and heightened our love of the scriptures. "Thou art a teacher come from God."[17]

Mission Home and Mission Field

As a missionary, a general authority, and a mission president, Duff was pleased to teach. As a missionary, Duff taught investigators every day. At the mission home in Salt Lake, for years he taught a course on "answering difficult questions" to thousands of missionaries on their way out to the mission field.

Rotary and Scouting

Duff came to love and respect the mission of Rotary International and was invited to speak and instruct at many Rotary training seminars around the world.

He also served on Scouting's highest level and like his experience with Rotary, it was not enough for him to serve in administrative roles—he taught the values and principles of Scouting at regional, national, and international trainings. He also came to love Philmont Scout Ranch in New Mexico, where the Boy Scouts of America trained many of its leaders.

New General Authorities

Over a forty-year period, Duff was pleased to be asked to train a multitude of his fellow general authorities. Such trainings took place in groups and in one-on-one lessons. Some were formal classroom-type training, but most were

15. Jeanne Davey Hardy to MDH, Apr. 2002.
16. Dorothy Schulz to MDH, 1965.
17. Plaque inscription: "In Grateful Appreciation, Your Class, Institute of Religion, 1964–65."

on-the-job experiences. This included newer general authorities being assigned to Duff's committees, and a large number of newer colleagues assigned to stake conferences, accompanying Duff as a junior companion. For example, Elder Marlin Jensen wrote to Duff saying, "Your interest and concern were touching indeed. For our entire adult lives we had admired you and hung on your every word, and then suddenly we were your associates in the work! You made us feel like we belonged and could measure up. This was critical to us in those early years."[18] Duff felt a mutual affection for Elder Jensen, handwriting on the letter, "Marlin Jensen is a dear, respected friend and associate."

Another representative letter will supply some background on his efforts. In August 1992, when Duff became an emeritus general authority, he received a letter from Elder Dallin H. Oaks that read: "Dear Duff, last evening I read the seventy's minutes of June 11, 1992, containing excerpts from your remarks. I was greatly inspired. No one outranks you in the ability to touch the heart and motivate the soul. For example, I will always be guided by the counsel you gave Russell Nelson and me, as newly called general authorities, on how to counsel couples and perform marriages in the temple. We miss you already, and we will miss you in the years ahead. But we will never be without you since a bit of you is built into all of us."[19]

At Maxine's funeral, in February 2018, Russell M. Nelson, newly called president of the church, said that he still has the notecard from his training with Duff hanging in his locker in the Salt Lake Temple.

In the scrapbooks that his secretary, Phyllis, prepared are many sweet expressions of gratitude from other church leaders that Duff was privileged to mentor or train in various aspects of their responsibilities. Included are letters from Russell M. Nelson, Dallin H. Oaks, Jeffrey R. Holland, Quentin L. Cook, Elaine Cannon, Richard G. Scott, David B. Haight, Elaine Jack, Neal A. Maxwell, Chieko N. Okazaki, Marlin K. Jensen, Ardeth G. Kapp, most of his colleagues in the Seven Presidents of Seventy, and scores of others.

WHAT HE TAUGHT

Provocation and Direction to Action

Early in his ministry, Duff decided that he preferred to focus his teaching on what he called the "lessons of life" that are found in the scriptures. That isn't to say that he was not extremely capable of teasing out complex doctrines or delving into detailed historical facts—he was. But he preferred to teach precepts that motivated change and improvement in the lives of his students.

He taught his classes a quotation from Ralph Waldo Emerson that he had written in the front of his scriptures: "It is not instruction, but provocation, that one can receive from another."[20]

18. Marlin Jensen to MDH, n.d.
19. Dallin Oaks to MDH, Aug. 27, 1992.
20. Ralph Waldo Emerson, "Graduation Remarks," *Harvard Divinity School*, July 15, 1838.

Duff said, "We are quite a disappointment to some who expect great academic scholarship here. That is possible, but for now I am very interested that you and I learn to love the book and get a feeling about it that will compel *action,* and *guide* what you are doing. If that happens, then we have accomplished something."[21]

Teaching in the Context of Faith

Inside one of his notebooks, Duff had typed these words to himself: "Teach in a context of faith, not doubt. Seek. Search. Knock. Ask. Yes! Question? Yes! But teach in the atmosphere of conviction!"

His Love of Teaching and Love of Students

Duff loved telling the story of John Trebonius, a humble schoolteacher in Germany many years ago. He was known for the unusually respectful attitude he showed toward the young people in his classroom. While it was the custom of the day for professors to keep their hats on, he used to remove his hat, explaining, "I do not know but that there sits among these boys one who will change the destiny of mankind. I take off my hat in deference to what they may become." Sitting in that classroom, under the influence of that wise and gentle man, was a young Martin Luther, whose courage and convictions did indeed change the world.[22]

Duff asked himself often, "Who is in your classroom that you may inspire?"

Duff had tender feelings about teaching. Here are some of those feelings:

"I love to be near university campuses, and particularly this one at this time of the year. The season's mix of apprehension, anticipation, anxiety, rejoicing, rush, and wait blends into an excitement that charges me. For more than twenty years I stood behind a teacher's table by a chalkboard and had my joy. But the years away from it have intensified within me the assurance that there is no greater or more rewarding work than teaching. I am reminded of it often as I meet those (and their families) with whom I had the blessing of sharing a classroom."[23]

He wrote, "I am honored to be in a small way an *instrument* of his love, an *agent* of his compassionate concern, as one who needs his mercy; a *teacher* testifying that 'in his will is our peace' and that he 'waits,' as the scriptures declare to be *merciful* when we come to ourselves, our better selves, and truly repent of our sins."[24]

"It has been a good day, as any day is when I am blessed to be able to teach. I love a blackboard and some chalk and a chance to teach. Maybe I will yet have that further privilege, which I would gladly now undertake, thinking that I might do some good in the process."

Preparation for Teaching

Duff understood the influence one good teacher can have on future generations. To make his point, he often quoted from a framed picture on his wall:

---

21. MDH-L to his students at the University of Utah institute.
22. Jeffrey R. Holland, "A School in Zion," BYU, Aug. 22, 1988.
23. BUW, 73.
24. MDH, handwritten note on yellow pad, no context.

You can count the seeds in an apple,
but can you count the apples in a seed?

He knew he wasn't teaching just one person but potentially hundreds of their future descendants by advance proxy. Because of that perspective, Duff felt it was his duty and his responsibility to diligently prepare for his classes.

It is hard to overestimate the tens, if not hundreds of thousands of quotations, articles, notes, ideas, and other writings that Duff collected over his lifetime. As he would come upon some piece of writing that intrigued him, he would pull out his marking pens and begin highlighting things that stood out to him. The margins of most articles were full of notes to himself and cross-references to other things he was reading or thinking about.

Due to his outrageous travel and work schedule, much of his studying came late at night after everyone else had gone to bed. His daughter Nancy captured his work with a poem that includes this stanza:

There was always light from my father's den,
cracking the door, warming the hall.
Sitting in darkness, washed in white
he read through the nights of my youth,
finding in words the secrets of sorrow,
the fruits of grief, the lessons of pain.[25]

The sentence "I cannot live without books" is widely attributed to Thomas Jefferson, but it could easily have been attributed to Duff. His study was his sanctuary. It was filled with books and magazines and articles and papers and a trusty typewriter. There were quotations and Dictaphone tapes and in-process speeches, and class outlines stacked up. Once when he was asked why he slept so little, he replied "Because I have so little time." His answer wasn't due to some sort of Protestant work ethic. It was him using every precious moment.

Application of Scriptures and of Principles

One of Duff's specialties in teaching came from 1 Nephi 19:22–23 in the Book of Mormon. Duff would write at the top of the blackboard,

"WHY STUDY SCRIPTURE?"

He would then list three answers from those verses:

"1. Know of the Lord's dealing with *others,*
"2. Persuade them to believe in the *Redeemer*, and
"3. *Liken them* (and apply) to our own situation."

Duff was an expert at pulling out from scripture, not only what they *mean* but

25. Nancy Hanks Baird, "Gate of Heaven," *The Shell in Silk* (Salt Lake City: Publishers Press, 1996), 34.

how they can be *applied* to our lives. Somehow, he could clearly see what he called "Lessons of Life" embedded in the scriptures.

Here are just a few examples from among hundreds:

> SCRIPTURE: The Book of Mormon begins in 1 Nephi 1:1 with these words: "I, Nephi, having been born of goodly parents ..."
>
> APPLICATION: Duff was keenly aware that the world was full of people who hadn't been born of "goodly parents," so he implored his students and readers to think about their futures by applying the scripture to themselves, replacing the words of the scripture with "I, Susie, who will someday *be* a goodly parent ...

> SCRIPTURE: In 1 Nephi 16:20–23, we read about Nephi breaking his bow in the wilderness. Faced with the prospect of starvation, even Father Lehi joined in murmuring against the Lord. Rather than murmur, however, Nephi made another bow, approached his father, and asked, "Whither shall I go to obtain food?"
>
> APPLICATION: Again, Duff would apply the situation to our lives: "A son who had strength enough, and humility enough, to go to his wavering father and say, 'You ask God, will you?' because somehow, he knew that this is how you make men strong, that confidence in men builds them. Lehi asked God, and God told him, and Lehi's leadership was restored."

Duff's daughter Ann summarized: "To Dad, each scripture was a lesson of life. We were taught to love books, love the scriptures, and to mark them. Most people have one set of marked scriptures. He had scores. He'd mark one for six months or a year, and then give it away, and start over."

Duff later explained, "This method is the heart of all the teaching I've done. We *read.* Then, we try to understand what God has taught his people in *other times* and how this helped them *believe* in the Lord their Redeemer—and then how to apply the lessons. Then you go and *apply* them."

From his early handwritten materials, Duff progressed to manufacturing pages on what he called his "roly-poly duplicator" (copy machines hadn't yet been invented.) Over time, the collection of materials he had prepared grew. By the time he was called as a mission president in 1961, Duff had consolidated them into a home-made collection he entitled, "KNOW THE BOOK," which began on the first page of the Book of Mormon to pick out important lessons and continued throughout the entire book.

The first thing Duff did was to ask each missionary to get a general overview of the Book of Mormon by reading an inexpensive edition in two weeks. At the end of the two weeks, they were to begin again, this time with a red pencil, marking every reference to Christ and the doctrines centering in Christ. He'd then invite them to read it a third time, marking those stories or instructions that had direct application to their own lives.

After reading it three times, every one of his missionaries in England then used "KNOW THE BOOK" in their daily study lessons. Eventually his students and missionaries became teachers and church leaders who used this method to teach. He said, "People are so kind. I have sweet temple workers who give me a big smile and remind me that they and their children and grandchildren are still using this approach and still have their scriptures with the markings in the margins. Just yesterday I got a letter from a woman who wrote to me and said, 'The day my life changed is the day I heard those words: "I, Donna, who would like to someday be a goodly parent." I knew I didn't have to follow the conduct of my own parents who showed no love—I could be the pivot point.'"

Effort Required to Learn

As I looked around the room at the Seventies week after week, I was pretty confident that Duff had forgotten more than most of the other Seventies ever knew.
—Elder Glen L. Rudd

Duff was particularly interested in his students putting forth the necessary effort to really learn and grow. He talked about the need to invest time and work into truly learning the scriptures. He believed that all engaged teachers needed to be engaged learners. The scriptures themselves describe the investment required by using words like *knock, seek, search*—each of which suggests a sense of investment in self.

He said, "Learning is not automatic. You don't automatically know how to read when you turn five years old. Most of us understand that we still have something to learn at every step of the way. It comes with seeking and searching, with reading and watching, with thinking, praying, and listening."

In dealing with those who were experiencing difficulty with their faith, Duff felt it imperative that all sides of an issue be given equal weight and effort in study. He counseled with people who had spent hours and hours investigating some negative aspect of the gospel or the church, but when he inquired how much time they had spent in the scriptures, there was a paucity of response. Equally prevalent were the numbers of people who had strong testimonies and commitment but had not expended much *recent effort* studying, instead relying on past education. He wrote a piece titled "Theological Illiterates," in which he quoted from Elder John A. Widtsoe's biography, and said:

> No one knows anything about Christ's work simply by being born a member of the church, and often he knows little about it after years of unmotivated exposure in meetings or classes. He must learn. And learning involves self-investment and effort. The gospel should be studied "as carefully as any science." "The literature of the church must be acquired and read." Our learning should be increased day by day. As we put the gospel truth to work in daily life, we will never find it wanting. We will be literate in the most important field of knowledge in the universe,

knowledge for lack of which men and nations perish, in the light of which men and nations may be saved.[26]

Duff once counseled with a woman, professionally qualified in her field, who was thinking of leaving the church because she had read about some problem in church history. Duff asked her when she had last done any serious reading about the church. She answered that it was in the ninth grade, studying the Book of Mormon in seminary, but that she had quit. And not long after that, she had quit living the principles of the church as well.

Duff asked the woman if she would like him to do what he could to help her get the interior design contract for the new Church Office Building being built. Would she like that?

"Of course!" she replied.

Duff answered, "There is only one catch. If you get the contract, you can only perform your specialty on that building based on what you knew about interior design when you were in ninth grade."

The point was made.

Saying "I Don't Know" and Teaching with Humility

Maxine and Duff taught their children that it is okay to question and wonder but that they should always look to the church to find answers. They also taught them that "I don't know" is a perfectly acceptable answer and that "not knowing" does not equate to "not being true." In the inside cover of his scriptures, Duff placed several yellow stickies to remind him of principles he wanted to emphasize. On one of them he had written simply, "*I know, and testify.*" Underneath that he had written "*I don't know.*"

Duff used the words of Alma speaking to the people of Gideon to illustrate this principle. Alma is asked about the coming of the Savior and when it will occur. Alma testified of what he *did know* and declared his faith that, "the time is not far distant that the Redeemer liveth and cometh among his people."

His next words are, "Behold, ... now as to this thing *I do not know.*" In other places, Alma bears witness and declares what he does know and repeatedly writes what he does not know. Here are some of the phrases he uses: "I do not suppose"; "I do not say, but let it suffice"; "I give it as my opinion" (Alma 7:8; 40:5, 17, 20).

Duff continued, "The principle is sure. What one knows, one testifies. What one doesn't know, one doesn't embellish, elaborate, stretch the truth, or invent. As a teacher, one must be willing to say, 'I don't know, but I will search for answers with you.' I am reminded of the story of the student who asked his professor a question by saying, 'Do you think ... XYZ?' The professor answered arrogantly, 'Young man, I do not think; *I know!*' To which the young student replied, 'Oh good, *I don't think I know, either.*'"

26. MDH-A, "Theological Illiterates," *Improvement Era*, Era of Youth section, Sept. 1969, 42, quoting from John A Widtsoe's biography, *In a Sunlit Land*.

In a 1985 training meeting of all the seventy, he reminded them that they were in positions they didn't apply for, positions recognized as having great significance in the eyes of church members and that carried a special responsibility to be modest, restrained, and correct in the counsel they provided and inspired to the extent they were prayerful. He summarized, "We each have a sense of our own limitations. We do not suddenly become all wise because we are a general authority, but the impact of our statements become greater and the more profound, and maybe we ought to prayerfully think again and again about doctrines we have decided on."[27]

Duff believed that teachers with confidence in their message should be willing to accept ignorance in unrevealed matters. If someone made a definitive pronouncement about this or that, he would quote Alma, "Now these mysteries are not yet fully made known unto me; therefore, I shall forbear" (Alma 37:11).

Duff often shared a talk by Anthony W. Ivins of the First Presidency, given on July 13, 1934, two weeks before his death. President Ivins spoke about teaching with humility and said, "There are many things I don't know and don't understand. I don't try to build up an idea or theory of my own and make it fit into something the Lord has said. If I don't see it clearly, I don't hesitate to say, I don't know. I don't argue with those who say the earth is only six thousand years old, or those who say it is six million. I know we are here on it, and I know the Lord has told us why we are here. The time will come when we will know all the rest."[28]

Duff also loved quoting President David O. McKay, who when asked to opine on some disputed doctrine, began his answer with "It would do no violence to my faith if..."

Teaching in All Settings

Duff chose to be a teacher all the time. The meetings he conducted, no matter the subject, always included some literature to learn or appreciate, some poignant story, or some scriptural principle.

"I recall many occasions we sat together in meetings where we were taught by you on many subjects," wrote Bruce Lake, a leader in the Church Educational System. "The teachings always went beyond the duties of the General Board. They pertained mostly to lessons of life and good literature."[29]

Duff wrote about a practice he often used when he had visitors in his home: "The most attractive part of the evening seemed to be the few minutes at the conclusion of our dinner when we read from the book *Prayers from the Ark.* Interestingly, people are deeply moved and vastly interested in such simple matters. They don't take time to do the same kind of thing themselves but seem to really enjoy it when others do. We enjoyed them."

27. MDH-A, "Meeting of the 70," Apr. 18, 1985.

28. Antoine Ivins, talk to seminary teachers, July 13, 1934, published in the *Deseret News*, Nov. 10, 1934.

29. Bruce Lake to MDH, n.d.

At his funeral, his daughter Susan said, "He took every opportunity to teach his children. He taught us to lead music. He taught us the gospel constantly, by working with us in the scriptures—teaching us to read them, mark them, and cross-reference them, by making connections ourselves. He would come to virtually every meal with some papers next to his plate. He would read to us from a book or an article he had read, or a letter he had received, or he would tell us about an experience he recently had. He was always teaching and sharing uplifting thoughts. He had files—binders and binders full of quotes, stories, and thoughts that he read, and that became a part of him. He loved Shakespeare, David Grayson, the great theologians, and many rabbis."

By the way, this was not always a pleasant experience. With twenty-three grandchildren and always a few of these "little people" present (as Duff would call children), Duff would try to hold court with the family, cover too much, and occasionally lose his patience. Often, it was a losing battle to get through the reading, but it never seemed to faze him, and he'd continue right on.

Duff also felt it important to teach, even when he didn't feel like it. Once after a long day at work, he finished the day counseling with a young woman who had committed adultery and then had an abortion. In his journal, he wrote something profound: "I spent an hour trying to build her up. This is a heartless job and one I do not relish, my having to listen to such stories. In the evening, I taught my class at the University, though I didn't feel very much like it spiritually and physically. It worked out well, as it usually does when you do what you're supposed to in spite of your own inclinations."[30]

Despite all of that, Duff's best teaching was probably his example. His oft-shared quotation from St. Francis could easily have applied to him:

"Preach the gospel all the time; when necessary, use words."

30. MDH-JE, Feb. 15, 1954.

11

Following Jesus Christ

Who shall separate us from the love of Christ? (Romans 8:35–39). The answer to Paul's question is that nothing can separate us from the love of Christ. Only we can do that. We may move; he will not—except to hold out the constant hand of support and love.
—Marion D. Hanks

In reviewing over ten thousand handwritten and typed documents in Duff's personal files, by far the number one topic, repeated over and over, typed, or in his distinctive handwriting, was the Savior, Jesus Christ.

"AN EXAMPLE OF THE BELIEVERS"

Your testimony of the Savior and knowledge of his teachings and ministry are legendary in the church.
—Elder John K. Carmack

Duff, you have the faculty of putting a person on a one-on-one relationship with the Savior.
—F. Burton Cassity

Duff was a believer. From an early age, he chose to follow the Lord Jesus Christ. He loved to quote from John 3:16 and then emphasize John 3:17:

"For God so loved the world, that he gave his only begotten Son, that whosoever believeth in him should not perish, but have everlasting life.

"For God sent not his Son into the world to condemn the world; but that the world through him might be saved."

This passage described the God that Duff knew and wanted others to know. Duff didn't choose to follow the Savior out of fear or a desire to be rewarded in the afterlife but rather because he knew that the Savior loves each of us and did not come to condemn us but came to heal us all.

Duff's love of the Savior will resonate through the generations. Said his daughter Susan: "The greatest legacy our father left to us was his complete and unwavering love of the Savior. He spent his life teaching and testifying of the

Savior in his rich, resonant voice. He lived his life following His teachings with no outward pretense or 'seeming to be.' It was simply the way he lived."[1]

Said son-in-law John Baird, "Elder Hanks has a particular quality of spirit and grace with the image of Christ in his eyes and in his manner."[2]

Duff's testimony of Christ was plainly delivered in myriad public sermons where he taught repeatedly of the Lord's love and mercy. He also chose to share his feelings in his personal writings:

> I have put too little in these writings of my *feelings*, and too much of my *doings*, but my feelings are reasonably well expressed in enough places, in enough hearts, that perhaps they are known. I wish to say here, however, that with all the problems and concerns that exist, the word of the Lord is sweet and delightful, bringing comfort to the soul and joy to the heart. The central core of that message is the Lord Jesus Christ and what He did for us. I love Him and love His name and love His sacrifice and His great forgiving heart. When I talk at general conference about the love of God and Christ, I will not do them justice, that is for sure, but neither will I do myself justice in this one thing—I do love the Lord.[3]

CHOOSING CHRIST AND TESTIFYING OF HIM

Duff loved to quote several lines from Tennyson's *Gareth and Lynette* in which he tells the story of the young man Gareth, who wants to join his brothers in King Arthur's court. His mother does not want him to go and tells him that if he stays home, she will arrange a deer hunt and find him a princess to be his bride. Gareth replies,

> How can you keep me tether'd to you—Shame.
> Man am I grown, a man's work must I do.
> Follow the deer? Follow the Christ, the King.
> Live pure, speak true, right wrong,
> follow the King, else, wherefore born?[4]

Perhaps Duff loved these lines of verse because they applied directly to him in several ways. He had so many opportunities to pursue secular gain and an easier, different life. But like Gareth, he could not imagine doing any of those things over the opportunity to follow the Savior and testify of Him. He wrote:

> With John of old I testify that "The Father sent the Son to be the Savior of the world." (1 Jn. 4:14.) My testimony is that Jesus Christ is the Son of God, the Only Begotten in the flesh, the Good Shepherd, our Exemplar; that he is our Advocate with the Father, our Redeemer, and our Savior. We rejoice in the wonderful welding in his life of *principle* and *performance.* The Savior taught precepts of spiritual

1. Susan Maughan, daughter, MDH funeral talk.
2. John K. Baird, letter to the author.
3. MDH-JE, Mar. 30, 1975.
4. Alfred, Lord Tennyson, *Idylls of the King* (1859–85).

perfection, and he practiced and applied them with perfection. He could with authority declare that he was the light and example the people should follow: "I have set an example for you. . . . I am the light which ye shall hold up—that which ye have seen me do." (3 Ne. 18:16, 24.)[5]

THE GIFTS OF OUR SAVIOR

All that is unfair about life can be made right through the Atonement of Jesus Christ.[6]

"We believe that through the Atonement of Christ, all mankind may be saved, by obedience to the laws and ordinances of the Gospel" (Articles of Faith 1:3). Duff believed that the gift of Jesus' life for us is the single greatest act in the history of the Earth—that His decision to save us began before the world was made, when he said, "I will go down and be the Savior." It is His grace that saves us.

Some have wondered why Christ was left alone on the cross for some period of time. Duff responded to this question, "Better than anyone else in all of history, Christ understands what it means to feel all alone. It was He who on the cross cried out, 'My God, my God, *why hast thou forsaken me?*' I know some of the theological implications of that moment of aloneness, but I confess that since I was a boy, I have harbored a private feeling of my own about it. Perhaps it came from my never having known my own father, from wondering about him, from listening to Mother talk about the gentleness of his loving heart. Thinking about my father, it seems to me that it is likely that the Father of us all had to *turn away* from that awful scene for a moment *to wipe away a tear.* Our Heavenly Father understands. The Lord Jesus Christ understands."[7]

Each Christmas, Duff would pen a letter to his friends and family. In 1981, he wrote from Hong Kong,

> We write from a world away, from hearts as near at hand as memory and affection and appreciation. Our thoughts at Christmastime are of who we love, foremost you, and Him of who it is written that He died to bring us reconciliation with God and to save us . . .
>
> *By his life.*—Romans 5:10
>
> We are thinking much of His life, and the strength of it and unselfishness of it, and the wholesomeness and generosity of it, and we are praying for you that you may build on Him and love Him and find reason and faith to hope and to give.[8]

THE UPLIFTING SAVIOR

Duff believed strongly that the message of the Savior was about uplift, love, and encouragement. Sometimes, when asked to share a favorite scripture, he

5. MDH-T, "The Royal Law," GC, Apr. 1992.
6. *Preach My Gospel* (Salt Lake City: The Church of Jesus Christ of Latter-day Saints, 2004), 52.
7. BUW, 84.
8. MDH-L to friends and family at Christmas, Dec. 11, 1981.

would respond by outlining the desperate and horrible things that were described in Moroni 9. After describing the depraved actions of the Nephites and Lamanites, Mormon then tells his son the following, which Duff loved to emphasize:

> "My son, be faithful in Christ; and may not the things which I have written grieve thee, . . . but may Christ *lift thee up*" (Moroni 9:25).
>
> The key is to not let life and all of its problems, all that is happening in the world and in one's own life, weigh us down. That isn't what Christ is all about, so we shouldn't let it all grieve us. *Let Him LIFT US UP!* And, let all that he represents rest in our minds forever.[9]

EXPERIENCING THE SAVIOR'S LOVE

Near the end of his life, Duff shared some of his insight and feelings about the biblical Job's experiences with Christ. In Job 19:25, Job says, "I know that my Redeemer liveth." Then later, in Job 42:1–5, Job, in effect says, "I've been saying that I *know.* But now, I *really* know."

What did Job see? What did he find out? What caused him to have this sudden humility? Job says, "I have heard of thee by hearing of the *ear,* but now mine *eye seeth thee.* Wherefore I *abhor myself* and repent in dust and ashes."

Duff asked, "Something changed, but what?"

Duff believed that Job saw the Savior on the cross several centuries in advance, that he was an eyewitness to the Savior's act of grace and love.

Some of the Savior's closest friends had left him. He was blamed for something he didn't do, and Father in Heaven seemed to have distanced Himself.

Duff said, "Like Job, I have been conscious of inadequacy, that the truths we are so earnestly teaching are too wonderful for me. All our lives we have heard of the Lord by the hearing of the ear. I believe that what Job saw, what humbled him so, was a Man in a Garden and then on a cross, offering that infinite and eternal sacrifice for the sins of all. It is this Holy One of Israel that I expect to see one day, he who is 'the keeper of the gate . . . and employeth no servant there.' The vision of Him in that garden and on the cross brings me a sense of penitence like Job's and the feeling to repent in dust and ashes."[10]

The theologian Karl Barth was said to have been asked, "What is the most important thing you have learned in a lifetime of study?" Barth allegedly answered by singing, "Jesus Loves Me, This I Know, for the Bible Tells Me So." Duff loved that story the moment he read it. Quite often, near the end of his ministry, Duff would sing a few bars from either that song or from, "I'm Trying to Be Like Jesus"[11] from the pulpit during a sermon.

---

9. MDH-A, "An Attitude: The Weightier Matters," *Ensign*, July 1981, 69.
10. MDH-T, personal notes.
11. *Children's Songbook* (Salt Lake City: The Church of Jesus Christ of Latter-day Saints, 1995), 78.

THE TEMPLE

Duff's somewhat unique teachings about the temple are explored in chapter 53 (pages 501–16), but here is a brief summary of what he believed and taught. He said, "As the mission of the church is to 'invite all to *Come unto Christ*,' so I believe, in its clearest and loveliest sense, that this is also the mission of temples."

Duff felt that the temple was all about Christ, from the moment we enter until the moment we leave. He taught that the endowment was our involvement in the *path* Christ followed on the earth. He believed that the Savior lived a life that demonstrated each of the covenants that we personally make in the temple, and that we should be willing to walk that same path.

NOT ENOUGH JUST TO READ ABOUT THE SAVIOR

It is not enough for our interest in the Lord Jesus Christ to be talking about Him, praising Him or even worshipping Him. We need to infuse Him into our souls and act on His will.

Duff loved to quote the opening stanza from a centuries-old hymn. It was also in a handmade, framed inscription on the wall of his office:

> Though Christ a thousand times
> In Bethlehem be born.
> If He is not born in <u>thee</u>
> Thy soul is still forlorn.[12]

One of Duff's favorite teachings on our need to *serve each other* came in general conference almost a ninety years ago:

> When the Savior came upon the earth, he had two great missions: (1) one was to work out the Messiahship, the atonement for the fall, and the fulfillment of the law; (2) the other was the work which he did among his brethren and sisters in the flesh by virtue of relieving their sufferings.
>
> He left as a heritage to those who should come after him in his church, the carrying on of those two great things: work for the relief of the ills and the sufferings of humanity, and the teaching of the spiritual truths which should bring us back into the presence of our Heavenly Father.[13]

The writer of a personal letter to Duff said, "I had not truly realized, as you said, that one of His great works was to help *alleviate* the pain and suffering in the world, and that this was our *obligation* to do so, also. Somehow, that had never really registered with me before."[14]

Duff wrote, "While one may be an immense help to the cause of Christ by being able to defend Him on an intellectual plane, he or she will be ten thousand

12. Lyrics translated from Johann Angelus Silesius (1624–77), "Though Christ a Thousand Times."
13. J. Reuben Clark Jr., GC, Apr. 1937.
14. Letter to MDH.

times more potent as a missionary if in their life there is evidence that Christ has made a change."[15]

The great Christian author C. S. Lewis wrote:

> The more we feel without acting, the less we will ever be able to act, and, in the long run, the less we will be able to feel.[16]

EMULATING THE SAVIOR

Heavenly Father's goal is to help us return to Him and to become like Him. "For behold, this is my work and my glory—to bring to pass the immortality and eternal life of man" (Moses 1:39).

The way to do that is to follow his Son, Jesus Christ.

President David O. McKay shared with us the importance of our thoughts and our sincere desire to become like Him. He said, "By choosing Jesus Christ as our ideal, we create within ourselves a desire to be like him and to have fellowship with him. If you think about him long enough, you will begin to act like him and if you act like him long enough, you will become like Him."[17]

Duff loved reading Thomas à Kempis, *The Imitation of Christ.* Here is one fitting passage he emphasized in his notes: "Whosoever will fully understand the words of Christ, must endeavor to *conform his life* wholly to the life of Christ. What doth it avail thee to discourse profoundly [about God], if thou be void of humility and art therefore displeasing to [God]? Surely, profound words do not make a man holy and just; but a virtuous life maketh him dear to God. I had rather *feel contrition* than to know the *definition* thereof."[18]

A FRIEND OF CHRIST

In his penultimate general conference talk, Duff told this touching story:

> As Easter time approaches, let me share with you the tender story of an eleven-year-old boy named Philip, a child with Down syndrome who was in a Sunday School class with eight other children.
>
> Easter Sunday the teacher brought an empty plastic egg for each child. They were instructed to go out of the church building onto the grounds and put into the egg something that would remind them of the meaning of Easter.
>
> All returned joyfully. As each egg was opened there were exclamations of delight at a butterfly, a twig, a flower, a blade of grass. Then the last egg was opened. It was Philip's, and it was empty! Some of the children made fun of Philip.
>
> "But, teacher," he said, "teacher, the tomb was empty."
>
> A newspaper article announcing Philip's death a few months later noted that at the conclusion of the funeral eight children marched forward and put a

15. MDH-T, mission president's training seminar, *Church News*, June 29, 1991.
16. C. S. Lewis, *The Screwtape Letters* (1942)
17. David O. McKay, GC, Apr. 1951.
18. Thomas à Kempis, *The Imitation of Christ.*

large empty egg on the small casket. On it was a banner that said, "The tomb was empty."[19]

One Easter Sunday, while sitting in church in his ward, Duff penned the lyrics of a poem that was later included in the 1985 LDS hymnal as hymn 198:

That Easter Morn

That Easter morn, a grave that burst
Proclaimed to man that "Last and First"
Had ris'n again
And conquered pain.

This morn renews for us that day
When Jesus cast the bonds away,
Took living breath
And conquered death.

Thus we in gratitude recall
And give our love and pledge our all,
Shed grateful tear
And conquer fear.

Text: Marion D. Hanks, 1921–2011. © 1975 IRI
Music: Robert Cundick, 1926–2016. © 1975 IRI

After Duff passed away, a friend described a last visit with him: "I sang him the song he himself had penned and which will extend his testimony through time as others sing it. He knew his Savior. They were friends. And he knew the truth which inspired those words."[20]

---

19. MDH-T, "The Royal Law," GC, Apr. 1992.
20. Margaret Young, "In Memoriam: Elder Marion Duff Hanks," *By Common Consent*, Aug. 8, 2011, bycommonconsent.com.

12

Searching and Knowing the Scriptures

I wish to thank my mission president, Elder Marion D. Hanks, who first introduced me to the profundity of the Book of Mormon and the majesty of Christ that lay hidden there. I know of no one who loves the Book of Mormon more than Elder Hanks, nor of anyone who has taught it with more power and conviction.

—Jeffrey R. Holland[1]

Duff read and marked his scriptures with a special emphasis on its chief message, the witness of the Lord Jesus Christ. He said that as he read, he too "felt to sing the song of redeeming love" of which the prophets spoke (Alma 5:26). Among other things, he found a multitude of sentences that were profound, beautiful, and worthy of any literature on earth.

Duff believed that the only way to understand the scriptures was to *invest the necessary time* with them. He taught, "I was thinking about what the scriptures themselves teach us about reading the scriptures. There are so many strong affirmations about searching and seeking and asking and knocking, and about the attitude with which we do this. Paul compared the people in two cities where he had taught. He reported that they in Berea were nobler than those in Thessalonica, in that they 'received the word with all readiness of mind and *searched the scriptures daily*' (Acts 17:11; emphasis added).[2]

"Christ himself answered the cynical question of the Sadducees concerning marriage in the resurrection, a resurrection in which they acknowledged no belief, 'Ye do err, not knowing the scriptures' (Matthew 22:29)." Duff added, "And so do we err if we do not know them.

"What men need is not so much to know what other men think or feel, but to know what God has said, what God has done, and what God wants us to do. But if we are wise and determined, we can learn it every day in the pages of the scriptures as we 'seek learning by study and also by faith' (D&C 88:118).[3]

"Many of us find ourselves slacking off. We have studied in times past and

1. Jeffrey R. Holland, *Christ and the New Covenant* (Salt Lake City: Deseret Book, 2009).
2. MDH-T, "An Attitude: The Weightier Matters," BYU, Mar. 25, 1980.
3. MDH-T, "An Attitude."

Duff with scriptures at a BYU devotional, unknown date.

probably remember it with joy, but haven't recently put in the effort—Alma responded to this situation by reminding the people of the faith and feeling they once had and then asking, 'Can ye feel so now?' (Alma 5:26)."

Duff taught, "We have to stay current and qualified in the things of God. It isn't enough to have once felt, when we were young, or when we were on a mission, or even a year or two ago. Life is full of changes and newness. We need the current companionship of the scriptures and the assurances they bring. Through constant connection to the Word of God and the truths found in the scriptures, we can find the strength and faith to accomplish God's purposes for each of us."

DUFF KNEW THEM

He searched and searched in the scriptures. He loved them. They were the most profound influence of his life. He cross-referenced them, loved all the books equally, and brought them together. He knew what was in them. He knew how they are all connected. This doesn't happen with internet searches. It goes way beyond footnotes. He was just remarkable.

Even today, Rich will be looking for a scripture and will be unable to find it using online search tools, because the need isn't word based; it is concept based. And then he will see some cross-reference that his Dad helped him with years ago, and there it will be!

At his funeral, his daughter Nancy said, "One day, not too long ago, I had a question about a contradiction in the scriptures. I was in his room, sitting quietly with him, and picked up his books, looked up one of the references, and there, written in big letters across the top of the page was my answer. I looked up at him and said, 'Dad, you are still teaching me.' He was watching me, and his eyes filled with tears."

Duff recalled, "Books I have long loved, especially the scriptures. Good literature became available to me in my home, and I read it as a youngster. The Book of Mormon was early read, though I was not a prodigy. I learned to understand something of its makeup and nature as a missionary and discovered a certain affinity for applying to myself and others the great instructions of the scriptures. That one blessing distinguished my personal enjoyment. All other good books attract me, especially the great Englishmen of earlier eras. For years, Shakespeare was a daily diet. I love him still."

Upon the publication of a new edition of the Book of Mormon, the Church Education team presented Duff a copy with the inscription, "We want you to have a copy of this new edition, since we consider you the greatest Book of Mormon teacher in the program."[4]

Duff didn't feel content to just increase his knowledge of the scriptures. When he discovered readings that touched his soul, he always sought to share them with his family and friends and the entire church.

---

4. Dale Tingey to MDH.

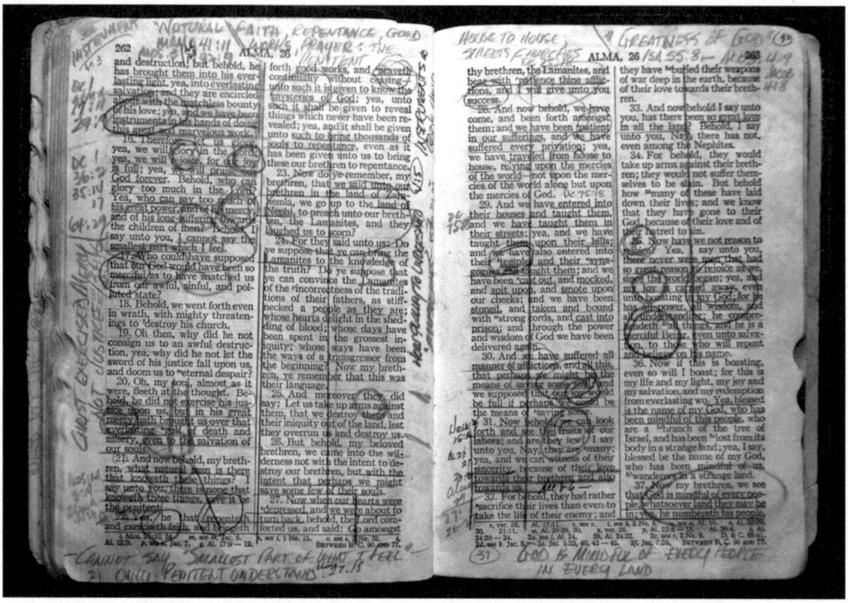

Two sample pages of Duff's marking style in one of his many sets of scriptures.

STUDYING AND MARKING

There was no neatness in Duff's method of marking scriptures. He felt no compulsion to keep the pages clean and readable. Instead, he would mark with multiple colors, circling words that he wanted to stand out, scribbling across the top and down the side margins, and writing cross-references to other verses—usually not the same as the ones in the printed cross-references at the bottom of the page.

Someone commented online, "Several years ago, I sat on the stand at a church meeting, next to Elder Hanks. I was close enough to see his scriptures, and my jaw dropped—never have I seen scriptures so marked, so color coded, so many handwritten notes on the verses, so many diagrams, and hand-drawn lines—vertical, diagonal, horizontal—whatever he needed to increase his understanding. I was in awe."

The overall results were well-worn, highly marked copies. This ties in well with the words he used to describe how a person can really get to know and love the scriptures—"mark, invest, digest, chew, absorb into your bloodstream."

Duff strongly encouraged his students to mark and cross-reference their scriptures and to take notes. He would quote the old saying, "The palest ink is better than the best memory."

LOVE THE PAINTING, INDIFFERENT TO THE FRAME

Instead of asking questions about the verses and wonderful teachings *inside* the Book of Mormon (the painting), many want to spend their time asking about how it got here, how it was translated, its historicity, and so on (the frame). This seems so unfortunate. When asked what verses or concepts they have learned from the scriptures, their answer usually demonstrates minimal investment in time spent actually reading and studying what the book itself says. Duff lamented this unbalanced approach throughout his life.

Shortly after he left the university to serve a mission, Duff received a letter from a professor of English who thought Duff was wasting his time and potentially hurting his future career. He enclosed a quotation from a significant literary figure concerning the Book of Mormon, which he thought might affect Duff's faith. Duff was shocked as he read it. Bernard DeVoto was recognized in the field of literature as an expert and had grown up in Ogden, Utah. This was the statement he made about the book: "It was a yeasty fermentation, formless, aimless, and inconceivably absurd... the estrus of paranoiac projected it into a new Bible."[5]

Duff wrote, "Formless, aimless, and inconceivably absurd? I was stunned. I set out with determination to discover why an expert should speak in so denigrating a manner about a book so important in my life and my mission."[6]

Duff read and read and prayed seeking to better understand the book, and he quickly came to understand exactly how the man could write such an assessment—he had not even read the book! He was judging it by the story of its unusual origin, presuming it to be a fraud based on the account of its authorship.

Far from being formless and aimless, Duff found the book to be "purposeful, complex, and sound," filled with so many marvelous sentences of such meaning that anyone who will read it with sufficient care "cannot escape being impressed by them, whether or not he obtains a witness of its divine origin."

BUT WHAT ABOUT THE FRAME?

While many people have genuine and honest questions about specific aspects of church teachings, or history, the truth is that Duff just didn't really think the "arm of flesh" stuff was all that important. He didn't really seem to care much about the historicity of the Book of Mormon, or any of the other scriptures, or about archeology, or word count analysis, or chiasmus, or any of those things. He would read about the occasional academic finding of this or that, but it didn't affect his testimony either way.

One time he was giving a speech at a hotel near Disneyland and went for a walk through what he thought was a children's playground. There was a great orange flying saucer-shaped object there, which turned out to be the latest lifeboat design. It was made of fiberglass, had small windows and a hatch, and could cross oceans of waves and remain intact. He wrote in his journal, "This unusual lifeboat might as well have had a plaque quoting Ether 2 and the story of the boat

---

5. Bernard DeVoto, "The Centennial of Mormonism," *American Mercury* (New York: Alfred A. Knopf, 1930), 5.

6. MDH-T, "It Speaketh of Jesus, and Persuadeth Them to Believe in Him," CES Symposium on the Book of Mormon, Aug. 15, 1986.

they made. Of course, this doesn't prove the Book of Mormon is true, but at least this particular detail no longer seems as foolish as some have sneeringly suggested over the years." That journal entry is one of only a few where he even entertains a discussion about the Book of Mormon outside of its spiritual teachings.

Duff also knew that the scriptures come to us in man's language. Someone once said, "The scriptures are adapted to man's weaknesses, his thinking, and his needs, therefore, they are sure to reflect something of man, as well as the inspiration of Deity."

Elder John A. Widtsoe had an interesting point of view on this concept: "The message of scripture is *divine*; the words in which it is clothed are *human.* Failure to make this distinction has led to much misunderstanding. Intelligent readers will separate the message of scripture from its form of presentation."[7]

The scriptures themselves contain the same idea: "For my soul delighteth in plainness; for after this manner doth the Lord work among the children of men. For the Lord God giveth light to the understanding, for he speaketh unto men according to *their* language, unto *their* understanding" (2 Nephi 31:3).

If Duff was inclined to point to someone defending the Book of Mormon, he would often quote Dr. Marcus Bach, noted philosopher, minister, and author, who wrote the following about the Book of Mormon:

> So, I paged through this American Bible wondering how many Protestants had seen a copy or read a verse out of any of the fifteen books. Wherever these auxiliary scriptures came from, whatever they were, they surpassed in magnitude and content my most extravagant expectations. The style was biblical, the references to Holy Writ were voluminous, the ancient story was tremendously involved. It was not the kind of book a man would read for pastime or write for profit. It was solemn and ponderous and heavy as were the plates on which it was inscribed. *No Vermont schoolboy wrote this* and no Presbyterian preacher tinkered with these pages. After wading through the first book of Nephi, I was ready to settle for the miracle of Cumorah and let it go at that.[8]

Duff was significantly more interested in the painting than in the frame.

CREATING TEACHING AIDS

As he studied more intently, Duff spent time creating one- or two-page teaching aids, monographs he could use to share the things he was learning. For example, he was struck by the interesting accounts of journeys between the major geographic centers of the time, Nephi and Zarahemla. He had been confused a bit as he read about the journeys, so he made up a chart to help him understand.[9] He said, "It was gratifying to learn with what credibility and consistency the complicated plot line was spelled out." Duff thought there was no way the Prophet

7. John A. Widtsoe, in Lowell L. Bennion, *Religion and the Pursuit of Truth* (Salt Lake City: Deseret Book, 1978).

8. Marcus Bach, *Faith and My Friends* (Indianapolis: Bobbs-Merrill, 1951), 295–96.

9. See appendix E, "Travels between Nephi and Zarahemla."

Joseph, in his early years and under intense pressures of the time, had been able to work out that complex a plot, let alone the vastly more important elements of religious doctrine and truth.

As previously mentioned, at the time Duff began teaching seminary there were very few materials on the Book of Mormon available as teacher's aids. If he wanted to produce handouts for the students, he would first have to research the subject and then make copies on his duplicator. For example, in order to understand and organize in his mind all the various plates involved in the Book of Mormon, he researched and drew out the different plates described in the book and their eventual place within its covers. Over time, the collection of materials he prepared grew.

READING AND GIVING AWAY

Another unique thing Duff did was give away his scriptures. Each year or two, he'd buy another leather set and start over again, studying and marking them up. At some point, he'd consider that set "finished," and he'd give it away. Over the years, quite a number of people have come up to me and said, "Hey, guess what? I have your dad's scriptures; would you like them back?" I suggest they keep them. I'm blessed to already have a set.

COME UNTO CHRIST—THE ULTIMATE REASON

Perhaps the most famous scripture in the world is John 3:16. It points to the ultimate reason for scriptures even to exist: "For God so loved the world, that he gave his only begotten Son, that whosoever believeth in him should not perish, but have everlasting life."

And it provides comforting assurance that because of the Savior, we can be saved. The scriptures themselves are also full of verses that tell us that if we are further away from God than we used to be, it is we who have moved, not He. Duff's prescription for our remoteness from divinity was to immerse ourselves in holy writ. He particularly loved this quotation from Spencer W. Kimball: "I find that when I get casual in my relationships with Divinity and when it seems that no divine ear is listening and no divine voice is speaking, that I am far, far away. If I immerse myself in the scriptures the distance narrows and the spirituality returns."[10]

10. Spencer W. Kimball, "Immerse Myself in the Scriptures," BYU, July 11, 1966.

HIS MINISTRY BEGINS

13

The Call and Beginnings

And so, the adventure begins.
—Marion D. Hanks

Maxine and Duff's life changed dramatically on October 4, 1953. On that Sunday morning of the church's general conference, president David O. McKay called Duff at 7:00 a.m. and asked if he would come down and meet with him in his office. At that time, Duff was serving as an assistant to Richard L. Evans, who was the director of Temple Square. Evans was also serving as a member of the First Council of the Seventy (later called the Presidency of the Seventy).

In the interview, President McKay asked Duff about Maxine, his missionary work, and his health. He then informed Duff that Elder Evans was going to be called as an apostle and Duff was being called as a general authority to take Evans' place in the First Council of the Seventy. Duff recalled, "His method of questioning me was so gracious and good that it has influenced my whole life."

Duff had been asked to give the opening prayer in the Friday morning session of general conference, which was a bit unusual because conference prayers were then typically offered by general authorities and stake, temple, or mission presidents. "The Spirit had whispered to me then," he said, "but I couldn't believe it and I was at odds with myself over this immodest inclination to believe that I was about to be called to an important office in the Church."[1]

After his interview with President McKay, Duff walked over to the lobby of the nearby Hotel Utah to call Maxine, who was home ill. When Duff told her that President McKay had called him to take Richard Evans' place, Maxine responded, "Well, that's very nice," thinking that Duff had been called as the new director of Temple Square.

"I really think you ought to come down to conference," Duff said, not being able to be more explicit because he was speaking in a public place. It was 8:30 a.m., and conference would begin at 10:00 a.m.

Maxine thought, "Why on earth does he want me to go to conference just

1. Joseph Walker, "General Conference Through the Years Is Different but the Same," *Deseret News,* Apr. 1, 2013; MDH-JE, Jan. 22, 1970.

because he's been called to take Richard Evans' place" on Temple Square? But with Duff's urging she got ready and went to conference on the day that would forever change their lives.

That day was momentous for another reason. "This is an epoch-making service," President McKay said as he opened the morning session, excitedly announcing that for the first time in the church's history, that day's conference sessions were being broadcast via television beyond Utah's borders—to California, Oregon, and Washington. McKay compared it in import to Brigham Young's sending President Abraham Lincoln the first message from Salt Lake City on the just completed transcontinental telegraph, in October 1861: "Utah has not seceded, but is firm for the Constitution."[2]

Throughout the afternoon session, McKay delightedly read telegrams coming in from church members on the West Coast, expressing their gratitude and wonder at being able to watch conference live on TV. Finally, toward the end of that concluding session, First Presidency member J. Rueben Clark read for a sustaining vote the names of the church's general authorities and general officers. Richard L. Evans was sustained as a new apostle and two new general authorities were called—Canadian Hugh B. Brown as an Assistant to the Twelve Apostles, and Marion D. Hanks as a member of the First Council of the Seventy, joining Bruce R. McConkie, Milton R. Hunter, S. Dilworth Young, Oscar A. Kirkham, Antoine R. Ivins, and Levi Edgar Young. In his talk after being sustained, Duff said, "I ask God to help me as I in humility seek to do a job which seems to me at this moment to be beyond my poor capacity to do."[3]

Duff was only thirty-one, Maxine only twenty-seven, and their two children just three and two years old. In comparison, the oldest and most senior member of Duff's new quorum, Levi Edgar Young, was seventy-nine.

Over the years, Duff was asked several times about the sacredness of his call to the ministry. In answer to one letter, he wrote, "I do have a story, that was an experience of a consequential nature. I knew about the call, through the Spirit, in advance and went through that torment which results from an honest mind dealing with a spiritual message it cannot handle. President McKay then invited me to his office, and called me, and the conversation was a sweet and beautiful one which culminated in his statement, 'The Lord has spoken.' My belief in his divine call and the integrity of his heart has made my effort in this great, but difficult, assignment, possible."[4]

One of Duff's former seminary students, Louise Sharp Davis, was visiting the home of her grandfather, J. Reuben Clark Jr., after the session where Duff's

2. Conference Report, Oct. 2–4, 1953, 97; Richard Neitzel Holzapfel, "The Civil War in Utah," in *Utah History Encyclopedia*, ed. Allan Kent Powell (Salt Lake City: University of Utah Press, 1994).

3. Conference Report, Oct. 2–4, 1953, 116, 131.

4. MDH-L to Lloyd Lamoreaux, Mar. 8, 1973.

Delivering his first general conference talk, October 1953. *Courtesy Deseret News*

calling was announced. Clark smiled at his granddaughter and asked, "Well, what do you think of your seminary teacher?"

"Oh, I think it's just wonderful!" Louise answered.

Then Clark became very sober and said, "It was his prayer that did it," referring to the prayer Duff had given to open the conference two days before.[5]

SETTING APART

On October 8, 1953—four days after Duff's calling was announced—the First Presidency and members of the First Council of the Seventy unitedly laid their hands on Duff's head as President McKay set him apart as a member of the First Council of the Seventy. Among other things, Duff was blessed to have an increased testimony of the divinity of the restored gospel of Jesus Christ.

Similar to his patriarchal blessing and a later blessing from President McKay that instructed him to "let his voice be heard," this blessing included the words,

5. Louise Sharp Davis to MDH, Feb. 6, 1984.

"We bless you that you may have freedom of speech, with your thoughts clearly comprehended."[6]

With gratitude to the Lord, Duff prepared to begin his ministry. He was excited about the opportunity but well aware of its challenges. He wrote a letter to three-year-old Susan and two-year-old Nancy:

> Someday, as you read this, girls, you will try hard to imagine your stodgy dad sitting at a desk and scrawling this out 20 years ago—staying awake past midnight to do it. I hope I am around to know you as young women and mothers. How I love you. Mom and I sometimes talk about our lives ahead. Probably you will never remember a time when your father was not a Church authority—and when pressure was not on you to conform. But believe it or not, we were young and carefree once—and we enjoyed it so! Not that we don't now, of course, but we are out of a normal pattern now and must pretty well surrender to a much-altered life.[7]

Duff was excited and humbled to have such a wonderful opportunity to serve others. People were kind and generous and patient. Congratulatory cards and letters poured in. His beloved mother was thrilled and so proud. His mission president and mentor, Leo J. Muir, wrote, "My Dear Marion D.—hereafter I shall address you as President Hanks—with genuine pride and satisfaction. I have expected this appointment, and I was exceedingly happy when my anticipation was realized."[8]

His friend Truman Madsen wrote from Harvard, where he was getting his PhD:

> Russ Nelson told me Sunday night that if it wouldn't look like favor-currying, he would write and tell you how thrilled he was with your new appointment. Ann and I feel the same way. Maybe the reason we both said some grateful things about you, at knee level, was that we know some of the thrusts and aches of your soul, and the searching range of alternatives that might have taken you in other directions. We have treasured your maiden Conference address sentence by sentence, rejoice in the pictures of you and your family, and exulted with Bill Jones and others here, with this tangible witness of approval.[9]

Hundreds of other letters and cards shared similar sentiments.

HOW AT SUCH A YOUNG AGE?

People often asked Duff how a thirty-one-year-old who had never been a stake president or even a bishop could possibly have been called to be a general authority at such a young and tender age. As he had done in his conference talk after being sustained, Duff would answer by describing his wonderful time on Temple

6. Minutes of the secretary to the First Presidency given to Duff, Oct. 8, 1953. See also Appendix C.

7. MDH-L to his daughters, Oct. 1953.

8. Leo J. Muir to MDH, Oct. 7, 1953.

9. Truman Madsen to MDH, Oct. 1953.

Square and his experience training new missionaries in the Salt Lake Mission Home. He taught a class there each week titled "Answering Difficult Questions" and taught the missionaries the fundamentals of the gospel. So he had some exposure to and acquaintance with church leadership through those responsibilities.

"It is sometimes strikingly significant to see how early in life the course and character of a man is manifest," newly sustained apostle Richard L. Evans wrote of Duff. "Duff is one whose early life indicated a definite direction. . . . Wherever he has gone, he has lived a well-rounded life, and the Church has been his chief interest. His life has followed a consistent course. His character and capacity were early in evidence. He is loved, and he has loved the Lord. May he be blessed with a long lifetime of effective and satisfying service."[10]

HIS COLLEAGUES

Duff came to love each of his colleagues in the First Council of the Seventy. He spoke of them with respect and a tender heart. All were older than Duff, some substantially, but they came to respect his ability and testimony. He paid tribute to each of his original colleagues.

Levi Edgar Young, seventy-nine, was the senior seventy. He was a former history professor who gave Duff books to read and prodded him to continue educating himself. He knew the scriptures and what they said about the seventies forming a quorum "equal in authority" to the First Presidency and the Quorum of the Twelve Apostles (D&C 107:26). "With Levi," Duff wrote, "there was a carry-over of early resistance to the direction of the Twelve, which had constrained the seventy for years. They had not been treated as 'equal in authority.'" For example, when Duff was called to the First Council of the Seventy (now Seven Presidents of the Seventy), they were not high priests, did not have the sealing authority, were expected to go to stake conferences, but were not able to ordain bishops or even set apart high councilors and stake presidents—only apostles could to that.

Humble and gentle Antoine Ivins, seventy-two, was the son of a former counselor in the First Presidency, Anthony W. Ivins. Once when Antoine was in the hospital, Duff visited him and, holding his hand, mentioned that he'd heard that President McKay had come to see him earlier. Elder Ivins said, "I do hope that my contributions have not been unacceptable to my brethren."

Oscar Kirkham, seventy-three, was a famous Scouter, loved building young men, and was probably the best-known Latter-day Saint on earth during his prime. He was also musically talented. As he began to decline cognitively in his late seventies, top church leaders stopped giving him assignments. Duff loved Elder Kirkham, and a couple of weeks before he passed away, Duff asked if he would accompany him for a talk Duff was giving at BYU. After the meeting started, Duff invited him to say a few words. Oscar stood and spoke to the students, including

10. Richard L. Evans, "Marion Duff Hanks," *Relief Society Magazine*, Dec. 1953, 810.

The members of the First Council of the Seventy when Duff was called as a general authority, 1953, (L to R): Milton R. Hunter, Antoine Ivins, Marion D. Hanks, Levi Edgar Young, Bruce R. McConkie, S. Dilworth Young, Oscar A. Kirkham. *Courtesy Church News*

this phrase, "Every day of your life, say the good word. As sure as the sun greets the morning, and rivers run down to the sea, a new day for mankind is dawning. Let us do well our part." Duff spoke at his funeral and later helped publish a book of Oscar's teachings, titled, *Say the Good Word.*[11]

S. Dilworth Young, fifty-six, was like nobody else. He was a poet, had lost a son in war, and had a wife who was an invalid. "Dilworth was up several times each night, taking care of her needs," Duff said. "When he went on his weekend stake conference assignments, a health worker helped, but Dilworth could not bring himself to surrender his wife to full-time public care. He had a capacity for uniqueness, individuality, loyalty, and unselfish love."

As Duff began his service, Elder Evans was still using the same corner office in the Church Administration Building that he had used before his call to the apostleship, and no one found an office for the newly minted Elder Hanks. "They let him wander in and out," a secretary wrote, "and nobody took care of him or anything."[12] If he had interviews or a setting-apart to perform, he had to look around for an unoccupied office. Finally, Elder Young asked Duff to drop by. "When I arrived at Dilworth's office," Duff said, "there was a man painting my name on the

11. Oscar Kirkham, *Say the Good Word* (Salt Lake City: Deseret Book, 1958).

12. Benson Young Parkinson, *S. Dilworth Young: General Authority, Scouter, Poet* (Salt Lake City: Covenant Communications, 1994), chapter 13.

door under Dilworth's name. Dilworth had moved his desk over and had brought in another desk, and we shared offices for a long time. That's the kind of man he was. He was as great a man as I ever knew."

Milton R. Hunter, fifty-one, had a PhD in history, was a seminary teacher, and wrote twenty-three books, mostly historical and religious in nature. One of his books was used for many years as a textbook in Utah schools. Elder Hunter had a deep interest in archaeology and spent years defending and trying to corroborate claims of the Book of Mormon. Although Elder Hunter's work was well researched and clearly written, he wrote for a popular local audience and from a Mormon point of view. He was known to be an unabashed defender of the faith and subjective in his review of anything LDS.

Bruce R. McConkie, thirty-eight, was the closest in age to Duff. "If there is a better man, I have not known him," Duff said. "He has been kind to me in speaking of my ability and effort and so forth. It is only that he is unguided by good counsel which surely would correct his tendency to speak unequivocally about equivocal things."[13] Over the next forty years, the two men disagreed multiple times over some of McConkie's declarative doctrines he pronounced in speaking and writing. Early in Duff's ministry, Richard Evans told him, "You're going to have the time of your life listening to Bruce build his bricks of logic. You will fill a role I have filled for years. When he gets it up fully, you just nudge one of the bottom bricks out and see [it fall]." As one example, Duff explained that Elder McConkie loved to quote Isaiah 2:2 in the Bible about the last days and the temple "in the tops of the mountains," which he said referred to the Salt Lake Temple. One day, in a discussion with Elders McConkie and Hunter, Duff pointed out that the previous verse, Isaiah 2:1, states that this was "The word … concerning Judah and Jerusalem." Milton Hunter jumped in and said, "Sure, but this is one of the Bible's misinterpretations." Duff replied, "Maybe, Milton. But 2 Nephi 12 and Section 133 [of the D&C] both use the same language."

In his 1968 journal, Duff wrote that while "no two men could have been more different than Bruce and I were when we first met after my call, he was always courteous and gracious, and I have seen some real changes in his viewpoint toward people and in his attitude toward what really matters over the past few years. I think he is a great young man."[14]

Duff talked with fondness about his years in the First Council of the Seventy. From his calling in 1953 until the formal reconstitution of the First Quorum of the Seventy in 1976, Duff watched as many of his dear colleagues in the council passed away, or were called away, and new members were called, including Elders A. Theodore Tuttle, Paul H. Dunn, Hartman Rector Jr., Loren C. Dunn, Rex D. Pinegar, and many others. He came to love these men and to trust them and their judgment and commitment to the Lord.

13. MDH-JE, and letter to family, June 26, 1981.

14. MDH-JE, Mar. 28, 1968.

Elder Marion D. Hanks with his wife, the former Maxine Christensen, and their two daughters, Susan Gay, 3; and Nancy Marie, 2.

The Hanks family, from an article announcing his call as a general authority, 1953. *Courtesy LDS Church*

GETTING STARTED

As a general authority in his thirties, Duff was energetic and surrounded by elderly men who had been on the road for many years and were tiring. Duff's strength and talents were put into action immediately. During the early years of his ministry, from 1953 until 1959, he functioned as one of the most consistent 'workhorses' among the general authorities. A sampling of his weekend stake conferences in just one year, 1956, reads like an extensive list of Utah and Idaho towns and counties, interspersed with a smattering of two- or three-week excursions to more distant parts of the country: Ensign, Garland, Heber City, Juab, Loa, Millcreek, Ogden, Panguitch, and Sanpete, Utah; Driggs and Soda Springs, Idaho; Inglewood, California; Lethbridge and New Brunswick, Canada; El Paso, Texas; Cambridge and Bridgeport, Connecticut; and Portland, Maine.

Maxine supported Duff in his callings, but she and their two little girls really missed him. During one extended trip, Maxine sent him a letter saying, "We wish you were here. Susan cried after you had to hang up the phone. Nancy wants to tickle your feet when you get home.... She and I read about it in her library book. It's a comfort to know you are safe and well and that you love me and miss me."[15]

His weekdays were full of counseling and meetings, along with his continued employment of teaching seminary in the morning, and serving as the Director of Temple Square. Two to three evenings a week were filled with talks, teaching institute, and other events. On occasion, he and Maxine would get a night out together.

Traveling on the weekends was usually by car and occasionally by train or airplane. His reunions with his family each weekend were looked forward to

15. Maxine to MDH, Nov. 14, 1954.

with anticipation and joy. Of one return trip from Idaho, he wrote, "The stake presidency got us to the Idaho Falls train station about 1:30 in the morning. We caught the train and went to bed. I awakened in the morning with LeGrand Richard's feet dangling from the upper berth. He had gotten aboard at Blackfoot, and I didn't hear him. We arrived home at 8:00 a.m. and I missed my seminary class for the first time. Maxine and the girls were at the train depot and thrilled me very much by their unexpected presence. Susan ran the length of the platform and jumped on me, with Nancy after her."[16]

Maxine and Duff were blessed with two more baby girls. Ann Elizabeth was born in May 1954 and Mary Linda joined the family in November 1956. Maxine had her hands full, and Duff was now outnumbered five to one. He adored their four beautiful little girls and loved to spoil them.

WORK OUTSIDE THE ROUTINE

Duff also stepped up his work in the community during these early years. In 1953, he chaired the Salt Lake County Cancer Drive and, as president of the Sons of Utah Pioneers, championed the funding of scholarships for deserving students. In 1954, he was honored with a Distinguished Service Award by the Utah Junior Chamber of Commerce. That year, he also gave the baccalaureate sermon at BYU's June graduation program. In 1956, he made special trips to speak at the LDS Institute of Religion in Los Angeles and to tour the church's New England Mission.

In 1959, the church planned a massive effort to reach its youth, with the purpose of stimulating greater faith and protecting them against tendencies toward delinquency. The program included a thirteen-week radio series aimed at reaching more than 5,000 fireside groups in the wards of the United States. The kick-off to the program was a massive fireside with the main address given by President David O. McKay, followed by twelve consecutive weeks of radio broadcasts. Stakes outside Utah received specially prepared tape recordings. Duff was the first speaker of the first fireside, on January 10, 1960.[17]

A NEW HOUSE AND NEIGHBORHOOD

On April 1, 1959, Duff and Maxine bought a new home at 1399 Butler Avenue in Salt Lake City. This was the principal house where they raised their children. They paid $23,500 for it.

Their last child was born on April 28, 1960. Maxine was mostly sedated, but she remembered Dr. Ellsworth shaking her, saying, "Wake up, Maxine, it's a boy!"

Because Duff and Maxine already had four girls, they assumed their fifth child would be another girl and "hadn't even thought of a boy's name," Maxine said. By the time the church service came in which Duff would give their son a name and

---

16. MDH-JE, Jan. 17, 1954.
17. Henry A. Smith, "Church Plans Massive Effort to Reach Youth," *Deseret News*, Dec. 5, 1959.

a blessing, they had narrowed their name choices to Richard or John. But until the name, "Richard Duff Hanks," came out of Duff's mouth during the blessing, it wasn't settled.[18]

The family home on Butler Avenue was next to the University of Utah, a terrific neighborhood for the kids. The "U" became a playground of sorts for the children, who rode bikes and skateboarded all over campus. In the winter, they went sledding on the grassy hills, or on Butler or First South when really big storms closed the streets. At the bottom of their street was Reservoir Park, where they played tennis and baseball and swung on the tricky bars. The only drawback was that their home was situated in the middle of the university's sorority and fraternity houses. Over the years, this resulted in several late-night, verbal tugs of war, as the family pled with their rowdy neighbors for peace and quiet.

The Hanks family was welcomed as members of the Federal Heights Ward, which became their ward for the rest of their children's growing up years. The ward met in a building just west of the university's Kingsbury Hall until a new, larger one was constructed further north, at the top of Virginia Street.

18. "First Son in Hanks' Family," *Church News*, May 7, 1960.

14

Reaching "the One"

No one has exceeded you in your gift to inspire and uplift those who have sometimes fallen short of the mark.
—Michael K. Fletcher[1]

Your ministry has been punctuated by your service to the disadvantaged, forgotten, and those that are lost.
—Elder Hugh W. Pinnock[2]

The mark of a great man is not just what he has *been* or *done* but what he has helped *others* to become. Duff was a builder of people—encouraging, strengthening, and lifting others. He had great confidence in the innate decency and goodness of people.

He also had an incredible gift to inspire others. He spoke from pulpits and podiums to large gatherings around the world, to groups of students at universities—including "intellectual students" at schools like Stanford and Berkeley. But it was his countless hours spent focused on the individual that truly defined his service. He made a conscious choice to defend the defenseless.

His daughter, Nancy, published a poem about him, whose verse reads:

> [he] with quiet ferocity rose from his desk,
> raged for the humbled, the voiceless;
> was gunner of senselessness,
> ally of the stricken.[3]

In his first general conference address as a general authority, Duff took as his subject "The Individual":

> We talk in multiples, and we think in numbers, and we teach classes with many people in them. But always there is the simple truth which we must understand:

1. Michael K. Fletcher to MDH, Apr. 17, 2004.
2. Hugh W. Pinnock to MDH, ca. 1992.
3. Nancy Hanks Baird, "Gate of Heaven," in *The Shell in Silk* (Salt Lake City: Publishers Press, 1996), 34.

> that the gospel of Jesus Christ is God's plan to get us home *individually*; and while we may teach classes, and while we may hold cottage meetings for groups, people come to faith and convictions individually. They enter the waters of baptism individually; individually they receive the blessing of the imposition of hands by those who have that authority; and when they seek to get acquainted with their Father in Heaven, and to go to the place he would like them to be, they do it individually.[4]

It is rare to find a man in such positions of leadership and authority in so many varied pursuits—religion, Scouting, Rotary, athletics, youth—who is able to focus in such a laser-like manner on the needs and concerns of each individual soul.

After years of his authoring and presenting "Doctor of Kindness" awards to those who deserved them, Duff's family and friends surprised him by awarding him a Doctor of Kindness award. Part of its declaration included this tribute: "What kind of person defends those who have no defense? Who gives attention to people ignored by everyone else? Who listens with patience to those who otherwise would have no voice? Only one who is authentically kind does those things. It requires one who has mastered kindness."[5]

THE INDIVIDUAL WORTH OF SOULS

Duff taught that the scriptures are replete and consistent in their emphasis on the individual: "Remember the worth of souls is great in the sight of God" (D&C 18:10). But he also knew that sometimes, the softer dimensions of a soul can take a backseat to easier-to-measure numerical measurements. However, as someone once said, "Not everything that can be counted counts, and not everything that counts can be counted."[6]

In a letter to Duff after his valedictory comments to the Seventy in 1992, Elder Spencer J. Condie wrote, "I was once again touched deeply by your sincere concern for all of our Heavenly Father's children, *individually,* not just as aggregate statistics. Thank you for all you've done and all you are."[7]

One of his favorite quotes by Joseph Smith made it clear where responsibility lies: "It is the responsibility of every Latter-day Saint to prepare himself for the vineyard, sparing a little time to comfort the mourners; to bind up the brokenhearted; to reclaim the backslider; to bring back the wanderer; to re-invite into the kingdom such as have been cut off.... Souls are as precious in the sight of God, as they ever were."[8]

---

4. MDH-T, "Response to a Call," GC, Oct. 1953, emphasis added.

5. From "Doctor of Kindness" degree bestowed on MDH by closest friends, Dec. 2000. For more detail, see page 240.

6. Attributed to Albert Einstein, also to William Bruce Cameron in his text, *Informal Sociology: A Casual Introduction to Sociological Thinking* (Ann Arbor: University of Michigan, 1963).

7. Spencer J. Condie to MDH, Aug. 1992.

8. Joseph Smith, "To the Saints Scattered Abroad," *Messenger and Advocate*, June 1835, 138.

Duff told the story of a man who accosted him belligerently on Temple Square. After speaking with him, Duff learned that when he was nineteen, a bishop's counselor had ejected this man from an LDS meetinghouse for some infraction. As he was being thrown out, another member objected, to which the counselor replied, "Oh, let him go; he's just one kid." Duff asked this man how many descendants he had. The answer was fifty-four! Duff asked if any were members of the church, to which he answered, "Huh, no, ain't any of them Mormons. They're a pretty hard lot."[9]

Speaking in an April 1966 general conference session, he said, "The individual, then, is the focal point of all the programs and performance of the Church—not the program itself, not the statistics. Not *institutional expansion*, but *individual exaltation* is the purpose of it all."[10]

And then, in October 1970 he said, "The objective of it all, then, is not counting the sheep but feeding them, not the proliferation of buildings or units or organizations or statistics, but the blessing of the individual child of God."[11]

When speaking about Christ, Duff would often teach how we come individually to the Savior to receive blessings and gain witness. Jesus blessed the little children "one by one." The multitudes saw and heard "every man for himself," then went "one by one" to feel the prints in His hands and side (3 Nephi 17:21, 25; 18:36–38).

APPROACHES TO CONTROVERSIAL ISSUES

Duff treated all alike. He focused a large part of his life and ministry on the disenfranchised, the underdog, the forgotten, the lost, and those on the intellectual and spiritual fringes. He treated those who were different from him with respect and dignity. He was a champion of people of color when that was not the prevailing sentiment in the country. He often expressed his sadness about the denial of priesthood and temple blessings for Black members of the church and had numerous conversations with other church leaders and hundreds of members and nonmembers about it. He wept with joy when church president Spencer W. Kimball finally received the revelation changing that policy.[12]

He never tried to dissuade individuals from entering into racially or religiously mixed marriages, but he did counsel individuals to be aware of what the future could look like, and the problems they might face along the way. Then he supported them in whatever decision they made.

Duff was particularly interested in helping solve problems between the individual and church policies. One such area was the negative impact on some parents and family members who were excluded from witnessing marriages in

9. BUW, 263–66.
10. MDH-T, "How Many Apples in a Seed?" GC, Apr. 1966.
11. MDH-T, "Bear Ye One Another's Burdens," GC, Oct. 1970.
12. See chapter 46, pages 427–40 for more details on this subject.

LDS temples because of the church's policy of only allowing fully active members inside its temples. While living in England, he had witnessed many marriages conducted civilly outside the temples, as legally required, followed by the sealing ordinance of the marriage in the temple. He advocated for such a policy to be implemented worldwide, believing it would alleviate the heartache, resentment, and lasting bitterness resulting from the existing policy. Unfortunately, his advocacy for such a policy did not come to fruition during his lifetime, but did change later.[13]

Duff was sympathetic to the plight of those who suffered under stereotypes and stigmas. He often counseled with gay and lesbian church members and their loved ones. In mid-July 1976, a newly minted BYU history professor, D. Michael Quinn, met with him at the insistence of his wife, Jan. Duff was Quinn's former mission president, and had performed the marriage ceremony of Michael and Jan in the Salt Lake Temple in 1967. Quinn described Duff as "the only general authority with whom I had a reciprocally trusting association." In that 1976 interview and with great trepidation, the thirty-three-year old Quinn revealed the homosexual feelings he'd had since the age of twelve and the resulting problems it had caused in his mixed-orientation marriage. "President Hanks was compassionate and supportive toward me," Quinn wrote. "He said that he knew of no cure for homosexuality and disagreed with LDS leaders who told young men that their desire for other men would disappear after they married."[14]

Several years later, in August 1984, Duff received a letter from Carol Lynn Pearson, a good friend and an LDS author and poet. Duff had performed her marriage ceremony to Gerald Pearson years earlier. Duff "wept over" the letter he received from Carol Lynn. Though she and Gerald had divorced in 1978 because of Gerald's homosexuality, she had taken him back into her home after he became seriously ill. Gerald had died in their home of AIDS the night before she sent her letter. Duff wrote, "She had read Walt Whitman to him, played Beethoven, and welcomed him to be surrounded by people who loved him as he died. Such Christlike and saintly virtue I cannot approach and can scarcely understand, but I take off my hat for it. She is a marvelous human being. I called her to tell her so."[15]

Duff didn't share or discuss personal conversations with people he counseled with, and he rarely documented them. The most detailed account Duff ever wrote of counseling with an LGBT individual described a several-hour talk with a man in the late 1980s. The man was about to be excommunicated for acting on his homosexual desires. Growing up with seven brothers, he had known as a young man

13. MDH-L to Grant Bangerter, Temple Department, Apr. 2, 1986.

14. D. Michael Quinn, *Chosen Path: A Memoir* (Salt Lake City: Signature Books, 2024), 336.

15. MDH-JE, Aug. 2, 1984. Carol Lynn Pearson wrote a groundbreaking and best-selling book about her and Gerald's story, *Goodbye, I Love You* (New York: Random House, 1986).

that he was different. He went on a mission, came home and married a young woman, and they had three children. Before getting married, he explained everything to her. He fulfilled his roles as a husband and father but ultimately was unfaithful to her. These challenges led to his mental collapse and attempted suicide and eventually his walking away from his wife and children.

Duff wrote that the man was "now adrift, afoot, completely heartbroken. My message to him was not one of criticism or judgment but of great compassion. It is plainly not his fault that he is like he is. We discussed abstinence and self-discipline and doing the best he can with what he has. I think he can do it. I don't know whether I could shoulder the heavy burdens I am laying on him. He has undeniable and undesirable problems, and I don't think he will succumb to them more than he seems to feel he had to. I hope there is room in the Church for one who, being different, can and will undertake to keep himself from acting out the tendencies which he did not ask for and cannot help."[16]

After Duff's death, a gay man blogged about his positive experience with him many years before. "My father was a stake president during my adolescent years," the man wrote, "and in those days the general authorities lodged with the president of the stake they were visiting." For one stake conference, "our visiting general authority was Elder Marion D. Hanks. Elder Hanks had a bit of a cult following in the Church due to his compassionate sermons, and I was eager to meet him.... The first thing I noticed was the total absence of the 'G.A. personality.' He looked into my eyes, and I immediately understood that he cared and that he was interested in who I was. We chatted about my college experiences. I was completely enthralled by the holiness and compassion of this man." He was nearly "the first person I ever came out to."[17]

Because Duff had complete confidence in God's mercy and was willing to lay all matters at the Savior's feet, when he counseled with LGBT individuals he came down on the side of love.

BEING ALL THERE

Duff taught himself to be completely present and involved with each individual before him. One of his most-used quotations was by the influential writer and scholar Mark Van Doren on "being all there": "There is one thing we can do, and the happiest people are those who do it to the limit of their ability. We can be *completely present.* We can *be all there.* We can control the tendency of our minds to wander from the situation we are in.... It is hard to do this, but it is harder to understand afterward wherein we fell so short. It was where and when we ceased to give our entire attention to the person, the

16. MDH-JE, Aug. 14, 1987.
17. "A Tale of Two Humanists," MoHoHawaii, Aug. 16, 2011, mainstreetplaza.com.

opportunity before us."[18] This quotation accurately describes Duff's approach in dealing with individuals.

The following passage by David Grayson, whom Duff loved to read, describes what an interaction with Duff Hanks was like: "Do not apologize, friend, when you come into my field. You do not interrupt me. What you have come for is of more importance at this moment than corn. Who is it that says I must plow so many furrows this day? Come in, friend.... We will invest our time not in corn, or in cash, but in life."[19]

When you were with Duff, you knew you had his undivided attention.

THE STAR THROWER

In his essay "The Star-Thrower," author Loren Eiseley tells the story of walking along a beach, passing by greedy shell collectors and coming upon a "star thrower"—a man picking up stranded starfish and flinging them back to life in the ocean. When the author pointed out that he couldn't possibly save all the starfish, the man threw another back in and replied, "True, but I helped that one."

Duff was a star thrower.

In his well-marked copy of Eiseley's essay, Duff highlighted the parts that struck him most forcefully:

"The stars," the man said, "throw well. One can help them."

"I understand," said the author. "Call me another thrower."

"[The star thrower] is not alone any longer. After us there will be others," wrote Eiseley. "The task was not to be assumed lightly, for it was *men as well as starfish* that we sought to save.... For a moment, we cast on an infinite beach together beside an unknown hurler of suns."[20]

It is fitting that the most repeated sentiment expressed in forty years' worth of letters is "Elder Hanks, you will never know the difference you made in my life." It was this ability to change the course of an individual life that best defined him. He was authentically kind and interested and believed that each child of God was worth saving.

Not surprisingly, an internet search shows that the most-cited quotation of all Duff's statements was this: "Every human being is trying to say something to others. Trying to cry out I am alive, notice me! Speak to me! Listen to me! Confirm for me that I am important, that I matter."[21]

SUFFERING WHEN OTHERS SUFFER

Duff's empathetic personality refused to let him turn away when others were suffering. Most of the time his response was private and personal. While

18. Mark Van Doren, "Your Magic Moment," *This Week*, Dec. 7, 1952, 2.

19. Ray Stannard Baker, *David Grayson: Adventures in Contentment* (New York: Doubleday, Page, & Company, 1922), 33.

20. Loren Eiseley, *The Star Thrower* (New York: Random House, 1978), 67–92.

21. MDH-A, "A Birthday for Ricky," *The Rotarian*, Dec. 1973.

introducing Duff as a speaker at Ricks College in 1979, Church Commissioner of Education Jeffrey R. Holland said of him, "His home is legendary as a way station for the heart-sick and homeless, as well as the happiest of young people. Unwed mothers, distraught fathers, frightened freshmen and struggling sophomores—blacks, browns, Jews, Gentiles—all have enjoyed hospitality in the Hanks home, which communicated to them that their names would always be safe there."[22]

Elder Richard P. Lindsay added, "Your example of service to the 'have-nots' of the world, from Africa to Salt Lake City, reflects a great love of people everywhere." And Bob Rees said, "It is always a strength to my faith to know that you are there and that you recognize the same kinds of problems that many of us see and are willing to acknowledge and talk about them. Please know that there are many of us who have been heartened by your courage."

LEAVING THE NINETY-NINE FOR THE ONE

Focusing on "the one" requires an effort to practice what one preaches, but it also requires the ability to notice and be aware of the needs to begin with. Duff had an unusual ability to sense a person's needs and then seek ways to help them. When a student named Aaron Dodini was impressed by a speech Duff gave at Ricks College, he lined up to shake Duff's hand afterward. Unfortunately, he had to leave early to get to his job as a lifeguard. Dodini's friend stayed in line and told Duff about Aaron who was really disappointed he didn't get to shake Duff's hand.

Dodini was sitting at his lifeguard post when Duff walked into the pool area, asking loudly for Aaron Dodini. When the young lifeguard raised his hand, Duff walked over to him and shook his hand. Dodini never forgot it.[23]

Duff's ability to comfortably move between large-crowd events and individual counseling was a constant throughout his ministry. His journals are replete with hundreds of days spent jumping back and forth between individual micro needs and the macro needs of the church. In August 1971, for example, with "excitement and joy" he spoke at an area conference in England, where 12,500 church members packed into a number of buildings to watch. Duff said, "I stayed after, talking to people, until they expelled us. One brilliant boy, an Oxford scholar, approached me in tears and expressed his love and appreciation." He wept and told Duff he had decided to go on a mission. "Another youngster wanted to know if I had ever felt inadequate in my life. We talked. It was all very sweet."

Later in London, Duff saw a girl walking in Hyde Park who looked like his daughter, Nancy.

---

22. Jeffrey R. Holland, introduction of Marion D. Hanks, Ricks College Baccalaureate Service, Apr. 24, 1979.

23. Dana Dodini, email to Richard D. Hanks, Aug. 22, 2015.

"American?" Duff asked her.

She was, and she was out of money and wanting to go home. She cried when Duff gave her five pounds. "I asked her to pass it on when she could," Duff said.[24]

24. MDH-JE, Aug. 1971.

15

Stay Inside and Lift

I've made it my policy to "lean into the Church."
—Marion D. Hanks

Due to his position in church leadership, but more so because of his empathy and willingness to listen, Duff was often the final sounding board for those who were deciding whether to leave the church or stay in. While he interacted with many who chose to leave their faith, he never assumed that transgression was the catalyst for a person's impending departure from the fold. Put another way, he didn't assume that someone's faith crisis was driven by personal weakness.

Duff's empathy for people's struggles came from his own experience dealing with faith issues as a young man. He was surrounded by intellectual friends at the University of Utah and afterward. Some of those friends eventually abandoned any religious belief. But before they did so, Duff engaged in many long-drawn-out conversations with them pertaining to the veracity of the Book of Mormon, the Atonement of Jesus Christ, the church, its doctrines and policies, and the weaknesses of its leaders.

Wayne Booth, the famous American literary critic, was one of Duff's favorite missionary companions and the two of them hit it off right from the start. Duff provided brilliant challenges to many of Wayne's ideas, radical and conservative, during their missions and afterward. Wayne chose what he described as "borderline straddling" in his approach to Mormonism. In his book *My Many Selves: The Quest for a Plausible Harmony*, he described himself as "never perfectly comfortable in or out of the fold." He wrote, "I choose to pursue the ground *shared* by the orthodox and the doubters, living daily with troublesome soul-splits."[1]

Alternatively, Duff chose to remain "completely in," albeit with accommodation to some issues. He wrote, "Over the years, I have refused to surrender what is very important to me, while at the same time, with some resignation, trying to live with some circumstances and people that are not always first choice for me. The years have authenticated the blessings that come with trying to do one's own

1. Wayne C. Booth, *My Many Selves* (Logan: Utah State University Press, 2006), 132–34.

best under circumstances of less than perfect quality. After all, Christ did all that he did knowing what lay ahead."[2]

As a young missionary and later a member of the military, Duff was always wrestling with some aspect of the church or the gospel. In 1945, at age twenty-four, he wrote: "My thoughts about the gospel and salvation ... are still in flux, and I presume they always shall be. I hope, by the way, that they will. I think a good gauge of an individual's real understanding of the gospel might well be his capacity to earnestly love and teach all men, knowing that they may never become fully indoctrinated Mormons and that they too may be saved."[3] Duff believed that bringing another person even one short step closer to Christ and His gospel constituted success in the ministry.

It would be fair to say that Duff's take on the church differed from many in that his focus over time became less and less about things specific to the church, and more on the Savior and the salvation of individuals. Duff did not shy away from openly questioning pronouncements that implied a "perfect church." He often quoted the following from renowned educator M. Lynn Bennion: "Religion does not teach us everything at once. It does not clear up all our difficulties. Some religious teachers have seemed to think that it is a reproach to religion not to be able to give a categorical answer to every question. They make assertions where the wise and reverent person often will be silent or recognize his lack of insight. There are many things which still are wrapped in wonder, and many ways in which we see God not fully, but only in glimpses, like sunshine through clouds."[4]

Characteristically, Duff's point of view regarding those who considered leaving the church or Christianity emphasized not only what they would miss out on but more especially that the Church *needed them* to stay and help it improve. He told them that regardless of their decision to stay or leave, he would love them. But if they stayed in the church, think of how much good they could do! Hence his frequent advice, "stay inside and lift."

EMBRACING THE QUESTIONER

To those who questioned, Duff often quoted President David O. McKay's statement, "Doubt is not to be condemned. Sincere doubting sometimes leads to truth, but to reject without sufficient evidence is fatal to the soul."[5]

To Duff, open dialogue and discussion of differing viewpoints was essential to creating an atmosphere of faith. He was consistent in this, both as a church leader and as a father. Leading child advocates have encouraged parents to celebrate questions from their children. That was certainly the case around the Hanks

2. MDH-L to George Turner, June 13, 1989.

3. MDH-L to home from sea, June 1945.

4. M. Lynn Bennion, "Creative Teaching," *Improvement Era*, Nov. 1946, 705. Dr. Bennion was a prominent historian, author, and superintendent of the Salt Lake City School District.

5. David O. McKay, "The Reality of Christ," *Latter-day Saints' Millennial Star,* Dec. 25, 1941, 821.

dinner table. "On so many occasions," Duff's daughter Mary remembered, "Dad would sit us down and teach us some principle and then invite us to ask anything we wanted about it."

In one particularly moving announcement, a former member of the church expressed on the internet his decision to remove himself from the church by saying, "The times of tolerance, respect for diversity, open-mindedness, and personal autonomy taught by men like President David O. McKay, Hugh B. Brown, and Marion D. Hanks are gone."[6]

While accepting the questioning heart and mind, Duff was also keenly aware of the need for those who were questioning their belief to "lean into the Church." That is, to assume good intent from the church and its leaders, to give equal time to the possibilities—both pro and con—of any specific viewpoint. This wasn't an attempt to stack the deck in any way but rather Duff's inclination to begin discussions about faith from the position of a believer rather than that of a disbeliever. He often repeated the simple phrase "Question everything, but stay on the path."

LIFE OF THE MIND AND LIFE OF THE SPIRIT

Over time, Duff's ministry seemed to migrate increasingly toward those who had intellectual, spiritual, or other faith concerns. When questioned, he responded that very few other church leaders were aiming their remarks at those struggling on the borders of orthodoxy, so he did.

In a 2003 newspaper article titled "LDS Intellectuals Tell Why They Don't Stray," Brigham Young University microbiology professor Bill Bradshaw described his decision to stay in the church, despite doubts, "because of certain people whose company I want to retain." He spoke fondly of Marion D. Hanks, an emeritus general authority, and his pleas for Latter-day Saints to embrace those on the "margins" of the faith.[7]

Because he had several friends in church leadership in California, Duff was invited multiple times to visit with some of the leading intellectual students at Stanford and Berkeley and the surrounding area. He would spend several hours with them, discussing and answering questions, then fly back home.

He would also hold the same type of event at universities in Utah. One evening in a class at the University of Utah, he answered "about every tough question that could be asked." Attendees included some detractors, some attackers, and some just curious. He reported that a few attendees were incensed because "Mormons teach their little kids not to play with non-Mormon kids." It was also [seriously] expressed that "some little Mormon kids are taught that Episcopalians eat children." Duff's tongue-in-cheek answer to that strange statement was "While this

6. Francis Nelson Henderson, "Exit Statement," Institute for Religious Research, Nov. 23, 2011, irr.org.

7. Carrie A. Moore, "LDS Intellectuals Tell Why They Don't Stray," *Deseret News*, Aug. 15, 2003.

was not general doctrine, there certainly were some of us who believed it!" In summary of the event, Duff wrote, "They were responsive, except for those who were hostile, and even they didn't put up much of a serious fuss. The professor and some others were pleased, and some of the non-Mormons stopped by afterwards to talk, so I suppose it was worthwhile."[8]

Duff knew that he was making a difference by the vast number of letters he received. One example said: "Brother Hanks, I do wish to convey, from the depths of my soul, an expression of gratitude for the service you render, unique among our general authorities, to so many of our people. We have so few who speak legitimately both the language of intelligence and the language of the Master. Those need not be mutually exclusive; too often they are made so. Thank you sincerely, for your witness that they should be complementary."[9]

One of Duff's more interesting hot and cold relationships was with Eugene England. Gene was a Latter-day Saint professor, essayist, scholar, and sometime burr under the saddle of the church. But then, Duff was a bit of a burr himself. Duff and Gene had a prolonged relationship, sometimes conflicted, but usually solid. They disagreed vehemently on the war in Vietnam, on appropriate ways to voice disagreement, and on other subjects, but they had mutual respect and admiration for each other.

In 1975, forty-one-year-old Gene applied for a teaching position at BYU but was rejected.[10] Duff wrote of a BYU Board of Education executive meeting, in which a possible teaching candidate was discussed, "a young man who has caused me considerable trouble and for whom I have exercised myself quite extensively." Though Duff did not name that individual, it was most likely Gene England.[11]

"One by one," Duff wrote, "the three others at the table abandoned consideration" of this young man because, they said, someone "in another forum" had "expressed lack of interest" in him.[12] Duff felt certain that this other forum was a Quorum of the Twelve meeting. Feeling his mind and stomach in torment, Duff responded with "an impassioned speech," declaring that it was "our responsibility as grown men, assigned a specific task, to express our views without reference to what others' views at other forums might be." He wrote, "I thought it a matter of considerable disgust that we could not fulfill our obligations as an executive committee and bring forth matters which we believe in, irrespective of the views of others."

8. MDH-JE, about Professor Jim Clayton's class on "conflicts between gown and town," Apr. 27, 1978.

9. Duane Jeffrey to MDH, Feb. 1978.

10. "Biography," The Eugene England Foundation, eugeneengland.org.

11. Terryl L. Givens, *Stretching the Heavens: The Life of Eugene England and the Crisis of Modern Mormonism* (University of North Carolina Press, 2021), 105–7.

12. Elders Hunter, Hinckley, and Monson.

The man who had brought up the "other forum" replied, "We three couldn't possibly vote [for the candidate] in view of what we have heard."

"That's too bad," Duff replied, "your vote ought to count for something."[13]

BYU did hire Gene two years later. When his outspokenness got him into hot water with top church leaders over the next twenty-one years, Duff went to bat to save Gene's job at BYU multiple times. After mostly positive experiences serving under the Dallin H. Oaks, Jeffrey R. Holland, and Rex D. Lee administrations, Gene was forced to retire from BYU in 1998—six years after Duff became an emeritus general authority.

Duff and Gene communicated off and on until Gene's untimely death from cancer in 2001, ten years before Duff's passing. Duff spoke at the memorial for Gene at Utah Valley University, where Gene had finished his teaching career.[14]

Despite a continual onslaught of doubters, critics, and those struggling with belief, Duff continued testifying, reaching out, and being accessible. But, as might be imagined, at times it wearied him. After prolonged periods of counseling and interacting with those on the periphery of orthodoxy, with a slightly sarcastic and tongue-in-cheek tone, a weary Duff would refer to a favorite quotation, attributed to Goethe: "Give me the benefit of your convictions if you have any, but keep your doubts to yourself, for I have enough of my own." One gets a clear sense, when reading through his journals, that despite his powerful testimony of the Savior and His gospel, Duff continued to struggle with some of the more human aspects of the church.

EMPATHY, YES, BUT EFFORT IS REQUIRED TOO

Because he spent much of his ministry with those having doubts, he was amused once at an acquaintance's presumption that Duff wouldn't want to spend time with doubting members. A great many of his close friends throughout a lifetime were "out there," living "the life of the mind" in universities and other places where Duff might well have found himself had he chosen a slightly different course. He had decided to stay in and try to help, rather than step out and contribute nothing to the church just because he didn't understand everything or believe everything exactly as other people did.

Duff also applied his faith toward helping those who felt they had "graduated from," or "outgrown" the church, as their intellect matured. He shared the story of a good friend who was about to write a thesis, in which he was going to describe his "emancipation" from the "provincialism" of the church. Duff listened carefully to his friend and then predicted he would never write it, "because you have no real idea what it is you think you have outgrown," Duff said. "Tell me about the Book of Mormon, or the Doctrine and Covenants, or the Pearl of

13. MDH-JE, Jan. 10, 1975.

14. "Biography," England Foundation.

Great Price, or the Bible. Tell me about the standard expositions of the doctrines of the Church. Have you really read any of them?"

Duff's friend answered, "No, not one." (Yet, he was going to announce to the world what he had overcome and left behind.)

Duff continued, "If you really go to work and discover what it is you are leaving behind, you will never write it, because I know what is deep inside you. If you do that much, you'll know."

There came a day when the man announced to Duff that he had decided to change his thesis.[15]

Duff felt strongly that a knowledge and testimony of the gospel required deep and concerted effort. At the young age of twenty-two, he wrote to a friend from his mission, "Are there things I'm not sure about? Yes, lots of them! I still question and doubt and worry. But my attitude is that I will someday be capable of understanding things that are now beyond my ken. Some might call that type of thinking blind faith—or perhaps intellectual dishonesty. Not so! I felt the same when I started to learn to read. I feel it now when I think of studying law or medicine. If I can school my mind to comprehend the things of science and art, why can I not look forward to a time of greater knowledge of things spiritual? If I want ... the assurance of knowledge, then I must go to the source of such knowledge and be willing to pay the price for obtaining it."[16]

Duff felt that many who listed grievances with the church or the gospel were enumerating things not always representative of what the church actually taught, or were cultural traditions or beliefs that individual leaders or members might have espoused but were not canonized doctrines of the church.

Duff became a well-known beacon for many who struggled not only with the church's teachings but also some of its leaders. A letter to Duff from a university professor friend said, "As I have struggled to reconcile my own convictions about the truth of the Gospel of Christ with the behavior of certain church leaders, I am humbled and inspired by your example. It has been hard to accept the fact that those called to lead the church can, at times, be narrow, petty, and even mean."[17]

A 1969 letter from a new BYU faculty member said, "I sense that there is something different about you, that you are speaking not only from conviction, but from conviction which has grown from understanding. I sense that you have also wrestled and struggled with the distressing human problems which confront us today, and I feel that the course you have chosen is a responsible course because it is based on understanding and faith, and not conviction alone. May the Lord continue to guide you."[18]

Occasionally, Duff could be quite stern with friends who, in their quest to be

15. BUW, 300–1.
16. MDH-L to a friend from his mission, 1943.
17. University professor to MDH, Sept. 1992.
18. BYU faculty member to MDH, Sept. 25, 1969.

a catalyst for change, chose to act zealously in public with an overabundance of criticism and finger-pointing. He frequently quoted a verse attributed to Spanish matador Domingo Ortega:

> Bullfight critics ranked in rows,
> Crowd the enormous plaza full.
> But only one is there who knows,
> And he's the one who fights the bull.

In a letter to Gene England, Duff wrote, "You know how to be happy and how not to be happy. Make up your mind and be happy. You know me well enough to know that I am not suggesting that you close your eyes or your mind, or that the road out isn't always going to be there. I am just suggesting that your highest happiness will be found lifting and deepening and broadening and loving, and not standing on the edge making noise or asking questions that any fool can ask, while others, with maybe fewer answers, are inside doing the work."[19]

In answering questions of a young member friend, he wrote, "I have never discouraged anyone from asking questions, but I am more impressed when the people who ask them are consistently contributing to the wellbeing of their fellowmen and willing to do the work that makes the church program go. We have perhaps been guilty of underestimating the mind and soul of man as we think up our better ways of doing things and wonder at the limitation and slow speed of those who govern."[20]

NEITHER THE BABY NOR THE BATHWATER

In a general conference address in April 1957, Duff said:

> Do you know that some of our wonderful young people of great potential intelligence and capacity are abandoning their faith and their way of life in the gospel, with all the strength and beauty of it, because they have questions for which they have not learned satisfactory answers?
>
> May I read you a statement from the pen of one of the most learned among us, who left us a legacy of scientific research and useful knowledge, and of great faith. Dr. Widtsoe said: "Wise men do not throw the Church overboard because they have not satisfied themselves concerning every principle of the gospel. Under the law of progression every principle may in time find lodgment in the inner consciousness of the seeker." To abandon the marvelous demonstrable truths of the gospel because there are some questions one cannot satisfactorily resolve would be foolishness in the extreme.... I plead with you ... not to abandon all that is good in your religion because there are some things you do not understand.[21]

19. MDH-L to Eugene England, Sept. 13, 1965.
20. MDH-L to JD, Aug. 8, 1990.
21. MDH-T, "Questions for the Iconoclast," GC, Apr. 1957.

KNOW-IT-ALLS AND SKEPTICS

While Duff was empathetic and sympathetic toward those who struggled with their beliefs, he was far less tolerant of those on the far ends of the spectrum, who either (1) "had all the answers" or (2) mocked others for expressing simple faith. Another favorite quotation of Duff's that made it into many of his sermons and writings was the following:

> **To the Skeptic and the Saved.**
> The world would be better off if every believer did not feel himself superior to every doubter in nobility of soul, and every doubter did not have the same attitude toward the believer on the score of intelligence. The doubter can also be an imbecile, and the believer a scoundrel . . . and vice versa.[22]

Smugness and a lack of respect for the differences between people was the antithesis of Duff's accepting and welcoming open-arms policy. He loved and earnestly believed in this wonderful statement of Brigham Young: "How it floods my heart with sorrow to see so many Elders of Israel who wish everybody to come to their standard and be measured by their measure. Every man must be just so long, to fit their iron bedstead, or be cut off to the right length: if too short, he must be stretched, to fill the requirement."[23]

BUT I CAN'T STAND MY LEADERS

To a friend who decided to leave the Church because of conflicts with its leadership, Duff wrote,

> I have read your latest letter, and it has been painful for me to have your intelligence, and capacity for love and leadership, sidelined while others you refer to in negative terms run the show. What a pity. What a loss!
>
> You have made a decision one way; a long time ago, I made it another way. I did not conceive it to be in the interest of good and truth to withdraw myself because I found some imperfections. Indeed, I discovered early that some who withdraw from the Church may be guilty of a greater unwisdom than those who conduct business from the limited standpoint of their parochialism or incapacity.
>
> Sure, there is plenty of ammunition and much to find fault. And you may be asking how you can find ways to do good and give leadership. I might even apply your arguments to my present situation and to what I observe going on day by day, but it would not be radically different. I never aspired to run the Church, but I did find many opportunities [to help].
>
> I say again that I love you and believe in you, and I am deeply saddened that you are not making the contribution you could to counteract whatever flaws there are in those who are in the driver's seats.[24]

---

22. Arthur Schnitzler, *Vanity Fair*, Apr. 1928.
23. *Journal of Discourses*, 26 vols. (London: Latter-day Saints' Book Depot, 1854–86), 8:8–9.
24. MDH-L to GH, Aug. 25, 1993; slightly paraphrased and summarized.

TO THOSE WHO DOUBT

In a letter to a young couple considering leaving the Church, Duff wrote:

> Dear Folks, your letter was beautiful and refreshing.... It carries a spirit and speaks its message in an unusually effective way. While I have deep personal convictions, I cannot answer for another. You must make that decision for yourself.
>
> I remind you of the basic principle spoken by Peter when certain of the disciples walked no more with the Lord, whereupon He said to the Twelve, "Will ye also go away?" Peter answered, "Lord, to whom shall we go? Thou hast the words of eternal life" (John 6:66–68).

Duff continued:

> It was this same Jesus who spoke to the Prophet Joseph and commissioned him.... Either this is true, or it is not. If it is not, we have the magnificent miracle of the Book of Mormon to explain, and I have not been able to do that in ways other than that declared by the Prophet.
>
> Long ago the Apostle Paul had to deal with the very questions that now concern you. Read, I urge you, 1 Corinthians chapter 8 and Romans chapter 14. Paul thought he could eat meat without any harm at all to his conscience or his faith. But he realized that there were others who might be upset by his eating of meat and therefore told the Corinthians that, while he felt this action would not harm *him* at all, he would rather starve to death than have *others* led by his example into harmful behavior.
>
> The bigger lesson is that Paul stayed with his flock. He remained inside, lifting and teaching and sacrificing and ultimately dying for the Lord and His children. So, I pray you will stay inside, considering not only your own satisfactions, but the drastic need of the infants in the faith to be taught by those who know, by believers. The road is not easy. I walk it with heartbreak on occasion, primarily a product of my own limitations. Yet, my decision is made to stay in and lift and love and recognize the utter indispensability of the institution as an instrument to get God's work done, particularly among those of weaker conscience.
>
> We love you yet, and always will, inside or out.
>
> Very sincerely, MDH.[25]

25. MDH-L to anonymous recipients, Jan. 1979.

16

My Specialty Is Mercy

The ultimate form of love for God and men is forgiveness.
—Marion D. Hanks[1]

To believe in God is to know that all the rules will be fair,
and that there will be wonderful surprises.
—Ugo Betti[2]

Duff's absolute devotion to the Savior and his testimony of Him permeated all that he did. He also believed that Heavenly Father's main goal was to help His children progress and return to Him. Puritanical attitudes toward sin were anathema to his compassionate beliefs. He also couldn't square them with what he read in the scriptures. The scriptures teach that Jesus took upon himself the form of man and was "touched with the feeling of our infirmities" (Hebrews 4:15). Duff added, "God loves us and believes in us and has done and will do anything he can to help us, but He will not impose on our free agency."[3]

Duff loved to quote from this description of Christ and his personal advocacy for us: "The keeper of the gate is the Holy One of Israel; and he *employeth no servant there*" (2 Nephi 9:41; emphasis added). This approach to the Judgment gave great personal solace to Duff, which he then shared repeatedly in his sermons and classes.

HIS "RIGHTS OF MERCY"

The last gospel discussion that Rich had with his dad was about Moroni 7:27–28, and Christ's role as the Advocate, especially verse 27, in which the Savior claims of the Father His rights of mercy: "Christ hath ascended into heaven, and hath sat down on the right hand of God, to claim of the Father his *rights of mercy* which he hath upon the children of men? For he hath answered the ends of the law.... Wherefore he advocateth the cause of the children of men" (Moroni 7:27–28; emphasis added).

1. MDH-T, "Forgiveness: The Ultimate Form of Love," GC, Oct. 1973.
2. Ugo Betti, *The Gambler*, in *Ugo Betti: Three Plays*, ed. Gino Rizzo (New York: Hill & Wang, 1966).
3. MDH-T, "Agency and Love," GC, Oct. 1983.

Duff asked a few questions to solidify what they had read together: Christ had finished his time on earth and then sat down on the right hand of God to claim—what? His prize? His godship? His inheritance? His reward? His accolades? His victory?

What kinds of things do we claim when we've finished a job well?

Jesus had finished His sacrifice on earth, and now it was his time to go back home and claim "his *rights of mercy.*"

Duff's specialty was mercy too. He practiced it daily.

MERCY IS "TWICE BLEST"

In his contribution to the book *Teachers Who Touch Lives,* Eugene England wrote: "For me, Elder Hanks has been one who best taught and embodied the unique Christian virtue described by Shakespeare's Portia in *The Merchant of Venice:*

> The quality of mercy is not strained;
> It droppeth as the gentle rain from heaven
> Upon the place beneath. It is twice blest;
> It blesseth him that gives and him that takes:
> It is an attribute to God himself.

Duff believed that God loves being God because it permits Him to be merciful, and He waits for us to open the door to His graciousness. He taught that in addition to repentance, obedience, and ordinances, we should manifest our discipleship in civility, in gentility, in kindness, in patience, refusal to condemn, and in forgiveness and mercy.[4]

ACTING ON MERCY

In a general conference talk, Duff said, "I am sure that everyone within the sound of my voice today is in favor of mercy. But mercy merely as a principle, impersonal mercy, is no more useful or virtuous than impersonal faith or impersonal repentance or impersonal love."

He then went on to describe a situation in which a "good and strongly opinionated man" wanted to discuss with him an error of judgment made by a young missionary. He demanded that "the young man must pay, and I must see to it."

The accuser leaned across the desk and demanded with intensity, "I want justice!"

Quietly Duff replied, "I want mercy."

Three times with growing force he repeated, "I want justice!"

Each time, Duff "responded to his crescendo with diminuendo, saying more quietly, 'I want mercy.' We parted with the agreement that it was my responsibility to handle the matter, to give justice its due, and to let mercy claim her own."[5]

Duff's teachings on mercy were consistently backed up by his actions. The

4. MDH-T, "More Joy and Rejoicing," GC, Oct. 1976.
5. MDH-T, "My Specialty Is Mercy," GC, Oct. 1981.

following letter to Duff is representative of many with similar sentiments: "Just ten months ago today, you interviewed me to go on a mission. I'll never forget the words you spoke to me, 'Maybe some of the older and wiser brethren wouldn't let you go, Elder, but I'm going to take a chance.' It has been ten months of hope and work, and I am realizing the joy of having brought someone else eternal joy. Thank you for taking a chance on a boy with a bleak background."[6]

One year, a very well-known and talented man was caught embezzling from two different employers in Salt Lake City. Most of his friends abandoned him when he was sent to prison. But Duff, knowing the stress this would put on his family, visited him in prison, gave his wife ten thousand dollars, and sent him a letter that closed with these words, "Publicly and privately, we will do everything to support and sustain you. No one, literally, no one, is in a position to cast the first or subsequent stones."

FAIRNESS AND TOUGHNESS WHEN REQUIRED

Even with his strong predisposition to forgiveness and mercy, while he was acting as a judge in Israel, complete exoneration was never a foregone conclusion. One of the responsibilities of general authorities who visit stake conferences each week is to restore the membership, priesthood, and temple blessings of those who had previously received Church discipline.

Rich told a poignant story: "I often picked Dad up on Sunday evenings as he returned home from far-away stake conferences. We would have lively and important conversations on the drive home. On one occasion, Dad was strangely silent and somewhat tearful. I asked him what was going on, and he told me that before leaving the conference, he had spent an hour with a man who had previously been excommunicated and was desperately trying to get back in. He had done horrible things to members of his family and had been out of the Church for seven years. But Dad said, 'Rich, I just couldn't do it.' He didn't say another word all the way home, and I could tell he was contemplating if he'd done the right thing."

On another occasion, he met with a young girl who had broken up a little family and a home by her actions, but felt no particular pangs of remorse about the whole thing. Yet she expected that the Spirit of the Lord would uplift and inspire her and that her testimony would remain clear. Duff wrote, "I mostly listened, but in the course of our visit managed to let her talk herself into an understanding of the vicious thing she has deliberately done and of the situation she has put this other lovely young wife in. I was a little bit harsh because she needed it. She was unrepentant and unhumble and I did what I could to help her realize the error of her position. I think she managed to arrive at a condition of humility before she left."[7]

6. Letter to MDH, n.d.
7. MDH-JE, Jan. 23, 1954.

PUNISHMENT AND SUFFERING

Duff didn't understand those who seemed to take delight in assuring the strictest and, in their words, "appropriate" punishment of the sinner. At that time, many in the church's leadership seemed to lean heavily toward punitive measures as a requirement for forgiveness from God. Duff felt strongly otherwise.

A letter from temple worker Lowell Leishman said, "It was our privilege to watch you minister and administer the affairs of the temple during your tenure.... We will never forget you teaching us: 'Sometimes the correction can be more offensive than the transgression.'"

In 1954 he wrote, "Our meeting emphasized ... that Brother McConkie and I are as far apart as the earth's poles when it comes to our attitude toward people. He is a fine and good man, and I sincerely love him. He has been very courteous and kindly and patient with me and has endured my consistent efforts to liberalize him with equanimity. I have a high regard for his faith, his loyalty, and his ability. I do not share his unforgiving attitude toward people, however, and I am unalterably opposed to any attitude which considers excommunication of people from the Church as any kind of victory to be exulted over."[8]

A January 1976 journal entry expressed his continuing disagreement with some of his peers on the topic of repentance. He wrote, "In particularities of doctrine, I am less content than ever. Some of my brethren are teaching things with which I just do not agree on the basis of my feelings, but more importantly, on the basis of what the scriptures and the prophets teach." The concept being emphasized was the needful "suffering," by the sinner, including formal Church action, with the punishment suffered not only by a broken-hearted, repentant sinner but, by association, everyone connected with him or her. Duff explained, "I am not aware of a need to measure how much a person has *suffered*, but rather how much they have *changed*." He continued, "It would seem to me that anyone whose own imperfections are remembered would comprehend that suffering isn't the product of some kind of court, punishment, or sanction, but is and will always be the personal consequences of sin."[9]

Duff was particularly bothered by the church's refusal to allow those who had committed certain serious sins to be considered for further leadership service in the kingdom. In June 1981 he wrote, "I spoke at BYU, emphasizing that God forgives sinners and sometimes even made egregious sinners president of the whole Church, such as Alma for instance." Duff found it strange that Alma could become president of the Church, but according to some of Duff's colleagues, "no sad sinner," even one who has "come all the way back sorrowing, can be a bishop today. I do not believe in this present view."[10]

8. MDH-JE, Jan. 21, 1954.
9. MDH-JE, Jan. 1976, emphasis added.
10. MDH-JE, June 1981.

HEAVENLY BOOKKEEPING

Some people harbor a certain animosity toward God in their youth, thinking that He is a "catcher," trying to catch us doing something wrong. Duff admitted to feeling that way as a young man but came to love instead what Isaiah says: "And therefore, will the Lord *wait*, that he may be gracious unto you, and therefore will he be exalted, that he may have *mercy* upon you" (Isaiah 30:18; emphasis added). Duff often shared this scripture, declaring, "God waits to be gracious. He loves to be merciful."

Duff taught that the specialty of the Father is mercy, and the specialty of the Savior is mercy, and that neither will give up on us. This manner of thinking leads into perhaps one of the most important pronouncements that he ever taught. After a full examination of the doctrine of the judgment, Duff summarized his feelings with this statement:

> *Salvation and exaltation are not matters of heavenly bookkeeping, but of the qualifying of the soul that comes with knowing the Lord.*
> —Marion D. Hanks[11]

To Duff, God won't be standing at the pearly gates with a clipboard record of our sins, but rather he'll be standing at the end of the race, encouraging us on. He believed, as the scriptures teach, of us going post-judgment to where we will be comfortable, and receiving what we are "willing to receive" (D&C 88:32). Similarly, Psalm 130:3–4 records, "If thou ... shouldest *mark iniquities,* O Lord, who shall stand? ... there is *forgiveness* with thee" (emphasis added).

Perhaps this change of thinking during his life, from "a catcher God" toward a Savior-administered but partially self-adjudicated personal judgment, informed Duff's determined commitment to mercy. Perhaps it was his own self-admitted shortfalls in living up to his potential. Maybe a little of both. In any case, mercy became a cause that he championed to the very end of his life.

DEGREES OF GLORY

Duff had a nuanced opinion of the three degrees of glory and what they mean. He felt the best description of the hereafter was that of us choosing the degree of opportunity we really want and preparing for it. It isn't a matter of somebody being better than somebody else, or God parceling so many into one category and so many into another pigeonhole. It is a simple explainable consequence of our choosing the opportunity we want. After a stake conference, he recorded:

> I have given few sermons on the degrees of glory, so called, but I spoke of it in a measure this morning. My view does not particularly respond to the notion of a stratified eternal experience, but rather of varying degrees of interest, involvement, and service and the preparation underlying these. I think of the degrees of

11. MDH-T, "Willing to Receive," GC, Apr. 1980. See also pages 379–80.

opportunity or levels of capacity, of preparations for eternal creative experience. In the 88th section of the D&C is recorded a statement about "that kingdom not of glory," and the standard by which those who arrive there are chosen. The words are simple and direct—we get what we are willing to enjoy and will not have imposed on us anything we are not willing to enjoy.

Thus, the enjoyment of opportunities is directly dependent upon our willingness to accept those opportunities, including faith and repentance and obedience and walking in the Spirit—in short, preparation for that kind of eternal, progressive, exciting, creative, learning experience. The people were responsive, and I had a fine time.[12]

CHURCH DISCIPLINE

In December 1977, Duff met with the First Presidency to discuss a church leader in Europe who had gotten himself into serious difficulty. Duff hoped to resolve the issue without having it be submitted to the weekly temple meeting where "some-hardliners would treat it with no blessing." Duff wrote, "The more I have to do with excommunications, the less I feel good about them. There may be cases where they are justified, particularly where public knowledge is involved, or people of great responsibility are involved, but generally speaking, I just do not believe in destroying the innocent with the guilty, and until our people learn how to respond to a repentant person, who desperately needs love and acceptance, then I could not feel very good about a harsh approach made in this matter."[13]

On another occasion, after meeting with a woman to restore her blessings, he wrote,

> I had the privilege of buoying her up and calming her fears, and of listening to a tragic story in which her own children have been all but destroyed and her own life so shamed that she is a shell of a person now. It is a fearful responsibility to say aye or nay to people in matters which are of great and lasting effect. I never take such occasion thoughtlessly or comfortably. I am not readily qualified to judge harshly. There just has to be a better way of operating Church discipline than to destroy and shame people, both the miscreant and the innocent. The Doctrine and Covenants supplies the formula—when a sin is committed in private, it shall be handled in private, but if it is public knowledge, then it must be handled publicly. This makes such great sense that I keep wondering why it is not applied.
>
> I have no desire to change the law, but only to understand and apply it in a way that will cease to destroy people. I cannot believe that destroying people in this world is any way to prepare them for eternity, and I do not believe it.[14]

Duff was greatly surprised by a report meeting held in the temple one day. President Spencer W. Kimball's compassion came through as he talked about a

12. MDH-JE, Mar. 13, 1977.
13. MDH-JE, Dec. 8, 1977.
14. MDH-JE, Dec. 1, 1977.

bishop who had given a boy an ultimatum to cut his hair or not hold the priesthood. President Kimball said this was not the spirit of the priesthood and that ultimatums are contrary to the Spirit of the Lord. Duff wrote, "I was astonished and thrilled to hear it and watched the faces of some who have not only issued ultimatums and taught others to do so, but have reported it with an almost gleeful tone to the rest of us. I have resisted this for years, heard President Kimball express his feelings in private twice now, and hope and pray that it has sunk in."

President Kimball also emphasized in the meeting that time should not be a factor in determining when someone who has committed a serious sin to be cleared to go to the temple. He noted that some could truly repent in twenty-four hours whereas others might not do it in twenty-four years. "He abominated the imposition of time penalties, teaching instead that true repentance is the issue."[15]

In setting apart bishops and stake presidents, Duff was quick to advise them that if mistakes were to be made, better to make them on the side of mercy, and the Lord would mete out justice.

OUR JOB IS TO FORGIVE

Duff felt strongly that "we must take people, where they are, as they are, in the imperfect conditions that so widely exist, in the personal imperfections which are universal." He taught,

> We cannot escape responsibility for our families and others whom we might touch, nor ever cease pulling for them, praying for them, and trying to help them. If they make wrong decisions, still we will love them and suffer with them and work with them, even as the father in the Lord's parable waited for the prodigal who finally came to his senses and headed home: "When he was yet a great way off, his father saw him, and had compassion, and ran, and fell on his neck, and kissed him" (Luke 15:20). We will watch and pray, even as the Lord himself waits with godly mercy, ... that he may be gracious unto you, and therefore will he be exalted, that he may have mercy upon you." (Isaiah 30:18).[16]

MERCY FOR ONESELF

All Church leaders eventually encounter individuals who will not forgive themselves or feel like they just can't measure up. In a masterful letter, Duff counseled with a young man who was suffering on his mission due to feelings of guilt and shame and low confidence in his abilities. Here are excerpts of what Duff wrote:

> Elder, there is nothing unusual about feeling inadequate in representing the Lord. There is really no other way to qualify yourself as a true disciple, except through meeting the tests that life brings you. And there is no greater battlefield than a mission.
>
> Don't cut yourself off from future opportunities by living sadly. You mention

15. MDH-JE, Jan. 29, 1975.
16. MDH-A, "Seeing the Five A's," *Ensign*, Nov. 1977.

a feeling of unworthiness. If these were disqualifying, none of us would be in service at all.

Remember, Isaiah said we will be forgiven, and even though our "sins be as scarlet, they shall be white as snow." All this attention to your past is wasted energy. Here's my advice … Buckle down and cease to worry about all this past history and get down to the work.

Repent of whatever problems you had in the past—if you haven't got that straight, then talk to your mission president. It's time for us to put aside nonsense, get on our feet early and late, work harder and harder, and get out the burdens we impose on ourselves by insistently referring to past failings. Your Heavenly Father and your Savior want you to make it. And so do I.[17]

CONTINUING TO TRY

Duff loved to root for the underdog. In basketball. In repentance. In life.

His was a ministry of long-term encouragement and uplift, without only focusing on the short-term outcome.

Duff believed that Heavenly Father does not prescribe a "win or lose it all" scenario for our lives. In fact, he believed that the opposite is true of the Lord. He therefore chose to teach from scriptures that emphasize the effort and the desire and commitment we can each feel, even if we fall short.

For example, the gifts of the Spirit are described as being "given for the benefit of those who love me and keep all my commandments, and him that *seeketh* so to do" (D&C 46:9; emphasis added). The Savior began his discourse to the Nephites, saying, "Therefore, if ye shall come unto me, or shall *desire* to come unto me" (3 Nephi 12:23; emphasis added).

Oliver Granger was an early Church member who always tried his best but evidently didn't accomplish everything he wanted to. The Lord said about him, "And when he falls, he shall rise again, for his *sacrifice* shall be more sacred unto me than his *increase,* saith the Lord" (D&C 117:13; emphasis added). In other words, the Lord seems to say that he is more concerned with his *effort* than his *results.*

As one writer relates, God is effectively saying, "I am more concerned with his labor to plant seeds in the garden, than how many ears of corn he picks."[18]

UNCONDITIONAL LOVE

Duff taught about a God that never gives up on us, as described in the Book of Mormon: "And now, my beloved brethren, seeing that our merciful God has given us so great knowledge concerning these things, let us remember him, and lay aside our sins, and *not hang down our heads,* for we are *not cast off*" (2 Nephi

17. MDH-L to a missionary.
18. Ted Gibbons, "At Least I Tried," *Meridian Magazine,* Oct. 22, 2013.

10:20; emphasis added). He also taught, "The Lord accepted others as they were without the intention to leave them as they were."[19]

Duff believed in the Savior's unconditional love for everyone and taught parents to have the same love for their children. "Our children have to learn somehow that they are more important than their mistakes; that they are worthwhile, valuable, and useful; that they are loved unconditionally. We cannot," he said, "condition our love [on] a beard or beads or habits or strange viewpoints. There must be standards enforced, but our love must be unconditional."[20]

One of the most powerful passages about Duff's mercy was written to him upon his retirement by Phyllis Peterson Warnick, his secretary of more than forty years. Phyllis worked with him almost every day, through good moods and bad, up days and down, health and sickness, while short-tempered or patient. She wrote:

> *Elder Hanks, of course none of us will be judged by man, but if we were, I'd be more than willing to be judged by you.*

19. MDH-T, "Be and Not Seem," BYU devotional address, Jan. 23, 1979.
20. MDH-A, "Love Unconditional," *Ensign,* Dec. 1971.

DELIVERING THE MESSAGE

17

Life as a General Authority

The hardest job I ever loved.
—Anonymous

Early into his service in the First Council of the Seventy, Duff was asked a question he came to expect often, "What's it like?"

Duff replied, "The job is difficult and the demands quite exacting, but the blessings are commensurately wonderful. I travel each weekend and spend considerable time during the week counseling people who need help. There is much to be done in the world in the way of encouragement and understanding."[1]

Being a general authority in the 1950s was far different from what it is in the twenty-first century. The population of the church was only 1.2 million, and there were only thirty-three general authorities, including the First Presidency and Quorum of the Twelve Apostles. There were no quorums of the Seventy, no area presidencies, and only 42 mission presidents.

By comparison, in 2024 there were 125 general authorities and 22 area presidencies around the world, with an additional 335 area authority seventies who live in each area and can respond directly to the needs of the local people. In addition, there are 415 mission presidencies worldwide. Church membership has grown to 17 million.

The mid-twentieth-century church was significantly more centralized, with authority and responsibility consolidated in a few dozen men in Utah. Every missionary, every bishop, and every stake president was required to be interviewed and ordained or set apart by a general authority. Added to those responsibilities was the ongoing crush of touring missions and presiding at stake conferences. The responsibilities took their toll on general authorities' physical and mental health.

There are other, more subtle things about being a general authority. For example, while most working men and women look forward to weekends as a respite and to retiring around the age of sixty-five, general authorities have only one day off a week (Monday) and travel most weekends to conduct stake conference meetings in some far-flung location. And, for the first thirty-eight years of Duff's

1. MDH-L, to Cal Cook, Jan. 1954.

ministry, the policy of general authorities becoming "emeritus" at age seventy did not exist. Maxine and Duff spent all that time believing he would serve in his calling until the day he died.

From a friend, he received a letter that included the following fairly accurate paragraph: "I have often wondered what it must be like [for you] to be totally at the grindstone at all times, to live in a fishbowl, be constantly monitored for signs of individuality—overtly and covertly—and be at the mercy of an apparently indifferent bureaucracy."[2]

Nobody wants to be a whiner, and Duff was no exception. But in his private journal, he did share his feelings, both good and bad, about his calling. He probably wouldn't approve of anyone even alluding to him feeling overloaded or unappreciated—he didn't. But he was human, and it is important to document this part of his experience.

SO MUCH!—THE ONGOING CRUSH OF VOLUME

The requirement that all senior church callings had to be administered by a general authority in those days meant that large numbers of people would be waiting to be set apart and/or ordained whenever a visiting authority came to a stake conference. Instead of flying home after the last meeting of a stake conference on Sunday, Duff would then perform priesthood ordinations, give blessings, dedicate chapels, and visit with members in need. After one conference, he wrote, almost in passing, "I should mention that I had more than thirty ordinations from stakes all over the place and worked hard and long this weekend. Spiritual enervation!"[3]

Asked in a letter what he did each week as a general authority, Duff responded,

> The general authorities serve full time, which amounts to far more of one's life than ordinary "full-time" employment. Every weekend we are away from home at a stake conference, with rare exception. That conference may be in New York, or Samoa, or New Zealand—as my forthcoming ones are. For my conference in New York, I will leave Friday at 5:30, conduct meetings all day Saturday and Sunday, speak or teach 5–6 times, interview, give blessings, set apart newly called people, dedicate a chapel Sunday evening, fly all night and get back to Salt Lake just in time to perform a couple of Temple Sealings on Monday morning.
>
> I am assigned to supervise the missions and members in Asia, like Japan, Hong Kong, Taiwan, the Philippines, Korea, Hawaii, Thailand, India, and including Vietnam where I have been twice this year.
>
> We get many letters, many of them very serious, many involving personal problems, many doctrinal problems, many just like yours.
>
> During the week, I work on church committees with many meetings dealing with spiritual and administrative issues. For instance, I serve on the Church Board of Education and the Board of Trustees for BYU, and the executive committees

2. William Bates to MDH, Jan. 24, 1990.
3. MDH–JE, June 16, 1973.

of both. I serve on the Scouting Committee of the Church, and I am in charge of the LDSSA.

I teach at the Institute of Religion one night a week from 6 to 9.

I try to do some civic things, like the Boy Scouts National Council, Rotary International, and other nonprofits.

Between times, I regularly give speeches at BYU, across the land for the Boy Scouts and as many youth meetings and conferences as I can work in.

I am tired [just writing] this account and hope it will be helpful to you.

Anyone who wants this job, should get it![4]

General authorities used to spend inordinate amounts of time touring the church's missions. In the early days, Duff would be gone three or four weeks at a time on these visits. Reporting on his 1954 tour of the Southern States Mission, he wrote, "Meetings were held from November 5–November 21. Our itinerary included the dedication of 9 chapels and the newly purchased mission home. I personally interviewed all 106 missionaries serving, and a number of local missionaries. We met with saints and investigators in each of the 12 districts and in a total of twenty-two different cities, holding some 36 public and missionary meetings. Wherever possible, we held meetings with servicemen's groups, and with various district presidents, councils and branch leaders of the 101 branches. The tour covered more than 4,200 miles in all."[5] By the 2000s, visiting authorities only spent two or three days touring a mission—teaching leaders and missionaries and interviewing a small sample of missionaries.

During Duff's first seven years as a general authority, he averaged thirty-five weekend stake conferences and forty weekday speeches each year. Including two general conference weekends, four weekend mission tours, and six Rotary or Scouting business weekends, that left an average of five weekends free a year, including the four he was supposed to take as vacation in July each year, but rarely did. Only after an increasing number of general authorities were called, including the reorganization of the seventy and area seventies quorums, did the workload decrease a bit.

CAN'T OR WON'T SAY NO

Some of Duff's challenges were of his own making. He just accepted too many speaking requests. He was always willing to say "yes" to one more request if he could bless the lives of others. But he was working himself to death—Maxine knew it, their kids knew it, and he knew it. But he had a hard time saying no, as a few of his journal entries over the years illustrate. "In the evening, I completed a very foolish week, too many assignments, too little will power in saying no—by going to the Davis Stake to talk to a Senior Aaronic priesthood group," he wrote in 1954. "The

4. MDH-L, to Bonnie Whittaker, Mar. 14, 1968.
5. MDH-A, "Report on Southern States Mission Tour," Nov. 1954.

experience was very enjoyable when all was said and done, and they had a very large group, some of whom, I think, or at least hope, profited from the experience."[6]

Two days later, he added, "In the evening, Maxine and I drove to Coalville, rather a long distance one would think to give a short talk, but I'm silly that way. It happened to be the Aaronic Priesthood ward night and so we went up and I talked, and it turned out quite well."[7]

One from 1972: "Did the usual job of failing to reject a request, so ended up talking to seminary kids at Skyline Seminary at 6:30 this morning. Nice experience—made it on time to the Church Coordinating Council and presented the concept for Young Adults and Young Adult wards."[8]

One from 1975: "I was busy and in meetings all day. At night I was off to Orem for a Fathers and Sons meeting and banquet. I don't say 'No' enough. It was a good night though, and Maxine went along and visited our daughters [at BYU] while I spoke. Lovely evening. I love kids and fathers."[9]

And one from 1977: "I was in meetings all day till 6:00, then went to the mission home to talk to the missionaries, then came home to prepare for talks Thursday in Orem, Friday in Washington, DC, Saturday to the missionaries in DC, then the young people in DC and then beginning stake conference Saturday and Sunday in the Norfolk Stake. Why do I do this to myself?"[10]

WORKING DESPITE ILLNESS

In an era when working through sickness was considered admirable, Duff would push through an illness to keep his commitments. One day in February 1954, he taught his early-morning seminary class in Salt Lake, drove to Provo to speak at a student body assembly, then drove back to Salt Lake to speak at a funeral of an eighteen-month-old child. After the funeral, Duff went to the cemetery with the bereaved father and mother. "They were grateful for our participation," he wrote. "I had had a serious siege of the flu and had not known whether I might make it to these appointments, but the Lord helped me, and it worked out all right."[11]

In February 1976, Duff and Maxine participated in the Samoa Area Conference, with numerous official visits, church meetings, and grueling travel. They had a pleasant experience, but not without health issues. "Maxine wasn't feeling very well from early morning on, and I have what seems like a broad infection in the head and have felt lousy myself, but we've both plowed on." He continued, "We were delayed out of Apia, but did arrive in Pago Pago in time to have a short rest overnight. President and Sister Kimball are heroic. Both are sick unto death

6. MDH-JE, Feb. 15, 1954.
7. MDH-JE, Feb. 17, 1954.
8. MDH-JE, Apr. 26, 1972.
9. MDH-JE, Nov. 20, 1975.
10. MDH-JE, Jan. 11, 1977.
11. MDH-JE, Feb. 9, 1954.

with high fevers and just punk health altogether. He had to stop and upchuck on the roadside because of the bug, but they are still moving and still functioning and are seeming to survive it all."[12]

BUT TRAVELING IS FUN, RIGHT?

Every Friday night, someone in his family would drive Duff to the airport on his way to a stake conference or other meeting. On Sunday night someone would pick him up, and Maxine would hang his suit outside on the clothesline to air out. Unfortunately, in those days, airplanes had so-called smoking and nonsmoking sections, divided only by a curtain, which meant that smoke filled the entire airplane. On one occasion, Duff wrote about "the sickening experience of having a really dissolute lout of a human being" sitting near him on a plane. Though the man was seated in the "no smoking" section, he "smoked one cigarette after the other until I had either to put up with it or punch him one. The airline crew didn't do much about it, and I nearly came to my own conclusion on the matter," Duff wrote. "This morning on the news, I heard it reported that more than 50 percent of all cancer is caused by cigarette smoke—self or others—and I felt by the time I got off the plane that I had enough to give me a dose of something."[13]

Doing so much traveling naturally brought Duff all kinds of experiences, from multiple airplane lightning strikes and engine flame-outs, to washed out bridges, to snoring seatmates. The vagaries of travel exposed him to an entirely different need for flexibility and patience. In fact, he used to tell people, with a smile, that he had a special arrangement with the airlines—If he wasn't there on time, they could leave without him. Duff wrote about a less dramatic but no less inconvenient circumstance he experienced: "At 8:30, Maxine and I drove for hours through a massive storm in order to dedicate a chapel for the Montezuma Creek Branch in southeastern Utah. By the time we got to Soldier's Summit it was a mess. We drove through Green River, Moab, and Monticello to get to Blanding where we rested for a couple of hours. As we transferred our belongings to another car, I asked Maxine if she had seen my suitcase—nope—I had left it at home."[14]

So Duff went shopping at a local Merc store, where he bought two white shirts and ties, shaving cream, deodorant, and a razor. Fortunately, he had hung his suit in the car. It was a reminder for him of the dangers of growing old in the service and forgetting the details.

SLEEPING IN STAKE PRESIDENTS' HOMES

In the early days of Duff's ministry, to save money, the general authorities rarely lodged in hotels, usually staying in the home of a member of the stake presidency instead. This made for some interesting, sometimes concerning, and sometimes amusing experiences. He never knew what his sleeping arrangements would be.

12. MDH-JE, Feb. 18–19, 1976.
13. MDH-JE, Jan. 14, 1977.
14. MDH-JE, Mar. 2, 1973.

Several times over the years, when the hosts had given up their own bed for the visiting general authority, Duff was awakened by a light switched on in the middle of the night by a sleepy young child coming in, looking for their parents.

Another time, he wrote, "I stayed in the home of the second counselor. They have five children and a modest unfurnished home. They were so kind to me." The parents put Duff up in the room of one of their kids, where he slept in a child-sized bed. "I had a perfectly miserable night, but survived it," he said.

One of Duff's favorite stories to tell was about a little boy who had just been served a bowl of soup. The father, who was the stake president, then announced to the mother that additional guests would be joining them. Realizing she didn't have enough food, she snatched the bowl away from the little boy just as he picked up his spoon, to which he inquired in a calm voice, "Mommy, have we already aten?" After forty years of staying in stake presidents' homes, Duff couldn't remember if that experience actually happened to him or to someone else.

Another favorite memory was told by Vernee Frame, Duff's cousin, "On one of Elder Hanks' trips to our stake," Frame wrote, "I persuaded him to bring Aunt Maude with him." As his two guests chatted with his wife in the front room, Frame slipped out to set the kitchen table. At each place the only thing he placed was a large white porridge bowl and a tablespoon. In the center he placed a stack of bread and a pitcher of milk.

"Duff, bring your mother and let's have a bite to eat," he called.

Not having told his wife what he was doing, she came into the kitchen with Duff and Maude with an expression of surprise on her face. What a supper for a general authority!

"Yet, I knew it would be a welcome respite," Frame said. "Our good saints often come near to killing our brethren with food or kindness."

On seeing the simple meal laid out for them, Duff put his arm around his mother and said, "Take a look at this, Mom. How many times in our life have we looked upon a scene like this? There is nothing I enjoy more before bedtime."[15]

DEALING WITH ANTAGONISTS, DETRACTORS, AND THE UNWELL

In harmony with his policy of walking arm-in-arm with those of different religions, Duff tried his best to be good-natured and accommodating to those who believed differently than he did. This proved easier for him when others were courteous and respectful. He even became friends with several protestors who stationed themselves outside of Temple Square's gates at each general conference, hoping to persuade general conference-goers of the error of their ways.

He had less patience dealing with those who were discourteous, uncivil, or antagonistic in their criticisms of him or the church. Though he typically just ignored those who were mean-spirited or ill-mannered, he became irritated with those who were persistent in their attacks, doctrinal and otherwise. Several

15. Vernee C. Frame, remarks at Maude Hanks' funeral, Oct. 23, 1967.

continued barraging him with letters throughout his ministry, frequently telling him what he believed, which was almost always incorrect. "Among the few things that have hurt me seriously over the year[s] is the superstition of a few," Duff reflected, "who do not believe that we individually love Christ as our Savior and worship him."[16]

Once, a young religion writer named David Virtue came to meet with Duff in his office. He was introduced as a "theologian with an armload of degrees, three years spent at the London University Divinity School, ministerial status, and the rest," Duff wrote. "He is also an arrogant young man with a great knowledge of church history and ecclesiastical history, and of the scriptures. We had quite a tussle before we were through. I was not inclined to accept the cynical and patronizing attitude he had. I think he was testing us to see if anybody could withstand the marvelous power of his logic. I haven't had this kind of workout for a long time, but thoroughly enjoyed it, and felt very good about it when it was over."[17]

Another fellow pestered Duff for many years. He was neither polite nor civil. Duff didn't spend much time responding to his attacks, but if the man became really rude, Duff would respond directly. "I have your dissertation on perfection," he wrote back once. "There are some things you come close to being perfect in. For instance, you come close to being perfectly arrogant, almost a perfect antithesis to the Spirit and example of Christ. (1 Peter 2:15, 16, 21–24, etc.) Over the years you have repeatedly told me what I believe, and you haven't come close to knowing what you are talking about.... You are certainly not perfect in humility or in understanding. Still, there is the possibility that if you endure to the end, as Jesus said, you might learn something. For the sake of all of us upon whose gentle eardrums you incessantly beat, I hope so."[18]

He met with and counseled with hundreds of enigmatic, perplexing, or mentally unwell people throughout his ministry. One example, "I met last night with a man who had received the commission from God to take over as Apostle #12, so they all can move up and Spencer Kimball can go home. He haunted me all day and finally cornered me at night. He is as batty as can be, and as calm and clever with language and thought as he can be. Sent him on his way telling him that his way is not the scriptural nor historical way. Tragedy."[19]

Harry and Amy McGimsey

Reverend Harry McGimsey and his wife, Amy, were evangelical Christians who traveled to the church's general conference for more than forty years, to hand out evangelical tracts to church members outside Temple Square. Unfortunately,

16. MDH-L, to Reverend and Mrs. Harry A. McGimsey, ca. Oct. 1980.
17. MDH-JE, Oct. 27, 1978.
18. MDH-L, Mar. 28, 1986.
19. MDH-JE, Jan. 31, 1985.

on occasion, they received verbal abuse from Latter-day Saint conference-goers. Once, Harry was even accosted and spat upon by members until he was rescued by another church member walking by.

Duff went out of his way to befriend and care for the McGimseys, and they returned the favor. After general conference sessions, Duff preferred to walk outside to his office in the Church Administration Building rather than use the underground parking lots and tunnels. Despite the crush of people at conference time, he preferred to be among the people. After walking out of one conference session, Duff encountered the McGimseys. "Harry warned me, both he and his wife in tears, that my life was in danger and [had been] threatened," Duff said. "He stressed that I should have extra security precautions taken. I told Church Security about it later. Harry was sincere, and I was touched because of his concern and tears." Duff and the McGimseys became lifelong friends, often speaking of their love for each other.[20]

In October 1980, Harry told the *Provo Daily Herald* that one year the verbal abuse they received outside general conference was so great that Elder Hanks gave a speech at BYU "telling the students about Harry and Amy by name and reminding them that Mormons also ask to be treated courteously and with love while serving their own missions."[21]

After reading that article, Duff wrote a letter from Hong Kong to the McGimseys, expressing his love and admiration "for their unselfish labor."[22] He also wrote a letter to Harold Wright, president of the Mesa Arizona Temple, another church leader mentioned in the article who had also befriended the McGimseys, inquiring about them.

"Regarding Reverend McGimsey, we hear from him quite frequently," Wright wrote back. "In fact, he has read *A Marvelous Work and a Wonder*, and the Book of Mormon, and a number of tracts. He still faithfully attends conference, but he no longer distributes anti-Mormon tracts. Whenever I visit with him in person, he always mentions your name with great fondness."[23]

Duff continued to correspond with Reverend McGimsey, sharing things they had in common, for many years.

Never a Dull Moment

Speaking of death threats, church security once informed Duff and the other church leaders that a mentally unwell man had manufactured a special "killing

---

20. MDH-JE, Oct. 1977.

21. John C. Speer, "Baptist Missionaries 'Attend' LDS Conferences for 36 Years," *Provo Daily Herald*, Oct. 8, 1980, 44.

22. MDH-L, to Reverend and Mrs. Harry A. McGimsey, ca. Nov. 1980.

23. L. Harold Wright to MDH, Dec. 9, 1980. LeGrand Richards, *A Marvelous Work and a Wonder* (Deseret Book, 1950) is a book about the doctrine and history of the Church of Jesus Christ of Latter-day Saints. Written as a missionary tool, it is believed to be among the best-selling books on Mormonism of all time.

knife" for each of the general authorities, inscribing their name on the knife blade intended for them. Duff thought it serious but also rather comical, wondering aloud to members of his family if the knife maker had etched in "Marion" or "Duff" on the knife slated for him.

Duff's family members weren't big fans of this type of news.

Seeking Common Ground

One holiday season, Duff accepted an invitation to speak to a group of adults from another church, answering their questions and explaining his religious convictions. He wrote in his journal, "One choice lady, perhaps confused by the contrast of what she heard from me, versus what she had been told we believe, rose from her chair and said, 'If I were to strictly follow the life of a believing Mormon, have all the ordinances, serve the church, and attend the temple every day, I could never return to God, except through Jesus Christ.'"

Duff responded, fully subscribing to her teaching and the rest of what the scriptures say that none of us could be justified by the works of the law but also that we are to work out our salvation in fear and trembling. Then he shared a sustaining verse from the Book of Mormon: "For we labor diligently to write, to persuade our children, and also our brethren, to believe in Christ, and to be reconciled to God; for we know that it is by grace that we are saved, after all we can do" (2 Nephi 25:23; emphasis added).

Duff then told her that "if she were to attend a conference at which I was presiding, I would be pleased to call on her and have her repeat verbatim the words she had just spoken. I would rise after her and confirm without reservation that she had just taught the truth of the gospel of Jesus Christ as I understand it."

Maintaining Faith

Duff was well versed on the "warts" of the church, its history, Joseph Smith's failings, doctrinal disagreements, archaeological challenges of the Book of Mormon, and so forth. None of it seemed to faze him, probably because his testimony wasn't rooted in men or their actions but rather in the Savior and His teachings. Many who leave the church say they feel betrayed because of the gap between their expectations and actuality. Duff never set those mythical expectations to begin with, so the gap for him, if any, was minimal. He didn't place church leaders (including himself) on a pedestal, so there was nothing to knock off. He didn't pretend to know the answer to every doctrinal point, so he had no mistaken doctrinal certitude to retreat from. He didn't confuse the church with the gospel of Jesus Christ, so the mistakes of the church and its leaders were not deal-killers for him. He was significantly more interested in *what* the Book of Mormon taught than in *how* Joseph Smith translated and published it.

But he wasn't like an ostrich with its head in the sand, either. Any time a tough issue surfaced, he dug in and researched it thoroughly. His files are brimming with research on everything from the "Adam-God theory" to the Mountain Meadows

Massacre to polygamy. He could stand toe-to-toe with scholars or agitators alike. But he just wasn't interested in either weakening or building his faith on things like church history or modern leaders.

JOURNALISTIC LIBERTIES AND BEING A CELEBRITY TARGET

It would be fair to suggest that 95 percent of journalists and their stories were fair and supportive of Duff and the kind of things he stood for. But he learned early in his ministry that a few journalists would unintentionally mistake his meaning, or misquote him, or rarely, intentionally twist words for their own purposes. Once after a talk at BYU, he received a letter from a student asking about the way he was quoted (out of context) in BYU's student newspaper, the *Daily Universe.* He replied to the author, "Thanks for writing. I have in mind perhaps dropping a gentle note to the newspaper to calm other students who may be misled by what they think they are reading. On the other hand, I suppose there is little value in that. In years of being quoted in public print, I have become somewhat reconciled to a different expression being presented than the one I thought I made."[24]

It wasn't just journalists who got Duff's words wrong. Church members occasionally misquoted him to another member, who then misquoted that quote further to another, and so on. In his files are a handful of letters he wrote saying, "No, I didn't say that. Here is what I said, and what I believe."

A couple of times over the years, investigative reporters would write a 'hit piece' on the church or its leaders and try to implicate Duff in some proposed wrongdoing. His attorney would write a letter to the publication, rebutting any inaccuracies and false accusations, and then urge Duff to sue for libel. But Duff preferred to turn the other cheek and just let the issues die.

After seeing and experiencing the problems that prominent people could face just by nature of being in the public eye, Duff eventually decided to never let anyone use his name for business purposes. But Duff's name was still occasionally used without his permission to try and improve someone's chances of selling a product. He wasn't usually aware of these attempts, but others were. For example, long after his death, Rich took an anonymous golf-cart sales tour of Wasatch Lawn Cemetery, where Duff and Maxine are buried. Despite the cemetery's assurances to him, years earlier, that they would not use Duff's name in any way to sell their product, the salesperson quoted a list of church leaders buried there, including Marion D. Hanks.

SCRIMPING ON THE LIVING ALLOWANCE

Contrary to some modern-day speculation that general authorities get rich through their service, nothing was further from the truth for Duff and Maxine. The general authority living allowance of just thirty-six hundred dollars a year meant that they struggled financially as they raised their young family of five

---

24. MDH-L, May 20, 1971.

children. They shopped at discount stores, rarely ate out, and occasionally drove to California for vacations. Duff was supposed to have one day off a week—Mondays—but for ten years he instead used that day to work as the editor of the "Era of Youth" section of the church's magazine, the *Improvement Era*, just to make ends meet.

Though this was a trying financial circumstance for Duff and his family, he wrote about it only once in his journal. In 1977 he was asked to referee a dispute between a church member and two general authorities in a complex business arrangement that had no clear-cut or legal solution. Duff wrote, "All of this illustrates another point all over again—that it is better for the brethren [general authorities] not to get entangled in businesses." But he also acknowledged that "unfortunately, there is almost a vital necessity to do so until one is old enough to get by on his own, given the small living allowance we are provided." For those general authorities still raising children to adulthood, "it is most difficult to manage on the available resources, without augmenting them. This, almost every [general authority] does, and since I have never known a more honest and good group of men, it is obvious that it would be better for general authorities to have their needs taken care of to the point where they could avoid outside business if possible."[25]

Older general authorities didn't seem to understand the financial pressures of those who were called to the ministry while they were still young and raising families. Most general authorities were called to full-time church service later in life, after having years to develop successful careers, savings, and sources of income. When he was called to the ministry, Duff was only thirty-one, recently out of law school, and supporting a young and growing family while teaching seminary and running Temple Square on a modest income. The difficult financial situation was not discussed, and the older leaders were not sympathetic to the economic plight of the younger ones. Finally, after Duff and Maxine spent twenty-five years scraping to get by, the church finally decided to raise the general authorities' living allowance to a decent amount, though it was still on the low end of the cost-of-living scale. Although Duff could have been making four or five times as much in the corporate world, this small adjustment put him in a position where he could finally sleep a little better at night, not worrying about how he would provide for his family.

COUNTLESS SWEET EXPERIENCES

Throughout his life, Duff conducted and spoke at thousands of enjoyable meetings. In hundreds of journal entries and letters, he expressed gratitude for wonderful experiences he had with the everyday members of the church he met all over the earth. He spoke often of their sacrifice, their commitment, and their loyalty to Heavenly Father and His son, Jesus Christ.

In one example, he wrote of "one of the dear times" of his life, going from church meetings in southeastern Idaho to the local bishop's modest home, heated

25. MDH-JE, Feb. 3, 1977.

only by a wood stove. "That night in a little lean-to on a wooden board, set up as a table, I met true civility and gentility." Duff's traveling companion was an employee of one of the church departments, professional and much experienced. "He spoke quite consistently from minute one," all through the night. Instead of showing irritation, Duff listened and spoke very little, "feeling no resentment at all."

"The dinner was good, the conversation enlightening, with almost no one else saying a word except the man of the hour." When the evening drew to a close, Duff expressed his appreciation to the bishop and his wife for the lovely experience of being in their home. "As we were leaving, the woman of the house hung behind, and so did I," Duff said. "Before I could speak, she took my hand in both of hers and tearfully said, 'Elder Hanks, thank you for teaching us what a true gentleman is.' I felt like crying.... I found gentility in a little country home, dressed in plain wear, aproned, and ordinary—except in the most important ways there are."[26]

On one trip, Duff and Maxine were visiting church members in the Pacific Islands. One afternoon, they had a remarkable experience in the village Sauniatu in Samoa. The village was deserted except for a few young children and one or two adults who had stayed home with them. The rest were working in the fields or at other tasks. Duff wrote, "As we walked between the rows of fales [houses], ... toward the new chapel and school, we heard singing—perhaps a half dozen children, none more than four years old, and they were singing with the sweetness of childhood a song we instantly recognized, "I Am a Child of God." We stood entranced, in tears. At the end of a long, tortuous road, on an island of the sea, we found tiny children, none of them having seen more of the world than their small village, singing what they had learned through the traditions of their fathers, the greatest truth in existence, save one: I Am a Child of God. That other truth? That there is a God who hears the voices of His children."[27]

After meetings at a stake conference in the Pacific Northwest in October 1985, he wrote, "They treat me so well I can't stand it. There are many of my former students and missionaries and others scattered across the countryside, plus a liberal number of Vietnam veterans or their families, plus the people who have been listening over the years, and who have found it not impossible to hear me again. One sweet lady said she would travel across the earth if she knew I was going to speak. She didn't say which direction."[28]

DUFF AND LINCOLN HANKS' MISSION TOUR

In November 1958, Duff was assigned to conduct a mission tour of the Gulf States Mission in Houston, Texas. He had previously taken part in many mission tours, and would conduct perhaps hundreds more in the following thirty-plus years. But this one was different, because the mission president was the former

26. MDH-JE, Apr. 1980, written about an experience in approx. 1960.
27. MDH-T, "The Tradition of Their Fathers," GC, Oct. 1968.
28. MDH-JE, Oct. 26, 1985.

president of the Salt Lake Stake, a formidable presence in his community and profession, and a well-respected leader. He also happened to be Duff's older brother by seventeen years, Lincoln Hanks.

After the tour, Lincoln wrote to their mother, Maude: "I have just had three glorious days, meeting Duff and being with him. He is one of the smartest and wisest and brainiest members of our church authorities that I have ever met. I am prejudiced as his brother, nevertheless, I have never seen anyone more able or capable of meeting any situation intelligently and fully and have the good will and joy of the audience and congregation like he has."

Duff likewise wrote a similar letter to their mother, extolling the greatness of his big brother.

WEARING DOWN

After a quarter of a century of church service, Duff's grueling schedule finally started to catch up with him. "More than ever, I am involved in other people's problems," he wrote, "more counseling, more listening, more praying with, more blessing, more preaching, more funerals, more love." Duff relished helping others, but missed his time in classrooms with smaller groups, where they could unfold the scriptures together. He also lamented not being able to spend as much time preaching to youth and other special groups, simply because "I don't have the strength any more to do what I have done for so long done." He wrote, "It isn't propitious to be away so much either, with Maxine alone. But I still have personal occasions to speak or teach, with multitudes more asking if I'll come, which I haven't been able to handle. My heart is with the need, but the resources are lacking to do all my heart would do."[29]

In the front of one of his notebooks, Duff wrote a noted quotation from the famous author Anne Morrow Lindberg: "My life cannot implement in action the demands of all the people to whom my heart responds." Below the quotation he added, "And M. D. Hanks!"

29. MDH-JE, Jan. 1, 1976.

18

Let Your Voice Be Heard

The only thing necessary for the triumph of evil is for good men to do [or say] nothing.[1]

Duff followed his conscience in speaking his mind. While he worked in a diplomatic role, he did not always choose to be diplomatic. A special blessing he received from President David O. McKay, and to an extent, his patriarchal blessing, both effectively told him, "Let your voice be heard, even in opposition to the status quo or accepted norms."[2] He did so, sometimes to his personal detriment.

While he was both a leader and a follower, he was never a blind follower and was willing to speak up and disagree with principles and positions he felt were not correct. On multiple occasions he expended his personal capital on an issue and was fearless of the consequences when the right course was before him.

A few mistakenly assumed he was doing this to raise himself up in the eyes of others or to take a maverick-type approach to initiating needed changes. Those assumptions were incorrect. He was less concerned with *who* was right than he was with *what* was right. His approach was always informed and catalyzed by those who would be affected by the issue at hand. He took many a courageous stand to ensure fair judgment of a person or problem. When he was granted emeritus status at age seventy, letters affirming this came pouring in:

J. Paul Jensen said, "You stand as one who has followed your conscience, always seeking the confirmation of the Lord to do what's best. You were fearless of the consequences when the right course was before you."

Robert A. Rees said, "You have been one of the few general authorities of my acquaintance who has been willing to be vulnerable, to be courageous, and to put a human face on what is often perceived as the removed, reserved, and even distant authority of the church."

And Elder Vaughn J. Featherstone added, "You have been one of the few brethren who has had the courage to speak up in meetings when you disagreed with something."

1. Attributed to Edmund Burke.

2. MDH-A, "How to Listen," *Improvement Era*, Mar. 1969, 16–17, and MDH-L, to his family, "A Life-Sketch," Nov. 7, 1980; see also Duff's patriarchal blessing in appendix B.

His courage didn't apply only to church issues. Once when Duff and Rich were at a professional hockey game, the guy behind them kept spilling beer down Rich's fourteen-year-old back. Duff turned around and politely invited him to discontinue. At the invitation of the inebriated man, he and Dad and Rich went outside. Rich could visualize the potential newspaper headlines, "Mormon General Authority thrashes drunken hockey fan." Fortunately, their interchange ended peaceably.

In 1977, he wrote to the editor of *Sports Illustrated*: "Dear Sir: I just read your publisher's letter about Bernie Fuchs and his tour of ten bars before he staggered to his car to drive away that night. I'll bet this humorous article encouraged a real belly-laugh in the families and friends of the 55,000 people who died on American highways last year from drunken drivers. You owe an apology to the multitude of American kids who take a cue from you, and to those maimed victims of behavior like that which you so charmingly salute. With no respect, Marion D. Hanks."[3]

SPEAKING UP AND SPEAKING OUT

It is impossible to know which of Duff's less-than-tactful responses were premeditated and which were simply his off-the-cuff responses to positions or approaches he disagreed with or to discourtesy shown by others. Nevertheless, his writings make it clear that Duff was aware of his diplomatic limitations and occasionally revealed his dissatisfaction with what he saw as his weakness.

At a stake conference early in his ministry, his traveling partner—a volunteer member of the church's Welfare Committee—expressed a viewpoint about the nature of prophets and revelation that differed from his. "I felt I did a fair job of shifting his viewpoint a little without being obvious about it," Duff commented in his journal, "which is better than my precipitate nature usually allows me to do in this kind of discussion."[4]

Sometimes Duff felt overwhelmed by a tendency of church leaders to focus on the negative aspects and the evils of the world and less on the uplifting and positive aspects of the gospel. In May 1973, at the weekly meeting of all general authorities, Elder Robert L. Simpson made a presentation on sexual morality. "Bob did a good job," Duff wrote, but "then others talked it into the ground. Each week it is the same. We are on a reign of terror against all kinds of evil (and the Lord knows we need to oppose it in every way), but there is seldom a word of strength and encouragement. All muck, all negativisms; we are instructed to carry it to the stake presidents and bishops.

"I was then asked to pray, and I did, as follows, 'Lord, bless us with the wisdom and strength to oppose evil, but not to be *preoccupied* with it. Help us to be

3. MDH-L, Oct. 6, 1977.
4. MDH-JE, Jan. 9, 1954.

instruments of thy Spirit, that thy children may have the Spirit of Christ poured in to flood out evil.'"[5]

The next week, Elder Ted Tuttle mentioned Duff's prayer, saying, "Duff, you are the only man in the whole church with the 'brains and courage' to have offered that prayer. Boyd Packer said the same thing as we rode together on an airplane to California." Duff wrote of Tuttle's comment, "The brains could be questioned, but perhaps not the courage."

In addition to his willingness to express his differing opinions, he also refused to back down from, and strongly resisted, the proud and the bully. His children were quick to note his love of the underdog and willingness to fight for those in inferior positions. They unanimously described him as being unafraid of any other human being.

While Duff was never afraid to raise his voice in expressing what he believed to be right, he also believed it should be done out of kindness and concern. "I am accustomed to speaking plainly and perhaps too freely, but never I trust with malice or venom," he wrote to his children. "I have no criticism of any man's or any person's frailties or fallibilities; only malice seems worthy of condemnation to me. I believe in reason and candor and integrity, but also in kindness and concern and love."[6]

Speaking at a temple meeting of general authorities in 1967, for example, Duff expressed great appreciation for fellow quorum member Antoine Ivins and his "marvelous qualities." Writing about the event in his journal, Duff alluded to some kind of mistreatment of the eighty-six-year-old Ivins. "I think everyone understood that I was expressing my own somewhat righteous indignation at the treatment of individuals who seem to have any ideas of their own." Duff described Elder Ivins' courteousness, his lack of personal aggrandizement, and great strength. "It was wonderful to pay him a bit of tribute and get some things said that needed to be said at the same time. Everybody seemed to get the message. Not everyone seemed to like it, but they seemed to get it." Antoine Ivins died seventeen days after Duff recorded this entry in his journal.[7]

FROM WHENCE THIS COURAGE?

Duff started letting his voice be heard at an early age.

In elementary school he was a pitcher for the Washington School baseball team. In those days, the teenage umpire stood behind the pitcher and was making what Duff thought were unfair calls. In total frustration, he said to the umpire, "You're a dirty cheater." The umpire picked him up by the collar and said, "You ready to fight?" Duff responded, "No, I ain't ready." So, he set him back down.[8]

5. MDH-JE, May 23, 1973.

6. MDH-L to family, June 26, 1981.

7. MDH-JE, Oct. 1, 1967.

8. MDH, oral history interview with Benjamin C. Sandel, Charles Redd Center for Western Studies, BYU, LDS Church Sports Oral History Project, Apr. 6, 2004.

On his mission, Duff wrote his mission president castigating him for something he said.[9] Afterward, Duff felt that while the content was correct, the way he presented it was not. He wrote home to his mother, "While sending the letter was definitely a mistake, it had its effect. What [I wrote] in the letter was too strong and petulant to a degree, but it was the truth, and I would still bank my mission existence on its pertinency. President Muir thought it was more impertinent than pertinent." Duff added this verse:

Low lies the record of Marion D.,
Who sank defending his "pertinency."
Now, he may have been right as he spoke his song,
But the mud's flown as thick as if he'd been wrong.

He concluded his letter, "The situation can pretty well be resolved in the old thought that unless an act is going to do someone some good, it had better not be done."[10]

In a letter he wrote as a college student to the editor of the University of Utah newspaper, Duff blasted the newspaper's decision to include tobacco ads. "We can have no quarrel with the millions of otherwise free American men and women who allow themselves to be enslaved by this powerful noxious weed," he wrote, "but we who are not addicted might plead for the continued opportunity of reading a few publications which do not seek to glorify a condition which is execrable to us."[11]

Where did Duff acquire the taste, bravado, and courage, for taking such stances? Perhaps he was born with it in his DNA. Perhaps it came from the bold stance he had to take with neighborhood bullies growing up, or from having the name 'Marion' on the playground. Whatever the case, courage lived powerfully within him.

When Duff was called as an assistant to the Twelve in 1968, he had to leave his formal association with his fellow members of the First Council of the Seventy, which saddened him. At that time, his colleague Elder S. Dilworth Young kindly remarked that Duff had been instrumental in "lifting the level of the seventy a bit." Duff's journal entry about the conversation reveals his inner feeling about himself.

"He is more impressed than he ought to be with what he thinks is my capacity to think clearly," Duff wrote of Elder Young's remarks, "but his chief emphasis of respect for me was based on what he perceives to be honesty and courage in speaking up and speaking out and in defending what I believe to be right. Since these happen to be the qualities I most covet in the world, I of course am touched."[12]

9. See details of this experience on page 55.

10. MDH-JE, Northern States Mission Journal, Nov. 9, 1943.

11. MDH-A, "Tobacco Ads Not Needed In Chrony, Student Asserts," *Utah Chronicle,* Dec. 12, 1940, 4.

12. MDH-JE, Mar. 28, 1968.

Daughter Mary said it best in a birthday letter to him: "As it becomes increasingly unpopular to stand up for what is right—I am so grateful for your character and integrity and willingness to love all men and to do what is kind and what is right."

As previously mentioned, two significant priesthood blessings informed his interest in that role and willingness to take it on. The first was his patriarchal blessing.

DUFF'S PATRIARCHAL BLESSING

In 1941, at nineteen years old, Duff went to receive his patriarchal blessing from Albert R. Lyman—a distant relative. It was not a positive experience for him. Much later, he reflected, "The experience had been an ordeal. Albert R. Lyman was a magnificent man and a true saint, but was in his advanced years. His wife typed out his patriarchal blessings as he spoke, but she was hard of hearing, and would repeatedly say, 'WHAT?' He would then patiently repeat. By the time I got out of there, I felt like saying, 'Just let me down, please. Let me out.'

"Mother said to me half a dozen times, 'Would you go pick up your patriarchal blessing?' and I said, 'Ah, I forgot. I will.' I finally went back and got it, and it turned out to be a blueprint of my life from that moment on."[13]

Of particular interest in Duff's blessing were these words, which he would live up to: "If you find that the thing to which the Spirit leads you is different to the way it has been done hitherto, and the way men think it should still be done, remember also that you are different, you have your own individuality, and your mission is that which has not been done in the same way before."

His blessing was also prescient in its description of how Duff would be received. It said, "You shall speak by the gift and power of the Holy Ghost, the righteous and pure in heart shall rejoice because of your words, even though the wicked may be angered and revile against you."[14]

A SPECIAL BLESSING FROM THE PROPHET

After Duff returned from being a mission president in England in 1964, President David O. McKay invited him to his office, where he gave him a special, personal blessing that included the same message as his patriarchal blessing:

> *"Let your voice be heard. Speak prayerfully, honestly, courageously. But let your voice be heard."*[15]

President McKay's blessing "was a massive spiritual moment in my life," Duff said. "Its contents have never been revealed and there seems little occasion now to suppose they ever will be. In part, it was a comfort blessing, unusual indeed. It had its effect. The rest of the blessing was based on premises I understood and

13. MDH-R, Nov. 8, 2000. See the full text of Duff's patriarchal blessing in appendix B.
14. MDH, patriarchal blessing, July 31, 1941.
15. MDH-A, "How to Listen," *Improvement Era*, Mar. 1969, 16–17.

have deliberately thwarted. Time seems to have made that course unwise, but only God knows. I am content to leave it that way."[16]

Duff let his voice be heard not only on doctrines, principles, policies, and programs, but also about individuals. Eugene England wrote, "Duff has been a teacher and friend with unusual courage: Probably more than any other general church leader, he has, in the name of Christian values, consistently espoused causes and defended people not generally popular in our culture. There are those who believe he has sacrificed opportunities for influence and advancement in the church that his obvious talents might bring, in order to defend unpopular causes and people."[17]

EXAMPLES OF "LETTING HIS VOICE BE HEARD"

A list of church doctrines, programs, policies, and people he grappled with and for would fill pages and pages. Some of the more interesting ones included mercy versus justice, progression between kingdoms after this life, the creation of singles wards, interracial marriage, Scouting, Blacks and the priesthood, church courts and discipline, required time minimums for repentance, institutional transparency, missionary Christian service, Bruce R. McConkie's *Mormon Doctrine* book and "The Seven Deadly Heresies" talk, the continuing status of professors at Brigham Young University, LDS fraternities and sororities and the Latter-day Saint Student Association, sending missionaries home early, civil marriages before temple marriages and nonmember parents at temple marriages, prying temple recommend questions, grooming requirements and other ultimatums for priesthood ordinations, and even more mundane things like the need for elevators for the press box of the BYU football stadium. Below are a few specific examples.

In October 1973, the executive committee of the church Board of Education and BYU's Board of Trustees met briefly to consider a request by BYU President Dallin H. Oaks for an individual to be hired as a professor. Several of the senior apostles spoke at length. Other members of the executive committee in attendance, including Duff and CES associate commissioner Joe J. Christensen—who was more knowledgeable about the candidate than anyone else in the room—were not asked their opinion before a vote was called for. When it was over, Duff said to Christensen, loudly enough for all to hear, "Joe, what is your feeling on this important matter? I did not hear you speak." Duff wrote of the incident, "I do not resent their presumptuousness, only their lack of consideration and their discourtesy."[18]

Duff found himself in the position of wanting to be deferential and respectful to those he worked with, but he also didn't equate "sustaining" with "conformity." He never felt constrained from "attempting to improve things or from being

16. MDH-L to his family, "A Life-Sketch," Nov. 7, 1980.

17. Eugene England, "The Quality of Mercy," in *Teachers Who Touch Lives*, compiled by Philip L. Barlow, (Bountiful, UT: Horizon Publishers, 1988), 54.

18. MDH-JE, Oct. 1973.

willing to try to accomplish some redress of grievances and some redirection of leadership."[19] And he refused to be intimidated or silenced by colleagues who ran roughshod over those who disagreed with their position. Over his lengthy years of service, Duff had numerous occasions to stand up, most often solo, against a few senior colleagues he described as "arrogant and obdurate," while others of his peers sat silent.[20]

After some particularly difficult meetings with the MIA executive committee on March 6, 1975, Duff was talking with Elder Gordon B. Hinckley, who notified him that one of the other apostles had told him that, "in Duff Hanks and Boyd Packer, he was working with two men who were diametrically opposite and opposed." Duff commented in his journal, "The description was, of course, valid, and it is equally valid of the man who made it, and of Brother Hinckley himself. Of both these things, I spoke, plus many others about which I would have been better to just shut up. At any rate it was said."[21]

On another occasion, Duff was in an April 11, 1975 meeting in which minutes were presented for adoption that did not accurately reflect the previous meeting. No one was willing to openly challenge them besides Duff, who commented that the minutes seemed like "Russian history." A fellow committee member, Thomas Fyans, asked if Duff meant that they shouldn't be adopted. Duff recalled, "I calmly responded that I didn't really mean that, unless they would like *true history* instead of fairy tales." Asked to explain, Duff then "spent a long time going back to several issues we had discussed that were absent from the minutes—the single sisters' meetings on Sunday morning (which were completely disowned by the so-called minutes), the athletic program including married men (which was completely disowned by the so-called minutes), and the discussion on family recreation (which the minutes said we had never been given any authority to deal with). When I was through, it was decided to try to adopt a statement that actually did reflect reality." After the meeting, James Faust came to Duff's office and quoted David O. McKay, saying, "Let your voice be heard!"[22]

In March 1977, Duff visited with Elder Mark E. Petersen concerning a couple and their excommunication. Petersen agreed with Duff that this was a "very bad judgment which should be reversed," Duff said. "I mentioned the stern and unyielding pressure [apostle] Harold B. Lee had put on people with problems, and the recent addition of a temple recommend question about any problem ever before experienced, which has caused great concern for many. The total effect of this conversation was to affirm Mark's strong feelings that 'things have gone far too far.'"[23]

19. MDH-L to George Turner, Mar. 22, 1988.
20. MDH-L to family, Aug. 9, 1980.
21. MDH-JE, Mar. 6, 1975.
22. MDH-JE, Apr. 1975.
23. MDH-JE, Mar. 5, 1977.

In another particularly difficult experience later that year, a senior apostle told Duff to release a man from his church assignment over a convoluted business deal gone bad. Despite pressure from above, Duff refused to release—and thereby shame—the other man until all the facts had been examined. In the end, the man in question was proven innocent, but Duff's standing with those above him had been damaged. He commented in his journal, "One may hurt oneself in the minds of resentful people, but that is nothing compared to getting the right thing done, and in this case, I have every confidence that the right thing was done."[24]

CALMING THE STORM

Letting his voice be heard was not always in response to conflict or differing opinions. In fact, it was more often about courage and courtesy. For example, he could not countenance rudeness in any fashion. If he were the guest speaker to an audience behaving poorly, it wasn't usually difficult for him to gain control because his presence was very forceful. But if he saw another speaker struggling to communicate over another's discourtesy, he could rarely contain himself.

One of his more public expressions of this disapproval of rudeness occurred in Vermont in 1962. He had flown across the country to speak to a group of teenagers brought together from the entire state. Duff watched as the young people responded "with contempt and discourtesy" to each speaker who preceded him, including local mayors and the governor. No one did anything to address it. The person who then introduced Duff was apologetic and embarrassed.

When Duff stood to speak, he said, "I'm sorry that most of you didn't hear the great talk that your governor just delivered.... You would have profited from hearing it, but you weren't listening. Let me repeat the theme of what your governor said. He talked about 'Vermont's Chief Asset, Her Teenagers.' ... If your behavior tonight is typical, if you've been acting as you really are, and if you are Vermont's chief asset, the Lord help Vermont." Duff then spoke for forty-five minutes to an attentive audience on the theme "moral courage," showing an increase of love towards them.[25]

Another experience involved a large LDS Boy Scout priesthood encampment in Letchworth State Park, New York, in July 1970. After a week full of activities, two thousand Scouts were gathered in the darkness on a shallow hillside, fronted by a large stage. Among the participants on stage were a group of teenage girls. Many of the boys began catcalling, yelling, and being rowdy. After the entertainment, the presiding bishop of the church, a mild and gentle man, John H. Vandenberg stood to speak, but the crowd of boys would not quiet down. Several hundred church leaders in attendance were appalled.

One eyewitness remembered, "We suffered with Bishop Vandenberg, and the indignity of his plight. How will this dreadful situation ever be brought under

24. MDH-JE, Dec. 2, 1977.

25. MDH-T, "Substance or Shadow," GC, Oct. 1962.

control? Bishop Vandenberg was also despairing, it was clear. Suddenly, from the wings, Duff stepped forward to stand by Bishop Vandenberg's side. He took the microphone and spoke in a low, calm voice using reason and love, and little by little calm was restored. Adult leaders and many more mature scouts in the crowd also helped quell the noise, but it all began with Elder Hanks' inspired example of priesthood leadership. Then he returned the microphone to Bishop Vandenberg. I found this to be, in so many ways, one of the remarkable experiences of my life."[26]

WHY NOT AN APOSTLE?

Elder Hanks, it has done me good to observe someone who did not seem concerned about position as much as about doing his part well. I pray that I may do the same.[27]

Called as a general authority at thirty-one, for nearly forty years Duff served in the seventy, then as an assistant to the Twelve Apostles, and then in the seventy again. Surely, despite any level of humility, the natural response would be to wonder, each time a position in the Quorum of the Twelve opened up, if he would be called to fill it.

What made this situation even more challenging was that numerous Latter-day Saints would write or call Duff, or even stop him on the street, to proclaim with confidence, "You'll be called as an apostle this time for sure!"

As one newspaper writer put it, "Elder Hanks was our idol. We were all sure that he was moving irresistibly toward an apostleship and eventually presidency of the church. Disappointment came with the calling and sustaining of others as apostles; all us Hanks partisans felt it was his turn."[28]

Letting your voice be heard does not always contribute to ingratiating oneself to those around you. Duff was keenly aware of that and sometimes wondered aloud how much his sometimes less-than-diplomatic attitude caused others to dislike him. Those who believe in the restored gospel tend to believe that God is in charge overall but that He also leaves room for man's involvement in earth-bound decision-making. Whether chosen by God to remain where he was or destined to be there due to actions of his own making, Duff simply put his head down and continued to serve.

In November 1971, following the unexpected death of apostle Richard L. Evans, he wrote the following: "So, Richard is gone, and some other will take his place. Many have been unwise enough to point at me again, but I am so far from any interest in this, or concern for its likelihood, that I hear them with total lack of response."[29]

26. John Arthur Taylor to MDH, Apr. 11, 1999.
27. J. Devn Cornish to MDH, Oct. 21, 1994.
28. Marden Clark, "Marion Hanks Endeared by Life of Serving Others," *Provo Daily Herald*, Aug. 3, 2002.
29. MDH-JE, Nov. 1971.

In a 1989 letter, Duff wrote:

> It is of interest to me that others wonder why changes have not occurred to put me in other assignments. The Lord is the ultimate controller, but I have observed that he leaves to our own dispositions and decisions much that affects the kingdom, and that he has intervened on occasions when it was necessary. I have no satisfactory answer to your question, except to say that perhaps two or three of the sweetest experiences of our lifetime were to be a mission president living in England, an [area president] living in Asia—responsible for initiating the church into the refugee services—and the Salt Lake Temple president. None of these could have occurred [if he had been made an apostle], and I would not have missed those experiences.[30]

Shortly after David O. McKay died, Duff wrote a glowing tribute to him in his journal:

> He called me to both the First Council of the Seventy and as an Assistant and gave me a magnificent blessing on my return from England, without my inviting it, but knew I needed it. I'll never forget those great hands on my head. I'll say no more about that now, and never will in writing, because it was personal and laid out some possibilities for me which I will not see fulfilled in this life, because of some deliberate choices I have made to follow courses that I have believed right.[31] Whether they are, I cannot know, but I do know that my own strength produces some weaknesses, as with all men, and that one of my weaknesses is to not fully know when I should keep silent in matters where my heart tells me something must be said in defense of a man or a principle. I feel no nobility in this, and no special pride, and in fact some sorrow, but I cannot be other than I am or do other than I have done. The future will perhaps bring this to a head, though I do not know the future, and the Lord does. We shall serve while we are permitted the privilege.[32]

Duff continued to serve in the position he had been called to, rallying around others he thought would do a great job in various positions. In 1973, for example, he journaled about a Church Board of Education meeting he attended: "Good meeting. [Church President] Harold B. Lee took a major part, others mostly responsive to excellent presentations of [Associate Commissioner of Church Education] Joe Christensen and [BYU President] Dallin Oaks. [Commissioner of Church Education] Neal Maxwell mostly engineers, seldom talks, does well when he does. I would feel good to see all three of those young men take over the leading spots in the general authorities as soon as possible. I think Neal will, and

30. MDH-L, 1989.

31. Others have speculated that President McKay ordained Duff an apostle in this blessing, but no formal documentation exists to corroborate.

32. MDH-JE, Jan. 22, 1970.

I hope so." Duff was spot on. Maxwell was called as an assistant to the Twelve one year later, Oaks to the Quorum of the Twelve in 1984, and Christensen to the First Quorum of the Seventy in 1989.[33]

When asked in person, Duff would usually respond to such questions by smiling and saying something like, "One serves in the Lord's church where and when one is called and for as long as one is called."

In later years, with a more philosophical bent and with many years of watching the unanimity expressed by the Quorum of the Twelve Apostles in its decision-making, Duff gave a different, if slightly irreverent, answer to the genuine queries of well-meaning people:

Question: Why aren't you an apostle?

Answer: "Because God knows me too well and He loves me too much."

While serving as president of the Salt Lake Temple, Duff wrote in his journal about "an interesting staff meeting at the temple, wherein certain dissatisfactions became expressed. One leader is downcast because he was not called to be my replacement counselor. I smiled and noted that I had been passed over more than the Israelites and had trained more apostles than any living man, and that I was content that it be so. He was not mollified, although he and his wife are faithful and unselfish."[34]

Speculation of Duff's becoming an apostle continued even long after he had been given emeritus status. In 2004, twelve years after Duff's release, Lavina Fielding Anderson wrote a blogpost in which she speculated on who might fill a vacancy in the Quorum of the Twelve. After handicapping various potential replacements, she wrote, "What if Marion D. Hanks, with his legendary compassion and progressiveness, were called out of retirement?"[35]

One of Duff's sons-in-law, attorney John K. Baird, wrote him the sweetest, insightful note:

> Dear Duff, here is a book that you will like looking through, possibly reading. In this book, is Benjamin Cardozo's response to a journalist who asked him which of his peers on the Supreme Court he considered the greatest American jurist. Thinking of Judge Learned Hand, Cardozo said, "The greatest American jurist is not sitting on the Supreme Court."
>
> Politics prevented what Hand deserved (and what everyone *knew* he deserved). It pained him, but he had a "revitalizing belief in the majesty of doing one's daily work well, regardless of what it may be." That is something you would say. I admire you greatly. With affection, John.[36]

33. MDH-JE, Feb. 1973.
34. MDH-R, Aug. 1, 1984.
35. Lavina Fielding Anderson, *Mormon Alliance Newsletter* 10, no. 3 (Sept. 2004).
36. John K. Baird letter to MDH, July 21, 1994, quoting Gerald Gunther, *Learned Hand: The Man and the Judge* (New York: Knopf, 1994), ix.

As time wore on, Duff vacillated between being glad he had been vocal and wondering how things might have been different if he had been less so. "I continue to stand on a platform of mercy, hoping to receive it and trying to give it," he wrote a friend in 1988. "I have not learned to control my mind or my tongue, but I wish to, when the desired outcome will be better accomplished in that manner. Shakespeare said, 'Tell the truth and shame the Devil.' I believe that, but I don't always tell all I know at any given moment to any given person."[37]

"I have had a fine opportunity to make a difference in some small ways," he wrote in his journal. "If I were less stubborn and rebellious and sinful, I might have made some bigger differences. But that is past."[38]

37. MDH-L to George Turner, Mar. 22, 1988.
38. MDH-JE, Mar. 28, 1985.

19

Speaking

When Cicero spoke, the people applauded and said, "How eloquent."
When Demosthenes spoke, the people stood and said, "Come, let us march."
When Marion D. Hanks spoke, the people wept and said, "Yea, Lord, I believe."
—Jeffrey R. Holland[1]

Next to teaching, public speaking is probably the activity that occupied the most hours of his ministry, with counseling a close third.

Duff was simply one of the best communicators around. When he spoke, you felt like he was speaking directly to you. His manner was relaxed and conversational. The moviemakers in the church loved to use him because he came across so naturally. Though Duff hated using teleprompters, the chief audiovisual tech for the church said he was the best and most natural at using it in general conference and other settings.[2]

He was often commended not only for the content he presented but for the way he made audience members feel when he spoke to them. A few sample commendations:

"One of the most articulate and eloquent speakers ever encountered, he uses language powerfully, always to lift people," said Sherman Clayton, one of Duff's British missionaries. "More importantly he was genuinely caring of all he encountered—beyond the words, there was content and character."[3]

"Elder Hanks, thank you so much for participating in Women's Conference," Carol Lee Hawkins, director of the annual BYU conference, wrote to him in 1991. "You lifted our sights from the mundane to the sublime. I found your talk very comforting and reassuring, and we have received so many expressions of joy and uplift from attendees."[4]

"Elder Hanks has a special way and demeanor that makes you feel like he is speaking to you and that he is your best friend. There is no way of telling how

1. Jeffrey R. Holland, Introduction of Elder Marion D. Hanks, Ricks College Baccalaureate Service, Apr. 24, 1979.

2. Richard D. Hanks, reminiscence of conversation at Duff's funeral reception, Aug. 13, 2011.

3. V. Clayton Sherman, *Pantheon of Giants*, section of ManagementHouse.com.

4. Carol Lee Hawkins to MDH, Apr. 23, 1991.

many young people Marion D. Hanks touched and inspired to live a better life. A whole generation was affected in the church."[5]

"When we were in Boy Scouts of America together, you were listed as 'One of the ten best speakers in America.' I still subscribe to that," popular youth speaker Elder Vaughan J. Featherstone told him.[6]

In his general conference address in April 1971, Elder LeGrand Richards quoted a story Duff had taught the regional representatives earlier in the week and then described Duff as a "wonderful storyteller." Later at a meeting with the general authorities and their wives, Elder Richards loudly announced that Duff was "the premier storyteller in the church." Since Elder Richards was one of the most famous speakers the church had ever produced, Duff replied, "Now, LeGrand, that would be like Shakespeare congratulating Joe Doakes[7] for his poetry."[8]

TO WHOM DID HE SPEAK?

Duff gave speeches in every state in the United States and in a multitude of foreign countries. Most were at stake conferences, but for years he gave scores of civic speeches, for which he never accepted any money. Speaking at Scouting and Rotary meetings took him all over the country and outside it, where he spoke at major forums and podiums and in training seminars. He spoke at multiple Scout Jamborees. His youth, fitness, and civic speeches number in the thousands. When Rich calculated the amount of money he was forgoing by giving all of these keynote speeches for free, he questioned Duff about it. Duff answered that he "didn't feel right commercializing whatever modest gifts the Lord had given him."

In addition to his ongoing stake conference meetings each weekend and general conference every six months, he also spoke at university commencements, devotionals, baccalaureates, funerals, graduations, trainings, military gatherings and building dedications. A short list of examples illustrates the breadth and diversity of his speaking assignments. In one short period, he spoke to the F-16 Air Combat Fighter Group, the Idaho probate judges' convention, the national PTA convention, as well as state PTA conventions in Nebraska and California. He spoke at the Orlando Tangerine Bowl football game, the mayor's prayer breakfast in Edmonton, Canada, the Boys Club of America convention, and the American Medical Association national convention.

After a speech at the White House Conference on Youth in March 1960, the conducting officer said at the conclusion of the meeting: "I reflected that Mr. Hanks comes from people that suffered bitter persecution for their ideals, driven to the far reaches of the country where they thought themselves away from all

5. Loren C. Dunn to MDH, ca. 1992.
6. Vaughn J. Featherstone to MDH, Feb. 25, 2000.
7. "Joe Doakes" was twentieth-century slang for "the average man."
8. MDH-JE, Apr. 14, 1971.

this. Now we have invited a leader of that people to come here to talk to us of the same ideals and principles for which we drove them away."[9]

MAJOR THEMES OF HIS SERMONS

Duff prepared individually for each speaking occasion. He never gave the exact same talk twice, but he did reuse favorite stories to support his thesis. A review of his published talks produces a list of some of his favorite themes in general conference:

- Christlike service to our fellow men
- Come unto Christ
- Mercy and love
- God loves us
- Choose God and love each other
- Individual worth
- The scriptures
- The temple

In 1954, when he was still a new general authority, he wrote, "I like to talk about people and the worth of man before God. My favorite theme is the worth of one man in relation to himself, his world, and his Father in Heaven."[10]

His talks were always intended to provide hope and encouragement. Many speakers tend to speak *at* people, delivering text that sounds good, but might not stimulate a response in hearts and minds. Duff always seemed to be speaking *with* people, about them and their needs. As one said, "Dear Brother Hanks, you have a special something that, quite frankly, no one else has, an empathy and ability to peer into the hearts of all of us and to recognize our weaknesses and needs, without offending us when you touch upon these tender areas."[11]

Duff's approach to leadership was to try and inspire others by edifying and strengthening them. He was no stranger to conflict, but he rarely came down hard on a stake presidency, preferring to quietly point out places where some changes might help them. Wrote one stake president, "Our stake members are still commenting on how uplifted and encouraged they felt from your talks. I especially appreciated your non-nagging approach to teaching."[12]

PREPARATION, OVERPREPARATION, AND AD HOC

Your ability to set things in order and command respect wherever you were assigned, or unassigned, for that matter, came from a lifetime of gospel study and devotion.
—Elder John K. Carmack

9. *Deseret News*, Mar. 29, 1960.
10. MDH-JE, Mar. 12, 1954.
11. Richard J. Marshall to MDH, Apr. 9, 1968.
12. Glen Hunsaker to MDH, Jan. 22, 1987.

Duff tended to prepare, then prepare again, and then over prepare. He had extensive recall of quotations and scriptures and stories that he could summon at will for whatever talk he was preparing. If he didn't remember something off-hand, it was sure to be in the voluminous library that he had been saving in filing cabinets for years. Anytime he heard or read something he liked, he'd write it down or have Phyllis, his secretary, type it up and catalog it.

He quite often could be found editing or crossing out ideas on his yellow pad or adding new thoughts right up until the moment he was to speak. And then sometimes, to use football parlance, he'd stand at a pulpit, materials at the ready, and call an audible. Many times, he'd begin his speech by saying something like, "I've prepared enough material for five hours, but I think I'll just speak from the heart." This wasn't some kind of ruse; he really did have five hours of material that he had probably been working on for weeks, but he felt inspired to go another direction. Usually, his intense preparation and research paid off. He would receive a nice note expressing someone's gratitude for helping them to improve in some way. One example: "Thank you for speaking at our Nebraska P.T.A. Convention. You should have seen the evaluation sheet. Only superlatives were used about you, such as: 'best speaker in seven years,' 'first time I've ever waited in fear that the speaker would finish,' 'inspiring,' and I could continue for 220 such comments turned in."[13]

HIS MASTERFUL USE OF LANGUAGE

He became the model for an entire generation of missionaries.
They emulated his style; they assimilated his values;
they adopted his delivery, his vocabulary, even his stories."
—Honorary Doctorate of Christian Service, BYU, April 22, 1993

Duff had a masterful command of the English language. He was able to string words together that both gladdened the heart and stimulated one's thinking. His manner of preparation and speaking provided fertile ground for the Holy Ghost to touch the listener's hearts. He was also quick to give Heavenly Father the credit. After a funeral in 1977, he said, "Perhaps it would not be inappropriate to say that there are a few occasions when one gets some help from above, and what could have been less than favorable, turned out in fact to be worthwhile. When it was over, a kind woman commented on my talk, describing its 'simple eloquence, without the clichés.'"[14]

J. D. Williams, a well-known University of Utah professor, hosted the national Phi Beta Kappa delegates in Salt Lake City one year, and asked Duff to speak to them in the Tabernacle.

William's follow-up letter to Richard L. Evans was priceless. He wrote, "Duff followed Alex Schreiner's organ recital with a masterful thirty-minute

13. Joyce Purtzer to MDH, May 1, 1967.
14. MDH-JE, text of funeral talk, 1977.

presentation of the philosophy, organization, and programs of our church. He was truly at his best! How it pleased me afterward to have these rather snooty Phi Beta Kappans come up to comment on Duff's matchless use of English, the extraordinary quality of his sentence structure, and the clarity and conviction of his presentation. As I said to him on leaving the Tabernacle, I just couldn't have been prouder of my church."[15]

Even in his old age, Dad continued to improve other's vocabulary. Speaking at his funeral, Rich said, "The nameplate on the door of his room at the care facility said 'Duff Hanks,' rather than his full name. One day, I was pushing him back to his room in his wheelchair and said, 'Here is your room, Dad.' He looked at his name on the door and said, 'Yes, that's my name, by a more familiar sobriquet.' (Dad was the one with Alzheimer's, and I had to go look up *sobriquet* in the dictionary—by the way, *sobriquet* means nickname.)"

Even something as simple as a Christmas card describing the gift of a little money was unusual in its construction and graciousness: "Dear Elizabeth: It is the season to once again petition your favor in accepting responsibility to help in the distribution of our slight surplus. This is for your personal and private shopping purposes."[16]

Often, we had to pull out a thesaurus or dictionary to figure out what he was saying. For example, he occasionally used two unusual titles to describe things—The Misunderstood Exclusionary Clauses and The Nonessential Insistencies.

His knowledge of the English language and grammar had some temporary drawbacks for the children. Both Maxine and Duff were happily willing to frequently correct their poor use of words. Heaven forbid that one of their children, or their friends, said something like, "*me and her* went downtown"—which seems to be acceptable speech today for some. (By the way, if you don't know what's wrong with the previous phrase, be glad Maxine and Duff aren't around.) They so indoctrinated their children with grammar rules that, to this day, they cringe if someone says something incorrectly.

His proficiency in language wasn't always serious. If you were doing something annoying, you might be threatened with a "blow to the chops" or "do that one more time and you'll pull back a bloody stump." If you were talking too much, you might be invited to "hud yer wheesht!" (Scottish for "hold your tongue").

HOW HE GOT HIS START

It's difficult to pinpoint how and when Duff became so proficient and so sought after as a public speaker. It began prior to his mission as he spoke at friends' farewells and his high school commencement and a few other church assignments. About one occasion, he wrote, "I went once to the ward where Elder Antoine Ivins was a member to give a name and a blessing to my friend Paul

15. JD Williams to Richard L. Evans, Sept. 28, 1961.

16. MDH to Elizabeth W. Hanks, Dec. 1990.

Sybrowsky's little baby. Neither parent was active in the church. Antoine listened to the blessing, then came up to me after and asked, 'Where did you fill your mission?' And I said, 'I haven't been on a mission yet.' He was one, I know, and Richard Evans another, who had some idea I might be able to talk without flubbing it, if need be."[17]

On his mission he was able to refine his speaking ability, as he spoke over seven hundred times with the singing missionary sextette—in addition to his standard missionary responsibilities. By the time he'd been home a couple of years, Duff was in high demand all over Salt Lake Valley, speaking multiple times a month including two or three weekends. He was also leading tours all day on Temple Square and most weeknights.

TOUCHING HEARTS AND SPIRITS

Elder Hanks, do you realize what this has done to the people of the East Pocatello Stake? You have strengthened their testimony and mine.
—A young girl's letter after stake conference

Someone once said his talks were eloquent but seemed effortless. After one stake conference in the Northwest, he received this note: "Elder Hanks, your presence in our stake conference this weekend brought a flood of light with you, warm and delightful and inspiring to us. We didn't want the meetings to end."[18]

Behind his rich, resonant voice was a man trying his best personally to live the gospel, even as he presented it to the world. I think this allowed people to see in him an approachability and sincerity that made him trustworthy. Letters from some of his peers reflect that feeling:

"Your words and example have lifted and inspired many people, including myself. You have a special way of knowing *when* and *what* to say in building people; and the *how* or method which you employ in communicating with others always leaves an enduring impression."[19]

"I appreciate so much being your companion this weekend. I've seen the relationship of long-term general authorities with stake congregations before, but it's been a long time since I've seen anyone who touches the heart strings of the people the way you do."[20]

FUNERALS

At Duff's funeral, Rich asked the following rhetorical question: "What does one say when he speaks at the funeral of the man that everybody wanted to have speak at their funeral?"

This was not an exaggeration. Duff spoke at hundreds and hundreds of funerals.

17. MDH-R, Sept. 26, 2000.
18. Beverley Burke to MDH, Oct. 27, 1986.
19. Carlos Asay to MDH, Feb. 25, 1980.
20. Cree-L Kofford to MDH, Aug. 27, 1991.

The old, the young, family members, fellow church leaders, those who committed suicide, his friends, his teachers, and so on. He felt it a solemn obligation to participate whenever he was asked.

None of Duff's funeral tributes was in any way "cookie cutter." He rarely used the same scriptures, which says a lot about his preparation. He would speak of the deceased's life and family and share a personal story or two about the person. He would share his love for them and for the Savior and His eternal plan. He talked about the Lord opening the door to the Resurrection for each of us and the promise of eternal life. His general approach was to give the person a sweet sendoff and to uplift and provide hope to those who remained.

At the funeral of someone who had died by suicide, he was quick to point out his deep-seated belief that they "were all right" and that they were "in a good place." In one such circumstance, he said, "In my mind and my heart, there is no question that there are explanations for this tragedy presently beyond our comprehension, and that when we know, we will certainly have no more criticism or blame in our hearts than we have today."[21]

Duff believed with all his heart in the continuity of the soul and the promise of a wonderful life after this. His sermons on behalf of those who had passed away emphatically reflected that.

APPRECIATIVE OF HIS FELLOW SPEAKERS

Despite his proclivity at public speaking, or perhaps because of it, he was genuinely appreciative of his fellow general authorities and receptive to the things he learned from their messages. After a temple meeting, he reported, "Delbert Stapley, LeGrand Richards, Boyd Packer, Neal Maxwell, John Vandenberg, Paul Dunn, Hartman Rector, and Vaughn Featherstone all spoke, and they all did a great job, particularly the latter and LeGrand Richards who were marvelous." Similarly, he often commented positively about addresses given by his colleagues at general conferences or other gatherings.

NOT EVERY TALK ENDED UP AS EXPECTED

Duff was particularly adept at changing a talk, presenting thoughts completely different than he had prepared. And while he was usually positive about his remarks, saying things like, "it seemed to be acceptable to the audience," occasionally, he would score his presentation as more modest in its delivery. For example, he wrote, "I was given such a lavish introduction that nothing I could have said would have been adequate. I did not disappoint them, falling flatly on my broad third chin, taking too long to do it, and not having enough fun in the process. I decided once again that you can do about as well in less time and that a spoonful of sugar always makes the medicine go down better. One of these days I will remember."[22]

---

21. MDH-T, Aug. 1, 1985.
22. MDH-JE, speech to Intermountain Electrical Association Convention, Apr. 20, 1978.

REACHING THOSE ON THE FRINGES

One of the main emphases of Duff's ministry, particularly near the end, was aimed at those on the fringes—whether intellectually, emotionally, mentally, physically, financially, or testimony-wise. His goal was to reach out and lift those who needed encouragement and kindness, who were discouraged and in need.

20

Author

Reading maketh the full man.[1]
—Francis Bacon

I cannot live without books.[2]
—Thomas Jefferson

Next to Rich's computer keyboard is a framed yellow sticky note in Duff's recognizable handwriting. It says simply, "Read!"

To appreciate Duff's prodigious authorship and writings, one has to start with recognizing the incredible effort he expended reading, studying, and marking. And no subject interested him more than the scriptures. His approach wasn't a "one and done" effort, either. Sometimes he'd read the same thing multiple times. Sometimes he'd read his own published talks and articles and mark them all up, as if he were reading them for the first time.

Duff was consistent and determined to keep learning and improving his mind. It is such a temptation to try and get by on what one learned years ago in school, or on a mission, or at university. But Duff was convinced it wasn't enough to once have known. In fact, he kept sending Rich a favorite quotation, over and over:

> *"One of the greatest temptations of bright young men*
> *is to get by on what they already know."*

The author was Marion D. Hanks.

LANGUAGE

Duff had an incredible mastery of the language, and he wanted his family to love words too. So the family memorized poetry.

Duff never used his knowledge of words and language to brag or underscore his ability, but his mastery of words was well known. He also stayed away from phrases that would draw attention to himself rather than to what he was trying to say. But he knew so many words and phrases that they came naturally to him.

1. Francis Bacon, *Meditationes sacræ* (1597).
2. Thomas Jefferson to John Adams, June 10, 1815.

Here's a fun example from his journal. Most of us would probably just say, "I pulled a muscle from overuse." Duff wrote in his journal, "It is the old high school problem still coming back when circumstances combine. The circumstances are physical weariness, and the muscle condition that results when there is too much sudden expression of what has been long quiescent."

In describing an athletic feat, he wrote, "I haven't done that often, but it was an expression of some determination and reasonable capacity."[3]

His sister Jeannette wrote in a letter to Duff: "Yesterday, Brother Lyman asked me if I knew Marion Hanks, a missionary. I replied that I thought I did know him a little. 'Well,' he said, 'I want to tell you that he wrote me a letter the other day and used language that would do credit to Shakespeare! Where did he learn the English language like that?'"

Duff never used his mastery of language to be cute or trendy. In fact, he preached the opposite. Two quotations he loved and repeated often come to mind. The first is by Solomon Bennett Freehof:

> Years ago, I preferred clever people. There was a joy in beholding … a mind … bearing thoughts quickly translated into words, or ideas expressed in a new way. I find now my taste has changed. Verbal fireworks often bore me. They seem motivated by self-assertion and self-display. I now prefer another type of person; one who is considerate, understanding of others, careful not to break down another person's self-respect.… My preferred person today is one who is always aware of the needs of others, of their pain and fear and unhappiness, and their search for self-respect.… I once liked clever people. Now I like good people.[4]

The second is the graffiti written on a wall at a Catholic university:

> Jesus said unto them: "Who do you say that I am?"
>
> And they replied: "You are the eschatological manifestation of the ground of our being, the kerygma in which we find the ultimate meaning of our interpersonal relations."
>
> And Jesus said, "What?"[5]

POSITION PAPERS AND SUPPORT

Duff led and served in just about every major department of church leadership and wrote talks and position papers on numerous subjects from the history of the church's position on Blacks, to the Adam-God theory, to the one mighty and strong, from full-time Christian service by missionaries, to the reconstitution of the seventy, to a structured approach to single members of the church, to the church's renewed focus on "Come unto Christ," and on and on.

---

3. MDH interview, Charles Redd Center, LDS Church Sports Oral History Project, Apr. 6, 2004, 2.

4. Solomon Bennett Freehof, *Richard Evans' Quote Book* (Salt Lake City: Publishers Press, 1971), 166.

5. *Los Angeles Times*, Jan. 19, 1974.

Duff was frequently asked to answer difficult questions in letters received by the First Presidency. Sometimes he would be asked to prepare ideas for the prophets to use in their general conference talks. As but one example, he supplied the idea and most of the background material for President Spencer W. Kimball's masterful talk in 1979 on Joshua and Caleb, entitled "Give Me This Mountain."[6]

LETTER WRITING

Duff was a prolific letter writer—to his mother, to Maxine, to his children, and to thousands of others. In his years serving a mission and on a ship during the war, he penned letters each week to those he loved. During the early years of his traveling as a general authority, he would carry a stack of onionskin paper and envelopes so that he could quickly communicate with Maxine and his mother.

He also became a master at using the Dictaphone.[7] His family could hear him late into the night talking into it, or handwriting notes and letters, or typing on his old trusty manual typewriter. A lot of credit has to be shared with Phyllis Peterson Warnick, his beloved secretary, who had to transcribe all of those letters, talks, and articles over a forty-five-year period. Because of his sporadic journal-keeping, much of the source material for this book comes from thousands of letters written by him or to him.

To make up for his prolonged absences, Duff wrote letters to his children, and later, his grandchildren. Getting a letter from their Dad was a red-letter day. They saved and treasure them. (Rich had a companion on his mission who jokingly said it wasn't fair that Rich could count reading his Dad's letters as scripture study time—though he never did.)

Duff felt that if someone had taken the time and made the effort to write him a letter, then he had a courteous responsibility to answer it. He had a special ability to touch one's heart strings through the thoughts and language of his letters. Elder Jeffrey R. Holland wrote: "Dear President Hanks, I once said that if you only *read* the classified ads, I would cry. I must now add that if you merely *sent* me the classified ads, I would cry. I wept openly when I read your remarks to the Seventy given on June 11, 1992. What is it about your power and influence and indelible imprint upon me? Surely, [Seventies secretary] Robert Tucker is not that good at taking minutes. And yet, I wept, and then wept some more."[8]

THE ERA OF YOUTH

Duff got his first taste of editing during high school when he was elected the editor of his school newspaper, the *Red and Black.* His advisor was Jennie Thomas, who recognized his talent and strongly encouraged him to continue writing throughout his life. She even spoke at Duff's missionary farewell.

---

6. Spencer W. Kimball to MDH, Nov. 5, 1979.

7. A Dictaphone is a small electronic device used to record speech for transcription at a later time. Duff used his Dictaphone for decades to dictate letters for his assistant Phyllis to type up.

8. Jeffrey R. Holland to MDH, Aug. 21, 1992.

Duff had been writing some pieces on occasion, for the *Improvement Era*, one of the church magazines, when he was approached by the Presiding Bishopric to start a section of the magazine aimed at adolescents, to be called "The Era of Youth." The first edition was published in July 1960.

Duff was the editor, with Elaine Anderson Cannon as associate editor. Elaine, who had worked with Duff on their high school newspaper and later became the church's general president of the Young Women organization, had been writing for the *Deseret News*. The two of them made a good team.

Duff wrote, "We used to spend Mondays working on 'The Era of Youth.' That was not particularly useful to my family since that was my only day off. But we just did what had to be done, and usually that took the full day. The two of us did quite a bit of the writing, but we had other wonderful writers, like Mabel Jones Gabbott, who wrote a number of the songs in the hymnbook. She was just a ray of light and sunshine, and she loved what we were doing."[9]

After several years, Maxine and Duff were called to England and left Elaine by herself to do most of the work. There were no faxes back then, but she would send a draft to Duff by the fastest mail method, and he would review it and return it. He also continued doing a little writing for the magazine from England.

Upon Duff's return in 1964, he resumed his pattern of working almost every Monday with Elaine to keep "The Era of Youth" going. In 1970, there began to be rumors that the church wanted to change the format of its magazines and that several leaders wanted to discontinue publishing anything for the youth. Duff and Elaine felt strongly that young people should have their own magazine and went to Spencer W. Kimball, who was then president of the Quorum of the Twelve, and made a proposal to him. He agreed.

In 1971, the church decided to make a wholesale change in its magazines, consolidating them all into three new magazines, one of which was called *The New Era*, patterned after "The Era of Youth" Duff and Elaine had been editing. Duff went back to his day job, and his family got to have their dad back for at least one day a week.

BOOKS AND MAGAZINES

Walking into Duff's study was like walking into a combination of a library and a newspaper editor's office. There were books everywhere, magazines, letters, yellow pads, and sharpened pencils. The kids liked it in there; it reminded them of him.

People were always encouraging Duff to write books. They begged him to write a book on the Book of Mormon and its "lessons of life." They wanted a book from him geared toward youth. They asked if they could compile a "best of" type book of his voluminous collection of quotations and articles on every subject imaginable. They asked him to flesh out his approach to marking and studying the scriptures. Later, they asked him to please write down his unique approach to understanding

9. MDH-JE, Jan. 11, 2002.

the temple and committed marriage. And so on. In his files were multiple letters from publishers, editors, and friends cajoling him in that direction.

His favorite response to such inquiries was always the same: "I write a lot of books, but I keep them in drawers where they won't hurt anybody."[10]

Eventually, three books came out with his name on them. All three are mostly collections of published talks he had given and articles he had previously written:

The Gift of Self	(Bookcraft, 1974)
Now and Forever	(Bookcraft, 1974)
Bread upon the Waters	(Bookcraft, 1991)

The main reason he didn't write more books was that he didn't want to misuse his authority. He worried that doing so might allow him to exercise undue influence over church members' thinking, simply by virtue of his position.

Much of the credit for prodding Duff to allow the three books to be published should go to Cory Maxwell from Bookcraft (and later Deseret Book), who persistently asked him for permission to begin collecting materials for a book.

Over the years, others of Duff's writings were included as chapters in books with titles such as *Women*, *Prayer*, *Teachers Who Teach*, and many others. A number of his talks were also turned into pamphlets such as *Gifts of a Mother*, and some were even made into videos and short movies such as *The Guilty*.

While he was giving speeches for over sixty years, he was also writing articles and texts and opinion pieces. Most of his writings were published in the magazines and papers of the church, including the *Instructor*, *Improvement Era*, "Era of Youth," *New Era*, *Children's Friend*, *Ensign*, *Liahona*, *Friend*, *Millennial Star*, and *Church News*. He also wrote manuals and texts for use in church instruction, such as the *M-Men & Gleaner Manual*, *Ensign-Laurel Manual*, *MIA Manual*, *Youth of a Noble Birthright*, and many others.

I suppose, like many good writers, Duff wasn't all that excited about someone else editing his speeches or articles for inclusion in a book or magazine. On one occasion, he wrote a handwritten note to the editor of a church magazine:

Dear Friend,
This is a good job of editing.
It effectively removes anything distinctive of my
—originality
—method of expression, and
—personality.
What it leaves, I am not sure.
Who loves an editor?
Regards,
MDH

10. MDH-R, Sept. 26, 2000.

There is no way to document the thousands of newspaper and magazine articles printed *about* him, but suffice to say he was quoted on every continent and in every type of publication. As a young boy growing up, Rich wasn't that interested that Duff was in national and local newspapers, like the *New York Times* or the London *Times* or even the *Deseret News*, but he thought it was particularly cool that his dad had been quoted in *Sports Illustrated*, even if the article had been printed before he was born.

Writing here about the kinds of pieces he wrote, and where they were published, is nowhere near as interesting or important as reading what he wrote about. Unfortunately, there is no way to include many of his talks and writings in a biography like this, but a quick internet search of his name brings up ten thousand hits, including websites with links to his fifty general conference talks, more than seventy-five talks he gave at Brigham Young University, and other public speeches. Of course, one will not find many of the thousands of talks he gave prior to widespread electronic and digital recording.

POETRY AND SONG

Duff loved poetry. He tried mightily to get others to love it too. In one talk, he quipped,

> Want to have more fun than some of you have been having? I can help. Have you known or heard the poem "Stretch Your Mind?" Listen to this brief repetition: "Stretch your mind, even as you stretch your arms, upward to the sky. Give it a daily task beyond its present strength and store it each day with treasure—poetry to say under your breath, knowledge newly acquired!"[11]
>
> Poetry? Aye, poetry! It is for more than just the English majors! All of us, each of us, could have our lives blessed by association with some good and uplifting poetry. But poetry, like the scriptures, should be occasionally read aloud, either to oneself or to others. Moses so taught us, as early as Deuteronomy.[12]

Duff was a very accomplished poet.

The main target for his poetry was Maxine. Many a birthday, holiday, anniversary, or other special event would produce a rhyme in her honor. Even giving her a book of poems for her birthday resulted in a kind of poetic love letter: "My Dearest, our son has revealed to all the world that I write love poems to my wife. Until a volume is published, I will share what *other* poets have expressed also. They too may have had such a feeling—though I doubt it—and think they had such a subject—though of course, they could not. This morning I give you love poems—theirs—and deepest love—mine. Duff."

He also showered her continually with love notes and letters of appreciation.

11. Maude Parker, to her daughters, "I Do Hereby Bequeath," *The Third Book of Words to Live By*, ed. William Nicols, Jan. 1, 1962.

12. MDH, personal notes on "Learning," n.d.

Reading through Mom's box of special things and letters is like reading through the love notes of Romeo and Juliet. It was really a simple fact—Dad loved Mom (and vice versa)—and we all knew it. Duff penned the following poem for Maxine in honor of her fiftieth birthday.

Fifty

If Columbia, the Gem of the Ocean
Celebrates proudly this year,
Proclaiming her birthday steadfastly,
Absent so much as a tear.

Why should Maxine, bubbling youngster,
Resist anniversary gold,
Knowing our fair lady nation
Is reaching 200 years old?

So, sing aloud, country and Chandler,
Announce on your several stage—
That heaven supplied us to cherish
These ladies of disparate age.

Our land we salute with full fervor,
Thank God for His generous store,
But heaven, take thanks without measure
For Mom—we love her even more!

A SPECIAL POEM—"THAT EASTER MORN"

Duff wrote what became his best-known verse on Easter Sunday 1972, on a rare occasion when was able to attend his home ward with his family. During sacrament meeting, he wrote a poem he titled "That Easter Morn" on the back of the meeting's program. On arriving home, he reworked it a bit on a yellow pad.

A few years later, knowing that Duff wrote poetry, Tabernacle organist Robert Cundick asked Maxine if she would provide one of Duff's poems that he could set to music. She sent him "That Easter Morn" to which Cundick wrote the music. It was later included in the 1985 hymnal.

Someone wrote the following commentary about the hymn: "In 'That Easter Morn,' Elder Hanks set himself an impressively demanding poetic task. Consider what must happen in the last two lines of each verse: the lines must rhyme with each other, they must include a form of the verb *conquer*, and they must advance the hymn's message in a natural way—all this in the space of only four syllables per line! Because of the poet's technical skill, the poem's beautiful message emerges in a fresh and significant form."[13]

13. Commentary on Hymn #198, "That Easter Morn," gospelink.com, Digital Library by Deseret Book.

That Easter Morn

That Easter morn, a grave that burst
Proclaimed to man that "Last and First"
Had ris'n again
And conquered pain.

This morn renews for us that day
When Jesus cast the bonds away,
Took living breath
And conquered death.

Thus we in gratitude recall
And give our love and pledge our all,
Shed grateful tear
And conquer fear.

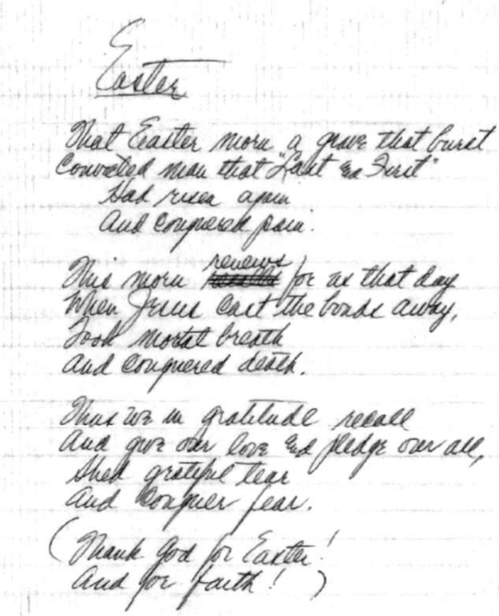
Easter

That Easter morn a grave that burst
Convinced man that "Last and First"
Had risen again
And conquered pain.

This morn renews for us that day
When Jesus cast the bonds away,
Took mortal breath
And conquered death.

Thus we in gratitude recall
And give our love and pledge our all,
Shed grateful tear
And conquer fear.

(Thank God for Easter!
And for faith!)

Duff wrote the lyrics to the hymn "That Easter Morn," on the back of a church program on Easter Sunday, 1972, then transferred the poem to a yellow pad, original shown on right.

Eugene England wrote the following critique of the text of "That Easter Morn":

> Elder Hanks has been shy about his poetry, though on the evidence of a unique occasion when he read a little to an English Department gathering at BYU, he is very skilled. (He sometimes claims his only shareable example is "I can't cope/ With hair on soap!")
>
> Fortunately, we have for the public domain his fine hymn, "That Easter Morn." He used a unique stanza form that he invented, an iambic tetrameter couplet (two rhyming eight-syllable lines, each with four alternating stresses), followed by an iambic dimeter (two stress) couplet. He handles this original verse form both fluently and imaginatively from stanza to stanza, to give us the great range of what Christ's resurrection did for us in the final lines of the stanzas, which are repeated as a modified refrain, with a different last word in each stanza."[14]

In March 1975, Duff was leading a large group of visitors on a tour of Temple Square, which included a visit to the Tabernacle to hear a Tabernacle Choir rehearsal. The choir surprised him and his visitors by announcing that they were going to sing three traditional numbers and then Duff's hymn, "That Easter Morn." Conductor Jerald Ottley addressed the packed Tabernacle, paying tribute to Elder Hanks and his work. Deeply moved, Duff called it "one of the sweetest experiences of a lifetime."

14. Eugene England, "The Quality of Mercy," in *Teachers Who Touch Lives*, comp. Philip L. Barlow, (Bountiful, UT: Horizon, 1988), 60–61.

THEIR ORDINARY LIVES

21

Just Dad

Those who love, should manifest their love when there is a chance to do so. If we are waiting for some later time when all imperfections are corrected and all frustrations pass away, then we are not wise.
—Marion D. Hanks[1]

In some ways Duff and Maxine's family was just like any other family. For example, they held family home evenings, irregularly, when they could. "In the evening, our family had a fine family night and I enjoyed it very much," wrote Duff. "We had a fire, of course, and everyone participated. Ann taught Mary a song she learned in school, and Mary picked it up immediately. Susan and Nancy also sang together, reading from a music sheet copy of 'Winter Wonderland.' They sang perfectly on tune and did a good job of it."[2]

While that description sounds idyllic, in reality (especially as the children got older), family home evenings were sometimes long and boring. And because Duff loved the scriptures so much, the family read a *lot* of scriptures—and the children did not always like it. But his efforts paid off in the future. For example, one day on Rich's mission, he was teaching an investigator about the Resurrection, and he turned to Alma 40, and it suddenly occurred to him that Duff had taught him that subject years ago and had helped him mark and cross-reference the scriptures. This scenario of delayed understanding has occurred repeatedly throughout the children's lives.

The little family prayed together almost every night. Much of the time they were praying for their absent dad and his travel and that he'd get home safely.

Like most religious, conservative men of the 1960s, Duff greatly disliked the Beatles, their music, their long hair, and all they represented. One day as he and Rich were driving along in the late 1980s, the song "Imagine," by John Lennon, was playing on the radio, and Duff was humming along. Rich asked him if he liked it. He said he did. When told who was singing, he said, "Well, I guess people can change." It's doubtful he would have liked many of the Beatles' other songs.

1. MDH-T, "Agency and Love," GC, Oct. 1983.
2. MDH-JE, Nov. 15, 1960.

The Hanks family on the steps of their Butler Avenue home in Salt Lake City, ca 1968.

VACATIONS

General authorities get the month of July off, but Duff rarely took the entire month. Each year, he somehow agreed to give several speeches during July. But they would still try to spend a week or two together as a family. When they were a young family, they didn't have any extra money to spend, so their vacations were usually local. Occasionally, Grandpa Christensen would pay for his grandkids to visit him and Grandma in Hawaii, but mostly they just stayed home or went to the cabin in Provo Canyon.

In later decades, every three or four years the family would venture out in their station wagon for a big trip to California. A favorite for the kids would be a week on the Balboa Peninsula at a friend's run-down beach house. The family would ride bikes, play in the ocean, and cross over to the other side on the ferry. Those were such wonderful times together.

They had some not-so-humorous mishaps along the way. One time as they drove down the highway, they realized that the blue tarp that covered their luggage on the roof was flapping all over the place. They pulled over, and all their luggage was gone! After backtracking for thirty minutes or so, they found their suitcases in the middle of the road, popped open, their clothes all over the place.

DUFF AS A DAD

At Duff's funeral, Rich said, "A young man could not have asked for a better dad. He was a man's man. He taught me how to kick, throw, shoot, swing, and hit. He taught me how to chop wood, saw logs, move streambeds, fix sprinklers, and swing a hammer. It's not the way the world knew him, but it's the way I knew him best."

For Father's Day one year, the *Church News* published a story called "Role Models for Fathers," in which Duff is quoted as saying, "The best 'handbook' for fathers is the Book of Mormon." He then quoted the opening verse of the Book of Mormon: "I, Nephi, having been born of goodly parents, therefore I was taught somewhat in all the learning of my father …" He continued, "This conscious responsibility of a father to teach, nurture, nourish and to share is a trait of good fathers in all places in all times."[3] Duff exemplified Nephi's description of a good father.

Duff was unusually wise beyond his years. That may have contributed to the way he treated his children. He always treated them as if they were ten years older than they were. It made them feel important and valued. But he could also be demanding and not particularly patient. He hated to be interrupted and could seem unyielding at times, refusing to negotiate away from his opinion. He never exercised unrighteous dominion or was domineering, but since he was in charge of almost everything he did outside the home, the family all knew who was in charge at home.

Because he didn't grow up with a father, Duff didn't really have much previous experience in seeing how other fathers parented. As a result, he could be a tough disciplinarian. Maxine did a lot of "wait until your father gets home" stuff. Rich remembered, "I don't ever remember him walloping us, but he didn't have to; the fear of disappointing him was punishment enough."

ABSENTEE FATHER

Duff's children all remember thinking, "If I was given a nickel for every time someone asked me, 'What's it like growing up as a general authority's child?' I could be rich." There were some very unusual things about growing up as children of a general authority.

Duff was gone almost every weekend of their childhoods, presiding at stake conferences or conducting mission tours somewhere around the world. But they never recall feeling that this was any kind of hardship. At his funeral, daughter Susan said, "We had a strong mother who never complained, and Dad genuinely felt that the Lord would watch over us and bless us, and He did."

On one occasion, Duff was going to be gone for an extended period to Southeast Asia. Rich was about six or seven years old and asked him, "Dad, why do you have to go again?"

"Because President McKay asked me to."

"Well, why doesn't he go?"

"Because he is too old."

"Well, so are you!"

---

3. "Role Models for Fathers in 'Handbook,'" *Church News,* June 9, 1990.

HAVING A GENERAL AUTHORITY DAD

The blessings of being a general authority's child, and specifically of being Maxine and Duff's child, significantly outweighed the few minor challenges the children encountered: they were treated kindly by so many who loved their Mom and Dad. And the halo effect from being around them sometimes provided respect and notoriety they didn't merit and blessings from others they hadn't earned. Of course, it made for interesting problems and challenges too.

One night at Brigham Young University, Rich kissed a pretty young woman he had been dating. The next morning, they went on another date, and after they parked at her apartment, she hugged not Rich, but the passenger window. It was obvious something had changed. He cautiously asked, "Did someone tell you who my dad is?" She nodded yes.

One of Duff's daughters had an experience with a boy at BYU who brought along a Book of Mormon to read together on their first date.

Such things were minor impositions but still had to be dealt with. Other happenings were more substantial. It wasn't always easy for his children to discern whether someone was giving them a leg up or if they had earned something themselves. As one example, when he was a senior in high school, Rich was approached to be the seminary president. He remembers going in to see the seminary principal and asking him point-blank if this opportunity was being given because of him or because of his father. Principal Davies smiled and, to his credit, said, "We don't do things that way here."

TRAVELING WITH DAD

The family had to adjust their life to his being in such high demand, but they did it. For example, with the ongoing crush of stake conferences, week after week, he'd occasionally take one of the kids with him (if he was driving.) These were some of their fondest memories together. In fact, Rich learned how to drive a manual transmission and clutch on a Saturday afternoon in Parowan, Utah—between Dad's stake conference meetings.

When Duff was assigned multiple mission tours and stake conferences overseas, lasting more than three weeks, he was allowed to take Maxine with him. When that happened, they would hire one or another of their single returned sister missionaries to watch the kids. Ruth Hughes was a particular favorite. She sent Maxine and Duff a letter in Tokyo, filling them in on how things were going. She wrote, "I have spent my first week with your children and have enjoyed every day so much." Your children are so completely trustworthy. Never do we wonder if they are doing anything but what they know they should. As Richard said in one of his prayers, 'Bless Mommy and Daddy, wherever that place is where they are. Much love, Ruth.'"[4]

4. Ruth Hughes to MDH and MCH, Oct. 17, 1966.

In preparation for one ten-day trip, Duff wrote this poem for Maxine:

Ten days, you say, why, that's a song,
We'll take it in our stride.
There've been many trips to last that long
Since she became my bride.
In winter's cold and summer's heat
With child, with pain, with fear,
But with no word of selfishness
And seldom with a tear.
Then why sit I with lava flow
Of moisture down my cheek?

AN ENGAGED FATHER

Duff took every opportunity he could to teach his children. He taught them geography from a set of books he had in his library. He taught them to lead music. He taught them the gospel constantly by working with them in the scriptures, by anecdote, and by example. At dinnertime he would share something he had read or heard that day.

Because his mother, Maude, grew purple pansies in their backyard, Duff always loved the Primary song "Little Purple Pansies." Because florists don't really sell pansies, Duff would occasionally buy a bunch of violets for his daughters when he was shopping at ZCMI.

With four beautiful daughters, Duff was also keenly interested in the boys who began hanging around. He was always introduced to his daughters' dates and friends. His firm handshake and direct look in the eyes could be a bit intimidating. Danny, one of Mary's friends from high school, rode his bike to the Hanks house late one evening wearing some incredibly short shorts. He and Mary were out front talking when Duff got home from work, and after pleasantries were exchanged, Danny was invited to go home and change "if he'd like to continue speaking with Mary." Danny became a professional public speaker and shared that story widely.

Duff would generally be awake when they got home from dates or some late-night event. The deadbolt latch on their front door on Chandler Circle made a notoriously loud click no matter how much Richard oiled it. So it was not unusual to come home from a date as quietly as possible, only to hear Duff's voice from his bedroom way down the hall, "Welcome home. What time is it?"

Duff didn't hold back anything in his support of his children. He wrote:

> My wife and I were in our ward when our only son was presented to the congregation to receive the Aaronic Priesthood and be ordained a deacon. At home that afternoon he was explaining the experience to his sisters. They asked if he felt scared standing with the bishop in front of the congregation when the sustaining vote was taken. "A little," he said, "but I looked down and saw Dad's hand higher

than all the rest, and I felt all right." It was true; my hand was held as high as I could reach. He is my son, and that's how I feel about him. I feel that way about his sisters, too, and the great generation the five of them represent.[5]

Duff was often away for big family events, both positive and negative. Things like school plays and football games were hit and miss. If they were being held on weekends, the odds were not good for him to be in attendance. This unfortunately also applied to emergency situations. He was in Taiwan when Rich tore up his shoulder bodysurfing in Hawaii. He was in Manila when his mother, Maude, passed away. One August day in Blackfoot, Idaho, he wrote, "The least pleasant part of this whole trip was the news that Nancy's Lissa had pulled over a boiling pan and been severely burned and is in intensive care in Honolulu. We are praying."[6] (Lissa recovered and is now a brain surgeon at Harvard.)

"I KNOW YOU LOVE ME"

One experience made a big impact on the family, demonstrating how young people need and want boundaries. In 1976, an exchange student from Brazil came to live with the Hanks family. Braulio was seventeen, didn't grow up with LDS standards, but knew that as long as he lived in the Hanks home he was required to live by their rules and standards: no smoking, no drinking, and keeping curfews. Duff didn't make Braulio go to church with the family, but he did have to attend *some* church. Sometimes he went to his church, but more often than not, he chose to go to their LDS ward with them. During the three months he lived with them, he strained under the bridle of rules.

After the three months were up, Braulio gladly left the Hanks and went to a Park City home, where he was given a car, a huge allowance, and zero rules. Following that home, he lived in another home with no rules and no boundaries. He seemed happy. He even became the kicker for the Park City High School football team.

One day there was a knock on their door, and there was Braulio standing on the porch, asking to speak with Duff and Maxine. Braulio shocked them by asking if he could spend his remaining two months in the United States with them. Duff responded, "Why, Braulio? You know the rules. You won't have all the freedoms, etc." To which Braulio replied, "I'd like to come back with you, please. *Because I know you love me.*"

FULFILLING HIS WARD DUTY

Despite his incredibly demanding life, Duff still found time to fulfill the occasional ward calling, including serving as Rich's home teaching companion during his most impressionable years. For a short and slightly unusual time, they were home

5. MDH-T, "The Sword of the Lord and of Gideon," BYU, Sept. 26, 1972.
6. MDH-JE, Aug. 23, 1977.

teachers to President Harold B. Lee and his wife, Freda.[7] Most of the time, Duff and Rich served as home teachers for the Vest and the Casto families. They both had fond memories of those nights when they would sit in the car and prepare, through prayer, to perform their priesthood duties. There is no teacher better than example.

INSTILLING A LOOK BACK AND A LOOK FORWARD

One of the ways Duff used to nudge his children was to have them memorize specific poetry or quotations that directed their thinking. For example, he never sat them down and gave them a lecture about how to behave as the child of a prominent person, but he did have them memorize specific quotes and repeat them over and over. Examples were Plutarch's "It is a desirable thing to be well descended, but the glory belongs to our ancestors,"[8] and Goethe's "What from your father's heritage is lent, earn it anew to really possess it."[9]

In a particular effort to prepare his children to think about what they could become in the future—what they wanted to be and how today's decisions affect tomorrow's outcomes—he had them memorize Harry Emerson Fosdick's statement "He who picks up one end of a stick picks up the other."[10]

And E. B. White's poem led to poignant reflections on future possibilities:

In the sudden mirror in the hall
I saw not my own self at all;
I saw instead a most familiar face,
My father stood there in my place,
Returning in the hall lamp's glare
My own surprised and watery stare.
In thirty years, my son shall see
Not himself standing there, but me.[11]

WORK

Duff believed that the key to temporal happiness includes hard work and going the extra mile. He would always say that doing good work brings out the best in people and creates a sense of pride, self-worth, and accomplishment. He told at least one audience, "Don't miss the joy that comes when you give everything that is expected and then a little more. You may only dig ditches or push elevator buttons, but seek to do it the best you can."[12]

---

7. This was unusual for several reasons—because President Lee was the prophet, but also because he and Duff had openly disagreed on several controversial issues over the previous two decades, and Duff felt that President Lee harbored animosity toward him.

8. Plutarch, *Of the Training of Children*.

9. Johann Wolfgang von Goethe, *Faust*.

10. Harry Emerson Fosdick, *Living under Tension: Sermons on Christianity To-day* (New York: Harper, 1941), 110–11.

11. E. B. White, "A Boy I Knew," *Reader's Digest*, June 1940.

12. MDH-T, "BYU 14-Stake Conference," *Daily Universe*, Nov. 8, 1982.

The thing about Duff was that he loved hard work the same way most people feel about going on vacation. After he and Maxine built their cabin, much of what little free time he had was spent there working with a shovel or a chainsaw or a broom. His love of labor was passed down to his children.

The Hanks family belonged to a neighborhood pool, and one week each summer they were responsible for cleaning it. Duff worked with the kids a few times teaching them what to do and then left it up to them to follow through.

About another occasion, Rich wrote, "I had been hired by our neighbors across the street to mow their lawn. I was thirteen and did a mediocre job, particularly on the edging. In those days, we didn't have weed-eaters; we knelt down and clipped the edges with scissor-like tools. The day before the neighbors returned from a trip, I was about two-thirds through edging when one of my friends talked me into going to play ball. I will never forget the next day, Sunday morning (one of the few Dad was home), looking out our front window and seeing him on his hands and knees across the street finishing the job for me. This was the only time I ever saw him work on the Sabbath. We had no further lessons on the subject, and I have never needed one."

"OUTLAWS" START TO JOIN THE FAMILY

As the girls grew older and one by one went off to college, boys started hanging around with more serious intent. Suddenly, the brownies and cookies made by Duff's four daughters in their kitchen, which had previously had some application to those at home, were being sent to those young men who stopped by or were brought up from BYU.

One by one, each of the girls got married, and four brothers joined the family. All of them—Paul Maughan, John Baird, Spencer Clawson, and Chris Clifford—are wonderful, good, and decent men. Each has served as a bishop and remained active and involved in the church.

One of the funniest parts of each of these four young men joining the family was watching them try to figure out what to call Duff. By the time he was in his seventies, they were all calling him Duff. But for the first decade or two, it was a struggle for them. Duff didn't make it any easier on them, never really suggesting what to call him, so they tried experiments: "Elder Hanks," "Duff," "Hey, you." It was all good stuff.

INTUITIVE DUFF

Duff was very intuitive in understanding his children's needs. He just seemed to know things. For example, on January 1, 1982, after a phone call from Hong Kong, Duff wrote Rich the following letter:

> Special Son:
>
> Why do I get the feeling that I was talking when I should have been listening in our phone conversation? Cars and tires and accidents were not really it, were they? Or am I wrong?

Duff and Maxine, June 1979.

This morning at 4:30 I awoke thinking of you. And Elizabeth. I really don't know Elizabeth, but I know you.

Has it happened to you? Have heads, and hearts, and spirits matched?

Practicalities, realities must be considered. But oh! the wonder and joy when it happens! Maybe not. You haven't said. But I wonder. Among the practicalities is that marriage is 24 hours every day from now on, whenever that is, and no turning back. And no turning away.

So, there must be thought. Thought and prayer and bouncing it off the solidest wall you can find.... Maybe Jeff, maybe Paul, maybe Homer.[13] Then maybe your dad. Ask what it is all about. Ask what is fair, what is wise. Consider answers, then consult your heart, spirit, mind. Ask what matters in the long run.

Ask if you are ready to give what marriage requires, from now on.

Maybe you will need to ask what I am talking about. I doubt it.

I love you. Dad.

Even from far away, across the world, Duff was absolutely correct.

FAMILY FOR THE LONG TERM

Duff wrote a loving tribute about his extended family after sitting in a room with Maxine, their five children, their eternal partners, and their (then) sixteen grandchildren. "I looked at twenty-seven other people," Duff said, "realizing that

13. Named were Jeff Holland, a family friend; Paul Maughan, Duff's son-in-law; and Homer Elsworth, a family friend.

my wife and I hadn't had a child for twenty-four years and would not again in this world. Yet twenty-eight of us were in the room, and there are others yet to come. What a remarkable vision it is to perceive continuity into the past and into the future; that all of us will find a place, ultimately, a loving place under the holy influence of Him whose sons and daughters we are spiritually and whose holy life and sacrifice brought us the blessings of these excellent hopes."[14]

14. BUW, 182–83. They ended up with twenty-three grandchildren.

22

Maxine the Great!

Those of us who are married are blessed to have been taught about marriage at least twice from Mom and Dad. Once, as we were counseled by them prior to the actual ordinance, and the second time over an extended period of observing their lives and the way they treat each other.
—Plaque for Duff and Maxine's fiftieth wedding anniversary.

Over the years, Maxine raised her children, supported her husband, and served with him as an LDS mission president in England, as an Area President in Hong Kong, as matron of the Salt Lake Temple, and in many other assignments. She was quietly and privately grounded and saw life clearly as she stood by Duff's side for over sixty-five years. She was a wonderful wife and mother and friend. She was a true believer in the gospel of Jesus Christ.

THRIVING DESPITE AN ABSENTEE HUSBAND

For most of their marriage Maxine raised the children alone, with an absentee husband and a small budget. Occasionally, thoughtful people would notice and share their gratitude. A stake president in Washington wrote: "Dear Sister Hanks and Children, we want to thank you for the privilege of having Elder Hanks with us in our stake conference. I am sure you would enjoy having him at home on weekends. But you really are serving in a fine way by sustaining him. It is surely true, 'They who wait, also serve.' God bless you."[1]

When questioned about her sacrifices, Maxine responded, "Yes, it is pretty lonely. You just have to decide—your children need at least one parent, and if you love your children enough, you are there for them while their father's gone. I think you have to decide early what is important to you and what isn't. I felt that they needed me. But there were a lot of lonely times, especially because I had no family near me."[2]

Duff knew how blessed he was. "There is not, and could not have been, a better wife in the world than Maxine has been for these long years," he said. "Not only has she not complained, but she has been unbelievably strong and generous

1. Stake president, Yakima, WA, to Maxine, 1960.
2. MCH-R, Dec. 10, 1988.

in her support. She's reared our choice children very much on her own, with little help from me, even when I was not away. That the children are as they are, is a tribute to her, and her alone."

Elder Marlin K. Jensen once wrote to her: "Sister Hanks, your example, and frequent encouragement to my wife, Kathy, about how to go on rearing a family with an absentee father and a tight budget often spelled the difference between happiness and despair. Just knowing you had done it for so many years and were so positive and affirming about life provided great hope and an optimistic outlook for our own future."

OUT OF THE LIMELIGHT

Maxine and Duff built a beautiful life together. With grace and poise, she let him shine because she loved him and knew he was everything she wanted. Others noticed. Menlo Smith wrote: "There is Maxine, usually in the background, often unnoticed, but always serving as a marvelous influence as she supports, encourages, and sustains her husband, while enriching, lifting, and loving her progeny—and others—in significant and special ways. This you do with grace and quietude."

FIERCE LOYALTY AND SUPPORT

Maxine was incredibly loyal to Duff, and he knew he had married above himself. In a 1973 journal entry, he expressed joy at reuniting after traveling: "My trip home was pleasant and concluded with a late arrival at home to find Maxine back from Hawaii feeling better and with joy for the blessing of being with her folks. She is a great and gracious soul, and it pleases me greatly that she can occasionally be with her parents. She is loyal, guileless, and a wonderfully loving daughter who is so genuine that she has no trouble at all being the kind of daughter any parent would want."[3]

LOVE AFFAIR AND BEST FRIENDS

Maxine and Duff had an ongoing love affair that they didn't need to either parade around or hide from anyone. It was just a natural thing. The kids also learned early not to mess with Maxine or they got to mess with Duff. In addition to their affection for each other, they also liked to tease each other. One of the funniest memories is of Duff arriving home after work or a trip. He'd walk into the kitchen, where Maxine would run to him and throw her arms around him. After a few seconds, he'd tilt his head back and holler loudly, "Put me down!"

Maxine's children paid homage to their mother for her love and devotion to Duff for all those years. Every Friday night she drove him to the airport with her little kids and then drove back out to pick him up on Sunday night. Then she spent the last seven years of Duff's life visiting him every day in a care center.

3. MDH-JE, Feb. 1973.

Duff and Maxine at a banquet.

This statement by fellow general authority Elder Loren C. Dunn is pretty accurate: "I can remember a few years ago when Duff and Maxine came to New Zealand. Their relationship was such a good example. In the quiet moments when they were talking with each other, you could tell they were not just husband and wife, but they were best friends. They spoke to one another with real interest, and they listened with real interest as well."

It was fun over the years to see stolen kisses, glances which spoke volumes, little love notes, and quiet hand holding. Duff saying to his kids, "Isn't she beautiful?" Maxine's eyes eagerly anticipating Duff's return home from travel.

They also complemented each other so well. A trip to the cabin always began with an unspoken division of chores. Maxine grabbed the broom, while Duff turned on the water and started the fire. Their work together as a team, their private understanding, and their demonstrated love set the example for their children.

Maxine framed Duff's love poems and placed them where she could read them every day. Here is one for Easter from an absent Duff across the Atlantic:

Easter 1970, with Roses
As only God can make a tree,
I cannot fashion one for thee.
But fools, 'tis said, can make a verse
To tell of love—or hurl a curse.

Thus, at this Easter, far from home,
I pen this missive, writ like poem,
Bursting with love as I compose,
I bring a flower, a blooming rose;
Though God alone can *make* a lily,
They can be *bought* at Piccadilly.
I love you, D.[4]

They functioned together as a team. There was never the slightest doubt of their enduring love and total commitment to each other.

THE HEART OF THEIR HOME—A TERRIFIC MOM

There were seven members in the Hanks family. One day when Rich was eight years old, Duff and all four daughters were in the kitchen and Maxine was running an errand. Rich came busting in the back door, looked at the other five, and said, "Hey, where is everybody?" Without Maxine, the house really was mostly empty no matter who else was there. She was "everybody" to them.

Maxine did all the things the best parents do. Her five children and twenty-three grandchildren adored her. She took special girls' trips with her daughters and exposed them to her love of the opera. She took them with her on trips to Hawaii and other places. She supported them in their extracurricular activities, such as Pep Club, politics, and musical groups.

With four older daughters and only one son in the family, one might think Rich was probably overlooked. Not so. Maxine was an ideal mom for him as a young boy. She helped him build scores of plastic models and rockets and then let him blow them up with firecrackers. She took Rich and his friends to the Silver Mine in Park City and made countless trips to the Hansen Planetarium, the Bingham Copper Mine, the Deseret Gym, and the Natural History Museum. They even went to the Great Salt Lake to see if they could really float in it. When the Blue Angels jets came to town, she took Rich and all his friends to see them at Hill Air Force Base in Ogden.

They all benefited from her love of swimming by being members of Waterhaven, a neighborhood swimming pool. The image of Maxine swimming in her mid-1960s swimming cap is ingrained in their memories.

One time, daughter Mary brought home a cigarette she found. Maxine helped Mary and Richard light it so they would never want to try smoking "those filthy things" again.

She gave her children freedom to choose and explore and the security of an accepting and loving home. She taught them to live the gospel. She taught them how to cope with life cheerfully. She taught them to be givers and not takers. She was loyal to them and trusted their judgment.

---

4. MDH-L to Maxine from London, April 1970.

FOOD

Maxine wasn't a master chef, though she went all out on holidays and Sunday dinners. She was a 'casserole queen' of the 1960s, and Campbell's Cream of Mushroom Soup was her best culinary friend. The family ate a lot of meat pies topped with watered-down ketchup. Eventually, with just one child left at home, she basically stopped cooking, except for holidays.

The family occasionally went out to eat at The Cinegrill or Dee's and, once in a blue moon, to the Hotel Utah. If they visited Duff downtown, they would beg to go across the street to ZCMI to get a hot dog. They really didn't have to beg much because Duff loved those hot dogs too.

A DOER

Maxine was an initiative taker and an organizer. She was bright, competent, straightforward, and unafraid. She created beautiful homes of refuge wherever she and Duff lived. Visitors were always welcome.

She was always doing, doing, doing. Upon arriving at the cabin, most people would want to relax. But Maxine would immediately get out a broom, begin humming, and start sweeping the deck. It was just a part of her DNA—both the doing and the humming.

LOVING TO LAUGH

One of Rich's absolute favorite things was to make his mom laugh uncontrollably. He could really get her going. She'd say, "Oh, Richard," and cover her mouth with her hand. And the children all loved to tease her. When she and Duff served in the Salt Lake Temple, her official title was temple matron. While that was a good and respectful title inside the temple, she wasn't that fond of it outside the temple. The children all got a kick out of telling her "Mom, you look so matronly today."

CREATING GATHERING SPACES

Maxine was adept at creating spaces to bring people together and build relationships. She was remarkably generous with her family. She envisioned the cabin in Provo Canyon and their small place in Hana, Maui, as places for holiday gatherings that brought her entire family together, solidifying family relationships and memories that will last forever.

Building the home in Hawaii was about more than just returning to her home after so many years away. It was her way of ensuring that the members of her family understood and were each filled with the spirit of aloha. Son-in-law John Baird wrote, "She didn't just build a house; she planted the islands in our hearts."

COUPLE FRIENDS

Maxine and Duff had some close personal friends, but not many. Perhaps this journal entry during his mission explains why: "I seem to have the unhappy knack of putting myself into a condition of social insularity which wards off advances of friendship. The condition is superficial because I simply don't feel that way. And yet, I think I dive behind the shield many times, [as] a means of escape, and sometimes, escape is what I'd like to do the most. Not that humanity bothers me any more than it does the average man. But sometimes I think I'd be more worthwhile to the world if I had a chance to be by myself and charge up once in a while. There have been times, lots of times, when the most desirable thing seemed to be a place where I could just sit, alone or with someone comfortable, and be quiet. I am a peculiar admixture of gregarious and hermit."[5]

Duff's desire to recharge alone, along with the periods he spent away from home, made forming and keeping close personal friends a challenging task. Maxine had dear friends growing up in Honolulu, including Joy Baird, whose son John married Maxine's daughter Nancy. Her dearest friend was Blanche Miles, whose husband Coy was a good friend of Duff's—their two families enjoyed numerous holidays together. Maxine and Duff also belonged to various study groups and social clubs over the years—Bonneville Knife and Fork, the Dinner Set, even Fort Douglas (for the swimming pool)—but they were never regular attendees.

HAWAII AND WATER

You can take the girl out of Hawaii, but you can't take Hawaii out of the girl. Maxine loved the ocean. Conversely, Duff wasn't a big fan of the water. In fact, family memories of Duff on the beach place him in a fold-out beach chair, hat on, with a long-sleeved white shirt, sleeves rolled up to the elbows, open collar (no tie), long khaki pants, white socks, and either boots or sandals (over the socks).

After a family vacation to California, Duff recorded in his journal, "Maxine was a sylph and a sprite in the water. Her children and grandchildren were much impressed, and she was much blessed by it all. Her natural habitation and life experience have been connected inextricably with water and sand through much of her life, and a renewal is rebirth. She was the hub of our vacation and every other activity involving her family."[6]

Maxine was an island girl through and through. She left the islands only for college and then her marriage to Duff. She had a deep connection and love for Hawaii. After traveling the world for forty years, the porch in Hana was their rest. She loved for her children to tell her how much they loved it also. The phone call to Maxine was one of the first things everyone did on arrival there.

Maxine was also adventuresome. The family would go to a waterfall or to the beach, and she, feeling at home, jumped right in—things her own children and grandchildren were more reluctant to do. At her funeral Rich told the story of their last time in the ocean together at Hamoa Beach on Maui:

---

5. MDH-JE, Aug. 25, 1942.
6. MDH-JE, about family vacation to Balboa, CA, summer 1984.

> Six years ago was the last time I got to be with Mom at the beach. She was 86 and a bit frail. One day there was rough surf, but she demanded that we get in the water. We held on to each other and bobbed between the waves, me kicking as hard as I could to get both of us up and over some pretty big waves. Frankly, it was hard to push both of us up and over, and I was wondering if it was worth it, but then I noticed the biggest smile on her face. I will never forget holding my mom up so we could giggle and laugh together in the waves, one last time.

Mary took care of her mother's garden for many years. Although she was very appreciative, Maxine lamented that she couldn't plant her beloved gardenias, anthuriums, or hibiscus in Utah's desert soil.

A trip to Hawaii is a vacation for most people, but for Maxine it was a visit home. However, she didn't get to do many normal 'home' things on her visits, because she was usually entertaining family members or at the beach. So, for her eightieth birthday, her five middle-aged children, (who had twenty-three children of their own), took Maxine to Hawaii for a special visit. They rented a minivan and drove Maxine to spots of her childhood. They walked around the Honolulu Tabernacle, and she pointed out where she danced with Duff and the spot where they first kissed. They drove by her schools and playgrounds and local shops, while she told stories of growing up—all the kinds of things that people normally share about their childhoods—when they're not on vacation in Hawaii. The children learned many things they had never heard before, and Maxine had a terrific time.

GRACE, BEAUTY, AND DIGNITY

Hebrews 1:9 offers a good description of Maxine: "Thou hast loved righteousness, and hated iniquity; therefore God, even thy God, hath anointed thee with the oil of gladness." She taught her children to love things that build character, things that uplift and inspire and radiate beauty. She loved museums, music and theater, opera, and poetry. She danced a graceful and dignified hula. She was wonderfully good at it. She loved warmth and sun and light. She was optimistic and cheerful.

Maxine was a beautiful woman. She was feminine and careful about her appearance. It wasn't just her appearance that made her beautiful though. It was also her grace. This grace was manifested in lots of ways. For example, when her children came home from school, *La Bohème, Madame Butterfly*, or some other opera would be playing on the record player as she did housework.

She was well read and loved improving her mind. She read more books in a year than most people read in a lifetime. If she liked something she read in a book or magazine, she would copy it or cut it out and then send it to her family.

She loved salads and turned up her nose at sugar. Her favorite treat was a ripe mango, a papaya, an apple, or a banana. From Hong Kong, Duff once quipped in a letter to his family, "Mom reads voraciously and eats wisely and is otherwise a splendid example for the rest of us."

Maxine Lehua Christensen Hanks.

AUTHENTIC AND REAL AND DIRECT

Maxine was always real. She had no pretense about her. She was filled with love and was straightforward, fearless, and spunky.

Maxine said exactly what she thought, and she could be a bit opinionated. But she was usually able to be direct and open without being offensive. She spoke her mind, sometimes without being invited to, but invariably people just smiled or laughed without taking umbrage.

When a family member visited Maxine with trendy, ripped Levi's, Maxine looked at her and said, "Meghan, do you need money?"

She replied, "No, why?"

"Because of the Levi's."

Meghan said, "Don't you like them?"

"No, they are the stupidest thing I've ever seen."

Maxine was also fearless in sharing her opinions outside the family. A grandson remembered one of his annual birthday trips with Grandma to buy new shoes. Maxine asked to speak with the store manager, a young man in his early twenties. She suggested to him that perhaps a couple of the shirts on display were not appropriate for children, and might they consider a different radio station to play that had more suitable songs to listen to.[7]

HELPING PEOPLE IMPROVE

Maxine just loved to help others improve, providing all kinds of advice and instruction, often without request. Rich remembered, "At 64 years old, I can still hear her saying, 'Sit up straight, chew your food, put your fork down between bites . . .' (And that was just before she died, and it wasn't even to me; it was to one of my friends!)"

Heaven help you if you tried to butter your entire roll without breaking it into pieces first.

Ask anyone in the family to state the correct grammar describing two people going downtown. Don't even think of saying, "me and him." The correct way is, "He and I."

And if one is going to eat soup, it should be done properly: "Like a ship going out to sea, I dip my spoon away from me."

Even now, when her kids and grandkids empty their washing machines, Maxine is there. One of the console labels uses the word "done." Maxine would *not* have liked that. Done is a cooking word. The wash cycle is *finished*, not *done*. Good thing for that Maytag product manager that he or she never met Maxine.

Some people loved Maxine's continual instruction. There are people who correct others for correction's sake. There are those who teach manners for manners' sake. But Maxine's reminders weren't for any of that. She just genuinely wanted to help people improve. She never stopped encouraging her children to be their best selves.

GENUINELY INTERESTED IN OTHERS

Maxine and Duff instilled a level of acceptance, interest, and genuine caring for other people. She treated everyone the same. Everyone was a "big shot" to Maxine. In conversations, she asked people questions about themselves. She had an uncanny way of turning conversations away from her toward *your* life and *your* experiences. She was genuinely not interested in talking about herself. Her ward bulletin noted, "She has met and mingled with famous people and important people, yet she does not distinguish them from the ordinary people she meets in her everyday life. She loves all people unconditionally."[8]

FAREWELL

After Duff's death, Maxine grew increasingly anxious to see him and be with him again. Her body slowly began to fail over a couple of years, but her mind and sense of humor remained sharp until the end. Only a couple of days before

7. Michael Maughan memories.
8. Holladay 3rd Ward, Relief Society bulletin, Apr. 21, 2002.

she died, her granddaughter Kristy was with her in her room when Maxine said, "Where's that light coming from, Kristy?"

Kristy wasn't sure exactly what she meant, so she said, "Heaven?"

Maxine replied, "Let's not go overboard, Kristy!"

After Maxine died, her obituary described a life well lived: "Maxine Lehua Christensen Hanks, beautiful and filled with unique grace and refinement, passed away on February 21, 2018, at the age of 92."

In the Old Testament it is written, "And [she] died in a good old age, full of days … and honor" (1 Chronicles 29:28). At her funeral, two grandchildren shared her impact on their lives: "She was really an incredible mother and grandmother. She filled our lives with beauty and grace. She was genuine, authentic, and kind, and it never occurred to her to be anyone but herself. She loved us with no conditions and never stopped encouraging us to be our best selves. She was never without a Kleenex, a loving correction, and a way to make you feel loved and important."[9] Maxine truly died in a good old age, full of days and honor.

9. MCH funeral, grandchildren Kristy Gaisford and Michael Maughan, Mar. 3, 2018.

23

Mr. Christmas

When no one can know that I can see the star, I will see the star.[1]
—Marion D. Hanks

Duff was enthralled with the traditions of the Christmas season. In his mind, there are just certain things one does at Christmas. If Duff could have had his way, Christmas would come around each month. Everything about it charged his soul and enlivened his spirit. The Savior, the good cheer, the lights, the literature, the service and humanity, the food, the traditions—the whole thing brought him joy.

A passage that he loved from David Grayson could have been written by him: "I sometimes think we expect too much of Christmas Day. We try to crowd into it the long arrears of kindliness and humanity of the whole year. As for me, I like to take my Christmas a little at a time, all through the year. And thus, I drift along into the holidays—letting them overtake me unexpectedly—waking up some fine morning and saying to myself: 'Why, this is Christmas Day!'"[2]

In fairness, Duff also loved Thanksgiving and would read from Deuteronomy 6 about vineyards and olive trees we did not plant, cities we did not build, and wells we did not dig. He taught that everyone should be full of gratitude because we enjoy so many blessings that we did little to deserve. But Thanksgiving was an appetizer. He was just getting warmed up for the main event.

THE STAR

From Thanksgiving to Christmas, and sometimes for months after, there was always a big white star above Duff's home. It wasn't just a decoration like the Christmas lights were, featuring those large, colored, incandescent bulbs you rarely see any more—oh, those were fun too!—but the star had so many meanings. It meant the Savior and tradition and love and family and continuity and so many more things. It was always the first thing to go up, proudly displayed on a high point outside wherever Duff and Maxine lived. Their original star is long gone, but it is succeeded by stars on the homes of their five children and now many more on the homes of their grandchildren.

1. MDH-L to family, Hong Kong, Jan. 2, 1982.
2. David Grayson, *Adventures in Friendship* (New York: Grosset and Dunlap, 1910).

Mr. Christmas, age 81, 2002.

Duff wrote several different articles and talks on the meaning of the star. One favorite was his comparison of the wise men and their travels toward Jesus with our own personal experiences. He wrote, "The Star of Christmas, multiplied countless times on trees and streets, in store windows, and story books, reminds us that God wants men to know His Divine Son and the Plan of Life and Salvation. The Star reminds us that we too, must travel far, and cross our own deserts and mountains, yet whoever we are and of whatever station, we will find Him and find happiness and peace through Him."[3]

The star was also brightly lit on special occasions, such as each of the five last nights they were together as a family before one of the children was getting married. In the middle of the summer, the night before Rich went into the Missionary Training Center to begin his two-year mission to Scotland, the family gathered, and Duff put up the star so all could see it. It was a night filled with emotion.

Duff summarized, "I suppose there are people lots more effective than we in celebrating Christmas, but I doubt it! At least, no one enjoys it more, the whole of it, and we are launching now into that enjoyment time. Actually, we have had our beautiful big white star on our balcony since Thanksgiving, and our lights burned first in the neighborhood and will burn the longest. We believe in Christmas."[4]

CHRISTMAS MUSIC

The music of Christmas played on the record player, then the cassettes, and then the CDs—the old classics and sweet sounds. Christmas Eve meant visits from carolers or visitors like the Arthur Nielsen family, the John Madsen family, and the Jeffrey R. Holland family.

---

3. MDH-A, "Shining Christmas Star Reminder to World," *Salt Lake Tribune*, Dec. 25, 1954, 1.
4. MDH-L to Steven Alldredge, Dec. 19, 1988.

The Hanks family had their own chosen song, "Merry Christmas from Our House to Your House," which each knew and loved and which is now loved by two more generations. Sometimes the family would go caroling to the neighbors. Every Christmas Eve, Duff and Nancy would sing "Mary's Boy Child"—Nancy playing the piano and Duff standing next to her. Their harmonizing was sweet and clear and became a family tradition for over twenty-five years.

On Christmas Eve, Fred Wolters, one of Duff's missionary companions, would visit, dressed in a big red suit with a white beard and a twinkle in his eye. He painted the children's noses red like Rudolph's, and everyone sang and laughed and loved.

CHRISTMAS STORIES

Christmas Eve meant a gathering of the family to read not just the biblical Christmas story from Luke, but the old and new classic stories Duff kept close at hand every Christmas. "Old and new" because he was always on the lookout for new material to read and share at Christmas. Stories included, "The Gift That Lasts a Lifetime," "Christmas Eve on the Desert," "Trouble at the Inn," "A Day of Pleasant Bread," "A Brother like That," "Holy Bread," "Prayers from the Ark," and many more.

No matter who was visiting, or how tired and cranky the little grandchildren might be, or the lateness of the hour, those at home would read—family and visitors alike. All these years later, the family still reads. But maybe not quite as long.

CHRISTMAS MORNING

Traditions on Christmas morning included lining up, youngest to oldest, eyes closed and hands on the shoulders of the sibling in front of them. Led into the front room, the kids would open their eyes to the delight of Christmas stockings and presents. In the toe of each Christmas sock there would be an orange and a dime to remind them how blessed they were, since that was the treat Duff had received each year in his stocking when he was a boy.

All would then gather in the kitchen to prepare the Christmas morning brunch, including eggs with cheese, massive amounts of fruit, waffles and ice cream, bacon and sausage, and on and on. In the Hanks family, it also included some fish—officially "Findon Haddock," but more commonly called "Finnan Haddie," which reminded them of their Scottish heritage and left the kitchen stinking. (One may still visit the village of Findon in Scotland to see the birthplace of this horrible, stinky tradition.)

The Christmas ball is a family tradition dating back to Maxine's childhood in Hawaii as passed down from her Danish ancestors. Maxine and the kids would buy all manner of small toys, gum, candies, and hair nets and then roll them up in crepe paper strips, forming a multilayered ball of fun. Sitting in a circle, each child would unwrap the Christmas ball until a prize fell out. The best memories include the look of horror and shock when a young boy would unwrap a girly thing like lip gloss or when a girl would unwrap a boy's toy.

As the number of grandkids grew and expanded, a full children's Nativity performance, complete with costumes of towels and robes, shepherd's crooks, and a baby Jesus, became a regular occurrence on the program.

DOCTOR OF KINDNESS AWARDS

The Hanks family had the most wonderful and meaningful tradition called Doctor of Kindness awards. Duff would compose a formal-looking proclamation on a scroll extolling the virtues of someone who had demonstrated a spirit of service and kindness to those around them: neighbors, good Samaritans, schoolteachers, church and civic leaders, and humanitarians. Similar to honorary doctorates conferred by universities, the award included a written proclamation and a medal tied on a ribbon to be worn around the neck. After the preparations were complete, everyone would jump in cars, along with longtime friends the Cannon and the Miles families, and then go and formally present the award to the honored recipients in their homes.

DELIVERING FOODSTUFFS

Duff would begin a couple of weeks early and take Rich with him to stock up on food to take to friends, neighbors, and others who were in need. He'd buy huge blocks of cheese at Brooklawn Creamery to be cut into smaller blocks, boxes of oranges and apples from the fruit wholesalers he knew downtown, boxes of nuts from Western Nut Company, and multiple turkeys, and other goodies, and they'd take them all home and repackage them into individual baskets for delivery. Then they would go delivering—so much fun!

"MORE BLESSED TO GIVE THAN TO RECEIVE"

Occasionally, Duff would learn of another family in need, and his family's barely opened, newly received presents would go to a new home. One year they had just received a new Ping-Pong table when Maxine and Duff told them about a military family whose father was overseas fighting in Vietnam and who didn't have much money. Maxine and Duff invited them over to the house, and they enjoyed the new Ping-Pong table so much that Duff presented it to them as a gift. The Hanks children never heard the details until the receiving family wrote it up in story form thirty years later.[5]

A VISIT TO SISTER CHRISTENSEN

One of their traditional stops was always to Sister Christensen's house. She was the mother of Duff's missionary who had been killed on his bicycle in London. They visited her every Christmas for decades until she passed away. Sister Christensen loved them and so looked forward to their visits. They would load her up with boxes of food and some cash and some caroling. One year the family

5. Laura J. Newby Clayton, *A Christmas Memory* (1997).

received a new TV from Santa Claus on Christmas morning, and Duff explained to the family that Sister Christensen didn't have a working TV. So they packed up their watched-for-only-thirty-minutes Christmas TV and took it to her.

TAKING IN STRAY VISITORS

Duff and Maxine always invited others to join with them on Christmas Eve—people who had nowhere to go or needed an extra boost or missionaries or people passing through Temple Square. Christmas after Christmas, they regularly took in strangers of all creeds and circumstances, usually people who were stranded in some way. When questioned about it, Duff said he did it because the scriptures say, "Be not forgetful to entertain strangers: for thereby some have entertained angels unawares" (Hebrews 13:2).

It was fun for family members to show up on Christmas Eve and be introduced to someone from somewhere around the world sitting at the dinner table. One year, two of the first Russian missionaries were invited. Another year involved some newly-arrived refugees. Elder L. Tom Perry wrote this brief note of appreciation: "I will never forget our arrival in Salt Lake as a new general authority. We had driven from Boston and were in a very small apartment for Christmas. You heard about our dilemma and on Christmas Eve we received an invitation to come to your home. As we were departing you gave us a small tree you had decorated. You have brought such joy into our lives."

A TYPICAL CHRISTMAS SEASON

Duff's journal provides a glimpse into a typical holiday season for him:

Sunday, December 21, 1975
I spoke twice on this date on Christmas themes, first for Bishop Robert Garff at the Val Verda 9th Ward in Bountiful, and then in my home ward in the evening. Both were lovely experiences, but especially among my own people. I don't know when I've felt more among friends and family. The response was sweet. It is wonderful to have a family and to have them nearby and to have them be supportive.

Tuesday, December 23, 1975
This was a normal day with Rotary presenting a fine musical program, followed by my preparations for the Doctor of Kindness degrees we are going to present tonight. In the afternoon, Rich and I undertook our Christmas visits to needy families with some remembrances and had a wonderful time and had a sweet experience as always. Later, the usual group took our Doctor of Kindness awards to Ted Jacobsen, Joe Henroid, Doug Sorenson, Alice Evans, and Dan Valentine. We then went home and had a lovely meal.

Wednesday, December 24, 1975
This afternoon we spent together in preparation for Christmas Eve. Richard and I had pretty well gotten the lights in order a few days ago, including the wrestle with the Star on the apex of our home. It looks great there. In the evening, for dinner, we

were blessed to have our family, plus Phyllis and her mom and sister, and two lovely Japanese girls who are away from home. For years we have had the wonderful blessing of having our family together, a privilege I know will one day be interrupted, and we have also had the blessing of some guests who honored our home each year.

DUFF'S CHRISTMAS WRITINGS

Duff's command of the English language, combined with the poetry that seemed to emanate from his soul, produced writings that were unique and beautiful and just plain fun to read. Here is a Christmas letter, in its entirety, that he wrote to his family from Hong Kong in 1982:

> Dear Uns:
>
> When I was little, I didn't know anything about time, much more, anyway, than I know now, but I knew Christmases came only once in almost forever, and New Year's hardly ever at all. Dates changing was a novelty not to be pondered; it just didn't happen often enough to worry, not like Halley's Comet, for sure, which came around like once in a lifetime, or so, and seemed to interest the old folks.
>
> In teen years there was worry; when will 16 come, 18, even 21: more than this was beyond conscious thought. The Christmases crept, and New Year's came, but almost never. And the progression of dates, mainly holidates [*sic*], even birthdays, could not yet comprehend the passing, the ending of a year.
>
> Mission and a war made it quicker to focus, and then marriage and children and the unavoidable reality of a family in transit, the journey measured in words and the way they were spoken, dresses, and who wore them, books, questions that became simpler and tougher as minds matured.
>
> Now Christmas is the comet, more's the pity.
>
> I love Christmas. I always shall. When no one can know that I can see the star, I will see the star, if I see anything as I now see. I will hear the sounds of Christmas, if then I hear anything as I now hear. And I will sing and smell and taste and swell in the heart and walk with those I love. Surely, there cannot be an end to the blessing of Christmas, whatever else changes.
>
> And the comet-years will fly; let them, they are much swifter than I know, those dragging "nevers," or almost "nevers." Every ten years, change two numbers.
>
> It has taken a long time to know so little about time.[6]

A journal entry shows how he pointed a grieving woman to Christ and how she responded:

> At Christmastime a long time ago, a beautiful lady came to my office with some personal grief. She needed help and I was in a position to turn her mind to the Savior and some things that happened to him. We talked for a while, and she went her way. She came back at Christmastime with a shadow box she had lovingly prepared. She herself had lettered these words,

6. MDH-L to family, Hong Kong, Jan. 2, 1982.

"Though Christ a thousand times in Bethlehem be born,
If he is not born in thee, thy soul is still forlorn."[7]

WHAT WE LEARNED AT CHRISTMAS

The Hanks children felt truly blessed to have a mom and dad who taught them the true meaning of Christmas with traditions and scriptures and Christmas stories. They experienced giving and giving and more giving. They had happy Christmas mornings and peaceful Christmas Eves. They had Santa, but they also had Christ. They had presents, but they also had prayer. They had laughter, but they also had love.

Long after the footballs and board games and clock radios were gone, the real presents they gave to their children remain. The children couldn't have experienced a better upbringing in the crucible of faith and the expression of Christian service in action. They experienced not only unconditional love directed toward the children, but unconditional love and acceptance directed toward others of God's children, regardless of their background or association. The children learned that differences in faith and life do not preclude people from worth and importance in the eyes of God or in the eyes of their parents. Richard wrote:

> Thank you for teaching me about feeling and not just having. Thank you for pointing out the "weightier matters." Thank you for demonstrating belief through actions, rather than just delivering words. And thank you for sharing your love of the Savior and implanting in us the desire to feel that way someday.

Duff's favorite Christmas poem was written by Harrison R. Merrill. Their family always read it, among the many other wonderful writings each Christmas Eve.[8]

Christmas Eve on the Desert
By Harrison R. Merrill

Tonight, not one alone am I but three—
The Lad I was, the Man I am, and he
Who looks adown the coming future years
And wonders at my sloth. His hopes and fears
Should goad me to the manly game
Of adding to the honor of my name.
I'm Fate to him — that chap that's I, grown old.
No matter how much stocks and lands and gold
I save for him, he can't buy back a single day
On which I built a pattern for his way.

7. Lyrics translated from Johann Angelus Silesius (1624–77), "Though Christ a Thousand Times."

8. Harrison R. Merrill, "Christmas Eve on the Desert," in *Utah Sings! An Anthology of Contemporary Verse* (Provo: Utah Academy of Sciences, Arts, and Letters, 1934).

I, in turn, am product of that Boy
Who rarely thought of After Selves. His joy
Was in the present. He might have saved me woe
Had he but thought. The ways that I must go
Are his. He marked them all for me
And I must follow — and so must he –
My Future Self — Unless I save him!

Save? — Somehow that word,
Deep down, a precious thought has stirred!
Savior? — Yes, I'm savior to that "Me,"
That thoughtful After Person whom I see!
The thought is staggering! I sit and gaze
At my two Other Selves, joint keepers of my days!

Master of Christmas, You dared to bleed and die
That others might find life. How much more I
Should willingly give up my present days
To lofty deeds; seek out the ways
To build a splendid life. I should not fail
To set my feet upon the star-bound trail
For him — that After Self. You said that he
Who'd lose his life should find it, and I know
You found a larger life, still live and grow.
Your doctrine was, so I've been told, serve man.
I wonder if I'm doing all I can
To serve? Will serving help that Older Me
To be the man he'd fondly like to be?

Last night I passed a shack
Where hunger lurked. I must go back
And take a lamb. Is that the message of the Star
Whose rays, please God, can shine this far?
Tonight, not one alone am I, but three –
The Lad I was, the Man I am, and he
Who is my Future Self — nay, more:
I am his savior — that thought makes me four!
Master of Christmas, that Star of Thine shines clear.
Bless Thou the four of me — out here!

24

Athletics, Sports, and Fitness

It is not often you can find a religious leader you can sweat with.[1]

If ya done it, it ain't bragging.[2]

As with many other areas of his life, Duff was an athletic Renaissance man—he did it all, from amateur boxing to college basketball to winning the All-Church Basketball Tournament to being the play-by-play announcer for football games at the university to being chairman of the Deseret Gym to winning multiple state championships, and to membership on the President's Council on Physical Fitness and Sports for five United States presidents. "From the ball fields at West High to the University of Utah," Duff said, "athletics has given me the opportunity to enjoy physical exercise, while enjoying the company of good men in active competition."[3]

TEAM SPORTS

While Duff's most successful team sport was basketball,[4] he occasionally wondered aloud if baseball was his best sport and what might have happened if he had been able to continue playing. He said, "I liked playing baseball. We played in the American Legion and then the Wheaties Leagues at the two White Park softball fields right across from the fairgrounds. I also played a lot of underhand pitch softball—it was so popular. I remember the time King Kong Kelly came to pitch in Utah. Had a wicked arm whip—he called all his outfielders in, and then struck every batter out. We'd never seen that kind of pitcher in the valley."

COMPETITION AND SPORTSMANSHIP

Duff was good, and he knew it. Even in his journal, where he sometimes feigned modesty about his athletic endeavors, you could read between the lines and feel his competitive spirit. He loved to be active, and he loved to win—not

1. Published article about a conference for religious educators held at the University of Texas.
2. Dizzy Dean, interview, 1934.
3. MDH-L.
4. See pages 27–28, 33, and 78–80 for more details on his basketball success.

a win-at-all-costs attitude, but more of an I'm-going-to-be-courteous-and-full-of-sportsmanship-and-still-take-you-down attitude. He wrote, "I freely confess, with a certain amount of exultation and some sorrow, that I take an unconscionable pleasure in winning on the heels of an unconscionable joy in playing at all. I really, really love the activity and competition."[5]

He described a typical contest in his journal: "This was a meeting day, until the late afternoon, when I had a fine squash match with Lowell Durham that went down to the wire. He didn't win."

Richard wrote, "As Duff's son, I occasionally wondered if he suffered from the old saying, 'The older I get, the faster I ran in high school.' After I got older—and usually if he was beating me—I would occasionally pester him about that. But then there are all those darn newspaper clippings that prove the stories are true."

Duff was always a good sport, tough but sportsmanlike. When one of his general authority assignments included supervision of the church athletic program, he pushed for greater spirituality and sportsmanship. Being a good sport was always a part of his life. In the finals of the All-Church Basketball Tournament, one of his teammates was called for a foul. They had only six players, so every foul was important. Duff, who was the captain of the team and personally knew the official, went over to the scorers' table to ask about the call. Duff remembered the referee explaining the call to him, quickly and emphatically, including why he called it, and "what business was it of mine, anyway?"

Up came Duff's teammate Myron Hale. "Myron was either fighting or cursing somebody most of the time, and he tried to reach the ref through me," Duff said. "I just held him off, saying, 'Stay away, Myron.' He said, 'We're not playing for fun, you know.' I blocked his path and held his arm and said, '*Yes, we are!* Let the officials do their job and we'll do ours,' and I led him away by his shirttail."[6]

SPORTSCASTING CAREER

When he wasn't playing, Duff was often asked to announce various games. In the early days of TV, Duff and a partner did the play-by-play commentary for the University of Utah football games. Duff would interview the coaches and players before the game. Then, after the game, a film editor would cut out all the huddles and time-outs, and Duff and his partner would announce the game after the fact. "They would cut the games down, and then I would talk into a live microphone, watching it play by play, and we'd turn it into a one-hour game. Ralph Hardy at KSL hired me to do that, and they paid me handsomely," Duff remembered. "We didn't have very much of a future financially at that moment, and it paid our rent. It worked out well."

A television review in the *Variety* section of the *Deseret News* reported:

> Football fans who like their pigskin without delaying action should go for KSL-TV's playbacks of the Utah football games. Aired the day after the game, these

5. MDH-JE, Jan. 29, 1974.
6. MDH-R, Sept. 5, 2000.

Duff catching behind Joseph Fielding Smith (honorary first batter) at the opening ceremonies of the 1959 all-church softball tournament. *Courtesy Deseret News*

sessions cut out everything but actual play and last under an hour. Duff Hanks comments during the game, calling attention to upcoming plays that pack a wallop. He stays calm, which, considering the fact that the outcome of the game is already known, is a good thing. All told, KSL is doing a good job of bringing viewers the thrills of football, without the delays.[7]

HIS MENTAL GAME

As he got older and team sports were less of an option, Duff migrated toward individual racquet sports. And he was a fierce competitor, not big on losing, gracious, but determined.

7. *Variety*, television reviews, Oct. 31, 1951.

When Richard turned seventeen, he was a pretty good tennis player and could finally beat his Dad. But Duff wasn't going to lie down easily. After he started routinely losing games to Rich, he would bring out his mental game, saying things like "Nice game, Rich. Is it okay if I play right-handed for the rest of the match?" Or he would wonder aloud if Rich's shoes felt too tight. Or he would ask if the net was the correct height. What a competitor!

CHEERING FOR THE UNDERDOG

Duff often chose to verbally root for the underdog, regardless of which team he favored. And he just loved a great play or player. That proved a bit embarrassing at Utah Jazz basketball games when he would sometimes cheer in appreciation of a wonderful play by the opposing team. Some of the Jazz fans didn't appreciate his equal-minded appreciation for talent.

Nowhere was that more evident than in his support for the University of Utah (his alma mater) and Brigham Young University, on whose board he served for twenty years and where he spoke almost every year. One year at the BYU–Utah football game in Provo, he sat next to BYU president Jeffrey R. Holland in the president's box. Duff stood and sang, "A Utah Man Am I, Sir." Boldly. Loudly.

At the rematch the next year, coincidentally, he sat next to Utah president Chase Peterson in the University of Utah president's box, and he stood and sang the BYU fight song, "Rise and Shout, the Cougars Are Out." Boldly. Loudly.

He felt right at home both years. Those of us with him were nervous.

HANDBALL AND RACQUETBALL

In his early adulthood, Duff loved playing handball. He had been hitting balls against walls since his childhood. He liked the toughness of the sport—all the equipment was part of your body—hands, feet, and head. Given his travel schedule, he played as often as he could and ended up becoming one of the best players in the state, playing in and winning both city and state championships.

Over time as he aged, Duff began playing more and more racquetball, although he never really considered it as good a sport or as difficult as handball. Until his introduction to squash years later, he focused on playing for fun and in tournaments with a wide array of friends and other members of the Utah Racquetball Association, in which he served as an officer. He recorded, "I played racquetball again with Cecil Thursday morning, and we had a better game. He is a rugged competitor. I played him left-handed and barely beat him, he not knowing [that I usually play right-handed]."[8]

THE DESERET GYM

"Three of my favorite games came together in the halls of the Deseret Gym," Duff wrote. "I have always enjoyed swinging a bat in court. My original love of court games probably sprang out from playing 'wall ball' many years before at

8. MDH-JE, Boise, Idaho, 1977.

Duff kept his handball game sharp, 1975.

Washington School as a child. Later as racquetball and squash gained in popularity, I picked them up and became quite proficient."[9]

After decades of playing sports there, Duff was appointed chairman of the board of the Deseret Gym, a position he held for many years. The church had constructed the original Deseret Gym in 1910 and a new version in 1965, to promote physical education. And for many years the old Deseret Gym was also home for University of Utah and LDS High School basketball games.

Duff tried to get to the Deseret Gym at least a couple of times a week at lunch or before going home at night. He loved to work up a sweat and try to keep his body healthy. When he did get a rare Saturday at home, he would often grab Rich, and they would play squash or racquetball.

To the dismay of a valley full of athletes, the Deseret Gym was torn down in 1997 to make room for the church's new Conference Center.

SQUASH

In the mid-1970s, Duff hired Rainer Ratinac to move to Utah and become the gym's in-house squash professional. Ratinac was from Australia and was one of the leading players on the North American squash circuit in the 1970s. Those were

9. MDH-R, June 20, 2000.

Duff pitching to grandson, Daniel, in Maryland, 1991.

fun days—the Deseret Gym had its own squash professional! A lot of young people became quite proficient, and enthusiasm for the sport skyrocketed in Utah.

Rainer was well connected, so he convinced the best players in the world to make stops in Utah for local tournaments and clinics. The local players got to meet and hit a few balls with members of the Kahn family, who were the top players in the world for decades.

Even in his mid-fifties, Duff wasn't content at being just an administrator at the Gym. He had picked up the squash bug too and added a squash championship to his handball and racquetball collection. "At eleven o'clock, I met Judge Aldon Anderson in a different kind of court, thank goodness—the squash court—where I defeated him for the Utah State Seniors Squash Championship," he recorded in his journal.

"It has been a long time getting around to the finals, but I was glad to have it over with. Unfortunately, it was not a particularly pleasant experience, since I got lashed to death with his left hand which he doesn't control well, but I won and got the trophy. I also got a lump on my elbow, one on my wrist, one on my hand and another on my forearm. The big bruise on my leg is sure to go away sometime also."[10]

PLAYING AT THE YMCA

In typical Duff fashion, while he was chairman of the Deseret Gym, he also continued to play squash and get the occasional steam bath at the YMCA, which was the Deseret Gym's only real competition. He really felt the need to reach out

10. MDH-JE, June 25, 1975.

to everyone in the community. The physical plant of the YMCA was significantly inferior to that of the Deseret Gym, but it had its own charm, with communal spittoons and dimly lit hallways to the squash courts.

Duff even petitioned the First Presidency of the church to donate twenty-five thousand dollars to the YMCA. "We have a highly constructive and pleasant relationship with the YMCA," he wrote. "We stand in similar position with them in the matters of taxation. They represent largely the non-LDS population of the city in their activities, though some of our people participate also." The First Presidency agreed and allowed Duff to make the donation to his friends over at the "Y."

TAKING ON ALL COMERS

Duff's reputation would often precede him to a city where he was going to speak. Groups would line up their best handball or squash players for a game, and he'd thrash them. Said one California church leader, "Elder Hanks was a man's man. He was an outstanding athlete and took great delight in schooling many who fancied themselves as great handball or squash players. During one visit to the Monterey Stake, I set him up with Gaylord Swim for a squash match. Gaylord was in his early 20's at the time and had the advantage of having his own squash court to practice on. Elder Hanks scarcely worked up a sweat in disposing of Gaylord."[11]

Duff commented on playing wherever he traveled: "While most of my playing time was spent at the Deseret Gym or at the YMCA courts, I also gained quite a reputation across the country. Sometimes, while I was traveling or giving a speech to a college or military group, I would get a challenge from a strong local player who might have heard that I could swing an arm or a racquet."

One of Duff's favorite memories was speaking at the University of Texas at a conference for religious educators. He spoke on Sunday night and then had to wait a few days to speak again. At the end of his first talk (on how church members felt about fitness), he asked some of the young men how they spent their free time. They mentioned handball. Duff told them he played a little. The next morning, three of them showed up to play, and he beat them all. Later, he teamed with a Methodist minister, and they topped the best doubles players at the school.

Henry Jacoby, who was co-chair of the event, wrote, "It was a surprise to us that a man in his position would take his religion out onto a handball court. He beat the boys. He beat the best player in our frat. Then he played Roger Tolar, the top player at the University and beat him. He beat us all, and he was 15 years older! Everybody liked him. It is not often you can find a religious leader you can sweat with."[12]

---

11. Correspondence between two friends, copy sent to MDH.
12. Article about a conference for religious educators held at the University of Texas.

Elder Marion D. Hanks fires opening shot as members of 14 BYU stakes take off on 4.5-mile run.

2,400 from Y. stakes run for fitness

Encouraging fitness at a running event, BYU, 1979. *Courtesy Church News*

EVANGELIST FOR FITNESS AND HEALTH

Duff became a leading evangelist for fitness, athletics, and health not only for the church but for the entire country. By 1959, he was speaking all over the country on fitness and athletics. As a member of President Dwight D. Eisenhower's Citizens' Committee on Youth Fitness, he was tasked to help improve the physical welfare of the nation's youth. Duff enlarged the conversation at every opportunity to include not just physical fitness, but also mental, moral, and spiritual fitness—including standards and values being reflected by youth.

In an article titled "Fitness for What?" in *Sports Illustrated*, Duff wrote, "The most important question we have to ask is not 'what fitness, but fitness for what?'" He continued, "Neither muscular development, intellectual brilliance, social competence, nor church attendance is itself our objective." What we really want for our young people is that they be fit to live meaningful, constructive lives. The young are like their parents. They are responsive to influence outside the home and susceptible to the environment. They can be guided toward moral behavior, but they quickly discern when conduct is not consistent with counsel."[13]

In a speech recorded in the *Congressional Record*, Utah Congressman David S. King added his support for a well-rounded fitness program, including intellectual, moral, and spiritual fitness as well as physical fitness. He wrote, "Just as man does not live by bread alone, so he cannot conquer his problems by muscle alone." He also quoted President David O. McKay, who observed, "Flabbiness of character, rather than flabbiness of muscle, is at the root of the problems of American youth." Congressman King then read into the record several lengthy quotations from Duff and then almost the full text of a speech Duff had given at the White

13. Quoted in *Sports Illustrated*, Oct. 26, 1959, 38–39.

House Conference on Youth the previous year. The essence of Duff's speech had been to point out the narrowness of any national fitness effort that focused on physical fitness alone. He pleaded with the country to teach our youth that the *kind of people* they are matters.

PRESIDENT'S COUNCIL ON PHYSICAL FITNESS AND SPORTS

In 1954, well-known New York City physician Hans Kraus published the results of a study showing that American boys and girls were woefully unfit compared to the children of Western Europe. The report created a national sensation and triggered a series of meetings culminating with President Eisenhower formally establishing the forerunner of the President's Council on Physical Fitness and Sports, called the Citizens' Advisory Committee on Youth Fitness. Duff was invited to participate, representing the church; there he met Shane McCarthy, a famous Catholic university professor and a close friend of the pope. McCarthy had a right-hand man named Ott Romney, who invited McCarthy to come to Salt Lake and learn from Duff how the church put on programs. McCarthy recommended that Duff be appointed to the President's Council on Physical Fitness and Sports, on which he served through the terms of five United States presidents. "It was a real privilege to serve on the President's Council on Physical Fitness and Sports and its predecessors," he said. "I was pleased to represent the church with some of the most famous athletes and leaders this country has produced. For many years I was able to rub shoulders with people of real quality and character, like Sammy Lee the Olympic diver, and Jim Lovell the *Apollo 13* astronaut. We made a lasting and important impression on America's youth by emphasizing the importance of fitness and athletic involvement, at a time when it was far less understood."

Duff believed that his duty as a member of the President's Council on Physical Fitness and Sports was an extension of his work for the church. He taught that the Council's emphasis on regular exercise, good living habits, and quality of life was in perfect harmony with the teachings of the church. He said, "The Lord has given us the rules; we must be wise enough to use them. Good health is often a matter of good judgment."

Among his peers on the President's Council, Duff became known for his ability to analyze a situation and compress the details of a lengthy discussion into a brief, concise summary. C. Carson Conrad, executive director of the President's Council, said, "Duff is the kind of person you want on your team. He is a man of great ability and deep convictions, and he is the kind of person who can do just about anything. He gets the job done."[14]

Another fellow member of the Council was Sammy Lee, an American physician and the first man to win back-to-back gold medals in Olympic platform diving. Sammy wrote to Duff, "You are a living legend of total fitness—physical,

14. PCOPFAS *Newsletter*, Washington, DC, Jan. 1976.

mental, and spiritual. If we practiced what you preach, our world would be a far better one when we leave, than we found it."[15]

In 1978, Duff received the Distinguished Service Award from the President's Council on Physical Fitness and Sports in recognition of his outstanding contributions to the national program of fitness over two decades.

Years later, Duff received a letter from Clark T. Thorstenson, a youth leadership professor at BYU, who had been invited to speak at the First National Conference on Fitness and Aging. He wrote that wherever he went he was greeted by comments such as "We know all about the Mormons—Elder Hanks served with us for years" or "Elder Hanks taught me well in his gracious way about your health code" or "You Mormons have it all together." Thorstenson summarized Duff's outsized impact: "There were numerous others who asked to be remembered and say how much they appreciated your Christlike influence. How wonderful it was for me to be there and realize that the church has had a magnificent 'forerunner' among so many influential and respected leaders of our nation."[16]

15. Sammy Lee's inscription in a copy of his book given to Duff.
16. BYU professor Clark T. Thorstenson to MDH, Sept. 28, 1981.

canyon. Duff was convinced that through heavy work and moving rocks around in the stream, they could successfully reroute it to ensure it didn't erode the dirt from the tree roots on either side. Consequently, the men of the family spent many hours in hip waders, not fishing, but lifting and moving "binnies" (rocks), as Duff would call them, from one side of the stream to the other. The next year they would assault the stream from the other side, tossing rocks and digging with shovels. He described those efforts: "We had good food and good work, including some rock shifting that made the spring run-off less fearful. It is pleasant to work with our four sons-in-law and Rich. We all put on hip waders and got into it with them. They are great men, each and every. I would not trade them for any."[2] One could suppose that over forty years, Duff and the boys touched every rock in that section of the stream.

WORK! FIRES! CHOPPING WOOD!

It seems that most people who own cabins go to them to relax. Not Duff. Three of his favorite things in life were at the cabin: working with his hands; building and enjoying fires; and splitting, chopping, and sawing wood.

Duff loved to work—any time, any place. But he especially loved working at the cabin. When he wasn't working, he was probably reading about working. He just loved reading books by David Grayson, as anyone who visited their cabin can attest. He'd invite the visitors in, sit them down, pull out a book, and start reading. Here is one of his favorite passages from David Grayson: "Happiness, I have discovered, is nearly always a rebound from hard work.... She loves sweat, weariness, self-sacrifice. She will be found not in palaces, but lurking in cornfields and factories and hovering over littered desks; she crowns the unconscious head of the busy child. If you look up suddenly from hard work, you will see her—but if you look too long, she fades sorrowfully away."[3]

No one will ever accuse Duff of being afraid to get his hands dirty. Some favorite pictures of him are taken in the middle of the stream, boots on, gloves on, with a look of determination. Family members were taught to work, really work, at an early age. Even when Duff had a little more money, he never hired someone to mow the lawn or shovel the snow. When he finally came home with a snowblower, Rich asked him, "Who are you, and what have you done with my dad?" Duff didn't get a power lawn mower for decades after his neighbors.

The cabin was the perfect place for Duff to hone his children's skills at labor. They dug and swept and shoveled and repaired. For the first five years or so, they would mush in through the snow in the winter to see if they could pry some of the deep snow off the roof with shovels and long poles. It was a real joy to him when a huge chunk of snow would come free and crash to the deck below.

One summer Duff and Rich were building a lean-to shed on the side of the

2. MDH-JE, 1977.
3. David Grayson, *Adventures in Contentment* (New York: Grosset and Dunlap, 1942).

Duff "adjusting" the rocks in the stream, Provo Canyon, ca. 1977.

cabin, and he let Rich lead the process. When Rich thought they were finished, because the outside looked pretty good, Duff asked how the inside looked. Then later, he had Rich read David Grayson's story of Charles Baxter. The village doctor had hired Baxter to make a table. He was observed finishing the under part of the drawer slides. The doctor asked, "Baxter, why do you spend so much time on that table? Who's going to know whether or not the last touch has been put on the underside of it?"

Baxter looked at the doctor in surprise. "Why, I will," he said.

Message received and remembered—even now, fifty years later.

Sometimes his family would wonder whether Duff really wanted to work that much or if he was just trying to instill a strong work ethic in his children. Perhaps a little of both. Getting him to take any kind of vacation was almost impossible. Even after the family arrived at their destination, he'd hang back from some of the activities to read, study, or prepare a speech.

Boy, did Duff love fireplaces! He always had wood-burning fireplaces in their homes, even when they were losing popularity—he didn't care. When he and Maxine built the cabin, he included a huge brick fireplace in which he could make the fire roar. Long before he had the cabin, he wrote the following journal entry: "Fireplaces have had a fascination for me unlike almost anything else in the world. Since I was a little boy, and lay hour after hour in front of our little fireplace at home reading books, I have delighted in sitting in front of a fire. We are greatly blessed to have a fine fireplace, and I observe with joy that my children are already as pleased to sit in front of a roaring wood fire as I am."[4]

Duff taught any of his grandchildren who were interested (and some that weren't) how to build a fire the correct way, with crumpled paper as the fuel, followed by kindling, followed by branches and sticks of increasing diameter until the fire was just right for the large split logs. And not to be forgotten was the strangely named "back log," which despite its name was placed by Duff at the very front of the fire to keep as much of the fire in the fireplace and not spark out into the room. Occasionally, someone could get him to cheat and use a Duraflame log, and only once or twice, when he was in a big hurry, was he caught spraying some charcoal briquet lighter fluid on the wood before lighting it.

Right after fires and fireplaces on his list of joys was getting out the chainsaw, the axe, the sledgehammer, and wedges. He just loved chopping and splitting wood for the fire. He would cut and split logs until the pile was huge, and then all would carefully stack the wood, get a drink, refill the chainsaw with gas, and start again. His hands would go numb, and Rich recalls seeing him shaking his gloved hands every few minutes. None of his family really understood why he did that. Now that they are in their sixties and seventies, they understand.

He wrote, "I am pleased for the opportunity to be at the cabin for a few days getting acquainted with the beauties of the valleys and mountains of the Wasatch. I discovered that my long-loved, two-bladed woodman's axe is still effective, that the chainsaws have their valued place, and the most fun of all—splitting logs with a sledgehammer and wedges. There are few sounds as exciting as a log splitting when the hammer falls and the wedge goes deep."[5]

FRIENDS

Duff had a few close friends he confided in, but he and Maxine really didn't have many close couple friends (see pages 231–32). His horrendous travel schedule and his sometimes reclusive nature made cultivating couple friendships difficult. Among his closest friends were Bob Thompson, Homer Ellsworth, Keith Garner, Paul Pehrson, and Coy Miles.

Bob Thompson and Duff grew up together, played on the All-Church Championship basketball team, and went to the same mission. They loved each other and could finish each other's sentences. They lifted each other up all their lives. Duff wrote, "Being with Bob and Donna Thompson emphasized the importance of friendships and love and gave us a new feeling of appreciation and gratitude for the sweet blessings of our lives."[6]

Homer Ellsworth was Maxine's obstetrician. He delivered Richard (and coincidentally, his wife, Liz) and became Duff's dear friend and later his counselor in the Salt Lake Temple presidency. Duff commented on his love for Homer: "After

4. MDH-JE, Nov. 15, 1960.
5. Handwritten note, n.d.
6. MDH-JE, Dec. 31, 1975.

a meeting, Homer and I went to Rotary and had a good time together. I love that big man and tremble to think of my world without Homer Ellsworth. I don't see him all that much, but I love him as well as I could a brother and have every confidence in the world in him, and a love that is unconditional. He is generous and warm and consistent, without being ostentatious or obnoxious. He is full of concern for his fellow men, and very generous in sharing his great personal and professional talents and is withal the kind of Christian all should be."[7]

Duff met Keith Garner when Keith was serving as a mission president in Hong Kong. Keith and Duff traveled throughout Vietnam during the war to comfort and uplift LDS servicemen. One could suppose that the statement "friends are made in foxholes" is a true one, because they remained friends the rest of their lives.

Paul Pehrson was twelve years older and owned Pehrson Hardware in Sugar House. The best possible outing for Duff was to get in the car and drive out to Pehrson's to look at hardware while talking with Paul. Unfortunately, Paul died thirty-five years before Duff. Duff described him as "a dear friend and as good a man as ever lived. I miss him constantly."

Coy Miles and Duff attended law school together, started and stopped a business together, and lived across the street from each other when their kids were growing up. Duff and Maxine's children called Coy and Blanche Miles "Uncle Coy" and "Aunt Blanche." Near the end of their lives, Coy wrote Duff a note that said, "Thank all the eternal powers that be—for you and your unquenchable willingness to oppose that which is wrong—your vision to see what really needs to be done—your valor to do the deed—without credit or recognition. Your forever identity with the right—the *champion* of the good, the noble, the beautiful. Your greatness has blessed me."[8]

CREATING ANXIETY

It is unknown if Duff suffered from anxiety or not, because if that was the case, he kept it well hidden. But he certainly created anxiety in some of his children with some of the things he did. Three things come to mind.

First, it was not unusual for him to read the obituaries, which he did every day, and then exclaim how he hoped he would go out with a "nice clean heart attack."

When he was leaving to go on long trips, he would tell his children where all the legal papers, wills, back-up cash, and family documents were located—"in case I don't make it back."

He also took his children with him many weekends to the LDS Hospital to visit people and give blessings. In Rich's opinion, ten-year-old children should not be exposed to that kind of suffering and illness.

Rich wrote, "There are very, very few things about Dad that I would change or that I regret him doing. But I was careful not to do those three things with my children."

7. MDH-JE, July 29, 1975.

8. Coy Miles, handwritten note, n.d.

OUTDOOR FUN

Duff really loved having fun in the mountains but was rarely able to enjoy it. He did get the occasional chance to ride motorcycles with Keith Garner in Heber City and to ride snowmobiles with his dear friend Ray Curtis. Duff wrote, "This afternoon I went snowmobiling with Ray. We had a delightful time, one of the happiest of my life. The machines are fast and reliable, and we went from Park City across the mountain to Brighton and back in three hours. I really love Ray, and we had a great time. He seeks me out for the occasional opportunity, and I am grateful. It really does something for me."[9]

PATRIOT

Duff loved America. Those with him stood at ballgames with hands over their hearts until the flag left the field, regardless of what others around them were doing. Don't even think of hollering for the home team before the national anthem is completed. And Duff always had the flag of the United States of America flying over his home. Another great memory is when Duff and Richard installed the flagpole on the city side of their house on Chandler Circle. There wasn't a lot of space around where the flagpole needed to go, and Duff wanted it to be buried deep in concrete. So they needed to dig a narrow but very deep hole. Duff held Rich by his knees and then later by his ankles while he lowered Rich's six-foot six-inch frame headfirst into the hole. Rich would then dig and fill up buckets until the blood rushed to his head.

Duff once wrote a letter to the First Presidency, expressing how beautiful the American flag looked on Temple Square and suggesting, "I wonder if our members would not respond to an invitation from you to fly the flag, and if it would be appropriate to offer that admonition."[10]

Duff was respectful of the final resting places of his family members. He'd take the family there and then tell stories. He also loved to tell stories about World War II and bravery and heroics and visit military cemeteries, "where the best men of this world lie." He wrote, "I was in Philadelphia, on my way to Valley Forge to speak to a group of Boy Scouts, and passed by the place where Thomas Jefferson wrote the Declaration of Independence. All the way there I thought about the marvelous declaration of conviction and commitment that had come from that unostentatious place. The Declaration of Independence is a great statement of principle. "This is what we believe," it says, "and this is where we stand. In defense of these principles, we commit our lives, our fortunes, and our sacred honor." … So it is with every major experience of life. There is the commitment and the opportunity to meet the subsequent tests. There is the declaration and the valley, and there is the inevitable triumph when courage and quality meet the tests.[11]

---

9. MDH-JE, n.d.
10. MDH-L to the First Presidency, July 8, 1969.
11. NF, 124–25.

Richard, Duff, and dog Pierre, at their home on Butler Avenue, ca. 1966.

SINGING

Duff loved to sing and sing vigorously. He'd belt out whatever song he was singing, and one always had confidence he'd be in tune. He had memorized all the hymns, but he'd open a hymnbook sometimes just to see if he could sing another part or harmonize with the melody. He loved the hymns of Zion and loved to listen to the Tabernacle Choir. He loved barbershop music. His family sang "Edelweiss," "Love at Home," "Merry Christmas from Our House to Your House," and "I love to go a-wandering ... val-deri, val-dera ..." He would often sing around the house—songs from the latest musical they had seen, or with Robert Goulet or Eddy Arnold, whose record albums he owned.

HARDWARE STORES

Duff never met a hardware store he didn't love, and when the big box companies like Home Depot started opening stores near him, he was thrilled. He wasn't a hoarder, but he did like to hang on to tools and supplies and other hardware items. He had boxes and toolboxes full of sprinklers from two houses ago, leftover supplies (just in case he needed them), and small glass bottles and cans of orphaned screws and nails and all manner of hardware. For white elephant gifts, family members would occasionally wrap up decades old items from his military days—MREs, canned water, and Kadota figs in the typical gray cans of the navy. There was no way to know how old those things were, and no one ever wanted to open them to find out, so the kids would rewrap them and save them to regift the next year.

ICE CREAM, MEAT PIES, AND CHEESE

Duff loved Italian food, ice cream, meat pies, and cheese—the more pungent, the better. He taught his entire family to love them. Meat pies were a reminder to him of the happy days of his youth when a Morrison meat pie, covered with watered-down ketchup, was all that his mother, Maude, could afford.

Duff also loved ice cream and cheese, and this was an area of his life where cracks occasionally showed in his discipline. There are great memories of a couple of late nights staying up until midnight with Duff, watching *Gunsmoke* and downing an entire half gallon of Snelgrove's burnt almond fudge or caramel cashew ice cream.

One time he wrote a major confession from a hotel in Idaho: "In the afternoon, I purchased a piece of watermelon and a jug of orange juice, and I consumed both before going to bed. This is a change from some of my ancient habits, though not much of an advantage in calories. The food provided the proper sustenance anyway, and I enjoyed it more than the ice creams and rolls of the past."[12]

And finally, anyone who really knew Duff knew that cheese was to be put on, or in, or around, almost everything—sandwiches, soups, eggs, crackers, vegetables, toast—anything and everything.

THINGS AND MONEY

"God promised the Nephite people as a community that if they would keep his commandments, they would 'prosper in the land,' taught Elder Bruce C. Hafen. "We ordinarily assume the word 'prosper'" in this context means material prosperity. I once heard Elder Marion D. Hanks offer an alternative interpretation; namely, that 'prosper in the land' means being within the constant influence of the Lord's presence. He derives this interpretation from the Lord's phrasing of his promise: 'Inasmuch as ye shall keep my commandments ye shall prosper in the land; but inasmuch as ye will not keep my commandments ye shall be cut off from my presence'" (2 Nephi 1:20).[13]

Duff's perception of the word *prosper* was indeed different from most. Neither Maxine nor Duff ever expressed much interest in buying the latest thing. Duff was simply the opposite of the word *accumulate*. He dressed nicely, but he wouldn't know a clothing trend if it smacked him in the face. In later years, he sometimes leased newish and nicer cars from his car dealer friends, but all the cars he and Maxine permanently owned were "beaters." But he did like to splurge occasionally and buy a brand-new chainsaw.

Frankly, Duff wasn't all that proficient with math and numbers—he didn't really care much about them. When Richard told him once that he was paying more than eleven percent tithing, he just smiled and invited him to mind his own business. Duff always seemed to be owed money from other people for emergency

12. MDH-JE, Idaho, Aug. 19, 1977.

13. Bruce C. Hafen, "Come, Come, Ye Saints," *BYU Speeches*, Aug. 28, 1995.

Duff in his favorite overcoat, at his desk in his study.

loans or bailouts he'd make to help someone in need. He was quick to let his kids borrow money for an activity, but it was never just handed over. Even asking him for twenty bucks for a date turned into a teaching moment. He would explain that he was pleased to help them, but that they should be grateful for everything God had given them.

Maxine's father, Elwood Christensen, who was very successful financially, promised to build her a new house, which he did in 1976. Whereas their previous two houses had been cozy and unobtrusive, this new home was much larger and built high up the mountainside in Arlington Hills in Salt Lake City. Duff never became accustomed to it—and he was uncomfortable because of its visibility. He was very pleased when they finally moved back to a more modest home in a modest neighborhood.

Occasionally, people will have the nerve to ask how they had the money to build cabins in Utah, and in Maui. The answer about the Utah cabin is that they made payments on it for many years, and it had been built at cost fifty years earlier by his friend Keith Garner, who was a developer. The answer about Hana is 100 percent Maxine's father, who owned the land, and when he died both the land and enough money to build on it passed to Maxine. Duff was pleased to have a place in Hawaii that Maxine could visit each year until the end of their lives. She had left her home and family forty-three years earlier to marry Duff, and he considered it a privilege to be able to partially make up for that by living in Hana each year for a few months.

GROWING AMIABLE RELATIONSHIPS

26

Community and Civic Involvement

Duff is one of those Mormons who is a bridge to the community. His friends are as wide and varied among non-Mormons as Mormons.
—Wallace F. Bennett, US senator[1]

Duff was a community bridge builder. And it wasn't just club luncheons. When he joined, he was all in. For years, he served as the strongest tie between the church and leaders of the non-LDS community in Salt Lake City and the state of Utah. Over time he was elected to regional and then national positions of various organizations and was a candidate to become president of two national organizations when he was unexpectedly called to be the executive administrator of the church in Asia, based in Hong Kong (see pages 456, 465, and 475 for more detail).[2]

As in most areas of his life, Duff tried to do what was right and leave potential politics out of the equation. As mentioned earlier, once he found out that the YMCA was in trouble financially, he would go play squash there—which wouldn't really seem all that unusual until you learn that he was chairman of the Deseret Gym, and the YMCA was their main competition.

One Christmas, he and a local Jewish businessman together rang the charity bell for the Salvation Army kettle in front of ZCMI, the church-owned department store. Between them, they knew a large number of those walking by, whom they would call over by name. They raised more money in three hours than the rest of the kettles in the state combined.

Duff explained his feelings about his civic involvement. He wrote, "I enjoy mingling a bit with the non-religious crowd in these occasional speeches. It is a pleasure to be involved in some measure in pursuits which are in a way temporal, but have great meaning in life."[3]

Duff's involvement with civic and community organizations began early in his career. At one time, he served as chairman of the Utah Committee on Children and Youth and was the keynote speaker at the White House Conference on

1. Scrapbook tribute upon Duff's being made emeritus.
2. The executive administrator title was later changed to area president.
3. MDH-JE, Nov. 1973.

Children and Youth in 1960. He was either chairman or a member of the United Fund, the Community Chest, the Salvation Army, the Speakers Bureau, the Bonneville Knife and Fork Club, the Salt Lake County Cancer Society, the Mental Health Society, the Crippled Children's Society, the Sons of Utah Pioneers, the Utah Council on Family Relations, the Governor's Council on Physical Fitness, and others.

As noted earlier, he was appointed a member of the United States President's Youth Fitness Committee, which was a presidential appointment. He served under Dwight D. Eisenhower, John F. Kennedy, and Richard M. Nixon, and under Gerald Ford and Jimmy Carter, when it was renamed the President's Council on Physical Fitness and Sports. When he retired from the council during the fourth year of President Carter's term, he was the longest-serving appointee. In scouting, Duff served on every level from the local council to the national executive board. He chaired numerous committees over the years and was approached to be a candidate for president of Boy Scouts of America in 1982 but had to resign when he was called to Hong Kong. He received every possible award that Scouting gives, including the Silver Beaver, Silver Antelope, and Silver Buffalo and was the first honorary recipient of the National Eagle Scout Association.

Duff joined Rotary International and was quickly tapped for leadership positions. He served as president of the Salt Lake Club, district governor, group leader and instructor at international conventions. He was nominated as a director of Rotary, in line to be elected the next president. He had to decline that opportunity when he was called to serve in Hong Kong.

In the academic world, Duff served at various times on the governing bodies of Weber State College, Snow College, Southern Utah State College, and Brigham Young University.

Duff's weekends were filled with travel and stake conferences. His weeknights were filled with firesides and other events and the chance to be at home with his family. But he still had time to squeeze in weekday speeches at various clubs and nonprofit organizations. And the invitations were constant.

Duff considered it vital that the church be represented as a participant in community and national arenas. Outside of a smattering of politicians, Duff was often the only church leader working with other faiths and traditions. He was sometimes criticized both to his face, and behind his back by some of his peers in church leadership for spending so much time on civic leadership outside of his church responsibilities. This type of viewpoint demonstrated the provincial and insular attitude shared by many members and leaders.

Duff's journals are replete with letters that both expressed gratitude for his service and asked him why more of his colleagues in church leadership didn't get more involved in external organizations, but remained so inward-centric.

Duff hoped to see the day that not only would church leaders become more involved in their communities but the entire missionary force of the church would be heavily involved in community service. He was pleased to see the church move steadily in that direction before he died (see chapter 47, pages 441–52.).

REPRESENTING YOUTH

One example of the power of Duff's involvement comes from a national conference held in February 1960. Duff was asked to act as a group leader in a workshop of Religious Leaders of Youth. Leading representatives of every large religious denomination in America, the chief of chaplains of every service and military academy, and many religion journalists would be attending. When he asked the First Presidency if he might attend, Duff was instructed to go to the Friday meeting in Washington, DC, but was not relieved of his assigned church responsibilities in Salt Lake on Thursday night nor his stake conference assignment in Las Vegas on Saturday and Sunday.

After flying all night, as he often did, he arrived at the Washington, DC, location, where Dr. Elson, minister of the national Presbyterian Church, was speaking. Elson announced that he had three parishioners he was particularly proud of because of their interest in youth—J. Edgar Hoover, Dwight D. Eisenhower, and Supreme Court associate justice Tom Clark, who would be the next speaker.[4]

Justice Clark opened his talk by quoting Paul to the Corinthians: "For if the trumpet give an uncertain sound, who shall prepare himself to the battle?"[5] Justice Clark then proceeded to indict religion and religious leaders as being inadequately interested in the young, saying that the problem with delinquency in America was with the adults, not the young. He noted that while he thought Dr. Elson was a great preacher, he hadn't observed in his church a Scout room or a recreation area where young people could gather and do things or where young and old would like to be. He then went on to charge everyone in attendance with a lack of leadership and courage.

When he sat down, host Shane MacCarthy went to the pulpit, motioned Dr. Elson away, and then said in substance, "I have high regard for Justice Clark, but I doubt that he will want his talk to go into the record, because it is not justified and not true." He then pointed out "Mr. Marion D. Hanks in the audience who had flown all the way from Salt Lake City and who represented a church that could refute point by point what Mr. Clark has said about recreation halls, Scout rooms, and so forth."

Mr. MacCarthy then asked Justice Clark to open the book in his hands, a copy of proceedings at the Air Force Academy in September 1959, to the page where the talk Duff had given at the academy was printed. MacCarthy then read some of the paragraphs, noting that Duff's talk had been a very well-organized statement of adult responsibility, just as Clark had pointed out. Then MacCarthy said,

4. J. Edgar Hoover was the first director of the FBI. Dwight D. Eisenhower was the thirty-fourth president of the United States.

5. 1 Corinthians 14:8.

"And just incidentally, Justice Clark, Mr. Hanks, like you, concluded his sermon with the same quotation from Paul to the Corinthians, 'For if the trumpet give an uncertain sound, who shall prepare himself to the battle?"

Duff recalled, "I have never seen an important public figure anywhere near as embarrassed as Mr. Clark was. He looked highly uneasy and soon excused himself and left before the meeting was concluded."

Following the general session, Duff and others led smaller groups in discussion, after which a number of attendees spoke confidentially and off the record about Duff's participation and especially about the church's attention to, and programs for, the youth. Duff continued, "My summation of this whole affair is to say that ... the church was the only organization represented that had a real program, and we were really the only ones there with much to say. This is not to be immodest—but only to recognize that lines are being slowly, but surely, drawn between this church and its programs and every other organization on the earth."

Following this remarkable experience, Duff flew all day to Las Vegas, where he conducted a stake conference, and then flew home.[6]

POLITICS AND OTHER OPTIONS

Politicians continued to try to interest Duff in running for public office. It might seem strange for a general authority to have been considered for public office, but there was precedent. Elder Reed Smoot was an apostle for forty-one years and a United States senator for thirty of those years (1903–33). Elder Ezra Taft Benson too was an apostle who served in the Eisenhower administration as Secretary of Agriculture, a Cabinet position, for eight of his fifty-one years of general church leadership.

Duff's name surfaced multiple times in political circles as a potential candidate, and he was announced in the press (without permission) as a candidate for US senator on at least two occasions. None of those times did the First Presidency offer him any encouragement. The closest he came to accepting such an opportunity was in 1976, but he ended up rejecting the approaches. Examples of some of the invitations to run for office or other professions are enlightening.

In 1961, Stan Darger reported, "I remember a member of a committee of the Republican Party calling on David O. McKay asking if it was possible to bring Duff home from England (1961–62), where he was serving as a mission president, to fill the position as an outstanding electable candidate for Congress. Not surprisingly, President McKay declined."[7]

In 1968, Duff told President McKay he had been approached again about leadership in youth fitness work. He reminded President McKay that years earlier, soon after the Kennedy administration assumed office, he was asked to accept the top position in youth leadership in the nation, but since this would have

6. MDH-JE, Feb. 5, 1960.

7. Stan Darger, in unknown newspaper clipping, 1961.

entailed much time in Washington, and possibly living there, President McKay told him not to accept it. About this later interview, Duff wrote, "He reaffirmed his feeling that I should not accept appointments which would require removal of residence, but he instructed me strongly to accept any invitation which would allow effective influence in behalf of youth. He said I must do this 'for the sake of the youth.'"[8]

In 1969, Duff was invited to become a university president. He reported that "President McKay seemed quite responsive as we discussed matters, including the possibility of my leaving church service to become president of a university. Feelers have come which I feel might be a way to contribute something else after many years here. President McKay didn't completely negate the idea of my leaving. He said that I must 'move slowly.'" Subsequently, Duff respectfully declined the opportunity.

In 1973, Senator Wallace F. Bennett decided not to run for the United States Senate again. Many potential candidates were rumored. In his journal, Duff wrote, "No one rumors me as an applicant (including me), but I wonder if it would be a good way to move to another career. Twenty years is a long time to have been here."[9]

In 1975, Richard saw his dad on television and called out, 'Hey, Dad, you're on TV!" Duff was surprised to see political commentators "speculating on my possible candidacy for the US Senate seat. They went on to quote (current senator) Frank Moss saying he would be 'scared if he had to run against Marion D. Hanks.' The whole thing left me cold."[10]

In 1976, Duff wrote, "I record for my own amusement that I allowed myself to think seriously about the possibility of politics this year and talked seriously with several about running for the office of United States Senator. President Kimball and President Tanner each inquired into my real feelings, as though they would seriously consider the possibility if I chose, and President Benson urged me to do it, but he didn't have in mind the complexities until we discussed them a bit."[11]

WEAVING DEVOTION BETWEEN CIGAR SMOKE

Duff purposely injected spiritual things into secular speeches he made at Rotary, Scouting, board meetings, and elsewhere. He didn't do this out of a compulsion to do missionary work; it just came naturally to him, and rarely was anyone offended.

About a speech to a Rotary district in Los Angeles, Duff wrote, "I was introduced by Harvey, who also introduced (daughter) Mary and Chris, who had been invited as his guests. They sat with the almost 100% non-LDS group and

8. MDH-L to Clare Middlemiss, reporting on a discussion with President David O. McKay, Dec. 24, 1968.

9. MDH-JE, June 25, 1973.

10. MDH-JE, Sept. 1975.

11. MDH-JE, Jan. 1976.

listened to me give a 'spiritual' message on that Sabbath morning. It worked out reasonably well, and I think all were pleased."[12]

On another occasion, he spoke at a Bonneville-Kiwanis Club luncheon to a lot of hard-headed businessmen who were always looking at their watches. When an attendee mentioned to those at his table that Duff's speech was going to be a tie-in to Easter, there was no great amount of enthusiasm evoked. He wrote to Duff, "Your masterful delivery and expressiveness and choice of subject matter changed the entire luncheon. My table full of anti-religious men were profoundly impressed, and one mentioned that he wished his wife had been there to enjoy it. What an outstanding meeting. Thank you again."[13]

Duff felt it important to pray in the name of Christ. He didn't make a big deal about it, he just did it. About a national Scout meeting in 1978, he wrote,

> I was asked to open with prayer, followed by dead silence when I finished in the name of Christ. This is not customary in Scouting, nor in other places, because of Jewish participants. So, few Christians do it. They have watered it down to keep from offending our Jewish friends. And the product of this is an abdication of conviction to pray in Christ's name. Another trend of the times is to change the words, "I believe," to "one does feel," but there are some good things worth believing and worth pursuing, not against good sense or sensitivity, but within those bounds, and that I will do.[14]

In one weekly report session of the general authorities, Elder J. Thomas Fyans proposed, and it was unanimously accepted, that Duff be "commended for the many outstanding services he renders for the church through his activities in the community." In particular, he was to be "celebrated for his recent presidency of the Bonneville Knife and Fork Club, which had invited Alex Hailey to be its keynote speaker, with Duff effectively using gospel principles and scriptures during the evening."[15]

12. MDH-JE, Apr. 7, 1979.

13. Keith C. Brown to MDH, Apr. 11, 1952.

14. MDH-JE, May 19, 1978.

15. Duff's notes from the meeting of the Presidency of the First Quorum of the Seventy, Oct. 12, 1978.

27

Humor

Laughter is the shortest distance between two people.
—Victor Borge

Duff loved to laugh, and he loved telling jokes, or "funnies," as he would call them—speech icebreakers, intellectual humor, funny replies to letters or questions he received, and on and on. And his humor wasn't always prepared for public consumption. Often, he'd just respond to ordinary inquiries or experiences with his legendary wit. One had to be on one's toes in order not to miss his clever responses.

ICEBREAKERS

Duff loved to begin his remarks with a joke or two. Usually, these would relate to the subject at hand. When speaking at a national educators' function, he told the story of a little girl who returned from her first day at school and said, "I'm not going back."

"Why not?" her mother asked.

She replied, "I can't read. I can't write. And guess what? They won't let me talk!"

Sometimes the joke had nothing to do with his remarks but just made Duff laugh, and he wanted to share the fun with others.

He told of a little boy sitting on the curb, smoking a cigar, when a police truant officer approached and asked, "Why aren't you in school, young man?" To which the boy replied, "Hell, Mister, I'm only four."

Like most people who love humor, Duff had jokes rotate in and out of his mind over the years, but he kept a few favorites to be repeated over and over. Here are a few (summarized) examples:

Did you hear about the cross-eyed discus thrower? Answer: He didn't set records, but he sure kept the crowd awake.

A golfer was having a brutal round. All his shots were off. He turned to his caddy, saying, "You, sir, are the world's worst caddy." To which the caddy replied, "No, sir, that would be just too much of a coincidence."

There is a bakery in England that put up this sign: "WE SELL THE QUEEN BISCUITS." The bakery across the street put up their sign: "GOD SAVE THE QUEEN."

Duff telling a 'funny' during a BYU devotional address, 1982. *Courtesy BYU*

Police officer questioning an injured man on the ground: "Can you describe the man that hit you?" Answer: "That's what I was doing when he hit me."

During a talk at Brigham Young University, he said, "I want to pay tribute to my wife, the mother of five extraordinary children and a wonderful person, the same way Duffy Daugherty of Michigan State paid tribute to his wife. He said that he often returned from the banquet circuit very late, very tired, but always, he said, 'to find things in perfect order in the home—dinner in the oven, slippers and jacket laid out, plenty of hot water. She hates to see me wash dishes in cold water.'"[1]

The story is told of the man who went to a psychiatrist for evaluation. When the doctor came to present the diagnosis the patient said, "That's what's wrong with me, isn't it, Doc? I have an inferiority complex, don't I?" The doctor said, "No, sir, that isn't your problem at all. You don't have an inferiority complex. You *are* inferior."

During another talk at BYU, he said, "There is the story about the boy who was having troubles with mathematics. The teacher, anxious to help him, brought him some physical objects and said to him, "Now, Tommy, if I have ten apples and I take five away, what's the difference?" Tommy answered, "That's how I feel about it, teacher. What's the difference?"[2]

After a talk he gave in Hong Kong, he wrote, "Sunday I spoke in our home ward in Kam Tong Hall, the Victorian Ward, and enjoyed myself. Only mothers who had babies to pinch left early."[3]

1. MDH-T, "The Banquet of Consequences," BYU, Oct. 3, 1967.
2. MDH-T, "Fuller Understanding," BYU, Nov. 16, 1982.
3. MDH-L to family, Dec. 27, 1980.

WITH FAMILY AND FRIENDS

On one occasion, he walked in late to a family dinner, and his daughter Ann asked him how his doctor's appointment had gone. He replied, "Dr. Metcalf told me my knee doesn't hurt anymore."

Once, Duff was interviewing a missionary, Elder Whitehead, in the British Mission home when Maxine walked in and asked Duff for twenty pounds to go Christmas shopping. Elder Whitehead got up to leave. President Hanks turned to him and under his breath said, "Don't leave, Elder, you might learn something here about how to deal with your future wife when she needs some money." Elder Whitehead recalled, "Well, I stayed, and they had their conversation, and she left with the twenty pounds, maybe even a little bit more. After she had gone, he turned to me and said, 'Well, I guess there was nothing for you to learn here after all.'"[4]

Duff also had a multitude of one-liners that were unique to him.

If a child was misbehaving, they would be threatened with a "blow to the chops from Iron Mike" (his right bicep). Just the threat, never carried out.

If someone told a joke that wasn't funny, he'd say, "Your humor is of the obscure variety, chiefly characterized by the absence of its presence."

Once during physical therapy after he had a knee replacement—on medication and being forced to exercise his knee—he said, "Your repetition is reducing the importance of my performance. I am left alone without companions, bereft of domiciliary and aficionados."

Maxine also had her own brand of humorous sayings, usually related to teaching her children or their friends or even complete strangers. If she saw someone chewing vigorously on a piece of gum, she would recite, "The gum-chewing girl and the cud-chewing cow—what's the difference? I know now. It's the intelligent look on the face of the cow!"

JOURNAL MUSINGS

His journal often reflected the humor he had shared in his most recent speech. After a speech at BYU in October 1967, he wrote, "My theme was 'Sin,' and I took a stand against it."

He told the wonderful story of the grandfather who started to take his wallet and picture album out, saying to his friend, 'Have I ever told you about my grandchildren?' To which the other replied, 'No, and I want to thank you very much.'[5]

After a BYU football game, he wrote, "It was Beat Baylor Day at Provo. When a BYU player got free and was being pursued down the field, I cried out with great feeling, 'ELUDE THEM, ELUDE THEM! PUNISH THEM SEVERELY AND REPROVE THEM!' We enjoyed ourselves, ate too much, and made ourselves sick."[6]

4. Richard Whitehead, missionary journal, 1963.
5. MDH-JE, Oct. 3, 1967.
6. MDH-JE, Sept. 8, 1984.

TROUBLES WITH JOCULARITY

Duff was known to tease a bit, particularly those he loved and trusted not to take offense. But this backfired on him a time or two. Usually those who spent a lot of time around him recognized when he was teasing, but not always. In today's day and age, some of what he said would not be taken well. In fact, some of it wasn't taken well thirty-five years ago.

On one occasion he received a searing rebuke from one of his returned missionaries from England, then in his mid-forties. Duff had earlier commented to another friend standing with them that the missionary had "taught him patience in England years ago." He also said that he was "one of the most mature of his missionaries." Knowing Duff, there is a 99 percent chance he meant his first comment in jest. The missionary concluded his stinging letter with, "I am writing this letter to request that when we meet on occasion, and you acknowledge our acquaintance, please say something positive, or don't say anything at all."[7]

Duff wrote back and apologized, saying, "I will accept and follow your counsel." On a yellow sticky taped to his copy of the letter he had written, "A lesson for me: Do not be so jocular."

Once, driving on a quiet street, he recognized one of his friends, who was stopped at a light just in front of him. Duff moved up gently and tapped the rear bumper of the other car with his bumper. Unfortunately, his friend didn't see the humor in it and came out with both guns (or more precisely, fingers) blazing. There followed apologies all around.

FUN WITH CHURCH MEMBERS

On occasion, he couldn't help but poke fun at some of the minor details that exercised the sensibilities of a few members of the church. In 1974 the *Church News* ran an article on health and fitness, and someone had the great idea to put Duff and Maxine on the cover. They invited Richard to join them. When it came time to take the pictures, Maxine chose to ride an older bike she was comfortable with rather than the more modern ten-speed Duff had given her years before. The photographer asked if she would "please ride the newer bike, in order to match the bikes that Duff and Richard are riding?" Halfway down the driveway, she fell and skinned her knee. Her reaction was to kick the newer bike and go back to the garage, where she grabbed and then rode her own choice of bikes, the one she had ridden for years.

Soon after the publication, a few well-meaning folks sent letters to Duff. One included some money so that he could "buy his wife a decent bike."

Duff's letter in response was typical of him in such situations. Courteous but firm. Teaching and correcting. Somewhat humorous.

He thanked the man for his letter and his money, which he returned. Then Duff wrote, "The one thing that interests me most about your response to my

7. MDH-L, Apr. 1986.

wife's bicycle is not the bright eyes that observe its bent basket and broken light, or the bulkiness of it, or the ancient nature of it, nor am I surprised with the attention paid to the equality of opportunity for the sexes; what really surprises me is that married people have discounted the possibility of *agency* in a woman." He continued, "Be comforted in the knowledge that a lovely yellow ten-speed rests in our garage (unless used by a daughter), while Sister Hanks, with determination and vigor, rides the bicycle *she wishes* to ride. Your interest and good humor have brightened the day."[8]

Occasionally, some rude but naive church member would innocently walk up and poke him in the chest, saying, "You're Paul Dunn, I just know it." Usually he'd politely correct the person, but sometimes he couldn't help giving in to temptation, saying something like, "Nah, he's better looking than I am," or he might poke her back on the arm, saying, "You're Mabel Smith … you're Mabel Smith."

Other church members would approach him and say, "Hello, Elder Hanks, you might not remember, but you married me." He would often reply, "Boy, will my wife be surprised."

People would say the funniest things to him. Once, after he had retired, a member walked up to him and said, "Hey, didn't you used to be Elder Hanks?" He wasn't sure how to respond.

Duff's brand of humor wasn't always overt. A temple worker told the story of a very wintry day when she was sitting at the reception desk, reading. All morning there had been no traffic, and then she heard someone whistling in the temple! This was not acceptable, but since she was new to the temple, she wasn't sure what she should do. She wrote, "As the whistler came nearer, I could tell it was coming from the general authority corridor, and then I could see it was President Hanks. I felt that I should say something about his whistling but wondered what to say to a general authority—it didn't sound too bad, and especially on that cold, silent, wintry morning—just like a ray of sunshine breaking through. Feeling my responsibility, I said, 'President Hanks, I bet you are the only general authority who would whistle in the temple.' He looked at me, rather seriously, and asked, 'How did you like it?' 'I loved it,'" I replied. "We smiled at each other, and the elevator closed."[9]

HUMOR ON THE FLY

Duff loved to share funnies with his associates at various civic clubs. On one occasion, he was asked to speak to visiting International Rotarians at the Alta Club in Salt Lake City. The afternoon went quickly with a lot of good talks and fine response. In his journal, Duff specifically mentioned Bill Lufburrow, a minister from Houston and president of the largest club in the world, who he thought was just delightful. Some of the talks were long, so after a while Duff invited

8. MDH-L, Aug. 1, 1974.
9. Caroline K. Berrett to MDH, June 5, 1985.

The First Council of the Seventy (former and current) at a BBQ: Bruce R. McConkie, Loren C. Dunn, Hartman Rector Jr., S. Dilworth Young, Milton R. Hunter, Duff Hanks, 1969.

everyone to stand up and stretch, raising one hand in the air and then the other to get the circulation going. "As we sat down, Bill said, 'Are we all Mormons now, Duff?'[10] There was a real burst of laughter." The church formed the major theme of the whole conference after that.

IT'S OKAY FOR THE BRETHREN TO LAUGH

While the general authorities need to take their work seriously, they are also known to share a quick witty exchange with one another. After a meeting in which Duff and his colleagues discussed their work and feelings, he then "gave Antoine [Ivins] a fast ride down the carpet in his wheelchair. Dilworth [Young] was worried. Antoine said calmly, 'I trust you.'"

Duff traded scores of letters with Elder Jeffrey Holland, most of which were serious in tone, but then there were some like the P.S. at the bottom of a letter from Elder Holland to Duff. Duff had thanked Holland for leaving him some food, 'some comestibles,' on his desk. Jeff wrote back, "P.S. As for comestibles, I was guilty of no such thing. Explosives of any kind are never carried on my person, nor left by me on or near church properties. However, I did leave some cheese." Duff wrote on the letter, "No comment could serve."

Duff once received a tongue-in-cheek letter from Elder Paul H. Dunn about an upcoming general conference that read, "Dear Duff, I would appreciate any notes you have on how to preside in the Assembly Hall." Duff replied, "Dear Elder

10. MDH-JE, Mar. 22, 1975.

Duff and President Spencer W. Kimball sharing a laugh, pre-1979.

Dunn, this being a serious matter, I undertake it in a serious vein, and with a serious salutation. This is no small thing. One who presides in the Assembly Hall must have been carefully selected for attributes essential to leadership in the dark." He then presented eight paragraphs of suggestions, including these gems: "My feeling is that one should never sit with his back fully exposed to the congregation," "I cannot tell you what degree of awakeness or somnolence should be practiced; this is a personal matter," and "refreshments should be of the quiet variety. I have personally discovered a certain amount of animosity from those who don't like to hear peanut shells cracking. You may have other preferences anyway."[11]

And then one day he was in a meeting discussing the pros and cons of continuing the tradition of having a baccalaureate service at BYU's graduation. He reminded the committee that he had delivered the baccalaureate at BYU two

11. Memos between MDH and Paul H. Dunn, Mar. 1986.

years earlier on a hot summer afternoon. The speaker before him had spoken for forty minutes and "covered every subject under heaven," he wrote.

> We were in those heavy robes, and everybody was roasting! By the time I got up to speak, I didn't feel like saying anything, so I told the story of the little Baptist girl whose mama dressed her like an angel on Halloween. At one door a man invited her in, heard about her costume, and said he knew just exactly what a little Baptist angel needed. He went and got an apple, and then dropped it ceremoniously into the sack she held. It landed with a thump. The little girl gazed for a long time into the sack after the apple and then looked up and said, "Mister, you just busted every damn cookie in my sack."
>
> Those who still had any sense of humor remaining in that soggy mess, laughed their heads off, and there are certain of the brethren who are still laughing. (Boyd Packer thought that was the funniest thing since Adam and Eve.) At that point, and when the word got around about the heat, baccalaureates ceased, and a banquet was introduced. To finish the other account, I did give an abbreviated speech, and afterwards got a letter from a young lady who said general authorities weren't supposed to swear. I answered her that I had been quoting.[12]

12. MDH-JE, Mar. 25, 1971.

28

Linking Arms with Others

Let's link arms with good people who have similar objectives.[1]
—Marion D. Hanks

Elder Hanks was a bridge builder between people of different faiths. He said, "I testify earnestly that we ought to join forces with good people who are seeking the same objectives we are and that we should walk with them as brothers toward those wholesome goals as far as we can go."[2]

He loved this statement by the Prophet Joseph Smith: "We ought always to be aware of those prejudices which sometimes so strangely present themselves, ... against our friends ... who choose to differ from us ... in matters of faith. Our religion is between us and our God. Their religion is between them and their God. There is a love from God ... which enables us to conduct ourselves with greater liberality towards all that are not of our faith, than what they exercise towards one another."[3]

Duff often quoted an experience in which apostle John A. Widtsoe was a panelist speaking on the subject of alcoholism. A man representing a large Christian denomination stood to speak and justified the use of alcohol in moderation, declaring that there is nothing wrong with such use. Another stood and with conviction announced that he differed with that viewpoint, saying that alcohol, used even in moderation, was a tool of the devil. Dr. Widtsoe, an internationally famous scientist, was the final speaker. He stood and said, "I think there is little need for me to add much today. *I link arms* with my young brother in what he has just said and walk with him." And then he added, "Because I am a scientist and know something of the effects of alcohol, perhaps I could talk a little about that." He did and let it go at that.

Duff wrote, "I have never forgotten the imagery and I have enjoyed the blessing frequently of trying to practice it. So, let's *link arms with good people* who have similar objectives and walk with them as long and as far as we can."[4]

1. MDH-T, "An Attitude: The Weightier Matters," BYU, Mar. 25, 1980.

2. MDH-T, "An Attitude."

3. B. H. Roberts, ed., *History of the Church of Jesus Christ of Latter-day Saints*, 7 vols., 2nd ed. rev. (Salt Lake City: Deseret Book, 1978), 3:303–4.

4. BUW, 281–82, and several other sources.

Duff was always pleased to meet others who professed a love for the Savior. Someone once described him as "a Christian first, and a Mormon second." His work with Rotary and the Boy Scouts and the President's Council on Physical Fitness and Sports and many other non-LDS involvements exposed him to a wide variety of high quality women and men of faith. For example, he reported, "I had a very pleasant time with a man and his wife, Mennonites who look forward to a missionary experience for their church when he retires from his farm soon. I sat by a young school superintendent and his wife who have seven children and who are pleasant, happy people. So were the others, and I enjoyed them very much."[5]

After a Rotary meeting in Cedar City, he received this note: "Dear Duff, just a short note to tell you that your visit to our club here was very well received. At the close of the meeting, I noticed Maurice C. talking to you. Heretofore, Maurice has been critical of the church, but I was told that he remarked to another Rotarian, that your talk was one of the best he had ever listened to and felt it very appropriate for a group of Rotarians where several religious faiths are represented."[6]

Unfortunately, some non-LDS folks in Salt Lake had little desire to associate with their LDS fellow citizens. Given the church's real or perceived control of the state and sway over politics, strict alcohol laws, and heavy proselyting, one can't blame them for feeling a bit irritated and even antagonistic. The history of the church, including its persecution by others and its proclaimed superior heavenly credentials and insular society, added to the discord.

Duff liked to approach this struggle head on, acknowledge it, and then look for areas of agreement and ways to link arms together to move forward. Duff could speak with authority on this type of issue because he didn't just give speeches about it; he lived it. He cultivated sincere and meaningful friendships across different religions, races, cultures, and economics. It came naturally to him.

One of his favorite stories was about a friend, Warren Bainbridge, whom he knew from a service group they both attended. They developed a strong affection for each other. Warren was the devoted leader of the Methodist church in Salt Lake City. One year, Christmas fell on a Sunday, and Duff and Maxine decided that after attending their own morning services they would take their two little girls and join Warren's congregation in worship that day. The Hanks family cheerily joined in with the congregation, singing Christmas hymns and reading together the scriptures of the holy season.

Dr. Bainbridge approached the pulpit to deliver his Christmas message, paused and began his sermon. His opening words were "My dear friend Elder Marion D. Hanks, a general authority of the Church of Jesus Christ of Latter-day Saints, shared with me a tender family story this week that I would like to share with you. His oldest child, Susan, had awakened in the night and begun throwing

5. MDH-A, visit to Aberdeen, Idaho, Rotary Club, 1977.
6. Elwood Corry, Cedar City Rotary Club, to MDH, Nov. 8, 1977.

up. Rocking in her father's comforting arms, Susan looked up into his eyes and said, 'Daddy, for a while, I thought I was losing the Christmas spirit.'"

At that moment, Dr. Bainbridge looked at the congregation, and his eyes fell on Duff's face. Startled, he adjusted his glasses and said, "Elder Hanks, is that you?" He then had Duff and his family stand to be recognized and warmly welcomed. It seemed to him an incredible thing that an LDS leader and his family would join with them to share the love they had for the Savior.

Later, Warren told Duff that, to his knowledge, his church had never had such a visit before. Duff said, "It was not with such a thought in mind that we had made the decision to be there that day. I had come to know the man and his character, so we went with no agenda other than to manifest our love for him and the Master whom he had served over a lifetime. Our family has been blessed for years by remembrance of that Christmas and the surprised delight he expressed, because we were there to worship with our friend and neighbors in another church." Just a few years later, Warren and his wife moved to another state to conclude his career among family and friends there. But Duff and Warren kept in touch for years.[7]

Just over a year after Warren Bainbridge moved away, Duff had an important experience with his replacement, Dr. Davis. In August 1969, Duff spoke at a luncheon of the Greek Orthodox Youth of America at their international conference being held in Salt Lake City. He wrote that they were gracious in their response, "particularly the archbishop, and many of the young folks in attendance." The next night at the Salt Lake Tabernacle an interfaith meeting was attended by about three thousand, including all the Greek Orthodox priests, Bishop Federal of the Catholic Diocese, Dr. Davis, who was the new pastor of the First Methodist Church, the new rabbi in town, and several others. Duff had a friendly discussion with each of his colleagues in the ministry.

Governor Cal Rampton and Senators Wallace Bennett and Frank Moss each spoke. Duff then spoke, giving a tribute to the Mormon pioneers and the principles they built on, suggesting that those principles and values are still needed today. He was moved by the response, particularly of his fellow clergy, who were gracious and warm—some even wept. At the report meeting in the Temple that week, Duff mentioned the experience, leaving out anything personal but mentioning Dr. Davis, who had been in town for a whole year and met a Mormon leader for the first time that night. Duff suggested that as church leaders, they might be missing an opportunity to meet in fellowship with some of the other religious leaders in the community. Duff wrote, "Mark Petersen took up the idea, and there is a current probability that we can plan some happy friendshipping experiences for the new pastors of the various churches as they arrive in town hereafter. It was worth bringing up, and the brethren responded nobly."[8]

---

7. MDH-JE; see Hanks, *Keeping Christmas* (Salt Lake City: Deseret Book, 1996).
8. MDH-JE, Aug. 25, 1969.

Duff received a kind letter from a member of the church who wrote, "I just finished watching a program on TV where you sat in the middle of a Catholic bishop, a non-LDS news reporter, and an Assembly of God pastor, and where you exemplified all that is true and good about the teachings of the one true church. Thank you for demonstrating the Christlike attributes of one who knows the truth but didn't need to shout it or intimidate another's integrity."[9]

Duff's example of reaching out toward one's neighbors and acquaintances, with no ulterior motive other than friendship and community, is worth emulating.

9. Letter to MDH, Aug. 1969.

29

Courtesy, Dignity, Authenticity, and Presence

Men fail in most part, not because they are not smart enough, but because they are not good enough.
—Stanley A. Hanks[1]

I cannot find language of sufficient energy to convey my sense of the sacredness of private integrity.
—Ralph W. Emerson[2]

Duff Hanks had a charisma and goodness about him that was almost palpable. On more than one occasion, people who had just met him for the first time commented on a feeling they had when they were with him.

"There is a remarkable kind of magnetism about Duff," said a close friend. "Among his associates, entire evenings have been spent exchanging what have come to be known as 'Duff Hanks' stories—items about his goodwill, his graciousness, his humor, his discernment, his keen mind, his good deeds."

COURTESY

Duff was taught by his saintly mother to be gracious and courteous. He wrote in the church's magazine for youth, "Manners are a manifestation of good sense and good breeding and consideration for others.... They are outward expressions of what we believe to be important, of our values. They reflect our attitude towards others; they show how we really feel."[3]

His commitment was evidenced in his actions. If you got to a door first and tried to hold it open, you'd get assisted through first. If you needed his help carrying something, he didn't ask—he just plucked it out of your hand.

Many a time, he would be walking down the street and come up behind a

1. Stanley A. Hanks, Journal.
2. Ralph Waldo Emerson, *Introductory Lecture on the Times*, read at the Masonic Temple, Boston, Dec. 2, 1841.
3. MDH-A, "On Manners in Church," *Improvement Era*, May 1962, 2.

fragile, elderly lady at a crosswalk. He'd slip his arm in hers and say, "Pardon me, I'm feeling just a bit shaky today. Would it be okay if you helped me across the street?" She would look up at him and giggle, "Oh, Brother Hanks . . ."

One time as a young boy, Rich accompanied his dad to visit President David O. McKay. As they approached the elderly, frail prophet, Duff whispered to Rich to watch carefully what President McKay did. As they got closer, President McKay struggled to push himself up, as if to say, I can no longer walk, but I will show you respect, even so. His strength barely allowed him to move less than an inch off his wheelchair, but the point was made and understood.

Duff was particularly well known for not being able to countenance rudeness, discourtesy, or bullying by others. This feeling extended even to those with whom he worked in church leadership day to day. The large majority of general authorities were refined gentlemen, but there were a few exceptions. After one particularly negative experience on a trip to Asia, Duff wrote, "The tour was generally a pleasant experience, but not all. [The apostle's wife] is a thoughtful and generous person; he is not. That is, his thoughts do not extend to the well-being of others. I express the hope, without rancor and without hostility, that I never have to have this kind of experience again."[4]

Duff was imbued as a child with what his mother called the "habit of helpfulness." It translated into his keen ability to notice when people could use some kindness or attention. "My mother was unable to come inside the temple for my marriage," wrote one convert. "Unlike most sealers who finish the ceremony and get back to work or temple work, Elder Hanks changed into his street clothes and went outside to find my little Catholic mother. When he found her, he took her to a quiet, shady spot and for 20 minutes he told her all about the ceremony, what was said, the feeling that was there, etc. My mother was so grateful, and so was I. My little mother passed away last week but had never forgotten that moment." This small, simple act by Duff was repeated literally thousands of times in different forms.

In 1976, Duff and Rich attended the Tangerine Bowl football game in Orlando, Florida. President Spencer W. Kimball sat in front of them on metal, backless bleachers. Duff scooted up and had the prophet rest his back against Duff's knees the entire first half and then against Rich's knees the entire second half. There was no pretense or announcement, just a simple act of kindness for an elderly man—who happened to be the prophet.

GENTILITY AND GRACIOUSNESS

Duff conducted thousands and thousands of interviews for various reasons—repentance, missionary, leadership, and employment. His journal described his desire to treat each individual with respect and dignity. He refused to probe details of sin unless it was absolutely necessary and strongly discouraged those he

4. MDH-JE, Aug. 27, 1982.

trained from ever using the language of the gutter or prying into a person's private life. In describing this approach, he often reflected on the manner and type of questioning President David O. McKay had used with him in interviews. He said that President McKay's method of questioning was so gracious and good that it influenced his whole life. Through his gentle questioning, the prophet was able to bring to light any issues, and he was able to do that with the gentle tone and graciousness of a gentleman. Duff wrote,

"I shall never forget the most important interview I had with the President of the church.... Note the nature of the questions and of the spirit of the man who asked them. It was a forthright interview, but it was also an exchange: For example, he didn't ask if I was faithful to my wife; he asked, 'Are there any improper alliances outside your home?'

"Each exchange was delicate and decent: 'Are you fully loyal to your family?'"

Duff remarked, "Who could resent or answer falsely such gentle and courteous questions?"[5]

DIGNITY OF OTHERS

Duff was predisposed to treat others with respect and accord them the dignity they deserved as fellow travelers on the earth. This was specifically expressed when he would say to someone, "Your name is safe in our home." He had learned this phrase from a fellow general authority he dearly loved, Oscar Kirkham, and it was the highest compliment he could give someone.

Duff believed in encouraging those church leaders he visited. On one occasion, while Rich was participating in a funeral, one of the visiting funeral employees asked if he could speak with him in his office, and then shared the following story.

> I was a stake president in the Midwest ten years ago, when we had a famous general authority come to visit our stake. He basically "beat us up" for two days and made us feel like worthless failures in our callings. Morale was so low that we all returned home with our heads down. A year later, your dad was the official visitor. We had the exact opposite experience—encouragement, uplift, praise. Sure, he pointed out some weaknesses and some things we could do better, but even those were presented in a spirit of love and appreciation. To be honest, when the first apostle left our stake, we all felt like we needed a bath; after your father left, we all felt like we'd had one.

Duff tried never to embarrass or shame others. His grandson told the story of Grandpa taking him aside and asking, "Mike, what is the greatest objective of human beings and their lives?" Mike thought for a moment and gave an answer. Duff's response was classic: "That is a good answer, and no one can improve upon it. But consider this ..."[6]

5. GS, 221.
6. Michael Maughan, notes.

The secretary of the Salt Lake Rotary Club wrote of Duff, "Rotary has given me innumerable opportunities to witness the kind and gentle ways of this remarkable man."[7]

BEAUTIFUL AND UPLIFTING THINGS

Duff sought after beautiful and uplifting things, (although he didn't really share Maxine's love of opera.) When he was granted emeritus status, the *Salt Lake Tribune* headline fittingly read, "LDS 'Poet-Soul' to Retire After 39 Years."[8]

Speaking to a legal conference, Duff said, "The one thing that every human being needs to do is continue to broaden his or her exposure to that which is delightful, good, and uplifting in this world, limiting, to the extent possible, the opposite. Perhaps you are acquainted with the ancient Jewish Proverb, 'God will hold us responsible for all the lovely things we did not enjoy in this world.'"[9]

In a letter sent to the children after Maxine's death, a friend used the following quotation to describe Duff and Maxine: "How delightful is the company of generous people, who overlook trifles and keep their minds instinctively gazed on whatever is good and positive in the world about them."[10]

Duff loved peaceful writings. The children memorized poetry. Rich remembered, "I can't count the number of times we'd be in a long car ride repeating lines over and over. Frankly, it made for some long car rides, but it expanded our exposure to good things. We were also invited to notice spectacular scenery, appreciate the Earth around us, and be grateful to God for it all. Perhaps there is no poem that captures this part of our upbringing better than this anonymous one that Dad repeated over and over our entire lives:

Enraptured by this glorious scene,
I gaze in meditation.
Like one lost in some sweet dream,
Amazed at God's Creation."

PRESENCE AND CONVICTION

Some people are accorded respect because of their position, title, or calling. Marion D. Hanks was accorded respect because of his dignity and integrity. One of the more interesting experiences of being the child of a famous man was to walk behind him or near him when people didn't know the child was there. People were taken by Duff's demeanor and could feel his presence, even if they'd never met him before.

On one occasion, Rich was with Duff in a room filled with military brass—several admirals—and many other leaders. He was standing behind two of them

7. Lila Perry, tribute, Salt Lake Rotary Club.

8. Peggy Fletcher Stack, "LDS 'Poet-Soul' Hanks to Retire After 39 Years," *Salt Lake Tribune*, Oct. 3, 1992.

9. MDH-T, "Truth a Shield to Memory," J. Reuben Clark Law School, Nov. 19, 1989.

10. Van Wyck Brooks.

against a window, when one admiral said to the other, pointing at Duff across the room, "That's Duff Hanks. You can just feel his strength."[11]

Another time they were walking down the street, and Rich fell behind, only to hear one passerby say to another, "There is just a transparent goodness about Elder Hanks, isn't there?"

After one of his many trips to California to speak to students, Duff received this letter:

> Dear Elder Hanks, Julie, who you spoke with yesterday, came into the institute this morning and indicated how deeply she was moved by your chat together last evening. She isn't a member of the church, but is struggling to find herself and get a testimony. She said that people who have tried to teach her about the church constantly say, "I bear you my testimony," when they are stumped. In her remarks to me this morning, she said, "When Mr. Hanks spoke, he didn't need to constantly say he knew; it was obvious by his power and inner conviction that he knew and I could see that he knew."[12]

Duff believed that courage and conscience in combination account for much that is good in the world. He spoke of Ulysses S. Grant, the general and later president of the United States. "Some talk of him patronizingly, which he may have deserved, but the story is told (perhaps apocryphal), that in the smoke-filled room of officers drinking to toast victory in the United States Civil War, one man rose, spoiling to get a filthy story off his tongue, and said, 'Is there a lady in the house?'

"No," said Ulysses S. Grant, "there is not a lady. But there is a gentleman."

The filthy story remained untold.[13]

While Duff told that story repeatedly, it could have just as easily been about him.

AUTHENTICITY

One of the first talks Rich ever gave in church as a young boy was titled "To Be and Not to Seem." Of course, Duff helped him write the talk, and in doing so, he taught Rich the story of the brave and good warrior who wrote on the inside of his shield, "To Be and Not to Seem." In addition to helping with a talk, Duff was teaching Rich an important lesson on the need to be an authentic and decent man.

Duff's courteous and interested approach was freely given to all. He did not privilege title or position over other attributes. From an article about him in the *Improvement Era* magazine: "Talk to building custodians, secretarial help, childhood friends, fellow general authorities, or the soldier just home from service, and you'll learn that Brother Hanks is loved because he has shown his concern for their welfare. Many a quiet battle he has fought to bring peace to his fellow man."[14]

---

11. Rear Admiral C. Monroe Hart about MDH.
12. Institute director serving UCLA students to MDH, Mar. 4, 1969.
13. MDH-T, White House Conference on Children and Youth, March 1960.
14. *Improvement Era*, Nov. 1967, 58.

Even people who didn't know him could sense his authenticity—this comment came from a newspaper article in Oregon: "Elder Hanks is a big man with a congenial personality, who leaves the impression of openness and candor in his discussions."[15]

MODESTY AND HUMILITY

Because of Duff's tendency to speak his mind (see chapter 18, pages 187–198), there are some who probably would not associate Duff with humility. But he really was humble in many ways. And if he wasn't feeling particularly humble, he'd remind himself with handwritten quotations in his scriptures or papers. A favorite was Thomas à Kempis: "Thou art none the holier if thou art praised, nor the viler if thou art reproached. Thou art what thou art."[16]

Duff was self-deprecating. One of the most confusing things he did was use the word 'we' instead of 'I.' He'd say, "We received this honor." Or "we spoke." It sometimes took a minute or two to figure out he was talking about himself.

A general authority colleague wrote about a stake conference they attended together: "I learn so much from you each time. Your opening statement at the Priesthood Leadership meeting in Oklahoma, 'We come, not claiming perfection, but knowing from whence the call came that brings us here,' was profound to me, and I have used the concept many times since."[17]

As he was being released from his calling, Duff was given the opportunity to address his fellow seventies in the Salt Lake Temple. One of his colleagues said, "He taught sacred principles. Not once did he lament becoming emeritus, nor start the 'Woe be unto me now that I'm being released,' or 'I'm going to miss this calling,' as did so many of the brethren before and after him. His dignity, bearing, and demeanor were so powerful that none who were in that meeting could but help experience what I felt. As far as I'm concerned, he set the tone for all general authorities who will be released from that sacred calling."[18]

In Duff's scriptures was this thought by John Ruskin: "I believe that the test of a truly great man is his humility. I do not mean by humility, doubt of his own power, but really great men have a curious feeling that the greatness is not in them but *through them*, and they see something divine in every other man, and are endlessly, foolishly, incredibly merciful."[19]

15. *Oregonian*, Aug. 8, 1970.

16. Thomas à Kempis, *The Imitation of Christ* (c. 1418–27).

17. Gene Hansen to MDH, 1993.

18. F. David Stanley, n.d.

19. John Ruskin, *The Works of John Ruskin*, ed. E. T. Cook and Alexander Wedderburn, 39 vols. (New York: John Wiley & Sons, 1903–12), 5:331.

SPIRITUAL STRENGTH

30

David O. McKay

We have met this morning, with our bodies cleansed and clothed in clean linen, our minds prepared, and our spirits subdued, to await the direction of the Lord.
—President David O. McKay

It is natural for one to hold in special regard the man whom God uses to call one to church leadership. But Duff's regard for the prophet David O. McKay went beyond that specific shared history to one of genuine regard, admiration, and almost reverence. To honor President McKay on his ninety-fifth birthday, Duff wrote a piece published in the *Improvement Era* in September 1968 titled "The Soul of a Prophet," in which he praised President McKay's Christlike character and genuine sincerity, his wholesome gentility, courteous demeanor, and love.

On one occasion in the temple, President McKay addressed all the brethren who had gathered, fasting and praying to prepare for general conference. The words he spoke deeply affected Duff, and he repeated them often. President McKay began by saying, "We have met this morning, with our bodies cleansed and clothed in clean linen, our minds prepared, and our spirits subdued, to await the direction of the Lord." Duff believed this would be a good pattern for living every day.

Duff loved to tell the story of the rough and famous labor union leader he escorted to an official visit with President McKay. The meeting was pleasant and informal. President McKay shared the story of a farm experience in his youth. He told how he and his brother had taken every tenth load of hay to the bishop to give to the Lord for tithing, only to be challenged by his father, who asked if the boys wouldn't like to go back to get some better hay for the Lord. The boys complained, saying that the Lord should take his tenth from every part of the field. Their great old Scottish father laughed, put his arms around the boys, and told them that might be all right for others, but for the Lord only the best was good enough.

"There was no posturing, or 'filling a role,'" said Duff of that visit, "just warm, friendly, and natural conversation and companionship." When the visit was concluded, this internationally famous man and his family were in tears and he said, "I have met with kings and rulers and seen leaders of many kinds in many lands,

LDS Church president David O. McKay. *Courtesy LDS Church*

but I have never met a man like that. I don't believe our generation will ever produce a man like that."[1]

On one occasion when Duff was with President and Sister McKay, photographers arrived to take photos for what ended up being their last anniversary together. They were in their nineties, and while sitting next to each other on a small sofa, they reached for each other's hand. "Just as the picture was snapped, the tiny frail hand lifted the big strong one to her lips," Duff said. "It was a spontaneous, beautiful expression of her love. The bodily powers were long since dissipated, but the love affair had been getting better all the time."[2]

Duff's article concluded: "In the clarity of his vision, the keenness of his intellect, the scope of his knowledge, and the depth of his wisdom, David O. McKay stands a paragon. Poets, philosophers, prophets, all are within his ken—their thoughts stored in his memory through hours invested and hard labors performed. His perceptive mind, his noble character, his generous nature, have translated, refined, applied, made wisdom the amalgam of his learning and his love. To him, the words of a friend seem particularly appropriate: 'I gave it and gave it and gave it, until it was mine.'"[3]

1. MDH-A, "The Soul of a Prophet," *Improvement Era*, Sept. 8, 1968, 3–5.
2. MDH-T, Manchester, England, Area Conference, Aug. 29, 1971.
3. MDH-A, "The Soul of a Prophet," *Improvement Era*, Sept. 8, 1968, 3–5.

31

Marriage

The solo ends; the duet begins.
—Marion D. Hanks

A common occurrence for the Hanks children has been for a complete stranger, or someone they've just met, to say, "Your dad married us." It isn't a mystery why that would happen—Duff performed the temple weddings (sealings for eternity) of hundreds, if not thousands, of individuals during his lifetime. He considered it to be one of his dearest blessings. He was also given the opportunity to counsel with many thousands of couples about marriage and its importance to a happy life. What follows is a synopsis of his advice on marriage.

IMPORTANCE OF MARRIAGE CHOICE

Married people should be best friends; no relationship on earth needs friendship as much as marriage.
—Marion D. Hanks[1]

"One of the most important choices any of us ever make in this life is our choice of companions with whom we shall share our lives.... Companions can do wonderful things for us," Duff said. "If they are happy, generous, thoughtful people, we will very likely be that way when we are with them.... If they habitually use clean and decent language, we will likely talk that way, too. If our companions are prone to kind and noble thoughts, they will in all likelihood help us turn our thoughts in that direction also. If they do things that are wholesome and constructive, we will likely go along."[2]

PREPARATION FOR MARRIAGE

Duff's approach to marriage was to have those entering into it understand the importance of working, really working, on their commitment to each other. He taught: "Marriage means some kind of a home and family. A good marriage means a good home and a happy family. But such a resultant marriage means

1. MDH-T, "Eternal Marriage," GC, Oct. 1984.
2. MDH-A, "Choose Well Your Companions," *Church News*, Jan. 30, 1960.

effort and maturity. It doesn't *just happen;* it requires two mature people who are willing to learn how to build such a marriage, and work on it day by day—it is an enterprise for adults."[3]

He began most of his wedding ceremonies with the statement that marriage is not two perfect people coming together to live happily ever after, but rather two *imperfect* people coming together and willing to *work* together to live happily ever after.

ACCEPTING THE WHOLE PERSON

Duff repeatedly taught that the commitments made in a temple are total and permanent, an acceptance of the current state—the assets, liabilities, quirks, and peculiarities—and that each participant in the marriage is prepared to "accept the whole person, *as is,* for the whole journey." That "neither person will remain as he or she is, of course; they will both grow and develop in a multitude of ways. But this marriage ceremony is without condition or reservation, save only the faithfulness of those who make it."[4]

LIBERTY AND UNION

Duff reinforced the importance of the chemistry that attracts two people—he thought it was a vital part of successful marriages. But he was also quick to point out that such an attraction is not all-inclusive of the love required for married couples. He reminded couples that one never falls into love; one falls into passion. One must climb into love.

Duff loved to quote a political speech by Daniel Webster, who spoke of the importance of *liberty* and *union.* Duff felt that this simple concept was also directly applicable to marriage—unity of the couple, with respect for the liberty of each spouse. For example, he said, "Nothing is more important than being a wife and a mother, but no woman can be one, unless she is regarded and treated as a human being by her beloved. In Ibsen's play *A Doll's House,* a husband declares to his wife, 'Before all else, you are a wife and mother.' And her response is, 'I believe that before all else, I am a human being.'"

Duff felt that the personality and individuality of each partner in marriage must be accepted and preserved if there is to be happiness. But he also cautioned that this liberty must be enjoyed in the spirit of a deep commitment to the building of the union—the marriage. Unless the union is strengthened often, at the expense of some individual wants, the union will not survive.[5]

Duff continued in his explanation of marriage:

- Marriage is an ordinance.
- Marriage is a companionship.

3. MDH, personal notes used in performing weddings, counseling, and speaking about marriage.
4. MDH-T, "Eternal Marriage," GC, Oct. 1984.
5. MDH-A, "More Than We Imagine," *New Era,* June 1971.

- Marriage is a friendship.
- Marriage is a love affair of sweethearts.

"Married people should be best friends. Friendship will motivate one to cross the room one day and say, 'I'm sorry; I didn't mean that.' 'I'm sorry' are healing words—use them often. Marriage will not pretend perfection nor demand it. It will not insist that both respond exactly the same in every thought and feeling, but it will bring to the union honesty, and integrity. There will be repentance and forgiveness in every good marriage—and respect and trust."

In the temple sealings that he performed, Duff always pointed out that spouses are responsible for their companion's success. He taught that it is the duty of each spouse to see that the other succeeds in his or her individual roles, and that each partner should think more in terms of *responsibilities* of marriage rather than *rights* of marriage.

He could pronounce the wedding, the marriage, and the sealing, but he could not pronounce happiness or maturity or courtesy or unselfishness or forgiveness or good humor—all of that is up to the couple, of their own free will and choice.

CAREFUL COMMUNICATION

Duff emphasized careful communication: "It is much more important for a man to prove that he loves his wife than to prove her wrong. He will get a very barren victory in the latter case but a wonderful victory in the former." Wrote one in response to his advice: "I credit my happy marriage to Elder Hanks, and his sage advice during our sealing ceremony: 'The cleverest things you think of to say, you must not say.' I have thought of a great many clever things to say to my husband over 22 years that thankfully never made it past my lips. What a remarkably wise man. Thank you, Elder Hanks."[6]

DISCIPLESHIP

And finally, Duff taught that marriage is discipleship; it is an ordinance of the gospel that brings together two children of God in his ordained way. As they have received each other, so they have covenanted to receive God in their marriage, home, and family. "As you commit yourselves to a relationship with each other and God there is the best friendship that makes life more warm and more wonderful, and there is discipleship which permits you to count on each other and to move together toward objectives that are unitedly shared and happily constructed. And you remain and become in a special, growing sense, sweethearts though all the years ahead."[7]

6. Online comment, Aug. 16, 2011.
7. MDH, personal notes used in performing weddings, counseling, and speaking about marriage.

32

Positive Attitude, Uplift, and Encouragement

There is no chance, no destiny, no fate, can circumvent or
hinder or control the firm resolve of a determined soul.
—Ella Wheeler Wilcox[1]

Duff's way of dealing with people was to praise, lift, encourage, and build up. He spoke in strings of positive adjectives full of praise and support. He savored the positive aspects of daily life. Here is an abridged version of one of his favorite passages by David Grayson:

> This is a well-earned Sunday morning. My chores were all done long ago, and I am sitting down here after a late and leisurely breakfast with that luxurious feeling of irresponsible restfulness and comfort of a clean Sunday morning. . . .
>
> When I first woke up this morning, I said to myself, "Well, nothing happened yesterday." Then I lay quiet for some time—and I turned over in my mind all that I had heard or seen or felt or thought about in that one day. And presently I said aloud to myself, "Why, nearly everything happened yesterday."
>
> I had walked among unusual events and had not known the wonder of them. I had eyes but I did not see. . . . It may be that our future life is only the reliving, with full understanding, the marvelous life that we now know.[2]

SEEING ONE'S POTENTIAL

Over and over, Duff taught the following from Goethe:

> If you treat an individual as he is, he will remain as he is.
> But if you treat him as if he were what he ought to be and could be,
> he will become what he ought to be and could be.[3]

---

1. Ella Wheeler Wilcox, "Will," in *A Library of American Literature: Literature of the Republic, Part IV, 1861–1889*, comp. Arthur Stedman (1891).
2. David Grayson, *Adventures in Friendship* (New York: Doubleday, Page, 1910), 173–75.
3. Johann Wolfgang von Goethe.

This attitude was one of the secrets to Duff's success. It was in his nature to treat people as if they *already were* what they wanted to *become*. When someone of his stature felt that you were more than you really were, you wanted to become that version of yourself.

It wasn't just "rah, rah, go team go" stuff either. It was a genuine encouragement and an incredible driver of self-confidence. One letter to him said, "I was a missionary when you visited our mission and asked us why we go to the temple. Then you explained that when you go to the temple, it is to worship the Lord, your God. The reverence and intensity with which that phrase struck me has stayed with me all of these 28 years."

Another letter read, "After this wonderful spiritual feast, I was called on to give the benediction, during which I wept. After the prayer, you took me by the hand, looked into my eyes, and said, 'There is something special about a man who can pray like that. May the Lord bless you.' I have recalled your words on many occasions when I have been filled with self-doubt and discouragement."[4]

To one of his missionaries at the end of his mission, Duff wrote, "We have not had one moment's worry about you or your performance or your faithfulness or the character of your work. We will always love you and be interested in everything you do. If our son grows up to be the kind of gentleman and devoted Latter-day Saint and human being that you are, we will be more than satisfied."[5]

In the movie *My Fair Lady*, Eliza Doolittle says, "The difference between a lady and a flower girl is not how she behaves, but how she is treated. I shall always be a common flower girl to Professor Higgins, because he always treats me like a common flower girl, and always will. But I shall always be a lady to Colonel Pickering, because he treats me like a lady, and always will."[6] Most people left Duff feeling as if they already were what they previously had hoped to someday become.

HAPPINESS IS A CHOICE

For years, Maxine had a piece of paper taped on the family refrigerator. It read simply, "Happiness is a choice."

Both Maxine and Duff chose to emphasize optimistic possibilities rather than historical or current negativism. Maxine almost refused to talk about or watch anything that was negative, especially the news. It wasn't just an avoidance on principle; in her soul she just couldn't really handle the sadness and difficulties of others. As usual, Duff had an entire bevy of quotations to pull out of his mind and share on the subject. One of his favorites was this: "The fountain of content must spring up from within the mind; and he who has so little knowledge of human nature as to seek happiness by changing anything but his own disposition

---

4. Blair Jones to MDH, Sept. 2009.
5. MDH-L to Richard Whitehead, June 15, 1963.
6. *My Fair Lady* (Warner Bros., 1964).

will waste his life with fruitless efforts, and multiply his grief which he proposes to remove."[7] He loved this one too: "Say you are well, or all is well with you, and God shall hear your words and make them true."[8]

Duff taught that we each have two compartments in our thinking ability. One he called the foyer, with thoughts and impulses passing through. But we have the power to kick out those unwelcome thoughts, just as we would an unwelcome intruder in our homes. The other part of our thinking is like the living room in our homes, and we need to invite that which is good and wholesome to enter there, to stay and visit.

Elder Quentin L. Cook remembered his mission president as a man who perpetually called for moral agency and correct choices. "Elder Hanks taught that people can't always control their circumstances, but they can control their spiritual reactions and make correct choices. He taught the importance of making the day-to-day decision to do the right thing."[9]

Duff proposed that life was much easier if one didn't take offense or hold grudges. He often quoted Brigham Young, who is reported to have said, "He who takes offense when no offense was intended is a fool, and he who takes offense when offense *was* intended is usually a fool." Duff continued quoting, "There are two courses of action to follow when one is bitten by a rattlesnake. One may, in anger, fear, or vengefulness, pursue the creature and kill it. Or he may make full haste to get the venom out of his system. If we pursue the latter course we will likely survive, but if we attempt to follow the former, we may not be around long enough to finish it."[10]

BUILDING FOR THE FUTURE

Duff was always pointing to the future. With regard to sin and confession and regret, his approach seemed to be, Okay, great, you've got that over with; now let's talk about the future. This attitude was incredibly helpful to those who were wallowing in the past. He once said, "The gospel as I understand it says to man that it doesn't matter a whole lot what you have been, if today you decide to be something else, and that something comes more nearly to being what you can be."[11]

In a similar fashion, he was continually directing others to look down the road and build for those who would follow. One of his favorite poems on this subject was "The Bridge Builder," by Will Allen Dromgoole. The poem is about an old man who has crossed a river and turns back to build a bridge. It ends with these words:

There followed after me to-day
A youth whose feet must pass this way.

---

7. Samuel Johnson, *Rambler*, Apr. 7, 1750.
8. Ella Wheeler Wilcox, "Speech," *Poems of Pleasure* (London: Gay and Bird, 1900), 17–18.
9. Quentin L. Cook, *Deseret News*, Aug. 13, 2011.
10. MDH-T, "Forgiveness: The Ultimate Form of Love," GC, Oct. 1973.
11. MDH-T, "Through the Eyes and Mouths of Children," BYU, Jan. 10, 1956.

This chasm that has been as naught to me
To that fair-haired youth may a pitfall be;
He, too, must cross in the twilight dim;
Good friend, I am building this bridge for him![12]

Another favorite example he often shared came from the scriptures. In the Doctrine and Covenants, the Lord told some pioneers that they would be given some land only "for a little season," but then he instructed them to "act on this land as [if] for years" (D&C 51:16–17). And they did. They planted crops they knew they would not be around to harvest.

Duff was constantly teaching others to "unpack their bags" and "bloom where they were planted." In another favorite verse of Duff's, John Ruskin wrote, "When we build, let us think that we build forever. Let it not be for present delight nor for present use alone. Let it be such work as our descendants will thank us for; and let us think, as we lay stone on stone, that a time is to come when those stones will be held sacred because our hands have touched them, and men will say, as they look upon the labor and wrought substance of them, 'See, this our fathers did for us.'"[13]

BETTER TO BE A BUILDER THAN A CRITIC

Given the position he was in and his willingness to stand up for what he believed was right, Duff served as a lightning rod for others who wanted to complain about this or that church leader or program or doctrine. While he always listened, and sometimes commiserated, he was absolutely consistent in his effort to turn the person's attacks around and attempt to persuade them to be part of the solution, rather than pointing out the faults of others.

He saw no reason to visit with a stake presidency, for example, and point out every single thing they were doing wrong or could improve on. He would briefly discuss needed changes, but recognized that most people already know where they can improve and harping on it doesn't speed up the process. Instead, he pointed out the positives he saw, and then he chose to let them discuss their own challenges and see if he could help or add value in any way.

Duff was constantly looking for ways that he could strengthen those around him. He was a builder of men. One of his missionaries recalled the calming effect of his encouraging words: "My first real meeting with President Hanks was at the London Temple, and we had a meeting in the chapel before. I went up to the stand to give the opening prayer and I guess I looked nervous, because he put his hand on my knee and said, 'Don't be afraid, Elder, just talk to the Lord.' It relieved my stress and taught me a lot about prayer."[14]

12. Will Allen Dromgoole, "The Bridge Builder," in *Father: An Anthology of Verse* (E. P. Dutton, 1931).

13. John Ruskin, *The Seven Lamps of Architecture* (1849).

14. Richard Whitehead, missionary journal, 1963.

SUPPORTING OTHERS IN THEIR CHOICES

When he noticed someone taking a courageous or noble stand, Duff was quick to send an encouraging note of support even if he didn't know the person.

In 1965, Bill Reeske was the football coach at the College of Southern Utah in Cedar City, now called Southern Utah University. He had suspended a number of starters and other members of his team because they broke team training rules. They had thought there was no way their coach would dare cut them off before a big, heavily publicized game. But he did. And their team lost.

Duff had never met the man and never did. But he wrote him a letter that read: "Dear Mr. Reeske, May I offer this simple note of appreciation and respect for your recent act in enforcing the rules by which athletes are expected to live. This took devotion and an uncommon sense of what really is important to young men. I commend you for it and offer my earnest congratulations."[15]

A year later, the coach wrote back, telling Duff that when he received his letter he was about as down a coach could get. His decision to put his foot down was rather unpopular with his critics. "I have had the ugliest threatening warnings—all kinds of letters from the other side, and two—yours and the college president's—that commended me. Because of those two letters, I stayed [coaching]."[16] The previous year, when the coach left most of their team home, the remainder of the squad took a 59–0 beating. The first game of the next season, they were victorious over the same team. The players said they wanted to win the game to prove they could come back after making a mistake. Duff commented that he had no grand ideas when he penned the note, but rather he was just honestly telling the coach how he felt as a human being.

He could also turn someone's act of courage or bravery into what we might now call a viral sensation. He could hear a story, tell it in a general conference talk, and many young people of the church would retell it in sacrament meeting talks over the coming years.

He repeated a particular piece of counsel many times with many different people. It involved how to approach the lengthy time commitment often necessary to complete worthwhile objectives. For example, one young woman was having a difficult time deciding if she should become a doctor and lamenting how long it would take—mission, college, marriage, family, then medical school, and earning enough to repay debts.

Duff's standard response was to ask, "Suppose you do all of that, how old will you be when you finish?"

Response—"36 or 37!"

Duff's return question, "That seems like forever, doesn't it?"

Answer—"Yes, it does."

---

15. MDH-L to Bill Reeske, Nov. 18, 1965.
16. BUW, 16–17.

Duff's response, "And suppose after all those years you don't accomplish any of those things. How old will you be?"

The point was made.

33

The Things of the Spirit

Some people are born with a craving for the infinite.
—Nancy Hanks Baird

Duff had a profound reverence for holy things. He once confided to his daughter that he was significantly more nervous to pray in general conference than to speak. When he prayed, he was speaking to God.

PRIESTHOOD BLESSINGS

An interesting thing experienced by Duff's family members over the years was unexpectedly meeting someone who had been named for him as a tribute to the kind of man he was. For instance, Duff's close friends, Homer Ellsworth and Bob Thompson, each named one of their sons Duff. And Elder Jeffrey R. Holland's son David has gone by the nickname Duff most of his life.

More often than not, these namesakes had been the recipient of a priesthood blessing from Duff. When he gave a blessing, Duff directed all recognition to God—he was well aware of who was really giving the blessing. For obvious reasons, this is a private and personal subject, one Duff did not discuss often and almost never in public.

Duff was frequently called on to provide priesthood blessings of healing and comfort to patients in the hospital. He took Rich along on so many weekend trips to LDS Hospital, near their home, that Rich had memorized the layout of the departments as a twelve-year-old.

What follows are some sweet, representative accounts of experiences with priesthood blessings.

"Brother Hanks, I called you from the hospital three years ago, at 11:00 p.m. A widow was near death and very much alone. From a medical aspect everything was against her. She wanted a blessing, so I tried to contact my bishop, but was unable to. This is when I called you. After you gave her a blessing, she recovered, much to the surprise of the medical staff. She is well and happy. We still keep in touch."[1]

1. MDH-JE, Sept. 28, 1967.

A friend wrote, "Dear old friend, yesterday in the funeral service for Denise McArthur, twice reference was made to you administering to her over forty years ago, when she was pregnant and undergoing heart valve replacement there in Salt Lake. You promised her in the blessing that she would survive to raise her children. All eight were present yesterday and she had passed her eightieth birthday. We shall miss this good neighbor."[2]

A grateful recipient wrote to Duff, "One fateful day in 1943 I was struck by a taxi in Chicago. A call was placed to the Northern States Mission to have missionaries administer to me. You came with your companion and gave me a blessing. I had been banged up pretty badly and I had the distinct impression of looking down at myself on that gurney and realizing that I had the choice of fighting to live, or just rolling over and forgetting it all. Your blessing made the difference, and I shall be eternally grateful to you for exercising your priesthood on my behalf at that critical moment."[3]

Duff wrote, "A lovely woman and her husband from Riverside, California, came to shake my hand. She reminded me that fourteen years ago in Idaho, I had given her a blessing. She was awaiting an operation on her back which had been diagnosed as cancer. She reminded me that she was so sick that she was lying on the floor in the stake president's office when we arrived. The next Monday the operation was not needed."[4]

Following a stake conference in Yellowstone in 1970, Duff recorded, "I was introduced to a little girl whose name is 'Marian Dee'—a little girl whose mother was having a desperate time getting her here, and I was asked to go and administer to her. I remember the night very well, and this little girl and her wonderful parents were quite warm and sweet and filled with emotion as we met ten years later."[5]

One day a sweet woman exited an elevator, breaking into tears. He wrote, "Twenty years ago, I gave her a blessing in the hospital just after the doctor had told her she had three months to live. She said, 'You gave me back my health, you gave me my life.' I listened with love and then corrected that carefully. I have no power to give anyone health or life, but ONE does, and did."[6]

In a letter to Elder Paul Dunn, Duff described a time when he and Elder Dunn gave a blessing to a one-month-old baby who lay dying with brain and heart problems. Years later, he had just met a normal, beautiful little girl. He wrote, "As I remembered the moment when our fingertips were laid so gently on that little hospital stocking cap, I wept inside at how little we know, and how humbly we must function when we represent the Lord."[7]

---

2. Letter to MDH, Aug. 27, 2000.
3. Bill Cannon to MDH, n.d.
4. MDH-JE, Aug. 11, 1984.
5. MDH-JE, 1970.
6. MDH-JE, Sept. 12, 1984.
7. MDH-L to Paul Dunn, July 22, 1985.

Duff regularly met with people he had administered to over the years. He wrote, "There are astounding stories about the one experience which most leaves me humble and helpless and causes me to rely solely upon the Lord. I have had some monumental failures, mostly in instances where I could not separate myself and my desires from my purpose and Priesthood. I sorrowed for these, but did not grieve, since I have never had and can never have the power of decision; I can only approach the Lord in broken heart, completely dependent, but joyfully so, upon Him."

Duff wrote, "Sometimes I write too casually and too critically about things. But behind all of this is the unrejectable fact that something is afoot here much bigger than my limitations and much better than my failings. The Lord has worked through me on many special occasions, and I am left to clearly see my absolute limitation and helplessness. He decides, not any man, not I. "If they die they shall die unto me, and if they live they shall live unto me" (D&C 42:44).[8]

In his quiet moments, Duff reflected on God's miraculous healing intervention in some situations and his silence in others. He wrote about one hospital visit where he went to administer to a man near death from cancer. He had a son on a mission and three other little boys, a beautiful wife, and everything to live for, and so wanted to live. Somewhat grimly he talked with Duff about the possible reasons for God taking him at this time. He could see little sense in it. After praying together, the man told his wife that he was reconciled to leave everything in the hands of the Lord. He died four days later. Duff reflected, "Such experiences for me are traumatic in the extreme, though I do my best to make them a part of an effort to do what I am called to do. Soon after I learned of his death, I also learned that the young wife and mother to whom I had administered in Hawaii recently had gone that weekend to the hospital for a cancer operation only to be told by an astonished set of physicians that she had no traces of cancer. They were mystified."

Duff expressed faith and humility: "I know the Lord heals, but I do not know when or why. Repeatedly, I have been involved in things that are as miraculous as any in the New Testament. There have been numerous incidents where people in the throes of mortal illnesses have been made well. Some of them are in my own family. On the other hand, some I love best have slipped away, despite my pleas and entreaties and earnest petitions to the Lord. I know the Lord can heal and that He does, but I do not know when He will, or why."[9]

LISTENING TO THE SPIRIT

No matter how bright or educated or capable a person may be,
he cannot learn the things of God, except through the Spirit.
—Marion D. Hanks[10]

8. MDH-JE, Sept. 12, 1984.
9. MDH-JE, Apr. 6, 1971.
10. MDH-T, New Zealand Area Conference, Feb. 22, 1976.

In addition to miracles related to priesthood healing blessings, Duff was blessed to experience numerous and ongoing interactions with the Spirit, providing intuition and inspiration to help him do his work.

"It is a very sweet pleasure to feel on occasion the warm impressions and expressions of the Spirit," Duff wrote. "I have had enough of those along the way to know when it is happening, and it happened Sunday ... with all of the concerns that exist, the word of the Lord is sweet and delightful, bringing comfort to the soul and joy to the heart. The central focus of that message is the Lord Jesus Christ and what He did for us.... I do love the Lord."[11]

Duff also had some unusually strong specific experiences. They were personal to him, and he shared them infrequently, so most are lost to history. But there are a few documented that are representative.

In December 1969, Duff and Elder Harold B. Lee spoke at an LDSSA convention in Salt Lake City. As the meeting closed, a young man gave the benediction, and the Spirit filled the entire room. Duff wrote, "It was a remarkable and unusual prayer that no one there will ever forget." As the conducting officer, Duff remained seated for several minutes and then stood at the pulpit in silence as waves of spiritual power swept through the room. Not a soul stirred for at least fifteen minutes.

In a temple meeting of general authorities in 1978, one of the apostles in attendance reported that he had seen a vision of "someone who looked just like Wilford Woodruff sitting in a chair above the organ, watching and participating.... He was perfectly rational and humble about it."[12]

In 1988, Duff presided at a stake conference in Des Moines, Iowa, and afterward received a letter from an attendee who shared from her journal, "Marion D. Hanks was conducting the conference, talking about fathers on Father's Day, and mentioning how he had lost his father as a child. I looked up at the podium ... with compassion ... and I gasped. There standing on either side of him, it seemed to me, were two personages—I believe they were his parents."[13]

A single mother described feeling alone at a meeting: "Everyone else was there with a companion, but I was there [alone]. Somehow you knew my situation, even though you did not know me. You directed a portion of your remarks directly to me, by mentioning your own dear mother and her long time in a mother-alone status. No one else knew it, and we did not speak. I am not even sure you knew what you were doing, or that I would understand. But it touched my heart and I have never forgotten."

Earlier in this book, I reported briefly on Duff's prior knowledge, by the Spirit, of some of his callings, and how on multiple occasions where, despite lengthy preparation for speaking about one subject, he felt he should put away his notes

11. MDH-JE, Mar. 30, 1975.

12. MDH-JE, 1978.

13. Letter to MDH, June 20, 1988.

and speak on a completely different topic. Only *after* his remarks did he discover that someone in the audience had been praying for him to speak about just that subject. For example, Duff received a letter from a young man who thirty-one years earlier had attended a fireside as a high school senior. After some opening remarks, Duff spoke about Alma 42:29, which is an invitation to let sins "trouble you no more." The man wrote, "Each word was balm to my soul." Duff then remarked that he hadn't planned to affirm this scripture but that someone in the congregation needed it. "Then you proceeded to deliver your prepared address, the substance of which I forgot. Every time I read Alma 42 I think of you, telling one young man in a chapel of a hundred, that the Good Shepherd loves him."[14]

Late in his life, Duff had long been in a care center when a letter arrived, addressed to Maxine:

> Dear Sister Hanks,
>
> I was raised in Salt Lake with some strong feelings against the church. When I joined, it was a decision I made with some opposition and ridicule. [As a new convert], I had just been taught that God and Christ were separate beings, when I read Mosiah 15:1–5 that said Christ was both the Father and the Son. I was filled with confusion and did not know what to do. A fraternity brother at the U invited me to go to a class taught by Elder Hanks. So, I went.
>
> There were about 300 people in attendance, and everyone was engrossed in the subject your husband was teaching. Then, in the middle of class, Elder Hanks stopped and said, "There is something I need to cover." I can still remember him closing the Doctrine and Covenants and opening the Book of Mormon. I had no clue what was about to happen. He turned to Mosiah 15 and read aloud the first five verses, then gave a brief explanation and a reference to the letter from the First Presidency in the appendix of the book *The Articles of Faith.* He then closed the Book of Mormon, opened back up the D&C, and finished the class. Often when things have seemed tough, I remember that experience. I will always be thankful he was listening to the Spirit that night.[15]

Duff was willing to improvise in situations where flexibility was required. Once, he took his son Richard to LDS Hospital to see Elder Paul H. Dunn, who was recuperating from surgery. After some moments of small talk, Elder Dunn asked Duff to give him a priesthood blessing. Usually, this would require two ordained elders, but Rich was only seventeen and not yet an elder. Dad went over to Elder Dunn to anoint, and Rich held back, at which point they both said, almost in unison, "Get over here, Rich." Rich reminded them that he didn't yet hold the Melchizedek Priesthood. And again, almost in unison, they both said, "Oh, get over here. God knows who you are." That was an important lesson in Rich's life in several ways. People are more important than procedures; surely God can allow us flexibility.

14. Stephen Snyder to MDH, 2004.
15. Bob Raybould to Maxine Hanks, Apr. 17, 2007.

PERSONAL RIGHTEOUSNESS

It is better to be good than to be clever.[16]

Duff put a special premium on his own personal righteousness. He knew he needed to keep himself in a position to hear the promptings of the Spirit, writing: "Maxine and I went to our once-a-year movie. The movie was supposed to be about the life of Franz Liszt—whose life turned out to be musically great and morally filthy. I did not enjoy the evening. I cannot afford to put myself into circumstances which minimize the possibility of the Spirit of the Lord being with us and which maximizes the elements in our nature which need no emphasis. Liszt apparently was a lecher and a libertine and a completely irresponsible, immoral man. His music will never mean quite the same to me."[17]

Duff was continually trying to improve his worthiness. On a well-worn card inside the front cover of his scriptures: "Paul teaches us that our lives are important in 'adorn[ing] the doctrine of God our Savior' and making it lovely and beautiful by our daily habits and tempers (Titus 2:10)."

Duff believed that sanctification as a process is just as important as justification, quoting, "Sound . . . doctrine is useless if it is not accompanied by a holy life. It is worse than useless. . . . It is despised by . . . shrewd men of the world as an unreal and hollow thing, and brings religion into contempt."[18]

President George Albert Smith visited the Northern States Mission while Duff was serving there. Duff was having a problem controlling his thoughts, thinking that as a missionary he ought to be able to live without unworthy thoughts. President Smith taught the missionaries that everyone has bad thoughts; identify them for what they are and get rid of them. He explained how important it was to not deliberately entertain them and toy with them. Duff later taught some missionaries, "I decided that if I could learn to control my muscles, I could learn to identify and expel thoughts I didn't want. I've been fighting ever since to do that and so will you. I mean we, not you. We."[19]

GRATITUDE AND REVERENCE FOR HOLY THINGS

I would rather feel compunction than know the definition thereof.
—Thomas à Kempis[20]

The Hanks children were taught to be grateful for everything the Lord has given. Duff loved teachings by Rabbi Abraham J. Heschel, who said, "Unless

16. MDH, on a sticky note in his desk, possibly quoting from *The Christian World Magazine*, vol. 8 (1872).

17. MDH-JE, Nov. 16, 1960.

18. J. C. Ryle, "Holiness: Its Nature, Hindrances, Difficulties, and Roots," in *Christian Classics Ethereal Library*, ccel.org.

19. MDH-A, *Success Messenger*, Aug. 1966.

20. Thomas à Kempis, *The Imitation of Christ*.

there is appreciation, there is no mankind. The real dignity of anything is in its relationship to God who created it. Unless we learn how to revere, we will not know how to exist as human beings."[21]

Duff taught reverence for holy things through his example and knew that reverence before God required effort, not just lip service. As someone once said, "No one ever drifted into holiness."

When he was asked to administer a priesthood blessing, if it was feasible, he would prepare by praying, washing his hands, and putting on a white shirt. Regardless of the time or place, Duff demonstrated through his actions that this was a special time. Family prayers, prayers at meals, father's blessings, and one-on-ones were all times where Duff taught the concepts of holiness through his actions. For a few years, Rich was Duff's home-teaching companion. Every time they went on their visits, they would stop and pray to the Lord to ask for his help and guidance before they went in to teach each family. By his actions, Duff taught his son that this time was different than the humdrum of normal life.

One late afternoon, they were called on to give Sister Vest a blessing. The Vests lived right in the middle of several fraternity houses just off the University of Utah campus. On arrival, two of the closest frat houses were blasting loud music outside. It was so loud as to be annoying. They prayed and went into the home, where all the windows were open. Just as Duff laid his hands on Sister Vest's head, the music stopped. When he finished the blessing and lifted his hands off her head, the music resumed immediately. Duff didn't notice, but Rich did. He was positive that it was the hand of God. Without discounting the miraculous as a potentiality, Duff offered a plausible alternative: perhaps the Spirit of God had touched the heart of some of the fraternity boys, who had recognized them as servants of the Lord on His errand and had stopped the music out of courtesy. There was no way to know the real cause, but either scenario was a marker of the importance of the ordinance they had gone there to perform.

Once while standing in a meal line at a jamboree, a man dressed in a Scout uniform took the name of the Lord in vain a dozen times until finally Duff turned to him and said, "That name is sacred to me." He spoke softly and courteously, and the man responded in the same way. Duff wrote, "As usual, he seemed not to know what he was doing and was embarrassed to hear it. Others looked at me a little peculiarly, but I think it was done with some taste, and there were no repercussions other than those I am pleased to bear."[22]

Matthew Arnold, a renowned British poet and literary critic, said that the greatest single line in literature was uttered by the famous Italian poet Dante when he said, "In Thy will is our peace." This quotation was scattered repeatedly throughout Duff's private notes and in several of his published talks.[23] Duff

21. Rabbi Abraham J. Heschel, radio interview, Jan. 21, 1968.

22. MDH-L unknown, July 1973.

23. MDH-T, "Follow the King," Mar. 11, 1986, speeches.byu.edu.

reminded us that God's wisdom and grace are infinite and well beyond our ability to comprehend. Therefore, when we submit to his will, we can be assured Heavenly Father will do what is best for us.

CHOOSING DALLIN OAKS AS BYU PRESIDENT

On many occasions, Duff felt the Spirit speak through him in choosing and calling people to positions. Some were very unusual experiences.

In March 1971, a search committee consisting of Marion G. Romney, Boyd K. Packer, and Marion D. Hanks was created to petition the Lord for the right man to serve as the next president of Brigham Young University, replacing Ernest L. Wilkinson. A number of strong candidates were interviewed. Duff recorded, "They were all outstanding, but Dallin Oaks made the strongest impression on me. He is a professor of law at the University of Chicago, is young and vital, very bright, very faithful, and a member of a stake presidency."

Meeting as a committee, they "prayed often and earnestly" and then cast lots, each voting for a different man. Elder Romney then led them in a discussion, where they talked about each candidate and presented their supporting positions. Duff wrote, "Dallin is the least well known, but the one I recommended. The other two are also fine men."

Three days later, they met again in Marion G. Romney's office to discuss the situation and recast their lots. President Romney joined Duff in voting for Oaks. Romney asked for suggestions on next steps. "Boyd answered that he felt we should go in united." Elder Romney had them each pray again, Elder Packer first because he needed the persuading, then Duff, then himself last. Duff wrote, "When we met in the afternoon, just prior to going into the office of the First Presidency, we were all agreed that the man we would recommend was Dallin Oaks."[24]

In November 1971, at the installation of President Oaks at BYU, Duff recorded, "It was a memorable event. This choice young man more than justified the recommendations of those who moved him into this present opportunity. He does not know that this is one instance where the Lord prompted a move, but for which, he would not be where he is. Far from wanting credit, I give credit where it is due. Brother Romney responded on the second ballot, and Brother Packer, reluctantly, also. It was obvious today that he is the one."[25]

CALLING NEW STAKE PRESIDENTS

When an LDS stake needs a new stake president, usually two general or area church leaders are assigned to visit the stake for a two-day conference. That time is extremely busy—all day Saturday, between thirty and fifty recommended men are interviewed to determine who the Lord would like to be the next stake president. That man is informed and chooses two counselors. Then on Sunday morning in

24. MDH-JE, Mar. 26, 1971.
25. MDH-JE, Nov. 12, 1971.

the large stake conference meeting, the outgoing presidency is released with a vote of thanks, and the new stake presidency is presented and sustained by the members of the stake. In forty years serving as a general authority, Duff was involved in calling well over a hundred stake presidents. He wrote, "I have never explained to others how the Spirit moved and how so many knew who was going to be a stake president, including the man himself. There is a kind of an unusual set of experiences often connected with this kind of business."[26]

Sometimes, the reorganization presented awkward challenges. On more than one occasion, an outgoing stake presidency, outside the approved process, had already decided in advance among themselves who the successor stake presidency should be. Nothing was said, but it was fairly obvious to discern: the man's entire family was gathered home for the dad's "coronation" (as Duff wrote in his journal). Sometimes Duff was given lodging in the man's home, ate meals with his family, and was driven back and forth to the meetings by him. And then after interviewing all day Saturday, when the inspiration of the Spirit suggested a different man, Duff had to inform them.

On several occasions, the individual being called was so overwhelmed that he chose to try to avoid the responsibility. Duff described an occasion where he and his companion finished interviewing many men, but after their prayers, no one felt right to be the new stake president. The two general authorities began to be a bit anxious because thousands of people were expecting to meet their new stake president the next morning. So, Duff asked for a list of all the high priests in the stake, and as he reviewed it, the name of one man—a complete stranger—clearly stood out to him. After asking if the man was active in the church, Duff asked to meet with him. The outgoing stake president said, "He usually attends all stake conference meetings, but I haven't seen him tonight." Duff asked for a car ride to the man's house. When his wife opened the door, Duff asked if her husband was at home. When she returned with him, he was looking down at the floor.

Duff asked the man if he knew why he was visiting. The man responded, "Yes, I've known I was going to be called as the new stake president for several days, but I thought if I just skipped the meetings, you would call someone else." After an interview together, Duff called the man to be the new stake president, he accepted the calling, and he served as an exceptional leader.[27]

Another example: Duff and Elder Vaughn J. Featherstone were inspired to set apart three men in a stake presidency, none of whom was on the original list for interviews. Elder Featherstone asked the new stake president how long he had known of his call prior to receiving it. He acknowledged that he had deliberately spent the day in the hills with his children because he had not originally been invited to the interviews and was attempting to reconcile the voice of the Spirit

26. MDH-JE, Apr. 16, 1978.

27. MDH-JE, n.d. See also Dan Peterson, "Jonah and the Reluctant Stake President," May 13, 2018, Patheos.com.

that had told him that he was to be appointed with the fact that he had not even been invited in to be interviewed.[28]

Duff was occasionally presented with the difficulty of needing to discern who the Lord wanted to be the next stake president when he was acquainted with one or more of the candidates. Perhaps no situation was as awkward as a time when he went to reorganize the stake presidency of the St. George Utah West Stake. Three of his beloved former missionaries were in the candidate pool he interviewed that Saturday morning. All three were repeatedly spoken well of and, in effect, nominated by the others being interviewed. Duff wrote, "The ultimate reality was that none of them was chosen, although all three were considered." He then spoke warmly about each and his desire that one of them could be chosen, "but that isn't the way it was with the Spirit. A choice presidency was launched. They will have their hands full but will faithfully and effectively do the work."[29]

PRAYER

Duff was often nervous to pray in public. He considered that feeling a thorn in his side. On his mission, Duff recorded feeling the same breathlessness when anticipating being asked to kneel in prayer after a mission conference, writing, "I can't quite reconcile myself to calling it fright, because I've never been bothered by the feeling in any other circumstance. Audiences of tens, hundreds, and thousands have not bothered me at all. But always the same breathlessness when I've knelt to pray with a group. Later, one of the other people in attendance told me that President Muir had said that there has never been a prayer equal to that in the mission home. I am grateful, but confronted with the knowledge of my own impotence and ignorance."[30]

HIS PERSONAL TESTIMONY

Duff's testimony of the Savior, His gospel, and the restored church came through like a ton of bricks. One could feel it in his presence and when he spoke. He lived his testimony in both word and deed. His testimony is best expressed in his own words: "I say to you that there are those who know for certain for themselves that God lives, that Jesus is the Christ, and that living his commandments and being honest with ourselves is the only way really to motivate the young.... I testify that I do know these things."[31]

He acknowledged that the witness of the Spirit feels different sometimes:

> I have felt that strong affirmation in my viscera and spine that constituted more than an emotional moment. The force and power of the truth rested upon me. In D&C 121:45, when it says, "Then shall thy confidence wax strong in the presence

28. MDH-T, "Principles and Procedures in Selecting a New Stake President," meeting of the First Quorum of the Seventy, Jan. 11, 1979, 6.

29. MDH-L to Bob Garff, Feb. 27, 1990.

30. MDH-JE, Oct. 4, 1943.

31. MDH-T, "Be Honest with Yourselves," GC, Apr. 1958.

> of God," I believe this is generally true of me. I have confidence as I talk to the Lord that He not only understands, but that He will respond in ways which his wisdom dictates, and I just leave it at that.
>
> The alarm bells and the burning bosom are not always present for me, and my long experience tells me this is true of others. There are those who seek to have a personal assurance on an immediate and conclusive basis that, generally speaking, are foreign to me. Daily I need help. I pray for that help in a modest way. The answers will come, and they will be the right answers. Of this, I have absolute assurance. But they may be different answers than I would like.[32]

He bore witness of the Father's plan of happiness and gospel teachings:

> I express my confidence that there is a living God and that He loves us and is our Father. He has a plan for us for a redemption, bringing mercy and opening the door to happiness. The heart of that plan is the Lord Jesus Christ. The commandments given of God through Him as part of the plan are essential to our happiness and to the enjoyment of our fullest eternal potential. That plan taught through the ages has been restored.[33]

A note in Duff's scriptures summarized his enduring faith in eternal truths:

> As sure as the sun greets the morning and the rivers run to the sea—
> God lives, and is good,
> Christ is our Savior and Redeemer.
> Life is eternal.
> Love is eternal.
> Relationships are eternal.
> Personality persists—Let us do well our part.
> —Marion D. Hanks

32. MDH-L to Jim Purdy, 1988.
33. MDH, First Quorum of Seventy meeting, Aug. 23, 1984.

A FOCUS ON FAITH AND DOING THE NEEDFUL

34

The 1960s, an Overview

The 1960s were a tumultuous decade defined in the United States and Europe by counterculture protests; the civil rights movement; the proliferation of rock music; the Vietnam War; and the assassinations of President John F. Kennedy, Bobby Kennedy, and Martin Luther King Jr. On the other hand, man landed on the moon, *Sesame Street* began airing, and smallpox was virtually eradicated.

Major happenings in the 1960s church included creation of the first non-English-speaking stake, a lowering of missionary age for young men from twenty to nineteen, the formalizing of family home evening, the change from ward teaching to home teaching, and the beginning of formal language training for missionaries.

For Duff and Maxine, the 1960s also meant significant changes in their lives. After four daughters, Maxine gave birth to a son, whom they named Richard. Duff's mother, Maude, passed away, as did his oldest brother.

Duff and Maxine were called to lead the mission in London, and along with the other members of the First Council of the Seventy, Duff was ordained a high priest and received the sealing power. He was called as the supervisor over the church's Southeast Asia Area and made a great effort to visit, on four separate occasions, the servicemen in Vietnam, traveling right up to enemy lines to meet with them. He also spent a lot of time with the missionaries in Korea and in Japan. Later in the decade, he was called to be an Assistant to the Twelve Apostles.

While in Britain, Duff participated in the creation of the first stake in Scotland, the land of his forebears, and in military leadership meetings in Germany. He began serving on the church's Board of Education.

Outside his church assignments, he continued to participate in the national leadership of the Boy Scouts, joined the Rotary Club in Salt Lake City, and served on the board of Beneficial Life Insurance Company. He also attended a couple of Scout Jamborees and the highly prestigious Army War College Strategy Meetings.

DEDICATING THE NEW CHAPEL AT KALAUPAPA

Just after Christmas 1965, Duff and Maxine traveled to Hawaii to Kalaupapa, Molokai, to dedicate the new chapel in the settlement, where patients had Hansen's disease, also known as leprosy. Duff dedicated perhaps hundreds of chapels over the years, but this was a special occasion. The chapel had dividers down the middle—patients were on one side and visitors on the other, with their own restrooms. The meeting was touching and included a double quartet of a few blind men and others leaning on them. Maxine said, "They sang with the spirit of angels." The patients were tragically impaired but full of the Spirit. Maxine and Duff felt it was one of the sweetest experiences of their lives.[1]

VISITING BEHIND THE IRON CURTAIN

In 1966, Duff visited the Swiss and Berlin stakes. In East Berlin, behind the Iron Curtain, he held a meeting with about fifty church members. He bore testimony and spoke with the people. He wrote, "They are depressed and much imposed upon, but still maintain faith and courage to meet together in the name of Christ. The stakes are not strong, but they are well led, and much strong effort is being made to lift them up."

NO CUTBACK ON SPEAKING SCHEDULE

Duff kept a rigorous speaking schedule during the 1960s. In addition to stake conferences virtually every weekend, he spoke at baccalaureate services and graduation commencements at Brigham Young University, Ricks College, Eastern Arizona College, Utah State, Church College of Hawaii, Weber State, and Dixie College. He also dedicated chapels and buildings across the country.

He attended and spoke at conferences in Tokyo, Hong Kong, Korea, Washington, DC, England, and countries throughout the Pacific, Australia, New Zealand, and South America and continued teaching his institute classes in Salt Lake City.

1. MDH-JE, Dec. 26, 1965.

35

Mission to England

In 1961, President David O. McKay invited Duff to his office and asked him if he would take on a very difficult job as the new mission president in London. He said they needed someone who could handle a challenging situation.

Duff replied, "Fine. We're ready to go."

But then First Presidency counselor Hugh B. Brown called Duff in and asked him to list the speeches and appointments he had already committed to. Duff explained his upcoming major speeches and the national committees he was serving on, including the President's Council on Physical Fitness and Sports. President Brown said his call would be postponed, but he was to take on no new appointments.

Three months later, President McKay called him in again and told him that he was officially being called to go to England to "stop the excessive baptizing of young people" and "to set the mission in order." President McKay said, "I told the brethren in the temple this morning that you were the only one among the general authorities who could take on this kind of job and set the missionary program there in order. They were enthusiastic and will support this call."

Duff asked, "When?"

President McKay replied, "Now."[1]

PREPARATION AND DEPARTURE

Maxine immediately began preparations to uproot their family of seven and move to London. Their farewell service was held on January 14, 1962, at the Federal Heights Ward on University Street in Salt Lake City.

Duff, Maxine, and their five children (Susan, Nancy, Ann, Mary, and Richard) arrived in London on January 22, 1962. President Hanks was forty years old; Sister Hanks was thirty-six.

Soon after their arrival, the *Millenial Star*, the church's official publication in England, published an interview with the new president. "I had always wanted to have the blessing of another missionary opportunity and was overjoyed to get this unexpected call," he told the *Star*. "The mission needs strong leadership and adult

1. MDH-R, Nov. 1, 2000.

The Hanks family departing for England, January 1962:
Mary, Ann, Duff, Richard, Maxine, Susan, Nancy.

members who are able and willing to accept responsibility. My prayer is that we may build some sound foundations in this respect.

... To the extent I am able, I would very much like to help the youth of Great Britain. I have been blessed with many opportunities to try to do this in America, and I hope I may have similar opportunities here."[2]

WAKE-UP CALL ON ARRIVAL

The Hanks family arrived in London amid what Duff called a "maelstrom of baptizing that had gotten out of hand, with contests, and competition, and unholy pressure." All these years later, some try to put a spin on this era of missionary work by saying things like, "Baptisms were high; quality and retention were low." Duff responded by pointing out that, in fact, the number of baptisms was off the charts and retention was near zero because most of those being baptized didn't even know they were now members of the church. Some thought they had joined the "MIA Club" and gone swimming.

Newspapers were running negative stories about missionaries rounding up young kids and baptizing them without asking their parents' permission. The British government had threatened the church with official sanctions, and it was not viewed in a good light. Things looked grim. There was no way to make "slight

2. MDH-A, *Millennial Star*, Apr. 1962, 84–86.

adjustments" or to "slide gradually" into the changes that needed to be made. Duff realized he needed to make major course corrections quickly.

President McKay sent Duff to England to put the place in order, without any instructions on how to do that except to rely on the Spirit of the Lord. Duff later recalled, "Things changed from the first hour after I arrived. Without reference to predecessors or previous procedures, we simply taught the program of the Lord—and added the small demand that every baptism for the first few months be performed in my presence. I never mentioned the previous mission president's name, except respectfully, but I changed everything he was doing."[3]

A HOUSE DIVIDED

Just when he thought things couldn't get any more challenging, Duff found out how really difficult a position he was in. Despite President McKay's personal charge to him and his own distaste for the excesses he was learning about, it seemed that not all the leading brethren at church headquarters understood what was going on.

On January 23, 1962, just one day after arriving in England, he recorded in his journal, "Today was our first mission meeting in Britain. Spencer W. Kimball and Howard W. Hunter were present, together with the Area President, N. Eldon Tanner, who conducted. The speakers included three of the current mission presidents in Britain: T. Bowring Woodbury, Bernard P. Brockbank, and Grant Thorn. When Spencer Kimball rose to speak, he gave credit to President and Sister Woodbury for 'opening the gates to a new era of missionary work.'"

Imagine the confusion those statements caused Duff, since they contradicted specific instructions he had received from President McKay to "fix the problems" occurring in the very same British Mission. His journal entry concluded: "This was an interesting meeting which left me cold and somewhat apprehensive, but greatly determined. It was immediately obvious that this is going to be anything but a picnic over here, and sometimes it will be very much the opposite. The Lord help me to do what President McKay said the Lord had called me to do, namely, 'set the British Mission in order.'"

INTO THE FRYING PAN

The British media and government immediately targeted the new mission president. One of his first exposures to the difficulty at hand was being called to a meeting across the street from 10 Downing Street (the prime minister's home) to listen to some of Prince Philip's friends mock the church. They had stacks of newspaper clippings and articles, with pictures of little kids dressed in white, their parents standing behind them, with headlines attacking the church. Duff recalled, "Here's this tough guy, one of Prince Philip's closest friends, letting me have it. I had an English stake president with me, and the two of us just stood

3. MDH-L to EB, Sept. 20, 1985.

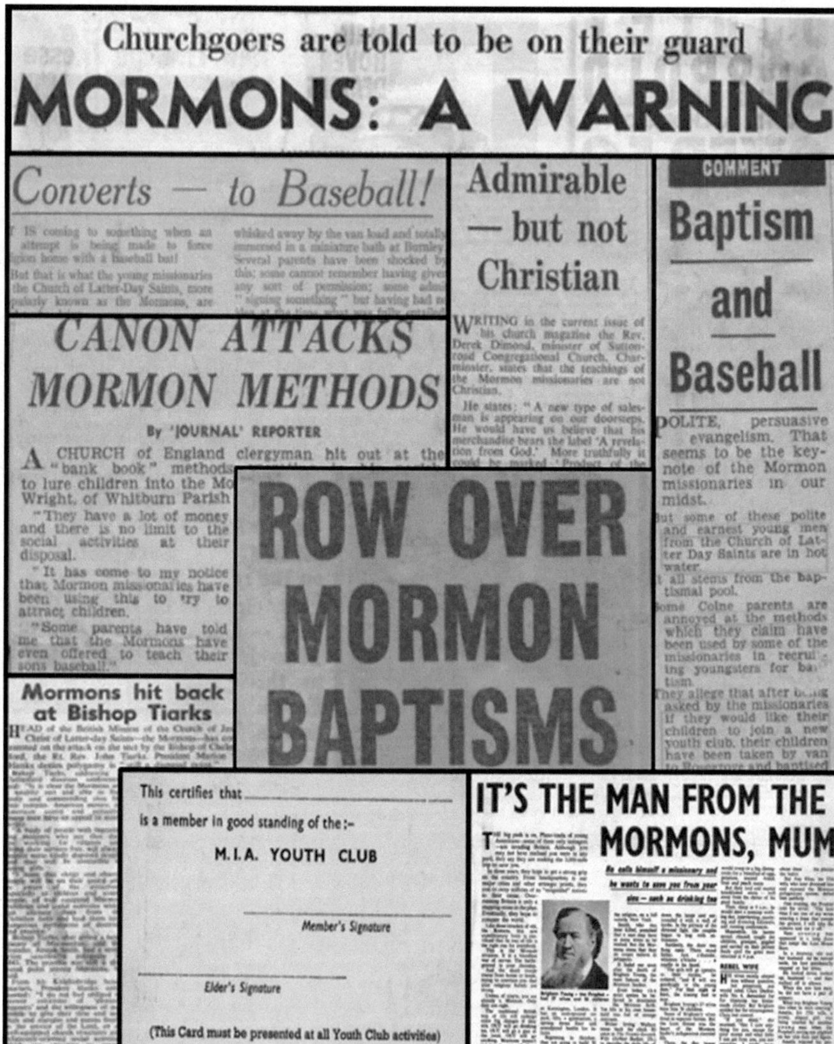

A collection of headlines from British newspapers about the Baseball Baptisms scandal.

there and took a beating. Then I spoke and told them that I was new, and I had the responsibility for stopping it." They brought out an article from *Time* magazine with a picture of Duff's predecessor and his wife with the caption "Have baptism, will travel."

Finally, Duff had had enough. "I faced the man that was giving us hell, and said, 'Look, I've listened to all of this I intend to listen to. You've heard now that I had nothing to do with this. If you get any more reports like this, they will not be valid. By the time you hear from me again, I will have spoken with every missionary in this mission, and we'll all understand that none of this is going to go on any longer.' They were talking about throwing us out of England, the Magna Carta country where the church had been for a hundred years!"[4]

HOW DID IT GET TO THIS STATE?

This book will not cover in detail the baseball baptism era of the late 1950s and early 1960s or its causes and collapse. It has been documented extensively elsewhere.[5] Nor will this book examine the alternative and sometimes contradictory views people have about missionary methods and approaches to acquiring converts. There are a few who hold different opinions whether what occurred before Duff arrived was good for the church, the missionaries and members, and the individuals who were baptized. What he believed is obvious to see in the actions he took.

Duff wasn't the first to encounter what was going on with such aggressive missionary programs in Britain and in other places around the world. Other church leaders had become aware of the excesses but had chosen to remain silent, some possibly agreeing with the methods being employed and others thinking that perhaps President McKay was aware of what was going on.

When President Henry D. Moyle was in Manchester in November 1960, he answered criticisms by telling the missionaries, "I have noted a little apologetic tone in some of your voices about baptizing too many young people. Well, don't you put on the brakes."[6]

A few mission presidents around the world were competing with each other to have the highest number of baptisms. For example, it was reported that in 1959, Great Britain and continental Europe baptized 9 percent of all convert baptisms in the LDS Church. A year later, Britain and Europe accounted for 36 percent of the church's convert baptisms.

As an example of how far things had gone, a contest was launched the year before Duff's arrival in which missionaries were told to honor their mothers by baptizing four people and that those who did so would be able to meet the prophet at the dedication of the Hyde Park Chapel. By implication, those not hitting quota had dishonored their mothers and would not get to see the prophet.[7]

DEFENDING THE INDEFENSIBLE

Many years later, Duff wrote: "Brought to my remembrance was a comment made to me by one of the apostles who was visiting us in London early on. After hearing and seeing the results of the past, he then said to me that he "hoped the

---

4. MDH-R, Jan. 11, 2002.

5. For example, see D. Michael Quinn, "I-Thou vs. I-It Conversions: The Mormon 'Baseball Baptism' Era," *Sunstone*, Dec. 1993, 30.

6. Gary Hansen, "A Firsthand Account of the New Era in Great Britain: 1958–1961" Aug. 6, 2015.

7. Vern Anderson, "Baseball Baptisms in '60s . . . ," *Salt Lake Tribune*, Aug. 15, 1993, C-15.

glorious records of the past could be maintained without the '*rumored excesses.*' Bah! The consequences of that time are still, and will eternally be, visited upon the church. Having looked at it for 12 years, I can't see one redeemable facet of it, and in fact it looks more ugly to me the longer I live."[8]

Early in life, Duff had Rich memorize a quote attributed to Abraham Lincoln: "You will never get me to support a measure which I believe to be wrong, although by doing so I may accomplish that which I believe to be right."[9]

In 1971, on his flight home from an area conference in Manchester, England, Duff reflected on his earlier time as a mission president in London: "The thoughts in my heart have been gracious and grateful ones. We made a difference here once, and people remember. We were honest and certainly brave enough, considering, and we did the right thing. And that must be it: not *who* is right, but *what* is right. We must try always to do that, with less grimness and more joy, remembering, not *who,* but *what* is right."

SLAMMING ON THE BRAKES

Duff immediately ended baptism quotas and stopped all the competitions and award systems that were driving the excesses. He also interviewed each missionary and explained the procedures that would be in place going forward. The previous administration's definition of a "family baptism" was any two individuals living under the same roof. This was changed to include at least one parent.[10]

As a result, the number of baptisms dropped precipitously, and Duff was soon criticized by President Henry D. Moyle, as well as by the presidents of some of the other British missions and a few local church leaders.

Thankfully, President McKay called Duff one day, saying, "I know what's happening there, and I want you to know I support you every step of the way." He then told Duff that President Moyle and Elder Gordon B. Hinckley were in London to meet with government officials. When Duff subsequently spoke with the two church leaders, President Moyle questioned him cynically, pointing out the huge drop in baptisms and rumors he'd heard that Duff was "teaching a seminary class with his missionaries."

Duff felt the need to defend his missionaries, who were working hard to serve the Lord. He had been there long enough to know them and the wonderful way

8. MDH-JE, Apr. 3, 1975.

9. Ida M. Tarbell, *The Life of Abraham Lincoln* (McClure & Phillips, 1900), 1:139.

10. The pressure to baptize is much less overt now, but subtle reminders remain—ranked lists of baptisms by mission, baptisms-per-missionary statistics, concerns expressed over "too much service" given by missionaries. Some people believe that the growth of the church is proof of its truthfulness. But if that were so, then God's reputation would depend upon how big we can make His church. The Savior gave the command to go into all the world and baptize, but he also focused on the retention of those baptized. For example, Matthew 28:19–20: "Teach all nations, baptizing them, . . . *teaching them to observe all things*" (emphasis added) and John 15:16: "Bring forth fruit, and *that your fruit should remain*" (emphasis added).

Maxine and Duff Hanks working in the London, England, mission office, 1962.

they had responded to the change in direction. He pointed out to President Moyle that though the number of baptisms was much lower than the previous year, they were, in fact, much higher than the average had been over the years before the "baseball baptism" programs. And no, he wasn't teaching a seminary class; he was helping the missionaries gain a testimony of what they'd been sent to England to teach.

Duff felt grateful for the loyalty of Apostle Mark E. Petersen, who as president of the West European Mission supervised all the European missions and was headquartered in another location in London. He spoke with every incoming group of Duff's missionaries and told them, "If you want assurance that the church is run by inspiration, then know that David O. McKay got up and spoke to us about sending your mission president here, because he's the only man who could do what has to be done."[11]

It took an abundance of intestinal fortitude for Duff to stick by his guns and continue with his chosen path in spite of some opposition, but he nonetheless moved forward, knowing what was right. To this day, there are still a few who say that what occurred in England prior to Duff's arrival "wasn't really all that bad." But, as has been said, facts are stubborn things. As but one example, eighteen months into Duff's mission, he received a letter from the Cambridge Branch president, saying, "I have completed a careful analysis of the 37 youth who came

11. MDH-R, Aug. 8, 2000.

into the church during the years 1960–61. Each received baptism as a condition of membership in the 'LDS Youth Club.' So far as I can ascertain, not one of them has any understanding whatsoever as to the ordinance of baptism. We have made a real effort to activate them and to interest their parents, without any success."[12]

Thirty years after his mission in Britain, one of his colleagues who was serving in the Europe Area Presidency wrote him, "During my mission in Germany in 1960–1963, word crossed the channel that President Marion D. Hanks, the newly called mission president in Britain, was emphasizing building the kingdom upon Melchizedek Priesthood leaders and families. That took great courage for you at that time to stand by your principles in the wake of a lot of countervailing pressure. Your example 30 years ago has been an inspiration and comfort to us presently as we have had to make some mid-course corrections in order to do the right things for the right reasons."[13]

A NEW PROGRAM: THE BOOK OF MORMON

Duff taught the missionaries that the focus going forward would be on conversion and retention, not just on baptism. Believing that one of the keys to real conversion was the Book of Mormon, he prepared his missionaries to teach and testify of it. The first thing he did was to ask each missionary to get a general overview of the Book of Mormon by reading an inexpensive edition in two weeks with a regular black pencil in their hands, putting question marks and notes for future reference. At the end of the two weeks, they were to begin again, this time with a red pencil, and, as they read, to mark every mention or reference to Christ and the doctrines centering on Him.

"At the conclusion of these two readings is when the miracle set in: They felt familiar with the book," Duff wrote. "They had a sense of the mission of Christ that they had never understood before. Then, we started a third reading, this time with no time frame. They were to read with a blue pencil, marking those stories or instructions that had direct *application* to their own lives. This third undertaking might occupy a lifetime, but the expectation was that the missionary would continue to read and expand his understanding and friendship with this great book."

Elder Hyrum Smith later wrote, "My mission president was Elder Marion D. Hanks—one of the greatest teachers on earth. I will never forget walking into his office for my first interview. He looked me steadily in the eye, and asked: 'Elder Smith, have you read the Book of Mormon all the way through, cover to cover, for yourself?' I said, 'No sir.' He then said, 'Elder Smith, I don't want to see you again for twenty-nine days. In that period of time, I want you to read the Book of Mormon twice. Then, apply the test you will read about in the book of Moroni. Do you have any questions?' Twenty-nine days later, I walked back into the office

12. W. Mont Timmins to MDH, Aug. 26, 1963.
13. Spencer J. Condie to MDH, Aug. 1992.

of President Hanks, a changed young man. He didn't have to ask me whether or not I had read the book twice. He could tell by looking at me."[14]

KNOW THE BOOK

To help the missionaries grow in their understanding and love for the Book of Mormon, President Hanks prepared a study program he called "Know the Book." Every missionary in the British Mission followed this study guide. A lot of bishops found out about it, and then other leaders in the British Mission started to follow along. It wasn't a comprehensive study of the Book of Mormon. Rather, it pointed out important lessons of life that are taught along the way. Over the years, Duff came across people who had used "Know the Book." They would smile and tell him that they still had their books with the markings in the margins, and their children were now using this approach.

BE INTERESTED IN WHERE YOU ARE

Duff wanted the missionaries to become more observant and interested in the things around them. When he thought a training meeting had reached the point of diminishing returns, he would ask the missionaries to go out in the street and come back with a lesson of life. He described what he learned from his missionaries as some of the greatest experiences of his life. One elder commented that from the upper floors of the Hyde Park Chapel he could see deep into a construction area—and taught a lesson about sepulchres, whitewashed outside, filthy underneath. Another young elder from ranch country talked about a stuffed greyhound in a glass case in the British Museum. He talked about not running faster than one has strength and compared his background to that of his companion by comparing his dog back home to the racing dog in the museum. He said, "My dog couldn't have caught that stuffed dog when it was alive, but in a battle with my dog, that greyhound wouldn't have lasted a minute." He said of his companion, "We're different. I can't talk. I can't memorize. I can't do any of the things he can do, but when he tires at 5:30, I can keep working hard, just as long as I need to."

Duff also encouraged the missionaries to read from great books like Shakespeare, and to attend cultural events on their weekly day off, called diversion day. One missionary wrote, "I'm also deeply grateful to you for instilling a love of learning in my life. Your quotes from the great books of the world and the lessons of life you taught opened up a whole new world to me."[15] One young missionary, Elder Quentin Cook, told of a day on his mission when President Hanks asked him to accompany him on a drive in the car. After about forty minutes of driving, Elder Cook asked where they were going.

President Hanks replied, "Elder Cook, you told me you wanted to go to law school, so I am taking you to Runnymede, where the Magna Carta was

14. From "Quotes about MDH," *MDH Mini-Book*, original source not available.

15. Virden J. Thornton to MDH.

Missionary dinner, British Mission, London, England, 1962.

signed. You can't be a good lawyer unless you understand the Magna Carta." Duff then spent an hour explaining how the Magna Carta played a part in the beginning of the rule of law we enjoy today. Elder Cook later concluded, "That was only one experience I had with Pres. Hanks. He truly cared about each of his missionaries."[16] Quentin L. Cook later became a lawyer and then a Latter-day Saint apostle.

STRIVING FOR "REAL GROWTH"

The focus of missionary work in the British Mission had now turned to conversion and retention—a concept they called "Real Growth." The missionaries focused on finding and teaching young families. They also met with people who had joined the church, continuing to teach them and lift them up long after they were baptized. Duff also instituted a rigorous program of trying to reclaim those who had joined the church in name only.

Duff was very clear and repetitive in his admonitions that missionaries be focused on the number of conversions rather than on the number of baptisms and that no one be baptized who had not experienced genuine conversion. In a March 27, 1962, mission bulletin, he wrote, "Whatever kind of missionary you have thought yourself to be in the past, be a good one now, and a better one in weeks to come. This is the kind of men and women we want to help you become. In doing so, you will find great joy and bring joy to many others."

Over the coming months, baptisms began to increase and, better yet, the

16. Quentin L. Cook to RDH.

number of people who stayed in the church improved tremendously. Perhaps equally important to Duff, the missionaries began to feel good about themselves and their work. Their consciences allowed them to feel positive self-worth and self-confidence as they taught the Savior's gospel and told people about the restoration of the Savior's church on the earth.

THE MISSIONARIES' RESPONSE TO CHANGES

The missionaries in Great Britain were incredibly, almost unbelievably, responsive. In a letter to all missionaries just two months into his presidency, Duff wrote, "We like your response to the challenge you've received—a new variety of challenge to some of you. A few have been bewildered in the absence of an external motivation. Some have gone on ticking away at their work, like clocks in a storm. All have learned that stretching can be painful, and that growing pains affect other aspects of the nature of man than his muscles."[17]

EVERY MISSION PRESIDENT A MISSIONARY

Duff didn't just send the missionaries out to teach; he went out teaching with them. He also had a standing practice to meet in the mission home with anyone who wanted to speak with him. And, of course, he spoke all over the mission. Many years later, after he died, a letter arrived addressed to Duff's children. It said, "Although my service in the British Mission was some years after your family had returned to Salt Lake City, President Hanks' reputation among the members in England was legendary. One district president, who joined the church after hearing your father speak, told me that the first time he listened to President Hanks address a large group of investigators at a fireside, he felt something unlike anything he had ever before experienced. That a church could produce someone as Christ-like and charismatic as your father, prompted him to listen to the message the missionaries delivered and to accept their challenge to read and pray and discover its truth for himself."[18]

The missionaries would bring the most challenging investigators to the mission home on Exhibition Road, where Duff was pleased to participate in the teaching and conversion of multiple people. Some took longer. In 1974, ten years after returning, he had the following experience, "I had a big surprise today, as Bishop George Jones showed up from the North of England. Bishop Jones is the stubborn man who gave his wife fits in England when she joined the church. I held her out for a long time, but she was finally baptized with her fine son, Julian. Three years ago, they came for a visit in which we talked very plainly to each other. Brother Jones went home then and joined the church. He is now a bishop."[19] Bishop Jones and his son Julian both later became stake presidents.

17. MDH-A, *British Mission Bulletin*, Mar. 27, 1962.
18. Roger Porter to the Hanks children, Apr. 2011.
19. MDH-JE, Apr. 7, 1974.

THE GLASGOW STAKE

On Sunday, August 26, 1962, over twenty-seven hundred church members and friends gathered in St. Andrew's Hall, Berkeley Street, Glasgow, to organize the Glasgow Stake—the first stake in Scotland. President McKay presided at the conference, and Duff spoke, sharing his love for that land. "It is about 100 years ago that my grandmother heard the gospel in Glasgow and shortly thereafter departed these shores for the United States. She blessed us with the great privilege of life in the gospel, and life in the church, a privilege for which I have been most grateful all of the days of my life. I am happy to be here and grateful to have come from that great old soul who lived into her 95th year."[20]

ELDER CHRISTENSEN'S DEATH

One night, a distraught missionary arrived at the mission home. Duff recognized trouble. The elder said, "Elder Christensen has been hit by a car on his bicycle, and he is in the hospital." Duff and the young man rushed to the hospital, only to find that Elder Christensen had passed away.

Elder Christensen was a fine missionary from Salt Lake. He had been out for just ten weeks and was the only son of a widowed mother. When the time came to go to the mortuary to dress the missionary's body in his temple clothing and prepare to send his body home, Duff decided to take three young elders with him. The first was his counselor. The second was Elder Christensen's companion. And the third was a former Marine who was struggling to decide if he should complete his mission. Duff gave them each a choice to participate or not. All three chose to do so.

The funeral director was nationally known. He had performed funeral services for the king of England and was very accomplished. He stood by while Duff and his three missionaries lovingly dressed their companion's body in his temple robes. Duff recalled, "There was no queasy feeling, nothing scary or objectionable. There was a spirit in that room such as I had never felt before, a particular spirit for that particular setting. I watched these strong, rugged young men, who loved this missionary, walk around him, adjust his clothing, then they would reach out and pat him just a little, just a touch. You see, we all knew that the 'real' Elder Christensen wasn't there, not in that form we could see."

When they finished, Duff invited the funeral director to join them in prayer. "And so, we knelt, and I talked to the Lord," Duff said. "When we stood up the room was filled with the sweetest peace I have ever known. When we left the room, the director said to me: 'President Hanks, this is the first Mormon funeral I have had anything to do with. I have heard a lot of things about you people, and I have misunderstood. For the rest of my life, I'll not forget what I felt in that

20. MDH-A, *Millennial Star*, Oct. 1962, 258.

room today.'" He didn't charge for his services and wrote a note to Duff that read, "The gain and the joy are all mine."[21]

The three missionaries who left that funeral home were likewise never the same again.

TWO ASSIGNMENTS AT ONCE

One day, Elder Mark E. Petersen, who presided over all the West European Missions, called Duff to say that he and his wife, Emma Marr, had to return to the States for a medical issue and that the brethren wanted Duff to take over until further notice.

In a letter home to his family almost twenty years later, Duff lamented his lack of journal entries during his overseas assignments. One of those periods was when Elder Petersen left Duff as acting president of the West European Mission while he was simultaneously president of the British Mission. It was two full-time jobs for about six months. He said, "I came near killing myself with absolute necessary-or-fail output of time and energy. I had no ability to run things *and* write about it."[22] Eventually, Elder N. Eldon Tanner arrived to replace him as president of the West European Mission.

THE ROMFORD STAKE

About thirty years later, Duff received a letter from Elder Jeffrey R. Holland, who was the visiting general authority at the Romford stake conference. During the Sunday morning session, he called on the patriarch, George Vousden, to bear his testimony. Brother Vousden stood and told the congregation about Elder Holland's earlier visit to the branch with President Hanks as a missionary. He reminded the congregation that President Hanks had stood at the pulpit and promised that the day would come when their parking lot wouldn't be able to hold the cars needed, that the young people of the stake would serve missions, and that the fledgling Romford Branch would one day be a stake.

Elder Holland wrote to his former mission president, "Three times during that session, the police gave us notice that cars needed to be moved or they would be towed. Almost all of the young men in the stake are going on missions, and we are very close to making another stake in the Romford area. I would love for you to have been there, but perhaps a brief note will let you feel some of their joy."[23]

HENRY D. MOYLE'S DEATH

On January 31, 1963, President McKay released President Moyle as chair of the Missionary Committee and replaced him with Joseph Fielding Smith, a strong opponent of Moyle-style missionary work.[24] President Moyle remained

21. MDH-T, Seminary S-Day, Jan. 26, 1974; BUW, 257–60.

22. MDH-L Nov. 7, 1980.

23. Jeffrey R. Holland to MDH, Nov. 25, 1992.

24. Gregory A. Prince and Wm. Robert Wright, *David O. McKay and the Rise of Modern Mormonism* (Salt Lake City: University of Utah Press, 2009), 249.

first counselor in the First Presidency. But without the missionary portfolio, which he had called his greatest work, he was an empty man. He confided to Duff, "I have been relieved of every responsibility except my title."[25]

On September 18, 1963, President Moyle died of a heart attack. Hugh B. Brown, the other counselor in the First Presidency, said, "He died of a broken heart." Duff wrote, "Henry Moyle's downfall and death have been spoken of with some connection to my course in England. We are all architects of our own future. I was not responsible for Brother Moyle's troubles, nor he mine."[26]

BECOMING A LITTLE BRITISH FAMILY

While Duff was leading the mission, Maxine was raising their family in a foreign country. The mission home was at 50 Princess Gate, on Exhibition Road in Kensington, one of the great streets of London, which led right into Hyde Park. Their home was just down the street from where John F. Kennedy had briefly lived as a young man. The Victoria and Albert Museum was down the street, and the Royal Albert Hall was a few blocks away. The kids were excited and nervous about this new opportunity—Susan was eleven; Nancy, ten; Ann, seven; Mary, four; and Richard, eighteen months.

Church for the family was just down the road at the newly completed Hyde Park Chapel, which has served as the central gathering point of church members in Britain since that time. The older kids began school at traditional British schools, complete with required uniforms. Corporal punishment was still in vogue, and Mr. Pierce, one of the teachers, would wander the classroom and whack the hands of any kids who were messing around.

The Hanks children added new life to the mission home. The kids loved the missionaries, and vice versa. One story involved a few elders trying to teach Susan some algebra. After a few days, the teacher sent home a message to Duff, saying, "Mr. Hanks, the teaching of algebra has changed in many ways in the years since you studied it, and we would prefer that you leave the teaching of that subject to our teachers."

Maxine introduced her children to the important sights of England. She immersed the family into things British, so they could all more fully appreciate the culture and the people they had been sent to serve. She routinely took the children to nearby castles, the ballet, theater, museums, and boat races on the Thames.

Occasionally, Duff would take one of the girls with him to a branch or stake conference, at which they would stand together and sing "I Am a Child of God."

About a month before Christmas, Sister Hanks, with help from her daughters and the office sisters, decorated the mission home for Christmas. There were beautiful pictures of Christ, a little village with cotton snow, and hanging handmade ball ornaments. On Christmas Eve day, nine districts came to the mission

25. MDH-L to family, Nov. 1980.
26. MDH-L to family, Nov. 1980.

home for a Christmas program. On Christmas Eve, the mission home elders and sisters had a special program with the Hanks family. The four Hanks sisters sang "I Saw Mommy Kissing Santa Claus." The main dish at Christmas dinner was a suckling pig with an apple in its mouth.

Duff and Maxine received an invitation from Queen Elizabeth II to attend an afternoon garden party at Buckingham Palace. Duff was enthusiastic, though not sure whether he should rent a top hat and tails or just wear a normal business suit.

Rich recalled, "One day, Dad and I were walking down the street, holding hands. I was three years old and don't remember this happening, but Dad said I did something wrong, and he was chastising me and trying to explain why I shouldn't do it again. Evidently, I looked up at him, and in a right proper British accent said, 'Father, do not scold me. I was behaving *prop-er-ly*.'" Duff went home and told Maxine they needed to get back to America soon.

DEVELOPING A LIFELONG LOVE FOR BRITAIN

Duff was never the same again after living in England. He relished the chance to return anytime he could. He loved the sights and sounds and smells and food. But he especially loved the people and the wonderful members of the church—many remained dear friends for the rest of his life. A love for all things British was also instilled in each of his children.

About it all he said, "I have had a serious and ill-disguised affection for Britain for many years. Whether that comes because my ancestors were born in England and Scotland, or from the wonderful blessing of having lived there for a time, I cannot say. My feeling is that it is a blend of these elements, a blend which confirms me as an anglophile for sure, and one incapable of not feeling deep and great emotion when I think fondly of my ties with the old countries."[27]

Duff often quoted from the English writer Samuel Johnson: "When a man is tired of London, he is tired of life; for there is in London all that life can afford."[28]

When Rich received his mission call to Scotland, Duff made sure Rich knew he had nothing to do with where he was being sent. But it was clear he was overjoyed.

GOING HOME

At the conclusion of his mission, President Hanks summarized the preceding twenty-seven months of steady church growth in Britain and could finally report that the place was in order. The missionaries were behaving like missionaries should. A letter from a stake president up north declared, "The day your family arrived on the shores of England, fresh breezes blew north. We were able to say after a few months, for the first time in years, 'I'm not ashamed of the gospel of Jesus Christ.'"[29]

---

27. MDH-A, thoughts on the 150th anniversary of the church in the British Isles.
28. James Boswell, *The Life of Samuel Johnson* (1791).
29. MDH-R, Dec. 10, 1988.

The theme of Duff's mission was "We Are Builders." His only statistical goal was to double the active membership of every functioning church unit in the mission and to increase worship and growth opportunities for the members. He wrote, "Missionary work in Europe is still difficult and demanding. Membership in the church often entails economic and social sacrifice and the severing of family and friendship ties. Notwithstanding this, there is a steady stream of converts from among the responsible elements in the communities. We have had the joy of seeing many of them come into the church, living the life, and giving service required by the church."[30]

Duff's missionaries grew in knowledge and testimony and confidence in the Lord and His gospel. They were able to return home with their heads held high, knowing they had served honorable missions. He wrote, "It was a top family adventure for us to serve as leaders of the British Mission. Our little children grew in that foreign country, and we had wonderful experiences. It was a tough assignment, coming directly from President McKay and forms a story of its own. It was a time of 'New Era,' when good sense died, and things got out of hand.

"I was sent to stop it. And I did."[31]

The family traveled back to America on the ocean liner *USS United States*—the trip took three or four days across the Atlantic.

LONG-TERM EFFECTS ON THE MISSIONARIES

A recurring theme written by his missionaries was the way he had changed the course of the mission, helped them regain their integrity, and yet, still strengthened their testimonies of the church and its leadership. One letter writer said, "President Hanks, I have been reflecting on that trying time in 1962, when it appeared to us that the church and isolated members of the Twelve and First Presidency were against us. I remember vividly your patience in teaching us as missionaries how the church is run, and that diversity among the brethren was healthy. In the end, your leadership brought about a change of direction. There were some discouraging times when all seemed lost, but as King Arthur once proclaimed, 'Right is might!'"[32]

After the mission was turned around, Duff was able to focus less on what needed changing and more on the missionaries, their testimonies, and the program going forward. His impact was profound. For example, Don Gull wrote, "Today I bowed my head and thanked God for you. Many days I say to the Lord, 'Please allow me to do for just one young man what President Hanks did for me.' You had a more profound influence on me than you can begin to measure. You were my spiritual mentor then and your memory continues to be my mentor today. God bless you."

30. MDH-A, *Millennial Star*, July 1964, 248.
31. MDH-L to family, Nov. 1980.
32. Robert Garff to MDH, Dec. 1981.

Richard G. Whitehead wrote, "President Hanks was the most incredible teacher and learner that I have ever known. He had the capacity to instill in everyone the desire to do their best."

James Pearce wrote, "I don't know if he will ever know or fully appreciate what a personal savior he has been to so many of us who were so damaged in England. We desperately needed a role model at that time. I still read and mark my scriptures as he modeled at that time. I love him!"

Michael Quinn said, "Under his leadership, the British mission was a cultural, intellectual, and spiritual paradise for young missionaries. It took me years to accept this fact, but, in 1963, there was no better mission in the world for me.... My personality and previous development were uniquely suited to gaining the most as a Hanks missionary. As he often said, 'If you convert only one person, let that convert be you, and your mission will be a success.'"[33]

Before returning home, Phil Pugsley wrote Duff a note: "I thank the Lord that I was called to this mission at this period of time. I'm thankful that we have not only been encouraged to do what I feel are the right things, but with a stimulus to do them for the right reasons. I don't think that it would be possible to overemphasize the importance of this latter, and I know that in future years, it will be even more evident in the position of the church here, and in the lives of those who have been privileged to be here."[34]

Duff loved and supported his missionaries. Some, such as Elders Holland and Cook, who became apostles, are well known. At least ten of his missionaries became mission presidents themselves; others were less well known but no less loved by him.

As the years rolled on, Duff continued caring for his missionaries. He made time for them, performed temple sealings for their children, spoke at their funerals, and loved them for the rest of his life.

One fun story involved one of his returned missionaries trying to teach his two-and-a-half year-old daughter how to flip a coin—the heads and tails sides of a quarter. He held up the front side and said, "Heidi, this is our first president. Do you know who he is?" She clapped her hands and said, "Yes! Yes! President Hanks!"

BRITISH MISSION REUNIONS FOR 40-PLUS YEARS!

For the next forty-plus years, the missionaries would plan and then hold a special reunion of those who served in the British Mission under President Hanks. One of the missionaries would plan it around the time of general conference, and they would meet in a ward building or a hotel and catch up with each other and then listen as Duff would teach them something important. That kind of longevity for a single mission is a telling achievement in and of itself.

33. D. Michael Quinn, *Chosen Path: A Memoir* (Salt Lake City, Signature Books, 2024), 119.
34. Phil Pugsley to MDH, Nov. 25, 1963.

36

Southeast Asia, Vietnam, and War

In grateful appreciation to Marion D. Hanks, patriot of the Vietnam era. His legacy of words and deeds, going in harm's way to visit, comfort, and inspire LDS military personnel and their families will endure through eternity in the hearts of all who cherish his dedication, friendship, and brotherhood.
—Presented by American servicemen in Vietnam, July 2, 1993.

In 1965, Duff was assigned by the First Presidency as the supervisor of the missions in the Southeast Asia Area. Four missions covered the entire area—Hawaii, Hong Kong, Japan, and Korea. Included in his responsibilities were the active combat zones in Indochina and the conflict in Vietnam, which was beginning to heat up.

In Korea, the church was achieving increasing acceptance. Spencer Palmer was the mission president, and the church was growing, with branches and districts being formed and the lone stake beginning to expand with strong leadership.

In Japan, the church was also beginning to grow under the direction of mission president Adney Y. Komatsu, with mission divisions and stake formations occurring over the coming years.

In both Korea and Japan were many American servicemen, including members of the church, who gave strength and support to the growing church. After a mission tour of those missions and the Hawaiian Mission in October 1965, Duff provided a full report to the First Presidency on his visit. His primary purpose in the tour had been to conduct lengthy interviews with every single missionary—which he did. There were more than five hundred missionaries in Japan, Korea, Hong Kong, the Philippines, Taiwan, and Hawaii. He loved and spoke highly of the young people who were serving and trying to learn difficult languages.

His report on the literature available to the missionaries and members was not as positive. Lack of literature was a major problem. The Book of Mormon was just becoming available to the people of Taiwan and Korea in their respective languages. Tracts, manuals, books, and teaching materials were all woefully undersupplied. To press the urgency of the situation, Duff quoted a young missionary's comments in his report to the First Presidency: "Why would the church send all these missionaries over here without materials to work with?"

Maxine and Marjorie Hinckley watch a snake charmer in Calcutta, India, 1966.

The more challenging part of Duff's new assignment was the Southeast Asian Mission, led by mission president Keith E. Garner, with headquarters in Hong Kong. The mission included not only Hong Kong and Taiwan but also Singapore and all of India, Indonesia, Vietnam, Thailand, Laos, and Burma. In late 1966, Duff and Maxine toured all of their assigned missions in Asia, along with Gordon and Marjorie Hinckley. In his report to the First Presidency in January 1967, Duff reported that they also traveled to Vietnam, India, Thailand and Singapore. This was Maxine's first trip to India, and while she was intrigued by the incredible cultural differences, her sensitive nature was deeply challenged by the difficulties faced by the poor in Calcutta and elsewhere.

Duff paid special attention to the servicemen everywhere he traveled. About six thousand members of the church were in service on military bases spread all over Thailand and South Vietnam, from the major centers to remote bush locations, from relative safety away from main fighting, right up to and including live combat areas.

"Hitchhiking" on a helicopter in Vietnam to meet with US troops, ca. 1967.

Over those three years, Duff visited Vietnam numerous times. He was in the company of President Garner of the mission and sometimes with Elder Gordon B. Hinckley. He took his responsibility for those in the military very seriously, even flying into hot combat zones and a few times behind enemy lines, to visit the Latter-day Saint soldiers and try to uplift them.

Only one VIP visit per year was allowed by the US military leadership, but other less-formal tours were permitted. The so-called VIP trips were planned by military commanders. On these trips, Duff visited each of the key areas of Vietnam, from Can Tho in the south to Da Nang in the north. Duff also visited with the leading generals, including General William Westmoreland, in order to support the LDS chaplains in their work. But because these visits occupied precious hours, Duff felt that the time was better spent out in the camps and in the bush among the men. On subsequent unofficial trips he would hitchhike from place to place with President Garner, flying in small-engine planes, transports, and helicopters, or riding in trucks and jeeps.

"THIS EXCHANGE OF LOVE"

Everywhere he went during the war, Duff expressed the personal greeting that the prophet, David O. McKay, had asked him to share with the servicemen. This was easy for Duff to do because he so revered President McKay.

On one occasion, prior to Duff returning to Vietnam to be with the LDS soldiers, he met with President McKay to receive his message for those serving there: "When we were through, that great hand reached out and touched me lightly on the knee, and he said something that seemed to me to summarize his noble lifetime. 'Please tell them of *this exchange of love,*' he said. It was not the words of love to which he was referring, but the feeling in his heart. I wonder if that isn't really what life is all about—to have the capacity to feel and the strength to communicate—to exchange love."

As he conveyed the prophet's love, Duff heard reciprocating testimonies of deep love and affection for President McKay—over and over, the men asked Duff to please convey their individual love back to him.

A PERSONAL REQUEST

Duff's involvement with members of the military became personal for him. Despite the long distances and time away from home, the unsafe environment, and difficulties of weather, Duff felt a pull toward the men he was serving. The following letter in 1967 is self-explanatory.

> Dear Brethren,
>
> I write this letter from a Marine Base in Da Nang, Vietnam. It is an important letter which I desire to dictate as I rest here for a minute, and which I am going to ask my secretary to send on to you, unsigned.
>
> I have not, to my knowledge, requested any personal favors or made any strong requests of the Brethren since I began to serve nearly 14 years ago. I now desire a favor, if it can be put in that category.
>
> I wish with deep sincerity to be permitted to work closely with the young men over here while this conflict is on. If some appointment—either military or civilian—could be made which would give me wider access to our men and let me travel on a high enough level to guarantee that I could get to the boys, I believe I could do some good. They deserve anything that can be done, and if I have any contribution to make any place, I think it might be here. Recognition of the kind I am talking about is available through civilian sources, and possibly through the military, and I request that inquiries be made which would permit me to undertake this assignment.
>
> I am certain you will not misunderstand my motives. There is nothing glorious or glamorous about this war or any part of it. It is a filthy, unattractive, tragic thing. The circumstances under which most of our men live are not good. This military base is about like the others, and the average Latter-day Saint marine here is living in very primitive circumstances in a tropical climate, and with danger at his elbow all the time. Many are being wounded and are dying. I want to do something to help them, and I believe that I can, with your authorization and blessing.
>
> —MDH-L, First Presidency, May 26, 1967

PERSONAL SACRIFICE FOR HIS FAMILY

While Duff was flying around Southeast Asia and Vietnam, Maxine and the kids were back in Salt Lake, missing him. He missed Mother's Days, birthdays, and kids' performances—all to be with the men in uniform far away from home.

While it was a personally unselfish thing Duff did to help others, it was a sacrifice for his family.

In a letter of condolence to a young married woman who had lost a baby, Duff wrote:

> When I left for Vietnam, to spend a month with our troops, Sister Hanks told me at the airport that she was carrying a baby, which, after a number of years trying, we thought would not happen. We shed a tear of glorious joy together, and then I got on the airplane and flew away, knowing that I could not hear from her for about a month. Each day, I sent my wife a note of appreciation and praise and expectation; we really wanted that child.
>
> I did not know until I got off the airplane in Salt Lake City, the day before Christmas 1966, that she had lost the baby only a few hours after I departed, and that she had been receiving all of those upbeat letters from me through the interim.[1]

During Christmas 1967, Duff was gone from home again. He dictated his traditional Christmas letter to his friends from Vietnam:

> This letter is dictated from a place far removed in distance and circumstances from the peaceful and pleasant occasion we usually enjoy together. Mortars and artillery and bombs and small arms fire are heard even here in the environs of the great city of Saigon. Tan Son Nhut Air Base is ringed with flares all night long and the bunkers and places of refuge stand nearby for everyone. At the base hospitals, the wounded are in profusion. The helicopters disgorge their loads, and the Quonset-hut operating rooms and intensive care wards bear little resemblance to the gleaming pleasant surroundings at home. Everywhere the hearts of mothers and wives and children grieve at the danger attending their loved ones. But in the midst of it all there comes the overwhelming message and purpose of the Prince of Peace.[2]

KOREA AND THE PALMERS

Duff came to really love the sweet and humble people of Korea. He made several visits in 1965 through 1967. During one of his trips through Korea, President Palmer wrote:

> We once again enjoyed the good sense of humor of this great man as we traveled through the many villages. A good leader of men makes those around him feel at ease. So it is with Marion D. Hanks. Thursday night, Elder Hanks filled in a speaking engagement for the American ambassador to Korea who could not be there. The people of the Lions Club in Incheon were very impressed and had their eyes opened to the potential of the Mormon people.

1. MDH-L, Nov. 16, 1994.
2. MDH-L to friends and family for Christmas, 1967.

> Friday, Brother Hanks was up early so he could finish interviewing the last of the 64 missionaries. Later on, he taught the missionaries the story of Elijah and his discouragement, and the Lord telling him there were 7,000 people who were ready. But the Lord didn't give Elijah their addresses; he had to go find them. He told the missionaries to help, build, and sustain each other. At 1:00, the Elders said goodbye, and sang the famous Korean folk song, "Arirang," to their beloved brother in the gospel.[3]

On another visit, Duff wrote in his journal about how impressed he was with a professor of Asian history he had met. He recorded this man's words: "Tonight, I am exceedingly happy to see Dr. Palmer and Dr. Hanks. In an old saying, there is an expression like this: 'How great your joy would be when you meet your friend who is from afar.' Dr. Hanks is here today not only as a friend, but as a great teacher. I was deeply moved when he was talking to the group of people at the meeting room this afternoon about the youth and their problems. Now, I feel a great desire to study about your faith deeply."

Duff remarked how well the Palmers were doing with so few missionaries. President Palmer was a scholar in Korean culture and had been accepted at the highest levels of leadership in Korea. Duff was impressed by both the missionaries and the members.

JAPAN AND THE KOMATSUS

In Tokyo, Duff and Maxine drove from the airport to the mission home with the Komatsus, the mission presidents, and found Elder Gordon B. Hinckley and Sister Marjorie Hinckley there. On his birthday, they took a day off to visit some of the sights of Japan—it was a rare recreational experience, and they enjoyed it immensely. The next day, the Hinckleys left for Osaka and Okinawa, while Duff interviewed missionaries all day and then spoke at a servicemen's conference that evening. Despite a miserable journey through Tokyo, they had a sweet and warm experience at the base where the services were held.

Duff wrote about the Komatsus, who became close friends, "They are modest and gentle people, gracious, entirely devoted, and much loved by their missionaries. The division of the mission is in the offing and should be accomplished as soon as possible. The leadership of such a huge mission is very demanding and hampers productivity."

Over the next few days, Duff dedicated several chapels, held a youth fireside, and interviewed the rest of the missionaries. They then flew to Sapporo, where they held a wonderful meeting in the old chapel there. Maxine met some members who had known her parents when they served as missionaries there forty years before. They shared pictures with Maxine, and she shed some tears as she thought about what this place meant to her folks.

---

3. Spencer Palmer, comments in a scrapbook.

THAILAND

On one of his visits to Thailand in the 1960s, Duff, President Garner, and Elder Hinckley met with a former Buddhist monk who was the government minister of religion and education. Their pleasant conversation with him resulted in acceptance of the church and permission for missionaries to officially work in Thailand. They also bought the piece of land where the Bangkok Chapel would later stand. On November 2, 1966, the three men, along with a small group, met in a quiet area of Lumpini Park in the heart of Bangkok and held a brief service. Elder Hanks offered the opening prayer and President Garner, the closing. Elder Hinckley offered another prayer, dedicating the land of Thailand for the preaching of the gospel.

VIETNAM AND THE SERVICEMEN

On Sunday, October 30, 1966, a group of soldiers and their families joined with Elder Hinckley, President Garner, and Duff on the rooftop auditorium of the Caravelle Hotel in the heart of Saigon to dedicate the land of Vietnam for the preaching of the gospel. Because of the war, it was deemed inadvisable to hold the service in a park, and it was not feasible to find a hill on the outskirts of the city. The three church leaders had conducted district conferences in Da Nang, Nha Trang, and Saigon on October 29 and 30, and the dedicatory prayer was offered at the conclusion of the Saigon conference.

Elder Hinckley gave the dedicatory prayer. Duff recalled, "There was a sweet peace and inspiration as Elder Hinckley opened the door to the work of the kingdom. Many tears were shed, many prayers were silently offered, many hearts were deeply touched at the historic occasion."

Before this meeting, the three church leaders had flown with Major Allen Rozsa, a pilot and the district president, to Tan Son Nhut airbase. Brother Rozsa gave them each a paper to sign, relieving the United States government from responsibility "in case something happened to them." It was so hot that the door of the plane was still open when they took off. As they were landing, the pilot mentioned, "If we are going to get hit, it will be right now, as we get lower in elevation." The pilot followed a helicopter in with a navy admiral onboard and all its weapons on high alert.

They held a sacrament meeting at the airbase with soldiers who had just come back from patrol. They then flew to Nha Trang for another testimony meeting and then to Saigon, where they held more testimony meetings and where Elder Hinckley offered the dedicatory prayer.

In May 1967, Duff and President Garner held a meeting with servicemen in Nha Trang, Vietnam. After the meeting, Duff walked quietly down an outside passageway. As he passed the back door, he peeked in and saw several men shielding the back part of the room from view. Beyond them, he saw three young men surrounding a fourth on a chair. "The three were dressed in flight suits, sweat

Duff, Keith, and military, after an LDS Church Sunday service in Vietnam, ca. 1967.

stained and reflecting the professional capacities of their wearer," he wrote. "Two of the young men had been on air strikes before the meeting, and one was preparing to go. The three were giving a blessing to a young man and setting him apart as a district missionary. For some reason, this sweet scene affected me more significantly than all of the priesthood sermons I've ever heard. Priesthood to them meant the right and the power to act in the name of the Lord and in his interests with their brethren. This is a scene I do not want to forget."[4]

In a meeting in the bush, Duff said to the gathered military leaders of the church, "The job you are doing is the most important thing there is to do in the world. When you represent your government in the great cause of the human spirit, and you in addition represent God Almighty and the cause of His priesthood, you represent the only causes there are in this world—because they include everything that is worth living and dying for—if you have to."

The Marine divisions at Da Nang were in daily contact with the enemy. Casualties were high and the circumstances for visitors like Duff and President Garner were not particularly encouraging. Nonetheless, they were welcomed and informed that about 250 Mormon troops would be available for a brief retreat to be held at China Beach that evening and on the morrow. Duff recorded:

> When we arrived, the men were gathering, arriving in troop transports, jeeps, in small buses, and on foot. They and their friends provided an air of expectancy that was not altogether engendered by the stacked arms, the guard surrounding

4. MDH-JE, May 1967.

Soldier on full alert, attending LDS Church services with Duff in Vietnam, ca. 1967.

us with automatic weapons, and the sound of war that filled the air. Mortar, artillery, aircraft, and even small arms fire peppered our meetings as men in battle uniform came to the front benches in groups and then stood one by one and bore humble testimony.

Brothers in the kingdom told of their love and gratitude and shared their longing for home and loved ones. A two-hour meeting stretched to four, and we visitors were not heard from. It was something incredible to feel the power and strength of these men as they spoke to each other and shared their personal feelings, far away from home, in a war-torn country, with battle raging all about us.[5]

Most of the time, the two leaders didn't know the outcome of their efforts with the men in uniform. Some testimonies were saved, some lives saved, some morale built up. For some, this would be the last church meeting of their lives; others would spend the rest of their lives trying to forget. Some had their lives altered in profound ways. "I was one of the fighter pilots flying out of Thailand in 1967," one pilot wrote to Duff almost thirty years later. "I was a young, scared pilot, without a strong testimony, needing the confidence of the gospel, and I

5. MDH-JE, May 1967.

can still remember the talk you gave in conference there. I believe that your talk was meant for me and gave me the personal assurance that God lives, that I had a purpose in this life, and that I would not be taken before my time. I finished my 100 missions and came through without a scratch. All six of our children have been married in the temple, and my wife and I are serving a mission in Oregon."[6]

Duff and Keith tried not to think about the danger. Colonel LaVoi Davis wrote, "They were on extremely dangerous missions. I guess they didn't think much about it. We were paid in the military to risk our lives, and after we'd done it for three or four wars, it was no big thing. But they didn't consider that they were in much danger, especially when compared to what the men in uniform were doing."[7]

The reality of war occasionally interrupted the peace of the church meetings. Colonel Davis explained that on one occasion they had a meeting set up for a regiment. They began the church meeting and had the opening song and prayer and the sacrament. Then the sirens began to wail. All the men raced to get their gear, the choppers came in, and the visitors were left standing as the entire congregation disappeared toward the battle zone.

In a general conference talk, Duff recounted the only humorous thing he experienced in all of his visits to the men in Vietnam. He had met with an LDS soldier who had finished his tour and was leaving for home. The soldier said, "I am leaving this place with mixed feelings—joy and gladness."

In December 1967, Duff went to Southeast Asia again. President Garner sent a letter to his bishop that captures the essence of their work together:

> Yesterday we put President Hanks on a plane for Tokyo. He spent ten days with us visiting several areas of the Mission. We held a district conference in Hong Kong, interviews, instructions, and conferences in Taiwan with both the Saints and eighty-five missionaries, and six days in Vietnam. It is estimated that there are about 6,000 LDS servicemen in Vietnam, and we met with some 1,200. In addition to our own men, we were kindly met by the chief of chaplains and commanding generals, including General Westmoreland (chief of all military forces in Vietnam), who extended an invitation to visit him. He was the pinnacle of gentility and spoke very highly of the LDS soldiers. He was very complimentary of our disposition as leaders to go where we've gone and meet directly with the men.[8]

During this and other visits, General Westmoreland expressed his confidence in Duff and President Garner because of their willingness to go out among the men, which in his eyes made them credible witnesses to what was really going on there. Duff and President Garner also met with the chief of chaplains in each

6. Robert Cardiff to MDH, Aug. 27, 2004.

7. Susan Stewart, *Pure Gold: A Behind-the-Scenes Look at a Builder of the Kingdom* (Salt Lake City: Promontory, 2003), 227.

8. Keith Garner to Bishop Dave Bacon, Dec. 13, 1967, and MDH-JE.

command, who spoke highly of the four LDS chaplains and the work they were doing. They were surprised to learn that the church had three large district organizations with sixty groups, each functioning with dedicated lay leadership.

The two leaders met with soldiers all over the land. Many came out of the bush with an M16 rifle slung over their shoulder or having just completed airstrikes that day. They would stack their guns and helmets in the back of the room to participate in the services. Duff wrote, "Everywhere our men were highly spoken of. Every one of the generals I talked to went out of his way to commend the Mormon servicemen."

The reality of war was everywhere, and the moral decay of the troops was alarming to the two leaders. President Garner reported that "sensuality and carnality is running rampant, and even our boys hardly escape, and then only through sheer moral courage. Abuse, invitation, and ridicule are present with them always." Duff wrote, "Out of all of this are coming men of steel and high caliber who will contribute much to the church and life wherever they go. One swells with pride at the experience of meeting so many true and faithful men, many of them volunteers, who are giving so meaningfully to their country and to the work of the Lord."

Wherever the two men went, they held testimony meetings so that about 150 servicemen had an opportunity to talk. Some of the men fighting in the remote sections could only get to church every two or three months, so this was their rare opportunity to share their feelings and love for God. The testimony meetings went on and on. In them, Duff and President Garner heard such heartfelt expressions as "I'm glad I'm here doing this work so that the missionaries in the field can be out doing the Lord's work" and "I am never going to be hard to live with again. If my wife spends an extra dollar, she won't get any complaints out of me again."

From a tough-looking but sweet young man, Duff heard a sentence he would repeat over and over the rest of his life: "I'm fighting a hard fight, but *my life can stand inspection.*"

For years, Duff used those words to teach others back home, including his family.

President Garner wrote, "It was a joy to be the companion of President Hanks again. He is a great soul. Full of love and charity for all mankind. It's rough for me to have to speak three and four times daily over a ten-day period, especially with the 'master of speech' as your companion, but somehow the Lord assists and the right things are said."[9]

EXPERIENCING SOBERING EVENTS

A number of sobering events occurred during Duff's visits. On their first visit to Vietnam, Duff and Elder Hinckley and President Garner flew in an old military aircraft the size of a DC3, nicknamed a "gooney bird." The plane was piloted by Major Allen Rozsa, who had been a fighter pilot in World War II and Korea

9. Keith Garner to Bishop Dave Bacon, Dec. 13, 1967, and MDH-JE.

and was also the district president for the church in the southern part of South Vietnam. Flying from Saigon to Da Nang, one of the plane's engines became compromised and had to be feathered.[10] The plane started to list heavily. Major Rozsa opened the cockpit door and looking back over his shoulder at the trio of men, smiled and said, "Don't worry, brethren. We still have one good engine." They flew over the enemy-filled jungle without serious incident and landed safely.

On one landing at the airbase in Da Nang, in an old workhorse airplane, they were met by a colonel at the airfield. He gave them directions and then apologized that he would have to leave shortly to pay special attention to a set of black helicopters that had just landed. In the middle helicopter were the chief of naval operations and the commanding general of all American forces. As they were walking, Elder Hinckley asked, "Did they fly up the same safety corridor we did?" The colonel looked at him quizzically, and said, "What corridor is that? No, sir, you've been over enemy territory every inch of the way."[11]

The realities of war affected everyone deeply. The soldiers were coming out of holes and off the mountains and out of the jungles to meet the church leaders. Duff said he would never forget visiting the morgue with an LDS mortician who told him that they averaged seventy-five men per day through the mortuary, including three LDS boys in the last three days. In a field hospital near Da Nang, he met with four LDS boys recovering from wounds, including one Hawaiian boy who had lost both his eyes. He wrote, "This is a vicious and costly war."[12]

For the rest of his life, Duff spoke about the courage of the men he met in Vietnam. He said, "I went there for as long as a month at a time in Vietnam, and we traipsed from one end to the other and met with these beautiful men, who worshiped and sang with us, many of whom were dead by the weekend. It was a terrible time. But they needed hope and concern."

FRIENDSHIP WITH PRESIDENT GARNER

They say friends are made in foxholes. Both Duff and Elder Hinckley developed strong friendships with President Keith Garner that lasted the rest of their lives. President Garner had been a real estate developer in Palo Alto, California, before becoming the mission president in August 1965. Because there were no functioning stakes yet in the Philippines, Hong Kong, or Taiwan, Keith was responsible not only for the five hundred missionaries and missionary work in those countries but also the ecclesiastical care of all members of the church residing in mission boundaries including India, Thailand, Malaysia, Singapore, Indonesia, Laos, Vietnam and beyond—a massive responsibility. He was effectively responsible for LDS church work among about half the world's population.

---

10. Feathering is employed if an engine must be shut down. The propeller's blades are turned pointing forward, resulting in lower drag.

11. MDH-JE, n.d.

12. MDH-L to Clare Middlemiss for David O. McKay, May 31, 1967.

Duff and Keith Garner, along with their escorts, Captain Bowring and Colonel Edmonds, departing Saigon, 1967

About President Garner, Duff recalled, "It took me about 30 minutes to begin to really appreciate the ability of this little dynamo, who moved swiftly and ran up stairs. He was wise and gentle and not arrogant. You knew and trusted the man." Duff's good feelings about Keith were reciprocated. After one of their tours together in 1967, Keith wrote to Duff, "The memories of your last visit and our transcendent tour of Vietnam will linger on and on. To enjoy the words of eternal life with you in this world is to taste the real—to come. Many thanks. Love, Keith."[13]

During his tenure, President Garner visited Vietnam more than fifteen times. The seeds he planted in each country continued to grow and develop, including the first district in Hong Kong, the Book of Mormon printed in Chinese, the first meetinghouse in Hong Kong, the Philippine Mission, the opening of Thailand and Singapore to missionary work, and the dedication of Vietnam for the preaching of the gospel.

WRITING LETTERS HOME TO THEIR FAMILIES

Duff was so touched by the courage and dedication and goodness of the LDS servicemen he met with that he decided to write letters home to their families to

13. Keith Garner to MDH, Hong Kong, Jan. 18, 1968.

Duff in Da Nang, Vietnam, dictating letters to the families of the servicemen he had met that day, 1967. *Courtesy Church News*

let them know that he had seen their son and try to give them some positive news. At first, Duff would dictate letters every spare minute he could find and then bring the tapes back home, where Phyllis, his secretary, would type up the letters and mail them to the parents and wives.

Word got back to Duff that on multiple occasions his letter had arrived after the parents or wife had already received word that their son or husband had been killed in action. One such letter read, "Dear Elder Hanks, thank you so much for your letter in which you conveyed my husband's thoughts to me. Sam wrote and told me of the very inspirational meeting which you held in Saigon, and how pleased he was to meet and talk with you. I was so thankful that he had the opportunity to attend this meeting, as four days later he was fatally wounded while carrying his injured men to safety."[14]

This outcome of events devastated Duff, so he decided he would write down the names of the servicemen he met each day, along with a few notes about each one, and then he would stay up until 3:00 or 4:00 in the morning dictating letters to their parents and wives. The next morning, the tapes were flown by pouch back to Utah. Phyllis would then quickly transcribe the letters and mail them out.

These letters were a real boost to the families of far-off soldiers in harm's way. In the book *Saints at War*, army colonel Russell Meacham wrote, speaking about the letter his family received from Elder Hanks, "I can tell you by experience in

14. Virginia Soloman to MDH, Jan. 7, 1967.

my own family that a letter from a general authority who has recently visited your 'loved one' in the field in Vietnam is a morale-builder."[15]

A second example out of hundreds of letters Duff received from parents and soldiers is this one from a chaplain: "I appreciate your prayers and guidance. We are still talking about the visit that you and President Garner made to the Ben Hoa area. Yesterday, the brethren were all talking about the letters their wives and parents received from you, Elder Hanks. I know how thrilled my own wife and parents were. It must be a tremendous amount of work for you—but to see how thrilled the brethren were because of your effort, would be worth all of it and more. Thank you."[16]

PERSPECTIVE ON WAR—IN GENERAL

Duff took no joy in war. He had seen things he wanted to unsee and lost old friends and new friends to the horrors of war. In a letter, he wrote, "I am leaving this week for [Asia] and another sobering and tearing visit to Vietnam. Nothing has ever affected me as deeply as has this series of adventures into these deep and complex and, to me, insoluble tragedies."[17]

But he was also a patriot and a lover of liberty and freedom, and he knew the costs that were required to sustain that freedom. "My pain at the thought of war is passionate, a passion perhaps reserved for those who have been there and maybe not possible for those who have not. I abominate the causes of war and the perpetrators and the agonies of war. But until the time comes when swords are beaten into plowshares and the spirit and influence of Him who will come again reigns upon the earth, it seems we must continue to make the terrible choice [to fight] for peace and honor and liberty."[18]

Duff recognized that the church will always be opposed to war and committed to peace. But on the basis of revelations, including the declarations of the President of the Church, it will sustain the responsibility of members of the church to support the laws of the countries where they are citizens. He quoted David O. McKay to confirm his position: "Even though we sense the hellish origin of war, even though we feel confident that war will never end war, yet under existing conditions we find ourselves as a body committed to combat this evil thing.... With other loyal citizens we serve our country as bearers of arms, rather than stand aloof to enjoy a freedom for which others have fought and died."[19]

Because of his great love for the United States and liberty and because he had seen so much of courage and bravery and death, Duff could not abide those who mocked war or those who had given their lives for freedom. He was once asked

15. Russell Meacham, in *Saints at War: Korea and Vietnam* (American Fork, UT: Covenant Communications, 2003).

16. Wayne E. Kuehne to MDH, June 5, 1967.

17. MDH-L to EH, Oct. 10, 1967.

18. MDH, notes in preparation for an undated talk to an unknown military audience.

19. David O. McKay, GC, Apr. 1942.

to respond to an antiwar essay and letter submitted for publication in the *New Era* magazine. In a scathing response, Duff thanked the author for submitting the essay and told him that his viewpoints seem sincere but were not acceptable for publication. He wrote:

> For one who has been in armed combat, who has seen vast numbers of good men die, and as one very familiar with the Vietnamese situation, who has stood in the field hospitals and morgues, and with many men who subsequently gave their lives, I not only have no sympathy for your views but weep at the tragedy of them.
>
> You have given your land nothing.... You have inherited, from the day you were born, the free air and free streets and free schools and free agency which this land presents.... Your references to the scriptures are unfortunate. You speak of the people of Ammon and the oath they took to nonviolence. You have neglected to note that their descendants had to later unearth their arms and preserve the land, else it would have been overrun and destroyed by barbarians.
>
> Your idealism is commendable. Go on and enjoy it, while decent men who know what it costs to keep a people free, go on giving.

The author of the essay had tauntingly written, "If you dig being closed-minded and at war, forget that I wrote this, and stand for the pledge to the flag." Duff concluded, "This is particularly ill-mannered and foul to one who has seen that flag bought at the cost of the bravest and best men I ever knew. God help you to reconsider your situation."[20]

As long as dissenters were civil in their opposition, Duff was more than willing to hear them out and listen to their point of view. Perhaps one of the most vocal pacifists inside the church was Eugene England, one of Duff's long-term protégés. In the winter of 1968, Duff met with Gene in Palo Alto to discuss the war in Vietnam. Gene was strongly against the United States' involvement in Vietnam, and he and Duff exchanged their different points of view. Duff told Gene that as long as he broke no laws, he should feel free to share his opinions on war through his teaching and writing. But they disagreed on principle. In an earlier letter to Gene about war, Duff had written, "You are entitled to your opinion, but to write an article like yours and to take a stand like yours is beyond my sympathy."[21]

PERSPECTIVE ON WAR—SPECIFIC TO VIETNAM

The Vietnam War was a lightning rod for conflict and disagreement not only for LDS church members but for the nation as a whole. Duff's perspective on Vietnam was that the United States went there to honor covenants made to help a struggling people. He wrote, "We were taken advantage of, were in an almost impossible dilemma as to what to do, we let the civilians run the war and our soldiers die, and then we abandoned them in the press."[22]

20. MDH-L to Mr. H., June 3, 1969.
21. MDH-L to Eugene England, Mar. 28, 1968.
22. MDH-JE, June 2, 1975.

The helicopter pilot who flew Duff around Vietnam wrote to him, "The war effort remains the same. Our cause is just, and we must stop the encroachment of communism. War is a terrible thing, but if fight we must, then let's get on with it, and put down this devilish plan."[23]

Duff said, "The only justification for war is in the defense of principles. Our scriptures, and even our belief in the war in heaven support the concept of active defense of correct principles. God knows that I hate war—in my short lifetime, I've been actively involved in three wars. I have been to Vietnam and Thailand frequently. South Vietnam is not faultless, and the Lord knows it. And America has made a lot of mistakes—maybe it was a mistake going over there in the first place, and then certainly escalating the war as it did. But the worst mistake of all would be to pull out now and leave the people we have committed to defend."[24]

In a return letter to a Brigham Young University student about the war, Duff wrote:

> You mention that you are appalled by our country's involvement in Vietnam. I have exactly the opposite observation and conviction. Peace is to be wished for, but before peace comes *freedom*—not just for me, but for all men. Also, before peace comes *honor* and *integrity*—and so great a concern for these qualities, that I will involve myself in a war against any enemy who could destroy them.
>
> We are there at the request of a beleaguered people. America's conscience could never be lived with if we refused to offer what help we can to keep men from the enslaving viciousness called communism.[25]

Duff expressed his feeling that the people who wanted to abandon Vietnam had been born a generation too late. The US had been committed by word and contract to preserving freedom since the Nuremberg Trials, and had committed not to let war criminals get away with killing innocent people. Therefore, it could not justify, with any degree of national integrity, abandoning countries that desire freedom.[26]

---

23. Louis T. Bowring to MDH, June 23, 1967.
24. MDH-A, in a newspaper clipping, near the end of the Vietnam War.
25. MDH-L to Andrew K., Aug. 12, 1970.
26. MDH-A, BYU, *Daily Universe*, Feb. 1, 1970.

37

Maude's Passing

Funny—when things look tough and I feel the need for help,
I still think first of the Lord and my wonderful mother.
Sufficient as I am expected to be, I am ofttimes still a lost and lonesome little boy.
—Marion D. Hanks, n.d.

The passing of one's mother is never an acceptable experience in this world, even with what we know about the future and notwithstanding the realities of mortality.

In October 1967, Duff postponed a trip to Vietnam because his mother, Maude, seemed unlikely to live long. But the military men were disappointed that he was not able to go, so he went to see Maude to explain the circumstances and to tell her that he was going to do what she had always taught him to do and fill that commission from President McKay. In a letter to a friend, Duff wrote, "She had lain unresponsive and mostly unconscious for many weeks, and would not respond to anyone, including me. Then, the day before I left, I visited her and told her of my departure, and held her hand and kissed her, and she opened her eyes and said the only words I had heard her speak in a long time. 'You go do your duty, handsome, and God bless you.' It was a mother speaking to her youngest boy one last time in this world."[1]

On October 19, 1967, Duff and Maxine flew to Manila in the Philippines, so Duff could attend a short conference there on his way to visit the troops in Vietnam; Maxine was going to fly on without him to Hong Kong. They went to bed in their hotel room in Manila and were lying in bed talking just past midnight when the telephone rang. At the other end in Salt Lake City was Phyllis Warnick, Duff's wonderful secretary, who through her tears and gentle heart, informed them of the death of Elder Antoine Ivins that day in Salt Lake. She caught her breath and then told Duff that his mother too had slipped away. It was not unexpected but came with the appropriate shock that such a sad message delivers.

Duff and Maxine sat and talked about Maude and Antoine. One of the most significant moments of his life occurred when he looked across the room at the

1. MDH-L, Oct. 1969.

Duff with his mother, Maude Frame Hanks, 1964.

contents of his briefcase stacked on the hotel desk: a stack of airmail envelopes, each with a single sheet of onionskin paper and pre-addressed to Duff's mother. It was his practice to write a note to her nearly every day while he was traveling, giving her just a word of greeting to let her know where he was and that he was thinking of her. Maude had followed Duff's travels with great joy.

Duff looked at that pack of envelopes and said to Maxine, "I will never be able to write her another letter on this earth." He said, "I have always been grateful to honor my mother and to speak of her with the most sincere and honest admiration and respect. She lived like a saint and was in fact a saint, and her children have everything for which to thank her."

Maude Frame Hanks had been the anchor to which her children could hold, even in the most trying conditions. She was a benevolent, loving mother with a great testimony of the Savior, grateful to be able to teach her children to love Him. She taught them about good literature, music, and poetry. But mostly she taught them about love, which she shared by serving all around her. Her children adored her.

Duff and Maxine talked well into the night, reminiscing and expressing gratitude to the Lord for his angelic mother. "Maxine and I decided that I had better go home. I hated to disappoint the men in Vietnam, but this was weighed carefully and considerately, and I decided to be with Mother this once more. We flew home and sat smiling through her funeral as one after another speaker thanked God for knowing her, and one who knew her well said of her, 'This noble lady gave her children everything that money *could not* buy.'"

Rich remembered, "I was just a little boy of seven years old, and I had never seen a dead person before, let alone my grandma, which was a bit unnerving. But the thing I remember best was holding my dad's hand as they wheeled out her casket and seeing him really cry discernibly for the first time in my life."

On learning of Maude's death, Jeffrey R. Holland, who had recently completed a master's degree at BYU, wrote a particularly sweet letter. "On one of our visits with your mom, she recounted the day of your departure for active duty [in World War II]. With tears in her eyes, she recalled the two of you standing by the old gate, in the pre-dawn hours—I think she called you her 'little-man grown-up' and how hard it was to let you go. As you walked off to war, she quoted a beautiful poem, the only line of which I now remember contained the phrase, 'my sailor with sea-blue eyes.'"[2]

Sixteen years later, in November 1983, the church hosted the executive board of the National Council of Women in Salt Lake City. The leaders of the Relief Society and the Young Women asked Duff to share some time with them, teaching about the church and answering questions. In a letter of gratitude, Elaine Cannon, the Young Women General President and Duff's friend since adolescence, wrote, "The comments of our visitors would have warmed your heart. Countess Paolozzi summed it up when she asked me, 'Such a remarkable human being—who nurtured him . . . who nurtured him?'"

Maude did.

2. Jeffrey R. Holland to MDH, Nov. 3, 1967.

38

Assistant to the Twelve

Before the general conference in April 1968, all the general authorities met, fasting and praying, in the temple for their usual meeting. Duff recalled, "I had had a very restive night for reasons I did not know intellectually, but knew, as I knew years ago when I was called to the seventy, that something was going to happen to me."

During the meeting, President McKay proposed that Alvin R. Dyer become a member of the First Presidency. He then announced two men to become part of the First Council of the Seventy. Then he fumbled a bit with his papers, and Duff thought to himself, "Maybe the Lord doesn't want that read, and we can all go home and forget about it for another six months." But President McKay read the name of Marion D. Hanks to become an assistant to the Twelve. Everyone voted affirmatively. Duff felt squeezes on his shoulder from Ezra Taft Benson, Spencer W. Kimball, and Mark E. Petersen. "Ted [Tuttle] and Bruce [McConkie] likewise responded, with the affection we have felt for each other."[1]

Duff had mixed feelings about the change in calling. He had no prior knowledge from any earthly source and was taken completely by surprise, although inside he knew that something was going to happen. The projected changes left Duff with a little sorrow at being extracted from a group he loved and was proud of and to which the Lord had called him. He had spent almost fifteen years in the First Council of the Seventy and was sad to leave the warm relationships with his brethren. He wrote, "I now find myself in the position of moving from a quorum, said by scripture to be equal in authority to the Twelve, to what Elder John Longden called the 'non-group.' The Assistants have no quorum, hold no meetings, have no esprit as such, and no group identity. They are fine men and are doing important work, but they are not a unit."

Duff had to remind himself that the same Source that called him before was calling him again and said, "I hope I may qualify for whatever opportunities or disappointments lie ahead. I do love the Lord and the church and would wish I were a better man than I am in the service of both. I will have to meet whatever comes and continue to serve where I am permitted to do so."[2]

1. MDH-JE, Mar. 28, 1968.
2. MDH-JE, Apr. 1968.

Thus ended fourteen and a half years of what Duff described as his choice association and brotherhood with those good and noble men.

BACKGROUND OF THE CALLING

Assistant to the Quorum of the Twelve Apostles was a priesthood calling between 1941 and 1976 of men who functioned as general authorities. When the first assistants were called in April 1941, J. Reuben Clark Jr. of the First Presidency explained that they had been called because of the rapid growth of the church. Thirty-eight men served the church as assistants to the Twelve before the office was merged with the seventy in 1976.

According to President Spencer W. Kimball in 1976, the calling of the assistants was "similar to that envisioned by the revelations for the First Quorum of Seventy," but "the scope and demands of the work at that time [1941]" did not yet justify the reconstitution of that quorum. After growth in many parts of the world led to the organization of the First Quorum of Seventy in 1975, the nearly two dozen assistants then serving became members of that quorum in 1976.

MOVING FORWARD

The newspaper headlines read, "Elders Dyer, Hanks Are Advanced." Duff later wrote that this new calling demonstrated trust and confidence in his abilities and efforts, but nothing really changed in his day-to-day activities and authority and responsibility. Plus, in his mind, the calling wasn't really scriptural. He had done a lot of research on the seventy and had hoped that the Quorums of the Seventy, as described in the Doctrine and Covenants, were going to be reconstituted, as eventually happened in 1976.

Once again congratulatory cards and letters came pouring in, and Duff was grateful for the kindness that people accorded him. Despite all the temporary adulation, he simply went to work and continued magnifying his calling.

39

The Church, the Gospel, the People, and the Culture

My view of the church was that it offered the standard around which one rallied, and the center about which one constructed a life.
—Marion D. Hanks[1]

I have so appreciated your blend of honest personal striving and relentless commitment to the institutional church.
—Bruce C. Hafen

Duff loved the gospel and the church and the priesthood. But he didn't have a problem distinguishing between them. He defined them and pointed to the ultimate purpose of each:

> *The Gospel of Jesus Christ.* The plan of God to bring His children back to Him—a plan of mercy and redemption and happiness. It centers on the Savior and His Atonement and love and service. Summarized by the Lord as love God and love our fellow man.
>
> *The Church.* An organization, an institution, whose purpose is to implement the plan. Sometimes called "the kingdom of God on earth." Led by good men and women who nonetheless have faults and foibles. A scaffolding around the gospel. Inspired by God, but not in every detail. The church provides a vision that centers in what one may *do* and *become* and *give.*
>
> *The Priesthood.* The power by which we work, delegated to us by God. It's the power by which the gospel is preached, and the church is organized and operated. For us, its chief purpose is to *serve* our fellow men.

While he believed in the good that the institutional church could do, he believed strongly that the purpose of it all was to improve the individual. Duff often asked, "Then what is the reason for these—why do they exist—the Gospel, the Church, the Priesthood?" His answer was—"THE INDIVIDUAL. All the

1. "News of the Church," *Ensign*, Nov. 1984.

organization charts, all the programs, all we do, should be to strengthen and lift the individual to help him or her to return to Heavenly Father."[2]

THE LIVING CHURCH

As a missionary, Rich wrote Duff asking him about the distinctiveness of the Church of Jesus Christ of Latter-day Saints. He replied with the following:

> We represent a *living God*, a loving, revealing, aware Father, the Father of the spirits of all mankind.
>
> The church worships a *living Christ,* born according to the prophecies, living according to His holy mission, being sent as He was to do the will of God, teaching what He had heard His Father teach, and doing what he had seen His Father do. He loved us so much that He died for us, was literally resurrected, ascended into heaven and is now on the right hand of God.
>
> We have a *living Church,* its pews and choir lofts and classrooms and recreation areas occupied by people who are growing with it, learning to be vibrant and alive as they turn from ways that little affected them, to a program that does.
>
> Ours is a *living Theology*, with revelation as a current and constant reality.
>
> We represent a *living Faith,* with tens of thousands of young men and women committed enough to it to leave behind their ordinary lives, and, at their own expense, share it with others. It gives purpose in life and meaning in living. It provides answers, a guide to conduct, and a witness of the truth and the way.
>
> Ours is a *living Religion.* It touches everything about us, even the food we eat and the clothes we wear. It includes emphasis on the fundamentals of decent personal conduct, eternal marriage, united families, and a future involving all of this.
>
> We work with *living Scripture,* where the lessons of the past are learned in the needful present, with the inspiration of God directing.
>
> Ours is a *living Brotherhood* and a *living Sisterhood,* with quorums and Relief Society and the support of our associates.[3]

Duff taught that vital religion cannot be maintained and preserved on the theory that God dealt with us only in the far past and that the Bible is the only evidence we have that our God is a living, communicating God. Quoting the great Quaker teacher and writer Rufus Jones, Duff taught, "If God ever spoke, he is still the great I Am, not the great He Was."[4]

THE THINGS THAT MATTER MOST

Duff loved the gospel and the church. But he knew very well that the church was led by imperfect men, because, as he said, "I am one of them." Duff had occasion to be faced with many instances in which he differed with an

2. MDH, notes in preparation for a presentation.
3. MDH-L to Richard D. Hanks, 1980.
4. Rufus Jones, "A Flash of Eternity," undated news clipping.

approach taken by the institutional church or some of its leaders. Because of his willingness to listen and care for the individual, he became a guiding light to many who didn't fit exactly into the mold of some of the church's doctrines and ideologies. Those who have what are now called "faith crises" flocked to him in droves. Those seeking mercy and some degree of hope for a future that included God's forgiveness sought him out. Those who believed that the church should take a more progressive stance on some issues hoped he would take their positions forward. Those who disagreed with the "we're right, you're wrong" approach to the Restoration of the gospel found a sympathetic ear for their concerns.

Confusion and concern about the church were felt not just by those on the fringes of activity. Committed Latter-day Saints also approached Duff for help in making sense of some things. One of Duff's most oft-repeated aphorisms highlighted an underlying principle that guided him throughout his life: "The things that matter most [should not] be at the mercy of the things that matter least."[5]

DOCTRINES AND DOGMA VERSUS FAITH

I am very comfortable with 'Come unto Christ.'
I am not so comfortable with doctrinal hocus pocus.[6]
—Marion D. Hanks

Duff was not personally inclined to focus on doctrine. He knew the scriptures as well or better than anyone around him. But he didn't really care as much about dogma and doctrine as he cared about getting to know the Savior. It just didn't matter to him "if the earth was created in seven days, seven years, or seven minutes." And his distaste for those who spouted "doctrinal certitudes" was legendary.

One of Duff's favorite stories was about a young priest who was about to leave his calling because he saw injustice. An older priest encouraged him to remain because he saw true Christian strength in the youth. He said to the younger man, "You have inquisitiveness and tenderness. You are sensible to the distinction between thinking and doubting. And best of all, you do not have that *bumptious security* which springs from *dogma* rather than from *faith*."[7]

Echoing this advice, Duff wrote, "I seek faith. I am uncomfortable in the presence of 'the bumptious security which springs from dogma,' and express my own strong feeling that it is of utmost importance that we value love, faith, repentance, obedience, morality, integrity, and walking in the Spirit, and that we never undervalue these principles at the expense of less essential matters which may

5. William P. Montague, *Belief Unbound: A Promethean Religion for the Modern World* (New Haven, CT: Yale University Press, 1930), 7.

6. MDH, note to himself.

7. A. J. Cronin, *Keys of the Kingdom* (Boston: Little, Brown, 1941), emphasis added.

preoccupy some. The only true tragedy any of us can ultimately experience is to be separated from Him, from Christ, and from our dear ones."[8]

Duff received myriad letters following his July 1981 *Ensign* article titled "An Attitude: The Weightier Matters," in which he outlined principles he had developed for wise teaching. The letters expressed deep gratitude for his straightforward and open discussion, especially on matters that hadn't been settled by the prophet. One particularly poignant letter was from a member, who when researching for her master's thesis felt some discomfiture on what she perceived was the church's opinion on man's origins. She wrote, "I have received startlingly hostile reactions from other members whose opinions on the subject leave no room for those who differ with them. You have pointed out that we must learn to say, 'I do not know,' and then proceed with our religious lives based on our faith in what we *do* know, . . . but it is hard to shore up one's faith against the condemnation of others. I felt like your article was written especially for me and will reread it when I feel the need to reaffirm my conviction that there is room for all of us."[9]

Duff was famous for question-and-answer sessions he would hold after stake conferences. One person, commenting online, remembered a time in 1970 when he was working at the Hill Cumorah Pageant. After speaking to all in attendance, Duff opened up the meeting for any questions. One missionary was bold enough to ask about wearing the temple garment *all* hours of the day, regardless of the activity. Duff replied, "Wear the uniform best suited for the event."[10]

DISQUIET

Like all who believe in a divine Father in Heaven and also believe in an organized, formal religion, Duff often found himself in the difficult dilemma of trying to reconcile his beliefs with some of the institutional and even cultural declarations of the church or its members. He just did not find an explanatory rationale for some of what he called, "the misunderstood exclusionary clauses" and the "nonessential insistencies" of the church. These (generally unofficial) positions have caused many people profound concern and interest. Most are related to the church's doctrines, or personal worthiness, or experiences with authority.

MISUNDERSTOOD EXCLUSIONARY CLAUSES

During an interview in the 1950s, a journalist asked Carl Sandburg, "What's the ugliest word in the English language?" He answered, "Exclusive." Exclusion builds walls. It tears people apart. It divides.[11]

Duff testified of the Restoration, the importance of saving ordinances, covenants, obedience, and following living prophets on the earth. But he did not

8. MDH-T, "An Attitude: The Weightier Matters," *Ensign*, July 1981, 70.

9. A. H. to MDH, July 6, 1981.

10. Online private blog.

11. Something that is *exclusive* is used or owned by only one person or group, and not shared with anyone else. *Collins English Dictionary*, s.v. "exclusive."

believe that having the truth created an exclusive club that left others out. This is a fairly easy point for people to agree with in principle, but it is far less easy to put into practice.

Duff well knew and testified of the saving ordinances (sometimes referred to as required, or exclusionary, ordinances),[12] such as the correct mode of baptism, and temple sealings, and the importance and power of the priesthood. But over time, he couldn't reconcile some doctrines with his idea of a loving, living God. Duff could not believe in his heart, for example, that a loving God would exclude his own children from eternal progression and joy.

On one occasion, he sat comforting the mother of a young boy who lay in a coma from a terrible accident. After a while, the mother expressed her concern that she wouldn't be able to be with her son after this life because she and her husband had not been sealed in the temple. Duff wrote, "I was faced with the dilemma of wanting to encourage her [to get sealed in the temple] and yet having the need out of my own convictions and tender heart to reassure her that if she will do all she can, there will never be any permanent separation between her and her son. I think that the Lord expects us to do all we can do, … but I have no question at all about whether in God's mercy and love there will be a tearing away of such relationships. We talked a long time and knelt in prayer together and I talked to the Lord on behalf of all of us. It was a tender and sweet time."[13]

Duff noted that there are also exclusionary people. Some people seem to really enjoy setting up rules and regulations and then lie in wait to catch the transgressors. Duff preferred to catch people doing good things.

A few other specific examples of misunderstood exclusionary clauses might prove instructive in explaining his feeling about them:

Myth: No Blessings If You Can't Keep All the Commandments

Duff frequently quoted a scripture describing the gifts of the Spirit: "For verily I say unto you, they are given for the benefit of those who love me and keep *all* my commandments, and him that *seeketh* so to do" (D&C 46:9; emphasis added). Whenever a teacher or speaker interpreted this verse as if the blessings would come only to those who keep *all* the commandments, Duff felt it important to point out the second half of the verse, which also promises the blessings to those who *seek* to keep them.

Myth: Must Have a Perfect Knowledge of Jesus to Be Saved

Whenever a leader felt to inform listeners that they couldn't be saved without their own personal testimony of Jesus, Duff shared the proclamation in the

---

12. MDH-T, "A Love of God and of All Men," BYU, Mar. 1981. A careful reading of his remarks shows that in this talk, Duff was referring to "exclusionary *ordinances*," not to "*misunderstood exclusionary clauses*." He was making the point that even essential ordinances are not enough; there is much more. We must, for example, serve our fellow man.

13. MDH-JE, Aug. 7, 1977.

scriptures that says, "To some it is given to know that Jesus is the Son of God" and "to others it is given to *believe on their words,* that they *also* might have eternal life if they continue faithful" (D&C 46:13–14; emphasis added).

Myth: You Must Know, Not Just Believe

When someone would set up perfect faith or lack of doubt as a requirement for exaltation, Duff would sometimes share the scripture in Mark, in which a man pleads with the Lord for the healing of his child: "And straightway the father of the child cried out, and said with tears, Lord, I believe; help thou mine unbelief" (Mark 9:24). Duff believed the Lord should be approached in faith and humility. He was genuinely impressed by those who would bear their testimony, sharing not only what they felt they *knew,* but also what they *believed.*

Myth: Burning in the Bosom Required of All

Despite having many sacred and spiritual experiences himself, Duff felt compassion for those who studied and prayed but felt that God was not confirming truth to their soul. Church members often quote Doctrine and Covenants 9:8 and seem to assume there is a blanket promise from the Lord that whenever we ask for direction, having done what we can to work it out, then we are going to have either a burning in the bosom or a stupor of thought that will conclusively settle the matter. When individuals would insist that God would provide this burning in the bosom to those who would study and ask, Duff would remind them of two points. First, this experience was given specifically to Oliver Cowdery about translating, and second, Oliver himself didn't always know when or how God was answering his prayers and had to be reminded (See D&C 6:14–15).

Myth: Parents Are Responsible for Children's Sins

Duff took seriously the Lord's instruction that parents should "teach their children to pray, and to walk uprightly before the Lord" (D&C 68:28) and that failure to do such teaching results in the "sin being upon the heads of the parents" (D&C 68:25). But in a general conference address in April 1967, Duff pointed out, "There is another side of this story that deserves compassionate consideration." He posed the following question: "What has the church to say to a sincere parent who, like all parents, has made mistakes, but who has really tried—only to have a child disregard his teachings and example and choose another way?"

In answering his own question, Duff first spoke of the many and persuasive influences on children besides parents. He then quoted from Ezekiel, whose people traditionally taught, "The fathers have eaten sour grapes, and the children's teeth are set on edge." Ezekiel told the people to stop misusing this proverb: "As I live, saith the Lord God, ye shall not have occasion any more to use this proverb in Israel" (Ezekiel 18:1–3). Ezekiel then taught that parents and children will not bear each other's iniquities, and he emphasized each person's individual responsibility before God (Ezekiel 18:4, 20).

Duff explained, "God requires that we each accept responsibility for our individual decisions; he deals with every man according to his own character." He then concluded, "To those to whom the sorrow of a child unresponsive to parental instruction has come, be comforted. God understands. He knows what it means to have a rebellious son and wayward children."[14]

The response from church members was overwhelming, and cards and letters came pouring in. One said, "Thank you for your talk and encouragement. We can now continue our activities in the church without such haunting feelings of guilt and failure, even though we have always done the best we knew how at the time. Your talk was mouth-to-mouth resuscitation for the spiritually expiring parent."[15]

Myth: No Heaven for Non-LDS and No Progression between Kingdoms

Concurrent with his strong belief in mercy, Duff did not believe Heavenly Father would ever give up on his children. While he clearly understood the law of the harvest,[16] he also could see in the doctrines of the church room for repentance, improvement, and opportunity for salvation for all God's children. Even though he was a temple president and believed in the sealing power, he couldn't accept that a husband and wife, married sixty-plus years and deeply in love, would be separated in the next life simply because they didn't have the opportunity to be sealed in a temple.

Similarly, Duff just did not agree with the assertion that there is no chance for progression between kingdoms after this life. He was well aware of the differing viewpoints on this subject held by church leaders over the years; compare Brigham Young's belief in progression and Orson Pratt and Joseph Fielding Smith's belief in no progression. Duff sided with those who believed that learning and growing continues throughout eternity. He wrote, "We who respond to the concept of eternal progression find no denigration or distress in the principle that we have much to learn, that every accomplishment is a new commencement, every challenge, every failure, every need for repentance a new opportunity of growth."[17] When pressed on the matter of progression between degrees of glory, Duff would supply copies of letters from the First Presidency specifically announcing that the church had not established a policy or viewpoint on the matter.[18]

---

14. MDH-T, "Be Comforted," GC, Apr. 1967.

15. Mrs. Harley T. Sandberg to MDH, July 13, 1967.

16. One reaps what one has sown.

17. Duff's undated notes in preparation for an unidentifiable talk.

18. "The brethren direct me to say that the Church has never announced a definite doctrine upon this point. Some of the brethren have held the view that it was possible in the course of progression to advance from one glory to another, invoking the principle of eternal progression; others of the brethren have taken the opposite view. But as stated, the Church has never announced a definite doctrine on this point." Secretary to the First Presidency in a 1952 letter and again in 1965, cited in *Dialogue: A Journal of Mormon Thought* 15, no. 1 (1965): 181–82.

Clearly, the genesis of these examples points to Duff's continual exposure to individuals' lack of confidence or their misunderstanding of church teachings, whether doctrine or tradition. His hours spent counseling with people led him to a profound sense of compassion for those who didn't fit into a particular mold of testimony or commitment.

On his becoming an emeritus leader, he received the following sweet letter from his friend Emma Lou Thayne: "Perhaps the saddest dimension to your not being there in that building, is the loss of what you brought dealing with the *exclusive*—your bold, deep, humane view that continues to be *inclusive.* Thank you for decades of bringing hope and light. You will be sorely missed."[19]

"NONESSENTIAL INSISTENCIES"

As a new deacon, Rich joined his parents at a church service at Aspen Grove, where he helped pass the sacrament. "I had seen the sacrament administered in only one way—the 'right' way—that is, my home ward's way," he said. "Suddenly, in the mountains, I was presented with a very different way to pass the sacrament. I asked the other boys, 'What are you guys doing?' I was incredulous and made it known that they weren't doing it correctly. Dad took me aside and helped me understand that it was okay."

That was Rich's first recollection of Duff explaining what he called the "nonessential insistencies." There are many examples of this in the church and its culture, such as: who sits where in meetings, what can be said in funerals or farewells (even what to call those meetings), which hand to use in taking the sacrament, acceptable facial hair, who can pray in meetings, perfection in delivering the sacrament prayer, hair length and shirt color worn by young men, what it means to be worthy, what "be ye therefore perfect means," use of the term "church broke," unwritten administrative rules, exactly where to walk in the temple, standing when a general authority enters a room, and on and on. Some make sense in certain circumstances; others just seem silly.

Duff felt the same way about some of the church's practices, policies, and interpretations of the scriptures. He once joked to a friend, "The church in general has too much *rigor* and not enough *mortis.*"

Duff was very pleased when the stake president, while ordaining Rich as a bishop, instructed him to "follow the *General Handbook*—unless you feel the Spirit is leading you otherwise."

Duff continually reminded those he loved against getting caught up in, "The thick of thin things."[20]

In October 1984, he was sustained in general conference as a member of the Presidency of the Seventy for the third time.[21] He mentioned in passing in his

19. Emma Lou Thayne to MDH, Dec. 6, 1992.

20. Attributed to the novelist Edith Wharton.

21. Duff's initial call was as one of the seven members of the First Council of the Seventy, comparable to today's Presidency of the Seventy.

journal that he was just fine sitting where he was and planned to continue there for the rest of the conference. After a break between sessions, he went back to his seat and found that his seat assignment had been made to a different row. He lamented in his journal, "I hate this stuff."

After so many years away from his wife and family, sitting on the stand during church services, on the rare occasion he was able to attend his home ward, he preferred to sit with Maxine in the congregation. Occasionally, an officious leader would remind him that he was presiding and was required to sit on the stand. He invited such folks to carry on without him; "I'll be in the audience if some need requires my attention." Tongue in cheek, he described the arrangement he had with his own bishop such that "when I don't sit on the stand, it won't be necessary to notify the people of my august presence."

In a journal entry in 1973, he wrote, "I may as well mention that Wednesday, another of the general authorities led an assault on beards, as if they were the most critical thing in the world. In the temple meeting on Thursday, as we discussed the Lord's return, I found myself wondering if He would have to shave to meet [the general authority] or to attend BYU. I don't mean to be cynical; I just mean to say our priorities are questionable."[22]

Duff was amazed at how far some members and leaders would take recommended church practices and expand them to their own liking. He received a letter about cola drinks and caffeine, which he forwarded to the First Presidency, per the author's request. He received a letter back from the First Presidency, "We have never taken the attitude that cola drinks could be included in the Word of Wisdom questions in the Aaronic Priesthood advancement interview."[23]

In a July 12, 1974, meeting with President Spencer W. Kimball, after finishing their scheduled business, Duff talked with him about some stake presidents who were making hair length a standard for worthiness in the priesthood. He wrote, "While I have not discouraged young men from following the counsel of their stake presidents, I have not pretended to believe in this kind of business. President Kimball encouraged me to talk with the stake presidents in a kind manner, without embarrassing them, and to set them straight."[24]

In a deeply insightful talk, Elder Stephen L Richards taught "Election, not compulsion, is the genius of the Christian Philosophy," adding, "It is the genius of the church to change its procedure and interpretations. The very elasticity of prayers, ceremonies and procedures is additional evidence of the adaptability of our religion to human needs."[25] Duff felt similarly.

---

22. MDH-JE, Dec. 7, 1973.
23. First Presidency to MDH, Mar. 3, 1972.
24. MDH-JE, July 12, 1974.
25. Stephen L Richards, "Bringing Humanity to the Gospel," GC, Apr. 9, 1932.

INVOLVING WOMEN

One of the main areas of concern for Duff was in the treatment of women. Throughout the entire world, both men and women had been living with unequal social mores for centuries, and change was slowly coming about. Even so, Duff came out of the darkness earlier than most. He included women on his boards and committees and asked for their input (when neither practice was common) and treated them with respect. He specifically pointed out the need to listen and learn from the women of the church. He loved it when others felt the same. After a meeting in 1975, Elder Marvin J. Ashton suggested to Elder Boyd K. Packer that the wives of stake priesthood leaders ought to be with their husbands at Saturday evening stake conference sessions. Elder Packer asked if a stake presidency couldn't hold a meeting without their wives present, and Elder Ashton said calmly, so we should tell them to say to their wives, "You will be alone again. I am going to a meeting to see a film of the President of the Church talking about missionary work. You don't have any business being there, so you can't come." Duff wrote that he was pleased to see Elder Ashton pushing back.[26]

While working on the creation of the church's young single adult program in 1973 in a meeting with Relief Society president Belle Spafford and her counselors, and later with the committee's advisors, Duff messaged his feeling that maybe "it was time to expand the whole concept of Womanhood throughout the church, restructure the Relief Society program and curriculum, and move to a new vista for all the women of the church."[27] There is no record of their response to his message.

Years later, after a difficult counseling session with a sister, Duff recorded his thoughts on the disparity between the way divorced men and women were treated regarding subsequent temple sealings. Duff wrote, "Abusive, hypocritical father. Divorce, then he [is] readmitted with another wife. She says he is beastly brutal in the name of the priesthood. I comforted her and may have gone too far in my comments—but I *feel* too far. This hierarchy of value with men at the top of the heap is just baloney, and rotten baloney to me. There is no preference for men in the heart of the Almighty, in my not so humble judgment in this matter. Over and over, we get it from the thoughtful and decent, the good and kind. I agree with them. A change could and should be made. I pray it will."[28]

IDEAS AHEAD OF THEIR TIME

In reading through Duff's journals, one can't help but be struck with the number of ideas and considerations that were discussed or suggested by Duff and a few of his colleagues that were years or decades ahead of their time.

26. MDH-JE, Jan. 25, 1975.
27. MDH-JE, Jan. 26, 1973.
28. MDH-JE, June 29, 1984.

Most of the suggested changes eventually occurred, yet some were never implemented. In addition to those discussed at length in this volume, such as teaching from the Book of Mormon routinely, emphasizing Christlike service by missionaries, "Come unto Christ" as the church's official mission, refugee assistance, changes in young adult programs, singles wards, family recreation, focusing more on conversion and less on baptism statistics, and institutional humanitarian service, there were many others. They include shortening church worship blocks, civil marriage before temple marriage, garment adaptation for hot and humid climates, a church "clearinghouse" of member skills, combining priesthood quorums to make better use of high priests, using social services professionals to help the bishops deal with mental health challenges, training courses for bishops, changing the direction and messaging of church discipline, focusing the temple experience specifically on Christ, the creation of emeritus status, reconstitution of the quorums of the seventy, and decentralization of church administration.

REVELATION FOR THE CHURCH

Dogmatic assertions do not take the place of revelation.
—Charles W. Penrose[29]

Duff was troubled by anyone, including especially his fellow general authorities, who felt it was in their purview to declare with authority what the church or Heavenly Father Himself believed about this or that subject. He was well versed in Doctrine and Covenants 28:2, 7, which declares the order of revelation for the church: "No one shall be appointed to receive commandments and revelation in this church excepting my servant Joseph Smith … *until I shall appoint unto them another* in his stead." Duff felt it was clear in the scriptures that only the prophet can receive revelation for the entire church.

In an address given at BYU titled "It Speaketh of Jesus, and Persuadeth Them to Believe in Him," Duff said:

> It is not in my capacity, nor yours, nor that of any man to break new ground in revelation or in any definitive declaration of what constitutes the official position of the church, where past Presidents of the church have not made that position clear. Let me note from President Joseph Fielding Smith a few lines which declare what I have just said: "Each of the apostles when he is ordained has conferred upon him all the keys and authorities which were given by Joseph Smith to the apostles before his death. These brethren, however, cannot exercise these authorities except when the occasion arises that they come to the presidency. Before that time, the powers lie dormant. This is one reason why they are sustained as

29. James R. Clark, comp., *Messages of the First Presidency of The Church of Jesus Christ of Latter-day Saints*, 6 vols. (Salt Lake City: Bookcraft, 1965–75), 4:264–65.

prophets, seers and revelators *in* the church, but there can be but one revelator *for* the church at a time."[30]

Elder Mark E. Petersen said in general conference to all who teach in the church: "I do not believe that the classrooms or the pulpits of our church are for laboratory purposes in which to experiment with new doctrines and speculative notions.... There is *only one man* in all the world who has the right to introduce a new doctrine to this church, and that man is the President of the church. So, teachers, until you become the President of the church, will you be willing to content yourselves with the present officially accepted doctrines of the church?"[31]

Five years after Duff joined the First Council of the Seventy, Elder Bruce R. McConkie published *Mormon Doctrine: A Compendium of the Gospel*,[32] which he described as "the first major attempt to digest, explain, and analyze all of the important doctrines" of the church. Church leaders were surprised by its publication, since they had not asked him to write such a book. The First Presidency called it "full of errors and misstatements."[33]

In June 1980, while on his mission, Rich sent Duff a copy of a talk given at Brigham Young University by Elder McConkie, entitled "The Seven Deadly Heresies," in which Elder McConkie pronounced that certain beliefs were "false and devilish" and heretical. Rich asked Duff if this talk was really doctrinally accurate and if he agreed with all the points of the talk. Duff's response was short and to the point, "No, Rich, I don't. I talked directly to Bruce, and I also met with the First Presidency about it." He included with his return letter to Rich a copy of a letter sent in 1952 from Joseph Anderson, secretary to the First Presidency. A member had asked the First Presidency, "Please inform me as to the teaching of the church regarding the possibility of a person progressing from one Kingdom to another after the resurrection?" (That was one of Elder McConkie's seven heresies.)

The answer was, "The Brethren direct me to say that the church has never announced a definite doctrine upon this subject."

After his meeting with the First Presidency, Duff wrote in his journal,

> I do declare that I love Bruce and believe in his character, but I think he sometimes lacks judgment. All he accomplished was to comfort a few close-minded people and put into disarray the position of teachers, substantially all of whom previously had copies of the documents I submitted to the First Presidency,

---

30. MDH-T, "It Speaketh of Jesus, and Persuadeth Them to Believe in Him," BYU, Aug. 1986, citing Joseph Fielding Smith, *Church History and Modern Revelation* (Salt Lake City: Council of the Twelve Apostles of the Church of Jesus Christ of Latter-day Saints, 1948).

31. Mark E. Petersen, in Conference Report, Apr. 1953, 83.

32. *Mormon Doctrine: A Compendium of the Gospel* (Salt Lake City: Bookcraft, 1958).

33. Erich Robert Paul, *Science, Religion, and Mormon Cosmology* (Urbana: University of Illinois Press, 1992), 179.

> including the one saying we have no position on organic evolution, and who now must equivocate, or shake their heads, or say this or that. All of this sounds like I care, really care, about such things. I do, but only to the extent that they exclude people, individuals, and that they seem to commit the church to unstable and unnecessary and even ridiculous positions. The question is, does Brother McConkie have the right to change declarations of the past presidencies of the church? And the answer is, that of course he does not.[34]

Elder McConkie later made forceful public declarations about whom we worship and whom we do not worship. His pronouncement included the words, "We do not worship the Son, and we do not worship the Holy Ghost."[35] Duff wrote, "I think that Bruce was trying to teach us what the scriptures also tell us—that we should worship the Father *in the name* of the Son. However, with our view of the absolute unity of the Father and the Son, and with our sense of the mission of the Savior, and with statements made over the years by many of the brethren concerning our worship of the Savior, how can we be in a position of announcing unequivocally that we do not worship him? We frequently sing Bruce's own hymn, 'I Believe in Christ,' which includes the wording 'I'll worship him with all my might.' The scriptures clearly declare the worship of him, and in general I cannot personally support the suggestion that we do not [2 Nephi 25:29]."[36]

In several notes in one of Duff's folders were these insightful words: "Church leaders should *not* speak unequivocally about equivocal things" and "Where doctrine is concerned, there is safety in counsel. When the *group* of apostles offer advice, better take it; where *one* speaks, consider it carefully."

"A MORE EXCELLENT WAY"

Duff disliked the "we're right, you're wrong" approach that some use to share the message of the Restoration. He preferred the words of Ether 12:11, which says, "In the gift of his Son hath God prepared a more excellent way." Duff chose to emphasize this description— "*the more excellent way*"—when he described the restored church.

All LDS missionaries are eventually faced with the problem of how they will message the restoration of the Lord's church to others. Investigators who are "mostly right" don't want to hear that they are wrong. They also don't want to hear that they have "inferior or invalid heavenly credentials," as one letter to the editor called it. Having more truth sometimes creates problems of superiority, ego, and inertia with those who try to teach it to others.

Here lies a dilemma: how to share with others that the truth has been restored, without implying or demanding that others are wrong. Of course, members could just mind their business and leave others alone, but then how would the church

34. MDH-JE, June 17, 1981.
35. Bruce R. McConkie, "Our Relationship with the Lord," BYU, 1982.
36. MDH-L to Daniel H. Ludlow, June 27, 1986.

fulfill the Savior's injunction to go into all the world? Duff mentioned a cartoon showing two missionaries at a slammed door. One is wearing a big button that says, "YOU'RE WRONG!" The other missionary says, "Elder, maybe it's your door approach."

Duff didn't feel a need to apologize for the Restoration; in fact, he felt the opposite. In a letter to Rich on his mission, Duff wrote, "Ours is a living theology with revelation as a current and constant reality. It has been restored and lives."[37]

He taught that truth had been restored and was *continuing to be* restored. And he often declared that "all roads don't actually lead to Rome," and that individual beliefs about a thing do not make it so. In a position paper titled "Questions for an Earnest Seeker of Truth," Duff laid out the scriptural case for there being only "one road" and "one true gospel." He made the argument that "it is not enough to be sincere in one's religious convictions; he must also have the truth."

Notwithstanding these beliefs, Duff chose to focus on the positives of the Restoration and its application to humankind, rather than on the negatives of another's beliefs. He would often read to visitors of other faiths from what Joseph Smith wrote in the dungeon in Liberty Jail, in which Joseph declared an attitude quite different from the strong language used to tell his story in the pamphlets the church distributes. He spoke clearly of his feeling that we must treat others who differ from us in religious viewpoint better than they treat each other.[38]

Duff would have loved the title of the book *You Don't Have to Be Wrong for Me to Be Right: Finding Faith without Fanaticism.* Duff's feelings about salvation allowed for a really big tent that would include a lot of souls. He would have enjoyed this more recently published description of salvation, because it echoed what he believed: "It is difficult to imagine that a few million, in a world of seven billion, can really be God's only chosen people and heirs of salvation. That's because they aren't. One of the most unfortunate misperceptions about Mormonism is in this tragic irony: Joseph Smith's view is one of the most generous, liberal, and universalist conceptions of salvation in all Christendom.... Mormons do not have a monopoly on righteousness, truth, or God's approbation."[39]

Duff taught, "One who believes or pretends that he or we have a corner on truth, or that we have all the answers, does not understand his own religion, which teaches that God not only is a living, revealing, communicating Father,

37. MDH-L to RDH, Jan. 1980.

38. "We ought always to be aware of those prejudices ... against our friends ... who choose to differ from us in opinion and in matters of faith. Our religion is between us and our God. Their religion is between them and their God. There is a love from God that ... gives scope to the mind, which enables us to conduct ourselves with greater liberality towards all that are not of our faith, than what they exercise towards one another." *Teachings of the Prophet Joseph Smith* (Salt Lake City: Deseret Book, 1976), 146–47.

39. Fiona and Terryl Givens, "Why It's a Myth That Mormons Have a Monopoly on Truth and Salvation," *LDS Living*, Mar. 7, 2018.

but that there is much of grave importance *yet to be revealed* pertaining to His work on the earth and in the heavens."[40]

DEBUNKING THE MYTH AND THE PEDESTAL

When placed in authority, some men grow, and others swell.
—Anonymous

The words *celebrity* and *celebrate* are obviously related. One could argue that anyone venerated by large numbers of people over a long enough period might be tempted to believe they are somehow better than others, influenced by the way they are constantly celebrated. That kind of arrogance bothered Duff when he encountered it in church leaders at any level. Conversely, he deeply admired the humility of the vast majority with whom he served.

As he grew older in tenure, he was often asked to train new general authorities or share his personal feelings with them. On these occasions, he strongly suggested that the new general authorities remain humble. He taught, "Surely a greater responsibility devolves upon all who are called, yet my own experience is that no 'cataclysmic cleansing' occurred by reason of my call, and that I still carried all the baggage I had had the day before."[41]

Having served both in the military and as a missionary, Duff learned to respect, follow, and obey those who had been assigned to lead him. But he couldn't stomach some of the accompanying tendencies that come with hierarchical leadership in any organization. Sometimes as he entered a hall to speak, the well-meaning church members in the audience would rise to their feet as a sign of respect. While he appreciated the gesture and their gracious intent, he would immediately wave them down, asking that they please sit. After a particularly difficult meeting, he wrote, "Status is never forgotten for a moment, which I cannot pretend to enjoy or believe in, and which I hope I do not really partake of. I don't like it much."[42]

When Duff became president of the Salt Lake Temple, his first act was to replace the pictures of church leaders throughout the administrative area of the temple and replace them with pictures of the Savior and other beautiful subjects. In one of his first memos to the thousands of Salt Lake Temple workers, Duff shared the text from one of his favorite cartoons. A few young boys are sitting in a treehouse and have finished hanging up a handwritten sign that reads,

"In this clubhouse, no one acts big, no one acts little, everyone acts medium."

Duff told another similar story, "Once a stake president told of his visit to a Primary class. When the visitors entered, they were made welcome, and the teacher, seeking to impress the significance of the experience for the youngsters,

40. MDH, talk preparation notes. n.d.
41. MDH-L to a newly called general authority.
42. MDH-JE, Apr. 1980.

asked a little child on the front row, 'How many important people are here today?' The child rose and began counting out loud, reaching a total of seventeen, including every person in the room. That is how Christ feels, and so should we."[43]

Duff loved to meet with and learn about people from all walks of life. From church security officers to the temple cafeteria ladies to the janitors he encountered, no one was outside Duff's interest or concern. He knew their names, their families, and their stories. There were no unimportant people to him.

TRANSPARENCY IN THE CHURCH

Duff was a big proponent of saying "I don't know" when that was the truth. He thought if it was good enough for Alma and Nephi, it was good enough for him. Unfortunately, others felt that admitting any ignorance as a church or by a church leader lessened the reputation of same. Some felt no reason to introduce into the narrative historical events that reflected badly on the church or its members. Duff had a different view. He believed that being transparent and telling the truth was the right thing to do, and that curtailing or hiding the truth would eventually result in harm to the church. Duff never purposefully obfuscated the truth or retreated from difficult subjects. In fact, quite the opposite occurred, as he was always willing to discuss difficult issues head on. (See the chapter "Teaching, Learning, and Education.)

While it is human nature to put one's best foot forward, history has proven that it is not the best strategy to tilt history toward only the good. Still, some church leaders have gone to great lengths to protect the members from overly negative events. Other leaders have given talks that actually denounce objective history.

Here is one example of a letter to Duff, among many, from a researcher writing about a difficult time in recent church missionary work. He had written what he thought was a trustworthy recounting of what happened in Japan during a certain time. Duff encouraged him to publish it as it was written. The researcher said, "I met with another church leader who suggested I edit it down (censor), because he was worried what President Hinckley and President Packer would think of it." Counter to the advice he had received from Duff, he cut the piece down, lamenting, "I don't have as honest a manuscript now. One of my friends said to me, 'You're not going to be in my book of *Profiles in Courage*, but I'll put you in my book of *Profiles in Wisdom*.'"[44] On that letter, Duff hand-wrote a note to himself: "Clear exposition of the historical viewpoint of some powerful and unwise leaders."

Duff wrote in a letter about this subject, "I have been around a long time, and I have never found occasion to compromise honesty or truth, and I am grateful for the restoration of the gospel and the assurance in my heart that

43. MDH-T, "Every Man in His Own Place," GC, Oct. 1972.
44. Letter to MDH.

what will ultimately happen will be in keeping with the will of the Lord." And he often quoted Shakespeare from Henry IV, who said, "Tell the truth and shame the Devil."

In recent decades, the pendulum has swung toward a more open approach to church history with the Gospel Topics Essays on ChurchofJesusChrist.org, the Joseph Smith Papers Project, and other efforts that embrace a more complete, objective history.

CHURCH LEADERSHIP AND AGE

After decades in church leadership, Duff broached the subject of retirement (emeritus status) for some of the general authorities who were getting old and losing some vitality, including himself. The concept of an honorable release for brethren approaching older age had been discussed as early as 1941 but was never implemented.[45] In the early 1970s, representing the Presidents of the Seventy, Duff presented to the First Presidency a proposal for emeritus status for general authorities, effective at age seventy.[46] On September 30, 1978, the First Presidency announced in general conference the new status of emeritus to be given from time to time to designated members of the general authorities.

He also was concerned about the weight of the burdens on the shoulders of the church's senior leadership, the effects of their advancing age, and the benefits of infusing the input of some younger leaders. He wrote, "I am of the solemn opinion that some younger voice of courageous reason is needed to balance and in some measure influence the thinking of three old men. In this there is no disrespect; it is how I feel and what I now observe after many years of respectful involvement."[47]

SOULS OVER STATISTICS

The problems of our day will be solved, not by formulas,
but by human beings who have the character to do it.
—Marion D. Hanks

Duff often quoted the saying "I've been in a statistics factory, and I know how statistics are made." While he wasn't opposed to statistics, goals, and key indicators, he believed that they were secondary to what was occurring *inside the soul* of each individual. He loved to quote James Stephens: "What the *heart* knows today, the *head* will understand tomorrow."

Perhaps nowhere was this more evident than in his feeling about the Final Judgment. Once, when asked to share some of his favorite scriptures, he surprised

45. Edward L. Kimball, *Lengthen Your Stride: The Presidency of Spencer W. Kimball* (Salt Lake City: Deseret Book, 2005), 258.

46. MDH-R, Nov. 29, 2000.

47. MDH-JE, Jan. 1, 1976.

the questioner by quoting Mosiah 2:36, 38 and 3:25 because they seemed so negative: "If ye should transgress and go contrary to that which has been spoken, that ye do *withdraw yourselves* from the Spirit of the Lord" (Mosiah 2:36; emphasis added); "A lively sense of his own guilt, which doth *cause him to shrink* from the presence of the Lord" (Mosiah 2:38; emphasis added); and "If they be evil they are consigned to an awful *view of their own guilt* and abominations, which doth cause them *to shrink* from the presence of the Lord" (Mosiah 3:25; emphasis added).

Consistent with his strong beliefs about mercy, Duff felt these scriptures were clear about our choosing to remove ourselves from God, not vice versa. Duff taught that a loving God would always be rooting for us. He felt, based on scriptural declaration, that each of us would get what we are "willing to receive" (D&C 88:32). He testified that, along with the Savior, who "employeth no servant there" (2 Nephi 9:41), we would, in effect, be partially judging ourselves and then take ourselves to a place where we felt comfortable. His view could be summarized by one of his most quoted statements: "Salvation and exaltation are not matters of heavenly bookkeeping, but of the qualifying of the soul that comes with knowing the Lord."[48] This made more sense to him than the clipboard view of the judgment, with its good deeds counted on one side of the ledger and sins on the other side.

Another area where statistics prevailed in LDS culture is the focus on baptisms in the missionary program. Driven hard by some general authorities (and sometimes counter to the counsel of those above them), the relentless push for baptisms is still an undercurrent in missionary work.

Because Duff was sent by President David O. McKay to England, specifically to clean up the mess of an overenthusiastic, numbers-driven mission president, it is not difficult to guess what his feelings were on the subject. After a mission presidents' training meeting sixteen years after returning home from England, he wrote: "The importance of integrity was emphasized. The 'bottom line' is still constantly playing on the minds of these mission presidents in a way which I think tragic. Some incentive is obviously needed by all men, but I would rejoice if that incentive could be the admirable one supplied by the Lord in revelations—the opening up for individuals of a vision of their highest and best potential. Instead, we are baptism-per-missionary oriented, and I suppose to some measure ever will be. Perhaps we even ought to be, if the condition were one people could live without overemphasis and improper perception."[49]

On another occasion, in April 1975, he sarcastically wrote in his journal: "Today was a meeting with the Regional Representatives. The emphasis was on missionary work—and it was all about numbers. We were assured that it is *not*

48. MDH-T, "Willing to Receive," GC, Apr. 1980.
49. MDH-JE, Feb. 26, 1978.

about numbers, but then there was a great deal of talk about goals and quotas. The great aggravation of no increase in baptisms was announced. However, this does not mean we are interested in numbers."

Maybe because so many of the general authorities have previously been leaders in business or maybe because it is just easier to count and measure discrete items, Duff often found himself surrounded by others who overfocused on charts and graphs and numbers and hard measurements and baptisms *at the expense* of some of the softer improvements in the human soul. On many occasions he tried to turn the church's rudder in this regard. The following two declarations by Duff are worth repeating: "The individual is the focal point of all the programs of the church—not the program itself, not the statistics. *Not institutional expansion,* but *individual exaltation* is the purpose of it all."[50]

And, "The objective of it all, then, is not *counting* the sheep but *feeding* them, not the proliferation of buildings or units or organizations or statistics, but the blessing of the individual child of God."[51]

ROLE OF THE CHURCH IN PRIVATE MATTERS

Duff believed that confession was a voluntary exercise and unless he specifically had to determine a candidate's worthiness for a church position, he would stay out of a person's private life. He also believed church leaders should not probe into the intimate expressions of a married couple's life. On one occasion, after an earlier meeting, he stayed to answer young people's questions. One young zealot approached him beforehand with a written indictment of those in the church who were preventing children, condemning birth control. As Duff answered questions, he invited the young man to mind his own stewardship. He commented, "Of course, only he and I knew that I was talking specifically to him, but I meant it. Butting into others' private business, judging and condemning, these are not fit concerns for any of us."

In a 1975 general authorities' meeting, somebody asked if a repentant person whose membership and temple blessings had been restored could hold high office. The answer seemed to be that he should not, with President J. Reuben Clark Jr. being quoted. Duff disagreed and said, "I do not comprehend such a practice in light of the scriptures (e.g., Alma in the Book of Mormon)."

A second question had to do with the intimate relations between husbands and wives and whether the bishop should give temple recommends to individuals whose marital relations seem unacceptable to some. Duff's answer was, "What business does a bishop have asking questions about people's private lives? One man has published his viewpoints all over the church in the matter, whereas I have heard two presidents of the church say that these affairs are the concern of

50. MDH-T, "How Many Apples in a Seed," GC, Apr. 1966.

51. MDH-T, "Bear Ye One Another's Burdens," GC, Oct. 1970.

the private individual alone, so long as [neither spouse] is being imposed upon, and the two are experiencing together that which is unifying and uplifting."[52]

After one temple meeting, Duff wrote, "We discussed a medical panel I have coming up and opinions on various issues—birth control, contraceptives, abortion, etc. Basically, we are all agreed that the church stands on the affirmative principles of the revelation, leaving *application* to the people. These are personal matters and should be left to the determination of the individual."[53]

AT CHURCH: GIVING, NOT JUST GETTING

Duff felt it is an individual's responsibility to study the gospel and improve church meeting experiences for others. He was often faced with people who complained that they "didn't get anything out of church." He believed, along with Brigham Young, "If any of you feel that there is no life in your meeting, … then it becomes your duty to go and instill life into that meeting and do your part to produce an increase of the Spirit."[54]

Someone once posted an online comment that would have rankled Duff. It read, "The Mormon Church just doesn't give me the ROI [return on investment] that it used to.… Who knows, maybe if the church demanded a little less from me, I might find myself going all the way back."[55] This kind of thinking annoyed Duff to no end. He thought such individuals were missing "half the fun of life," that of learning to give and to serve others. He believed firmly in Joseph Smith's teaching that "a religion that does not require the sacrifice of all things never has the power sufficient to produce the faith necessary unto life and salvation."[56] In the eternal perspective, the blessings obtained by sacrifice are greater than anything that is given up.

---

52. MDH-JE, Jan. 29, 1985.

53. MDH-JE, Sept. 7, 1967.

54. Brigham Young, in *Journal of Discourses*, 20 vols. (Latter-day Saints' Book Depot, 1854–86), Liverpool: 10:309.

55. Online comment, Feb. 10, 2007.

56. Joseph Smith, *Lectures on Faith* (Salt Lake City: Deseret Book, 1985), 6:7.

CHANGE AND GROWTH

40

The 1970s, an Overview

The 1970s were full of vim and vigor and exertion for Duff and Maxine. On the home front, all four daughters were married, bringing four sons-in-law into the family. The cabin in Provo Canyon was completed, collapsed after several years, and was built again. They moved from Duff's dream home into Maxine's dream home. And they became empty nesters.

The world was dealing with Watergate and the post–civil rights era. The Vietnam War was winding down, and the Cold War continued.

The decade of the seventies was full of milestone events and significant changes in the church, highlighted by the revelation giving Black men the priesthood. President David O. McKay died, and three other prophets served after him during the decade. The quorums of the seventy were reconstituted, and the emeritus designation for general authorities was announced. Temple building began to ramp up, and the church issued new editions of the scriptures.

Duff's life was no less busy. He and his committee led the complete restructuring of the singles program for the church, creating young single adult wards and the young adult and special interests organizations. Later in the decade, he led the complete reorganization of the Young Men and Young Women programs, including the creation of Young Men presidencies at all levels of church hierarchy. He worked hard to create the first activities committees of the church. During the 1970s he also served as the area advisor for multiple areas of the world, including Southeast Asia, the South Seas, Canada, the West and East Coasts of the United States, and the Utah Area.

Duff continued his collegial association with his fellow church leaders. On February 9, 1977, just a few months after he was called to the Presidency of the Seventy for the second time, he wrote in his journal, "The meetings of the First Quorum are good. The spirit is growing and I think in some considerable measure because there is a spirit of honest brotherhood and a sense of unity that is increasing in its virtue regularly."

The 1970s were the decade of Duff's most significant contribution to the national leadership of the Boy Scouts of America and of Rotary International—both of which were actively pursuing him to become president of their respective organizations. His work on the President's Council on Physical Fitness and Sports continued, and his involvement with the United States military increased.

Other interesting events of the 1970s also affected Duff specifically.

DEATH OF RICHARD L. EVANS

On October 25, 1971, Duff received word that Elder Richard L. Evans was in the hospital, unconscious and critically ill. Duff visited his mentor and friend each morning and night. He wrote, "Posterity will neither read, nor if it did, would not understand the depth of my love for Richard Evans. The opportunities I have enjoyed trace primarily back to him. There is nothing I could say but good about the man." Because of *Music and the Spoken Word*, which Evans wrote and presented for over forty years, Duff felt that no one person ever had, or ever would reach so many people inside and outside the church with such effectiveness. Duff said, "For many years on Temple Square, I believe I was his closest friend and confidant. To have been his friend was one of my greatest blessings."[1] Duff and others spoke at his funeral.

DEDICATION OF THOMAS L. KANE STATUE

Major General Thomas L. Kane was one of Duff's—and Utah's—heroes, for successfully mediating the Utah War.

In 1858, United States president James Buchanan sent a 2,500-man army to the Utah Territory to quash a fabricated rebellion. Church leaders had had enough persecution and were determined to hold their ground.

When Thomas Kane heard about it, he traveled under an alias at his own expense by steamship to Panama, crossed the Isthmus overland by rail, boarded a ship for southern California, then rode horseback to Salt Lake City to meet with Brigham Young, his lifelong friend. Together they worked out a deal for a compromise, and Colonel Kane personally escorted the new federal governor into Salt Lake City, averting the war. He earlier had written a letter to Brigham Young containing the famous words "Give way. Go on giving way, the whole summer through."[2]

Thomas Kane built a church in Pennsylvania in 1883 and was later buried in front of it. In May 1971, after the LDS Church purchased the building, Duff represented the church at an open house honoring Thomas Kane. A year later, Duff returned to Kane, Pennsylvania, to dedicate a statue of Major General Thomas L. Kane, copied from the one in the rotunda of the Utah State Capitol.

FOR WHAT PURPOSE?

In a memo dated February 17, 1971, the First Presidency asked the brethren to stop holding question-and-answer sessions following stake conference general sessions. Duff was the only one holding these on a regular basis; he had been

1. MDH-JE, Nov. 18, 1971.
2. Kane to Young, July 5, 1858, Kane copy, Kane Papers, BYU, box 3, folder 6.

holding these sessions, primarily for youth, for many years. The two principal reasons given in the memo were that the impromptu answers might be contrary to instructions given by the church and such sessions might cause parents to have to wait longer to get home from church. Duff was reserved in his response but not his tone. He wrote on the margins of the memo, "What a day! Spencer Kimball later apologized, and after the meeting Boyd [Packer] came to tell me he was ashamed of the decision by the twelve to cancel my question-and-answer sessions with the kids. He said Gordon Hinckley had been the one to kill it; others agreed. I was pleased that Boyd would come."[3]

THE ACTIVITIES COMMITTEE

Duff was always interested in promoting physical activity by members of the church. On May 2, 1974, he met with the Presiding Bishopric to discuss the possibility of having *family recreation* become a concept for the church.

In "A Challenge from Elder Marion D. Hanks," he wrote, "Think of what we would do with a recreation program in each ward or branch of the church that would involve the entire ward family in wholesome activities—members of individual families participating with other families. Singles, married, divorced, widows and widowers, the active and the less active, all joined together in opportunities that would recreate and regenerate—that would bring rich social, physical, and spiritual benefits to those involved. What a remarkable blessing would come to so many who need something enjoyable to do and, please don't forget, someone to do it with."[4]

Duff's advocacy, along with others, was finally accepted, and in 1977, the church announced the creation of a churchwide activities committee, signaling an increased emphasis on both cultural arts and physical fitness in the church. Duff called Keith Engar to be the first (and only) chairman of the church activities committee with seven committee members in the specialties of arts, sports, dance, fitness and family recreation, women's sports, girls' camp, and camping.

Each ward was also to call a three-person activities committee, including a chair, a cultural arts specialist, and a physical activities specialist. The local activities committees were to encourage opportunities for cultivating skills and talents and to develop and implement cultural arts and physical activities that would cross organizational lines. The purpose of these committees was to relieve the quorum and auxiliary leaders of the responsibility for ward or stake activities, allowing them to focus their energies on the duties unique to them. While changes have been made to the activities committees over the years, the concept of family recreation that Duff championed was never formally adopted on a churchwide basis.

---

3. MDH, handwritten notes in margins of the memo, Feb. 17, 1971.
4. MDH, "A Challenge from Elder Marion D. Hanks" (manuscript, unidentified time or context).

THE FOUR HANKS DAUGHTERS GET MARRIED

During the seventies, Maxine and Duff were thrilled to welcome four terrific young men into their family.

Susan married Paul G. Maughan, from Las Vegas, Nevada, in August 1971.

Nancy married John K. Baird, from Honolulu, Hawaii, in August 1973.

Ann married Spencer H. Clawson, from La Jolla, California, in August 1976.

Mary married Christopher J. Clifford, from Arcadia, California, in June 1976.

All four women met their husbands at Brigham Young University. Duff performed all four sealings in the Salt Lake Temple. The family expanded significantly, and Rich finally got to have brothers. In June 1983, Duff performed Rich's sealing to Liz Winters, also in the Salt Lake Temple. The family has been blessed that each of the five marriages has been strong and lasting and gave Maxine and Duff twenty-three grandchildren to love.

41

Singles, LDSSA, and Young Adults

Elder Hanks took the responsibility to develop a singles program, which today has proven to be of inestimable value for the single members of the church—to know that they are valued and loved in our church, in our society, and by their Savior.
—Elder Robert D. Hales

For his entire ministry, Duff was focused on the youth and young adults of the church. In April 1968, Duff was called to be the managing director of the LDS Student Association (LDSSA). He served in that position until he was called as the managing director of the newly formed Melchizedek Priesthood Mutual Improvement Association (MIA). The LDSSA eventually numbered two hundred thousand students on five hundred college and university campuses around the world.[1] By April 1969, Duff had visited with LDS students representing about 175 campuses. In a report to the First Presidency, he noted their commitment to the church and "not one single instance of real dissidence among them," which would have been highly unusual for the rest of the country in the troubled late 1960s.[2]

In early 1968, Duff attended a convention with fifty-five university level LDS students from all over Great Britain and a few representatives from Holland and France. The British students had established locally the basic principles of the LDSSA without knowing what was being planned on the general church level. Duff commented that it would be a simple transition to involve them in the LDSSA and solidify their relationship with church headquarters. That year, Duff also attended a meeting of the Association of Governing Boards of American Colleges and Universities. He mentioned the concern he felt from the attendees due to the general discontent across campuses and noticed "a general feeling of apprehension and fear on the part of governing boards and administrations of American universities."[3]

1. First organized in 1960, LDSSA sponsored religious, social, entertainment, and recreation activities for LDS students attending college. Its purpose was to help students balance secular and religious experience and to coordinate church activities for college students. A chapter of the LDSSA still exists in many locations where an institute of religion of the Church Educational System has been established.
2. MDH-L to Clare Middlemiss for President David O. McKay, Apr. 28, 1969.
3. MDH-L to Middlemiss.

In May 1969, Duff was joined by Elder Harold B. Lee at a meeting of the LDSSA in San Jose. Duff noted that this was the first time he and Elder Lee, who was one of the apostles advising him regarding LDSSA, had ever been together around any youth. Duff had been traveling for many days most weeks, holding meetings all over the United States, with no encouragement or positive comments from his advisors. That was typical of Elder Lee's interactions with Duff.

Together, they spoke to a couple of thousand students at LDSSA conferences in San Jose and Oakland, California. These experiences were completely different from Duff's prior interactions with Elder Lee, who on this occasion was cordial and gracious and even went to Duff's room to pray with him. Duff wrote, "Whatever anyone else's faults are, my own are adequate to occupy my attention and I am grateful to have had this sweet occasion with Brother Lee. What could have been a disaster turned out to be marvelous and I am deeply appreciative of the experience."[4]

LDSSA CONFERENCES

In December 1969, after months of planning, the first general convention of LDSSA was held in Salt Lake City. One of the most unusual experiences of Duff's life happened during the conference. Duff and Elder Lee each spoke, followed by a closing song and prayer. As briefly mentioned in an earlier chapter, the young man giving the closing prayer spoke from the heart and in such a way that there was not a dry eye in the room. Duff wrote, "Halfway through his prayer, he abandoned the formal language of prayer, and cried out in great anguish of spirit to the Lord, pleading with the Lord to let President McKay feel the fervor and sincerity and faith of these people. It was a remarkable and unusual prayer that no one there will ever forget."

As the conducting officer, Duff remained seated for several minutes and then stood at the pulpit in silence as waves of spiritual power swept through the room. Not a soul stirred for at least fifteen minutes.

The next year, 1970, a second conference was held, this one on the campus of Brigham Young University. The church-sponsored fraternity and sorority, Sigma Gamma Chi and Lambda Delta Sigma, held their annual conventions in conjunction with the conference. Conference attendees met in discussion groups to discuss national and church issues.

The keynote speaker, former governor George Romney, then serving as the United States Secretary of Housing and Urban Development, shared some nuggets of wisdom and received a standing ovation. Duff was honored with a special tribute for his longtime service to youth. The conference was proclaimed successful.

Over the following years, the LDSSA grew and strengthened, as Duff and his board worked diligently to address the needs of the church's members who were students. But those needs were much broader than just students; they included all single adults in the church.

---

4. MDH-JE, May 3, 1969.

Meeting with LDSSA youth leaders at Aspen Grove, 1969.

YOUNG ADULT PROGRAM AND SINGLES WARDS

He had such concern for the single adults of the church. He literally went head-to-head with other leaders, advocating special wards and programs designed to meet the needs of the singles, which was not particularly popular with some who wanted to force them into regular wards.[5]

The first youth-oriented stake had been created in January 1956, when Elders Henry D. Moyle and Adam S. Bennion of the Quorum of the Twelve organized more than eight thousand BYU students into the first student stake. Duff worked with Elder Bennion and Elder Richard L. Evans to create the twelve student wards that made up that stake. But because only apostles could organize stakes at that time, Duff was an observer when the units were officially organized.

While the student wards filled a part of the need, students were just a small part of singles in the church. Over the years, Duff became cognizant of a gaping hole in the church's approach to its single members. A significant portion of his individual counseling sessions involved single adults. He listened to them, empathized with them, and cried to the Lord with them. The number of single adult members was steadily growing as a proportion of church membership, and although the traditional nuclear family remained the ideal situation, the needs of this growing segment of the population who didn't fit into that traditional mold were not being met. All too frequently, single church members reported being treated as if they were "broken and needed fixing." At that time, the word *single* was often interpreted to mean young unmarried students, yet there were all kinds of others who were single, including

5. John Stohlton, online tribute after Duff's death, Aug. 2011.

those divorced or separated, newly returned missionaries, single parents, older singles, widows and widowers, young single adults, and people with disabilities. Duff felt that each was important to the Lord and valued members of the church and should not be looked on as "less than" members of the body (1 Corinthians 12).

BREAKTHROUGH! BUT WAIT . . . WHAT?

After decades of advocating for the single members of the church, on May 4, 1972, Duff made a presentation to a group of apostles composed of Elders Hinckley, Monson, and Packer—where he presented a case for (1) singles units in local stakes and (2) creation of a churchwide young adult program. At that time, the latter was accepted and became the program of the church; the former was rejected. Duff wrote, "Following that rejection, Elder Monson suggested that I would not want to submit my report to the Presidency until I knew what their [the apostle advisors] report said. I rejected that kind of thinking and submitted my report, which was opposite to theirs.[6] Despite the lack of complete acceptance of both ideas at that time, Duff was pleased, writing, "Some ground was made—I was appointed Chairman of a Committee to work on it."[7]

Six months later, in November, Duff was called into a meeting with the First Presidency, at which it was announced that the MIA[8] was to be divided. Youth under eighteen would become part of the Aaronic Priesthood MIA. Those over eighteen would be in a category called Melchizedek Priesthood MIA[9] and further divided into Young Adults (eighteen to twenty-five) and Special Interests (twenty-six and over). Duff was overjoyed. Single church members would finally be getting the attention they needed.

During the formal announcement in the temple meeting, on November 9, 1972, President Harold B. Lee, then president of the church, told all the general authorities gathered that there was no more important matter in the whole church. The program presented was essentially what Duff and his team had pioneered through LDSSA and had been adopted nearly everywhere they had organized a student group. President Lee mentioned in the meeting that Elder Hanks would be particularly pleased, "since he had been involved with Elders Bennion and Evans when the student wards were initiated," over fifteen years earlier. Duff was especially happy that special interests individuals would also be getting some specific attention.

---

6. MDH-JE, May 18, 1973 (looking back to a year earlier).

7. MDH-JE, May 4, 1972.

8. The Mutual Improvement Associations (MIA) were created in the late nineteenth century to provide recreational and faith-promoting activities for youth. At times, the age limit for the program was very wide in scope. For example, the Church History Topics essay explains that in 1913 men aged twenty-two and older were "advanced seniors" in the program. By 1970, youth in most LDS wards spent one night each week attending MIA.

9. The initial titles of Aaronic Priesthood MIA and Melchizedek Priesthood MIA proved rather cumbersome, and by 1977 the programs were simply renamed Young Men, Young Women, and Single Adults.

President Lee then announced that the new organization would be led by Elder James Faust with Duff Hanks and L. Tom Perry as assistant directors. When the announcement was made, many eyebrows were raised. Those assignments came as a surprise to Duff and others, because Elder Faust had just been called as a general authority the month before and Duff had two decades of institutional and recent knowledge of the pertinent issues. As they departed from the meeting, Elder Faust whispered to Duff that his brains and experience would be the heart of what they were going to do. But it was still a major shock.

Duff wrote, "This came as a real crunch to me. But I was soon able to get philosophical about it, knowing that such matters are very personal, and that the affairs of the Kingdom are more important than any individual man's sense of disappointment."[10]

The three leaders got right to work, getting concepts clear and the program underway. Thankfully, most of the groundwork had already been worked out during Duff's leadership of the LDSSA. Elder Faust asked Duff to take the lead in 90 percent of the working meetings as they fleshed out the new program. Duff felt that the personal relationship among the three general authority leaders was good. And the members of their working committee were each outstanding and extremely talented individuals. Over the coming months, they "polished, refined, interviewed, and refined some more." They met with their advisors (Elders Monson, Packer, Ashton, and McConkie) multiple times and then with the entire Quorum of the Twelve on January 25, 1973.

Duff wrote, "The meeting with the 12 was good, questions being pushed by Elders Hinckley and Petersen." A subsequent meeting that afternoon was held with the First Presidency and the Quorum of the Twelve, where the committee's entire proposal was "accepted fully and without question."[11]

Looking back fifteen years later, Duff wrote, "There are frustrations. And, yes, there are levels and layers of sieves that all proposals have to go through. The singles program got clogged up at the second level, and then, the top officers of the church came out and just overruled them, really, and said, 'This is what we want,' and they even liberalized our recommendations, went beyond what we had been willing to recommend, because we didn't think they would ever get passed."[12]

Along the way, they selected a permanent board, with Jeffrey R. Holland as the director. Duff wrote, "I am so proud of him, but trying not to smother him. Jim Paramore has emerged as a friend, John Covey as a choice brother. The future is interesting."

On February 1, 1973, the three leaders met in the temple with all the general authorities and presented an update, including the names of the new Melchizedek Priesthood MIA staff.

10. MDH-JE, Jan. 26, 1973.
11. MDH-JE, Jan. 26, 1973.
12. MDH-R, Dec. 10, 1988.

May 18, 1973, was a historic day as they met in Elder Faust's office with several stake presidents, during which the formation of new singles units in their stakes was announced. Duff wrote, "Both the Young Adult program, and singles wards are now accepted, and we are authorized to go ahead. In other words, what I presented a year ago, is now the program of the church, though I was not thought able enough to lead it. Ironic, but fortuitous. I get to work on the program, while being free from the hat-in-hand waiting that the manager has to do. Jim [Faust] can do it; I cannot, nor do I want to."[13]

Every chance he could, including special meetings at his stake conferences each weekend, Duff solicited feedback on how to help the single members of the church. One representative example: "I met early with Ron Hyde, now President of one of the BYU Stakes. We talked about their adaptation of the MIA program in their student setting. Wonderful man, good ideas."[14]

On September 27, 1973, Elder Faust and Duff presented a report at the temple meeting. Duff recounted the history that had brought them to this point: the creation of institute in the 1920s, student campus wards and stakes in the 1950s, LDSSA in the 1960s, and now the young adult and special interests programs in the 1970s. He specifically mentioned five developments underway: (1) the establishment of singles branches in the Salt Lake Valley (three so far), (2) the area conference concept, (3) family home evening groups for singles, (4) meetings on Sunday mornings for single women, and (5) singles meetings for Sunday School on a ward or stake basis.

Duff then repeated his main hope, which was for his colleagues to have vision and patience, and not revert back to the old ways. He said, "I expressed the hope that they might all possess the vision of the prophet in this matter—it cannot be done in old ways, in old methods, through old programs. Our objective is to help the ONE, based on three principles:

"1. A genuinely concerned priesthood leader on every level,

"2. Genuine peer leadership by the young adults themselves, and

"3. Local flexibility, including allowing singles to choose where to attend church."[15]

PUSHING HARD TO CARE FOR SINGLES

Despite opposition on many issues, Duff continued to work with his colleagues and the board, moving the program forward. He was well aware of how the institutional church did things—he'd been trying to get something going with young adults for twenty years—but he was encouraged by the support he was feeling for the new programs aimed at the single adult members of the church.

Unfortunately, some other church leaders just didn't have the same feeling he did. In a December 1973 meeting with the committee's advisors, Duff discovered

13. MDH-JE, May 18, 1973.
14. MDH-JE, June 14, 1973.
15. MDH-JE, Sept. 27, 1973.

that they had decided against permitting young adults to have social time together on Monday nights after family home evening. Elder Packer told them they could hold a meeting for one hour, but then they needed to go study. Duff wrote, "This is unrealistic. These are good kids, and the kids he is trying to hold down are innocently and determinedly getting together, as they will continue to do, whether he authorizes them to or not. I had to remind Boyd that any rule that has a hundred percent breach needs some looking into. It was submitted to his committee for further consideration."[16]

On January 31, 1974, Duff learned that Elder Packer had prepared a letter explaining to the Melchizedek Priesthood MIA committee why he had put the Denver Stake in trauma by declaring their Sunday morning meeting for single women inappropriate. The stake leaders called Duff in heartbreak, saying it was their most successful effort with their young people. It seemed like two steps forward, one step back. That erratic process would continue.

The board continued submitting additional adjustments to their advisors; for example, the age split didn't seem right. Duff had heard repeatedly from single members statements like "We are needed just as much as married people. We are not 'different' or second-class members. Stratification by age implies that we are." Similarly, the debate over allowing singles to choose whether to attend a family ward or a singles ward, or "forcing them" to attend a family ward continued. Duff had written almost three years earlier, "We do not consider the needs of a student adequately, if we arbitrarily insist that he remain in his home ward. Some parents and leaders are making these young people feel that they are committing a sin if they attend student wards and activities."[17]

He told a friend, "It has been a real heartache for me to see singles units established and people excited about them, and then they get sent back to their home ward because they don't live in a certain place, or qualify by age, or some other thing."

In a journal entry on February 1, 1974, Duff wrote that some momentous decisions occurred that day in a meeting with Elders McConkie and Packer (two of the then-current advisors). The basic decisions were as follows:

1. Singles branches could divide when they reached appropriate numbers, following the church's regular pattern,
2. Where available, Melchizedek Priesthood holders from in or out of the local stake could be called to work in the branches, and
3. The units could cross over stake lines to use facilities that were not being fully used.

Duff was thrilled, because the intent behind each of these suggested changes was "getting the *individual* served wherever that can be done. It was a very good meeting, and we all enjoyed it very much."

16. MDH-JE, Dec. 7, 1973.

17. MDH, report on stake conference, May 5, 1971.

Despite the occasional challenging issues, they kept pressing forward. By October 1975, the Sunday morning meeting of young women had sprung up all over the church, meeting a significant need. But the attitude of the Relief Society General Presidency was that the young women of the church should be shepherded by the Relief Society and that the Relief Society's exclusive territory was being infringed on. Duff was always amazed at things like that. He wrote, "Seems a strange thing to concern oneself with jurisdictional matters when Rome is burning, but that happens. Hope it can be worked out. On paper, it seems ridiculous."[18]

ONGOING LEADERSHIP

Over the succeeding years, guidelines and principles continued to be developed to meet the needs of the single adults of the church. The managing directors (Duff and Jim Faust) worked with a director and a board of thirty outstanding specialists to develop methods and programs that worked. Where needed, adjustments continued to be made. For example, in some areas, an age subset called young special interests was created.

This new approach for the single members of the church was different in that the single adults were now given the charge and responsibility to be the *architects* of and *lead* their own activities and programs, with local church leadership beside them if requested. This approach was a huge departure in a church that was accustomed to operating on a top-down, command and control, here's-what-we're-going-to-do basis. This flexibility was meant to permit local and individual needs to drive the success of their own experience. Additionally, a main strategy was to involve single adults in things that they enjoyed and could participate in. For example, it was noticed that the bigger the event, the fewer people could actually be involved in planning and executing it. So, while there were still a few large-scale events, like firesides or conferences or dances, the new emphasis was on meeting the needs of most single adults with many smaller, locally-based activities, such as home evening groups, service projects, and hobbies.

Duff felt it incredibly important that single adults should be focused on *serving others* as a way of life. He also believed that physical and cultural *activities* were important as well as social activities, so that single adult church members would stay involved and active. Over time, the Melchizedek Priesthood MIA was also given responsibility for adult athletic and recreational activities for the church. It was from this "side assignment" that Duff later helped create the activities committee of the church.

DIVORCED PEOPLE AND SINGLE PARENTS

One of Duff's greatest heartbreaks over the years was his association with wonderful people who had experienced divorce and were living with the difficulties that come with that and with single parents left to raise children alone. He had counseled

18. MDH-JE, Oct. 3, 1975.

thousands of people in these situations and felt that the church needed to do something specific for them. Comments of divorcees from his notes included these:

> "I have failed at marriage, but I don't intend to fail at divorce."
>
> "The usual approach of the church is to assume I don't exist, to isolate me, or to wonder what sins have brought me to this pitiable condition."
>
> "Divorce is like having a disease that others don't want to catch, so they try to immunize themselves against me."
>
> "Members say right to our face, 'When you got divorced or widowed, did they take away your temple recommend?'"
>
> "I had a teacher say, 'If everyone lived the gospel, there would be no divorce.'"

Duff also struggled with some of the rules pertaining to divorce and the temple. On a trip with President Spencer W. Kimball in late 1975, Duff repeated instances of distress from worthy divorced women who were being denied a temple recommend at the time they needed it most, until divorce clearances came through. He expressed his concern that individuals in those circumstances almost uniformly felt that the church had no place for them. He sent a follow-up letter to President Kimball and wrote, "I am wondering if there is anything to be done about this, and if you wish any further input from me on the subject?"[19]

President Kimball requested more information, and Duff submitted a further analysis of problems and suggestions impacting divorced LDS women and the temple. His main suggestions were:

> That a previously sealed, divorced female be given the right to apply for a cancellation of sealing after an appropriate time following a civil divorce whether or not she has made present plans to marry again.
>
> That inquiries made about past mistakes should be limited to those which have occurred after baptism into the church, and then only to those matters "not properly resolved in accordance with normal church procedure."
>
> That if a letter from a former spouse is deemed necessary, a clearance or cancellation should not be delayed because of arbitrary refusal of a spouse to write such a letter. Perhaps if a letter is required, a time limit of thirty days should be placed upon their reply.[20]

In a meeting of all the general authorities in May 1976, Duff again brought up the plight of divorced people and single parents in the church. He began by reading from 1 Corinthians 12:26: "And whether one member suffer, all the members suffer with it." Duff then summarized the comments of single and divorced people in

19. MDH to Spencer W. Kimball, Jan. 22, 1976.

20. Undated document. File note in Duff's handwriting says, "Submitted by MDH to Pres. Kimball 1976."

the church: "Divorced members feel they are suddenly considered inferior and not accepted. Children feel rejected by the departed parent, or feel resentment toward the remaining parent, or feel guilty for having caused the breakup. Single mothers feel concerned about children not having a male image to relate to. Coping with loneliness is one of the greatest challenges. Affection. Financial problems. Daycare. Finding time to relax. Not being a family in the church. Fear of remarriage. All these and more." Duff wanted to give his colleagues a realistic personal feeling for this difficult problem. He continued campaigning for the changes he believed would help. And then, eight months later, came a change he couldn't have anticipated.

MAJOR ORGANIZATIONAL CHANGES—A NEW OPPORTUNITY

On December 3, 1976, apostles Gordon B. Hinckley, Marvin J. Ashton, and L. Tom Perry called together the heads of all the organizations to explain a major change in priesthood responsibility. There was to be an adult program, headed by James A. Cullimore; a youth program headed by Duff Hanks; and a curriculum program, headed by Dean L. Larsen. All three leaders were Assistants to the Twelve.

This meant that simultaneously Duff was to be the managing director of all youth programs for the church, director of the Aaronic Priesthood (temporarily), chairman of the General Scouting Committee, and managing director of Military Relations.

After almost a decade of incredibly demanding work and leading a radical change in the way the church treated single adults, he was leaving the leadership of single adults (over eighteen) and was now in charge of leading all youth of the church (under eighteen.) In the meeting, Elder Perry shared his and others' great affection for Duff and said aloud, "Can you imagine how it will be when the church learns that Brother Hanks is going to run all the youth programs?"

Once again, Duff experienced bittersweet feelings. Sad at having to leave his previous assignments, but excited to work on new opportunities, because he loved the youth of the church so much.

Over the coming decade other refinements were made toward helping single adults in the church. In May 1978, student and singles branches were made into wards. In 1986 the groupings and names were changed to young single adults (YSA) for single individuals up to age thirty and single adults (SA) for individuals over age thirty. Each ward was to call a mature married couple as YSA advisors. Guidelines allowed for flexibility for age divisions and home evening groups across ward boundaries.

In 2011, just months before Duff passed away, the church enlarged the singles program even further by doing away with the remaining exclusive student units and merging them into YSA wards, which are now a part of all-singles stakes.

INTERMISSION

Ten years passed from 1976 to 1986, during which Duff was called to other responsibilities (covered later in this book), leading the youth program of the church, moving to Hong Kong as president of the Church's Southeast Asia Area, serving with Maxine as the president and matron of the Salt Lake Temple, and so on.

YOUNG ADULTS, PART TWO

Then, in December 1986, while still serving as one of the seven Presidents of the Seventy, Duff was called to be the executive director of the Priesthood Department, including all members of the following committees: Melchizedek Priesthood, Single Adults, Military Relations, Family Home Evening, and Home Teaching. Those assignments put him right back in the middle of the single adult issues of the church.

Despite no official responsibility for single adult church members for the previous ten years, Duff had continued to feel drawn toward helping them. He once read aloud a letter to a priesthood training group that quoted the sad words, "I am 31, single, and miserable." The letter was a plea for help from a woman who felt that her fondest dreams were vanishing with the years.

About another occasion, he wrote, "The most sweet and uplifting part was the response that came all day Sunday from singles, single parents, family heads, the downtrodden who felt that there was no place for them in the church. There is such a large body of these, and I weep for them. They are so rejoiceful over any little bit of attention."[21]

By May 1988, there were 1.3 million single adults over eighteen in the church. That was more than the total membership of the church when David O. McKay became president of the church in 1951. In 1988, 6 percent of single church members were in singles units, both student and nonstudent.

Duff was pleased with the growth and acceptance of singles wards, but he also knew that only a small proportion of adult church single members were served by them. The growth of most single adults would occur in conventional wards and stakes. For example, Phyllis Warnick, his secretary, was single much of her adult life but chose to attend a traditional ward. Because of her experience and others', he believed that flexibility by area and local leaders of the church would be required to assist singles, making sure they were invited to responsible leadership and service callings on the same basis as any other faithful, worthy member. He also said, "Do not rob them of their independence and self-reliance, rather, help them to turn their minds from '*what I need*' to '*where I am needed.*'"

He also continued to teach members to welcome single people into their homes without reservation, treating them normally, giving them callings, and allowing them to contribute to the well-being of others. In a 1988 training meeting for regional representatives, he presented a document, summarizing the needs of LDS singles (See appendix E).

21. MDH-JE, after a California stake conference at which his subject was "singles."

THE SINGLES FIRESIDE

On February 26, 1989, a historic event happened when a churchwide fireside for and about LDS single adults was held. Duff had engineered the meeting, created the video, and moderated a panel, composed of single people in different circumstances.

Feedback on the fireside was 99 percent positive. The choice of panelists was applauded. One representative letter said, "As a regional singles leader, I sat in our chapel amid the shattered lives and broken dreams to hear the broadcast. All throughout the broadcast I heard quiet but audible comments such as: 'That's right,' and 'I've had that happen too,' and 'I feel that way also.' As different reasons for singleness were mentioned, different people could be seen dabbing their eyes, appreciating someone who finally understands. And to end with the challenge to give service was excellent. Thank you for caring."[22]

Another single person wrote, "Last Sunday night I started to laugh inside myself. Your announced video panel discussion was at first received as another pathetic attempt to sanctimoniously pacify the singles' need to be a participant in an unreal proposal to jump on a mythical bandwagon. WOW!! Was I humming the wrong tune! This ended up being the most valid and consistent demonstration of effectively and honestly discussing a current issue 'being single in our church' that I have ever witnessed."[23]

WALKING THE TALK

As usual, Duff wasn't inclined to let meetings, strategy sessions, speeches, and leadership titles be his only contribution to the effort. One summer, Duff approached Glen Parker, the director of the Aspen Grove Family Camp near his cabin, with the idea of providing a camp for single-parent families. In response, the Aspen Grove staff designed a program they launched in the summer of 1996. Duff contributed some materials and his own financial support to the cause. The response was terrific and heartwarming. Duff's niece, Becky, who was widowed and raising young children, talked about how experiencing Aspen Grove as a family was especially meaningful. The letters and cards that came in from attendees were warm and hopeful and full of gratitude.

22. "From a single sister in the gospel," Feb. 28, 1989.
23. HPH to MDH, Feb. 28, 1989.

42

Serving the Youth

The Youth of America could ask for no greater advocate than Marion D. Hanks.[1]

Duff had a great love for the youth and rapport with them. He was a favorite among the youth of the church, especially in the early years of his ministry. He had a special ability to tie together principles and examples that were meaningful to young people. When he was called as a general authority, he was incredibly popular as a fireside speaker, noted for his attention-holding style of speech and his rapport with audiences, especially teens, to whom he taught gospel principles using vivid stories and life experiences.

Elder Loren C. Dunn said, "Elder Hanks had a special way and demeanor that made you feel like he was speaking to you and that he was your best friend. There is no way of telling how many young people Marion D. Hanks touched and inspired to live a better life. A whole generation was affected in the church."

Elder Bruce C. Hafen said, "During the early years of my life, Elder Hanks was the first general authority voice that fully rang the bell of my spirit."

Duff had a strong conviction about young people. He was convinced "we habitually *underestimate* their intelligence and *overestimate* their experience. We expect them to act like miniature adults, and yet we don't teach them."[2]

The praise wasn't just from members of the church, as evidenced by this representative letter: "Dear Sir, I live in Detroit, and Sunday, April 7, 1968, I witnessed the conference of the Mormon Church on television. To say the least, Elder Hanks, it was certainly very informative. I am a Christian and a Black American. Your words were inspirational to me, and I wanted you to know that I agree that our young people are crying out for believing, belonging, giving, and loving. After the broadcast, I called my two teenage sons to me, and we recommitted ourselves to the faith of our fathers. I am pleased to let you know that Christ rules supreme in my life."[3]

1. Boy Scouts of America, Silver Buffalo Presentation, San Diego, California, May 20, 1988.
2. MDH-T, "Substance or Shadow," GC, Oct. 1962.
3. Mrs. Gross to MDH, Apr. 8, 1968.

LEADING THEM

For the first ten or so years of his ministry, Duff had four main pulpits from which to speak to the youth of the church. He was the editor of the *Era of Youth* magazine, he spoke in general conference every six months, he held special youth meetings at stake conferences around the world, and he accepted invitations to speak at youth meetings almost every week.

He also served America's youth on the national level. He spoke at several White House conferences on children and youth and served on the United States President's Citizens Advisory Committee on Children and Youth, on the President's Council on Physical Fitness and Youth (under five US presidents), on the executive board of the Boy Scouts of America, and in many other leadership positions related to serving youth.

Inside the church, over time, Duff led every major department that touched the youth of the church. His committee developed the Young Men and Young Women programs and the Activities Committee, he was a member of the Board of Education, director of church athletics, managing director of youth programs, managing director of the Latter-day Saint Student Association, managing director of the Melchizedek Priesthood Mutual Improvement Association, chairman of the Scouting Committee, and managing director of Military Relations—each of which affected the youth of the church. Additionally, he wrote literally hundreds of articles for the "Era of Youth."

Despite all the administrative leadership roles he had in serving youth, it was in his in-person speeches, question-and-answer sessions, and one-on-one counseling sessions that he felt the most able to make an impact. Duff knew it was incredibly important to *teach*, not just *talk at* the youth. Rousseau said, "It is not enough to say to the citizens, be good; they must be taught to be so."[4]

CONNECTING WITH THEM

Duff's general observation about the youth of the church was that their primary need was to be reassured, encouraged, and strengthened. They needed to know that the church was led through inspiration by men who had personally experienced and understood what they were going through in their lives. He observed that the young people of the church (and the country) responded better to a real leader who had overcome real problems, rather than one who carried a facade of perfection. Repeatedly, he heard young people say that the "middle management" of the church (that is, the local leaders) were more concerned about appearance, statistics, and image than they were about individuals and their honest questions about the gospel.

One young single adult wrote, "Brother Hanks, I am a college student. When I graduated from seminary in 1955, you were the speaker. You talked about when you were our age, which didn't seem impossible because you understood us so

4. Jean-Jacques Rousseau, *A Discourse on Political Economy* (1755).

well. In fact, it seemed to me that you were almost one of us, instead of a teacher. You taught us to live with greater confidence and trust in God, and because we trust you, many of us will."[5]

Duff's approach was to treat the youth as if they were adults. He was approachable and genial, and they trusted him. But he wasn't cutesy or wishy-washy. He didn't talk down to them and he didn't dilute his messages. He was absolutely convinced they were ready to accept responsibility for the choices that they made. He talked to them plainly about the consequences of choices. One of his favorite lessons for youth came from the saying,

> "He who picks up one end of the stick picks up the other. He who chooses the beginning of a road chooses the place it leads to." [6]

He taught that we may or may not intend the consequences of our decisions, but we follow the paths that led to them. And it is not only our own course we are affecting when we choose the beginning of a road; we inevitably travel with others, and sometimes we bring anguish or happiness to those we love.

Duff also spent a lot of time trying to get the youth to understand that success is a function of consistent and continuous action, not flash-in-the-pan exertion. He loved to quote Edmund Vance Cooke: *"The true test of greatness is the way one meets the eternal Everyday."*[7]

Duff spoke often about our inability to control circumstances, but our sure ability to control our reaction to those circumstances. He had every missionary that was sent to England with him memorize a poem:

> There is no chance, no destiny no fate,
> Can circumvent or hinder or control
> The firm resolve of a determined soul.[8]

Duff truly believed that young people could accomplish anything if they put forth the effort. During the 1960s, when the country was bashing and degrading the young people in America, Duff chose to speak to them directly, full of love and affection, without coddling. He was aware of their problems, and he was convinced that youth will rise to the opportunity if inspired, will learn if effectively taught, and respond if called on.

He quickly gained a reputation for connecting with the youth throughout the country and was in high demand. Herbert Hoover, former president of the United States, invited Duff to speak to the national convention of the Boys Club of America, saying, "I hope very much that you will be able to accept this invitation on the subject, 'Building Values in Boys.'"[9]

---

5. Hy Coon to MDH.
6. Harry Emerson Fosdick, *Living under Tension: Sermons on Christianity To-day* (1941), 110–11.
7. Edmund Vance Cooke, "The Eternal Everyday," in *Impertinent Poems* (New York: Dodge, 1907).
8. Ella Wheeler Wilcox, "Will," in *Literature of the Republic*, part IV.
9. Herbert W. Hoover to MDH, Feb. 6, 1961.

One journalist spoke in appreciation: "Elder Hanks was our idol. He always seemed to be speaking on a level we could understand and about problems and questions that were central to our religious lives. He demonstrated a profound sense of caring for all of us. And, he retained his own youth far longer than most of our leaders do."[10]

ABOUT YOUTH

Duff described five things that are generally true about youth:

1. They are usually like their parents and the homes from which they come.
2. They are heavily influenced by other adults and friends outside their homes.
3. They are responsive to their environment. They see, they hear, they absorb, they imitate.
4. Young people are inclined to hero worship and to image emulations. It may be a celebrity or not, but they will likely choose someone to follow.
5. They are quick to spot deception and lack of sincerity. They are sensitive to the phony and resent it. They are more likely to follow a sincere cynic than an insincere "saint."

With that knowledge in place, Duff fashioned speeches and teachings and trainings aimed at lifting and encouraging and saving youth.

BUILDING YOUNG MEN'S AND YOUNG WOMEN'S PROGRAMS

In December 1976, after a decade of demanding work instituting single adult wards and a new young adult organization, Duff was pulled from that world and put in charge of leading the organization and programs of all church youth under eighteen years of age.

On December 3, he met for the last time with the Melchizedek Priesthood MIA Board, which was responsible for single adults. The next few days involved kick-off meetings with the Young Women and Aaronic Priesthood leaders and then with their committees. When they were finished, the women told Duff it was the first time they had been listened to in four years."[11]

During the first week of his new assignment, he met with nursing students from Ricks College, flew to Oklahoma for meetings, met with the United Way officers, spoke at the Institute of Religion at the University of Utah, met with the Military Relations Committee, met with Deseret Book employees, set apart several chaplains, and counseled with four or five individuals.

The following week he met with the rest of the departments now reporting to him, including the Primary General Presidency and the Sunday School General Presidency. His comments about the kick-off meetings with the Sunday School General President are interesting: "The president of the Sunday School is Dr. Russell Nelson, a fine and bright man and a great surgeon. I continue to have a certain

10. Marden Clark, *Daily Herald*, Provo, Utah, Aug. 3, 2002.
11. MDH-JE, Dec. 1976.

discomfort at seeing such a [talented] man sitting in meetings, when his tremendous capacities and life-saving skills are so needed in so many places. But, as he has said to me before, he can't operate all the time. He performs his [church job] very well."[12]

For the next three months, Duff worked with the various presidencies reporting to him, with special time and attention given to the Aaronic Priesthood and Young Women boards. In the youth departments, the boards suggested that the name of the Young Men program be changed and that a presidency be created at the ward and stake levels as there were for the Young Women, the Sunday School, and the Primary. That had been shied away from in the past because it was assumed that the presidency of the Aaronic Priesthood was all a ward needed.

Near the end of the first quarter, Duff started making presentations to each of the needed levels of church administration, soliciting feedback, answering questions, and incorporating approved changes.

SUCCESS!

On March 30, 1977, Duff wrote in his journal, "This morning the whole package was presented to the First Presidency and the Twelve, and again passed with flying colors and no reservations. It is fair here to say, that while we have labored for many months on this program, and hundreds of meetings and thousands of hours, and that it has passed through the layers of the sieve slowly, yet as it came out, it was substantially what we gave them months ago. All of the principles have been tested by every [level], up to and including the [First] Presidency, even the august people of correlation, and it ended up where it began."[13]

After the meeting, Elder L. Tom Perry put his arm around Duff and said, "First, the new Young Adult and Special Interest program was yours, and now [this reengineering of the Youth Programs] is yours, because you were talking about all of this clear back then.... I would like to write the foreword to a book you write, so the people [of the church] could know." Duff responded, "Tom is quite guileless and full of integrity. We had a pleasant talk."[14]

At regional training meetings held in June 1977, the main features of the restructuring they had been working on were explained, including the formation of corresponding Young Men and Young Women adult presidencies at the general, stake, and ward levels. A combined Young Men–Young Women committee was also formed at each level. Both the Young Men and the Young Women presidencies in a ward would now serve under the direction of one counselor in the bishopric rather than all three members of the bishopric, who were previously involved in activity night programs. This member of the bishopric was given responsibility for all youth programs in the ward. The former weekday youth activity night would now be referred to as Mutual.

12. MDH-JE, Jan. 19, 1977.
13. MDH-JE, Mar. 30, 1977.
14. MDH-JE, Mar. 30, 1977.

For the rest of the year, the new programs began to be implemented. Duff was thrilled for the youth of the church and the difference the new approaches and leadership would bring.

SUDDENLY, IT WAS ALL OVER

On May 4, 1978, after the general authority temple meeting, Duff was invited to meet with President Ezra Taft Benson, President of the Quorum of Twelve Apostles. He thought he would probably be relieved of his Military Relations responsibility. He was surprised when President Benson told him that the First Presidency wanted to relieve him of some of his duties, and therefore he was being relieved as managing director of the Youth Department, including chairmanship of church Scouting. He was told that the Presidency wanted him to focus on his work outside the church and on his church geographic supervision because "they didn't want me to work myself into the grave, as Elder Richard L. Evans had done."[15]

Duff was to remain on the executive board of the BSA and all his committees in that organization and continue with his work as district governor of Rotary. Inside the church, he remained a member of the Presidency of the Seventy, managing director of Military Relations, zone advisor for Canada, Australia, New Zealand, and the South Seas area, and a member of the bishops nominating committee.

Duff thanked President Benson warmly, expressing gratitude that he could have a part in the development and fashioning of the Young Men and Young Women programs and the activities committee and that he was pleased to continue working in Scouting.

HIS CONCERNS EXPRESSED OVER THE YEARS

Duff felt a special concern for parents of wayward children who had done all they could and still their children had chosen a different path. He testified, "They are never completely lost, and we should never give up on them. Heavenly Father knew them long before you met them, and he loves them too. And he is significantly more forgiving and loving and merciful than we can understand."

He was concerned with the "progressive" idea that directing kids down certain paths was a form of brainwashing and that kids should be allowed the freedom to choose without any direction. Duff became increasingly concerned as he saw parents abdicating their responsibility to direct their children toward good, wholesome, and decent things. One trend that was growing then and is even stronger now is the tendency for parents to say, "I'm going to let my children decide for themselves." This was nonsense to Duff. It reminded him of the old

---

15. Richard L. Evans was Duff's mentor. He wrote and delivered *Music and the Spoken Word* on radio and TV each week for forty years while serving as the director of Temple Square, and fulfilling his heavy duties as a general authority of the church. In addition, he served as the president of Rotary International, and was an author, narrator, and editor. He was known for his incredible work ethic and high productivity. His death at only sixty-five years old from a viral infection was sudden, and he worked right up to the end.

adage – if a gardener allows his strawberries to grow with no weeding, no direction, and no help—they will grow weeds every time.

THE POTENTIAL OF YOUTH

Duff realized the important potential in each of Heavenly Father's children. And he had seen the devastating effects of someone declaring, "It's only one kid." He knew that every single interaction with a young person was going to affect not only one life but perhaps thousands of their descendants as well.

Duff was continually willing to overlook faults and weakness in youth in order to emphasize their potential and lift them toward improvement. He had confidence in their eventually making correct choices. He taught, "The marvel to me is how many choice young people see through the mists and choose a wiser way."[16]

Duff felt that the way youth are treated by others has a direct bearing on how they act. Young people tend to meet the expectations set for them. If they are perceived by others to be intelligent, loyal, and trustworthy and they know it, they will generally seek to justify that perception. He believed that when we perceive good things about our youth, we should let them know we do. Duff spent a lifetime doing just that.

16. MDH-T, "Every Man in His Own Place," GC, Oct. 1972.

43

Elders Holland, Cook, and Others

My mission was the closest thing in my life to a new star appearing in the heavens, after which all else would be dated. For that experience I have the Lord and Marion D. Hanks to thank.
—Elder Jeffrey R. Holland[1]

Jeffery R. Holland was one of Duff's missionaries in England. He had already been there a good while when Duff arrived, but they soon discovered a mutual chemistry. Elder Holland had served the first part of his mission during the previous administration with all the contests and pressure and so forth. So, when the Hanks family arrived, he was primed to appreciate the complete change of direction.

For the rest of Duff's life and beyond, Elder Holland stayed very close to Duff and Maxine and their children and treated them as if they were an important part of his family, and he part of theirs. Even after Duff died, he continued to love and care for Maxine. He performed the marriages of many of their grandchildren, gave them priesthood blessings, and showed genuine interest in them. He has been loving, loyal, and committed.

At Duff's funeral he said the following: "Just seven weeks ago, I addressed 120 new mission presidents and their wives at the Missionary Training Center. Trying to relieve some of their understandable fears and anxiety about winning the hearts of their missionaries, I put up a theater-sized photo of Marion D. Hanks and said, 'I love this man with all my heart. He taught me the gospel of Jesus Christ and thus changed my life forever. We named one of our sons after him. After 50 years he is still my President—the title I always use when addressing him. I still go to see him regularly. I still seek his counsel and approval for the life I am trying to lead. My undying gratitude for his influence in my life can never be fully expressed, but neither will it ever be diminished.'"[2]

There is no way to adequately present fifty years of communication and the feeling between the two of them. Here is a sampling of their expressions of love

1. Jeffrey R. Holland, introduction of Marion D. Hanks, Ricks College Baccalaureate Service, Apr. 24, 1979.

2. Jeffrey R. Holland, Aug. 13, 2011.

Jeffrey R. Holland, using his mission president, Duff, as an example while teaching new mission presidents, 2021. *Courtesy Church News*

for each other: Shortly after he became president of Brigham Young University, President Holland wrote to Duff, saying:

> Things are going reasonably well, here. I face my first commencement this weekend. We are trying to feature Dallin [Oaks], and the President of the church is going to be in attendance, so I will probably put my foot in a potted plant.
>
> You will not remember writing it, but while going through some old papers, I ran across a letter you had written for me to the BYU Scholarship people, in the early 1960s, shortly after my mission. After some generous and considerably exaggerated comments about my few virtues, you wrote, "It would be wise to help this young man attend Brigham Young University, inasmuch *as he will probably be president of the school one day.*"
>
> I read that line and exploded into tears. It has been a tender time for me anyway feeling my inadequacies and knowing my limitations. Yet to think that for all these years you have believed in me and helped me and cared for me is more than I know how to say in return.[3]

From another one of hundreds of letters between them: "Thank you for loving and teaching me. Thank you for giving me the Book of Mormon and for introducing me to the Savior. Thank you for seeing something in me I couldn't see."[4]

3. Jeffrey R. Holland to MDH, Aug. 18, 1980.
4. Jeffrey R. Holland to MDH.

As his mission president, Duff saw some exceptional qualities in young Elder Holland and made him part of a traveling team of trainers whose assignment was to help other missionaries become disciples. He said that Elder Holland "blossomed into discipleship, centered in Jesus Christ," and responded diligently to his mission president's call to teach from the Book of Mormon. He noted that Elder Holland's love for that book and his ability to teach from it have grown continuously stronger through the years.[5]

Elder Holland has been singled out because he and Duff had so much interaction and communication. But there were many, many others whom Duff mentored and loved and shepherded. Elder Quentin L. Cook was also in England as a missionary leader when Duff arrived. In fact, Elder Holland and Elder Cook were companions for about two weeks. Elder Cook has also been gracious and kind to Maxine and Duff and the family all these many years since then. He wrote, "Winston Churchill, in writing about an admired colleague said, 'He lighted beacon fires which are still burning; he sounded trumpet-calls whose echoes still call stubborn soldiers to the field.' Elder Hanks was such a leader for those of us who served under him or who have heard him teach. I can honestly say that except for my parents, my brother Joe, and Mary, no one in my life has had as much influence as President Hanks."

Duff sensed Elder Cook's qualities right away. On one day in 1975, Duff wrote in his journal, "I had a visit from Quentin Cook. It was quite a satisfaction to see this fine young man in his role as an outstanding lawyer. He is a bishop, and on his way to fulfilling what I felt very sure of when he was an outstanding missionary in England. He has been a man all his life, and somehow that makes a very big difference."[6]

Imagine Duff's happiness at seeing two of his missionaries become apostles.

It is dangerous to single out just a few of the many people Duff loved and tried to mentor over forty years. Elder Holland and Elder Cook, as apostles, would be the most well-known, but there were hundreds of others.

If Duff were writing this book, right about now he would direct our attention to Alma 48:17 *and* 19. Verse 17 describes young and valiant Captain Moroni, who was strong and well-known. But then, verse 19 reminds us, "Now behold, Helaman and his brethren were *no less serviceable* unto the people than was Moroni." In other words, even though Helaman was not as noticeable or famous as Moroni, he was just as important and as useful as Moroni. Duff would make sure that the reader knows that about his less-famous missionaries.

Maxine once counted ten of their missionaries who had served as mission presidents and many more who had been called as Relief Society presidents, stake presidents, or bishops, or faithful home or visiting teachers. A few chose to leave

5. Don L. Searle, "Elder Jeffrey R. Holland," *Liahona*, Aug. 1995, 26.
6. MDH-JE, Jan. 16, 1975.

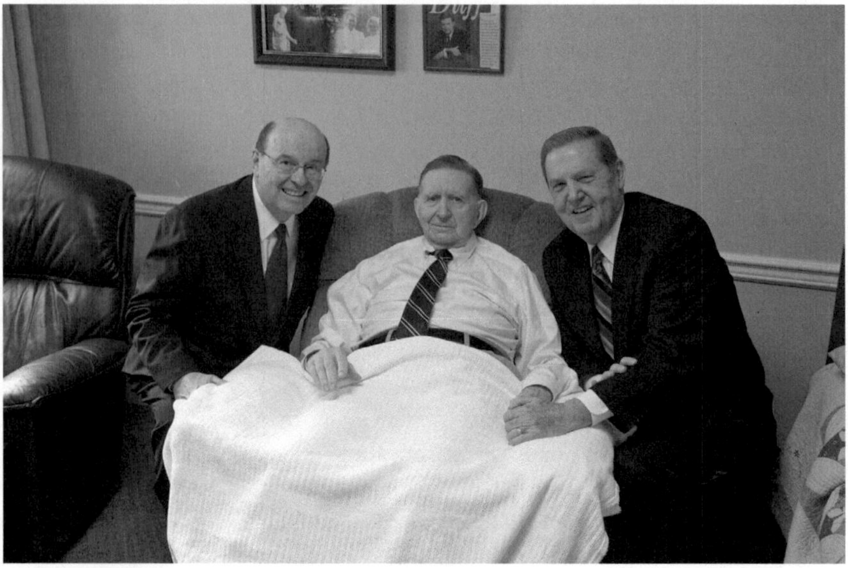

Elders Quentin Cook and Jeffrey Holland visit with their mission president, Marion D. Hanks, in his memory care center, 2007. *Courtesy Church News*

active involvement in the church, but that didn't diminish them in Duff's eyes or his efforts. They were "his missionaries" for life.

As he got older, Duff got more and more satisfaction out of seeing his students and protégés progress in testimony and in leadership. After one weekend on the East Coast, he wrote, "Both regional representatives, Elder Rossiter and Elder Tingey, are my former students. Three of the stake presidents involved were also my former students, President Waite in Syracuse, President Dalton in Rochester, and President Miller in New York City. I left the place with some genuine feeling of personal encouragement."[7]

The same was true of those he was blessed to serve with on church committees or in Rotary, Scouting, or his high priests group.

7. MDH-JE, Apr. 11, 1980.

44

Church Military Relations

I never witnessed one who demonstrated a love for and devotion to the military members, particularly our chaplains whom I felt you loved like sons, more than you.
—J. Paul Jensen

As a patriot, a veteran, and a father, Duff had a keen love and concern for those serving in the military, in harm's way, willing to defend their country, often alone and in trying circumstances. He served as the executive director of the Church's Military Relations Committee on two separate occasions. He braved the battlefields of war to visit personally with the LDS men fighting in Vietnam. He spoke at bases all over the United States and Germany as well as in Southeast Asia.

Despite his ability and willingness to perform leadership roles in these organizations, it was once again with the *individual* where he found his greatest joy and contribution. He had great empathy and sympathy for the servicemen themselves, because he had been one. His love for the chaplains was powerful because he had been one. The fears and stresses of war and being shot at were real to him, because he had lived them.

MILITARY RELATIONS COMMITTEE

The Church's Military Relations Committee had two principal functions in those days: first to work with and support the LDS men and women in the military; and second, to function in the selection, endorsement, support, and training of chaplains, who represented the church in representing Christ.

The issues covered by the Military Relations Committee included things like chaplain relocations, military promotions, health issues of spouses, potential chaplains at VA hospitals, advising service academy cadets planning to resign their commissions to go on missions, training, annual chaplain's conferences, and base fraternization policies affecting home teaching, and so on. Before Duff's assignment to this committee, the Church's Military Relations Committee had been focused solely on United States servicemen on bases around the world. The church was just then beginning to investigate augmenting the Military Relations staff to begin to fulfill the needs of LDS servicemen from other countries.

Because of the constantly changing scenarios the military deals with, the church has to be prepared to mobilize and organize church units to accommodate current situations. For example, in January 1991, eleven LDS chaplains and eighty-four group leaders were put in place in Saudi Arabia and the Middle East. Where the size of the congregations permitted, a nearly complete branch or ward organization was implemented.[1]

VISITING THE SERVICEMEN

Duff invested time and energy during his ministry to visit servicemen and, in later years, servicewomen all over the United States, Europe, and Asia. His many visits with servicemen in Vietnam and Thailand, in particular, are discussed elsewhere (see pages 345–55).

In a report to the First Presidency in January 1967, Duff wrote, "We held servicemen's meetings also at bases near Tokyo, Seoul, and Bangkok, and met others in Berlin and Hong Kong. Where we have the chance to reach these young men, we are achieving outstanding results. Our mature and faithful Latter-day Saint service people are doing outstanding work. Tragically, large numbers of our choice young people are being lost for want of being able to reach them. There is a desperate need for a more successful approach to our young servicemen."[2]

Duff knew that when members of the church enter the military, they are thrust into an environment that is totally alien. At that point they can choose to follow the norms of the military, many of which are contrary to the gospel, or to be active in the church. The goal of the church is obviously to hang on to as many of these choice young people as possible and keep them active during their military years. Duff felt it important that church leaders spend face-to-face time with military members as often as possible, hence his many visits over the years to military bases all over the world.

After his funeral, Maxine received this letter, typical of many similar letters:

Dear Sister Hanks, Elder Hanks never knew this story, but he had a tremendous influence on me in my decision to join the church in 1971.

I was a young Army captain and Vietnam veteran, when I was asked, one summer, to be his guide and escort at Ft. Lewis, Washington, even though I wasn't LDS. I told my commander that there were Mormon officers who would like the opportunity, but the commander said Elder Hanks wanted to meet a Vietnam veteran, so I was it.

What followed was a delightful day of conversation—me driving the jeep and Elder Hanks riding with me. We talked of family, friends, war, service to the country, and even religion. His countenance, sincerity, friendliness, and kindness left a positive, lasting impression on me and when I finally studied the gospel and asked to be baptized, I thought that I hoped I could be as good a member as Elder

---

1. MDH, update on Military Relations at a meeting of the Seventy, Jan. 17, 1991.
2. MDH-L to First Presidency, Jan. 18, 1967.

Hanks. I will miss him, but I know that someday, we may again ride around in a celestial jeep talking about things that matter.[3]

Everywhere Duff visited with servicemen, he took personal notes of the important things he both heard and felt. These notes could fill a thousand-page scrapbook. One that stands out is something a captain said at a testimony meeting in Vietnam: "Some of us know what it means to be separated from our families temporarily. I sure don't intend to be separated permanently."[4]

BERCHTESGADEN

Berchtesgaden was the site of Hitler's Eagle's Nest, a complex of bunkers that he intended to use as his last stronghold in World War II. But for LDS military members in the 1970s, it was the site of the annual servicemen's conference.

Duff spoke at these conferences multiple times over the years, rallying the troops and commending them on their sacrifice. In 1976, he took Maxine with him to Germany, and both of them spoke several times. Duff began one of his talks by quoting a verse by Clarence Day that he had just learned (it was amazing how he usually seemed to have just the perfect quotation or scripture for every occasion):

When eras die, their legacies
Are left to strange police.
Professors in New England guard
The glory that was Greece.[5]

He then spoke of Hitler and this place he had built at enormous cost of money and labor and how he did so much damage in the world. But now, in a strange turnabout, a group of Mormon young people came each year with their chaplains and their brethren, speaking of Christ and the virtues of the human soul.[6]

CHAPLAINS

Duff had a special place in his heart for LDS chaplains, who represent the church in each of the branches of the military. LDS military chaplains provide vital priesthood leadership to LDS men and women in uniform while also serving people of all faiths. Duff recognized the sacrifices that chaplains were making to serve their brothers and sisters and applauded them for it.

One of the challenges in recruiting Latter-day Saints to become chaplains was the requirement by the service branches that LDS chaplains be prepared to handle multiple religious faiths and services and "take part in general Christian worship services and in teaching, preaching, counseling, marriage and family support, etc." This requirement caused some to feel like they were not being loyal

3. Chuck Akerlow to MDH, Aug. 2011.
4. Unidentified captain's testimony from Vietnam, 1966.
5. Clarence Day, "Thoughts on Deaths," in *Thoughts without Words* (New York: Knopf, 1928).
6. MDH-T, untitled, European Servicemen's Conference, Berchtesgaden, Germany, Nov. 6–8, 1962.

to the church and its claims of restoration. In a letter to one chaplain, Duff wrote, "With you, I regret that some people back away from becoming a chaplain, somehow feeling compromised in their convictions. I do not feel this way, and never intend to. My life has been spent pretty much on the frontier where the church meets the world and I have rejoiced in the blessing of trying to share the good things we have, without contention or turmoil, finding arguments to be unfruitful and pressure to be inappropriate and unacceptable."[7]

Duff's admiration and love for the chaplains was expressed in his personal friendships cultivated over many years. They were welcomed in Duff's home and met his children, who were taught to love and respect them.

TOP-TO-TOP RELATIONSHIPS

Another of Duff's responsibilities was to maintain strong relationships with military leaders across the service branches. That entailed numerous visits to Annapolis, Maryland; West Point, New York; and Colorado Springs, Colorado, as well as numerous speaking engagements at events, both on and off base, over many years.

In addition, when top military leaders visited church headquarters in Salt Lake, Duff was often the general authority who had previously met them and had the best relationship. For example, General William Westmoreland was the top allied commander in Vietnam. Duff and Keith Garner had visited him in that country during the war, so when he made a visit to Salt Lake in February 1970 to speak at a National Guard recognition evening, Duff already had an established friendship with him.

Duff took General Westmoreland in to meet with the First Presidency, where the general was most generous in his recognition of Mormon servicemen. He also toured the Tabernacle, which he loved, being an engineer, "calling it one of the most remarkable things I have ever seen." They toured the Temple Square Visitors' Center and viewed the movie *Man's Search for Happiness*, after which General Westmoreland said, "This is something my wife and family must know soon." Duff commented, "He was personally so warm to us and the church."

Duff recalled visits of many others, including the chief of chaplains of all military branches. One of his favorite experiences was the visit of John O'Connor, archbishop and cardinal, a "brilliant and modest man." Duff recalled, "I had the blessing of escorting Chaplain O'Connor to a meeting with President Spencer W. Kimball, then in advanced years. I watched these two men respond to each other, charming, gracious, witty, respectful, and then stood by as Father O'Connor departed, after having asked for a blessing from President Kimball."

Part of Duff's responsibility included establishing relationships with the members of the Chaplains Endorsing Committee, composed of representatives of the major religious groups. After one of many meetings in Washington, Duff recalled, "We discussed the problems chaplains are having across the world. While

7. MDH-L, Mar. 14, 1989.

at first, I wondered what I was doing there, it became evident that the church needs to be represented there by someone who can associate with and relate to the others who are there. These are the 'chaplains to the chaplains,' who control the major denominations. I think it will be harder for one of them to permit disrespectful treatment of our boys or chaplains after we have become personal friends and they have gained some consciousness of our integrity and ability."[8]

ARMY WAR COLLEGE AND OTHER CONFERENCES

In an unprecedented occurrence, Duff was invited six different times to attend the National Strategic Seminar at the Army War College in Pennsylvania. He was able to attend four times.

Every year, about two hundred command level officers, the cream of the army officer corps, would spend nine months in concentrated learning and then spend a full month preparing a national strategy for the next fifteen years for the United States government. Each year a few civilians were invited to sit with them and discuss the plans they had made. Each of the top-level commanders of the various armed forces, including the chairman of the Joint Chiefs of Staff and the Secretary of Defense, attended, spoke, and answered questions, under top security. Duff was incredibly impressed with the character, integrity, and knowledge of both the military brass and the civilians he worked with. He called his first week, in 1966, the most rewarding of his life in making him aware of the country's responsibilities and plans with the rest of the nations of the earth. He was also able to become friends with many senior military leaders, as well as the chief of chaplains. He was the only one of the civilians in attendance who had actually been in Vietnam and met with the troops.

FEELINGS ABOUT WAR

Duff's feelings about war, previously discussed in more detail in the chapter on Vietnam and Southeast Asia, matched that of the scriptures: we should be willing to fight for our own liberty and freedom and should be willing to fight to save others' liberty and freedom when necessary.

Duff hated war and everything that went with it, but he knew it was sometimes required to save freedom and liberty. All the standard works and even our belief in the war in heaven support the concept of active defense of correct principles.

In 2011, after his death, the Veterans' Association for Service Activities Abroad, a group of LDS military members, presented a plaque to Maxine recognizing Duff's lifelong commitment to the LDS military. In the introduction, they said: "Through the history of Saints serving in wars, church leaders knew that the fighting forces would need spiritual guidance. In every era, from the church's founding in 1830 to the present, certain men of God became giants of spiritual strength to those in uniform. Such a one was Marion D. Hanks. Legion are the stories about

8. MDH-JE, Mar. 18, 1976.

his care and love of those who went in harm's way. He walked the walk; he talked the talk. He was our minister, our chaplain, our brother, our friend."[9]

THE BIGGEST CHALLENGE OF ALL

By far, the most difficult thing about serving on the Church Military Relations Committee was having to see strong and courageous young men in the prime of life go off to war and give their life for freedom, liberty, and country. He never got used to it, and it never got easier to deal with. In an August 1968 letter, Jeffrey R. Holland, home only five years from his church mission himself, wrote an anguished letter to Duff describing a sweet and decent young man, twenty years old and engaged, whom he had interviewed just a few weeks before. He relayed that his stake president had called him that morning to say that "the young man had been killed in the middle of some leech-infested bog, near a base he probably couldn't pronounce.... When will we learn?"

Despite Duff's knowing about the greater good, the individual sacrifice was a nearly impossible pill to swallow.

9. Plaque from Veterans' Association for Service Activities Abroad.

45

Reviving The Seventy

The Seventy are to act in the name of the Lord, . . . building up the church and regulating all the affairs of the same in all nations.
—D&C 107:34

In 1835, the Prophet Joseph Smith called the first seventies in this dispensation, organizing the First Quorum of Seventy just after calling and organizing the Quorum of the Twelve apostles. Both of these quorums, one with twelve members and the other with seventy, were formed from men who had been on the Zion's Camp march to Missouri from Kirtland, Ohio. At that time, no one had any idea of what a seventy was or how to organize them. They did know there were references in the Bible where the Lord sent out "other seventy" who had returned rejoicing.[1] The prophet also organized two and a half more quorums of seventy, making a total of three and a half quorums. They were presided over by seven presidents of the first quorum.

Over the years, the calling of the seventies developed to meet the changing needs of the growing church. Eventually, each stake had a seventies quorum, which was not what the scriptures delineated. Why the explicit instructions in the Doctrine and Covenants were not followed is not known. In a 1932 letter, Elder B. H. Roberts wrote, "Since the days of Nauvoo, more than eighty years ago, the First Quorum of Seventy has had no real and fully organized existence; by which I mean they have never met in their quorum capacity and have not been allowed to function in their place and station in the church. Why, I do not know."[2]

Over time, members of the church adopted an inaccurate understanding of what a seventy was. Elder Antoine Ivins wrote, "The organization of the seventies is one that sits off on the side in a special assignment. It does not come between the office of Elder and High Priest at all. It does not come in that category any more than the office of patriarch does. It is a specialty. And we hope to succeed in re-establishing what the Lord plainly taught to the people about the calling of the seventy."

In the October 1975 general conference, President Spencer W. Kimball announced the reconstitution of the First Quorum of the Seventy and announced

1. See Luke 10:1–17; see also Exodus 24:1, 9; Numbers 11:16.
2. B. H. Roberts to S. S. Simpson, Aug. 30, 1932.

the calling of four men to serve as seventies. A year later, in October 1976, all the Assistants to the Twelve were assigned to the First Quorum of Seventy, and Duff was called again to be a member of the seven Presidents of Seventy. In 1986, the seventies quorums in each of the stakes around the world were discontinued. In 1989, a Second Quorum of the Seventy was organized. In 1995, the calling of regional representatives was discontinued, and local officers above the stake level, now called area seventies, were called.

Between 1997 and 2020, the First Presidency added additional quorums, bringing the total number of quorums of the seventy to twelve as of 2024.

Duff played a role in each step of the revival of the quorums of the seventy.

DUTIES OF THE SEVENTY

The scriptures are not brimming with an abundance of information on the seventy, but they do have very clear instructions on what their duties are.

"The Seventy are also called to *preach the gospel,* and to be *especial witnesses* unto the Gentiles and in all the world" (D&C 107:25; emphasis added).

"The Seventy are also to act in the name of the Lord, under the direction of the Twelve or the traveling high council, in *building up the church* and *regulating all the affairs* of the same in all nations" (D&C 107:34; emphasis added).

The Twelve are "to call upon the Seventy, when they need assistance, to fill the several calls for preaching and *administering the gospel,* instead of any others" (D&C 107:38; emphasis added).

The Seventy are "instituted for traveling elders to *bear record of my name* in all the world, wherever the traveling high council, mine apostles, shall send them to prepare a way before my face" (D&C 124:139; emphasis added).

DECENTRALIZATION OF AUTHORITY

Duff participated in general church leadership long enough to see substantial improvements made in the decentralization and pushing of responsibilities lower and lower in the organization. When he was first called, so much work had to be done by the general authorities that it staggered the imagination and, frankly, wore many of them out. He wondered why so many things had to be done centrally or by a few leaders, when the Doctrine and Covenants was so clear about the decentralization of leadership and the work of the seventy. In his journal, he often wrote of his hope of continuing decentralization of church leadership. He couldn't understand how the church would survive its incredible growth without decentralizing its leadership.

Later in his ministry, after a stake reorganization on the East Coast, he remembered the old days:

> These stake re-organizations are pleasant, but ponderous in their implications, and the total effect is to leave a person very much enervated. Pouring out the Spirit in settings-apart is a throw-back to the old days, when we were under obligation to exhaust ourselves—tragically sometimes, considering Richard L. Evans,

for instance—we now don't do a tithe of the things we used to do. Stake presidents have suddenly become competent to interview and set apart missionaries, to ordain bishops, to ordain seventies, to ordain high councilors, and in general run their stake in the way they should. They can do it at least as well as we can, and a lot better considering they know the local members and are on the scene and must live with them after the whole thing has been launched. It is a new day. One wonders what the next day offers of expanded responsibility and opportunity.[3]

PUSHING FOR THE RECONSTITUTION OF THE SEVENTY

From the beginning of his ministry, it became clear that the then current organization of the seventy did not align with the revelations in the Doctrine and Covenants. In a letter to the Council of the Twelve in 1954, Duff's quorum, the First Council of the Seventy, listed sixteen items they felt needed to be adjusted, given the current organization. They then wrote a seventeenth item that read, "The First Council of the Seventy are particularly desirous that the seventies of the church be organized and that they function for the best interests of the church, according to the revelations, and subject to the direction of the Council of the Twelve."[4]

Elder John A. Widtsoe had researched and written extensively about the seventy and the First Quorum. He wrote: "The duties of the Twelve and the seventy are nearly identical, almost word for word, in the revelations. This identical function of the Twelve and *Seventy seems to have been overlooked, and therefore weakened the use of the First Council in furthering the interests of the church.* It is clear that they are to build up the church and regulate all the affairs of the same in all nations" (D&C 107:33–34). He went on to say, "The growing church of Christ needs more 'administrative' workers. The Assistants to the Twelve do not meet that present need. The present organization is wholly insufficient. The work is not being done as well as it might be. Men are being worn out before their day. However, the First Quorum of Seventy is already provided for in the revelations. As it is gradually filled, it would become a reservoir of power to carry on the work of the Lord."[5]

Even after the church began to pass more authority down the line to the stake presidents and bishops, it was difficult for many leaders at the top of the organization to relinquish control. As but one example, Duff recalled an instance in which the Utah governor had not wanted to pay for a float in the inauguration parade of Jimmy Carter as president of the United States. The church decided to help by asking some wards and stakes in Washington, DC, to put together a float. Duff quietly asked in a meeting who had chosen the specific stakes and wards to do the job. Gordon B. Hinckley, the apostle in charge, said, "I did." Duff

3. MDH-JE, May 21, 1977.
4. First Council of the Seventy to Quorum of the Twelve, Mar. 11, 1954.
5. John A. Widtsoe, personal research on the Seventy, n.d.

again quietly asked if the area supervisor or the regional representative had been allowed to participate or at least were informed. There were some grim looks and an embarrassed smile as people realized what was happening.[6]

Duff continually petitioned the senior brethren about the need for a reconstitution of the First Quorum of Seventy and the assumption by the seventies (from the apostles) of much of the leadership of the church across the world—matching what the scriptures described.

In a lengthy March 1968 letter to the First Presidency and the Quorum of the Twelve, the Seven Presidents outlined the scriptural organization and authority of the seventy, including the following conclusion: "The revelations provide for a First Quorum of Seventy and specify the duties and powers of such. There is at this time no First Quorum of Seventy, and as far as we are advised, no determination has been made as to how this quorum should be organized under the conditions that exist today."[7]

In a letter to President Harold B. Lee, dated May 26, 1971, Duff wrote about "the selection and use of certain men as members of a reactivated First Quorum of Seventy." He had spent a good amount of time thinking about the issue and had collected all of the materials on the Seventy that he could find, including much written by Elder Widtsoe, as well as all of the scriptural references. There was further discussion about how to choose and train such men. Duff wrote, "It would seem a strong step could be taken if members of the (new) First Quorum could be called from among the large body of high-quality, experienced men who have served missions or in stake Presidencies, and who have had extensive church experience and would be thrilled with such an assignment."[8]

Even after the First Quorum of the Seventy was reconstituted, many adjustments remained to be made. On March 24, 1977, he wrote in his journal, "I spent nearly an hour with the President of the Church this afternoon. I delivered to him the book on the First Quorum of Seventy that I have been preparing, having written much of it, and copied much material from Dr. Widtsoe's collection and other sources, putting it all under one cover to meet President Kimball's request that I give him what I had presented some time ago."[9]

Notwithstanding the need for changes, Duff knew that the church moved slowly and carefully. Looking back, he wrote, "I've never felt uneasy that it takes time to get around to these things, but when we do get around to them, we function. Now we have our Seventies in groups of three as area presidencies all over the world. And they are on the front lines, and they really carry the load."[10]

---

6. MDH-JE, Jan. 5, 1977.

7. First Council of the Seventy to the First Presidency and Quorum of the Twelve, Mar. 6, 1968. Author not named, but it appears to have been Duff.

8. MDH-L to Harold B. Lee, May 26, 1971.

9. MDH-JE, Mar. 24, 1977.

10. MDH-L, 1995.

"EQUAL IN AUTHORITY"

One of the more challenging issues related to the reconstitution of the Seventy centered around wording found in the Doctrine and Covenants 107:26, which describes the Seventy as a quorum with equal standing to the Twelve Apostles and the First Presidency. That's the word the revelation uses: *equal.* Specifically, it says that the Seventy "form a quorum, equal in authority to that of the Twelve special witnesses or apostles just named" (D&C 107:26). Some have suggested that this means that the Seventy have all the power and authority necessary in the unlikely case that the First Presidency and the Twelve are all killed; but that isn't what the scriptures say – it isn't a hypothetical or conditional equality. Instead, the section directly declares the two groups to be of equal authority. In researching this point, Duff wrote, "If the Twelve have power and authority over the Seventy, and not the other way around, this is something that we know from some other source than the scriptures."

This had been a sticking point for members of the Seventy for decades, long before Duff was called as a general authority. It is hard to really understand how challenging this issue was back then, given the major changes that have been made since. But, as a bit of background, the Seven Presidents of Seventy, although called as general authorities, were not even ordained as high priests. They did not have the sealing power; they could call a bishop but not ordain him; they could not ordain high priests or set apart high councilors. They could not organize or reorganize stakes. The following is a lengthy but important piece of background from Duff's journal in 1967:

> We met with the new "regional representatives of the Twelve." These are 70 men appointed to be kind of junior varsity general authorities over areas of the church (above the stake president level). I rejoice at their calling. The only real misfortune about it all is that Brother Lee quoted from material he had relating to the seventies - quoted from Lorenzo Snow and Wilford Woodruff to the effect that the seventies were apostles, and that the Twelve and the Seventy should be directing the affairs of the church. Brother Lee also quoted the scriptures that say, when the twelve apostles need assistance, they are to send the Seventy *instead of any other.* He then completely ignored all of that and went on with great emphasis about the Twelve and their calling these men (regional representatives) who would report directly to them. In effect, the First Council of the Seventy and the Assistants to the Twelve were shoved back a great big length, which in all honesty is what ought to happen to the Assistants, but certainly should not happen to the Seventy. It should be made clear here that I have no personal resentment or resistance to whatever the leaders of the church want to do with the Seventy, but it ought to be done with the knowledge that the scriptures are being ignored and the processes being followed are those of the leaders and not the scriptural revelations. All of the leaders of the church up to President McKay today have understood what the Seventy is supposed to be but have apparently done little about it. I repeat that I

> have plenty to do, and that I would be content to be doing whatever is wanted. But I am not content to see the scriptures ignored and the teachings of the prophets overlooked without explanation or apparent understanding.[11]

Much later, at a meeting of the Seventy in April 1991, Elder Dean L. Larsen said, "The verse in section 107 that speaks of the Seventy as having the same authority as the Quorum of the Twelve. I don't take that to mean we are competitive in any way, but it does seem clear that the Seventy have the authority to do anything that the First Presidency and Twelve direct them to do. In recent years, that area of responsibility has been tremendously expanded and will continue to expand."[12]

ARE THE SEVENTY APOSTLES OR NOT?

Another issue surrounding the seventies has to do with whether or not they are apostles. Joseph Smith, Brigham Young, and other early brethren in this dispensation taught that there were two apostolic quorums in the church: the quorum of the Twelve Apostles and the quorum of the Seventy Apostles. Doctrine and Covenants 107 describes the duties and powers of the Twelve and the Seventy using almost verbatim wording. On December 2, 1835, Joseph Smith wrote: "This day, the Council of the Seventy met to render an account of their travels and ministry since they were ordained to that apostleship."[13]

In an April 11, 1991, meeting of the seventy, Duff explained the need for quorum members to be wise in using the term "seventy apostles." He told them that this was not a new title, it had been used in the early days of the church and was included on some seventies' certificates of ordination. Duff taught them that the significance of that authority is, fundamentally, to witness for Jesus Christ. He also cautioned "it would be well if members of the seventy would feel a comfort, and praise God for that sweet blessing, and act in that authority, but, in order to avoid confusion, not talk about it."[14]

HISTORIC MEETINGS

In a letter to the Missionary Executive Committee in June 1976, the First Council of the Seventy (with Duff's authorship), responded to a request made of them to describe future scenarios for expansion of the church. The letter said,

> The fact was clearly established that the First Quorum was to assume the function assigned in the 107th Section. The rest is history. The First Quorum now stands as it should, next to the Twelve, and none others are called on to regulate the church. One can readily see the hand of the Lord in it. Prior to this time there were no seventies in the church with enough experience to regulate the church in all the world. The years served by the Assistants have been a period of preparation

---

11. MDH-JE, Oct. 1, 1967.
12. Dean L. Larsen, Duff's notes from the meeting of the Seventy, Apr. 1991.
13. B. H. Roberts, ed., *History of the Church of Jesus Christ of Latter-day Saints*, 2nd ed. rev., 7 vols. (Salt Lake City: Deseret Book, 1978) 2:346.
14. MDH-T, meeting of the Seventy, Apr. 11, 1991.

The First Council of the Seventy when Duff was called in 1953. *Courtesy Church News*

> for them, so that when the First Quorum was organized, they were ready to regulate in all the world. The regional representatives are being trained too. What will be their future function? One can almost foresee where we are heading—quorum 1, quorum 2, etc. as the church increases.[15]

Eighteen months later, during the week of December 19–22, 1978, meetings were held during which President Ezra Taft Benson announced significant changes in the duties and responsibilities of the First Council of the Seventy, now to be called the Presidency of the Seventy. He indicated that this was one of the most significant historical events in the past thirty-five years: after a transitional period, the Presidency of the Seventy would be assuming the major ecclesiastical administrative responsibilities heretofore held by the Quorum of the Twelve.

All these years later, the importance of this substantial change may have been lost to history. This was a significant shift. Individuals previously reporting to the Twelve would now report to the seventy. For example, Duff would now act as the church's top military representative without oversight. The Seven Presidents of the Seventy were given authority to train their quorum members. And the Seven Presidents were instructed to act as a presidency in a fashion similar to that of the Council of the Twelve, with a senior leader who conducts and presides.

15. Presidency of the Seventy to the Missionary Executive Committee, June 30, 1976.

The Presidency and Quorums of the Seventy just before Duff was granted emeritus status, ca. 1992. *Courtesy Church News*

MORE CHANGES

Following the reconstitution of the First Quorum and its absorption of the Assistants to the Twelve, the church's governance morphed over time to more closely match that detailed in the Doctrine and Covenants. In 1986, seventies quorums in the stakes were discontinued. Additional quorums of the seventy were organized, and area presidencies, now composed of members of the seventy, were called.

Duff was pleased to see the steady movement of the church toward matching the organization revealed in the Doctrine and Covenants. Issues remained to be addressed, however. For example, Duff wrote to President Howard W. Hunter in 1991, "So long as the First Presidency and the Twelve are responsible for calling the seventy, and making their assignments, and directly supervising the work in area presidencies, the Seven Presidents are relegated to an advisory role with their own quorum members. To direct the Seven Presidents to act as though they have jurisdiction is both a contradiction and a futility as long as quorum members know otherwise and are interfacing regularly with members of the Twelve on the most significant aspects of their calling."[16]

The photograph above illustrates the growth in the leadership numbers that Duff witnessed during his ministry—from the seven members of the First Council of the Seventy when he was called to be a general authority in 1953, to the large number of seventies in place when he received emeritus status in 1992.

16. MDH-L Presidency of the Seventy to Howard W. Hunter, president of the Quorum of the Twelve, May 8, 1991.

46

Blacks and the Priesthood: "This Momentous Event"

Hallelujah. I thank God I lived long enough to see this day.
—Marion D. Hanks, revelation on the priesthood, June 9, 1978

On June 9, 1978, the First Presidency called a special temple meeting of the general authorities. All general authorities in Salt Lake that day were asked to attend. Duff arrived and began greeting his colleagues. When he reached Boyd K. Packer, they shook hands and Elder Packer, with tears in his eyes, said, "It is good for us to be here. Today is an important day."

Before the meeting started, Duff leaned over to Elder Paul H. Dunn and said, "'This is about [Blacks and the priesthood.]' I knew that from looking into Boyd's eyes, he and I having discussed the matter on many occasions, and he having hinted periodically that something of consequence would happen one day before too long."

The meeting began with the hymn "We Thank Thee, O God, for a Prophet." President Ezra Taft Benson gave the opening prayer and prayed emotionally, three times referring to "this momentous event." President Spencer W. Kimball then rose and told the assembled leaders that for some time he had been struggling with the challenge of the priesthood for all members of the church, discussing it with his counselors and the apostles and specifically in the temple by himself. He then asked Francis Gibbons, secretary to the First Presidency, to read a statement that had been drawn up. It read:

> [God] has heard our prayers, and by revelation has confirmed that the long-promised day has come when *every faithful, worthy man* in the church may receive the holy priesthood, with power to exercise its divine authority, and enjoy with his loved ones every blessing that flows therefrom, including the blessings of the temple. Accordingly, all worthy male members of the church may be ordained to the priesthood without regard for race or color.[1]

1. Official Declaration 2, ChurchofJesusChrist.org.

Before Brother Gibbons had read two lines, Duff began to weep. He immediately thought of all the men he knew who had been affected all these years. Some were still alive; some had passed on. Ruffin Bridgeforth and Monroe Fleming, who were still living, came to mind, and especially his dear friend Len Hope. "I thought of his death and funeral and of the loss of their faithful children because they could not hold the priesthood."

President Kimball invited anyone to stand who wished to make a comment. Elders LeGrand Richards, James E. Faust, and Bruce R. McConkie each stood and spoke.

Then Duff stood and through his tears said, "I thank God that I have lived long enough to see this day." He continued, "There have been two thoughts in my mind—the first of faces and lives I have grieved for and prayed for, and secondly that the cynics and the critics will have at us again for this, but having with complete loyalty sustained the position of the church through the years, I care not for what any critic might do. The good news has been delivered, and I am full of joy and rejoicing."

Following Duff's remarks, most of the other brethren spoke. After that, the general authorities stood and raised their hands to the square at President Kimball's invitation and agreed to support the revelation. Together they then sang "The Spirit of God," and President Romney gave the closing prayer.

Just outside the door, Elder Ted Tuttle approached Duff, and they hugged each other in a tight embrace. Elder Packer did the same, as did the others. It was a day of rejoicing for their friends and brothers who had chosen to stay with the church and follow its teachings despite not being allowed to hold the priesthood.

Duff wrote:

> Throughout the day, telephone calls came from many people, all of them rejoicing in this significant event. I have anguished for a lifetime, fasted and prayed a multitude of times, defended the church under harassment on many university campuses, faced people on many fronts in all walks of life and suffered, wept on my pillow many times, and grieved with choice souls who had broken hearts over this, read all I could, written much at the behest of prophets, and now feel that the matter is done and I could only weep and rejoice and thank God.
>
> Of course, we have only barely begun. What lies ahead, no one knows. Only the Lord only knows how many times I have answered that question on Temple Square and in classrooms and on campuses and across the earth, and I never have answered it without grieving in my heart.
>
> Praise the Lord![2]

BRIEF HISTORY OF THE PRIESTHOOD BAN

There was rejoicing all over the world. Before that momentous day, despite the church and its canonized scriptures declaring that "all are alike unto God"

2. MDH-JE, June 1978.

(2 Nephi 26:33), from 1852 until 1978, persons of Black African descent were excluded from holding the priesthood, which was conferred on worthy males of every other race.

During the first two decades of the church's existence, a few men of Black African descent were ordained to the priesthood.[3] In 1852, however, President Brigham Young announced that Black African men would no longer be ordained to the priesthood, nor could Black African men and women receive the temple endowment or sealing ordinances. Subsequent church presidents continued the restrictions. Nevertheless, small numbers of Black African converts continued to join the church through baptism and reception of the gift of the Holy Ghost. Over time, church leaders and members advanced many theories to explain the priesthood and temple restrictions. None of these explanations is accepted today as the official doctrine of the church.[4]

During the decades of the priesthood ban, prophets spoke about its eventual lifting. Wilford Woodruff wrote, "The day will come when all of that race will be redeemed and possess all the blessings which we now have."[5]

President David O. McKay said, "Sometime in God's eternal plan, the [Blacks] will be given the right to hold the priesthood."[6] President McKay often prayed fervently to the Lord for permission to rescind the exclusion.

President Harold B. Lee spent years thinking about the issue. Just before he died, he spent days in the upper room of the temple fasting and praying earnestly to the Lord for guidance on the matter without receiving an answer.

THE HOPE FAMILY

While Duff was serving as a missionary in what was then the Northern States Mission, he regularly visited the home of Len and Mary Hope, a Black family living on the outskirts of Cincinnati, Ohio.[7] The family had not been welcomed into the meetings of the local Church branch. Duff recorded that when Len Hope was told branch members didn't want a Black family worshiping with them, Len responded, "Can we still pay our tithing?"[8]

So the missionaries went to the Hopes' home on the first Sunday of each month to hold a sacrament and testimony meeting with their family. It was also arranged that every three months, when the district conference was held, the Hopes could attend. This went on for nearly two decades. Duff, Len, and Mary became dear friends during his time in Cincinnati.

---

3. Black men were given the priesthood during Joseph Smith's lifetime. W. Paul Reeve, *Let's Talk About Race and Priesthood* (Salt Lake City: Deseret Book, 2023).

4. "Race and the Priesthood," Gospel Topics Essays, ChurchofJesusChrist.org.

5. First Presidency Statement, Aug. 17, 1949, cited in *Neither White Nor Black: Mormon Scholars Confront the Race Issue in a Universal Church*, ed. Lester E. Bush Jr. and Armand L. Mauss (Midvale, UT: Signature Books, 1984), 221.

6. David O. McKay letter, Nov. 3, 1947, cited in *Church News*, June 17, 1978, 4, 6.

7. See also pages 56–57.

8. MDH-R, Nov. 2003.

Duff as a missionary, with Len and Mary Hope, Cincinnati, Ohio, ca. 1942.

A few years later, in 1947, Len and Mary Hope visited Salt Lake City. When no hotel in Salt Lake would allow them to stay, they stayed at Duff's mother's home. Despite the hotels' refusals of service, they enjoyed their visit so much that they decided to move to Salt Lake. Duff voiced to them his concern that they would have even more negative experiences in Utah, which was less than 1 percent Black at the time. Nonetheless, Duff and others helped to fix up a home for them in Salt Lake, and they were welcomed and accepted by their ward.

Len died in 1952, and Mary then moved east to Philadelphia to be near one of their children. She continued to attend LDS meetings there as her health allowed. When she passed away in 1971, her body was flown back to Salt Lake and buried beside Len's.[9]

THE PHOENIX COLLEGE CHOIR

Another experience stood out in Duff's mind. That experience occurred long before the nation in general came to a more compassionate understanding of racial differences. He and Maxine were living in an apartment in the home of a dear couple, the Romneys, who owned a motel on North Temple Street in Salt Lake.

9. MDH-R, May 1, 2001; MDH, note on the Hope family.

Duff was giving tours on Temple Square when a college choir from Arizona visited. Among their number was one Mexican boy and two Black boys. After the tour, the choir director told Duff that no hotel in the city would allow these three boys to stay, including the Newhouse Hotel and the Hotel Utah.

Duff called Brother Romney on the phone, asking for help, thinking it would be a simple request, but Brother Romney paused and said, "If we do that, our Triple-A sign will be down by Monday morning." Duff was astonished but told Brother Romney he didn't want to put their livelihood at risk. So Duff called his mother, Maude, and with no hesitancy she had the boys stay in her house. The next morning, Duff delivered them to their bus to return to Phoenix. He said, "These young men discovered a benevolence and a Christian kindness in her act, which made them truly love her and which stimulated in them, as it has done in me, a greater desire to be a brother to all men."

He continued, "I took [my daughter] Susan with me to the bus station, and these two big young Black men stood there and wept and held her in their arms—they had eaten at our little apartment and slept and eaten at Mom's house. We remained friends for years and years."[10]

DUFF'S PERSONAL HISTORY INVOLVING THE BAN

Duff believed that the ban would be reversed in his lifetime. Even so, he wasn't content to just sit back and wait. Over the years, he spoke frequently to the prophets, but publicly continued to defend the church's position, even though he didn't agree with it or understand it. He was in a difficult position, because he had a rock-solid testimony of the restoration of the gospel and its leaders and authority, but ironically, he spent much of his life struggling to explain a policy he didn't believe in. He said, "All my life this has been a big sorrow for me, but I did my best to sustain the policy since I knew enough about the scriptures to understand that God has always selected certain people to do the things he needed to have done." It was not a matter of "superior" or "inferior."

In describing Duff and the rest of the faculty at the Institute of Religion at the University of Utah, Eugene England wrote, "When they told us to be patient about the church's denial of priesthood to the Black people and that such a practice did not prove either that God was a racist or that Christ's Restored gospel was untrue, we trusted them."[11]

Duff also couldn't agree with those who, in searching for an answer, landed on such ideas as premortal choices, or birth into certain lineages, or some assumption of Black inferiority. He didn't think any of these were satisfactory explanations, and yet he read in both the Old Testament and the New Testament where God chose certain of his children to receive blessings before others. For example, Christ didn't allow the Gentiles to hear the gospel at first but did at a

10. MDH-R, Jan. 11, 2002.

11. Eugene England, "The Achievement of Lowell Bennion," *Sunstone*, July 1988, 24–30.

Missionary Duff in a Cincinnati Park with "my pals" on preparation day, 1942.

later time. A question Duff raised in this regard was, "Does God's selection of a chosen people and chosen leaders connote superiority and thus demean all other men?" Or does His selection of a chosen people connote a "selection to service," with the purpose of elevating and lifting all other men? He wrote:

> The whole pattern of the early ministry of the Savior revolves around the instructions of Jesus Christ, not to teach the Gentiles, but only to go to the lost sheep of the house of Israel. And so, He used this process of selection. God chose Abraham and not everybody else—Isaac and Jacob and Joseph, and not everybody else. That could be used to suggest that this is what was happening with the Black people, that it was not the Black, so much as the White who needed the time of preparation for the general bestowal of the priesthood upon all worthy people, i.e., until the White folks get spiritually mature enough to accept people and meet the change with grace and goodness.[12]

Duff refused to believe that the verse in 2 Nephi 5:21, which described a skin of blackness associated with being "cut off from the Lord's presence," was related to anyone other than those people at that time. If someone tried to explain that scripture as being some kind of justification for the priesthood ban, he would ask them to turn to 2 Nephi 26:33, which reads, in part, "And he denieth none that come unto him, black and white, bond and free, male and female; and he remembereth the heathen; and all are alike unto God, both Jew and Gentile." He

12. MDH-R, May 1, 2001.

was always quick to point out that if this was the reason for the ban, it was never a matter of superior or inferior—it was always a matter of the Lord's timetable. If anyone expressed any feelings of racial superiority around him, Duff invited them to repent immediately.

When Duff was asked to summarize his position on the race-based priesthood ban, he responded, "The Whites aren't ready, or good enough, yet. The Blacks will hold the priesthood when the Lord is ready."

He once was speaking at the University of Montana, when a faculty member stood and questioned him: "How do you have the guts to come here and teach educated people, when you don't even let the Black people hold the priesthood in your own church?"

Duff responded, "Well, for one thing, you're not a very courteous guy, are you, to put us on the spot like this? But I'll give you an answer. When the church, and its White leaders, learn to handle this, the rest will be able to handle it all right."

The questioner went away mad and cursing.

It bothered Duff to have to adopt an attitude of suspended judgment on this issue and rely on (and wait for) the prophet to receive revelation that would remove the priesthood ban. But he was a believer, and he felt that when the time was right, the prophet would receive the instruction to change things.

What follows is a small sampling of papers, letters, and experiences that Duff wrote about the priesthood ban over the decades:

1947—Discussions with Lowell Bennion at the Salt Lake Institute

In August 1993, Duff spoke at a tribute to Lowell Bennion. He remarked, "I have had an eye and an ear open to Lowell Bennion since the day about 36 years ago that I mustered freshman courage and with an associate had a conversation with Lowell. I was eager to meet this young teacher of whom I had heard so much as to intellect, training, and Christian behavior." Duff's friend wanted to contend over the issue of excluding Blacks from the priesthood. Bennion did not oblige him, but did make a lasting impression on Duff by responding forthrightly that he was not sure he could help them on this issue but that he knew that good men were praying earnestly about the matter and that more light and knowledge were needed and would be received some day.

Duff left rejoicing and enrolled soon thereafter for further instruction from Bennion. His friend departed, muttering, and never returned. Duff wrote, "There is a scripture which for me fits Lowell Bennion in principle: 'So he fed them according to the integrity of his heart; and guided them by the skillfulness of his hands.' (Psalm 78:72)."

1951—West High Seminary Handout

In 1951, Duff published a position paper for the West High seminary class he was teaching. He began the paper by quoting Elder John A. Widtsoe: "The cause of the black skin … is not known.… There is no evidence, as far as found, to justify the belief that [black individuals were] neutral in the great council in heaven before the foundations of the earth were laid, or that he has been punished with a black skin."[13]

Duff pointed out that there are many aspects of our birth that are not understandable based on this life only. He refused to speculate as to why and invited his students to likewise refrain from speculation. And he taught them that those with black skin have the promise that what is now denied them, they may receive later, if they are worthy. He also reaffirmed the church's teaching that if any change is to be made, it will be by revelation from God through the prophet, who stands at the head of the church.

1954—With Harold B. Lee

> At 5:30 a.m. left for Rexburg, Idaho, to attend Stake Conference there. On the train we had a fine set of companions. Harold B. Lee, LeGrand Richards, Alma Sonne, Bruce McConkie, and I, together with our respective Welfare agents. We practically had a "Mormon special" [train car.] I talked with Brother Lee at some length about the [Black] issue. He had a file on the matter which I was privileged to look into to some extent, though not fully. We read something of Brother [Elijah] Able, the black man who was ordained to the priesthood in Joseph Smith's day, and discussed that situation. Apparently, Brother Able was ordained to the priesthood, but was not allowed to exercise ecclesiastical authority [after 1852].[14]

1965—From a Letter Duff Wrote to a Convert in England

In the letter, Duff explained that Heavenly Father clearly has a timetable, and His timing is not our timing. Christ himself did things which might have seemed un-Christian to observers—things like telling the woman at Canaan that he was sent only to the Lost Sheep of Israel. She came for help, and Jesus wouldn't listen. "He later makes a rather uncomfortable suggestion that the children's bread should not be fed to dogs. The plain implication is that she and her people were not to be fed, yet."

To Duff, it was clear that Jesus was following God's timetable. One group had the first opportunity, not because they were superior, but because they were chosen to serve. Their blessings had only been temporarily postponed while the Lord prepared them and prepared His chosen people to accept them. "Of course, none of us are more valuable in his sight than others. And there is no reason for any of us to be derelict in our responsibility to treat every man like a man and a brother."[15]

1966—From a Letter Duff Wrote on Behalf of the First Presidency

> Dear Brother, you are aware that many of those who have written for the church have referred to the passage in Abraham that seems to indicate that the reservation

13. MDH, position paper, 1951.
14. MDH-JE, Jan. 16, 1954.
15. MDH-L, Sept. 13, 1965 (Matt. 15:22–28).

of the priesthood [from Blacks] traces back to certain incidents relating to Ham. I confess that I have never taken much satisfaction in this approach and am comforted in reading the writing of Dr. Widtsoe and others who didn't agree with it either.

In these days of foment and thoughtful inquiry, perhaps additional investigation is justified. I wrote a letter to a man recently, which I sent to the First Presidency as an answer on the [Black question], and it came back with the approbation of the President of the Church. In it, I did not mention Cain, or the pre-existence, but simply noted that God had from the beginning apparently invoked a timetable for His children. He selected certain ones to serve their brothers, designating them and giving them the authority to do so. This was true from the beginning.[16]

1968—Answer to a Letter

"Anyone who knows David O. McKay must understand that if any man on earth would by nature be led to alleviate the [issue of Blacks and the priesthood], it would be David O. McKay. I do not say this because he is President of the Church. I say it because I know the man. I am sure he has shed more tears and cried out with more anguish in this matter than the rest of us put together, yet he has not been guided to change things."

Duff assured the recipient that he would never cease weeping and praying and hoping for change. He declared that he was never comfortable with answers involving Cain and curses, and he believed that any limitation imposed on any people by God is for the good of those people, since only that which is good comes from God.

"I believe that there will come a time when [Black people] will get every opportunity that anyone will ever have as a member of the church. I believe that many of these good people will be far ahead in capacity to lead and to create and to be considerate and Godly. When that time comes, only God knows, and I believe he will reveal it to the prophets."[17]

January 1969—From a BYU Trustees Meeting

We met with the BYU Trustees and again, had the interesting experience of hearing Ernest Wilkinson plead for a little help on what to do about the [Black] situation. Some of the brethren were again in favor of hiding their heads. Brother [N. Eldon] Tanner, in his characteristically honest and highly intelligent way, noted that we could not long run away from this or refuse to face it. There was some shifting of the feet still, until I stated openly and rather loudly that I agreed one hundred percent and that it was unfair to Ernest to keep him silent in the face of all the attacks, that the issue will not disappear, that the students will not

16. MDH-L to Philip R. Kunz, Feb. 3, 1966.

17. MDH-L to LaVema L. Bringhurst, July 30, 1968.

be quieted, and the faculty will not let them. This was a frontal assault on the position of my good friend Elder [Richard L.] Evans and Elder [Delbert L.] Stapley, and I would presume Elder [Harold B. Lee.] Nonetheless it had to be said. At that point action was taken to authorize Ernest to present his statement to a committee of the Twelve and then to the First Presidency to be made available to the students of BYU so they may know where things stand.[18]

January 23, 1969—Letter to a Member in Tennessee

God bless you. I for one will not submit to the notion that I cannot treat my brother like my brother, and I will not be bullied by those who feel otherwise. For many years I have attempted to sustain in faith and practice the view of the church toward [Blacks] and the priesthood, at the same time I have earnestly attempted to express the true feelings of my heart for every man in whose life I have the blessing of some involvement. The color of his skin or the nature of his status was and is of no importance in that respect. I will use your intelligent and humble statement of facts to try to get a vision of the breadth and seriousness of this problem a little more firmly before at least some of the brethren.[19]

April 1969—Meeting with President McKay

Despite his advancing age, President McKay seemed quite responsive as he and Duff talked alone together for forty minutes. "Then we talked about the [Blacks and the priesthood] issue." Duff said. "He was not talkative, but did respond that this had been an issue for a long time, and I then told him about the intensity of the matter and the statements being made, the athletic games being cancelled, the pamphlets being passed out of ancient stuff written by President [Joseph Fielding] Smith and others. He seemed sorrowed by all of this and I do not know what the result will be."[20]

December 10, 1969—Harold B. Lee and Hugh B. Brown

"Brother Lee said he has been working on the matter all day, by which he meant the document on the [Black issue] (that I didn't like and said should be recast). I told him about the letter I had written to a new member in England in 1965, a letter which the Presidency had read, and which President McKay had authorized. He asked for a copy. Phyllis finished a modified copy which I took to him before closing time."

Just when Duff arrived at Brother Lee's office, President [Hugh B.] Brown exited, looking very gray and very red in the face. He and LeGrand Richards and Joseph Anderson had been in Brother Lee's office, and Duff suspected that President Brown had been hearing things that were not to his liking.

18. MDH-JE, Jan. 10, 1969.
19. MDH-L, Jan. 23, 1969.
20. MDH-JE, Apr. 24, 1969.

Right about this same time, Duff and Maxine received a letter from Maxine's mother, reporting on a radio interview she heard in which President Brown had said that the [priesthood ban] was not a principle, but was a policy, that it could be changed any time, and that it likely would be changed soon. He later put similar sentiments in a four-page letter to the vice-president of Stanford University, a letter which was widely circulated.

Duff wrote, "It will be interesting to see what comes out of this. What I suspect is that a letter much like the draft which Brother Lee sent to me, will be published. I think this is unfortunate, but of course I can do nothing about that. I have every reason to suppose that if his attitude is as it was, my letter will not please him, but I am more interested in getting it said and considered than in having it please anybody. I think it is right and that is all that concerns me at the moment."[21]

December 13, 1969—Official Statement

Duff attended a training session for regional representatives all day. During the meeting, President Tanner read a statement on the [Blacks] that said that the church is helpless until the Lord tells the prophet to change. He also included references to the church's beleaguered past, its feeling for constitutional rights and civil rights, and the thought that if people are really concerned with our situation, then those who believe God is running the church will join it and shut up, and those who don't believe that we have the priesthood, will not join and shut up. Duff wrote, "I've tried this approach many times as a last desperate measure and it [quiets] some people, but never wins anything in the exchange. I should note that when I was in Brother Lee's office the other day he was working on this statement and noted that we must have further light from the Lord on both (1) the [Blacks and the priesthood issue], and (2) the seventy. I mentioned my letter to the man in England about the [Black] issue, and he had me submit it to him. Not a line or recognizable thought from it [was included] in the final document read in the meeting."[22]

March 1970—Threatened Violence against Church Leadership

> The [situation with Blacks and the priesthood] is tough, with lots of play now. Police guards are in the Church Office building. Courting death in a cause which is in my judgment unworthy of the life of anyone. We owe a duty and ought to do it. If it really is the Lord's will that we be in this situation, then it will be made known, I'm sure. My faith is that we ought to do something about the problem now.[23]

21. MDH-JE, Dec. 10, 1969.
22. MDH-JE, Dec. 13, 1969.
23. MDH-JE, Mar. 5, 1970.

June 1971—Visit to the Hattiesburg Stake

Duff was assigned to the stake conference of the Hattiesburg Mississippi Stake. While there, he agreed to speak at a high school commencement service in Liberty, Mississippi. Upon his return to Utah, he wrote a letter to the First Presidency, alerting them to the civil unrest that was occurring in the South and the serious problem in Mississippi, where over 144 private schools had been established to avoid the integration orders of the federal courts.[24]

December 1973—President Lee in the Temple Meeting

In the weekly general authority temple meeting, President Lee was particularly touched and asked the brethren to pray for him with the promise that he would do everything in his power to live to merit the blessings of the Spirit. He stated that he couldn't sleep much lately, lying awake thinking about the problems which beset the church. President Lee mentioned going to his counselors for help in a question concerning the sealing of Black babies to White parents through the priesthood and that they had counseled him that there is only one source through which that information could come. Duff wrote, "He spoke of President McKay and said he must now get the right answer to this question since so much depends on it. His presentation was very mild and humble and filled with expressions of love."[25]

October 1974—Visit with Lester Bush

After a regular day of meetings and conversation, Duff met with Dr. Lester Bush. He had last met Dr. Bush in Vietnam, and described him as "a brilliant young man with a very curious and inquiring mind, mixed with a strong conviction in the church. I enjoy him very much. He published in *Dialogue* and passed on the full body of his research on [Blacks and the priesthood] to Boyd Packer, who turned it in to the First Presidency, who have apparently buried it in the Church Historian's Library or elsewhere. The account was purely historical and does not attempt to tell anyone how to run the church, and it would have seemed to me to be a strong and useful help to the brethren.[26]

1975—Letter from Lester Bush

Lester wrote to Duff, "I was especially encouraged to hear that my earlier work may have had at least a marginal effect. Most especially, thank you for your words of encouragement. I'm sure it is no surprise to you to learn that such an expression to me was without precedent among your colleagues."[27]

March 1976—Genesis Group

A meeting was held in Elder Packer's office with Ruffin Bridgeforth and Jim

24. MDH-L to the First Presidency, June 1971.
25. MDH-JE, Dec. 6, 1973.
26. MDH-JE, Oct. 22, 1974.
27. Lester Bush to MDH, Aug. 22, 1975.

Dawson, the leaders of the Genesis Group,[28] expressing discouragement over dissidence within the group. Duff reported that "interestingly, the men in the group can handle the priesthood deprivation, but the women cannot, and are egging the men on to make trouble—and the group is decreasing in membership."

There was free interchange, and at the end, Elder Packer asked that they pray together. Duff recounted:

> We knelt, and he wept his way through a sweet discussion with the Lord and asking for assistance. When we stood, Boyd and Ruffin and I were all weeping. They are [in a tough situation] and I for one am heartsick that little can be done about it. There was real tenderness and real concern by all.
>
> Boyd said two things as we left: "Someday, someday, something will happen here," and "Ruffin Bridgeforth has done more to bring the priesthood to the Black than all of the protesters put together."[29]

November 1976 and April 1978—Interracial Marriage

In 1976, Duff met with the parents of a young lady Duff had previously counseled who was planning to marry a Black man. "They left with the plain suggestion that they are not wise in turning away their daughter. We talked about unconditional love and the rest."[30]

In April 1978, Robert Stevenson, an African American Mormon, married Susan Bevan, a White Mormon. They had met at BYU, but her family questioned the viability of the relationship. Stevenson later noted, "Everybody from the garbage man to the stake president had told her that marrying me would be to her eternal detriment." They met with Elder Boyd K. Packer, who invited Duff to attend. "According to Stevenson, 'Elder Packer squared off on one side, and Elder Hanks squared off on the other.' Packer argued that Stevenson 'could accomplish [his] mission in life and be more effective without being married to a white woman.' Hanks said, 'I think it's the best thing in the world that you marry Susan. I think that you'll be more effective, and you'll be able to break down racial barriers easier.'"[31]

1993—Commentary a Year After Becoming Emeritus

Looking back fifteen years after the announcement, Duff wrote, "All of us had the sense of discomfort at the continuing policy that kept good and honorable people from the blessings of their possibilities. For all the years I was a general authority, and for years before that, I answered thousands of questions on tours

28. The Genesis Group was established in 1971 by the First Presidency of the church with Ruffin Bridgeforth, Eugene Orr, and Darius Gray in Salt Lake City, Utah, as a dependent branch to serve the needs of African-American Latter-day Saints.

29. MDH-JE, Mar. 23, 1976.

30. MDH-JE, Nov. 18, 1976.

31. Quoted at onthisdayinmormonhistory.blogspot.com.

at Temple Square. I had to find ways to respond to what was a troubling reality that there were worthy and wonderful people who were not yet permitted to hold the priesthood. One can't respond to questions about this for so many years and know that the Lord tells us that He 'esteemeth all flesh in one' (1 Nephi 17:35), and not look forward to a change."

47

Missionary Service and Convert Retention

What if we tempered our aggressive proselyting with aggressive Christianity?
—Marion D. Hanks[1]

Duff spent a lot of energy trying to help the church go into all the world to teach and baptize those who believed. He loved missionary work because he loved the gospel—it was a part of his makeup. But his vision of the future of missionary work entailed the joining together of Matthew 25 with Matthew 28.

> Matthew 25: "Inasmuch as ye have done it unto one of *the least of these* my brethren, ye have done it unto me" (vv. 31–46; emphasis added).
>
> Matthew 28: "Go ye therefore, and teach all nations, *baptizing* them .... teaching them to *observe*" (vv. 19–20; emphasis added).
>
> In other words, called to *baptize* AND called to *serve*.

Duff viewed both of these directives by the Lord as being equal in weight and nonnegotiable commands of the Lord for all members of the church, not just missionaries. The Lord described *both* as prerequisites for gaining eternal life.

This chapter discusses Duff's tireless lobbying for more Christian service from missionaries, but his broader hope for the global church was that the entire membership would adopt the Savior's command toward serving "the least of these" (see more discussion of this hope in chapter 55, pages 523–33).

His vision was that someday the church's worldwide missionary force would be lifting boxes into U-Hauls, providing meals to the homebound and homeless, helping the Red Cross, volunteering at the local veterans hospital, helping local residents weed, plant, and paint. But this had not been the church's historical approach.

It seems difficult for some leaders of the church to embrace the concepts embodied in Duff's hoped-for vision of missionary work. Even within recent years, while serving as a mission president, Rich heard such interesting criticisms as, "We are sent *only* to baptize!" and "We aren't the Peace Corps, you know," or "Those missionaries are doing *too much service.*"

1. MDH-JE, Oct. 1, 1981, quoting from his remarks in a temple meeting that morning.

Sometimes, Duff felt alone in his effort to push the church toward missionary Christlike service. It would probably not be too far off the mark to suggest that the large majority of his general authority colleagues were far more accustomed to talking about Matthew 28 than about Matthew 25.

In 1985, Lowell Bennion, Duff's dear friend and colleague at the Institute of Religion at the University of Utah, gave a talk subtitled "Serve, Then Teach." Bennion said:

> I am concerned that we don't balance our proselyting efforts with a greater emphasis on service in word and deed.... I am not so naïve as to believe that the church can solve all the world's problems. But we could develop some pilot projects which might demonstrate some solutions. Some church farms, for example, could be a wonderful setting for senior citizen living, or a place to redeem alienated youth. The church is committed to taking its message to the world. I believe it can be done most effectively if it is a message from a people who are living a Christian life of service toward others. Maybe someday we will send missionaries out to serve [first] and then to teach. The results would bear watching. [We could call it,] "Go Ye into All the World': To Serve and to Convert."[2]

On his printed copy of Lowell's remarks, Duff highlighted that section and wrote in the margin, "NOW!"

IT'S GOING TO BE A LONG ROAD

Duff was well aware of the church's snail-like pace in making changes, and despite that knowledge, he continued to push for any kind of movement.

Elder James M. Paramore, one of his colleagues, wrote, "One of the great things Duff did over the years was to bear his testimony repeatedly asking for the missionaries to be able to do service. Now, all these years later, thousands of missionaries have opportunities every week (even if only for a few hours) to serve others, beyond their proselyting endeavors."

In a newspaper story about Duff's life were these comments: "Among Hanks' lasting legacies, BYU professor Warner Woodworth believes, is his suggestion to help the poor without proselyting. Now Mormon missionaries are required to do weekly humanitarian service."[3]

While the wheels of change in the church ground slowly, Duff kept advocating for the kind of changes he envisioned, while continuing to work and teach within the then-current paradigm of missionary work.

His exposure to missionary work began, of course, during his youthful mission to the northern states. After his mission, he began his decades-long love affair with Temple Square, where he could teach daily and testify of Jesus Christ and His restored church. After his call as a general authority, he began four decades

2. Lowell Bennion, "Serving or Converting?" address at Sunstone Symposium, Aug. 1985.
3. Peggy Fletcher Stack, *Salt Lake Tribune*, Aug. 2011.

of setting apart new missionaries, lengthy mission tours, mission president seminars, trainings at the mission home, and then the Provo Missionary Training Center, serving as a mission president in London, and doing his own missionary work with individuals. At the same time, he continued his personal efforts to serve his fellow man.[4]

HIS PERSONAL MISSIONARY EFFORTS

Duff had his own commitment to personally share the gospel. There are numerous accounts of his teaching and baptizing people interested in the church. One of his early missionary efforts was on board a ship in the middle of the Pacific Ocean during World War II. He wrote home, about a young sailor who Duff taught about the restoration over several months. Duff remarked that he "believed so much of Mormonism that he wanted to believe the rest. He is a remarkable man and someone I'd be most happy to see accept the gospel. He has read and digested more church literature in the past three weeks than I have in the past six months.[5]

CONVERSION, RETENTION, AND ACTIVATION

Duff felt ill at ease with a focus solely on baptism. The Lord had instructed His disciples, "Go and teach all nations, *baptizing* them in the name of the Father, and of the Son, and of the Holy Ghost." But the Lord required more than just baptizing. The scripture goes on to say, "*Teaching* them to *observe* all things whatsoever I have commanded you" (Matthew 28:19–20; emphasis added, see also pages 330, 445–49, 521).

The past thirty years have seen a moderate shift in the church's approach toward retaining converts. Of course, this isn't recent to the Lord. In John 15:16, the command is "Go and bring forth fruit [baptism], and that your fruit *should remain*" (emphasis added).

In Moroni 6:4 we read, "And after they had been received unto baptism, ... they were *numbered* among the people of the Church of Christ; and their names were taken, that they might be remembered and *nourished* by the good word of God, to *keep them in the right way*" (emphasis added).

Many other scriptural passages say the same thing.

Perhaps influenced heavily by what he inherited as a mission president in London, Duff began a crusade to balance missionary proselyting and baptizing with conversion, activation, and retention of new converts. He was never a fan of statistics and numbers and chest-beating convert baptismal metrics. His belief mirrored that of another Christian minister, who said,

---

4. I don't want to imply in any way that Duff was alone in giving Christlike service, but he often felt quite alone in his attempt to *move the institutional church* toward complete adoption of the principles.

5. MDH-L to home from ship, Dec. 17, 1945.

> God does not want His church to seek its strength in mere numbers. We are making that mistake today.... [trying] to make Christianity a big thing in a way that will make everybody like it. The result is a "Best-seller" religion, calculated to win a large following. And it does. It builds beautiful statistics. But, this is not the church that was bought with the blood of the Son of God. This is a church that is counting its members instead of weighing them.... We ought to be ashamed ... aping the method of salesmen and showmen, competing for an audience and "counting the house." This is far beneath our dignity as Christians, for we are serving one whose people are more numerous than the sands on the seashore and the stars in the sky.[6]

Duff wrote, "The Lord directed that his sheep be *fed,* not *counted.* We seem to have a widespread concern for continual expansion of numbers without reference to what then happens, and I believe we will be punished for this. There should be in our minds and hearts a *spiritual vision of progress for individual* children of God, for 'establishing the Church' in the hearts of the individual."[7]

CALLED TO *SERVE*

Duff lamented the fact that church members call what missionaries do "missionary service," when our missionaries really didn't do much service at that time. The records of the councils he attended, his journal entries, and numerous letters attest to his unwavering commitment to balance proselyting with Christlike service.

His concern could be summarized by one paragraph of a letter from a young missionary to his father, who forwarded it to Duff: "Dad, there is an anti-service attitude among missionaries that really frustrates me. There are so many people that need help, but they aren't members, or won't commit to baptism. We were driving home yesterday and I saw a guy stalled in his car. He was trying to push it up a hill, and obviously needed a hand. So, I asked my companion to pull over so we could push, but he said, 'No, we haven't got time. We still have to contact 1 ½ hours before we are ahead of the other district in contacting hours.' Everyone is so caught up in the business of being a missionary, they forget what we are really here to do—serve."

It was Duff's dream, and long the dream of many who have served the Lord as a missionary, that the term "called to serve" would be a valid description of what missionaries do as part of a broader vision beyond "called to teach" or "called to baptize."

Duff explained, "The Lord's command in Matthew 28 is clear, '*teach* all nations ... *baptizing* them, ... teaching them to *observe* all things whatsoever I have commanded you'; what did the Lord expect newly baptized people would be taught to observe? Surely it would include the instructions he gave in the parable

6. Peter Eldersveld of the Christian Reformed Church.

7. MDH, undated position paper.

of the sheep and the goats in Matthew 25 which he declared to be a key to everlasting punishment, or life eternal."

Neither of the commands in Matthew 25 and 28 seems to be optional, nor subordinate to the other. But as recently as 2024, the church's website included these words for missionaries: "Keep mission priorities in order. Service is important, but it should not interfere with your *greater purpose:* finding, teaching, baptizing, retaining new converts, and activating less-active members. As a missionary, you will engage in planned service each week. You should not spend more than 10 hours per week in community service without permission from your mission president."[8]

The church of the twenty-first century is starting to lean and move toward missionary service. But it's been a slow change. Old habits die hard.

A BRIEF HISTORY

What follows is a sampling of Duff's writings over the decades, documenting his prodigious efforts to move the church and the missionary program toward conversion, activation, retention, and Christian service.

1971

On May 6, at the weekly temple meeting, Duff stood and talked about his concerns with the missionary program. He expressed his opinion that historically missionaries were able to participate as teachers and speakers and branch presidents and so forth, but these opportunities were now largely absent. Previously, missionaries learned the gospel and also learned what it meant to be a member of the church.

He noted that "our policy for some time now has been for missionaries to learn the six magic lessons and then do nothing but proselyte for two years. We are preparing them to do something they probably will never do again, and failing to prepare them for that which they are expected to do forever after. No enthusiasm greeted my suggestions, but I had not expected that it would, since what I said went in direct contrast to the philosophy of recent years."[9]

1980

It was frustrating for Duff to watch as quotas and goal setting and pressuring members to do proselyting missionary work was reintroduced over and over and over again across the years. He wrote:

> At 10 o'clock, I met with the First Quorum of Seventy in a meeting which all of us survived. In it was introduced another shot at the missionary program that assigns bishops and other officers to *get a family,* and *report* on them within a *given date,* collecting statistics. I sat in sorrow. With this I am in total disagreement. After the meeting, Dean Larsen shook his head also, feeling the same. It seems the critic in

8. Community Service Guidebook: JustServe Supplement, ChurchofJesusChrist.org.
9. MDH-JE, May 1971.

me surfaces as I write these journal entries, but in fact, I cannot conceive that these bright men would again undertake to warm over a five-year-old effort that was a failure and do it again. It will not work, it has not worked, it is not the right way.[10]

1981

On September 18, 1981, over the signature of the First Presidency, a letter went out to all leaders of the church authorizing the full-time missionaries to "teach inactive members." Previously, missionaries had been instructed not even to talk to inactive members. Duff was overjoyed with the change and on his copy of the letter wrote, "HISTORY! An incredible change of direction—years late. [Missionaries] have become one of our greatest resources to strengthen and build the church." The change in direction allowing missionaries to work with less-active members gave Duff renewed strength to keep campaigning for missionary Christian service.

On October 1, 1981, in a temple meeting for all general authorities, Duff suggested how great it would be if the church tempered its aggressive proselyting with some aggressive Christianity and how lovely it would be if thirty thousand missionaries all over the earth were doing acts of Christian service part of their time. He told them it was his conviction that if they did so, there would be a strong upsurge of institutional credibility and strengthening of the kingdom, not to mention the enhancement of the feeling of people for the church. And most importantly, it would be what the Savior taught.[11]

1984

Four years later, he wrote, "Early morning meeting with the 70's. Then the Temple meeting, where I presented the idea that I've been developing for 30 years: that Matthew 25 is at least *as important* as Matthew 28. "Go ye into all the world,' yes; but do it 'unto one of the least of these,' ... each of these [instructions] with eternal life as its outcome, and the opposite consequence if we ignore the Lord's summons. Some there believed me."[12]

1985

In a letter to Duff from a serving mission president, Duff highlighted the following text:

> I am well aware of the most obvious measurement of my work as a mission president—how many people did we baptize this month? The pressure to baptize overrides the whole process of finding, teaching, and fellowshipping and therefore *the processes are short-circuited to get the baptism.*
>
> Is it possible that "building the kingdom" has little to do with baptizing people? Teaching love and allegiance to priesthood leaders, being true to sacred

10. MDH-JE, June 17, 1980.
11. MDH-JE, Oct. 1, 1981.
12. MDH-JE, Oct. and Dec. 1984.

covenants, preparing men to honor women, nurturing the spirit through scripture study, understanding the Atonement and the Savior—are not these all dimensions that reach far beyond baptism? I believe it is more likely that "building the kingdom" is really about "establishing the church *within the individual* through ordinances and covenants that happen after baptism. One hasn't really participated in building anything except the membership rolls until he himself participates in personal kingdom-building activities like those I've just described.

Occasionally, Duff would see some light at the end of the tunnel on this particular issue: "Tomorrow, I am to meet with the managing directors of the Missionary Department to discuss Community (alias Christian) Service. This is a beginning, and I am impressed that it got by the committees and the Twelve and is to be given a hearing. I must get ready and prepared to be heard."[13]

He added, "On March 7th, we met with the general authorities in the Temple. Good meeting, generally. Russ Nelson, back from China, emphasized Alma 17 and 22, when the sons of Mosiah undertake to give service, *no gimmicks,* before they share the Good News with the King and associates. They were wonderfully successful in their sharing of the gospel, because they were living and serving and had their minds off the 'bottom line.' He did so well, and in fine spirit and strength, perhaps there will be more of a listening ear."[14]

1987

In a letter to one of the mission presidents who formerly reported to him in Asia, Duff wrote: "I have been up all night trying to prepare materials for the brethren to consider, which would change in some measure the vision of missionary work. The concept is simply that every missionary ought to be a member of the church, while he is a missionary, and be a true disciple of Jesus Christ by offering, not only the *word* of the Lord, but the *works* of the Savior as indicia of his devotion."[15]

In April 1987, the First Presidency sent a letter to all church leaders around the world again authorizing the limited use of full-time missionaries to assist local leaders in activating less-active members when there were not enough holders of the Melchizedek Priesthood. While there were some qualifiers attached, it was still movement in a better direction.[16]

1988

Finally, Duff started to observe the beginnings of a change. President Gordon B. Hinckley, then a counselor in the First Presidency, speaking at a regional representatives seminar, said, "One of the great and glaring tragedies of this work is the terrible loss to inactivity and even apostasy on the part of converts. It need

13. MDH-JE, Feb. 25, 1985.
14. MDH-JE, Mar. 1985.
15. MDH-L to Garth Andrus, Feb. 4, 1987.
16. First Presidency letter to all Church leaders, Apr. 3, 1987.

not happen. It should not happen. It must not happen. As I grow older, I have less and less interest in the number baptized and a growing interest in the number who come into the church and remain true and faithful. What shall it profit us if those who have been baptized drop away after a month or a year or five years?"[17]

1989

Finally, after decades of prodding, in 1989 Elder Robert L. Backman, Duff's colleague in charge of missionary work for the Presidency of the Seventy, presented a document that Duff had primarily authored, to the Missionary Committee of the Church, and they approved the official beginning of LDS Missionary Christian Service. A later article in the Church's *Ensign* magazine said:

> Along with their proselyting efforts, missionaries now also show their love for others by putting shoulders to the wheel in community service for half a day a week.... This new practice follows a letter sent by the church to Area Presidencies and mission presidents on 11 May 1989, giving guidelines for missionaries to become involved in service in their communities. The letter urged missionaries to give "Christian service" and contained suggestions for doing so.
>
> The guidelines stress that the service should come from a sincere desire to help others rather than as a means of obtaining teaching appointments or gaining publicity for the church. This emphasis on service is helping missionaries feel greater love for those they help and is giving them good feelings about being in the service of the Lord.[18]

1990

In a meeting of general authorities on October 2, 1990, President Gordon B. Hinckley outlined the church's critical problem with retaining new converts. His presentation and the direction of his remarks surprised everyone. The content of the data was certainly not new, but the direct summation of the problem and implicit and explicit counsel to the general authorities was.

In a letter to the Presidents of the Seventy, Duff wrote, "President Gordon B. Hinckley has finally openly acknowledged this critical problem that has bedeviled us for many years." A few of the things Duff summarized in the letter included:

> Some missions are engaged in a numbers game. Missionaries are given badges and honors for winning scores, instead of winning souls.
>
> It is easier to love and strengthen converts at the time they come in, than later.
>
> Yes, there will be some losses. (Heavenly Father lost a third part of the hosts of heaven.) But baptism is a serious thing, a covenant with our Father; it is more than a rite of passage.[19]

---

17. Gordon B. Hinckley, regional representatives seminar, Apr. 1, 1988.
18. Giles H. Florence Jr., "Called to Serve," *Ensign*, Sept. 1991.
19. MDH-A, meeting notes, Oct. 1990.

TWO STEPS FORWARD, ALMOST ONE STEP BACK

Unfortunately, just a few months later, some of the general authorities were once again trying to minimize the problem. Despite President Hinckley's noticeable change in attitude toward conversion and retention, many of Duff's colleagues continued to press for baptism statistics. Duff was asked to review a draft of a position paper on missionary work to be signed by the Seven Presidents of Seventy. Duff reviewed the draft and then wrote a fairly scathing letter to the other Presidents of the Seventy, chastising them for "missing a magnificent opportunity to do something meaningful" to change the church. His review included the following comments: "President Hinckley was shocked with what he saw on his recent trip to Europe. In our October meeting, he shared his strong feelings about what is 'really going on' with missionary work and called for a change in focus." And "How can any of us be immune to the reality of the pressures, subtle or overt, that are exerted on mission presidents to produce baptisms? They exist all around us. Even the monthly reports showing percentage increases or decreases of baptisms, with the ranking of individual missions, clearly tell a mission president what really matters to the church leaders above him."

While Duff was pleased that some focus had shifted toward retention, he pointed out that the scriptures emphasize teaching people correctly *before and after* they were baptized in the first place. Moroni 6, D&C 20, and Mosiah 18 all effectively say the same thing as Matthew 28:20: "Teaching them to *observe* all things whatsoever I have commanded you" (emphasis added). In other words, baptism was not the only goal described in the scriptures—the goal also included a person's *conversion* to the gospel and to the Lord Jesus Christ.

Part of the draft letter also suggested that prescribed service and activation efforts by the missionaries were "not making a difference." One could almost see Duff's face as he responded, "Not making a difference?!? It has scarcely begun! It has not been tried and found wanting! It has generally not even been tried, because it is not understood, or because there exists the perception that doing it would 'cost baptisms!' Where it *has* been tried, it has produced remarkable results."[20]

It must have been incredibly frustrating for Duff to hear the man who was essentially leading the church at the time make an about-face, shine a bright light on an issue that everyone knew was a problem, read the scriptures that are clear in their declarations, and then watch his colleagues essentially do nothing, conceding to the status quo. Duff's letter to them said, "I cannot believe that we would be willing to ignore this call from [President Hinckley]. If after reviewing what he said, and the scriptures I've presented, if you individually do not think it important, then I am at a loss to pursue it further. Should we not be teaching our young men and women correct principles, trying to help them arrive at an

---

20. MDH-L to the Presidents of the Seventy, Oct. 19, 1990, in response to a draft letter.

honorable approach to building the kingdom? The consequences of our inaction at this point, or of our modest declaration of truth at this point, may significantly affect the whole church and the future."[21]

1991 and Afterward

The final version of the letter was delivered to President Howard W. Hunter, President of the Twelve, on January 30, 1991. It was substantially different from the draft version. It clearly reflected Duff's changes. The letter contained an answer to the question of why so many new members were falling away after baptism. The answer was straightforward: An undue emphasis on new baptisms, including content and style of reports, direct contact by the missionary department expressing displeasure at diminishing baptisms, and overall pressure from the leadership felt strongly by all mission presidents. Other problems discussed included shortened teaching time of converts in some missions and not enough emphasis on the spiritual side of missionary work. For each problem listed, the letter outlined suggested recommendations—the most controversial of which suggested (1) bringing a better reporting balance between baptisms, sacrament meeting attendance, priesthood ordinations, and temple attendance, and (2) changing the reports to emphasize retention. Another candid suggestion was that Doctrine and Covenants 20:37 (qualifications for baptism) be adhered to more carefully and augmented with increased emphasis on Doctrine and Covenants 20:68 (having "sufficient time to expound all things concerning the Church of Christ.")

Included in the letter was this insightful sentence: "Adhering carefully to the Lord's instructions may result in a short-term reduction in the number of baptisms, but the long-term effects upon the Church, as well as upon the lives of new members, would be very beneficial." Duff kept things moving forward.

Elder Jeffrey R. Holland wrote to Duff while Elder Holland was serving as Area President in England:

> I want to let you know what is happening in England. Following President Hinckley's rather remarkable statement six months ago, no one could have been more willing to implement that attitude in Great Britain, than Elder Ballard has been. Given his past experience in the Missionary Department, I wasn't sure that would be the case, and it has been both a relief and a joy to see it firmly taught. I have found it wonderfully pleasant to teach this new emphasis on *activation* and *retention,* along with some *community service* wherever possible. Our experience in several wards has also allowed us to teach it in a way that suggests that baptisms will go up, not down.[22]

Donald McArthur, president of Utah Salt Lake City Mission, wrote, "As we've encouraged our missionaries to reach out to the less-active, I've seen their view of

21. MDH-L to the Presidents of the Seventy, Oct. 19, 1990, in response to a draft letter.
22. Jeffrey R. Holland to MDH, Apr. 12, 1991.

their calling expand significantly, resulting in more members helped toward full activity, and a deepened appreciation of true conversion for their converts. I'm sure that their learning to render '*no-strings-attached service*' has a corresponding benefit to the missionary's perspective, as well as benefiting the recipients, and improving the image of the church."[23]

One more example of scores of letters he received on this subject: "Dear Elder Hanks, we would personally like to extend our gratitude for your implementing community service into the missionary program. We really believe it broadens the perspective of our missionaries. The value it brings to the community is undeniable and greatly needed. When I was a missionary, I always felt an imbalance in my life. I felt that giving more of my time to humankind, whether or not they were interested in the gospel, would strengthen not only me, but the understanding of what we stand for."

Some have compared the difficulty of changing large organizations to trying to turn a battleship. As Duff reminisced on his decades-long attempt to push the institutional church and its missionary program toward true Christian service, emotions rose in his voice. He was glad to see that some results were beginning to show, but he refused to take credit when several journalists called to get his side of the story. He said, "It would be inappropriate for me to get any credit. All I did was act as a burr under the saddle. Everything we're doing is in the Good Book, in Matthew 25. The brethren understood the scriptures long before I introduced the concepts."

Others in the know didn't agree with Duff's deflection of recognition. Said one former mission president, "I suppose most of all, I loved Elder Hanks' example of service and concern for others. He fought for and finally won the battle over allowing missionaries to devote substantial hours each week to service. There were some among the Twelve who opposed the move, but Elder Hanks carried the day. A lesser man would have given up in the face of powerful opposition, but I believe that he had the Lord on his side in the debate."[24]

It is clear from the records that Duff pushed and prodded and prayed the church and specifically its missionary program toward the Savior's command to perform true Christian service for our fellow man. He taught that when missionaries perform Christlike service, they are living the principles they teach. They are not only proclaiming the Savior's words, but they are also emulating His works. And while bringing others to a knowledge of Christ, they are coming closer to Him themselves.

The church's missionary efforts have continued to move toward Christlike service. Over the decades since Duff was granted emeritus status, encouraging steps have been taken and impactful changes made. Have the changes incorporated all

23. Donald McArthur to MDH, 1992.

24. John Stohlton, online tribute after Duff's death, Aug. 2011.

of Duff's vision—what he hoped and worked for? Probably not. But in the more than thirty years since, the church has been increasingly involved in humanitarian relief and development activities throughout the world. In some missions, missionaries are being allowed to perform more service than the maximum ten hours per week prescribed in *Preach My Gospel.* Instructions for missionary service in the JustServe program are refreshingly straightforward, "We are not providing service to proselyte." In addition, special full-time church service missions have been created for young people better suited to that type of mission experience.

48

Rotary International

Duff joined Rotary in 1968, not long before Richard L. Evans died. Elder Evans had been the worldwide president of Rotary International, while serving as an apostle, and for years had urged Duff to join. Upon joining, he was invited to serve on several committees and enjoyed the experience as he got acquainted with others. He also loved the vision of Rotary and its strong service component. It closely matched his own feelings for community and church service.

It didn't occur to him that Rotary would become an important part of his life, but he enjoyed making a broader set of friends. He said, "I had been on many community enterprises, but the association was not lengthy enough or close enough to form real friendships. Rotary was different."

As time passed, Duff formed consequential and respectful friendships with individuals who were not members of the church or not active in it. They came to recognize his sincerity and the service he was committed to.

Duff was elected a vice president of the Salt Lake Club several years after he joined and then served from 1974 to 1975 as president of that club. In May 1975, he was elected district governor nominee. The circumstances were unusual because he hadn't submitted his name and had been out of town at a stake conference during the candidate interviews. Members of the Salt Lake Club had presented his name in absentia, and he was voted in as district governor nominee. After some time of training and shadowing other leaders, he was inducted as the district governor and he wrote in his journal, "A pin was pinned on me, testifying that it is so."

MEMBERSHIP IN THE SALT LAKE CLUB

As a member of the Salt Lake Club, men he had known only peripherally became close friends. For example, he wrote, "In this period, Bob Groesbeck became a good and lasting friend. I came to love and appreciate him and Shirley very much. They are far away from any kind of church commitment and the good they might do there, but they need no defense, being outstanding people of high quality who do very much that is good in this community."

His exposure to a broader audience also grew. "After a day of meetings," he wrote, "I was again on the program as master of ceremonies for a banquet that evening. We laughed a lot, there was a lot of humor beyond jokes, there were serious parts and a pleasant evening, and the encouraging result was that people like John Lowe, and Bob Arnold, not members of the church, came to say they had never laughed so hard, or had so much fun as they had that evening. I was very pleased, since this was the first time that I'd appeared in this type of guise with them."[1]

PRESIDENT OF THE SALT LAKE CLUB

During his year as president of the Salt Lake Club, it grew in membership and in camaraderie, especially in LDS and non-LDS relationships, which had always been strained. The service aspects of the club were also strengthened, with the club completing several local projects and contributing to several international projects, including a dialysis center in Bolivia. The members also got behind a project to build a cover over the swimming pool in Salt Lake's Central City, committing $25,000 to do that (about $160,000 in today's dollars).

DISTRICT GOVERNOR

During his service as Rotary District Governor in 1977, Duff spent six months traveling all over Utah and Idaho to big towns and small, sleeping in motels and driving from town to town or occasionally flying. He became acquainted with some terrific people from all walks of life—farmers, postmasters, architects, realtors, dentists, plant managers, and so forth. He visited and evaluated fifty-four diverse clubs, located across two states, with different levels of understanding of Rotary's cause and commitment to it.

INSTRUCTOR AT INTERNATIONAL MEETINGS

Over the coming decades, Duff was a trainer, instructor, and keynote speaker at many Rotary International worldwide meetings. Although it was hard work, he really enjoyed it. As but one example, in February 1977, Duff was a keynote speaker at a zone institute meeting in Kona, Hawaii, involving district governors and their prospective successors. He said, "I gave an inspirational talk on Sunday morning, teaching the gospel and doing it in an unvarnished way. When I was through, Harvey Christen was so moved that all he could say was, 'The spirit of Richard Evans is here.'"

His exposure allowed him to reach a wide and influential set of leaders. For instance, he served as an instructor at three international assemblies—Boca Raton in 1977 and May 1980, and Nashville in 1986—at which all new district governors from 156 countries were brought together to be trained.

THE MESSAGE

Duff's message in his Rotary speeches and trainings over the years was somewhat similar to topics he presented in his other speeches. There was a bit less focus on religion and a bit more focus on serving one's fellow man as well as on the ideals of Rotary. He emphasized the important service that Rotarians were

1. MDH-JE, July 1974.

doing around the globe and the opportunity to do more. He counseled them, "Let's not just be proud of Rotary; let's be part of it. Mere membership doesn't mean anything; you have to do something."

He recommended that each Rotarian, in the vocation he pursued, keep the highest ethical standards. He told the story of a man being interviewed for a job who was asked, "If I hire you, can I count on you to be honest." The response? "Sir, you can count on me to be honest, whether you hire me or not."

Duff taught that Rotary was far more than a social luncheon club and networking. He explained that Rotary is unique in its members' diversity of vocation, with a particular capacity for *usefulness* and *service* to communities it draws from. Duff particularly enjoyed quoting Rotarian leader, John Dalton, who said, "Don't merely attend luncheons, salute the flag, and slap each other on the back. Plunge into the true meaning of Rotary—the nobility of serving others."[2]

A published report about his August 1977 visit to the Boise club is representative: "With an engaging style, District Governor Duff Hanks told a joke or two, shared heart-warming experiences of his own, quoted Marshall Petain, Tom Dooley and Rudyard Kipling, admitted that Rotary was not the most important thing in his life, confessed failure, and left us admiring the man for his candor and his ability to focus on the principles on which Rotary is based."[3]

Reflecting on his Rotary service, Duff said, "Rotary is a good cause, though I often wonder what I am doing when I think about how far away I am from home and other important matters. The program involves some high principles and noble objectives and some very good people, which is why I affiliate."[4]

NOMINATED TO BECOME PRESIDENT OF ROTARY

Rotary International supports more than forty-six thousand clubs worldwide. It is governed by a board of directors that includes the president, the president-elect, the general secretary, and seventeen zone directors. The nomination and the election of each president are handled in the one- to three-year period before he or she takes office, making the whole process before becoming president a multiyear, pay-one's-dues, effort.

Duff rose quickly through the ranks and by the end of 1979 had been nominated to the Legislative Assembly and as a candidate for director. He was on his way, he was told by many senior leaders, to becoming the president of Rotary in a couple of years. He never ran for office but was repeatedly nominated by others.

Richard L. Evans, Duff's friend, mentor, and fellow general authority had served as president of Rotary from 1966 to 1967. Elder Evans was beloved by Rotary. Duff was being treated in the same way, and he was following the same path as Elder Evans.

---

2. John Dalton, Rotary International.
3. Boise Rotary Club Bulletin, Aug. 1977.
4. MDH-JE, June 5, 1977.

CARRY ON

In meetings in April 1978 with President N. Eldon Tanner and on May 4, 1978, with the entire First Presidency, Duff was instructed to continue his work with both national Scouting and Rotary. He was told they were so important that he should concentrate on them and represent the church and continue to do the immeasurable good he was doing there.

On November 14, 1979, Duff met with the First Presidency on another matter and told the brethren about his upcoming opportunity with Rotary to become its president and a similar opportunity to become the next president of the Boy Scouts of America. No member of the church had risen that high in Rotary since Richard L. Evans thirteen years before, and no one in the church had ever been president of the Boy Scouts of America.

Duff described for the Presidency the hefty commitment these opportunities would require over several years and asked for their counsel. All three were united—President Spencer W. Kimball spoke first and said that Richard Evans had done tremendous good for the church and that if it were possible to duplicate his performance, he would like to see it done. President Tanner declared that he thought Duff's participation and contribution were unique, that there was no other future in Rotary except through him, and that he thought Duff should continue. President Marion G. Romney also said he thought Duff should continue to do what he had been doing and that it was a unique opportunity of great importance.

Duff reiterated that if he were to continue in this direction, getting to these two positions would require several years of a kind of apprenticeship and that he would need to be indulged during that time. In the meantime, he didn't think these activities would unduly interfere with his service in the Presidency of the Seventy. Duff expressed to them his "willingness to either continue functioning as described, or to withdraw from them completely, as the First Presidency thinks best."

After discussion, the First Presidency commended him for his excellent service in these activities and agreed that he continue with them. Duff left the meeting to carry on.[5]

ROTARY PARK—SERVICE ABOVE SELF

At the top of City Creek Canyon in Salt Lake City is the Rotary Park Picnic Area, the uppermost section of which is dedicated to Marion D. Hanks as the "Service above Self" area. It was dedicated on September 10, 1996. The large plaque there recites significant highlights of Duff's life, including leadership positions with the LDS Church, the Boy Scouts, the US President's Council on Physical Fitness and Sports, and of course Rotary International.

Part of the plaque reads, "Duff's service has been basic in his worldwide experience. The life of Marion D. Hanks lends special meaning to the motto of Rotary International: "SERVICE ABOVE SELF."

---

5. MDH-JE, Nov. 14, 1979.

49

Scouting

"On my honor"—what an ennobling phrase!
Three short words, but the summation of all we call character.[1]
—Ezra Taft Benson

The ideals of the Boy Scouts of America (BSA) in the twentieth century almost perfectly meshed with the principles and values that Duff held dear. Building youth, teaching honesty and integrity and discipline, loving God and helping one's fellow man, loyalty, and patriotism—these along with other traits were the backbone of Duff's vision of what was right with America.

Duff became a Scout at twelve years old in 1933, and he served as an assistant Scoutmaster at seventeen, later becoming a member of the Great Salt Lake Council and its vice president. Over the next six decades he supported Scouting in any way he could. After a short hiatus from official connection, he began accepting numerous speaking invitations at various Scouting events. Soon he began to participate in the national leadership of Scouting, serving on the National Explorer Committee and on the BSA National Council Public Relations Committee. Eventually, Duff advanced to become chair of several powerful Scouting committees, including the Property Committee and the Camping Committee, and became a member of the National Scouting Executive Board. Duff was awarded every high-ranking award given by the Boy Scouts, including the Silver Beaver (1968, for local service), the Silver Antelope (1970, for regional service), and Silver Buffalo (1988, for "nationwide service to the BSA, and the youth of America"). Duff's entire family went to San Diego, California, to watch him receive the prestigious Silver Buffalo award.

He was also the first honorary inductee of the Eagle Scout Association (1973), on the senior staff at multiple jamborees, and he participated on or chaired the LDS Church's Scout Committee for many years. He was also responsible for creating the Family Life merit badge.

Duff didn't usually make a big deal of getting awards, but he seemed really pleased at being recognized for his many years of trying to improve America's young men. One can often tell what individuals value in life by what they hang

1. Ezra Taft Benson, "On My Honor," address at Boy Scout Encampment 1988, Island Park, Idaho, Aug. 1988.

on their office walls. Duff always had his Scouting pictures front and center for all to see.

STARTING OUT

Duff was involved in Scouting with Troop 59 of the Nineteenth Ward from 1933 to 1939. His first Scout hike was to Lake Blanche, a 6.5-mile round trip from its trailhead in Big Cottonwood Canyon. He was twelve, he loved his bishop, Eli LeCheminant, and he had a good Scoutmaster (see pages 29–30).

Duff's recollections of that first hike included the addition of canned food to each boy's pack, which became so heavy that none of the Scouts could lift his pack off the ground. He said, "So they'd have to lift it up on my back, and this was also true of the other kids. The big strong boys could probably handle it. I remember feeling so embarrassed because I couldn't lift that pack."

Other adventures on that hike remained fresh in his mind. A convict had escaped from the Utah State Prison and was rumored to be up in the hills. The assistant Scoutmaster had an axe and told the boys, "Well, I hope he comes here. I'll split his skull with that axe." Duff wrote, "The guy didn't come, and so all our mystery and adventure were dissipated. We did everything that was good on that hike. We had a nice rainstorm, and so we had to dry our equipment over the lines they put up. It was a memorable experience, my first and one of the best."[2]

His youthful journal (written with a vocabulary of a sixty-year-old man) describes a July 1939 trip to Lake Steiner Boy Scout Camp ninety miles east in the high Uintas. He invited his buddy Sterling Paul to accompany him. After they arrived at the camp, they prepared lunch and discovered their entire eight pounds of hamburger was "quite thoroughly infested with fly eggs," so they had to toss it all out. The rest of their time was full of typical Scout camp experiences and adventures with fires, and hikes, and rowing contests.

Duff's most memorable part of the experience was the wisdom imparted by top Scout executive Don Carlos Kimball: "Never pattern your life or character after just one man. Pick out the best traits and qualities of men as a whole to mold your character." Sixty years later, Duff still remembered all of what this man taught him on those hikes and at that camp.

LOCAL INVOLVEMENT

Duff began his involvement in Scouting leadership above the unit level when he worked for a short time as a Scout leader on his mission and later when he accepted positions as Council Explorer Cabinet Advisor and vice president for the Great Salt Lake Council of the BSA in 1959, as a member of the BSA Region 12 Executive Committee, and as vice president of the Western Region from 1969 to 1970.[3] After years of serving at the local and then the regional level, Duff was

---

2. MDH-R, June 20, 2000.
3. *Deseret News*, Feb. 10, 1959, 12A.

Showing scouting mementos for a newspaper article on the church and scouting, 1978. *Courtesy Church News*

elected to membership in the National Council. That was his initial foray into Scouting's national leadership, where he would serve for the next three decades.

SPEAKING AND TRAINING

Duff served for many years as a member of the Boy Scouts of America Speakers Bureau. That took him all over the country giving speeches. In January 1977, Duff gave a speech at the BSA Western Region Conference in California that rocked the Scouting world from coast to coast. In it, he spoke the unvarnished truth, including the boys' need for role models among men. Duff didn't hold back any punches. He talked about the complete lack of credibility of any drunken Scoutmaster and questioned how Scout leaders could indulge in habits and substances that they knew were not good for them, which they would not let their own kids use. Duff recounted, "There was some stirring, but I [delivered] it with laughter and good fellowship, and I think it was all right. John Clarehout came up after and said my words would be remembered long after this meeting. I hope so."[4]

The letters came pouring in, expressing gratitude for his willingness to address the issues head on: "Duff, your talk touched everyone there that night. You said things that needed to be said. We left inspired to do a finer job back in our individual communities."

4. MDH-JE, Jan. 1977.

Duff participates in a scout disability awareness training, Moraine State Park, Pennsylvania, August 1977. *Courtesy Church News*

His journal recorded, "Scout meetings, mostly across the West have been my biggest extracurricular activity this fall and winter. I've been to many of them and have had remarkable experiences. Stanford, Las Vegas, Richmond, and Reno have all been good."[5]

NATIONAL EXECUTIVE BOARD

In early 1977, Duff was elected to the Boy Scouts of America National Executive Board. He had been nominated fifteen years earlier, but he had felt at that time it was more important for an apostle to be on the board for the sake of the church's visibility and for the influence of the Quorum of the Twelve on Scouting, so he deferred and nominated Thomas S. Monson in his place. At any rate, in 1977 the following press release was issued about his election: "A leader of the Church of Jesus Christ of Latter-day Saints (Mormon)—one of the prime sponsors of Scout units—today joined former president Gerald R. Ford and two others as new members on the National Executive Board of the Boy Scouts of America."[6]

Duff's tenure on the executive board did not really change his continuing leadership of various committees, on which he had been participating for twelve years. He enjoyed his involvement, feeling that he was really making a difference. In his journals he commented on various decisions regarding specific issues. For example, in December 1979, he wrote, "The meetings were generally very good.

5. MDH-JE, Mar. 5, 1970.
6. BSA press release, Feb. 17, 1977.

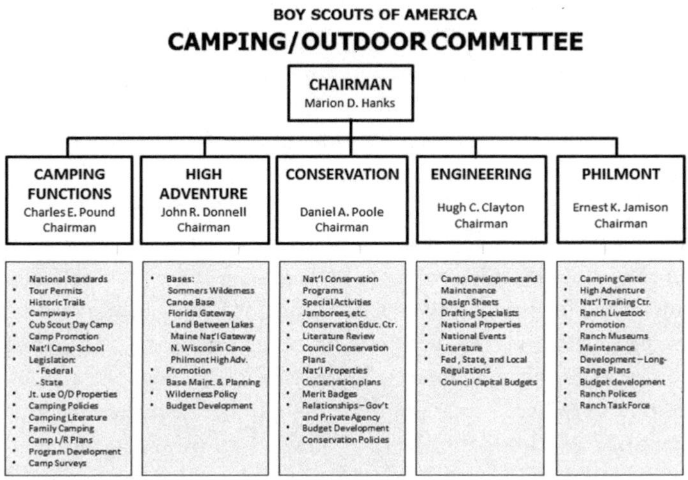

Organization chart of one of the scout committees Duff chaired, demonstrating the complexity of work in running such a large organization.

The toughest is the study committee for High Adventure. These involve six major bases and many millions of dollars. They serve only a few young men, but those young men are at an age where we are otherwise not able to reach them."[7]

Duff served on the executive board until 1980.

COMMITTEE PARTICIPATION AND LEADERSHIP

Over the years, Duff served on many committees of the Boy Scouts of America, including

- The National Council
- The Public Relations Committee
- The High Adventure Task Force
- The National Exploring Committee
- The Finance and Investments Committee
- The Jamboree Site Selection Committee
- The Special Task Force to relocate Scouting HQ to Texas (Chair)
- The National Properties Committee (Chair)
- The National Camping/Outdoor Committee (Chair)

The complexity of operating a nonprofit with 5 million young members and over 1.5 million leaders was extensive. For example, the organization chart above outlines the multiple responsibilities of the Camping and Outdoor Committee of the Boy Scouts, demonstrating the requirements of leading such a big and complex organization.

7. MDH-JE, Dec. 1979.

FIGHTING TO KEEP LDS SCOUTING ALIVE

Unfortunately, one of Duff's main tasks was to repeatedly defend Scouting to a few of the senior LDS leaders who did not like it. On many occasions, Duff had to resist others to keep Scouting alive in the church. He wrote, "To continue to fight the whole program of Scouting is unfortunate. They fight against it from the same basis—ignorance and inexperience."[8]

In April 1978, he wrote in his journal, "The day started with the General Scouting Committee meeting at which point I ran back for another meeting with the Young Women's Presidency. Then, I talked with Boyd [Packer] about several topics, including Scouting, and singles branches. I just frankly told him that I find myself repeatedly at odds with him on both issues and would like very much to hear his rationale on the subjects. Before we were through, he announced that he would not try to hurt Boy Scouting, although the reason he invited me to talk in the first place was to warn me he was going to hurt Boy Scouting economically, by saying we could no longer afford it. At the end, he changed and said he didn't intend to harm Scouting at all, so I don't know where we go from here."[9]

Duff bristled at the need to defend the church's participation in Scouting. He couldn't understand how others, who themselves had zero exposure to Scouting, could challenge the value of Scouting in a boy's life. Since the concerns were almost always to do with money, he said, "One wonders how our preoccupation with the small amounts paid to sustain Scouting stands alongside the reality of problems with our young people today—drug treatment, delinquency, custodial costs, and more, all run to large amounts of money. It becomes a matter of deep concern that Scouting is constantly on the defensive in these times."

In a lengthy 1989 letter addressed to Elders Marvin J. Ashton and Neal A. Maxwell, Duff wrote about the importance of Scouting, including the following thoughts:

> The church is one of the largest sponsors of Scouting units, second only to the PTA and School Boards. The members of the church in leadership constitute a large percentage of Scouting at every level. Our people make important contributions. If we minimize or constantly attack it or put it on the defensive, we endanger our influence with multitudes of men and boys in Scouting across the country. We would deliver a serious blow to Scouting if we ever backed away. I believe we have a great responsibility to our own people and to the youth of this nation. Who will do the work if Scouting is phased out?[10]

Twenty-nine years later, in 2018, after more than a century of partnership, the church officially severed ties with the BSA and pulled four hundred thousand young people (about 20 percent of its membership) from Scouting. While

8. MDH-JE, May 3, 1972.
9. MDH-JE, Apr. 19, 1978.
10. MDH-L to Marvin J. Ashton and Neal A. Maxwell, Oct. 30, 1989.

LDS youth may still join Scouts, the church as an institution stopped sponsoring troops and began its own youth initiative in 2020. Reasons given include the need to have a uniform program around the world and diverging values between the two organizations.

JAMBOREES

Duff attended national Jamborees in 1964 (Valley Forge, PA), 1969 and 1973 (both in Farragut, ID), 1977 (Moraine State Park, PA), and in 1979 he attended the international Jamboree (Sweden).

After visiting his first Jamboree in 1964 as a church representative, he was invited by the Scouting leadership to accept a more integral role as a senior staff member at future jamborees.

He served as assistant camp chief, director of relationships, chaplain general, and many other positions. But his main enjoyment came from speaking and teaching the scouts. Said Duff, "My chief joy in Scouting ... is meeting these young men, whom I've been privileged to visit in their camps and along the paths of the jamboree."[11]

In 1973, Rich attended the Jamboree in Idaho. Duff wrote, "Maxine was fully compatible with the decision for me to accept being senior staff at the jamboree, since it involved my being with Richard in this once-around-the-course opportunity for him." Rich and Duff had very little time together but did manage to sneak away a few times briefly.

Duff really enjoyed the experience, and found it impressive to watch 30,000 young men and leaders pour into the jamboree. Chief Scout executive Alden Barber arrived, greeting Duff and saying, "It wouldn't be a jamboree without you, Duff."

The next morning, at the opening ceremony, tens of thousands of kids grouped together around marvelous flags of various kinds. He later wrote:

> "No place that I know of outside of military compounds is the great experience of the flag raising with a marvelous band playing, quite so moving. It made me weep, and many others also, when the great flag went up.
>
> I smiled to myself today as I thought about an afternoon at the national Scout Jamboree when, sloshing through the rain, soaked myself, I saw a youngster sliding down a mud bank into a mud puddle. He was as wet and muddy as anyone could get. I said to him, "Son, you don't look unhappy with the rain."
>
> He said, "No, sir."
>
> I said, "You don't wish you were home, then?"
>
> "No, sir. They would never let me do this at home!"[12]

One of the most challenging situations Duff faced at a jamboree occurred when a young Scout from Santaquin, Utah was struck by lightning. The lightning bolt struck, breaking into branches along the ground in all directions, and pinned

11. "LDS Official Visits Scouts at Farragut," *Idaho Statesman*, July 16, 1969.
12. MDH-T, "Seeing the Five A's," GC, Oct. 1977.

With Rich at the National Scout Jamboree, Farragut, Idaho, 1973.

fourteen-year-old Cal Armstrong to the ground. The impact of the main bolt was so intense that several Scoutmasters in nearby tents were thrown against tables.

When the lightning hit, Duff and several Mormon chaplains raced to the scene. While Cal was attended to by the medical staff, Duff gathered together the frightened young boys who had witnessed the incident, hoping to calm and reassure them. Despite the storm that continued to rage outside, peace filled the tent. Duff told the boys that this experience would help them grow up in a hurry, if they hadn't already begun the process. "Mortal life is temporary," he said. "We need to appreciate the gift of life and the importance of living it well. What each of you can decide today," he said, looking intently at the young men in the tent, "is that life has great meaning that goes beyond this world. And so, we want to be living in a way that will make us feel comfortable with our Heavenly Father when that time comes."[13]

Duff notified Cal Armstrong's parents. Sister Armstrong caught the next available flight to Pittsburgh and stayed with her son at the hospital, where Duff met with them and where, still comatose, Cal passed away four days later.

13. Undated newspaper clipping.

ASCENSION, THEN RESIGNATION

Duff loved everything about Scouting and America. As time went on, Duff rose to higher and higher positions of leadership. Historically, senior LDS Scout leaders had a reputation of not being willing to pay the price and roll up their sleeves. Duff destroyed the stereotype by pitching in on numerous committees, eventually becoming chair of the powerful Properties Committee and then the Outdoor Camping Committee. He wrote, "Suddenly, to them, I'm smarter than I look, and I'm a Mormon who actually shows up. To them, I was a Mormon leader who showed his intent through his actions."[14]

And then in May 1978, Duff was approached by several leaders at the National Scout Conference asking if he would accept the job as national president.[15] They were prepared to nominate Duff to be the head of the Boy Scouts of America, a position no other Latter-day Saint had ever come close to.

Duff had visited with the First Presidency about his being in the queue to become both the president of Rotary International and the president of the Boy Scouts. He had been clear about these two opportunities and what they would mean for the church and its reputation. He had explained that he didn't want to either hold them off or encourage them unless the First Presidency felt it would be worthwhile for him to accept. Duff had not coveted nor sought after either of these nominations, but he was pleased that others had thought well enough of him to nominate him.

Then one day, out of the blue, he received a call from President N. Eldon Tanner, informing him that he was being called to be the executive administrator for the church (now called Area President) of the Southeast Asia Area, with eleven missions and multiple countries to lead. Duff accepted the call and then brought up the subject of his upcoming Scouting and Rotary presidencies: "Two months ago, at your approval, I told the leaders of these organizations that I was in for the long-haul. President Tanner said, 'Oh, my goodness, I forgot about that. We'll [need to] call another man. Don't do anything until I can speak with the First Presidency.'" Duff went for a walk and decided he should accept the Lord's calling. He sent President Tanner a note to let him know.

The next day, President Tanner reiterated the decision and assured Duff that the First Presidency felt it was the right one. He told Duff that if they had remembered their previous instructions, they would not have extended the calling. That was comforting to him. President Tanner then conveyed that the Presidency wanted him to go on with his civic assignments, feeling them to be indispensable and of great value but still felt that he should take the appointment in Hong Kong. Duff wrote, "I chuckled a bit, and explained that these two commandments were mutually exclusive, and that the opportunity for the church to have someone be the president of these two organizations would be gone for decades."

14. MDH-R, June 27, 2000.

15. National President (changed to National Chair) was the title of the Boy Scouts of America highest volunteer position until the title was changed in 2018.

In February 1980, Duff wrote one of the saddest letters of his life, tendering his resignation from Scout leadership due to his assignment to live in Asia for the next two or three years. He wrote, "I intend to plan on working in Scouting as long as I am mobile and would be pleased to look forward to a resumption of some of my pleasant associations when we return from Hong Kong."[16]

He received scores of letters expressing sadness and encouragement from Scouters within and without the church—at all levels of the organization, from the chief Scout down to a young Scout whose parents helped him write a letter.

NATIONAL ADVISORY BOARD AFTER SERVICE IN ASIA

After his return from living in Asia, Duff served again on the Boy Scouts National Advisory Board. Unfortunately, his opportunity to be president of the Boy Scouts had passed him by, but he continued to serve and gave multiple speeches supporting Scouting around the country.

In his speeches, Duff would often ask Scout leaders if they were teaching young men of their own self-worth. Have they been inspired in developing the best in them? Have we been direct in motivating their talents and contributions? Have they caught a glimpse of what a man can be? Duff spoke directly to the future of these young men. He would tell them, "We expect of you that you be young men intelligent enough and strong enough to get ready for the future by meeting present challenges. This country is going to need you."

Duff worked with the Scouting Relationships Committee and Church Scout leaders to create the Family Life merit badge. "The *Family Life Merit Badge,* recommended by the family task force under Duff Hanks' leadership, was presented to the Scout Advancement Committee on February 4, 1991, which, the next day, recommended to the Boy Scout Committee that it be adopted. That committee approved it as a new merit badge, and the pamphlet is scheduled to be released to the field in the fall of 1992."[17]

MARION D. HANKS SCOUT CAMP

A few years after Duff's death, one of his missionaries, Hyrum Smith, spearheaded a fund-raising effort to build the first Scout camp in southern Utah. The camp was to be named the Marion D. Hanks Scout Camp at Quail Creek. In his pitch to donors for money, Hyrum wrote: "Elder Hanks was known internationally for his work with Scouts. I had the life changing experience of serving as one of his missionaries in London many years ago. I promised that I would not get involved in any more fund-raising campaigns. But I am breaking my promise for this." In June 2016, the multiuse center at the Scout camp was officially opened.[18]

16. MDH-L to James L. Tarr, Feb. 13, 1980.
17. Duff's notes from the minutes of the Relationships Committee, Feb. 18, 1992.
18. Newspaper clipping, St. George, Utah, June 2016.

THE THINGS THAT MATTER MOST

50

The 1980s, an Overview

The 1980s began with Duff and Maxine picking up their lives and moving to Hong Kong—far away from kids and grandkids.

In the months previous to their move, Duff was released from everything he was in charge of, including being a member of the Presidency of the Seventy, a member of the Church Board of Education (after eighteen years), chairman of the Deseret Gym, a member of the executive committee of the Boy Scouts of America, and a legislative delegate for Rotary.

After their return from Asia, Duff and Maxine were called to the Salt Lake Temple presidency. In October 1984, he was called to again serve in the presidency of the Seventy. By that time, he was almost sixty-three, was exhausted, had served half his life as a general authority, and was the oldest and most senior member of the quorum.

For eighteen months, beginning June 1985, Duff served as the executive director of the Correlation and Evaluation Department and Chairman of the Communications Coding Committee.

And then in 1986, Duff was called as the executive director of the Melchizedek Priesthood Department and as a member of the Priesthood Executive Committee. A year later he was also called, for the second time, as executive director of Military Relations. He held all these callings until he was given emeritus status in August 1992. And of course, he continued his heavy load of speaking at stake conferences, mission tours, firesides, and so on. He visited India again, as well as the South Seas. He served on the board of Deseret Book, dedicated the site for the new Primary Children's Medical Center, and fulfilled a whole slew of other engagements. Duff had always performed a substantial number of marriages and spoken at funerals, but as he and the people around him aged, the number of requests for him to speak at funerals continued to grow.

Administrative changes in the church during the decade included instituting the three-hour block of church meetings on Sunday, transferring responsibility for building costs from local congregations to church headquarters, and installing over five hundred satellite dishes linking church headquarters to the world.

Church President Spencer W. Kimball passed away late in 1985 and was succeeded by Ezra Taft Benson as the prophet and president of the church. Four years later, in 1989, the Second Quorum of the Seventy was created.

Duff and Maxine's family life also saw significant changes. They became empty nesters in 1983 when Richard was fortunate enough to marry Elizabeth A. Winters.

Conservative politics held sway when Ronald Reagan was elected president of the United States. Sandra Day O'Connor was appointed the first female US Supreme Court Justice, video games gained popularity, new computer technology emerged each year, and the Berlin Wall came down. Other LDS events of the 1980s closely affected Duff.

GENEALOGICAL REVIEW

In late 1979, the Quorum of the Twelve asked the Presidency of the Seventy to undertake a review of the Genealogical Department because of concerns with its work of name extraction, a program in which names for temple ordinances were supplied by members. Working at stake or multi-stake sites, thousands of record extraction workers copied information and dates from microfilmed records of many countries, followed by data entry workers entering this information into large computers. Despite being significantly more efficient than previous methods, a few general authorities were concerned that the extraction program weakened the spirit of "turning the hearts of the children to the fathers" when compared to the traditional method of members seeking only their own ancestors and family lineages (see D&C 110:15).

Duff was assigned to do the bulk of the work and to write the report to the Twelve. His response to the assignment in his journal read, "It is interesting that this assignment fell to me, since no one—no one—was more ignorant of genealogical matters than I. I've had occasion to read and refer to principles, but I have never had much to do with the genealogical department. With this assignment, it became necessary that I know what I am talking about and so I undertook to learn, spending many hours listening and investigating, and coming to some comprehension of what they are trying to do."[1]

Duff wrote the report, shared several drafts with the other six Presidents of the Seventy and with Genealogical Department leaders, and then submitted the formal answer from the Seven Presidents to the Twelve. Duff's report said that name extraction was felt to be highly productive and had generated considerable excitement in the church, did not diminish the spiritual fervor traditionally associated with direct personal research efforts, and was becoming a significant influence for good in the church. The day after the report was submitted, each of the general authority leaders of the Genealogical Department called Duff to express their heartfelt gratitude for his help and openness and support.[2]

1. MDH-JE, Feb. 13, 1980.
2. MDH-JE, Feb. 4, 1980.

NATIONAL COUNCIL OF WOMEN IN UTAH

For the first time in its hundred-year history, the executive committee of the National Council of Women held its monthly meeting in Salt Lake City at the invitation of Elaine Cannon, the church's general Young Women president. As a part of their visit, Duff spent time with them on Temple Square, teaching them about church beliefs and answering questions. Sister Cannon's follow-up letter to Duff began, "It seems that we are forever thanking you and thanking God for you. Each visitor expressed to me her personal surge of hope and sweet feeling about the Savior because of your remarks and your urbane demeanor."[3]

WELFARE SERVICES IN DEVELOPING COUNTRIES

During Duff's work with the members of the church in Southeast Asia in the early 1980s, he felt the need to find a way to help members in his area improve their living conditions. He worked with the Church's Welfare Services to further develop and implement a set of lessons on basic living practices already in development. The lessons included five units on disease prevention, nutrition, personal hygiene, home health care, and gardening. First tested in the Philippines in July 1982, the program expanded to 112 wards around the world by 1985.

CONTINUAL COUNSELING AND HEARTACHE

All the while, Duff continued to be involved with individuals' specific problems. For example, in a heartbreaking journal entry from a visit to Indonesia, Duff wrote, "Much of the day was spent at the hospital with a family whose mother, a Relief Society president, was killed riding on the back of her husband's motorcycle. What a sad story. Great couple. Eleven children; she a community leader. He, a former military hero. He was drastically injured; all the children were at the hospital while we prayed and then administered to him. He was partially conscious, having just learned of his wife's death. It was a touching and terrible time."[4]

MELCHIZEDEK PRIESTHOOD DEPARTMENT

In December 1986, Duff was called as an executive director of the Melchizedek Priesthood Department and as a member of the Priesthood Executive Committee. He defined his role as being responsible to look out for the well-being of four groups:

1. Less-active church members wanting to retain at least nominal affiliation.
2. Male members not holding the priesthood office they should.
3. Individuals formally separated from the church.
4. Individual members not known to leadership or not wanting to retain affiliation.

Duff met with Elder Neal A. Maxwell, who had been asked to chair a committee exploring new ways to work with those less involved with church activity.

3. Elaine Cannon to MDH, Nov. 21, 1983.
4. MDH-JE, Aug. 6, 1981.

In that meeting, Duff expressed his feeling that the only way to deal with such individuals is on a person-to-person, one-on-one basis and that the current structure and programs of the church made doing so unlikely. Right off the bat, Duff offered two convictions about his new calling:

1. Combine the elders and high priests into one quorum.

He believed that many of the issues that beset wards were caused by too much pressure and responsibility being put on the elder's quorum president at a time in life when he is newly married, with a young family and a young career, and inexperienced in church leadership. He wrote, "If the Melchizedek Priesthood in a given ward were grouped together in one quorum, the combined capacities of the elders and high priests could be more effectively put to work. We're not talking of one lost sheep. We are talking about 33 or 34 men, often who do not have the priesthood and who need warm and loving attention. They are not getting it now, and never will under the present system." He supplied more detail, "Suppose that men released from church callings return to the elders quorum and give their attention to matters at hand. If they joined together there would be a great advance of strength. This would provide leadership to the quorum, and give the high priests, often still young men, something to do other than talk in their quorums about things that are removed from their real life."[5]

Thirty-two years later, in March 2018, the church announced that high priests and elders would be combined into one quorum in each ward. This restructuring was made to "increase unity and effectiveness."

2. Use full-time missionaries to serve and build.

Duff continued to press for using full-time missionaries in Christian service to build the kingdom. He wrote in his journal, "Suppose the extreme emphasis on baptisms were mitigated, and instead of having the reputation as proselyters only, all our missionaries were sent out with the understanding that they were to build the kingdom. They could find and teach people and baptize them and stay with them, circling them and their friends and families with the warmth and light of the gospel. I reference our dear friend President Bob Sackley, who took a weak and threatened branch in Baguio, Philippines and turned it into a stake during his brief leadership, almost exclusively using that pattern."

Duff believed that these two changes would increase unity in the priesthood, with young missionaries learning better how to work with priesthood leadership to build a branch or ward and in more effective use of priesthood resources and leadership. He wrote, "My solemn judgment is that if the above two major adjustments were made, there would be no negative consequence, and there would be a strong and growing increase in the very matters where we now have distress and threat for the worldwide church."[6]

5. MDH-JE, Dec. 19, 1986.
6. MDH-JE, Dec. 19, 1986.

As mentioned previously, in 1992 the church established a program requiring all missionaries to spend four hours a week in community service. That was later increased to ten hours.

TEMPLE DEDICATIONS

Duff was invited to speak and participate in several temple dedications in the 1980s: for example, the Tokyo Japan Temple in 1980, the Boise Idaho Temple in 1984, and the Chicago Illinois Temple in 1985. The Tokyo Temple was particularly important to Maxine and Duff because Maxine's parents had served as a missionary couple there for a few years before Maxine was born in 1925. Although Maxine's mother, Arva, had recently passed away, her father, Elwood Christensen, was still living, and he paid for all his children and their spouses to meet together in Japan to celebrate a temple finally being built in the land of the rising sun.

51

Hong Kong

I'll go where you want me to go, dear Lord,
Over mountain or plain or sea.
—Mary Brown, Hymns, no. 270

In early 1980 Duff and Maxine began preparing to move to Hong Kong, where he would function as the new executive administrator (now called area president) for all the countries of Southeast Asia and the Philippines.

When the announcement of his calling was made in the weekly temple meeting, his colleagues were astounded. For the next few days, Duff was again inundated with kind and sweet compliments and congratulations. Each of his peers in the Presidency of the Seventy expressed their personal sadness with his departure. His family was stunned but supportive. In his journal, Duff wrote, "Maxine feels good about the proceedings. Our children responded uniformly with encouragement and joy, but also with some tears."[1]

On February 28, Duff was invited to give his farewell to the First Quorum of the Seventy and then begin to unwind his responsibilities in preparation for the move to Hong Kong.

"BANISHED"?

Duff received numerous letters and private inquiries about his sudden departure to Southeast Asia and his having to give up the prospective Scouting and Rotary presidencies. People were surprisingly direct in their questions about his personal life. One individual wrote, "I mentioned to friends that I hadn't heard much from you lately. One of them said he heard you had been 'banished' to Hong Kong. If this is the case, may I say that I have long been impressed with your candid and honest approach to the gospel. It's too bad that church leaders such as yourself must bow down before the less tolerant of your ranks."[2]

In response to another writer, who effectively asked the same question, Duff wrote, "Yes, I was extracted from the potential of becoming the president of the BSA and Rotary Int'l, and then shipped off to Asia. Some offended friends wrote

1. MDH-JE, Feb. 4, 1980.
2. J. D. to MDH.

asking about our 'banishment.' But, we left—to *the most important service* we have ever given, in the refugee camps and missions of Asia. Never mind the motives; we can make something good out of the whole thing!"[3]

In a third letter he wrote, "It has been my dream for many years to see the church take its rightful place in acts of Christian service, to add to the great work of proselyting, and welfare services among its own members. When the brethren concluded to support this effort, I knew why I had been taken from some very important assignments in the United States to work in Asia again. This undertaking in the refugee camps is the direct expression of my own conviction."[4]

FIRST EXPOSURE TO HONG KONG

If the first chapter of their Hong Kong experience was the calling from President Tanner, the second chapter began when Maxine and Duff flew from Salt Lake City to Hong Kong for a preliminary visit. When they arrived in Hong Kong, they were met by Elder Jacob de Jager, the outgoing executive administrator, and Bruce Opie, director of Temporal Affairs, with whom Duff would be working closely.

The next day they were given a brief tour of the island and Duff's office at Kam Tong Hall, the first church site in Hong Kong. Duff was shown around a bit and hoped he could find an apartment near enough for him to walk to the office and where Maxine could stop by to see him. He had been flying to Asia regularly over the years but had been staying in hotels for a few nights here and a few nights there. Now they needed a more permanent place.

Duff jumped right into the new job, participating in a lengthy area council meeting, which he described as "very useful, with subjects of prime and immediate importance." The issues ranged from inappropriate student visits between mainland China and Taiwan, to securing facilities for upcoming area conferences, to politically sensitive issues in multiple countries. Many principal issues were not new to Duff, given his previous leadership assignments over the area, but some were new and pressure filled. For example, for the retranslation of the Book of Mormon, members in Taiwan wanted to use traditional Chinese symbols rather than simplified Chinese symbols, often used in mainland China and its communist government. Others had the opposite opinion.

Afterward, Duff and Maxine visited with the Opies and Elder de Jager, discussing details of apartments and grocery shopping and so forth, before visiting the Hong Kong Mission Home and the stake center and driving through parts of Hong Kong to get acquainted.

A month later they were living in Hong Kong full time. Duff quickly came up to speed with the work, while Maxine worked on the apartment and getting accustomed to life in one of the busiest cities on earth. The ward members were

3. MDH-L to "Ed," no last name, n.d.
4. MDH-L to Mr. and Mrs. Delmer L. Edmonds, Jan. 14, 1981.

kind and welcoming. The sight of Hong Kong harbor from their apartment window was spectacular. But the news in the papers each day quickly awakened them to the formidable task before them.

Duff wrote, "We will be traveling much through the territory in the next few months. It is a brooding and sobering part of the world. We hear almost daily of trouble here or trouble there, like coups and overthrows and expulsions of missionaries, and influxes of refugees. More than most parts of the world, it is a collection of temptation for the missionaries, and it is a wonder how well they do."

Duff tried to take a quick walk every day. He saw the elderly doing their tai chi every morning. The sights and smells of the street were overwhelming. About the weather, he wrote, "The heat has been an interesting discovery. With humidity near 100% and temperature high, the air is like walking under Niagara Falls. To and from town or work is a soaking experience. The Chinese go around wiping their faces, using umbrellas, keeping in the shade, and walking very slowly. We are not so bright."[5]

FIRST VISITS TO REFUGEE CAMPS—THAILAND

Right away, Duff felt a calling toward involving the church in helping with the huge problem of refugees. He wrote, "On July 16, I took off for Bangkok with Bruce Opie and renewed my taste of that city and my first view inside a refugee camp. Bruce and I made the trip alone, with refugee work in mind. I believe I have been pulled here, in major part, to do something about this."[6]

The church had a widespread reputation of being interested only in its own members and proselyting more new members. Because of that, church members and missionaries were not welcome in any of the refugee camps. Duff wrote, "They do not understand. But frankly, neither do we. All of my ministry I have been pleading and trying to lead us toward acts of Christian service and have been looked at as odd and extreme—'strange case, old Duff'" (For more on refugees, see chapter 52, pages 487–500).

When Duff arrived in Hong Kong, he received a letter declining the church's request to rent the Queen Elizabeth Stadium for upcoming regional meetings with the prophet. The letter said, "The Queen Elizabeth Stadium and building are constructed for the use of those who contribute significantly to the community. We cannot count among them the Mormons, who are known to be aggressive proselyters, but make no contribution of any kind to our community."[7]

When the church tried to buy a parcel of land in Hong Kong, everything was going smoothly and then the answer came back by letter, saying in effect, you can't buy the land. Where is your hospital wing? Where is your school going to be?

Duff wrote detailed notes about this trip to Thailand, commenting on all on the

5. MDH-JE, July 1980.
6. MDH-JE, July 1980.
7. Rejection letter from a government agency, Hong Kong.

variety of things he saw, including back roads, water buffalo, small businesses everywhere, and the miniature elaborate spirit "houses" in front of each home. He then wrote, "It is into this setting that our great young missionaries trudge the streets, trying to tell people about Joseph Smith and Jesus Christ or other strange people in whom they are uninterested and care to know nothing. There must be other ways."

TAIWAN

Duff's next trip was with Maxine to various cities in Taiwan, meeting with mission presidents Miner, Baker, and Powelson and the missionaries. He visited missionaries in the hospital and attended to matters with the embassy in Taipei.

He wrote, "We heard from a great group of young people working under hard circumstances. The cities are behind the times. Traffic is unbelievable. We had a long taxi ride from the airport which was made on two wheels mostly. Maxine was sick. So was I. When I paid the bill, I was sick again. Too weak to argue."[8]

CULTURAL FUN

Back in Hong Kong, Duff's new secretary was totally unabashed in sharing her thoughts. He wrote, "She started what I thought was a philosophical discussion about the size of things here. Says I, 'I am used to small things, small beginnings.' She grins and says, 'I was thinking of *your* size, particularly your elephant fingers.' Unabashed, she was, in saying that, totally unabashed."[9] He became accustomed to the mostly innocent put-downs.

SINGAPORE AND INDONESIA

Maxine and Duff then visited Singapore and Indonesia. When he had last been there, fifteen years earlier with Keith Garner, there wasn't one local member, only a few British and Aussie servicemen. Now there were seven hundred or so, with a few expatriates mixed in. President Talmage Jones was on his second stint as a mission president, and he and Duff hit it off right away. They worked together in a mostly unbroken demanding pace of meetings, teachings, and effort.

Singapore was clean, progressive, and vital. Indonesia was much different—old, dirty, and struggling. Day versus night in comparison. The missionaries were working without visas and with no replacements on the horizon, so they lived in an atmosphere of pressure. In Singapore, only a mission president and one non-native missionary were allowed by the government. Neither the Singapore nor Indonesian missionaries could proselyte in those countries, so instead they thought up creative situations where individuals could approach them. Health was also a continual problem. And yet they soldiered on, proclaiming the word.

MISSIONARIES IN HONG KONG

Duff described the Hong Kong missionaries as "full of fire and functioning properly." On one Sabbath day, he drove all the way into the New Territories to

8. MDH-L to family, Sept. 1980.
9. MDH-L to family, Aug. 1980.

Yuen Long, where the Saints of the Hong Kong District were waiting. The building was filled and mission president Mitchell and Duff each spoke, and then Duff moved to the blackboard to do some training. He remarked, "This mission had me walking into a situation designed to emphasize 'the myth.' The missionaries all leapt to their feet, and I was supposed to proceed to the stand like the prophet does at general conference." Instead, Duff insisted on going through the crowd and shaking hands with everyone—something he much preferred to the standing ovation.

MISSION PRESIDENTS

One of the advantages of being closer to the area was getting to know the various mission presidents and their wives much better. Duff had such respect for these good couples and the sacrifices they were making to lead their missions. He watched with gratitude the love they felt for their missionaries. Several times a year, Duff gathered all of them together for training, with the high point of the conference being the sharing of testimonies. One interesting testimony was given by President Doug Powelson of the Taiwan Taipei Mission, who shared that many years before, Duff had set him apart as a young missionary to Hong Kong and told him things in that blessing that had come to pass. He also told the others that when Kam Tong Hall, where they were meeting, was purchased by the church, he lived there in a decrepit back room, combating rats and bats and fears, never dreaming that he'd be back, years later, speaking in the same room as part of a mission president's seminar.

THE ETERNAL EVERYDAY

Duff continued learning and leading as he went. Occasionally he wrote a letter to his children trying to explain day-to-day events. He wrote, "Yesterday I was on the telephone with five mission presidents, went to speak to 200+ of our young people meeting at a youth conference at the Chinese University of Hong Kong, many letters, many large and small meetings, sent telexes, tried to get copies of mission budgets from two tardy missions, one of which had sent it in by mail weeks earlier and the other paralyzed by the inability on the part of the young elder to understand the complex forms, etc. Finally, I got some work done and walked home, arriving at 7 p.m. or so."

In the meantime, Maxine, without knowing the language, worked on making their apartment a pleasant place for them to stay. Duff called her a genius in getting things done.

Duff's letters home described busy days and never-ending challenges. One day, for example, included calls from three of the eleven mission presidents: one berserk missionary, one excommunication, the heart attack of a mission president, and a missionary missing for ten days who turned up in Los Angeles. "Had Area Executive Committee meetings with the department managers coming in to report to Bruce Opie, their boss, and me. They didn't know I'd arrived. This is an incorrect system, me having ultimate responsibility, but the non-ecclesiastic side not aware of that. My secretary is helpful and sweet and intelligent, but the language isn't—even though, in theory, she 'knows' English. She asks me, 'What is "back in the harness"? What is "safe at home"? What is "cart before the horse"?' She tries. Mostly I do it myself on my electric typewriter at work."[10]

Duff was pleased to find out that Spencer H. Osborn was coming to live in the Philippines as a full-time, unpaid regional representative. Duff described him as "one of the best men on earth." Their friendship blossomed over the coming months. Years later, when they were both home and Duff was called as the president of the Salt Lake Temple, he called Spencer to be his counselor.

Things never really got any easier. With eleven countries, there were always issues needing attention. At one report meeting in Salt Lake City of the executive administrators from all over the world, Duff stood and reported tongue-in-cheek that he hadn't had any missionaries thrown out of any countries since the previous month in Indonesia and had not had an overthrow of a government for about three weeks.

MAXINE KEEPS THE HOME FIRES BURNING

Maxine's letters home were typical of her—upbeat, self-deprecating, loving. One example included: "I miss you all so much. I don't like being 'preachy,' but I feel impressed to ask you if you're having your family nights and your family prayers? The longer I live, the more I realize the simple, sweet experiences in our own homes in life are the most important.... The meetings were great. We shook over 200 hands—calluses. They even asked for autographs—me! Imagine!! Love to all."[11]

In another she wrote: "Thanks for the pictures. I feel so lucky. We can hardly believe all your snow. What's the due date for your baby? Is it May? Dad just got home from dedicating another chapel in Taiwan. The aircraft carrier *Coral Sea* is here, so we had lots of servicemen at church. We are going to Bangkok on Tuesday for two days to go with David Kennedy to meet the Queen. Then Dad goes to India and two days later we go all over the Philippines. We love you!"[12]

THE PHILIPPINES

The Philippines was exploding with missionary work. A single trip in August 1980 involved eight days, four missions and three stakes. Duff had pleasant visits all over the country and presided and spoke at stake conferences on weekends. He loved the Filipino people—some of the most able, devoted, loving, capable people in the world. But the country was challenging, full of graft and corruption and constraints on the average person. On top of that, they had been visited with every natural disaster one could think of—earthquakes, volcanoes, and typhoons.

The members were incredible and willing to sacrifice for their families and the church. One bishop, in a meeting with Duff, told him that he couldn't stay

10. MDH-L to family, Aug. 1980.
11. Maxine to home, 1981, unknown location.
12. Maxine to Susan, Hong Kong, Jan. 31, 1982.

a bishop for much longer, explaining that he was trying to feed himself, his wife, eight children, his mother, and a crippled brother. He lived in a one-room dwelling built on stilts above the filth. He taught school six days a week and made the equivalent of eighty-three American dollars a month. But transportation cost so much that he and his wife had to decide whether the family would have a second bowl of rice that day or go to church.

Duff spent a lot of time in the Philippines. During his time there he created many new stakes and reorganized several more; each occasion was a blessing to meet with such decent and faithful people who loved the Lord.

Another important thing happened in the Philippines. Duff set up a test program with John Hill of the Benson Institute at Brigham Young University to go to Manila among LDS members and teach them how to kill intestinal worms. Nearly 100 percent of them had worms. The test program was a huge success and several years later was expanded to other countries.

The growth of the church in the Philippines has been incredible—there are now twenty-three missions, 123 stakes, and fifty-six districts of the church!

GENERAL CONFERENCE—THROWING DOWN THE GAUNTLET

In late September 1980, Duff and Maxine returned to Utah to attend general conference. While there, he held several meetings, including one that would prove vital to the future of the refugee program he had launched.

On October 6, Duff presented a formal refugee proposal to the Presiding Bishopric, and on October 9, he made the same presentation to the Welfare Services Executive Committee. He didn't hold back anything. In his journal and in a subsequent interview with BYU researchers, he said, "I stood before them and told them that while I was going perform my standard leadership duties, it was also my intent to take missionaries from various missions and place them into some of the refugee camps all along the border of Cambodia, Thailand, and the Philippines." Duff described how people were being killed as they fled for their lives and that the Vietnamese refugees were coming by boat, getting slaughtered and raped—and that the church needed to DO something about it. He told them about the letter denying the church's use of a stadium because "we are selfish and contribute nothing to the communities where we work."

One of the brethren asked, "How many baptisms will this cost you?" Duff replied, "*All of them.* There won't be *any* baptisms. We will do *zero proselyting.* And if anyone asks to be baptized, we won't baptize them, but we will send them to a free country where they can find and learn about the gospel. But.... we will be doing the work of Christ." He continued writing, "I wanted them to know that this was going to be different than it had been."[13]

They asked questions and deliberated and finally offered commendation and authorization to proceed. No negative votes. It was a huge day for Duff, but now the real work needed to begin.

13. MDH-JE, Oct. 9, 1980.

INDIA

India was in a category all by itself. Missionaries were not allowed in India. Religion was acceptable, but not foreigners, not missionaries, not proselyting. Duff wrote that, in effect, the Indian government was saying, "We've had 200 years of you and your Christian missionaries. Please excuse us from your further blessings."

Duff had taken Maxine on a trip to India fifteen years earlier, and she had vowed never to return. The sight of so much suffering and degradation had been too much for her to handle. She had thought she was managing okay, and then she was told that many of the children she saw begging had been intentionally maimed by their parents to make the begging more productive. It was a surprise for her children to learn that she had accompanied Duff on another trip to India. In a February 15, 1981 letter, he wrote: "Your very own mother and father have survived India and have returned to testify: We testify; we are glad to have been to India. We also testify; we are glad to be out of India. One of us will never go back. The other one will."

Duff had work to do and recommendations he wanted to provide to Salt Lake about the pioneer members in India who had been ignored or had waited far too long for decisions that were postponed. On his visits to the few struggling branches, he was pleased to mingle with the wonderful people there. For church services, the children sat in the front on the floor; behind them, the men; and behind them, the women. "They ask, 'Why do you come only every six months or year? When shall we have more teachers, books, support, teachings of Jesus? You come from President Kimball? Who is he? What message shall you deliver? We will listen.'"

Some people traveled six hundred kilometers, all night, to greet the visitors from the church and petition again for baptism. They went so far as to find out where Duff and Maxine were staying, and knock on their hotel room door, saying, "We believe. Please baptize us, so that we can teach our children with the Spirit and can baptize them." In one city, a teacher wrote a three-page essay, asking, "Why must I wait longer, when I believe, when I have read every page of the Book of Mormon and can quote from it freely?"

They traveled to Delhi, to Goa, to Bombay, to Hyderabad, to Coimbatore, and to Madras, and then to Colombo in Sri Lanka. Everywhere they went, they were approached by people who requested baptism. One man had composed a pageant for the church. Another showed Duff his Book of Mormon, notes and cross-references on every page. He had five sons who were well-educated professionals. He wanted to be baptized and to preach and teach and testify.

Along the way, they also met with Duff's Rotarian friends. One of them owned a university in Coimbatore, and Duff set the stage with him for a professor swap with BYU.

They traveled from big cities out to small branches, all with the same segregated church congregations, women in the back, men up front. Duff spoke at each stop.

Vera Jean Jones, Duff, and Maxine Hanks with members
of an LDS Church branch in India, ca. 1981.

In a few small communities, there were rudimentary LDS buildings. They were all oblong, one-story chapels. One had an organ somebody had sent to them. A nail had been put through one of the keys to hold it in place. Nobody could play the organ, so they just pumped it with their feet, "Whang, whang…" Whatever the song was, it had the same one-note accompaniment.

One of the more unusual things Duff learned was that once these people were baptized, they lost burial privileges, so members who died had to be buried in a sandbar, where the animals would then dig them up. He gave them instructions to immediately buy a piece of land sufficient for burials.

At one stop, there was a woman with her foot up and knee exposed, the flesh full of maggots. They were eating her alive, and Duff asked the mission president, "What are you doing for this lady?" He replied, "We can't take care of everybody in this condition." Duff took out thirty dollars and paid personally for a taxi to take her to the hospital.

Trying to figure out the unofficial leaders of the church in India was sometimes confusing. Duff and Maxine visited the home of one of the most famous unofficial "Mormon evangelists," in which they found candles burning before the Virgin Mary and four photos of a famous Indian guru.

The longer-term church members were full of warmth and gratitude. Some had been educated in other countries, joined the church, and then moved back home to India. A few sisters had met and married non-LDS Indian men in the United States and then moved to India—all were overjoyed to meet with church leaders.

In many cities, they met with senior couples working ostensibly on the cause of microfilming. These couples were having the time of their lives, both good and bad. After several weeks away, Duff and Maxine concluded this maiden trip back to India and returned to Hong Kong.[14]

Duff returned to India many more times, but Maxine, although willing to travel with him everywhere else, could not bring her sensitive spirit to accompany him there again.

PING PONG BALL

After the considerable effort made to move Duff and Maxine to Hong Kong, some leaders wanted him back in Salt Lake. Duff wrote, "After several months, I got a call from Mark Petersen inviting me to return home. I said, 'To do what? Resume flying out here every few minutes?' That would surely cost way more than living here. I told him that we had leased our apartment for two years, and that was the minimum we were staying. He was very kind to me and very supportive."

Duff had already been the leader for this part of the world several times before, and now, after living there, he didn't think the job could be done from thousands of miles away in Utah. Before Duff's calling to Hong Kong his predecessor, Elder Jacob de Jager had lived in Hong Kong, serving without counselors, and now Duff was doing the same. His viewpoint was captured in the old aphorism "You can't win a war working in the Pentagon." He later wrote, "I was living out there, and I spent about 20 hours a day trying to stay ahead of all the economic, political, and ecclesiastical problems. Not to mention coups, attempted bribes, real estate transactions, etc. Half the people in the world are out here!" Duff was vocal in his disagreement with the notion that all church leaders should live in Utah. He strongly believed that the church needed to decentralize its leadership and that the executive administrators (today's Area Presidencies) need to live in the area over which they presided, "He can't know what he is talking about when attempting to [lead] and instruct people living 8,000 miles away."

Despite those feelings, two years later the church had Duff's successor, Robert L. Simpson, resume leading the area from Utah, again without counselors and traveling back and forth. Eventually, the concept of Area Presidencies evolved over the decades, and today, the church is led by twenty-three Area Presidencies worldwide, each made up of three men who live within the geographical area they supervise.

MISSIONARY CHRISTIAN SERVICE

Duff continued to pursue his goal of encouraging the eleven missions of the Southeast Asia and Philippines Area to adopt and move toward true Christian service. Every missionary was given a personal invitation to do something useful for the people they came to know. Duff told them, "This isn't about one-time punch and cookies at Christmas or singing a song. It must be a consistent,

14. MDH-L to children, India, Dec. 1981.

enduring, dependable commitment." In a letter in January 1981, Spencer Osborn wrote to Duff about missions in the Philippines that were having success with this new emphasis: The missionaries in Baguio were using the evening of preparation day to take a branch member to visit inactive members, and all the wards and branches in that mission were participating in an effort to teach the members how to look after the lost sheep. Additional success stories flowed in from other missions. For example, two sister missionaries in the Singapore Mission were working with the Singapore Association of Retarded Children to set up a home-based training program for preschool children. The sisters felt they were having great success in doing Christ's work and in improving the credibility of the church by dispelling the people's fears and prejudices toward it. They wrote, "For us, this has been a different type of mission. Frequently, we have been bombarded by well-meaning individuals from home who have asked us repeatedly, "Have you had an opportunity to do any real missionary work?" Our replies are always the same: "We do real missionary work, all day, every day! This IS missionary work! This is the work of the Lord, described in Matthew 25."

A HOMECOMING IN HONG KONG

In July 1981, Rich finished his mission in Scotland and went to live with his parents in Hong Kong. Dad invited Rich to travel with him as he did his work in various countries, so they became companions for six weeks in the summer of 1981. They traveled to Bangkok, Chiang Mai, and Korat for meetings with missionaries and members in Thailand.

One of the meetings was held in a chapel that Duff had purchased with Elder Gordon B. Hinckley fifteen years earlier. One night, while teaching a principle, Duff mentioned an old aphorism, "Flowers leave part of their fragrance in the hand that bestows them." The next night, the mission president repeated that sentiment to a different audience, rendering it as "When you hold flowers, your hands smell." Funny misquote. It happened to Duff frequently.

Duff and Rich then flew to the Philippines, first to Manila and then to Baguio—meetings everywhere they went. Then they went on to Jakarta, Indonesia, where they escorted the last foreign missionaries out of the country by order of the government. This left twenty-five local missionaries in the country to do the work. A scary encounter took place at the airport when one of the expelled missionaries tried to smuggle a four-foot machete down his trousers as he went through a metal detector. Duff and the missionary were in a back room with the police for two-and-a-half hours trying to straighten things out, explaining that the boy was young and immature and simply wanted a souvenir of their wonderful country. They eventually let the traveling party depart (without the machete).

Then on to Singapore and then Kuala Lumpur, Malaysia—more meetings with missionaries, members, and government officials. In his journal, Rich wrote, "Dad was in meetings all day, every day on most days. Not just to attend them either! He is the main event everywhere he goes and is expected to perform to perfection each time. I feel sorry for Mom and Dad sometimes. Often, during our trips I felt like shaking the people and saying, 'Leave them alone!' But they just continue to give and give."

RELEASED

After a couple of years spent traveling through some of the most difficult conditions on earth, Duff wrote to his children, "There is still magic for me, increasing magic, in the glowing vision of a future, where inequities and injustices are no longer purposeful and tribulation no longer necessary or normal, and when 'The tabernacle of God is with men, and he will dwell with them, and they shall be his people, and God himself shall be with them, and be their God. And God shall wipe away all tears from their eyes; and there shall be no more death, neither sorrow, nor crying, neither shall there be any more pain'" (Revelation 21:3–4).

In a letter from President Ezra Taft Benson dated August 19, 1982, Duff was notified that he was being released from his duties in Asia. It was the end of an era. Duff and Maxine moved home to Salt Lake City.

52

Refugees

The world has Albert Schweitzer, the LDS Church has Elder Marion D. Hanks.[1]

"We visited the Bataan Refugee Camp in the Philippines. There we heard all about your pioneering work and it taught us the importance of service to the needy, whether in the church or out of it."[2]

During his visits to Southeast Asia over many years, Duff had become acquainted with the problems of refugee camps there. He was overwhelmed with the plight of those displaced from their countries, their homes, and all they knew and loved. He tried to convince other church leaders that doing Christian service should be as important for the church as proselyting. He also made the most senior leaders aware of how poor the church's reputation was in that area of the world. While other churches were building hospitals and schools and pouring money into refugee and other humanitarian needs, the LDS Church was considered to be full of self-serving proselyters. This view particularly bothered Duff because he felt there was no greater entreaty in the scriptures than the one found in Matthew 25 about serving "the least of these." And to him, there wasn't anyone more deserving than those in the large and growing refugee camps of Asia.

His vision to pioneer the church's work in Asian refugee camps extended the boundaries of Christian service beyond the membership of the church, and included the promise that *no proselyting* would be included in the church's efforts—straight Christian charity with *no strings attached.*

As things started moving forward during his full-time service in the Southeast Asia and Philippines Area, he recorded his excitement: "I've been working so hard to get this accomplished and I want to see it really move, so the church will not just read the scriptures about Christian service, but will do it, where it is needed most, in the way the Lord described."[3]

---

1. Warner Woodworth, as cited in Peggy Fletcher Stack, "Marion D. Hanks, Longtime Mormon Leader, Dies," *Salt Lake Tribune*, Aug. 15, 2011.
2. H. Burke Peterson to MDH.
3. MDH-L to family, Dec. 6, 1980.

REFUGEE CAMPS IN THAILAND

After Duff and Maxine had settled into Hong Kong for a few weeks, he and Bruce Opie traveled to Thailand to visit two refugee camps. At the Lumpini Resettlement Camp, they saw a teacher in a small room with thirty-two people inside, trying to teach while a loudspeaker was blaring in the background. He wrote, "Little children hung on our hands, legs, waists, and feet from the moment we got there. They got down on their hands and knees to look at the stockings the ladies wore, innocently looking up at the stockings to see how far they reached. The camp was reasonably clean, tragically endless, and mostly empty, but not for long."

It was in Lumpini in the mid-1960s that Duff had been with Gordon B. Hinckley to dedicate Thailand for the preaching of the gospel. Now it was a refugee camp with about two thousand people in transit. After persuasion, patience, and prayer, they began a small test there with the mission president's wife and three Welfare Services missionaries teaching grammar school classes.

They also visited Phanat Nikhom in the Chon Buri Province, another camp out in the desert being constructed to hold hundreds of thousands of people. They toured the camp with the United Nations director, a young Swiss man named Mario Howard, who listened to Duff's plans and was frank to speak about opposition from other churches, "who look at you Mormons as raiders who don't ever give humanitarian help. You have no support from the other agencies." As they walked along, Duff expressed the church's strong interest in helping the people. Mario wasn't very interested because of the church's proselyting reputation. Duff gave him his word, eye-to-eye, that this effort would be about loving the refugees in the way the Savior taught, that there would be no proselyting, no strings attached. He told Mario that the church would be preparing a video and other resources, that they would provide well-educated workers, and that they could be counted on to provide Christian aid without trouble from any of the other groups. He gave him his personal phone number, told him he lived in Hong Kong, and told him if there was ever an issue, he would fly there immediately.

Mario seemed impressed by Duff's sincerity and his personal commitment. He said he would give it serious consideration and talk to his supervisors. Within a week, Mario called, saying, "I'd like to have you come, and I'll provide an area for your people."

For the sister missionaries they built small little shacks the size of lean-tos. There were no indoor toilets, and the sisters had to get water out of a horse trough to wash. It was rudimentary at best. But it was a beginning.

FINDING THE PREPARED SISTER MISSIONARIES

It was time for Duff to find the right missionaries for the camps. During Duff's first visit to Taiwan, he spoke at a missionary meeting in Kaohsiung. He asked the mission president to please call on several missionaries to speak. President Baker suggested six. After those six spoke, President Baker asked Duff if he wanted to

Robert Taylor and Duff with refugee children at Lumpini refugee camp, Bangkok, Thailand, 1980.

hear from others. Duff said "No, unless you feel to." President Baker also said no, then reconsidered, and invited one more sister to come forward—Karen Gerdes, a convert from Florida. She went right to the point, saying she had felt direct revelation twice in her life, once when she had known the gospel was true, and again last night. She said she knew she was to speak and had been bewildered when not initially called on. It was a moment of high spirituality and lack of pretense.

Duff then spoke to the missionaries, using the blackboard. He noticed one pair of eyes that seemed far away. When the meeting finished, the eyes and her companion left, while all the others came forward to visit. The eyes and her companion returned later, and Duff asked her to please stay.

The eyes belonged to Rita Edmonds. Duff asked her what she was doing on a mission, and she replied that she was a Welfare Services missionary. Duff said, "Yes, but what are you doing on a mission?" This round of questioning was repeated two more times. Duff then asked what she did prior to her mission. She had several degrees and a PhD from Columbia in family education and community education (the very degree that was needed). Duff then asked, "Shall I tell you what you are doing here? You are here to open the work of LDS Christian service in a refugee camp in Thailand." Sister Edmonds burst into tears. When she regained control, she said she'd waited years and had been preparing and praying for eight months in Taiwan for this to happen. It was her special interest, her promised blessing. Sister Edmonds was perfect for the role in terms of

Duff and Maxine with Rita Edmonds, first Welfare Services missionary assigned to refugee camps, Thailand, 1980.

preparation, ability, and credentials. Duff transmitted her credentials to Mario, which strengthened his resolve to let the church in.

After the modest labors they had performed at Lumpini Park, Duff had solicited help from Salt Lake City to supply missionaries he could use in Phanat Nikhom, but they had no recommendations for missionaries with qualifications to lead the effort. And yet here she was, already serving in one of the missions in Duff's area. What are the chances that after the church could not find any qualified candidates, after weeks of looking, that the very type of missionaries Duff was looking for were all there, right in the area, over culture shock, with some language skills, and were high functioning, competent people?

At lunch, Duff asked the Bakers how they'd feel about losing their star lady missionary. They replied, "No, not Sister Gerdes!" Duff said, "No, Sister Edmonds, but I like your suggestion. Can we use them both?" The two were notified to get ready, and they became the pioneers of the first program.

Subsequently, Duff found two great sisters in Manila, three in Hong Kong, another at an area conference in Korea, and two returned Thai missionaries, and the group was formed. In one single tour of the missions, he had found the needed sisters. They each stood out from the crowd and were prepared and waiting for a special assignment. Duff wrote, "Thus began the first efforts of the

Phanat Nikhom Refugee Program of the church, directly through the inspiration and assistance of the Lord."

WHO WERE THE REFUGEES?

The refugees were made up of several different ethnicities: Vietnamese boat people escaping communism, Cambodians who were spilling across the border from Cambodia into Thailand, and Laotian people. Most had suffered terribly. Of the boat people, around fifty percent died en route, with 90 percent of the women raped or otherwise abused sexually during their escape and internment. Before the war in Vietnam erupted in the late 1950s, there were approximately nine million people in Cambodia. Pol Pot, their communist leader who came to power in 1976, terrorized and murdered his own people, and then in 1979 the Vietnamese communists invaded, pushing thousands more to search for a better life. Cambodia's population had fallen to around four million by 1980.

THREE OBJECTIVES

Duff repeated over and over the three main objectives of their refugee program:

1. To do good humanitarian work for those in need, following the Savior—with no strings attached. No proselyting. These are God's children who need help.
2. To enhance the credibility of the church as givers of service. Not credit, credibility.
3. To build the kingdom the right way, Jesus' way.

When it was time for him to leave his assignment in Southeast Asia, Duff wrote, "I can say with assurance that we have succeeded in these objectives. We have done good, unselfish things, in an effective way, for a lot of people. The 'we' means the fifty or so outstanding young women who have accepted the responsibility of these camp jobs under my direction. I found them in all the missions of Asia and have brought them together in some remarkable teams."[4]

PREPARING TO SERVE

In September 1980, Duff made two telephone calls to Elders Gordon B. Hinckley and Thomas S. Monson to ask if they would step in and break a church political logjam and help make at least one video for the sisters to use with the refugees. As a consequence, Bonneville Productions began making a teaching video called *A New Home*, on subjects such as cultural acclimation and language. Church Welfare Services began helping too. Duff wrote, "We are seeing the beginnings of a miracle; now what we need is to perform the miracle of going in and *doing some good.* I believe we have the people to do just that."[5]

A couple of months later, Duff wrote to his two colleagues, thanking them for their help and enlisting their continued help: "Dear Gordon and Tom, because of

4. MDH-L, July 1982.
5. MDH-L to family, Sept. 1980.

your great support in our beginning refugee efforts, we seem to be moving on steady ground. The video you helped create is being shown widely with complimentary reactions, including the wife of the American ambassador to Thailand, who said, 'This is the first time a program has been so well prepared before its start in the camps. You were ready with a plan, excellent personnel, with materials and equipment.'"

Despite early opposition, the United Nations High Command for Refugees took the courageous step to assign to the LDS missionaries the entire responsibility for the orientation process. This was good for all involved—the church, the missionaries, those who could open doors, and especially the large numbers of refugees who were helped.

Duff was pleased that their early efforts were favored by the Lord. He wrote, "We are well prepared. We need continuing creative thought, continuity of personnel, a couple to help with supervision, and qualified teachers in the pipeline now so they can be ready to replace our current group. Again, thanks. Good and Godly blessings, Duff."[6]

PHANAT NIKHOM TRANSIT CAMP

Around September 16, 1980, Sisters Edmonds and Gerdes arrived in Hong Kong from Taiwan. They had been called as the program director and assistant program director at Phanat Nikhom, which was the hub of all refugee activity in Thailand. It was the central place for the movement of all refugees from border camps to eventual resettlement in their new country.

In another miracle, the LDS sisters were given the responsibility for education, cultural orientation, and survival English, which meant the most direct contact with the refugees. Other agencies were assigned immigration, medical care, clothing, food, sanitation, recreation, and post office duties.

In addition to the video produced in Utah, which all the other agencies envied, the sisters were able to scrounge together a 'model home.' This was their version of a Western house filled with used furniture, appliances, bedroom, bathroom with a bathtub and toilet, and a kitchen with a refrigerator and stove, all of which were used to teach the refugees about the Western world.

The sisters named their organization the Welfare Services Unit for Refugees in Thailand (WSURT). They brainstormed ways to teach, eventually creating and implementing a full curriculum. Later, the United States government hired full-time specialists who spent six months developing curriculum for refugees that was no better than that developed by WSURT.[7]

"WE COULDN'T PREACH, BUT WE COULD LOVE"

In a March 1988 *Ensign* magazine article, returned refugee missionary Annette Stevenson noted, "We couldn't preach, but we could love." Along with not

6. MDH-L to Gordon B. Hinckley and Thomas S. Monson, Nov. 11, 1980.

7. Cindy Bateman, "A Very Exciting Mission: History of Refugee Camps Early 1980s," unpublished MS, Oct. 23, 1988.

Welfare Services missionary teaching English street signs to refugees in preparation for their relocation to the United States, 1980.

forcing North American cultural traditions on the refugees, Duff had to continually remind both the sisters and anyone visiting, that the church was not there to proselyte. Not 'wink, wink, nod, nod' but … nothing! "He was very stern about not proselyting," said Maryan Myres (later Shumway), one of the missionaries working with refugees. "He taught us that we should work with 'no strings attached,' that we should just do the work, because it needed to be done." She wrote, "As Elder Marion D. Hanks, who instigated missionaries to work in refugee camps taught us in the 1980s: 'Serve with no strings attached—without looking for any credit. Our purpose is to serve in a way that exemplifies pure religion. As you teach and visit with the refugees, you are sitting in proxy for the Savior.' None of us would ever be the same. How could we be?"[8]

Another sister, Cindy Bateman, wrote, "When asked by the refugees about our church, we simply told them that we belonged to The Church of Jesus Christ of Latter-day Saints, and if they wanted to learn more, they should find the missionaries when they were settled in their new country. Many asked us what it was that made us different from everyone else in the camp and pled with us to share the gospel with them. But we adhered to our commitment to the United Nations."[9]

Henry B. Eyring, then commissioner of the Church Educational System, wrote to Duff to thank him for explaining the direction of humanitarian work in Thailand: "I feel better about our experience in trying to help people in Thailand

8. Maryan Myres Shumway, as quoted in Peggy Fletcher Stack, *Salt Lake Tribune*, Oct. 3, 1992.
9. Bateman, "A Very Exciting Mission."

than about anything else I have done in a long time. Thanks for helping me lean in the right direction."[10]

BUT THIS ISN'T MISSIONARY WORK!

Letting go of traditional missionary work was a challenge for many missionaries and church leaders. In reading through thousands of pages of letters and Duff's journals, one can't help but note what 150 years of tradition had ingrained in the minds and psyches of members of the church. Some people just didn't seem to understand the importance of Matthew 25 and Matthew 28. It would almost be comical if it wasn't so sad. Before the missionaries arrived in the camps, for example, a single missionary, away from his sick companion, wandered through one camp. When asked if he were there to visit with Mormon refugees, he replied, "No, but they all soon will be." That was one of the tamer things he was reported to have said, which quotations were then relayed to the local government and the US embassy, causing a headache for Duff.

On December 6, 1980, Duff recorded another incident in his journal. "In the first week of December, an inconsiderate and uninformed member visited Bangkok, was somehow alienated by the mission president, and left vowing he'd use his influence with the 'brethren' to see that those missionaries get back to proselyting where they belong!" This kind of thing irritated Duff immensely. The man didn't visit the camp, didn't know a thing about the sisters or their qualifications, including that they were never proselyting missionaries in the first place. Duff wrote, "He is lamming his lumps around. If I catch him, I'll give him some more to lam."[11]

EXPANSION

While things were progressing in Thailand, President Garth Andrus in the Philippines Manila Mission sent a few sisters from his mission to serve as part-time volunteers in the inner-city refugee camp in Manila. President Bob Sackley of the Baguio Mission called on May 15, 1981, to tell Duff and Bruce Opie about a large refugee camp within his mission at Bataan (place of the infamous World War II death march). In June 1981, Rita Edmonds and Cindy Bateman flew from Thailand to the Philippines, where they spent five days networking. In Palawan they visited a camp of five thousand Vietnamese boat people. Providentially, the very person they needed to convince that Mormons were useful for the camps was seated next to them on the plane. She was the person who later decided that perhaps the LDS missionaries *could* be trusted and should have a place in the camps.[12]

Before returning to Thailand, they visited the Philippine Refugee Processing Center (PRPC) in Bataan, with seventeen thousand refugees. After some more preparations, Cindy Bateman and Maryan Myres left Thailand in November

10. Henry B. Eyring to MDH, Dec. 15, 1980.
11. MDH-JE, Dec. 6, 1980.
12. Bateman, "A Very Exciting Mission."

1981 to set up a program in the PRCP. And Sister Ruth Bemer was sent from Thailand to work with one of the sister missionaries from the Philippines Manila Mission to develop a program on Palawan.

At the PRPC, the only job not filled was the responsibility to teach refugees fifty-five years and older, so the sisters took it. They met with Duff, Spencer Osborn, and President Bob Sackley to plan for this new adventure. They chose the name Mormon Christian Services (MCS), proclaiming who they were and affirming that they were Christians. They did not initially know when they arrived that they would be living many miles from the nearest telephone, with no office, housing, or classrooms. Although the strict non-proselyting rules in Thailand did not exist in the Philippines, the sisters chose to continue their promise to do no proselyting among the refugees.

They began by trying to make friends with all the other agencies in the camp, from the smallest to the largest (with five hundred staff members and teachers). Then they got to work, made themselves a place to stay, organized classes, and overcame resistance from the other agencies. After Duff's next visit to the camp, the camp leaders helped the sisters convert some leftover lumber and supplies into classrooms and improved living quarters. In a short time, the church's contingent of refugee workers grew from two unknown, untested young women, into a fully staffed, well-functioning cultural and educational agency.

At roughly the same time, the work at the refugee camps in Hong Kong continued. In the camps right in the heart of the city, a few elders were permitted to visit on their preparation day. They would come in and teach all kinds of sports and musical instruments. After about a year of service in the Hong Kong camps, the church was permitted to offer some service in recreational leadership, driven by the discovery of a missionary in Taiwan who had taught recreational science at Brigham Young University. Despite heavy opposition from the other agencies and churches, she and her companions set up a recreation program at the Kai Tak North camp.

WINNING OVER THE OPPOSITION

Over time, in each camp, the most vigorous resisters became fans, offering apologies and the warmest kind of acceptance. One letter from the International Red Cross said, "These poor people are bewildered and overwhelmed by the mere act of survival. Your [missionaries] have given them a few moments of respite, a hope for a future where they can pick up the shattered threads of their lives. Working together with you, we've all become more understanding, moved closer together, and become more tolerant. We will all miss you."

When Rita Edmonds finished her mission, the church received a customized letter from the United Nations High Commissioner for Refugees, expressing how sorely she would be missed and calling her a "pioneer—capable, full of enthusiasm, cooperation, hard work, and talent."[13]

13. Nellie Chan to the church, May 21, 1981.

When Cindy Bateman left the Thailand camp to start operations in the Philippines, she received a similar letter from the same person, who wrote with warmth and affection and appreciation for all she and the others had accomplished.[14]

Duff considered the sister missionaries working in the camps and the senior couples assisting them as nothing less than true modern-day heroes. He tried to stay in touch with them and show an interest in them for the rest of his life. For example, years later, when Cindy Bateman graduated from medical school, he wrote to her, "I am more proud than I have any justification to be at what you have done and what you are. I cannot think it chance that you were where you were when you were. You did a great work and I remain proud of you. The Lord bless you now as you undertake the next phase of your continuing contribution and preparation."[15]

SWEET EXPERIENCES

The stories coming out of the camp were incredibly touching. "Imagine a young sister missionary on her knees, totally unconscious of the fact that there are hundreds of refugees watching her," Duff wrote. "She's got a little baby in her arms and a diaper on the floor. None of the refugees have ever seen a diaper before. She kisses the little baby and gently puts on the diaper and holds him up for all to see. The women crowd in and treat her about like they would have treated the Lord, if they understood Him."[16]

One of the missionaries wrote, "What a blessing this is. We've watched an unhappy, droopy-headed little girl that constantly cried, turn into an energetic, happy little helper who smiles and carries herself proudly. We've seen a little boy turn from a fighting little monster into an affectionate tease. We are surrounded by these children constantly, and they know we love them."[17]

One of the most meaningful incidents from the refugee camps occurred at Christmastime, when the sister missionaries put on a Nativity and explained the circumstances of the Savior's birth. Rita Edmonds played the part of the mother, holding the baby Jesus. Afterward, a woman came up to Rita and innocently asked, "The story of Mary, Joseph, and Jesus is a refugee story, isn't it?" Everyone was stunned by such a profound statement.

Rita Edmonds summed up her feelings about the refugee program: "Dear Elder Hanks, I remember how many times you talked of how the refugee program could make a major change in the direction of the church. I believed you but didn't understand. I am beginning to understand. The successes in the camps have turned the tide. It can be done now because it has been done—non-proselyting, international outreach by the church."[18]

14. Nellie Chan to Cindy Bateman, Nov. 3, 1981.
15. MDH-L to Cindy Bateman, May 27, 1987.
16. MDH, unknown origin.
17. Terri Ferguson to MDH.
18. Rita Edmonds to MDH, Apr. 13, 1982.

There was a feeling about the missionaries—the way they behaved and cared for the refugees. Even the hard-core detractors and initial enemies could feel it. Victor, the UN administrator, said, "There is still a great deal of fear among the other agencies that the Mormons will proselyte." Then he said, "Even if you don't ever talk about your religion, *your values come across like a ton of bricks.* And that scares people. *You live what you believe*—therein may lie your problem [with the others]—especially when it brings such inner strength, peace, and confidence."[19]

SO, WHAT HAPPENED AFTERWARD?

Efforts to help refugees continued to grow. In a letter to Duff, Maryan Myres described its impact after she and Cindy Bateman began teaching its principles in the Missionary Training Center: "Cindy and I were constantly amazed at your leadership ability and mostly for your philosophy of service—'no strings attached.' Cindy and I are now training couples and sisters in the MTC to teach refugees. How this work has spread!"[20]

It seems that the church has no way to exactly measure the influence of the refugee program on the number of baptisms. Since that was never Duff's primary motivation, he never pushed for such a measurement. Plus, it just seemed so obvious that the long-term result of Christlike love and service would be to draw people to the Savior and his church. As the wife of the Consulate General in Hong Kong said, "I expect you will attract more people to your church through your refugee efforts than you would proselyting."

A few surveys were conducted whose results demonstrated incredible growth, and the anecdotal stories began to flood in. Here are just a few of hundreds of examples, including some from many years later.

In June 1983, Joan Dixon, a former refugee missionary, completed an analysis of LDS Refugee Branches for a class at BYU. Her findings included the following:

- 65 Asian branches were found to exist, 50 in the US and Canada.
- Of those returning her survey (28), the average branch size was 85 members—biggest was 350, smallest was 7.
- More than half the branches reported church attendance over 100%, due to investigators.
- The average branch had been created in the last 18 months—the oldest was 3 years old.
- The average number of refugee leaders per branch was 4.[21]

Cindy Bateman wrote, "We adhered religiously to the commitment Elder Hanks had made to the United Nations, that is, no proselyting. Yet, in the six

19. Victor Dannet to Rita Edmonds, June 26, 1981.

20. Maryan Myres to MDH, Aug. 1982.

21. Joan Dixon, "Analysis of LDS Refugee Branches," CB679R, Independent Practicum, June 16, 1983.

months after my return, the number of refugees being baptized throughout the world was greater than the highest baptizing mission in the church. The thousands of refugees that were exposed to WSURT and MCS knew without a doubt that we were striving to serve them as disciples of Jesus Christ. That was the greatest miracle of all."[22]

A mission president wrote, "Elder Hanks, I thought you'd be interested in an experience enjoyed by our Vietnamese language missionaries here in Australia. They were walking down the street when they were stopped by a young man in his early twenties who told them he had recently arrived from one of the refugee camps in the Philippines. He told them he wanted to hear about the gospel. When they asked him why he was so eager, he told them that he recognized the name badges—the same ones worn by the sisters in the refugee camp, who were so kind and helpful."[23]

In December 1987, Duff received a sweet note from an elder serving in the Texas Houston Mission. He had been working with the YMCA International Service to translate for newly arrived Vietnamese. He said that the YMCA connection had been the source of twenty-five baptisms, including a new family of eight who immediately accepted the missionaries and the church. The family had been sent to the refugee camps in the Philippines and felt the spirit of the missionaries there.[24]

"Elder Hanks, I thought of you last Sunday as I heard a young Vietnamese girl bear her first testimony," wrote former mission president John Stohlton. "She said she first encountered the missionary sisters at a refugee camp in the Philippines, ten years ago. She spent six years in the camp and was so impressed with the love and service of our sisters, that when the missionaries knocked on her door, she immediately recognized their name tags and invited them in."[25]

REMAINING INTERESTED AND SUPPORTIVE

Although not formally involved following his release as Area President, Duff continued his personal campaign for the cause of the refugees and for institutional church involvement in acts of Christian service.

He mentioned refugees and Christian service in general conference talks in October 1981, October 1988, and April 1992. At a fireside at the Salt Lake Institute of Religion in December 1984, he told the story of the sister missionary teaching hundreds how to put on a diaper.

In May 1987 and again in February 1988, the mission president in the Philippines Quezon City Mission wrote Duff letters updating him on the Bataan camp and baptisms and telling about dedicating a small chapel there. He praised

22. Bateman, "A Very Exciting Mission."
23. John Stohlton to MDH, July 24, 1993.
24. Michael Morgan to MDH, Dec. 1987.
25. John Stohlton to MDH, July 24, 1993.

the impact of refugee missionaries on proselyting and thought Duff would be pleased. That was not necessarily so.

Duff wrote to the Area Presidency, voicing his concerns and expressing the view that the great successes they had were precisely because they did *not* proselyte during his tenure. He said, "It sounds like the present circumstance diminishes our greatest asset. We have again become aggressive proselyters. We intrude into the lives of these refugees at a time when they are in no position to make careful and measured judgments. I am deeply apprehensive about the ultimate effects under those circumstances. I think it will cost us hard-won credibility and much ultimate real growth."[26]

In May 1988, Ray Hillam from BYU wrote to him, updating him on the creation of a first-class group of scholars on international development, saying, "I often think of how you personally would be pleased with what we are trying to do. The church is making important steps along the lines you have been urging for years ... to assist church and non-church members with third-world problems."[27]

Duff continued to lobby for church involvement in Christian service. In a July 17, 1989, letter to Elder Neal A. Maxwell, he talked about energizing four main "assets" the church could use in volunteer Christian service: each priesthood quorum, every full-time missionary, twenty-three thousand Boy Scout units, and the auxiliary organizations of the church. He said, "And, in terms of reactivation, we could fashion the best and most practical activation that we have yet had. Those less active who do not respond to other advances, may well be motivated to service responsibilities offered."

The three essential goals underlying their work in the refugee camps repeatedly surfaced: Christlike service, credibility, and real growth, including true conversion. Those who participated in those early days in the refugee camps gave service they were proud of, with an almost universal response being "This is the most decent thing I have ever done. My life will never be the same again."

In September 1989, Duff brought up the topic again in a Melchizedek Priesthood Department meeting. He outlined the many opportunities for the church to participate in volunteer service within a community, including matching needs with church member skills, officially assisting with the homeless, implementing basic hygiene programs that were amazingly successful in Southeast Asia, getting the young adults involved, and teaching the Aaronic Priesthood young men to be of service not only to the church but to the community as well.

Duff continued advocating and petitioning for the refugee programs and institutional and individual Christlike service until he died. "At the end of Elder Hanks' life," wrote Maryan Myres Shumway, "I called Sister Hanks and asked if I could visit him. She cautioned me, 'He may not know you; sometimes he's

26. MDH-L to George Cannon, Area President, June 28, 1989.
27. Ray Hillam to MDH, May 25, 1988.

lucid and other times he's not.' As I walked into his room, I could see as I looked into his eyes that he did remember me. At the end of our visit, I asked him, 'Elder Hanks, what is the most important thing we can do with our lives?' In his true sage-like way, without missing a beat, he looked at me and said, 'You already know. *Service*.'"[28]

Since then, the church has significantly increased its efforts to provide assistance to those in need. It has been actively involved in humanitarian relief and development activities throughout the world, including disaster emergency relief assistance and humanitarian programs that strengthen self-reliance. Church-sponsored programs and websites like Just Serve "coordinate volunteer opportunities for people from every walk of life in the community to help and get involved."[29] As noted on the church's website, "There are many people in virtually any community in the world who struggle to meet their basic needs. The Church seeks to help as many as possible."[30]

28. Maryan Myres Shumway, online tribute to MDH, Apr. 17, 2016.
29. JustServe, justserve.org.
30. Humanitarian Programs, Church of Jesus Christ of Latter-day Saints, churchofjesuschrist.org.

53

Temples and the Savior

We go to the temple worthily seeking perfection, not professing to have already achieved it.
—Marion D. Hanks

He taught us to bring Christ to the center of the temple.
—Homer Ellsworth[1]

Duff's view of the temple placed all the focus on the Lord Jesus Christ.[2] He said:

Heavenly Father has provided this wonderful place for us to visit. A place where several things are going on simultaneously, each of which derives from and *points to the Savior.*

While in the temple:

We are *separated* from the world for a time, where we can quietly *review our status* before him and learn more of his expectations.

We participate in sacred *saving ordinances,* that by their very nature direct us toward the Savior and prompt us to walk the very path he walked.

We come in humility and meekness and gather together to learn through repetition the concepts of *accountability* and stewardship and returning to report our efforts to him.

We even dress in a manner that *removes the concepts of class and status* that the Savior so abhorred while he was here on the earth.

After we have been through the temple for ourselves, the rest of our experiences there are *acts of service* for others—service was Christ's main message while he was here on earth.[3]

Duff believed that the temple is a place of instruction. He often quoted President Spencer W. Kimball, who said, "The house of the Lord is *functional.* Every element of the design, decoration, atmosphere, and program of the temple contributes to its function, which is to teach. The temple teaches of Christ. It teaches of His ordinances. It is filled with His Spirit. There is an aura of deity."[4]

---

1. Homer Ellsworth to unnamed recipient, copy to MDH.
2. Recent changes to temple ceremonies have made the temple experience significantly more focused on the Savior than it was during the twentieth century.
3. Duff's personal notes on the temple.
4. Edward Kimball, *The Teachings of Spencer W. Kimball* (Salt Lake City: Bookcraft, 1982), 53.

WALKING THE SAVIOR'S PATH

The Lord declared that the temple is a place where "the Son of Man might have a place to manifest himself" (D&C 109:5). But many people come and go without paying much attention to the Lord's declaration. Many commented that the Savior didn't seem prevalent in the temple.

Duff felt the opposite—that the overall purpose of the temple is for us to learn more about the Savior and to learn how to become more like Him. He said, "As the mission of the church is to 'Invite all to Come unto Christ,' so I believe, in its clearest sense, that this is also the mission of temples, where we not only undertake the sacred service of work for redemption of the dead, but where the choice opportunity exists to learn of Christ, and to come to know Him, and commune with Him, and to purify our own hearts."[5]

He wrote, "I try hard [to teach] without delving into the arcane and mysterious, about which everyone would like to know. I neither know nor care, being satisfied with the lovely reality that the principles, clothed by the covenants, constitute the *central points of the Lord's life.*" In effect, Duff believed that, like the men on the road to Emmaus, we walk with the Lord and learn of Him and make covenants that, in concept, tie us to Him.

People were responsive to Duff's gentility and education in the temple.

THE COVENANTS ARE ALL ABOUT THE SAVIOR

Duff taught that the covenants we make in the temple match *the central principles of the Savior's life* and the path He trod. In every covenant we make, He is there. "Who best lived a life that demonstrated each of the covenants that you and I make in the temple?" Duff questioned. "The obvious answer is the Son of God. Was His not the most obedient, unselfish, and completely committed life to ever grace the earth?"[6]

Duff summarized the merging of the covenants we make in the endowment with the path of the Savior:

- "First, the *initiatory ordinances* are completed in His name and are efficacious through His shed blood. We receive a symbolic cleansing—a washing. Then, we are blessed and anointed, clothed, and given a guide to help us make wise choices.
- Next, the endowment begins with the symbolic presentation of the *Creation and the Fall*, with Christ fully involved.
- *Obedience.* The Savior came to do the will of his Father. We promise the same.
- *Sacrifice.* His life was geared to giving and to sacrifice. We promise the same, knowing that we may be led to a point of great sacrifice, as it did with Him.

---

5. MDH-A, "Christ Manifested to His People," in *Temples of the Ancient World: Ritual and Symbolism*, ed. Donald W. Parry (Provo, UT: FARMS; Salt Lake City: Deseret Book, 1994).

6. MDH, notes and outlines for speeches about the temple.

- *Love, the law of the gospel.* The law of the gospel is never fully explained, but Duff believed it refers to the Savior's desire to love God and love his children, as we must do also. He *loved* in a way perhaps only He and the Father understand. Similarly, we promise to love God and others and to be a true neighbor.

- *Discipline and purity.* Jesus demonstrated loyalty, fidelity, and purity, unmatched. He refused the things of this world. We promise to live a life of purity, fidelity, and discipline, especially relating to sexual expression. And finally,

- *Consecration*. The motivating power of His life was in seeking first the kingdom of His Father and being willing to give all for it. No one gave more. We too promise a willingness to lay it all on the altar for Him and His cause—consecration is unselfishness in its most holy and magnificent sense.[7]

- In the *sealing ceremony,* which is the culminating covenant of the temple, sweethearts kneel at an altar, and *receive each other* in a way that again, *points to the Savior,* how he died, the pain He suffered, the love and magnificent concern he will always feel for us."[8]

Thus, in the temple, is distilled for worshippers the pattern of His exemplary life.

PREPARING TO ATTEND

Duff explained, "many who come to the temple never come again. That which is supposed to happen to them apparently does not happen. Perhaps we could do more to prepare those who are missing the blessings."[9]

Mere temple attendance is not enough. "We come too often in a hurry," Duff lamented, "without pondering or preparation, bringing shallow vessels to dip in the deep well of our Lord. Preparation requires effort."

Duff also believed that when one understands that the temple is really about the Savior, it makes a significant difference in the way a person worships there. He explained that ritual can become dull and routine unless the *heart* is in it, and long ago the Lord told us to "lift up our heart with our hands unto God" (Lamentations 3:41). We need to have our hearts in these ceremonies. If not, things can become dull and not very instructive. Duff believed that temples are at least as much for the living as for the dead, and when we go there, we are having a "refurbishment that ties us to Christ and that ultimately will bless us with His presence." He continued, "I must tell you; I don't really worry that much about sentinels along the way. What I think about is the Holy One of Israel, who standeth at the gate, and 'employeth no servant there.' That's what concerns me."[10]

Church leaders are sometimes disturbed because they hear of missionaries

7. For the church's official description, see *General Handbook of Instructions: Serving in The Church of Jesus Christ of Latter-day Saints*, 27.2, ChurchofJesusChrist.org, accessed May 2024.

8. MDH, notes explaining the temple and its covenants.

9. MDH-A, "Christ Manifested to His People," in Parry, *Temples of the Ancient World*.

10. MDH-T, "Things of My Soul," June 11, 1992.

baptizing people before they understand the gospel. Duff wondered if it is any less disturbing to urge people to go to the temple in ignorance of the facts and place them under covenants they are not prepared to accept. He believed strongly that we must help them prepare for their temple experience.

PREPARING TO GO FOR THE FIRST TIME

Rich clearly remembers the time he spent with Duff before going to the temple for the first time, and he remains extremely grateful for his instruction and clarity.

The first thing Duff explained was that it was normal to feel a little nervous—this was going to be a new experience. And not only would this be a new experience, but much of what Rich was going to learn would be taught using a method of worship that he had not really experienced much—that of symbols and ceremony.

The second piece of advice Duff gave was to listen specifically for application to the Savior—particularly in the covenants Rich would be making—to listen to the covenants carefully and to focus on the promises he was making because this was the only time that those promises were being made by Rich, for Rich. He also told him that there would be physical elements of the endowment and new things to memorize and that he should focus *less* on these and more on the promises he was making personally to the Lord.

Duff then had them read together the story of Naaman, one of the most powerful stories in the scriptures for someone preparing to go to the temple:

Naaman is the powerful captain of the armies of the king of Syria. But he contracts leprosy, the most horrible of diseases. A little maid is captured and serves Naaman's wife. The young lady effectively says, too bad Naaman isn't in Samaria; our prophet would cure him. Eventually the message gets back to Elisha the prophet in Samaria, and he sends for Naaman. "So Naaman came with his horses and with his chariot, and stood at the door of the house of Elisha. And Elisha sent a messenger unto him, saying, Go and wash in Jordan seven times, and thy flesh shall come again to thee, and thou shalt be clean" (2 Kings 5:9–10).

Naaman gets angry because Elisha's instruction is for him to perform a simple action, repeated over and over. Naaman essentially says, I thought it would be a great thing, like striking his hand on my body, or some kind of wand waving or fabulous blessing. Instead, he tells me to go and dip in the River Jordan seven times. Naaman's servants then say an insightful thing to him: "If the prophet had bid thee do some great thing, wouldst thou not have done it? how much rather then, when he saith to thee, Wash, and be clean?" (2 Kings 5:13).

So Naaman does as he is told. He dips in the river seven times, and the scriptures record that "his flesh came again like unto the flesh of a little child, and he was clean" (2 Kings 5:14).

In summary, Duff taught that as we prepare to go to the temple for the first time, we should focus on four things:

- The Savior.
- Symbolism.
- Covenants, for ourselves.
- Naaman's experience of repeatedly performing a simple ritual to demonstrate his humility and obedience.

WHAT OUTCOME FROM ATTENDING THE TEMPLE?

Duff taught that we should be *changed* by our temple worship. He loved sharing the story from Acts 1–5, where, after the Savior was crucified, something incredible happened to the surviving disciples. Pentecost—the coming of the Spirit—occurred, and those who had wavered stood strong in testimony and testifying of Jesus. Periodically, they were brought before the council, where they were warned and beaten and released. The end of chapter 5 describes how Gamaliel intervened with his associates to give the disciples yet another chance. They are once again warned, beaten, and told to cease teaching and preaching Christ. Then they are released.

The scriptures say they departed, "rejoicing that they were counted worthy to suffer" for Christ's sake. And then it says that "daily in the temple, and in every house, they ceased not to teach and preach Jesus Christ" (Acts 5:41–42).

Something had happened to them at Pentecost. Duff commented, "In a similar way, something should *happen to us* as we depart the temple after having felt of the Spirit. We read: 'Therefore, go ye unto your homes, and *ponder* upon the things which I have said, and ask of the Father, in my name, that ye may understand, and *prepare* your minds for the morrow'" (3 Nephi 17:3; emphasis added).

QUESTIONS AND ANSWERS ABOUT THE TEMPLE

The following questions and answers were condensed from scores of pages of talks, teachings, and notes that Duff wrote about the temple and temple worship that are not covered elsewhere in this volume.

Q: What am I entitled to *feel* as I attend the temple?

A: His "holy presence may be continually in this house; … that [we] may feel [His] power" (D&C 109:12–13).

Q: Should I *learn* something every time I attend?

A: "Some say they learn something every time they go to the temple. But what does that 'learning' entail? Is it from a continual *dissection of the endowment* itself? Perhaps. But my experience has been a little different. I liken it to the great scripture 'Be still and know that I am God,' which I believe is more than a suggestion, it is a declarative commandment. 'Be still and know that I am God.'" Duff continued, "The symbolic approach of the temple is not, to me, in deep and hidden things, but as a way to teach the gospel, the principles, the ordinances and covenants of God's plan."

Q: Are there less-well-known scripture stories about the temple?

A: One of the most unusual stories of loving the temple is the story of Jonah, where he talks about *the temple and "his vows."* Even in the belly of the fish he looked to the temple for restoration and spiritual future (Jonah 2).

Q: "Multiply and replenish" is all about children, right?

A: "Yes and no. It certainly has to do with children, but it also might have to do with talents and generous hearts. The dictionary notes that the word is rarely used in the context of children, but rather to increase, or amplify, or spread. These are other ways of multiplying. For instance, in Acts 12:24 we read, 'The word of God grew and multiplied.'

"*Replenish* refers to filling or repletion, but may also be referring to filling the soul, the heart, of another person with inspiration, reassurance, strength. Maybe this latter meaning has something to do with preparing the earth to ultimately become the celestial kingdom."

Q: Does Christ visit the temples?

A: Yes. "I will manifest myself to my people.... Yea, I will appear unto my servants" (D&C 110:7–8). Elder John A. Widtsoe made a wonderful statement about that scripture. He said: "It is a great promise that to the temple God will come, and that in temples man shall see God. What does this mean? Does it mean that once in a while the pure in heart may see God there; or does it also mean a larger thing, that the pure in heart who go into the temple may, by the Spirit of God, always have a *rich communion with God?* I think *that* is what it means to me and to most of us. We have gone into these holy houses, with our minds freed from the ordinary earthly cares, and have literally felt the presence of God. In this way, the temples are always places where God manifests himself to man and increases his intelligence. A temple is a place of revelation."[11]

Q: Is temple work just for the benefit of the dead?

A: No. Elder John A. Widtsoe taught: "There is a feeling abroad that the benefits of the temple are primarily for the dead. This is not so. While the dead, if repentant, are able through our efforts to enter into a larger salvation, yet the work itself has a most beneficial effect upon *the living,* who serve as proxies for the dead. The response of the spirit of man to the ordinances of the House of the Lord stimulates every normal power and activity and ... we rise to higher levels of thought and action."[12]

PRESIDENT AND MATRON, SALT LAKE TEMPLE

Duff and Maxine were called to be the president and matron of the Salt Lake Temple on July 19, 1982. He later wrote: "I smiled in the eyes of the leaders and told them I probably had an accumulation of ignorance on this subject equal to

11. John A. Widtsoe, "Temple Worship," *Utah Genealogy Magazine*, Apr. 1921.
12. John A. Widtsoe, "Beginning of Modern Temple Work," *Improvement Era,* Oct. 1927, 1079.

President Marion D. and Sister Maxine C. Hanks at the Salt Lake Temple, 1982.

anyone's. Thereupon, President Tanner suggested that might be the reason I was being appointed."[13]

Duff and Maxine absolutely loved this opportunity to serve. He spoke often to his friends and family about the many opportunities that temple service offered. He pointed out that every day there were opportunities to be kind and giving.

Duff felt that no one could have better counselors than he was blessed to work with. Spencer Osborn, Collins Jones, and Homer Ellsworth were a mighty force for good, and he had literally no worries with those fine men on the job. He wrote, "We have been completely consonant in our melody here, and the generous appraisals I hear daily from many sources confirm that love and respect and courtesy work to make the atmosphere and experience a lovely one for people."[14]

Duff treated Maxine as being vital to everything they hoped to accomplish in their leadership of the temple. Despite her having her own full list of duties, he also wanted her to be a full partner in all major decisions and communications.

13. MDH-L to Menlo Smith, June 1997.
14. MDH-JE, Nov. 6, 1984.

She signed each of the instructions and memos that went out over the temple presidency's signature and was invited to express her opinions on all major issues.

DEDICATED TEMPLE WORKERS

One of the first things Maxine and Duff noticed in the temple was the love and devotion of the temple workers, who came from every walk of life and socio-economic class. They came early and stayed late. They routinely sacrificed food or attention to personal issues while they were working their shift. Duff was continually impressed by the commitment and sacrifice they exhibited—through snow and rain and sleepless nights. Since many of them were elderly, this was particularly impressive to him as a new temple president. Here is a journal entry about an incredible interview:

> Today I met with Don Kirk as a prospective ordinance worker. Sightless, Don is a rare human. He traveled from Magna alone, no dog, no person. Came here and waited a while, then quietly shook my foundations with his remarkable story. Aviator, submariner, expert in cryptology, Sioux Indian who spoke no English until he turned 16, Bataan Death March after being rammed by a Japanese cruiser off Subic Bay, volunteer flower planter on Temple Square, incredible senses. The first day he worked, he noted from the back row, that a person in front had dropped his apron. What a man![15]

Duff loved and honored the commitment he saw from the workers every day in the temple. One day he arrived at the temple at 4:30 a.m., grateful that he had made it through a huge snowstorm. In a secluded room, Duff chanced upon an older, deeply admired temple worker dressed in white, sitting thoughtfully and leaning on his cane, ready to begin his shift. Duff asked him what he was doing there so early in the morning. He replied, "You know why I am here, president." Duff responded by wondering how the man had traveled all the way from Heber City, since the news had just reported that the I-80 freeway in Parley's Canyon was closed with snow." He replied, "I have a four-wheeler that will climb trees—and about those barricades, I have known many of those highway officers since they were born. They know that I must get through [to the temple], or I might just try to go overland. They also know my truck and my experience, and so, they just move the barricades." He was there, faithful and loyal, at 4:30 a.m. through a blizzard, from fifty miles away.

A PERSONAL COMMITMENT

Duff and Maxine also sacrificed. Here are a few journal entries about the experience:

> It perhaps should be noted that we are constantly interviewing, recommending, releasing, and calling workers, sealers, veil workers, and other personnel. The job is never-ending and never-descending; it provides the same level of energy all the time.

15. MDH-JE, Mar. 15, 1985.

Salt Lake Temple Presidency: Collins Jones, Duff Hanks, Homer Ellsworth, 1985.

> My experience here is like my experience on Temple Square years ago. I am here until at least 8:30 each night, and usually a little later. After speaking at the evening chapel session, I usually collapse in the office and try to clean up a little of the desk. Much of it gets hidden for another time, while I struggle home and try to eat a bite, put on the pajamas, read the paper, and notice it is now near midnight, after which I try to sleep, so that I can get up in a little while.[16]

Duff and Maxine decided it would be good to meet in the evenings each week with stakes and wards and other groups in the temple chapel for some instruction, followed by a temple session. While these specially created events took a toll on them physically, it was a terrific opportunity to involve more people in temple worship in a special, warm atmosphere. Scores of groups had a wonderful time together. He wrote, "I've exhausted myself vigorously, but we are gratified at the people's kind response."[17]

16. MDH-JE, Feb. 16, 1985.
17. MDH-JE, Jan. 14, 1984.

CHANGE IS GOOD

Duff and Maxine wanted to emphasize the Spirit in the temple. A few of their goals were to focus on the Savior, decrease the hierarchical feeling of rank among the workers, teach graciousness, make the temple experience less rigid and more personal, and try to ensure each patron left feeling the spirit of love.

He tried to remove as much of the military-like hierarchy from the almost three thousand temple workers as possible. He started by removing the nameplates on the doors and ID badges of the temple presidency, replacing the monikers "first counselor" and "second counselor" with simply "counselor."

To say that changing the daily habits of thousands of mostly elderly and set-in-their-ways temple workers was a daunting task would be an understatement. But slowly there was a change in the attitude of almost all the workers.

OFFICIAL, NOT OFFICIOUS

Duff and Maxine wanted temple patrons to leave feeling uplifted and spiritually fed. That goal required adjusting the natural tendency of some older temple workers to focus on the minute details of the ceremonies or even on some administrative items, such as where patrons should and shouldn't walk, whether it was OK to hold hands, or wear jewelry or perfume. Duff's temple presidency taught the workers that they should preside with kindness, not the letter of the law. He invited the leadership of the temple to "bring the gospel back into the temple" and remember that "the *ordinances* are revealed, but the *procedures* are flexible."

In a letter to all Salt Lake Temple workers dated June 13, 1983, and signed by Duff, his counselors, and Maxine, he wrote:

> Beyond the exactness and uniformity which are indispensable for the success of the work, there is ample room for individual expression and involvement. Chiefly, this is in the radiation of the Spirit, which reaches out in kindness and patience and consideration and concern, and helpfulness to the patrons and fellow workers. So,
>
> 1. Be EXACT in performing the ordinances.
>
> 2. Seek UNIFORMITY of procedure. If you feel there is a more effective way, share it with supervisors and temple administrators.
>
> 3. Reach out in INDIVIDUALITY, using gentility and kindness in every element of temple service. Be helpful, be patient, be supportive.[18]

TEACHING CORRECT PRINCIPLES

Duff found out that some old dogs don't like new tricks, particularly in the Salt Lake Temple: He wrote:

> Today I spent two hours with four sealers. They just don't understand, and the meeting turned out to be fruitful. One of them thought that the woman gives

18. Salt Lake Temple Bulletin, June 1983.

> herself to the man in the sense of surrender to his priesthood. I told him that was antediluvian, [Attila the] Hun-style, and not useful in the temple or the kingdom. She is no man's chattel, no husband's plaything, no patsy. The priesthood is a commission to *service*, in the spirit of Him after whom it is called. They seemed to learn and said they were grateful.[19]

Some pushback was inevitable. Another day he wrote:

> I met with the sealers today. We discussed procedure and it was not as high and holy a feeling as I'd have liked. One man announced that he had been a sealer in three temples and had been a supervisor and he didn't like my instruction. I thanked him. He then stood again and repeated it all. He came to my office after to repeat it all a third time.
>
> Other matters were cleared up and some muddied up and it all took a little longer than it should. My responsibility—I should have shut him up and shut up myself. Next time.[20]

NOT ATTENDING AN AUCTION

Duff was not a fan of the auctioneer-like speed with which some proxy ordinances were being performed. He spoke by letter to the Church's Temple Department, expressing his observation that he was uncomfortable with the "manner, and the speed and lack of personal involvement of the ordinance worker and proxies" and said that watching it was "a sad experience for me." From that point on, his presidency, including Maxine, attempted to evoke a personal meaning to every ordinance performed.

In a letter to all supervisors in the temple, dated January 28, 1983, he emphasized:

> We give service in the temple, not for "names" but for individuals—living, unique persons who have passed through the veil and are "dead" only in the vernacular of this mortal time. Every action performed on their behalf should be personal, respectful, unhurried, dignified, and spiritually motivated. In the book of Nehemiah an account is given of the manner in which the prophet Ezra and his associates taught the people: "So, they read in the book in the law of God distinctly, and gave the sense, and caused them to *understand* the reading" (Nehemiah 8:8). The spirit of this scripture is what we desire as we officiate in the ordinances of the temple. True communication will be the result.

Again, in another reminder letter to the baptistry workers twenty months later, he repeated the message that the recipients of the ordinances as well as those performing them are each individually significant. "We are not in a hurry to get a certain number of baptisms accomplished. To sacrifice the sweet sense of the

19. MDH-JE, Oct. 27, 1983.
20. MDH-JE, June 10, 1984.

spiritual service for expedience in the interests of time is inappropriate. Please take time to dignify the experiences."[21]

TURNING THE CORNER

With their combined effort, some habits began to change. Duff wrote, "This morning I performed the marriage of a young couple. They were lovely and responsive. Peace reigned in the halls of the temple today, better than I've known it, and I'm glad. We are accomplishing something in this respect. A few workers resist, but most can take a lively interest in the patrons without seeming to pressure or to shush."[22]

On the other hand, some habits were slow to die off. He wrote, "Life goes on in the temple, just as unusual. I just dictated an [apology] letter to a lady who was ordered to remove her small pierced-ear earrings by a worker, who acknowledged to another worker that it was not temple policy, it was *her* policy. This is the second such letter in a few weeks, and I am discouraged. The issue has been taken up again and again."[23]

But despite two steps forward, one step back, the overall movement was to the positive: "Cal Smoot came back from a wedding this day to say something so solemn it made me weep. He thanked us for bringing the 'gospel back into the temple.' This was not a criticism of the past, only gratitude for the reemphasis of the Savior and His program in the temple worship experience. Seems strange to be congratulated for that, but in fact that is what we are trying to accomplish."[24]

Duff received a letter after an experience in the baptistry: "We love the spirit of kindness, the openness, the not being constantly corrected for walking down the wrong aisle accidentally, etc. In fact, part of the reason the temple is so much more pleasant is that there seem to be so few hard and fast rules, so we are no longer afraid of inadvertently breaking them. It seems like the temple is now a wonderful and joyous place for the living as well as for the dead. The loving care you are taking in your temple stewardship is blessing thousands of us."[25]

NEVER A DULL MOMENT

Duff wrote, "The last two years in the temple, has been a remarkable place to be, and it needs no exposition of its beauty and joyfulness, but it also is a collection point for problems, particularly if one is willing to listen, and I am. It is also a marvelous place for sanctuary from coarseness and crudity and the minimization of things which are too much with us on every television set and all about us. We are all susceptible, and the effort has to be calculated, deliberate, persistent, and consistent. The temple is a real sanctuary."

21. MDH-L Sept. 14, 1984.
22. MDH-JE, June 8, 1984.
23. MDH-JE, Feb. 16, 1985.
24. MDH-JE, Mar. 15, 1985.
25. Sherry McMullin to MDH, June 9, 1983.

Here is one journal entry, demonstrating the roller-coaster pace of his temple leadership experience:

> The crisis of the day was a call from the sealing office that a girl had fled the altar at the moment of her response. Couldn't find her at first. I directed the search, and then sat with her for an hour trying to help. She was undecided. Both returned missionaries, northern bound, she had begun to think of the Arctic nights alone while he carpentered on oil rigs for six weeks at a time. Also, she didn't want to tell the kids their daddy couldn't go to church on Sunday because he was working.
>
> The families and a large group waited in the sealing room while I spent time making it clear I wasn't trying to persuade her, but would simply give her some standards of measurement by which to decide. She said she didn't have the spiritual assurance she thought she should have. Neither have many of the rest of us, I convinced her. Ultimately, they went back upstairs and through with it. Hope it is right and good. No persuasion on my part.
>
> Then K's sister called to see if I could get her cleared from her dead husband. She didn't love him and didn't want anything to do with him in the great beyond, and wants to marry C. in the temple—for permanent. Told her we'd look for the records, and did, and found them.
>
> The rest of the day went at a fast pace. The building engineer came for consultation, along with many others. I met with a man from Mauritius at Rotary. Hurried back to meet Dallin Oaks and Russell Nelson, two new members of the Twelve Apostles, sent by the First Presidency for my instruction and some more acquaintance with the temple. They were eager and respectful listeners for two hours. Excellent and special men, and I enjoyed a pleasant experience with them.[26]

Occasionally, Duff had to engage with the Temple Department over various issues. Near the end of 1984, there were several back-and-forth communications concerning an imbalance of male and female names in the baptistry and some rumored potential changes, including some statistical goals and quotas. Duff wrote, "We have been blessedly free from quotas and allotments in this temple and have been repeatedly thanked and extended strong appreciation by priesthood leaders for that approach."[27] The rumored quotas never materialized.

MAKING PHYSICAL CHANGES TO THE TEMPLE

Any attempt to make changes to the physical nature of the Salt Lake Temple, the central hub of the kingdom of God on earth, was obviously not going to be met with open arms. Some things about the temple hadn't been touched in the almost ninety years since it was dedicated. Others had been added along the way but had also become sacrosanct. Nonetheless, Duff and Maxine saw things that could be better if they were adjusted a little bit.

---

26. MDH-JE, June 5, 1984.
27. MDH-L to the Temple Department, Nov. 7, 1984.

In a letter to the Temple Council in August 1982, Duff suggested changing a few things to facilitate the movement of elderly and disabled people through the endowment ceremony. These included replacing stairs with ramps in several places where there were one or two steps, including the bottom of the grand staircase, and installing ramps leading up to the veil. These suggested changes were accepted and were made.

As the temple workers and patrons began to feel more at ease providing feedback, practical ideas for improvement flowed in. A few examples of changes made, include:

- Replacing the large painting in the terrestrial room of Joseph interpreting the dreams of Pharaoh's butler and baker with a painting of Christ.
- Removing the photo of the First Presidency in the bride's room.
- Removing some statuary from the celestial room.

MARRIAGE AND ETERNAL MARRIAGE

Behold, I give unto you power, that whatsoever ye shall seal on earth shall be sealed in heaven; and whatsoever ye shall loose on earth shall be loosed in heaven; and thus shall ye have power among this people.

—Helaman 10:7

The sealing power brought Duff some of his most wonderful experiences. He said, "Nothing I have done seems more important than those few moments in the temple with a great young couple who are prepared to kneel, take each other by the hand in a way that points them to the Savior, and help them understand what is about to happen. To me it is the most sacred and sweet teaching moment of a lifetime."

One example of the hundreds of marriages he performed: "I performed two choice marriages this morning, the first for the daughter of Arthur Neilsen. Large group, good spirit, fine experience. For such young couples, I concentrate on the simple principles of the ceremony, encouraging not many homilies and humors, but the principles of acceptance 'as is,' together with the blessed and continuing obligation to help each become what each can be."[28] (For greater detail on marriage, see pages 295–97.)

MIRACLES IN THE TEMPLE

Some feel the temple experience should be shrouded in mystery and miracles. Duff felt similarly, but his definition was a bit different from most. While he absolutely believed that the temple is a place where the Lord reveals Himself, he felt that most of the time the miracles come as we feel His Spirit and receive revelation for our personal lives.

He also didn't understand those who felt that "learning in the temple" meant

28. MDH-JE, June 19, 1984.

a "continual dissection of the endowment." He thought we should individually learn something each time we went to the temple and that miracles were all around us—we just didn't always notice them.

This didn't mean that he wasn't aware of supernatural miracles, large and small, and even some more mundane miracles that occurred in the temple. One day Duff received an urgent message to go to a sealing room where an infant suffering with terminal cancer had just died. He had been brought to the temple directly from Primary Children's Hospital to be sealed to his parents and had died just as the officiator concluded the ceremony. While the required legal arrangements were in process, Duff went to the foyer to meet with the family and brought the grandparents from the waiting room back into the annex to be with their little grandchild and his parents. Duff said, "We talked together there of sacred things, and they were touched by the Spirit. I stood at the door sometime later as they left and linked my arms with them for a moment. I said to them that as the temple president I had escorted them past the recommend desk because their children needed them; I would be honored to be here when you come back with your recommends to receive the blessings of the temple for yourself."

A little more than a year later, Duff stood in the sealing room as they received the higher ordinances leading us to Christ.[29] These types of occurrences were miracles to him.

SUMMARY AND RELEASE

In summary, Duff often asked, why do we build temples?

Answer: To walk the path the Savior walked and to do the will of the Father:

- Washing and anointing
- Endowment and covenants
- Sealing
- Work for the dead
- That the Son of Man might manifest Himself unto His people

"The temple reminds us who we are, and who makes us, and to whose pasture we belong, by whose stripes we are healed; who paid the price for us, who bought us with his love and life."

All church callings come with a built-in release. And so, after three years, Maxine and Duff's time in the temple ended. They received so many gracious thank-you letters from temple workers and patrons that they filled several scrapbooks.

Here is one specific to Maxine: "Sister Hanks, you two are so exemplary in your devotion to each other. As I've observed you walking through the corridors hand in hand, the beauty of it almost makes me catch my breath. You have made so many sweet changes—a special restroom, drapes, mirrors, a table here and a chair there for comfort—all up and down the corridors I see evidence of you

29. MDH-T, Regional Representatives Seminar, Apr. 3, 1987.

having been there. Some people want all the honors. You are the opposite. How precious you are."[30]

Duff summed up their experience as follows: "God be praised; I believe we made a difference here. We are content with our effort and the direction that came, sometimes from others, and often from the Spirit. I know there was inspiration involved because as I was teaching I learned from what I said. It went beyond my poor knowledge and my poor ability. Clearly the credit goes to the Lord."

Duff and Maxine learned of their release, and on June 9, 1985, they happily, if a bit emotionally, ended this chapter of their lives. Duff wrote, "For now, the chapter endeth, and we are grateful and thankful. Daily, in the temple, and in every house, may we cease not to teach and preach Jesus Christ."[31]

30. Caroline Barret to MCH, June 5, 1985.
31. MDH-JE, June 9, 1985.

54

Come unto Christ

In this folder is the foundation of a four- or five-year effort to try and get the church to unite on our real mission, 'To Invite All to Come unto Christ.'
—Marion D. Hanks[1]

In April 1986, Duff submitted a document to President Ezra Taft Benson recommending that the church begin to focus on the scriptural teaching to "Come unto Christ" and to focus on "the individual" and move away from programs and statistics. He wrote, "If we have the wisdom and courage to forget the numbers and concentrate on our real purpose—then, we can succeed in those purposes with far greater numbers than we now see."[2]

While he had been trying for years to push the church down that path, he knew that his time and influence were diminishing, and he began a formalized, concerted effort to move the church in that direction.

Duff believed that the individual should be the center of all efforts and the incremental "movement forward" of each individual toward God—determining where each member stood and then moving each one ahead—should be the church's goal. He quoted from the scriptures that speak of that maturing process as "growing up in the Lord" (Helaman 3:21; Ephesians 4:15; D&C 109:15).

This approach seems fairly obvious in today's context, but back then the church was well on its way down the path of focusing on discrete statistical measurements and programs rather than on individual improvement. This emphasis on measurement was manifested in decades of churchwide focus on baptisms, attendance at meetings, home teaching statistics, and the number of temple ordinances—all of which today have finally taken a back seat to ministering to the individual.

Duff expended years and years of personal energy trying to get church leaders to focus less on baptism statistics and more on helping new converts stay in the fold, to focus less on home teaching statistics and more on the spiritual and

1. MDH-A, handwritten note on a folder.

2. Addendum materials on "Come unto Christ," submitted with a letter to President Ezra Taft Benson, Apr. 1986.

physical needs of the people visited. He quoted numerous scriptures that are clear in their message: "The 'fruit should remain' (e.g., retention; John 15:16) 'after baptism, their names taken that they might be nourished … and [kept] in the right way' (e.g., nurture and retention; Moroni 6:4)," and so on.

Among areas where Duff felt there could be significant improvement was in retaining new converts, recovering those who had gone inactive or were separated from the church due to church action, and focusing on ministering to individuals.

To him, both the Melchizedek Priesthood quorums and the full-time missionaries were significantly underused resources that could be put into action in these causes.

The document Duff gave to President Benson was lengthy, but a few summary points demonstrate its suggested direction:

- NO NEW programs.
- Bishops to use *underutilized priesthood holders* to do much of the work in the ward—less responsibility on the bishop, more responsibility on the Melchizedek Priesthood quorums.
- Full-time missionaries to *stay with and teach new converts* much longer.
- Full-time missionaries being allowed to teach *inactive members.*
- Emphasis on *individual* progress, ministering, and nurturing.
- *Wives* going home teaching with husbands.
- More attention on *advancing* male converts in the priesthood.
- Home teaching focused on those who *need it most.*

Frankly, Duff sometimes became discouraged as he made proposal after proposal to the First Presidency and emphasized the Savior in meeting after meeting. Inertia is a difficult thing to overcome. But he stuck with it, believing it to be the right thing. And then the ship started to slowly turn.

President Howard W. Hunter, in training the regional representatives in 1987, said, "Keep in mind the purpose: to *invite all to Come unto Christ.* I bear my testimony as King Benjamin of old, that 'there is no other name given nor any other way nor means whereby salvation can come unto the children of men' (Mosiah 3:17). This must be the ultimate vision of every priesthood and auxiliary leader. The whole purpose of the church operating smoothly at the local level is to qualify individuals to return to the presence of God."[3]

And at the conclusion of the October 1987 general conference, President Ezra Taft Benson said, "Once one is convinced, through the Book of Mormon, that Jesus is the Christ, then he must take the next step; he must *Come unto Christ.*"

And in April 1988, President Benson said, "May we all go to our homes rededicated to the sacred mission of the church as so beautifully set forth in these conference sessions—to '*invite all to Come unto Christ*' (D&C 20:59)."

---

3. Howard W. Hunter, Regional Representatives Seminar, Apr. 3, 1987; Apr. 5, 1991.

THE CHURCH'S MISSION

But isn't the church's mission a list of three or four things? No. It isn't.

When Duff would hear someone state that the mission of the church was three of these or four of that, he would quietly remind the speaker that the actual mission of the church is to invite individuals to "Come unto Christ" and that the three or four areas were a tactical subset of "Come unto Christ." As he described it, "The church has only one mission, with multiple dimensions. The mission of the church is to '*Come unto Christ.*'" He thought it incomplete when someone would say that the mission of the church was missionary work, temple work, and perfecting the Saints—and not even mention the Savior.

Duff pushed hard. Writing and sending numerous position papers, letters and quotations to the First Presidency suggesting that the church adopt a unifying theme of Come unto Christ but specifically focusing on the key concepts of nourishing, nurturing, shepherding, ministering, and allowing flexibility. He reinforced the traditional dimensions of preaching, saving, and perfecting and often quoted Elder Marion G. Romney's October 5, 1956, conference talk in which these areas were first proposed.[4] But he saw a real need to bring the church and its members away from the distractions of statistics and key indicators and more toward the Savior.

It was obvious to Duff that the Lord Jesus Christ is the center of all we are doing and trying to accomplish as a church. But at that time (and maybe even today), if you randomly asked 100 members what the mission of the church is, most would skip over the part about the Savior and His grace and Atonement and list the three or four areas of work.

There were other problems with the traditional approach of a three- or fourfold mission statement. The church often found itself supporting "self-contained silos," in which people worked only in the area to which they'd been assigned. This created a separated division of labor, as if the three efforts were discrete and unrelated. In a ward, for example, that could mean the bishopric would be the only ones talking about how all areas should mesh. By having a unity of effort, the focus on statistics is diminished and a focus on individuals increased—less emphasis on "administering" and more focus on "ministering."

REACTION

Anyone who has been a leader in the church knows that it is easier to simply focus on statistics, forms, and reports rather than spend the time necessary to nurture and nourish the members under one's stewardship. The change of focus away from "administering" toward "ministering" can be more time-consuming and difficult. But local church leaders were very positive about the change in focus.

---

4. "It has been said that the major responsibilities resting upon the membership of the church may be classified under three heads: (1) Preaching the Gospel, (2) Performing vicariously the saving ordinances of the Gospel for the dead, (3) Perfecting the Saints." Marion G. Romney, GC, Oct. 5, 1956.

After a stake conference, a bishop handed Duff a note: "Brother Hanks, when I think of coming unto Christ, I think of a full day of attempting to administer the complex problems of my holy office; and then, at the end of my day, *ministering* to the needs and expressing the love of my heart for my people, that is when I enjoy the fullness of what that great invitation means—*Come unto Christ.*"

KEEPING THE MOMENTUM GOING

Duff was aware of the need to keep the momentum going—human nature often causes people to revert back to what they are used to doing or to what is easiest to recall from history. For the entire church to come together in a theme that would be universally accepted and applied would require a change in mindset, accompanied by continued instruction by the general authorities over a long period of time. In an October 1987 meeting of the First Quorum of Seventy, Duff taught again the "Come unto Christ" vision and cautioned the leaders about the need for consistent repetition and reinforcement by telling the following parable.

There was a gathering of all animals, fish, and fowl. The lion was in charge and tried to get each animal to change its ways—the hyena to quit being so frivolous, the giraffe to stop being so haughty, the pike to stop living off the work of others. When they were dismissed, the wise old owl, observing from a tree, remarked:

> The sermon now ended, each turned and descended.
> The eels went on eeling, the pikes went on stealing.
> Much delighted were they, but preferred the old way.

Duff continued teaching his colleagues. "In a way that may never have been possible before with a growing church and wide implication of such assignments that have now been given to the seventy, has there been a chance to get our minds set on what we are really all about, as the scriptures repeatedly teach."[5] He then walked his colleagues through what just a *few* of the scriptures say:

> "Yea, *come unto Christ,* and be perfected in him" (Moroni 10:32; emphasis added).

> "*Come unto me* all ye ends of the earth" (2 Nephi 26:25; emphasis added).

> "And now, my beloved brethren, I would that ye should *come unto Christ,* who is the Holy One of Israel, and partake of his salvation, and the power of his redemption" (Omni 1:26; emphasis added).

This line of invitation continues in Alma 31:34–35; Ether 5:5; Helaman 5:12; D&C 20:59; 2 Nephi 2:6–8; Matthew 11:27–28; John 14:1–6; and Hebrews 7:25.

He then reminded them that the changes being made were not just semantic and that certain members needed special attention:

---

5. MDH, notes of the meeting of the First Quorum of Seventy, Oct. 8, 1987, 3–4.

- Less-active
- Single adults
- Those separated from the church by church discipline
- Missionaries who return home early
- Those not yet endowed

He then repeated the valedictory words of a loving father to his son: "My son, be faithful in Christ; and may not the things which I have written grieve thee, to weigh thee down unto death; *but may Christ lift thee up*"! (Moroni 9:25; emphasis added.)[6]

REAL GROWTH

Change-management professionals are well aware that continual, sustained repetition is imperative to making changes in any large organization. Sometimes it's two steps forward, one step back. To fight that entropy, Duff continued to train every group he met with, including in general authority training meetings each year from 1986 to 1992. In Duff's mind, the next step was to begin to strengthen the church and develop new converts. After the introduction of the true mission of the church, Duff convinced the senior brethren to talk less about baptisms and more about "real growth," which he defined as conversion, retention, activation, and ordination.

At a general authority training meeting on March 27, 1990, he outlined the recent history of pronouncements by the leaders of the church:

> In 1985, the First Presidency issued an invitation to "*Come back.*"
>
> In 1987, the theme was "Accomplishing the true *mission of the church.*"
>
> In 1988, the call was to continue ministering, emphasizing "*real growth.*"
>
> In 1989, the emphasis was on *quorum committees* in accomplishing the mission of the church.

Looking back many years later, Duff wrote in a letter, "The major thing I have helped change, I suppose, is to focus us on the real mission of the church which is to 'Come unto Christ.' This language was not in the official statement of the mission of the church just a few decades ago. The First Presidency's understanding of the mission would be no different than my own, but somehow there seemed to have been a willingness to keep from language relating to Christ which [might possibly] seem to tie us to fanatics and saved-from-abovers and so forth. I think after all these years and all this effort, that this scriptural message of our true mission has swept the church in a way that will never again suffer containment."[7]

6. MDH, notes from the First Quorum of Seventy meeting, Oct. 8, 1987, 7.
7. MDH-L to GH, Aug. 25, 1993.

TODAY?

The description in the 2024 *General Handbook of Instructions* shows that the church continues to emphasize the message of "Come unto Christ" and maintains as its principal goal the advancement of the *individual* toward salvation and exaltation.

A graphic on the church's website declares:

The Work of Salvation and Exaltation
We come unto Christ and assist in God's work by:
- Living the gospel of Jesus Christ.
- Caring for those in need.
- Inviting all to receive the gospel.
- Uniting families for eternity.

The church has also continued to adapt and refine the mission as new inspiration has been received. Duff would be pleased to see the church has added a fourth area: "Caring for those in need," since he spent the last half of his life trying to get the institutional church to focus on true Christlike service to our fellow man.[8]

8. Caring for Those in Need, Church of Jesus Christ of Latter-day Saints, ChurchofJesusChrist.org.

55

True Christian Service

[We are] to feed the hungry, to clothe the naked, to provide for the widow, to dry up the tear of the orphan, to comfort the afflicted, whether in this church, or in any other, or in no church at all, wherever [we] find them.
—Joseph Smith[1]

If you were put on trial for being a Christian, would there be enough evidence to convict you?
—Anonymous

Apart from his testifying of the Lord Jesus Christ, nothing consumed more of the life and ministry of Marion D. Hanks than the Savior's injunction to serve "the least of these." In a previous chapter, we explored his strong belief in missionaries performing Christian service. This chapter will focus on Duff's efforts to have each of us include Christlike service in our daily lives.

WHAT HE BELIEVED AND TAUGHT

While Duff loved the Lord's commandment to teach and baptize, he was far more interested in *aggressive Christianity* than he was in *aggressive proselyting.*

This declaration from Duff in general conference sums up his feeling: "Nothing would seem more clear than the high premium the Savior put upon selfless service to others as an indispensable element of Christian conduct and of salvation. Helping, giving, and sacrificing should be as natural as growing and breathing."[2]

Duff loved this statement of J. Reuben Clark Jr. and used it often as the basis for his presentations on Christian service: "When the Savior came upon the earth, he had two great missions: One was to *work out the Messiahship,* the atonement for the fall, and the fulfillment of the law. The other was the work which he did among his brethren and sisters in the flesh by way of *relieving their sufferings.* He left as a heritage to those who should come after him in his church the *carrying on* of those two great things: work for the relief of the ills and the sufferings

1. Joseph Smith, *Times and Seasons*, Mar. 15, 1842, 732.
2. MDH-T, "The Royal Law," GC, Apr. 1992.

of humanity, and the teaching of the spiritual truths which should bring us back into the presence of our Heavenly Father."[3]

Duff explained, "In the most personal of his parables, the Savior identified himself fully with the hungry, the thirsty, the naked, the homeless, the sick, and the imprisoned. 'I was an hungered, and ye gave me meat: … I was a stranger, and ye took me in' (Matthew 25:35). The promise of Christ's mercy is sure and certain to those who find Him and trust Him. And we as His agents are not only to *declare His word,* but to *represent Him* in doing unto the least of His brethren that which He Himself would do were He now here."[4]

Duff often taught that the role of one who gives service is to be God's hands. Jesus did what only He could do in performing the Atonement. But as His disciples, we are supposed to help Him with His other great mission, that of relieving suffering. He needs instruments of His love, and He needs *us* and *our hands* to carry His love and make it meaningful and personal in the lives of others. As a wise and loving person once said,

The best way to make room for Christ is to make room for others.
When we open up the door to others, He rushes in with them.
—Liz Hanks

To Duff, the sweetness of Christian service was often experienced in obscurity—in quiet rooms in homes and hospitals and in military barracks and refugee camps, and in other places far from public attention. Often such service is unheralded, but reflects the standard set by the Savior for those who will "inherit the kingdom prepared … from the foundation of the world."

The main text for Duff's fervor came from Matthew 25: "For I was an hungred, and ye gave me meat: I was thirsty, and ye gave me drink: I was a stranger, and ye took me in: And the King shall answer and say unto them, Verily I say unto you, Inasmuch as ye have done it unto one of the least of these my brethren, ye have done it unto me."

This statement was then followed by "For I was an hungred, and ye gave me no meat: I was thirsty, and ye gave me no drink: I was a stranger, and ye took me not in: naked, and ye clothed me not: sick, and in prison, and ye visited me not. Then shall he answer them, saying, Verily I say unto you, Inasmuch as ye did it not to one of the least of these, ye did it not to me. And these shall go away into everlasting punishment: but the righteous into life eternal" (Matthew 25:35, 40, 42–43, 45).

On another occasion, Duff said:

> One day, there may in fact be a reunion of the Savior with those who follow Him and are able to hear Him say, "Inasmuch as ye have done it unto one of the least

3. J. Reuben Clark Jr., GC, Apr. 1937.
4. MDH-T, "My Specialty Is Mercy," GC, Oct. 1981; emphasis added.

of these my brethren [and my sisters], ye have done it unto me" (Matthew 25:40). We say that periodically, and we love it at Christmas—but we ought to believe it *every day.* . . . The Lord gave the three parables that ended with the one where the goats were on the left hand and the sheep were on the other. Those represented by the sheep on His right hand were invited to be with Him in 'eternal life'; those on the left were assigned 'eternal damnation.' The distinction had to do with *the way they had behaved toward their fellowmen.*[5]

The story is told that Heber C. Kimball was once asked to expound on the "Mysteries of the Kingdom." He is reported to have said, "I am well qualified to preach them and shall do so. Sister Jones has been cutting her own stove wood for six months, even though she has a broken ankle. Apparently, that is a mystery of the Kingdom. Brother Johnson has been serving on a mission for over seven months without proper clothing. Perhaps that's a mystery of the Kingdom."

He continued for an hour, saying, "The mysteries of the Kingdom are that there are individuals sitting right next to you that need your help, and the only way you can receive help yourself is to help another."

Duff wrote, "President Spencer W. Kimball taught that to lighten your own burden, you should lift another's. It is a sad thing to go through life and miss those wonderful opportunities to assist our fellow man. And the opportunities are all around us."[6]

Albert Schweitzer, sometimes described as the greatest humanitarian of the twentieth century, said, "Just do what you can. It's not enough merely to exist. It's not enough to say, 'I'm earning enough to live and support my family. I do my work well. I'm a good father. I'm a good husband.' That's all very well, but you must do something more. You must give some time to your fellowman. Even if it's a little thing, do something for those who have need of help, something for which you get no pay but the privilege of doing it."

Duff loved the story of Dr. Schweitzer refusing to spend time with a group of high-society young physicians visiting him in the jungles of Africa. He did not want to come out of his office to encourage them in the riches they all anticipated in the drawing rooms of Manhattan. When he finally emerged, he said to them, "I don't know what your destiny will be, but one thing I know: the only ones among you who will be really happy are those who will have *sought and found how to serve.*"

HIS PERSONAL SERVICE EFFORTS

Love is not all; it is not meat nor drink nor slumber nor a roof
against the rain; nor yet a floating spar to men who sink.
—Edna St. Vincent Millay[7]

5. MDH-T, "The Three A's: Atonement, Agency, and Accountability," BYU, Apr. 16, 1996.
6. MDH, Notes
7. Edna St. Vincent Millay, "Love Is Not All," in *Collected Poems* (1931).

To Marion D. Hanks:
The focus of a lifetime of Christian service was ever to be putting his Heavenly Father's will before his own.
—Honorary Doctorate of Christian Service, BYU, 1993

Although he was presented with many honorary awards, there was really nothing "honorary' about Duff. He walked the talk. He personified what being a disciple of Christ means: reaching out to lift up the poor and downtrodden, standing up to the proud and the mighty, sharing testimony of Christ at all times and in all places, rendering service whether recognized or not, giving liberally to worthy causes. Duff practiced the "habit of helpfulness—the ministry of service—the useful interest in the welfare of others." He learned this at the knee of his widowed mother. He wrote, "Some are born less interested, less responsive, or less sensitive, but *we can each learn.*" He cultivated his gift of personal service. Simple, but concrete examples abound:

1. He lived on a cul-de-sac. On garbage day, he'd place his cans farthest out on the main road so his neighbors wouldn't have to walk as far to place their cans.
2. When it snowed, Duff would shovel his own walks and then just keep on shoveling down the street for all the neighbors.
3. He knew all the secretaries and security people at church headquarters by name, their families, and their lives.
4. He had an old Ford Bronco with four-wheel drive. Duff would drive home from some event in a blizzard, change his clothes, grab Rich, and they would go back out to drag out cars stuck in the snow.

From Duff's journal: "Rich and I cut and trimmed our lawn, fixed the garage, and then mowed the lawn of the Miles and the Swensens [neighbors] without telling either. The other day, I saw Dr. Swensen out looking at his lawn with great puzzlement. I didn't say a word."[8]

One morning Phyllis, his secretary, called to say that another elderly general authority had not arrived at the office. Duff rushed to President Antoine R. Ivins' apartment, where he found him lying on the bathroom floor wedged between the toilet and the wall. He'd been there thirteen hours. Duff questioned, "Antoine, what are you doing there? The reply was, "Waiting for you. I knew *you* would come." Duff called it the "greatest compliment of my life."

As a poor graduate student on Christmas break, Truman Madsen was at the Keith O'Brien department store on Third South when Duff bought him a new suit. Truman said, "I doubt he had many more nickels than we did. But he insisted. And then pledged me never to say a word about it. But I didn't promise that I wouldn't write it."[9]

8. MDH-JE, July 26, 1975.
9. Truman Madsen, Oct. 26, 1953.

BYU English professor Margaret Young recalled a time when her husband Bruce, also a BYU English professor, asked Duff what could be improved in the church. Elder Hanks responded quickly, "More service." She said, "He was not only willing to help, he also prepared himself for the opportunity. He pulled troubled souls from various mires, using physical ropes or spiritual ones. He was a servant of God until the end, seeking to soothe the afflicted and liberate any who had gotten stuck, whether in a muddy ditch, or in the middle of their own wildly mapped egos, or in the tangle of deceit."[10]

Duff wrote about returning home after a long day of meetings when he stopped to pick up an elderly man waiting for a bus: "After a few miles, I discovered that he is the brother-in-law of Louise Lake (a dear friend). He is 84, infirm, and not competent to be by himself. I was glad to give him a ride."[11]

Duff was at a stake conference in California, when up came a friend who had come to their home twenty-one years earlier as a beautiful little unmarried mother. When she joined the church, she had been expelled from her home, had no one to turn to, and came to Duff and Maxine fearful and bitter. Duff said, "The battle for her life was one we were really not prepared to undertake, but Maxine and I tried to give her a home and make her feel loved. Our little children really won the battle. Susan and Nancy wore down the abrasives and warmed and loved her. She stayed with us through her confinement and went to the hospital with Maxine to have her baby. Maxine held her hand, loved her, counseled her, and mothered her. I was privileged to help for some time after, when her baby was adopted."[12] They kept in touch with her for some time, she writing to the children and sending them birthday gifts for many years.

A final story showed his remarkable capacity for ministering to the one. "My husband and I met Elder Hanks in the Honolulu airport in 1970 where we had met for his R&R from Vietnam," wrote one woman. "My infant child and I then got on a flight, along with Elder Hanks, to San Francisco, but mechanical problems kept us on the tarmac for two hours. We landed just before my SLC flight was to leave. I gathered up my infant, child seat, bags, etc. and started across the airport, thinking we wouldn't make it. Running back in my direction was Elder Hanks. He had sprinted all the way to the SLC flight right into the cockpit to ask the pilots (who hadn't been notified about us) to wait. Then he came back and helped us to the gate."[13]

Lowell L. Bennion summarized Duff's life this way: "He gets down to real religion, practicing what he preaches."

---

10. Margaret Young, "A Fitting Funeral for a Great Man," *Meridian Magazine*, Aug. 25, 2011.
11. MDH-JE, Nov. 16, 1979.
12. MDH-JE, Jan. 19, 1975.
13. Janet S., online comment, Aug. 6, 2011.

NOT ALL SERVICE IS HELPFUL

Sometimes Duff's commitment and loyalty to serve others was questionable. For example, during all of Richard's childhood, Duff was completely loyal to a barber who worked in their neighborhood. He stayed loyal to this man, whom he knew personally, even though many of his fellow clients migrated to newer, updated barber shops. And then the man developed a tremor as he aged, a big, noticeable tremor. Duff soldiered on, loyal to his friend, but Rich felt like his ears were in danger every time they went to get their haircuts.

CHURCH HISTORY—WHY SO INWARDLY FOCUSED?

There are several potential reasons why the church may have been so inwardly focused over the years. Soon after the organization of the church in 1830, its leaders established bishops' storehouses, places where grain and other commodities donated by members as free-will offerings were stored and distributed to help members in need. Once inside the fold, converts belonged to a church that focused on both the spiritual and economic needs of its members. Suffering intense persecution over the years surely solidified the feeling among members that the outside world was Babylon. At the same time, the church was young and economically shaky, and most of its scarce resources were spent on missionary work and operating the church. Additionally, most of the converts were poor, humble people now living in an insular society and trying to survive themselves, let alone provide assistance outwardly.

In April 1936, the church formally organized a welfare program to help church members suffering from the devastating effects of the Great Depression. President Heber J. Grant stated that its primary purpose was to "set up a system under which the curse of idleness would be done away with, the evils of a dole abolished, and independence, industry, thrift and self-respect be once more established amongst our people." The church's welfare system was a real blessing to the members, but it still had an inward focus on the church's "worthy poor." The church became stronger and better in its ability to serve its own people but was still less inclined to look outside its circle.

As the church moved into the twentieth century, the missionary program continued to provide an increasing number of new converts across the world in third-world countries, and the church became less parochial and more worldwide in its scope. With the growth of the church in all of these new countries, large amounts of capital were required to build church buildings, facilities, and programs for new converts who generally lived in poverty. Once again, with finite resources and huge demands on those resources, the church didn't focus much on helping those outside our faith.

The church's focus on aggressive proselyting, resistance to join any ecumenical movements, and dearth of humanitarian aid promoted a reputation that the church was not Christian in its expression of beliefs.

PLEADING FOR INSTITUTIONAL HUMANITARIAN EFFORTS

We are doing this, no strings attached; simply because it is the right thing to do.
—Marion D. Hanks[14]

No one I am acquainted with has demonstrated greater concern for Christian service than you.[15]

The state of affairs for most of the twentieth century was that the church had no formal humanitarian efforts and very little outreach to the poor and needy outside of its own insular religious society. It is no exaggeration to say that Duff spent more than fifty years trying to convince the institutional church to spend its resources on "the least of these" regardless of their faith or lack of one (Matthew 25:31–46).

This effort began early in his life when he chose to participate (while a general authority) with various nonprofit entities such as the Salvation Army, Salt Lake County Cancer Drives, Crippled Children Agency, and Mental Health organizations. Later, he initiated the church's pioneering effort with refugee camps in Southeast Asia, and finally after he retired from active church leadership, he became involved in three major nonprofit efforts around the world (see pages 540–44). But it was not an easy road to travel.

In a meeting with the First Presidency in the mid-1950s, Duff asked if they might discuss the problem of indigents and stranded travelers in the Salt Lake Valley who were being sent to the Salvation Army to obtain food and refuge. Duff was on the Board of the Salvation Army and decided to approach the First Presidency to ask if the church would help. President J. Reuben Clark questioned, "Salvation Army! Isn't that another church?"

Duff responded, "Well, if it is, President Clark, I haven't joined. I'm still a member of the same church you are. But they are doing a great good in this city," adding, "President Clark then commented that 'the church takes care of its own—let them take care of theirs'—and my response was that there are no 'theirs' and 'ours,' since this is our city too, and these travelers come here."[16]

President Clark was not pleased with Duff's bold response. But things turned out favorably. Duff wrote, "President McKay saved the situation by asking what was needed, and then authorizing the church to supply it. He was a wonderful, wonderful man."

On another occasion, perhaps twenty to twenty-five years later, Duff wrote, "On Wednesday, Melvin Lyman came in to see me and wail about the lack of church interest in working in third-world countries. He is my cousin and a physician who has given many years overseas. He's also a great missionary and cannot

14. Marion D. Hanks, as quoted in Peggy Fletcher Stack, *Salt Lake Tribune*, Oct. 3, 1992, in addition to multiple memos, letters, and presentations over the years, where Duff used these words.

15. Robert A. Tucker, longtime secretary to the First Council of the Seventy, to MDH.

16. MDH-R, Nov. 25, 2003.

see why the church cannot see the connection between Christ-like service and proclaiming the gospel."

Duff responded, "Neither can I."[17]

During a discussion with Gordon B. Hinckley in 1985, Duff spoke again about directing resources overseas, reminding Elder Hinckley about the refugee programs Duff had initiated there. Duff remarked, "I do not understand why we have not established ourselves as an agency qualified legally to do some good for people."

Unfortunately, Elder Hinckley responded "with some heat" that "he knew why, he knew why, he knew why; it is the 'we take care of ourselves principle.'"

Duff told Hinckley the story of Rita Edmonds and the refugee program and wrote hopefully, "Maybe something will come of [our meeting.]"[18]

During his many trips to Asia, Duff saw again and again, the vast number of God's children who needed aid. After touring the Asian missions in 1966, he wrote in his report letter to the First Presidency, "I spent the month of October in the three [Asian] missions.... One of the most sobering aspects of my visits to this indescribable part of the world, was to note the unselfish and very effective social service being rendered by other churches, in contrast to the almost total lack of it on our part." He went on to describe schools and hospitals in each major area provided by other churches.

To drive the point home, Duff commented that when our LDS missionaries got ill in Asia, they went to Seventh-day Adventist hospitals, were treated by Seventh-day Adventist doctors, and ate food grown on Seventh-day Adventist farms. He wondered earnestly when the church would get around to doing something medically for the people.[19]

In a follow-up meeting to his trip report, Marion G. Romney and other leaders in the room remarked that they "hated to see the church *compared* unfavorably with any other institution." Duff replied that "he didn't like to see the church *acting* unfavorably compared with other institutions." This statement was deeply resented by many in the room, but accurate.

His final summary: "We proselyte and bring people into the church, period. Our programs are rudimentary or nonexistent, our literature negligible, our interest in their personal welfare unexpressed. We need to find a way to permit us to express our Christianity in Asia."[20]

Duff continued his appeals for institutional involvement. But it wasn't just an academic effort; he continued to work with non-church agencies to support them, and he also continued to perform personal acts of service in his daily life.

After years of giving presentation after presentation and writing paper after

17. MDH-JE, Feb. 13, 1985.
18. MDH-JE, Mar. 27, 1985.
19. Trip report letter to the First Presidency, Jan. 17, 1966; see also MDH-JE, Feb. 4, 1971.
20. Trip report letter.

paper, when he got called as president of the Salt Lake Temple, he sent one final letter about Christian service to the Presidency of the Seventy, concluding it with these words: "Perhaps you will accept these humble suggestions as a kind of valedictory from me since I have no intention of continuing to pursue them further unless and until some inquiry is made."[21]

Over time, other church leaders began to share Duff's long-standing enthusiasm for Christian service. "Our Seventies Quorum meeting in the temple today centered in Russ Ballard's trip to Africa," he wrote three years later. "Good news to see the church reach out to do something in this special way of thoughtfulness and concern for our fellow men. Biggest message he got was that in the world there are many of God's special children who are way ahead of us with respect to our relationships to Christ and our fellow man. I sat and smiled. I am glad to see some progress toward practicing Christianity by the institution. Many of our people are wonderful, but the institution has not taken its part. Russ came back telling this story. Richard Scott laid his hand on my arm as the talk was given. He understands."[22]

Eventually, because of the efforts of Duff and others, the church began to morph and serve the less fortunate of the earth as an institution. It pleased Duff to see the church move toward "serving the least of these." Over the final decades of his life, he witnessed the creation of LDS Charities, Humanitarian Centers, Emergency Response Aid, the Just Serve program, and many other programs. He would clip out articles in the newspaper or *Church News* or in the church magazines and mark them up with a highlighter and a ruler—all with a smile on his face.

When Duff became emeritus, a dear colleague in church leadership wrote to him: "Dear Duff, I remember you, as the 'lone voice in the wilderness,' pleading that Christian service be integrated into the very fabric of the church.... It is interesting to note that an initial rejection of an idea fades as understanding builds upon proper and eternal principles. Thank you for this and many other lessons your life has taught and demonstrated."[23]

PRESENTING PRACTICAL SOLUTIONS

If someone needs help carrying their cross, may I give them your name?
—Anonymous

As Duff continued working with the refugee efforts in Asia in early 1982, he verbally submitted several ideas to the First Presidency suggesting two additional changes that the church could implement immediately: (1) substantially increase missionary Christian service (less proselyting) and (2) create an institutional clearing house, or matching, of church member skills with needs.

21. MDH-L to the Presidency of the Seventy, Nov. 4, 1982.
22. MDH-JE, Mar. 28, 1985.
23. Thomas J. Fyans to MDH, Oct. 1992.

In an April 22, 1982, letter submitted through official church channels, Duff formally suggested a determined effort to get all missionaries to perform "acts of Christian service" as an indispensable part of missionary work, and establishing a small church agency that would (1) inventory needs across the world, focusing on things that the church might best help with, and (2) inventory the skills and resources in the church and its members, and then pair 1 and 2 together to help Heavenly Father's children. The letter ended up in the Missionary Department and was not circulated further.

When he received no response to his letter, he followed up with another letter, dated May 27, 1982, to President Gordon B. Hinckley and included a copy of his previous letter.

MISSIONARY CHRISTIAN SERVICE

Ever since his time as a missionary in the Northern States, through his time as a mission president in England, through thousands of missionary interviews all over the world and heavy leadership involvement in Asia, Duff concluded that the best possible missionary work in the world involved more Christian service.

One might question Duff's ability to sustain an almost indefatigable push toward institutional Christian service over a forty-year period, and it eventually wore him down. Years later he wrote: "Boyd Packer passed me on the elevator trail and said Christian service and missionary work are to be discussed in the meeting of the Twelve today, so I sent him a letter that I wrote after we'd returned from Asia, which apparently nobody ever read. I've talked all I care to about it all and have a worn esophagus and a tired psyche. Matthew 25 and 28 go together for sure! When we learn that, we may make some headway"[24] (see pages 441–52).

MATCHING SKILLS WITH NEEDS—LDS CLEARING HOUSE

Duff pitched the idea of matching member skills with humanitarian needs over and over and over. A few months after writing his second letter to the First Presidency, Duff wrote to the Presidency of the Seventy reiterating his previous suggestions and adding, "I do not believe that the execution of a small agency [a clearing house matching member skills with needs across the world] can be done through the Missionary or Welfare Departments. A dentist or physician who goes out to provide service for a month is really not in the line of missionary or welfare services supervision. What they do need is someone who can go into an area and ascertain needs, resolve legal and temporal realities, and prepare the way for our people to do the work."[25]

The following is a reply to a church member dentist who asked Duff why the church didn't have organized programs to work in other countries:

Thank you for your excellent letter. I have submitted an application for consideration of a church effort on a wider scale to enlist the skills and strength and

24. MDH-JE, Jan. 31, 1985.

25. MDH-L to the Presidency of the Seventy, Nov. 4, 1982.

faith available to help people. Your thoughtful letter and practical suggestions will help if and as we get a chance to pursue that idea.

I hope for the day when our fine people will be doing good things for the Lord's children under the banner of the church. I am fully supportive of the wonderful work done by so many people over many years when we were institutionally absent. I am anxious that the church establish credibility as an institution that really helps people at the level of their needs and through the depths of our humanity. When that reputation becomes the chief scepter of recognition, rather than our aggressive proselyting, then I think we will need less of the latter and will have the best and sweetest kind of consequences.[26]

CONCLUDING WISDOM

While doing research for this chapter, and searching through his files, the following card, in Duff's handwriting, fell out of one of his briefcases. It is a fitting summary to this topic:

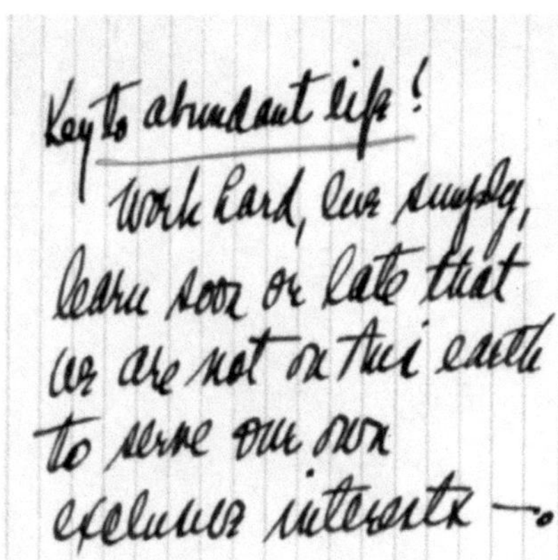

Key to an abundant life!

Work hard, live simply,
learn soon or late that
we are not on this earth
to serve our own
exclusive interests —.

— Marion Duff Hanks

26. MDH-L to Dallas Murdoch, June 18, 1982.

NEW WAYS AND NEW REALMS TO SERVE

56

Emeritus and After Emeritus

He never did figure out that emeritus could mean "slow down."[1]

Duff was granted emeritus status (which he jokingly pronounced *em-er-eye-tus*), on October 3, 1992, just a few days before his seventy-first birthday. Typical of his approach, with a complete lack of self-congratulatory sentiment, he began his fiftieth and final talk in general conference with these words: "Anyone who has been permitted to serve as we have is honored beyond personal merit. We know that, and are grateful."[2] That was it. That was all he said about his church service after almost forty years.

A perceptive friend wrote to him, saying, "In 1953, while a student at BYU, I read your first general conference address. I still remember the humble acknowledgement you made in that first talk. Your opening remarks this last Sunday reflected those same qualities. What struck me most about your remarks was that rather than focus on you and your experiences, you concentrated on what we needed to hear—the need to reach out to others and, as always, to emphasize the positive. We left thankful for one more patient reminder of the 'things that matter most.'"[3]

What isn't well known about that day is that Duff was initially informed that the previous general conference (April 1992) would be his final general conference talk. He had chosen at that time to speak about the Savior and "the royal law" (James 2:8) and "Thou shalt love thy neighbor as thyself" (Galatians 5:14).

Duff's departure was noteworthy. One of his coworkers wrote, "A significant chapter in church history closes today as you leave your office for the last time. I cannot foresee that the institutional memory you carry will ever again be duplicated. I hope you find time to write and publish. Please know that your influence will continue to linger not only here at church headquarters, but throughout the earth in the individual lives of all who have been touched by your words and ways."[4]

---

1. A family member.
2. MDH-T, "A Loving, Communicating God," GC, Oct. 1992.
3. Roger Porter to MDH, Oct. 1992.
4. Hoyt W. Brewster Jr. to MDH, Aug. 1992.

The Salt Lake Tribune
RELIGION
Religion Desk: 237-2045
SATURDAY, October 3, 1992

LDS 'Poet-Soul' Hanks To Retire After 39 Years

■ Continued from A-1

named to the Quorum of Seventy.

He often has told Kent Miles, Coy's son, that, "when placed in a position of authority, some men grow and others swell."

He grew.

In the early 1950s, he took black visitors into his home after no hotels in Salt Lake City would receive them, says Eugene England, who was one of his students at the University of Utah.

His oldest daughter, Susan Hanks Maughn, says Elder Hanks even gave away several family TV sets to people who needed them.

In the 1960s, Elder Hanks visited war-torn Vietnam, where he stayed up all night sending notes to the parents, wives or families of LDS soldiers he met there.

Elder Hanks always had a particular fondness for the youth of the church. He was active in Boy Scouts, receiving the highest awards that Scouting offers.

He also served the nation on the President's Citizens' Advisory Committee on Youth Fitness from 1957 to 1963, and on the President's Council on Physical Fitness and Sport from 1968 to 1980.

Elder Hanks wanted to have good relations with the embassies and the U.N. personnel in the area. During his visits to Vietnam, he became acquainted with the problems of refugee camps there. He convinced LDS leaders that doing Christian ser-

Lynn R. Johnson/The Salt Lake Tribune

Marion D. Hanks, retiring as an LDS general authority, is shown, at left, speaking in 1970, and with wife Maxine in 1990.

Friends, Colleagues Pay Tribute to Inspirational Hanks

Wallace G. Bennett, a fellow member of Rotary Club in Salt Lake: *"Duff is one of those Mormons who is a bridge in the community. His friends in*

ly not an ecclesiastical politician."

□□□

Kent Miles, son of Coy who

pretentious but unstinting sharing of self."

□□□

Maryan Myers Shumway, a

LDS 'Poet-Soul' Hanks to retire after 39 years. *Courtesy Salt Lake Tribune*

A FLOOD OF GRATEFUL LETTERS

Hundreds of congratulatory and appreciative letters began pouring in. People were kind and generous toward Duff and his contributions. The scrapbooks Phyllis kept were bulging.

One letter writer said:

> Emotions ran high yesterday after the final session of general conference. We met as a family and discussed your release. One of my sweet daughters-in-law said, "How can the church get along without Elder Hanks?" Truly, you have been a beacon of light to all who have known you, both in and out of the church. Your bearing commanded respect. You were ever impressive in your speech and provocative in your thoughts expressed. We have benefited through the years from your devotion to your calling and your innumerable contributions to the cause. Thank you so much.[5]

And another example:

> It was never my privilege to meet you, but for forty years you have been a shining example to me and my family, and have conducted yourself like one of God's true noblemen. If "no one is indispensable," there must be one exception to this rule—Marion D. Hanks. Your conference address was exactly as one would have expected

5. Unnamed person to MDH.

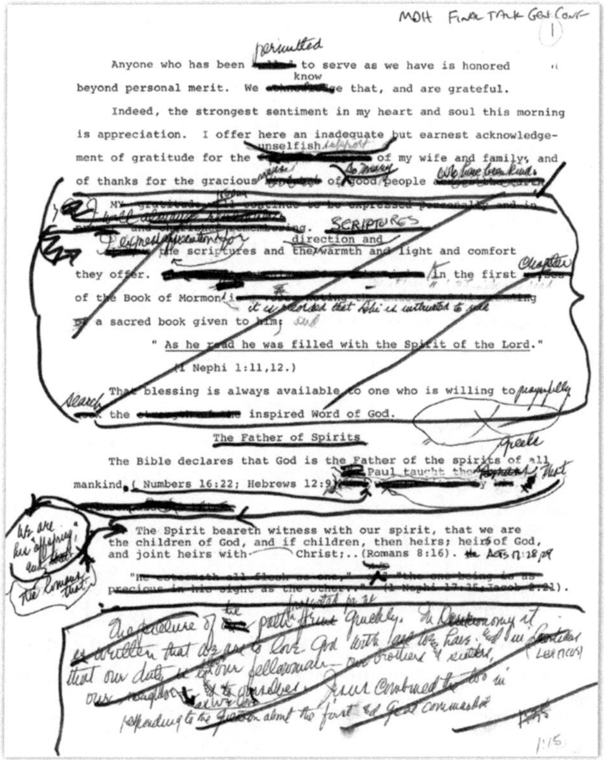
MDH FINAL TALK GEN CONF

Anyone who has been permitted to serve as we have is honored beyond personal merit. We know that, and are grateful.

Indeed, the strongest sentiment in my heart and soul this morning is appreciation. I offer here an inadequate but earnest acknowledgement of gratitude for the unselfish support of my wife and family, and of thanks for the gracious [illegible] of good people [illegible]

[illegible] SCRIPTURES direction and [illegible] the scriptures and the warmth and light and comfort they offer. [illegible] In the first chapter of the Book of Mormon [illegible] a sacred book given to him:

"As he read he was filled with the Spirit of the Lord."

(1 Nephi 1:11,12.)

That blessing is always available to one who is willing to [illegible] the [illegible] inspired Word of God.

The Father of Spirits

The Bible declares that God is the Father of the spirits of all mankind. (Numbers 16:22; Hebrews 12:9) [illegible] Paul taught the [illegible]

The Spirit beareth witness with our spirit, that we are the children of God, and if children, then heirs; heirs of God, and joint heirs with Christ;..(Romans 8:16). Acts 17:28,29

"He esteemeth all flesh as one," [illegible] "the one being as precious in his sight as the other." (1 Nephi 17:35; Jacob 2:21).

Page one of an early working draft of Duff's final general conference address, October 1992.

> from you—a sincere, earnest plea with the Saints to do better, a comfort to those of us who try so hard, the expression of a fervent testimony, and—so typical—devoid of any reference to your own person and your many accomplishments. God bless you, dear Elder Hanks, for your wonderful, selfless, and caring ministry, and for always having been a champion for us humble and simple people.[6]

And one more:

> I want to express my thanks and good wishes regarding your "graduation" to emeritus status. Thank you for your graciousness during my college years, and for writing me encouraging words when I felt particularly endangered by some things I was reporting on.... I have some sense of how much richer and enlightened the church has been due to your presence and perception; now I find myself hoping that *you* have survived spirit and soul. And may God grant you the years of peace and light you shared with me and with others.[7]

6. Max Zimmer to MDH.
7. Linda Sillitoe to MDH, Oct. 5, 1992.

FEELINGS ABOUT BEING EMERITUS

Duff was pleased to accept emeritus status. He and Maxine had had a wonderful and choice experience over many years. They had been able to rub shoulders, work with, and come to love some of the finest men and women in the church—members and leaders.

But forty years is a long time. At the beginning of his ministry, Duff's and Maxine's expectations were anchored around his lifetime appointment as a general authority, but their expectations were amended with the change announced in September 1978 that all general authorities except the apostles would be granted emeritus status at age seventy. They began a new life together. Duff told his children, "It's your mother's turn now to do what she wants."

A NEW WORLD

Duff refused to slow down after leaving full-time church service. He didn't seem to be able to figure out what *emeritus* meant. Someone said, "Marion D. Hanks just wasn't cut out for retirement."

As soon as his responsibilities to the church were completed, he set up shop in a small office in the Judge Building in downtown Salt Lake. Phyllis graciously agreed to go with him as his secretary on a part-time basis. He wrote to a friend that he was incredibly busy doing "everything except resting and rusting."

In the months before he became emeritus, Duff was inwardly trying to decide what he would do to stay active. After forty-three years of Maxine's following Duff around, he was quite sure he owed her the chance to follow some of her dreams. He also had the Hanks Foundation to run, but what else? Decades before, he had memorized something Joseph Smith had said shortly before his death: "A man filled with the love of God is not content with blessing his family alone, but ranges through the whole world, anxious to bless the whole human race."[8]

With that in mind, he turned his focus towards seven major areas, including the leadership of three nonprofit organizations:

Ouelessebougou Utah Alliance (OUA). Duff served as chair of this nonprofit organization that provides the means of self-reliance to villages in West Africa. Duff and Rich went on two trips to Mali after Duff was seventy years old. They met with villagers, physically dug gardens, and tried to survive the mosquitos at night.

Enterprise Mentors International. Duff was chair of this nonprofit headquartered in St. Louis, Missouri, that taught business skills and self-reliance to small entrepreneurs. He traveled to meet with aid recipients in the Philippines and Guatemala.

The Marion D. and Maxine C. Hanks Foundation. Duff was chair of this nonprofit group that helps individuals in acute financial need and crisis.

8. "Letter to Quorum of the Twelve," Dec. 15, 1840, Joseph Smith Papers, josephsmithpapers.org.

A modicum of public speaking. Duff continued to accept a few engagements as a public speaker.

Family time. Duff was able to spend more time with Maxine and the grandkids.

Personal acts of service. Duff continued practicing "Habits of Helpfulness" all around him, searching out people to help in any way he could.

Hana, Maui, Hawaii. Duff and Maxine returned for a few weeks at a time to allow her to enjoy her homeland after she lived elsewhere for more than fifty years.

OUELESSEBOUGOU UTAH ALLIANCE (OUA)

Your example of service to the "have-nots" of the world, from Africa to SLC, reflects a great love of people everywhere.
—Elder Richard P. Lindsay

The Ouelessebougou Utah Alliance (OUA), now called The Ouelessebougou Alliance (OA), was founded in 1985 by five Utah men who traveled to East Africa to see if they could help after major droughts there. They found all kinds of nonprofit organizations in East Africa, but hardly any organizations were helping in West Africa, especially Mali. So that's where they focused.

Duff served as chair of the board of the Alliance, supporting a four-fold program of service to numerous villages in Mali, including digging freshwater wells, developing village gardens, providing health care, and constructing schools.

Sitting in board meetings and raising funds for the Alliance was not enough for Duff, even at age seventy-one. So, in November 1992 and again in 1994, Duff traveled to Mali to participate personally in the operations there. Rich went with him.

Despite entreaties by his wife and others, Duff wanted to sleep at the Alliance compound in Ouelessebougou rather than in a hotel in Bamako, the capital of Mali. At that time, the Alliance compound was very rudimentary—the toilet was a hole in the ground, the mosquitos were hostile, and the 'shower' was a hose attached to a used car radiator hung by some wire.

He visited many villages, observing the ongoing construction of schools and wells. He also spent much of five days working alongside the local villagers, bent over, hand-digging furrows for village gardens, which led Rich to mention in his report to the executive director of the Alliance that "future expeditions going at this time of year should be composed of hearty, strong individuals with a disposition to work hard and get dirty, but probably not in their 70s."

Duff concurred with a joint comment from the members of the expedition that this was the "most rewarding, most worthwhile thing I have done in years." He wrote, "Few of my life's experiences have been as tender and satisfying as those few days toiling with the people of the villages, preparing and seeding their gardens during the day, and then meeting with them at night with one ancient kerosene lamp, as they learned reading and writing and arithmetic. We joined them in pulling up, hand over

Duff and Richard with village men as they rest from making bricks for a school in Mali, West Africa, 1992.

hand, the stitched goatskin buckets from wells that now for the first time in their lives provide sufficient year-round water for their crops and personal needs."[9]

While the work was tiring and the days were long, the rewards were spectacular. Both the young and the old, who weeks before were illiterate, stood with some anxiety and proudly read basic sentences aloud to their fellow villagers and solved simple math problems on an old, cracked chalkboard.

As they entered one village, the ninety-one-year-old village chief said, "You are like a rope lowered from heaven to help us with what we really need."

Rich wrote:

> Our travel to Mali was eye-opening. Arriving in Mali, we got off a huge, modern airplane and walked down the stairs into a little ancient building where none of the passengers followed generally accepted rules of human separation. I lost Dad in the room and couldn't see him because if I turned my head, I would have kissed the man next to me, he was that close. I called out, "Dad, are you okay?" He replied, "Yes, but I am learning an entirely new definition of the term 'personal space.'" He was okay, and we survived. Things were a bit iffy later, when the immigration folks wanted to know details of the huge suitcase I had been asked to transport, which was full of replacement eye lenses (I think). On the flight back to Paris, a lady on the plane started to build a little stack of wood kindling on the

9. MDH-T, "The Contribution You Can Make to an Ailing World," BYU commencement speech, Apr. 22, 1993.

Duff visiting with entrepreneur shoemakers in the Philippines, 1993.

floor of the plane and was going to make a fire because she was cold. I rang the flight attendant button with some urgency.

The eye surgeons traveling with the alliance changed people's lives immediately. And the gynecologist-obstetricians were miracle workers. The repair surgeries the medical professionals performed were mostly inexpensive and returned their patient's lives to normal, giving them their lives back. That is the kind of lasting effect the Alliance has.

Duff loved the Alliance and continued his involvement with it through formal and then informal means to the end of his life. He was extremely complimentary of the leadership of the nonprofit, including executive director Michelle McFarlane, his dear friend Addie Fuhriman on the board, and many others in both Salt Lake and Africa. Even though Maxine and Duff are gone, the extended Hanks family has remained involved in the cause of the Alliance.

ENTERPRISE MENTORS INTERNATIONAL

Thank you for teaching us that the only time you can be happy is when you're quietly helping others. For always battling to champion the underdog. For caring so much for the little people.[10]

Duff also served as the chairman of Enterprise Mentors International (EMI, now simply called Mentors). Founded in 1990 by returned mission president Menlo Smith and a few friends, EMI was created to assist economically and

10. Mac Christensen to MDH.

educationally deprived people in three large cities in the Philippines and has since grown to include centers in countries all over the world. Its goal is to transform generational poverty into sustainable self-reliance through programs such as mentoring, training, small-scale business loans, microenterprises, and assistance to family-owned businesses.

As chair of EMI, Duff split his time between traveling around the United States giving cottage meetings in wealthy donors' homes, leading board meetings, and traveling to the target countries to visit with recipients.

EMI's guiding principles are similar to those of the OUA, including the importance of providing a hand up rather than a handout, aiming for self-reliance as the end state. For most EMI clients, regular employment in the formal sector of the economy is not available because of a lack of skill, literacy, and resources. This means that they must often be self-employed as vendors or peddlers, leaving them subject to the whims of local loan sharks, bureaucratic red tape, bribes, and corruption. The EMI programs provided alternatives, teaching entrepreneurial and basic business skills, and giving microloans at low rates.

Duff said, "For those who understand what Enterprise Mentors is doing far away, in terms of human good for God's children, there is a strong sense of satisfaction in the vital help and hope being given there."

THE MARION D. AND MAXINE C. HANKS FOUNDATION

Your ministry has been punctuated by your service to the disadvantaged, forgotten, and those that are lost. Your work in humanitarian ways has inspired many of us to follow in your footsteps.[11]

In 1996, led by Hyrum Smith, the Hanks Foundation was established and funded by a few of Duff and Maxine's British missionaries so that Duff and Maxine and their posterity would have money in perpetuity to help those in need. Maxine and Duff had been doing that all of their lives already, with their own modest means. But now, with this sweet gift from their missionaries, they were able to help many more people.

The foundation focuses on helping individuals or families in difficult circumstances—a widow in Albuquerque, a family of a convicted felon in Provo, a family of three boys, each with spina bifida, who needed a special van—just trying to fill the gaps in life. The Hanks Foundation and the good it has done brought an incredible amount of joy to Duff and Maxine and has been a blessing to their entire family, as three generations have been able to provide help to those in acute distress.

A MODICUM OF PUBLIC SPEAKING

Duff also continued to accept a few engagements as a public speaker, although

11. Hugh W. Pinnock to MDH.

Duff and Maxine at Aspen Grove, Provo Canyon, Utah. Left, ca. 1965, right ca. 2000.

the volume of his acceptances fell in his later years. Still, he would occasionally agree to do favors for close friends or family. For example, in 2002 he gave a talk titled "I Do Not Do My Work in the Spirit of Benefaction but of Atonement" (a quotation from Albert Schweitzer), at Utah Valley State College in Orem.

After his retirement, he gave eight speeches at various venues at Brigham Young University, dedicated buildings on several university campuses, spoke to the servicemen at Fort Hood, Texas, spoke at Rotary zone conferences in three states, and wrote a few pieces for magazines and other people's books. He continued to perform sealings in the temple and speak at a ward now and then, several stake conferences, and a few fundraising dinners. He also continued to respond to the capacious but diminishing volume of letters he received. Eventually, he felt he'd spoken enough.

FAMILY TIME

A congratulatory letter to Duff from a friend said, "I hope your retirement brings you and your 'first love,' Maxine, the opportunity for time together that has been in such short supply these past forty years."

It may have taken them a while to get used to being around each other so much, but the family never heard about it. It seemed like they were even more in love and were pleased to be able to spend more time together. One minor issue was that Duff was sick of traveling, but Maxine suggested they might travel a bit.

They compromised and didn't travel much, except to Hawaii and Aspen Grove. They did, however, have more time to spend with their grandchildren, attending some athletic games with them and teaching them. Maxine was pleased to have as many of her family as possible come to her house in Salt Lake or in Hawaii just to be with her.

PERSONAL SERVICE

In the pattern of the Lord he loves, he goes about doing good, only a little of which is known.
—Maxine C. Hanks

As Duff aged, his desire to help others did not decrease. His ability to perform physical acts of service, such as towing cars out of the snow and mowing lawns diminished, but he replaced them by writing letters of encouragement and giving monetary gifts from his own pocket and from the Hanks Foundation to those in need.

HANA, MAUI, HAWAII

If I take the wings of the morning,
And dwell in the uttermost parts of the sea;
Even there shall thy hand lead me,
And thy right hand shall hold me.
—Psalm 139:7–10

The famous aviator Charles Lindberg chose that scripture from Psalms to be inscribed on his headstone. He is buried not far from Maxine and Duff's home on Maui. When you're there, it's hard not to believe you are on the right hand of God. For Maxine and Duff, Hana meant seclusion and quiet serenity. It was a place where they could relax, watch the ocean, go for walks to nearby waterfalls in the peaceful mornings, or go to the beach. Maxine could wander around their small garden of beautiful flowers and bushes that she had chosen, placed, and planted. Duff could do some physical work by trimming back the plants and picking a papaya or a stalk of bananas.

Background

Eastern Maui has a rich heritage of battles and sieges as the Kingdom of Hawaii was becoming unified. Muolea, right below the Hanks home, was the summer residence of King David Kalakaua. Hana's fame grew in the late twentieth century as marketers labeled it "Far from Waikiki," and songs began describing the winding road that takes people there. It still has only one school, one gas station, no stoplights, and some of the most wonderful people in the world.

Maxine's father, Elwood Christensen, was a successful real estate broker in Honolulu, and after a planned development in Hana didn't go through, he purchased the lot in Muolea (Hana) in May 1947. When Elwood died and his assets were divided, Maxine used her inheritance to purchase the lot from her siblings and to build a small home on the half-acre lot. The house and tenant apartment were completed in 1993. They named it Hale Maluhia I Ke Kai (Peaceful House by the Sea).

The Road

Arguably, today's eastern Maui is most famously known for how to get there—The Road to Hana. For some, this is simultaneously the most beautiful and most miserable road on earth. It is a two-to three-hour drive with stunning waterfalls and vegetation, fifty-four one-lane bridges, and hundreds of winding curves that are either fun or not so fun, depending on one's stomach and disposition. Duff described it as only he could: "There are some, like Maxine, who have made the trip scores of times and have solved a little bit of the bilious experience by taking half a Dramamine tablet. Others, like my own poor self, though a graduate of the mighty deep in war time, have no reaction to the Hana highway. It is simply a road with some bends and bridges and waterfalls, and sheer beauty that is incredible." About 10 o'clock in the morning, the first tourist cars begin to pass by on their way to the Seven Sacred Pools (there are more than seven, and they are not sacred). Duff wrote, "Every car that jousts with the world-famous Hana Highway passes our place. Many pause to catch their breath and assure themselves they are headed to the fabled Seven Pools and to the burial place of Charles Lindbergh. (One carload asked if we knew where the Wright Brothers are buried!) We send them on, faith restored, to learn more about this great aviator and far-away place."[12]

Hana Time

Maxine was transformed in Hana. She was happy everywhere, but especially so in Hawaii. Duff would read and type letters and some journal entries and conduct the business of the nonprofits he was involved with. He fashioned bamboo flag poles so he could fly his United States and Hawaiian flags. Together, he and Maxine would drive into Town to buy groceries or supplies and the daily newspaper from Hasegawa's store or some vegetables from the farmer's market.

They were pleased to share the house with their family and a few friends. In a letter to friends who would be staying in their home, Duff wrote a four-page, single-spaced tome expounding on everything from light switches to the ice maker to the friendly geckos to the mooing cows next door. But his description of one part of the house is classic:

"The beautiful and major surprise is the *outside shower.* It should be noted that there are those, living and dead, whose chief regret in life is that they were somehow not attracted to that outside shower. It becomes a lifesaver several times a day and is pure unadulterated fun. If you shower at night, please pick up the wooden mat when you are through and sweep the excess water on the concrete slab with the broom hanging there. Maxine is afraid I am dictating too much in this letter, but I have hardly begun."[13]

Maxine and Duff were welcomed as family in the Hana Branch of the church and loved their many friends in that unique setting. Maxine supported the town's small historical museum, and they participated in funding for local addiction recovery, elder care, and conservation.

12. MDH-L to Michelle Macfarlane, Mar. 1996.

13. MDH-L to Macfarlane.

A New Life Begins

So Duff and Maxine began a second life together, serving others in new, formal ways, spending more time with each other and their family, and trying to unwind more than fifty years of nonstop activity.

57

Decline and Death

Everybody needs his memories. They keep the wolf of insignificance from the door.
—Saul Bellow[1]

In May 1974, at age fifty-three, after a health scare with an elevated heartbeat, Duff wrote in his journal a sentiment his wife and children would hear him voice repeatedly as he aged:

"The thought of invalidism would give me pause.... A sharp, clean departure from this sphere would be a blessing and benefit, though I am not pushing for the privilege right away."[2]

Duff often repeated this thought, hoping his exit from earth would happen, to use his words, with a "nice, clean heart attack." The cruel irony of his verbalized desire for a quick exit from this life, juxtaposed with his final seven dementia-plagued years, is one of the unanswered questions of Duff's life.

DEALING WITH ADVERSITY

The rain falls on every house.
It's the foundation of the house that determines the outcome.
—Marion D. Hanks[3]

Why Duff had to suffer so much at the end of his life, after all those decades serving others, is a question his family is interested in asking the Lord. Although, in reality, it wasn't him suffering as much as it was those who loved him, particularly Maxine. When asked about the purpose of Duff's slow dementia-driven demise, a dear family friend responded, "Maybe it was your family that needed to learn something."

At any rate, whenever the question intrudes, one's mind goes straight to Duff's teachings on the subject. Because of all the counseling he did with people suffering problems, one of his most studied topics, with voluminous folders of talks and quotes and scriptures, was the topic of "Affliction and Adversity."

1. Saul Bellow, *Mr. Sammler's Planet* (New York: Viking Press, 1970).
2. MDH-JE, May 3, 1974.
3. MDH-A, "God Will Consecrate Affliction," in *Know the Book* (self-pub., 1962).

As always, Duff turned to the scriptures for answers to the problem of affliction. Here is a sampling from his myriad materials and speech preparation on the subject:

All suffer afflictions:

- "God has not promised immunity from affliction. He loves us and believes in us and will do anything he can to help us, but he will not impose on our free agency."
- "He maketh the sun and rain to fall on the just and the unjust" (Matthew 5:43–45).
- "Be patient in afflictions, for thou shalt have many" (D&C 24:8).

What, then, are His promises?

- The Lord visits people in their affliction (Mosiah 24:10–14).
- He will support us in our trials and lift us up at the last day (Alma 36:3).
- "All these things shall give thee experience ... for thy good" (D&C 122:5–7).

Preparing for a speech, he wrote on his yellow pad: "Do you really want to tell God that if he loves you and if he is just and if he is fair and if he is kind, then he will keep you from those experiences that made him and his Son what they are? *No, God does not deny us the very experiences we came here to have.* He does not insulate us from tribulation or guarantee immunity from trouble. But he will support us, and he will help us improve throughout our difficult experiences."

Duff then asked a teaching question: "The issue is not why good people have trials, but how shall good people respond when they are tried."[4]

As he frequently did, Duff had a lesser-known scripture story to illustrate his point. The prophet Habakkuk felt that he could bear anything, meet any test, with absolute confidence in God *if* he could understand the purpose or meaning of the suffering. Duff wrote,

> Nevertheless, he would not yield. He built his watchtower of faith and waited for the clouds of distress and affliction to lift. Hear his testimony, "Although the fig tree shall not blossom, neither shall fruit be in the vines; the labor of the olive tree shall fail, and the field shall yield no meat; the flock shall be cut off from the fold, and there shall be no herd in the stalls. Yet, I will rejoice in the Lord, I will joy in the God of my salvation" (Habakkuk 3:17–19).
>
> For the heroic folks with disabilities, for those who endure the buffetings and buffeters of mortal anguish, and for the heroes who serve and nurse and care for them, the courage and faith of this ancient prophet should yield fruits of comfort and reassurance, of renewed fidelity in the face of difficulty.[5]

One of Duff's dearest friends was a courageous woman named Louise Lake. Louise had contracted polio in her early thirties and, though disabled and in a

4. MDH-T, "A Loving, Communicating God," GC, Oct. 1992.
5. MDH-T, unpublished talk. See also MDH-T, "Trust in the Lord," GC, Apr. 1975.

wheelchair, became a beacon of hope for others similarly situated. She taught people with disabilities how to live again. She was named the first "Handicapped Person of the Year" by President Eisenhower, and she authored a book titled *Every Day a Bonus*.

At her funeral in January 1982, Duff summed up her life with these words, "That one who has been confined to a wheelchair for all these years and has suffered much heartache, should radiate so much of healing and motivate in others so much gratitude and renewed determination, is unassailable witness that God can indeed consecrate our afflictions to our gain."[6] The example of Louise Lake and hundreds more like her gave Duff and his family courage to deal with the difficulties that awaited him.

CHANGES

In a 2002 letter to a friend in another state, Duff wrote, "We moved five years ago from Maxine's 'dream home' on the hill, where we lived for about 25 years. We're now out in Holladay, where all five of our children are now living, within five minutes of each other. So, we have a modest place behind gates. My eleventh year of emeritus will soon begin, and we have membership in a wonderful, regular ward with good people, whom we can help teach and be partners with."[7]

In 2003, about eight years before his death, the family started noticing Duff's cognitive abilities begin to slip. It started slowly and wasn't at first distinguishable from what they thought was normal aging. But then unusual things started to occur. For instance, he started to believe and comply with the TV infomercial hawkers when they said, "Get out your credit card now!" A couple of unneeded new vacuum cleaners and a portable air conditioner showed up from UPS.

One night Rich was awakened by his phone ringing at 3:30 a.m. Maxine and Duff's wonderful neighbor Dave Robertson asked if Rich could come right over. Rich wrote, "When I arrived, I found Dad, all dressed in his suit and ready for the day, banging on the locked gate of their cul-de-sac. I said, 'Hi, Dad, whatcha doing?' He replied, 'I have a missionary meeting downtown this morning, son.' I said, 'Dad, you are retired from the church, remember?' I gently led him back to bed."

For the next eighteen months, gentle caregivers came to the house to help take care of him. And the family learned that while the attention is usually on the patient, it is the main caregiver, Maxine, who was suffering the most.

Eventually, as he became weaker and more dependent, the family decided they had to move him to a memory care center. During those final years of Duff's life, Maxine was a saint in her devotion to Duff. For seven years, she went every single day to see him, with rare exceptions. She continued to be there for him throughout his prolonged illness with devotion, passion, and love.

No matter what else dementia took from him, he never stopped expressing his

6. MDH-A, *Deseret News*, Jan. 1982.
7. MDH-L, to a friend, 2002.

love for Maxine. Just a month before he died, as he was visiting with a grandchild, he began to cry, saying, "Do you know why I'm weeping?"

The boy replied, "No, Grandpa, why are you weeping?"

And Duff said, "Because I love ... my wife."

Church services on Sunday were a new experience, with about twenty-five wheelchairs in one room. The branch presidency and their wives were gentle and responsive to Duff and to his entire family. During his illness, the family encountered many health-care angels that live on the earth.

Many kind people would come to visit. President Thomas S. Monson would drop in about every two weeks on a Monday, and he and Duff would sit and visit or just sit. His missionaries, some of his colleagues, friends from his youth, all would visit occasionally. Someone from the family, in addition to Maxine, was there every day. His daughters would take him raspberries and cream; others would drop by with a hamburger or cookies. Rich would sneak him a Frosty ice cream from Wendy's. The nurses told the family to be extra careful about giving him sugar because of his diabetes, and then one day they just looked at each other and said, "What are we doing depriving him of the joy of ice cream and cookies when he is almost ninety and suffering from dementia?" Ice cream went back on the menu.

Duff's illness was a kind of dementia that cycled up and down for the first few years. This meant that on some days Duff seemed almost normal, and the very next day, it was like someone else was inhabiting his body. Some days Rich would walk into his room, and he would ask who "the tall man" was. The very next day he'd walk in, and before a word was spoken, he'd say, "Hi, Rich."

At the end of July 2011, Duff's body started to fail. For his last few nights, Maxine and the children squished into his room and tried to sleep in chairs and on the floor. At the end, when he couldn't seem to escape his body, they decided it might be because he didn't want to leave Maxine. One of them took her outside the room, and Duff slipped away on August 4, 2011.

FUNERAL AND CONDOLENCES

His funeral was held in a stake center. Frankly, it would have been nice to have held it in the Tabernacle or the Assembly Hall on Temple Square, given his decades of service there. But at his death, he had been emeritus and out of the public eye for almost twenty years. Plus, most of the people who knew him best were already deceased. The stake center worked out just fine. It was overflowing.

The funeral was sweet and represented him well. The opening song was sung by Duff and Maxine's grandchildren. Children Nancy, Susan, and Richard spoke, and then Nancy's daughters performed a sweet musical number. They were followed by two of his beloved missionaries, Elder Quentin L. Cook and Elder Jeffrey R. Holland of the Quorum of the Twelve Apostles, and then President Thomas S. Monson. They then sang "How Gentle God's Commands," which Duff had wanted as the closing hymn.

Duff's casket carried out of his funeral service by his grandson pallbearers, August 13, 2011. *Courtesy Deseret News*

In her talk, Susan said, "He spent his life teaching and testifying of the Savior in his rich, resonant voice. He lived his life following His teachings with no outward pretense or 'seeming to be.' It was simply the way he lived."

Nancy said, "This is the image of my father—inclusive of all peoples, all faiths, all races. Men and women. Giving the understanding of the word. And teaching of the Word, who came, 'mighty to save.'"

In his remarks, Rich commented, "Dad was a good man who honored God with his life. His absolute devotion to the Savior and his testimony of Christ permeated all that he did."

Elder Cook said, "He was always willing to share his rich testimony of Christ, and his life was defined by his faith in the Lord."

Elder Holland shared, "The scriptures were the hammer and tongs he used to forge our souls. He taught me the gospel of Jesus Christ and thus changed my life forever."

President Monson said, "We have had in our midst all these years Marion D. Hanks—an honorable man, a man of God. He accepted in full the Apostle Paul's challenge to be 'an example of the believers.'"

Sons-in-law Paul Maughan and John Baird gave the family prayer and dedicated the grave, respectively. There was a military salute and a Scottish piper. It was a sweet day.

The Hanks family with Maxine at Duff's funeral, August 13, 2011:
Paul and Susan H. Maughan, Chris and Mary H. Clifford, Liz and Richard Hanks,
Maxine Hanks, John and Nancy H. Baird, Ann H. and Spencer Clawson.

58

The Gift of Self

Marion Duff Hanks was "one of those rare souls who see sermons in stones and books in brooks and the bright light of God over everything. Across a reverently gentle lifetime, he has had eyes and ears to hear music which most of us miss.[1]

Marion Duff Hanks dedicated his whole life to God, Christ, and his fellow man. In a letter to his mother during the war, Duff wrote, "When I think back over my first 24 years, I am not sure that I have done anything worth speaking about above a whisper. If I listed the activities of my life so far which might be regarded as constructive and worthy of mortality, I believe I could name three things:

1. The Lord's work, and the church has always come first in my life, wherever I've been or whatever the circumstance.
2. I tried to be a good missionary and worked hard at it.
3. I love my family dearly and would hope fondly to be able one day to do for them and theirs what they have done for me.

I am hopeful that my life, while unmarked by great success or unusual achievement, might be a satisfaction and a joy to you when you look back over the eternities.[2]

Sixty years later he wrote, "My approach has always been that, with whatever talents and whatever limitations I may have, my purpose was to try to serve the Lord and be helpful to His work and to those who carry the burden of it. So, I have tried to share, and encourage, and strengthen, and lift to the extent I could."[3]

IN THE END, WHAT HAD HE LEARNED?

The theologian Karl Barth, when asked to summarize what he'd learned in a lifetime of learning, is reported to have said, "Jesus loves me, this I know, for the Bible tells me so."[4]

---

1. Daughter Susan Maughan at Duff's funeral, quoting from Duff's description of President David O. McKay, "Soul of a Prophet," *Improvement Era*, Sept. 1968, 3, possibly paraphrased from William Shakespeare, *As You Like It,* 2.1.12–17.
2. MDH-L to Maude, Oct. 13, 1945, from Pearl Harbor.
3. "News of the Church," *Ensign*, Nov. 1984.
4. Karl Barth, as reported by Billy Graham, "A Simple Message," BillyGraham.org.

Aldous Huxley was asked in his eighties what advice he had to share. His answer was, "Be a little kinder to each other."[5]

When asked what he had learned in his life, these two sentences became his two most frequently spoken answers and Duff shared them often as he approached the end of his life.

"I've learned some simple things, I think. I don't know much more than I knew fifty years ago, but I know some things very well," he said. "And the first and most significant thing I know, is that if your life does not merit the reasonable approval of your own conscience, then you are not happy. And if it does, then hell or high water may flow upon you, and you will still be all right—*if* your relationship with other people is reasonably good. The rest is incidental to those relationships."[6]

Duff Hanks was an anchor for many. They knew he was a true believer. He may have grumbled about some excesses and human failings in the church, but it never translated into his faith wavering. He never neglected the weightier matters, and he served God and his fellow man not only in name, but in deed.

Even those who left the church usually expressed positive feelings about him. Once, when commenters on the *Salt Lake Tribune* website were stirring each other up against the church and its leaders, one of them wrote, "To you haters. Do not lump this man in with others. Marion D. Hanks was real, genuine, intelligent, open-minded, and loving. He embodied everything positive about the LDS Church. He was, in a very pure way, a Christian first and a Mormon second."[7]

When asked to describe the secret of a happy life, Duff replied, "Work hard. Be honest. And be generous. And be aware that there are people who have less than you have, and that a way to enjoy your own life is to share what you have with them."[8]

A friend of one of Duff's granddaughters spent some time with Duff and Maxine in Hana. At his death, she wrote something profound:

- This man stood for Jesus Christ all over the world.
- This man loved God.
- He knew God.
- And he knew how to love like God.[9]

DID HE MAKE A DIFFERENCE?

Duff's colleague Joe J. Christensen wrote, "Dear Duff, this would be a very different church without your valuable input at so many levels and in diverse ways. Your sensitivity to human problems and needs causes us all to try harder."[10]

5. Aldous Huxley, *Moksha: Writings on Psychedelics & the Visionary Experience*, ed. Michael Horowitz and Cynthia Palmer (Stonehill, 1977).
6. MDH-R, Dec. 10, 1988.
7. From an online comment, n.d.
8. Enterprise Mentors video.
9. Catherine K. Arveseth, "A Man to Remember: Elder Marion D. Hanks," *Meridian Magazine*, Aug. 21, 2011.
10. Joe J. Christensen to MDH, Dec. 19, 1974.

At his death, an online commenter said, "As I grew older, and learned from others more about the organization, and the tensions and rewards of being a servant of the church, repeatedly Elder Hanks' name came up: he'd been there, he'd done that, he'd been everywhere and done everything. No specialist he, but rather one who truly spoke with 'general authority.' He will be missed."[11]

Over his remaining years, Duff was pleased to see that many of the changes and improvements he had worked on tirelessly were coming to pass. It's true that many of them took decades to be implemented. But that's par for the course in the church and most other large organizations. Most great men in history have been a bit ahead of their time.

He reflected in his journal, "I have not really sought the honors of men. I have, however, sought to contribute to the *lives* of men, and in the few awards I have received, I was gratified that each citation mentioned, not my positions, but referred to *contributions.* I have loved the opportunity to serve others. People have been gracious enough to point to a few things we've accomplished over the years. Some have called attention to something I've done, or some effort I've led, and my loving effort at teaching. The implication is that I have made some contribution, and with that possibility, I am pleased."[12]

A PRACTICAL PROBLEM

The family had a practical problem when Duff died: What should they put on his headstone? How could they summarize the incredible lives of their mom and dad in just a few words? So they paraphrased a sentiment Duff loved from one of his honorary doctorates:

Serve others. Wherever they are. Whatever their faith.

That's a pretty good description of their lives.

FINAL GIFTS

During Duff's final years in the care center, the family wrote down meaningful things he said during their visits. Here are a few representative exchanges:

May 7, 2007: (To Mary)
Mary: "Dad, when you look at your hands, what are you checking?"
MDH: *"To see if they've done any good today."*

May 20, 2008: (On a lucid day—during a hug goodbye.)
Rich: "Dad, is there anything you'd like me to do?"
MDH: *"Be a good man."*
"Learn what the Lord expects, then do it."
"When something is wrong, do the right thing to correct it."

11. Russell Arben Fox, comment, *By Common Consent*, bycommonconsent.com, Aug. 9, 2011.
12. MDH-JE, June 21, 1979.

Duff's last official portrait, 2005. *Courtesy Silver Pelican and Nancy Baird*

And on one special, important day, after years in a mental fog, he was unusually alert. The words he spoke in one of his last family prayers perhaps best represent the gift of his life. He prayed, "Father, grant unto me peace and purpose in this current situation. Grant unto me that I may be useful to thee and to a few people while still on this earth."

THE LORD JESUS CHRIST

The scripture Dad quoted most near the end of his life was Job 42:3–6: "Therefore, have I uttered that I understood not; things too wonderful for me, which I knew not. . . . I have heard of thee by the hearing of the ear: but now mine eye seeth thee. Wherefore I abhor myself and repent in dust and ashes."

Daughter Nancy said, "I can hear his beautiful voice quoting Job. I can hear it echoing down the halls of the Salt Lake Temple. Our father understood the truth of what Job was seeing, as he understood the truth of most things. The thing is, he applied it to himself. He kept repenting. He knew who Job saw. He understood what had happened in the garden and on the cross."

Dad's absolute devotion to the Savior and his testimony of Christ permeated all that he did. He was a believer.

He declared, "My strongest desire is to qualify to be a friend of Christ."

I think he has. I think he is.

APPENDICES

A

MDH Life Timeline

Oct. 13, 1921	Born in Salt Lake City, to Stanley A. and Maude Frame Hanks
June 8, 1939	Graduated from Salt Lake City West High School
1939–42	Attended University of Utah
Jan. 19, 1941	Ordained an elder by Eli LeCheminant
July 31, 1941	Received patriarchal blessing from Albert R. Lyman
Feb. 17, 1942	Received endowment, Salt Lake Temple
Mar. 1942–Feb. 1944	Served as a full-time missionary, Northern States Mission
May 5, 1944	Ordained a seventy by Antoine R. Ivins
May 1944–Apr. 1946	Served in the US Navy, Pacific Theater, World War II
1946–54	Seminary teacher and principal, West High School Seminary
1946–65	Temple Square guide, assistant director, director, and counselor in the mission presidency
1948–49	Began teaching the first-ever early-morning seminary class
Apr. 1947	Played on winning team, All-Church Basketball Tournament
July 1948	Graduated from University of Utah law school
Aug. 1949	Married to Maxine Lehua Christensen in the Laie Hawaii Temple
July 22, 1950	Birth of daughter Susan Hanks Maughan
Aug. 23, 1951	Birth of daughter Nancy Hanks Baird
1951–53	Vice president, Allen-Duff Associates (advertising)
1950–70	Instructor, Institute of Religion serving University of Utah
Oct. 8, 1953	Called as a general authority by David O. McKay
Oct. 1953–Apr. 1968	Served as a member of the First Council of the Seventy
May 26, 1954	Birth of daughter Ann Hanks Clawson
Nov. 4, 1956	Birth of daughter Mary Hanks Clifford
July 1958–Apr. 1978	Member of President's Council on Physical Fitness and Sports and its predecessor organizations for five US presidents
1960–70	Editor, "Era of Youth" section of the *Improvement Era* magazine
Mar. 1960	Addressed White House Conference on Children and Youth
Apr. 28, 1960	Birth of son, Richard Duff Hanks
July 27, 1961	Ordained a high priest by President David O. McKay
Jan. 1962–Apr. 1964	Served as president, British Mission
1962–80	Member, Church Board of Education and BYU Board of Trustees
July 6, 1964	Received the marriage sealing authority from David O. McKay
Feb. 1965–Feb. 1977	Member, National Council of Boy Scouts of America (BSA)

1964, '69, '73, '79	Leader, BSA Jamborees: Pennsylvania; Idaho (two times); Sweden
May 1965	Supervisor, Oriental [Asian] and Hawaiian Missions
1966, '67, '70, '75	Attended US Army War College National Strategy Seminars
Apr. 1968–Oct. 1976	Served as assistant to the Twelve Apostles
Apr. 1968–Jan. 1973	Managing director, LDS Student Association
Dec. 1969	National president, Delta Phi Kappa
Dec. 1970	Speaker, White House Conference on Children
Feb. 1971–July 1980	Deseret Gym Board; chair, 1972–80
Apr. 1971	Participant, White House Conference on Youth
May 1971	Supervisor, LDS West Coast Area
May 1971	Advisor to YMMIA and YWMIA
May 1972	Completed cabin near Aspen Grove, Utah
Nov. 1972–Dec. 1976	Associate managing director, Priesthood Department
Nov. 1972–Dec. 1976	Managing director, Melchizedek Priesthood MIA
July 1974–July 1975	President of Salt Lake Club, Rotary International
1974	Published *The Gift of Self* and *Now and Forever*
May 1975	Director, Church Activities Committee and Church Athletics
Jan. 1976–Jan. 1979	Managing director, LDS Military Relations
June 1976–June 1977	Supervisor, Central Utah and Atlantic North Areas
Oct. 1976	First Quorum of Seventy created, Assistants to the Twelve reassigned
Oct. 1976–Apr. 1980	Second time serving in Presidency of the Seventy
Nov. 1976–May 1978	Managing director, Church youth programs, including Scouting
Feb. 1977–July 1980	Served on the BSA National Executive Board
July 1977–July 1978	Served as district governor, Rotary International (Utah, Idaho)
July 1977–July 1980	Zone administrator, Australia, New Zealand, Hawaii, Canada
May 1980–May 1988	Served on BSA National Advisory Council
July 1980–Sept. 1982	Executive administrator (area president), Southeast Asia
July 1980	Initiated LDS Church involvement in refugee programs
July 1982–July 1985	Served as president, Salt Lake Temple
1985	"That Easter Morn," hymn no. 195 included in LDS hymnbook
Oct. 1984–Aug. 1992	Third time serving in the Presidency of the Seventy
May 1985–Dec. 1986	Executive director, Correlation and Evaluation Department
May 1985–Dec. 1986	Chair, Communications Coding Committee
Dec. 1986–Aug. 1992	Executive director, Priesthood Department
Oct. 1987–Aug. 1992	Executive director, Military Relations, second time
May 1988	Received BSA Silver Buffalo Award
1991	Published *Bread upon the Waters*
Oct. 1992	Given general authority emeritus status
1992+	Chair, Ouelessebougou Utah Alliance, Chair, Enterprise Mentors International, Chair, Marion D. and Maxine C. Hanks Foundation
1993	Completed house in Hana, Hawaii
2000	Family began to notice cognitive difficulties
2004–11	Resident at Silverado memory care facility
Aug. 5, 2011	Death at age eighty-nine, Salt Lake City

B

Patriarchal Blessing

Salt Lake City, Utah—July 31, 1941

A blessing given by Patriarch Albert R. Lyman upon the head of Marion Duff Hanks, son of Stanley Alonzo Hanks and Maude Frame, born October 13th, 1921, in Salt Lake City, Utah.

Dear Brother, Marion Duff Hanks:

Having been called and authorized to bless, I place my hands upon your head and give you a patriarchal blessing.

You are descended through a chosen line of ancestry, even from the loins of Ephraim, the grandson of the patriarch, Israel.

You are a chosen vessel of the Lord to bear His name, speak by the authority of His priesthood, and build up His kingdom in this important age of the world. Before you will open the pathway to this special labor as the thing to which you have been ordained and sent into the world.

There is no other course which you can devise or to which you can be directed by the wisdom of men which will give you the perfect and complete satisfaction which is possible to you in this line which you have been sent here to follow. Therefore, do not suffer the popular styles and conventions of the world to change this program to conform with their notions of how it should be done.

If you find that the thing to which the Spirit leads you is different to the way it has been done hitherto, and the way men think it should still be done, remember also that you are different, you have your own individuality, and your mission is that which has not been done in the same way before.

The adversary will try to dissuade you from your purpose, but the Spirit of the Lord will enlighten your mind and you will have great wisdom along the line of your assigned labors. In the due time of the Lord, you shall be given a choice helpmeet, and you shall stand at the head of a noble posterity, for you are a natural heir to the priesthood and it will be your right to exercise it in great power and authority; even to the accomplishment of wonderful things in the cause of Zion.

You shall speak by the gift and power of the Holy Ghost, the righteous and the pure in heart shall rejoice because of your words, even though the wicked may be angered and revile against you. I bless you that you may be made equal to all the difficulties and responsibilities of life; that your name shall be held in honorable remembrance throughout all the generations of your posterity, who shall be led by a consideration of your good works to glorify God with labors of righteousness.

Be of good cheer and let not your faith fail, for glorious things are awaiting you when you have magnified your calling and finished your mission here on earth.

I seal these blessings upon you through your faith and faithfulness by virtue of the Holy Priesthood in me vested, and in the name of Jesus Christ, Amen.

[signed] Albert R. Lyman

C

Settings Apart as a General Authority and Member of the First Council of the Seventy

Salt Lake City, Utah—October 8, 1953
The Brethren of the First Presidency [David O. McKay, Stephen L Richards, and J. Reuben Clark], and of the First Council of the Seventy then unitedly laid their hands upon the head of Brother Hanks, and President McKay was voice in giving him the following blessing and setting apart:

Brother Marion Duff Hanks, dear fellow-laborer in the Cause of Christ, by virtue of the Holy Priesthood, and the authority in us vested, we, your brethren, servants of the Lord, unitedly lay our hands upon your head, and set you apart as a member of the First Council of the Seventy in the Church of Jesus Christ of Latter-day Saints, and confer upon you every right, privilege, power, and authority pertaining to this holy office in the Melchizedek Priesthood.

We bless you, dear brother, with an increased testimony of the divinity of the Restored Gospel of Jesus Christ.

We bless you with a sense of the reality of the existence of our Heavenly Father, of the divine Sonship of the Lord Jesus Christ, and of the restoration through those divine personages of the gospel, as given by our Savior and Redeemer. The gospel was given when men assumed the responsibility of mortality to gain experience. The gospel today is restored and the Church and the Kingdom of God set up, nevermore to be thrown down or given to another people, and you are a special messenger to declare these truths to the world.

The Lord bless you and endow you richly with his Spirit.

We bless you that you may have freedom of speech, with your thoughts clearly comprehended, and your testimony such that it may be expressed to the convincing of the honest-in-heart, at home and abroad. You have magnified your special calling as a Seventy. You have touched the hearts of thousands and tens of thousands in your missionary work on Temple Square, and in other places. You have inspired the youth in your seminary teaching. Now may your influence be extended, be more influential, because of this added responsibility, for you now become one of the General Authorities of the Church.

We bless you with a sense of the mission, the distinctive mission of the Seventy. May the Lord magnify you in the minds of the people. May you gain their confidence, and having gained their confidence, may your words sink deeply into their hearts to inspire them to more righteous living, and to induce men and women outside of the Church to make investigation of the principles of the Gospel of the Lord Jesus Christ.

We bless you that your home life may continue to be sweet, that you may find an encouraging and uplifting influence always when you enter the sanctuary of your home, and may that homelife radiate such ideals as will influence your neighbors to have better homes and to live better lives.

We bless you with increased influence when you stand before the pulpit and declare the message of the Restored Gospel.

These blessings will be yours through your faith and faithfulness, for the Lord requires of his servants upright living, clean living, clear thinking, and as your thoughts are pure and your feelings in harmony with the gospel, the Lord will reveal to you those things which you need in in order to magnify this important calling.

Go forth, dear Brother Hanks, with confidence in your leadership, with confidence that you are the Lord's servant in spreading the gospel, with confidence that through the Holy Ghost you will receive that guidance which each one of us needs in order to succeed. We cannot succeed in our own wisdom nor in our own judgment. This is the Lord's work, and we are dependent upon him. Go to him in secret, plead with Him for His guidance, plead with Him to reveal to you your duties, and having them once revealed, plead with him to give you power to perform your duties in humility, and thus expressed you will find a consciousness that by your side he is walking with you by his Holy Spirit, to warn you of dangers to come, to show you things ahead, and above all, to reveal to you His mind and will.

These blessings, with others that the Lord sees will be for your good, we bestow upon you, with this setting apart, in the name of the Lord Jesus Christ. Amen.[1]

1. Transcript of blessing, Oct. 8, 1953, in the author's possession and CHL.

D

Obituaries of Marion Duff Hanks and Maxine Christensen Hanks

Marion Duff Hanks died August 5, 2011, at the age of 89, in Salt Lake City, Utah, of causes incident to age. Elder Marion D. Hanks was one of the great souls born to this earth. He lived his life by the teachings in the Holy Scriptures, with which he was intimately acquainted and which he loved so deeply and taught as no other. He was a teacher, a scholar, a defender, a great intellect, and a servant, but above all, he was a man of God.

Elder Hanks was born into poverty but was unfailingly generous with his time, money, and spirit to all who needed him. He was fatherless from his babyhood but was a mentor, counselor, protector, leader, and father to innumerable others.

He believed the words of the Savior and chose the weightier matters of life—judgment, mercy, and faith. He felt that he personally needed to feed the hungry, take in the stranger, clothe the naked, defend the defenseless, and comfort those who mourned. He loved his family and was kind and courtly, courteous and generous to everyone he met.

Elder Hanks was commanding and charismatic. He was an advisor to five Presidents of the United States, serving on the President's Council on Physical Fitness and Sports, beginning with Dwight D. Eisenhower. He was a local, national and international leader of many organizations including Rotary, Ouelessebougou Alliance, Enterprise Mentors, Boy Scouts of America, Salvation Army, Utah Boys Ranch, Salt Lake Cancer Society, Sons of the Utah Pioneers, and numerous others. Elder Hanks was a consummate community bridge builder. He spent many years on the Board of Trustees for Brigham Young University.

He possessed a strong mind with a deep capacity for language and thought. He was serious from his childhood. He resisted the proud. Elder Hanks succeeded in many arenas, but the focus of his life was the Kingdom of God and all of God's children.

Elder Hanks was born October 13, 1921, in Salt Lake City to Stanley A. and Maude Frame Hanks. He was married to Maxine Lehua Christensen in the Hawaii Temple in 1949. They are the parents of five children. He graduated from the University of Utah Law School, served an LDS mission to the Northern States Mission, and served in the US Navy in the Pacific during WWII.

At the age of 31, Elder Hanks was called by President David O. McKay to serve as a general authority for The Church of Jesus Christ of Latter-day Saints. He spent the next 40 years serving others across the earth with Maxine. He served as a member of the Presidency of the Seventy on three occasions, as an Assistant to the Quorum of the Twelve, as a mission president in London, England, Area President/Supervisor in Hong Kong, the Pacific Isles, Central Utah, South America, and the Atlantic Northeast Areas, editor of the *New Era* magazine, Director of the Correlation Committee, Military Relations and chaplains, the Priesthood Department, and President of the Salt Lake Temple, to name but a few. He traveled on multiple occasions to Vietnam during that war, in order to comfort and meet with LDS servicemen. He stayed up late into the night dictating letters to the families of servicemen he had visited. In Asia, he was the catalyst for the creation of the refugee programs for the Church in Thailand and the Philippines.

Elder Hanks influenced the lives of thousands of students as a teacher of the Book of Mormon in seminary and institute classes for many years. He was always willing to say "yes" to one more request and filled innumerable speaking assignments. He loved the temple and was beloved by all who worked with him there.

He was a gifted athlete who loved sports and excelled in basketball, handball, and squash. He loved his country deeply. He also loved literature and books and would often quote long passages of Shakespeare. He loved to chop wood, shovel snow, move rocks in the stream at Aspen Grove, and occasionally go home to the Hawaiian Islands with Maxine.

His wife and partner in all things, Maxine, has taken care of Duff throughout his long illness with devotion, passion, and love.

His five children love and honor him and are so grateful to have had such a kind, wise and remarkable father who gave each of them the gift of unconditional love.

Elder Marion Duff Hanks is survived by his wife, Maxine, and their five children: Susan (Paul) Maughan, Nancy (John) Baird, Ann (Spencer) Clawson, Mary (Chris) Clifford, Richard (Liz) Hanks, 23 grandchildren, and 38 great-grandchildren. His parents; brothers, Lincoln and Bruce; and sisters, Jeannette, Maurine, Beulah, and Maude May, all preceded him in death.

Elder Hanks' family would like to thank the many friends who continued to visit him, some of whom could scarce afford the time, and the caregivers who loved and respected him and treated him with such kindness, respect and compassion.

Funeral services will be held Saturday, August 13, 2011, at 11:00 a.m. at the Holladay South Stake Center, 4917 Viewmont St., Salt Lake City.

Visitation will be held Friday, August 12, 2011, from 6:00 to 8:00 p.m. and Saturday, August 13, 2011, from 9:00 a.m. to 10:30 a.m., also at the Holladay South Stake Center.

Interment at Wasatch Lawn Memorial Park (3401 Highland Dr, Salt Lake City).

In lieu of flowers, contributions may be made to the Marion D. and Maxine C. Hanks Humanitarian Foundation, P.O. Box 9672, Salt Lake City, Utah 84109.[1]

Maxine Lehua Christensen Hanks, beautiful and filled with unique grace and refinement, passed away on February 21, 2018, at the age of 92.

Maxine was born on November 4, 1925, in Honolulu, Hawaii, to Arva Eunice Boothe and Elwood Lowell Christensen.

She was an island girl, through and through, and left the Hawaiian Islands only for college and then her marriage to Marion Duff Hanks (Duff). Mom had a deep connection and love for Hawaii, especially Hana, Maui. After traveling the world, the porch in Hana was their rest. She longed to hear of family telling her how much they also loved it. The phone call to her was the first thing we all did on arrival in Hana.

Maxine met Duff when he was in port in Honolulu during WWII. They took a hike to a waterfall in Manoa Valley and when Maxine's little sister Janet got tired, Duff carried her. When he didn't mind Janet's muddy feet getting on his navy whites, Maxine knew he was the one. They were sealed in the Laie, Hawaii, LDS temple on August 27, 1949. He died in 2011.

After attending the University of Hawaii, Maxine graduated from the

1. Marion D. Hanks obituary, *Deseret News*, Aug. 5, 2011.

University of Utah with a BS in elementary education. She taught school briefly before she and Duff began to raise a family.

Maxine and Duff built a beautiful life together. With grace and poise, she let him shine because she loved him and knew he was everything she wanted.

Maxine created beautiful homes of refuge wherever she and Duff lived, whether it was Salt Lake City, London, Hong Kong, Hana, or Aspen Grove. Visitors were always welcome.

She was an initiative-taker and an organizer. She was bright, strong, competent, straightforward, and unafraid. She loved to laugh, and she deeply loved her husband, her children, grandchildren, and great-grandchildren. Maxine was rarely sentimental, and she didn't look back. She loved beauty and uplifting things. She danced a beautiful hula.

There were always piles of books wherever Maxine was—history, biography, commentary, novels. She loved the symphony, the theatre, and the opera.

She loved salads and turned up her nose at sugar. Her favorite treat was a ripe mango, a papaya, or an apple banana—although she loved a good hot dog. Dad once said in a letter to us from Hong Kong, "Mom reads voraciously and eats wisely and is otherwise a splendid example for the rest of us."

Maxine served with her husband as LDS mission president in London, England, as Area President in Hong Kong, and as Matron of the Salt Lake Temple, and many other assignments. She was quietly and privately grounded and saw life clearly as she stood by our father's side for over 65 years. She was a true believer in the Gospel of Jesus Christ.

Mom left a legacy of five children: Susan (Paul) Maughan, Nancy (John) Baird, Ann (Spencer) Clawson, Mary (Chris) Clifford, and Richard (Liz) Hanks, 23 grandchildren and 69 great-grandchildren. She was preceded in death by her parents; her brothers, Lowell and Paul; her sister, Janet; her grandson Greg Clawson; and great-grandchildren Laird Thomas and Isaac Carlston.

Our family would like to thank Mom's many caregivers for their loving and gentle care. Also, the dear friends and neighbors who have helped Mom over the years. They have become family to us.

Funeral services will be held Saturday, March 3, 2018, at 11:00 at the LDS chapel located at 4568 S. Holladay Blvd, Holladay, Utah. Visitations will be held at the chapel on Friday evening, March 2, from 6:30 to 8:30 P.M., and also on March 3 at the chapel from 9:30 to 10:30 A.M.

Interment in Wasatch Lawn Memorial Park (3401 S. Highland Dr., Salt Lake City). In lieu of flowers the family suggests contributions be made to the Marion D. and Maxine C. Hanks Foundation, whose purpose is to financially lift those in need.[2]

---

2. Maxine C. Hanks obituary, *Deseret News*, Mar. 1, 2018.

E

Examples of Duff's Teachings

GUIDES TO TEACHING

Marion D. Hanks

1) I will never teach students anything they will have to unlearn.
2) I will learn how to say "I don't know."
3) I will memorize and apply Alma 37:11—"Now these mysteries are not yet fully made known unto me; therefore, I shall forebear."
4) I will memorize and try to apply Alma 39:11—"For when they saw your conduct, they would not believe in my words."
5) I will teach the first principles of the gospel, whatever the subject.
6) I will try to understand and teach the principle of revelation.
7) I will try to inspire students with the world mission of the Church—and not focus on meaningless details.
8) I will try to teach the greater commandments—the "weightier matters"—as well as the letter of the law (Matthew 23:23).
9) I will teach students to join forces with those who seek similar ends.
10) I will, whatever my subject, teach "Jesus Christ, and him crucified."

Early in his days of being a teacher, Duff wrote what he called his "Guides to Teaching"—ten truisms he believed were essential to teaching.

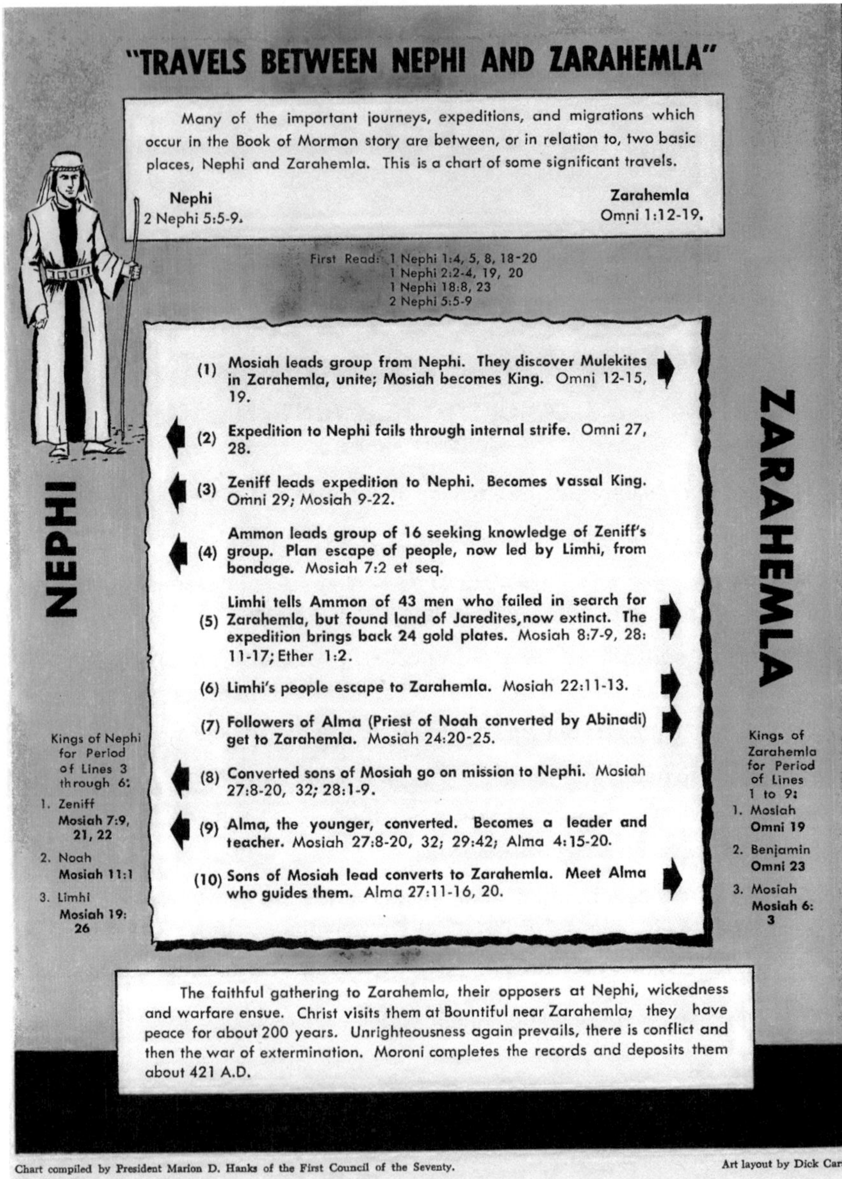

"TRAVELS BETWEEN NEPHI AND ZARAHEMLA"

Many of the important journeys, expeditions, and migrations which occur in the Book of Mormon story are between, or in relation to, two basic places, Nephi and Zarahemla. This is a chart of some significant travels.

Nephi 2 Nephi 5:5-9.

Zarahemla Omni 1:12-19.

First Read: 1 Nephi 1:4, 5, 8, 18-20
1 Nephi 2:2-4, 19, 20
1 Nephi 18:8, 23
2 Nephi 5:5-9

NEPHI | **ZARAHEMLA**

(1) **Mosiah leads group from Nephi. They discover Mulekites in Zarahemla, unite; Mosiah becomes King.** Omni 12-15, 19. →

← (2) **Expedition to Nephi fails through internal strife.** Omni 27, 28.

← (3) **Zeniff leads expedition to Nephi. Becomes vassal King.** Omni 29; Mosiah 9-22.

← (4) **Ammon leads group of 16 seeking knowledge of Zeniff's group. Plan escape of people, now led by Limhi, from bondage.** Mosiah 7:2 et seq.

(5) **Limhi tells Ammon of 43 men who failed in search for Zarahemla, but found land of Jaredites, now extinct. The expedition brings back 24 gold plates.** Mosiah 8:7-9, 28:11-17; Ether 1:2. →

(6) **Limhi's people escape to Zarahemla.** Mosiah 22:11-13. →

(7) **Followers of Alma (Priest of Noah converted by Abinadi) get to Zarahemla.** Mosiah 24:20-25. →

← (8) **Converted sons of Mosiah go on mission to Nephi.** Mosiah 27:8-20, 32; 28:1-9.

← (9) **Alma, the younger, converted. Becomes a leader and teacher.** Mosiah 27:8-20, 32; 29:42; Alma 4:15-20.

(10) **Sons of Mosiah lead converts to Zarahemla. Meet Alma who guides them.** Alma 27:11-16, 20. →

Kings of Nephi for Period of Lines 3 through 6:
1. Zeniff **Mosiah 7:9, 21, 22**
2. Noah **Mosiah 11:1**
3. Limhi **Mosiah 19: 26**

Kings of Zarahemla for Period of Lines 1 to 9:
1. Mosiah **Omni 19**
2. Benjamin **Omni 23**
3. Mosiah **Mosiah 6: 3**

The faithful gathering to Zarahemla, their opposers at Nephi, wickedness and warfare ensue. Christ visits them at Bountiful near Zarahemla; they have peace for about 200 years. Unrighteousness again prevails, there is conflict and then the war of extermination. Moroni completes the records and deposits them about 421 A.D.

Chart compiled by President Marion D. Hanks of the First Council of the Seventy.

Art layout by Dick Carter

Over the years, Duff created numerous teaching aides from scratch, like this example from *The Instructor* magazine, January 1957.

STEPS TO LEARNING

Marion D. Hanks

READ: "Reading maketh the full man," said the sage. So, READ. Starting now! Isaiah 34:16: "Seek ye out of the book of the Lord and read."
See also Deuteronomy 17:19; Acts 17:11; 1 Nephi 1:12; 2 Nephi 25:26.

LISTEN: Ah, there's a rare exercise. Don't be like the student who couldn't explain what he just read because he wasn't listening. Be still. Listen.
Doctrine and Covenants 88:122: "Let one speak at a time . . . and let all listen."
See also Proverbs 1:5; Isaiah 55:3; Mosiah 2:9; Mark 4:24.

MARK: Read (or listen) with a pencil in your hand. Annotate. Ask questions in the margin. Write a meaningful word so you'll be familiar with the terrain.
Luke 4:17: "Opened the book [and] found the place where it was written."
See also Luke 24:27; 2 Timothy 4:13.

ORGANIZE: Read widely enough to get a good understanding of the principle involved. Pursue the subject in other scriptures and books. Make an outline.
Acts 17:11: More noble because they received the word and searched it daily.
See also Doctrine and Covenants 88:118–19; 90:15.

THINK: Concentrate. Invest your full attention. Use your imagination to explore. Enjoy mulling over the thought. 3 Nephi 17:3: Go home. Ponder. Pray.
See also 1 Nephi 1:12; Doctrine and Covenants 138:1; Psalm 119:15–16.

DIGEST: Blow away the chaff and chew on the grain. Absorb it into your bloodstream so it's yours. Deuteronomy 6:3 and 31:11-13: Hear—Do!

APPLY: Use it. Put its teachings into operation in your daily life.
1 Nephi 19:22-26: Liken to self and apply.
See also Mosiah 4:10; Ezra 7:10; Deuteronomy 31:1-13.

SHARE: Tell others what you've learned. Teach your family and friends.
Deuteronomy 6:7 Teach children– in house, as you walk – day and night.
Also: Nehemiah 8:8, Alma 38:15.

Over time Duff codified the steps he believed were vital to "learning and learning to love to learn."

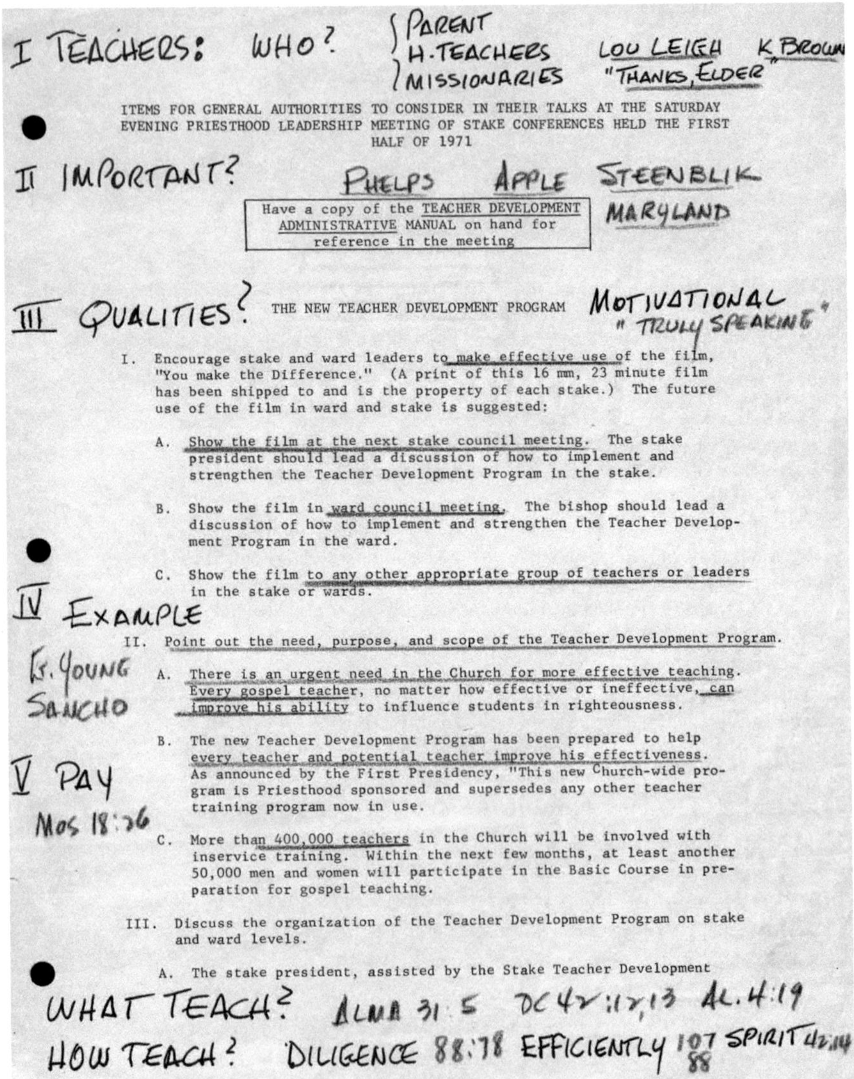

I TEACHERS: WHO? { PARENT H.TEACHERS MISSIONARIES   LOU LEIGH   K BROWN "THANKS, ELDER"

ITEMS FOR GENERAL AUTHORITIES TO CONSIDER IN THEIR TALKS AT THE SATURDAY EVENING PRIESTHOOD LEADERSHIP MEETING OF STAKE CONFERENCES HELD THE FIRST HALF OF 1971

II IMPORTANT?   PHELPS   APPLE   STEENBLIK   MARYLAND

Have a copy of the TEACHER DEVELOPMENT ADMINISTRATIVE MANUAL on hand for reference in the meeting

III QUALITIES?   THE NEW TEACHER DEVELOPMENT PROGRAM   MOTIVATIONAL "TRULY SPEAKING"

I. Encourage stake and ward leaders to make effective use of the film, "You make the Difference." (A print of this 16 mm, 23 minute film has been shipped to and is the property of each stake.) The future use of the film in ward and stake is suggested:

A. Show the film at the next stake council meeting. The stake president should lead a discussion of how to implement and strengthen the Teacher Development Program in the stake.

B. Show the film in ward council meeting. The bishop should lead a discussion of how to implement and strengthen the Teacher Development Program in the ward.

C. Show the film to any other appropriate group of teachers or leaders in the stake or wards.

IV EXAMPLE

II. Point out the need, purpose, and scope of the Teacher Development Program.

B. YOUNG   SANCHO

A. There is an urgent need in the Church for more effective teaching. Every gospel teacher, no matter how effective or ineffective, can improve his ability to influence students in righteousness.

B. The new Teacher Development Program has been prepared to help every teacher and potential teacher improve his effectiveness. As announced by the First Presidency, "This new Church-wide program is Priesthood sponsored and supersedes any other teacher training program now in use.

V PAY   MOS 18:26

C. More than 400,000 teachers in the Church will be involved with inservice training. Within the next few months, at least another 50,000 men and women will participate in the Basic Course in preparation for gospel teaching.

III. Discuss the organization of the Teacher Development Program on stake and ward levels.

A. The stake president, assisted by the Stake Teacher Development

WHAT TEACH?   ALMA 31:5   DC 42:12,13   AL. 4:19

HOW TEACH?   DILIGENCE 88:78   EFFICIENTLY 107 88   SPIRIT 42:14

The margins of most articles and papers were full of notes to himself and cross-references to other things he was reading or thinking about.

Book of Mormon Lesson of Life
President Marion D. Hanks

1 Nephi 1:1 **"GOODLY PARENTS"**

READ First Nephi 1:1 **"I, Nephi, having been born of goodly parents…"**

Who were Nephi's parents? Why should he be grateful for them? What did he owe them? How could he repay them? What did they really want from him?

What if our parents are not living as we think they should? What if one parent (or both) is dead? Do we have any obligations? What do we owe? To whom?

1. EACH OF US OWES A DEBT TO OUR FATHERS... OF OUR FAITH, OUR FREEDOM, OUR FLESH.
"When you drink the water, don't forget the spring from which it flows."

2. WHAT RESPONSIBILITY DO CHILDREN HAVE TO THEIR PARENTS?

Exodus 20:12	Honor them. (The first commandment with promise)
1 Tim 5:4,8	Take care of them. Provide for them.
Proverbs 6:20	Follow their counsel. (Ephesians 6:1; Obey them.)
Alma 39:11	Keep faith with them. Support them spiritually.
1 Nephi 16:20-25	Strengthen, rather than criticize, if they waver.

3. WHAT DOES A PARENT OWE HIS/HER CHILDREN?

D&C 68:25	Instruction, guidance, concern, example
Alma 36:3	Faith, confidence in God, goodness
Alma 39	Reproof, discipline, counsel
Ephesians 6:4	Rear them in nurture and admonition of the Lord.
Jacob 2:35: 3:10	Example
Mosiah 4:11-15	Take care of them temporally, morally, spiritually.
Deuteronomy 5:27-29	Fear God and keep His commandments, that it might be well with their children forever.

4. WHAT ABOUT A PROSPECTIVE PARENT? DOES HE/SHE OWE ANYTHING TO THE FUTURE?
See #3 above.

5. WHAT DOES A NORMAL PARENT WANT FOR HIS/HER CHILDREN?

1 Nephi 2:9,10	That they may be strong, humble, obedient.
2 Nephi 1:16, 21-23	Be men, united; amount to something!
2 Nephi 2:28,29	Accept Christ. Choose righteousness, not evil.
Alma 37:32-37	Learn wisdom in youth. Be prayerful, spiritual.
Alma 38:10-15	Work, serve. Be filled with love. Be humble.
1 Timothy 4:11-16	Be an example of the believers.

IF WE HAVE GOODLY PARENTS, WE ARE FORTUNATE, BUT THIS IS OUT OF OUR CONTROL. WE CAN ALL BE GOODLY PARENTS. OVER THIS WE HAVE CONTROL.

"Lesson of Life" example from Duff's Book of Mormon guide, "Know the Book."

UNDERSTANDING THE NEEDS OF LDS SINGLES

There are important things that singles need to hear.

(1) God loves them, individually and personally and always.
They may sometimes feel lonely, but they need never be alone.

(2) Church leaders love them and are aware of their special needs.
This includes unmarried single adults, and those into whose lives have come the sorrows of death or divorce.

(3) There is a place for them in the Church.
We must continue to emphasize the importance of families, but we are well aware that at least 25 percent of the Church membership is composed of singles. The principle is to involve every individual in determining needs, making suggestions, and being an active participant in meeting those needs.

(4) The Church is aware that single adults have special challenges.
But it is also true that tribulations, afflictions, and problems are all part of living. The Lord has not promised us immunity from difficulty, but has promised to help us meet our challenges with courage and faith.

(5) There is a key to a rich and abundant life for every single person, and that is to fill his or her life with worthwhile interests—service to others, volunteer work in hospitals, with youth, with the elderly, with underprivileged or disabled people. Self-improvement programs, classes, activity in cultural pursuits, association with others in similar circumstances—all will bring joy and fulfillment. Change your mindset from "What I need" to "Where am I needed?"

Marion D. Hanks

In a 1988 training meeting for regional representatives, Duff presented this document summarizing the needs of LDS singles.

Glossary of Terms

Area Presidency: In each area of the world, a general authority seventy is assigned by the First Presidency and Quorum of the Twelve Apostles to serve as the area president. Two counselors, who are general authority seventies or area seventies, are assigned to assist the president. They determine how to apply general church policy and direction to meet the needs in their area.

Apostle: A "special witness of the name of Christ in all the world" (D&C 107:23), usually a member of the *Quorum* of the Twelve *Apostles*, the presiding body second in authority only to the *First Presidency*.

Bishop: Local lay leader who presides over and acts as pastor of a ward, typically serves for several years on a part-time basis with no financial remuneration.

Bishopric: Group of local leaders composed of a bishop and his two counselors.

Book of Mormon: Scripture used by Latter-day Saints, taken from records of the ancient inhabitants of the Americas and compiled by a prophet-historian named Mormon, translated by Joseph Smith through "the gift and power of God" (D&C 135:3). Companion to the Bible, it contains "the fullness of the gospel" (D&C 20:9), has the purpose of testifying "that Jesus is the Christ," and is known as "Another Testament of Jesus Christ."

Branch: Local congregation, smaller and less completely organized than a ward. Presided over by a volunteer church leader called a branch president.

Branch president (see *branch*, *ward*)

Doctrine and Covenants (D&C): Volume containing revelations through Joseph Smith and his successors as heads of the church, accepted as scripture by Latter-day Saints.

Fast Sunday: On the first Sunday of each month, church members voluntarily go without food and drink for two meals to grow closer to God. The church encourages members to take the money they would have spent on food and donate it as a **fast offering** to the church to help the poor.

First Presidency: The highest presiding council in the Church of Jesus Christ of Latter-day Saints, having worldwide jurisdiction, composed of the prophet and president of the church and his first and second counselors, or assistants.

First Council of the Seventy (1844–1976): An administrative unit in the Church of Jesus Christ of Latter-day Saints with priesthood authority to preside over quorums of the Seventy as a whole. Made up of seven general authority seventies. Replaced by the Presidency of the Seventy.

General authorities: Presiding officers of the church worldwide, they include the First Presidency, Quorum of the Twelve Apostles, Quorums of the Seventy, and Presiding Bishopric.

General conference: Worldwide gathering at church headquarters covering two days each April and October at which church business is conducted. *General authorities* and others speak. It is carried worldwide by means of satellites and other media; it is a time of expounding gospel principles, exhortation, and spiritual renewal.

Mission: (1) Large geographical unit in charge of proselyting and service by full-time missionaries; it sometimes supervises *districts* and *branches*; (2) period of full-time missionary service, often two years, by church members. Typically, young single adults or retired couples serve as missionaries.

Ordinance: A sacred rite or ceremony such as baptism or confirmation (normally performed outside of temples), as well as endowments and sealings (performed in temples).

Patriarchal blessing: A blessing given by the laying on of hands to members of the church, through priesthood authority (by an ordained patriarch) typically once during a person's lifetime. These blessings include inspired counsel, reassurance, admonitions, and other insights to guide the recipient's future life. The blessings are considered sacred and private but are recorded and transcribed for the recipient.

The Presidency of the Seventy: A group of seven general authorities of the church who preside over all members of the Seventy and oversee the work of the Seventy throughout the world.

Priesthood: The power and authority of God, and also the formal authority to preside or officiate in the church, it consists of two orders or divisions: the lesser (Aaronic) Priesthood, generally held by male youths, focuses on temporal affairs, or "outward ordinances"; and the higher (Melchizedek) Priesthood, held by adult men, deals primarily with spiritual matters, including ordinances and blessings of healing, comfort, and guidance. Holding the priesthood is not a status symbol but rather an opportunity for service.

Prophet: An individual who is authorized to speak for God, the president of the church is regarded as a prophet and the only person authorized to declare new doctrines, positions, or interpretations officially for the whole church.

Relief Society: Latter-day Saint women's organization, emphasizing education and compassionate service; organized in 1842, it is one of the oldest and largest women's organizations in the world.

Restoration (of Christ's gospel): The return of the doctrines and authority of the New Testament church to the earth by means of heavenly messengers and divine revelation.

Setting apart (to be set apart) Setting apart is a ritual or priesthood action in the Church of Jesus Christ of Latter-day Saints where a person is formally blessed to carry out a specific calling or responsibility in the church. The blessing gives recipients direction and power to act in their callings.

Stake: Geographic group of local congregations (wards and branches), similar to a diocese; this term is taken from the comparison of God's work being carried on in a large tent in which the surrounding tent posts or stakes are sources of stability and strength (see Isaiah 54:2).

Seventy, Seventies: Group of men holding the office of seventy in the Melchizedek Priesthood whose name is taken from Christ's appointing seventy men to serve under the Twelve in spreading the gospel (Luke 10:1). There are currently eight quorums of the Seventy. Each quorum may have up to seventy members. Some of the Seventy are assigned to headquarters administrative functions, but most live and work within a specific geographic region of the Church. This calling earlier was held by men at the local level.

Singles: Men and women who have not yet married or who are divorced or widowed make up a significant portion of church membership. **"Single members"** refers to all adult members of the church who are not currently married, further broken down into **"young single adults"** (eighteen to thirty), and **"single adults"** (thirty-one and older.) Most single members attend a geographic unit with members of all ages. In some geographies, special young single adult or single adult wards are created. In this case, eligible members may choose to attend singles wards or their geographic ward.

Temple: Sacred building (separate from local meetinghouses) dedicated as a "house of the Lord," where church members receive ordinances (including baptism and marriage) and make covenants with God. Temples are thought of as a place of revelation where heaven and earth meet. They can be entered only by church members meeting standards of worthiness.

Temple work: Ordinances performed in temples, for the living and also for those who have died. Marriages performed in the temple are called sealings and hold the promise of a couple being married, or "sealed," for eternity. Ordinances performed for the dead are valid only if the deceased individuals accept them in the hereafter. LDS belief in vicarious ordinances for deceased ancestors is the driving force behind church members' commitment to researching family history.

Ward: Local congregation, part of a stake; generally consisting of a few hundred members in a specific geographical area. Larger and more completely organized than a branch. One of multiple units comprising a stake. Presided over by a volunteer church leader called a bishop.

Ward teachers (home teachers): Individual members of the church are assigned (usually in pairs) to watch over a few members of their local congregation, visiting them as requested and performing service.

Index

I

N

About the Author

Richard D. Hanks is an author and retired senior business executive, having served at several of the largest multinational companies in the world, including Marriott, PepsiCo, and Price Waterhouse. Also a successful serial entrepreneur, he was named by Ernst & Young as Entrepreneur of the Year in 2010. Rich obtained his bachelor's degree from Brigham Young University and his MBA from Northwestern University and taught as an adjunct professor at Cornell for ten years. He has served as a board director of profit and nonprofit organizations and as an in-demand public speaker and well-regarded lecturer at many universities.

Rich and his wife, Liz, raised their family in Texas, Maryland, and Utah, and now reside in Salt Lake City. He is active in his faith, having served as a missionary in Scotland, a youth leader, a bishop, and a mission president in Alabama. Rich loves being with his family, and in his spare time enjoys sports and woodworking. He adores his wife, Liz, loves their three terrific children and their spouses, and spoils his eleven grandchildren.